King Football

King Football

Sport and Spectacle in the Golden Age of Radio and Newsreels, Movies and Magazines, the Weekly & the Daily Press

Michael Oriard

The University of North Carolina Press

Chapel Hill and London

© 2001

The University of North Carolina Press

All rights reserved

Set in New Baskerville, Meta, and Champion types
by Tseng Information Systems, Inc.

Manufactured in the United States of America

The paper in this book meets the guidelines for
permanence and durability of the Committee on
Production Guidelines for Book Longevity of the
Council on Library Resources.

Library of Congress Cataloging-in-Publication Data

Oriard, Michael, 1948–

King Football: sport and spectacle in the golden
age of radio and newsreels, movies and magazines,
the weekly and the daily press / Michael Oriard.

    p. cm.

Includes bibliographical references and index.

ISBN 0-8078-2650-2 (cloth: alk. paper)

1. Football—History—20th century.   2. Mass
media and sports—History—20th century.
I. Title.

GV950 .O73   2001

796.332′09′041—dc21   2001041459

05   04   03   02   01   5   4   3   2   1

FOR ERIC SOLOMON

Contents

Illustrations

Preface

To reconstruct the narrative and visual universe of football from 1920 to 1960 in newspapers, magazines, radio, newsreels, and feature films, it was critical to be as comprehensive as possible, within reasonable limits and the constraints of available sources. The daily press could only be surveyed selectively, but for a range of regional newspapers I examined the full run of eight newspapers—the *New York Times* and *New York Daily News, Atlanta Constitution, Chicago Tribune, Dallas Morning News, Omaha World-Herald, Los Angeles Times,* and *Portland Oregonian*—supplemented by dozens of other small-town and metropolitan papers where needed. Against these I read through forty years of football coverage in the *Chicago Defender* and *Pittsburgh Courier,* and in other black papers more selectively; several Polish, Italian, Jewish, Greek, Lithuanian, Hungarian, Slovak, and other ethnic papers from the 1920s and 1930s; and the *Daily Worker, Young Communist Review, Milwaukee Leader,* and a dozen more labor and radical papers over their variously brief runs.

Among the five major newsreels, two—Hearst's *Metrotone News* (later *News of the Day*) and *Universal News*—were available, the former at UCLA's Film and TV Archive, the latter at the National Archives in College Park, Maryland. Complete synopsis sheets of the Hearst newsreels and program notes for the Universal reels made fully documenting their football coverage possible. I had access to limited viewing of the Hearst footage and unlimited viewing of the Universal newsreels as well. Some newsreel footage has been completely lost, and the sound tracks are damaged for much of what survives, but these two newsreels are an invaluable resource for scholars. For the other three newsreels I was dependent on a database listing the programs for Pathé and Paramount, and an in-house compilation of the surviving footage from *Fox Movietone News.* Radio broadcasts are considerably more difficult to study comprehensively. My newspapers provided the listings of football games for each city in the study, but no radio broadcasts of football games before 1935 apparently exist. The collection of NBC broadcasts at the Library of Congress includes eleven football games from the late 1930s, eleven more through 1945, then nearly weekly games from 1946 through 1954, in addition to a smattering of other football programming. I paid particular attention to the earliest broadcasts. I was able to view 63 of the 120 football movies; for the rest I had to depend on secondary material. The periodical press posed the fewest difficulties. I read all the football journalism in the *Saturday Evening Post, Collier's, Life,* and *Look,* and more selectively in other magazines; and all the fiction in the *Post, Collier's,* the pulp magazine *Sport Story,* and the juvenile periodical *Boys' Life,* along with a sampling from other mainstream and pulp magazines. (Of the 133 short stories and serials in the *Post* and *Collier's,* just one was published outside the months of September, October, November, and December. It is possible that I missed other out-of-season stories.) Finally, the Joyce Sports Collection at the University of Notre Dame provided access to a wide range of additional print materials, most notably an extensive collection of football programs from throughout the period.

Directors and staffs at numerous libraries provided information or made my research easier. My thanks for help on site or by correspondence to Linda A. Horner, at the National Scouting Museum, Murray, Kentucky; Carolyn A. Davis, at the Syracuse University Library; Howard Hayes and Clarence Fong, at the UCLA Film and Television Archive; Laura Kaiser, at UCLA's Powell Library; Dennis Lien, at the University of Minnesota's Wilson Library; Steve Nielsen, at the Minnesota Historical Society; Bill Hennessey, at the Sherman Grinberg Library in New York; Roger Bell, Executive Director of Library Services at Twentieth-Century Fox; Charles De Arman, at the Motion Picture, Sound, and Video Branch of the National Archives; Joe Horrigan, at the Pro Football Hall of Fame Library in Canton, Ohio; Lyle Minter, at the Government Publications and Periodical Section of the Library of Congress; Madeline Matz, at the Motion Picture, Broadcasting and Recorded Sound Division of the Library of Congress; and George Rugg, director of the Joyce Sports Collection at the University of Notre Dame. I am also grateful to Raymond Fielding, dean of the Florida State University film school, for sharing his database on the newsreels; Stephen T. Miller, for providing me a list of sports pulp titles he had compiled, long before such information was widely available; and Bill Plott, for tracking down articles in the *Birmingham News* and *Birmingham Post* for me.

Closer to home, Doris Tilles and her staff in Interlibrary Loans at Oregon State University's Valley Library — particularly Heidi Weisel and Thelma Evans — performed with astonishing good cheer a sometimes daunting task of locating and acquiring the hundreds of reels of microfilm that made this book possible. My friend and chair of my department, Robert Schwartz, provided both institutional and personal support; Diane Slywczuk and the office staff — Wendy Novak, Aurora Terhune, and Catherine Showalter — attended to countless details with unfailing cheer. Henry Sayre helped me read the artwork on football programs. Norma Rudinsky and the sadly late Viola Jonas helped me with translations from immigrant newspapers. Over the years a number of my undergraduate students—Stefanie Hargreaves-Dyer, Darren Noble, and Heather Shannon—photocopied materials in the library, and I am grateful to Heather for her original research on the first black players at Oregon State. Three wise and good friends in my department—Kerry Ahearn, Jon Lewis, and David Robinson—read the manuscript in its entirety (when that entirety was much longer than it is now) and offered invaluable advice for revisions.

Travel grants from osu's Valley Library and grants from osu's Research Council facilitated my work, and a term at osu's Center for the Humanities provided much-valued time at a key stage. The Research Council and the Edward Smith Memorial Endowment made the large number of illustrations possible. Most important, a fellowship from the National Endowment for the Humanities provided the opportunity for a year-long immersion, through which I was able to complete a first draft of the book. May future U.S. Congresses have the wisdom to continue funding NEH and NEA.

The often frustrating process of acquiring permissions for illustrations was made easier by helpful individuals at archives and publishers: Rebecca Armatis, Tamar Chute, Trina Cieply, Tom Gilbert, Martin Hackett, Meridth Hammer, Carolyn McMahon, Lois Reed, Carla Rickerson, Cherie Sommers, Michael Stier, Rick Van Brimmer, Donald Walker, and Linda Wobbe.

To the anonymous readers for the University of North Carolina Press I am grateful for many useful suggestions, most fundamentally to reorganize my material thematically. At the press itself, the editorial guidance of David Perry and the copyediting of Eric Schramm have made this a better book. To them, and to the entire staff at UNC Press with whom I have worked, I offer my thanks as well.

One note on the text: in the chapters that follow, I have routinely used a number of conventional abbreviations: NYU for New York University, CCNY for City College of New York, LSU for Louisiana State University, SMU for Southern Methodist University, TCU for Texas Christian University, USC for the University of Southern California, and UCLA for the University of California at Los Angeles (as well as Cal for the University of California at Berkeley and Pitt for the University of Pittsburgh); NCAA for National Collegiate Athletic Association, ACC for Atlantic Coast Conference, SEC for Southeastern Conference, SWC for Southwest Conference, and PCC for Pacific Coast Conference; NFL for National Football League, AFL for American Football League, AAFC for All-America Football Conference; AP for Associated Press,

UP for United Press, INS for International News Service; and *SI* for *Sports Illustrated*.

Any book of long gestation marks a period in its author's life. Over the years of researching and writing this one, my wife and I have watched our older son blossom into a high-school and small-college basketball star and our younger son take to football with the same passion I remember as a boy. A father's pleasure in his sons' startling athletic elegance and exuberant tenacity has confirmed my own sense that sports can still offer positive experiences, without blinding me to the ways that sports can also do harm. My book is neither an indictment nor a defense of football but an attempt to understand what it meant to a broad range of Americans during the period when it assumed a major presence in the national life. As always, I share this book with Julie, Colin, and Alan, the ones who matter most, but I formally dedicate it to the teacher and scholar who introduced me to the study of sport, and who, through his wisdom, friendship, and personal example, has guided me through a quarter-century of my professional life.

King Football

Introduction

In 1932, a book titled *King Football* indicted the big-time intercollegiate sport for commercialism, anti-intellectualism, distorted priorities, fraud, hypocrisy—the full range of charges currently in the air. The author was Reed Harris, who had been the editor of Columbia University's campus newspaper until March of that year, when the administration expelled him for his attacks on various university practices including its sponsorship of a big-time football team. Harris was reinstated on appeal (after a student strike and intervention by the Civil Liberties Union) but declined the privilege and wrote *King Football* instead.

A few years later, another radical critic, James Wechsler, appropriated Harris's title for discussing the sport in his own book about student militancy and administrative repression. Wechsler was sympathetic to football players, who toiled for little pay, but he despised the institutionalized game as a reactionary force on campus.[1] For Harris and Wechsler, "King Football" was a vulgar, bloated, mead-swilling pretender.

For the editors of the pulp magazine *Sport Story*, welcoming the 1932 season with a hearty "Hail, King Football!" His Majesty was a jolly and benign ruler, presiding over three months of festivity. This was the majority viewpoint. An article in 1933 in the *Literary Digest* by the *New York Sun*'s George Trevor worried about how "King Football" was faring in the Depression. The following season, a six-column cartoon in the *Portland Oregonian* captured the merry monarch in all his gaiety—"Here Comes King Football, the Popular Old Rascal, to Demand the Attention That Is His Due This Time of Year"—as did the program for the Ohio State–NYU game in 1936.

By 1938, "King Football" was among the clichés of the sport satirized by a writer in the *Atlantic Monthly,* but the sportive monarch easily survived such mockery. An editorial in the 1939 inaugural issue of *Football News* joyfully proclaimed, "At this time of year we look to King Football to wear the crown in his royal manner." A history of the sport in a magazine published by the Dow Chemical Company in 1947 had the title "King Football." His Highness still ruled as late as 1963, when a history of the high school sport celebrated the rise of "King Football in Texas."[2]

THE REIGN OF "KING FOOTBALL"

My book is a study of "King Football" from the 1920s through the 1950s, a period mostly marked by the enthusiasm of the editors of *Sport Story* and the *Football News*, but rarely without the censure of a Reed Harris or James Wechsler. My underlying question will be a simple one: what did football mean to the actual millions who followed it, whether casually or passionately, during this period? The book continues an investigation I began several years ago in *Reading Football: How the Popular Press Created an American Spectacle*. Football was born on college campuses in the Northeast in the 1870s and reached its first maturity, its acceptance as a spectator sport, by the 1890s. Popularity by no means meant unambivalent embrace, however; football's early decades were marked by hyperbolic condemnation as well as praise. Controversies over "professionalism," "overemphasis," and, above all, brutality provoked periodic efforts at reform, culminating in major revisions of playing rules and institutional practices in 1906, 1910, and 1912. Having begun as a version of rugby, American football developed in the 1880s and 1890s along the lines of infantry warfare, as the first generation of coaches devised various strategies for massing the offensive attack on a vulnerable point in the defensive line. What pleased coaches appalled critics of the resulting mayhem and, more pragmatically important for football's future, risked boring its newly won fans. Those fans were drawn to the game, in large part, by the sensationalized coverage in their daily newspapers, inaugurated by Joseph Pulitzer and his rivals in New York who created the modern newspaper. With the game uneasily established as both an extracurricular activity and a great public spectacle, the rule makers opened up play, most significantly by legalizing the forward pass, and largely completed the transformation of American football from its rugby beginnings to the game we know today.

Football thus reached its second maturity on the eve of the Great War in Europe. A handful of schools had dropped the sport for its brutality, and Cal, Stanford, and some other West Coast universities had briefly abandoned American football for the less-brutal rugby version, but otherwise intercollegiate football was now played throughout the country, and high schools everywhere were adopting the collegians' game.[3] Professional football had as yet no formal organization or even social acceptance, but former college stars had played for pay as "ringers" on athletic club teams since 1892, and by the early 1900s professional teams were forming in many midwestern towns.[4]

The outbreak of war interrupted football's development, only to spur it to greater growth afterward. Football's "Big Three," Harvard, Yale, and Princeton, were among the colleges that suspended their football programs as the United States was drawn into the conflict, while others scaled back and the game's promotional engines were geared down. Walter Camp named no All-America team for 1917, and the Rose Bowl in 1918 and 1919 featured service teams instead of collegians. But the war also turned out to be an impetus to the tremendous growth of football in the 1920s. Walter Camp helped organize a service-football program that introduced the game to thousands of young men. An editorial in the *New York Times* in 1919 declared that "football owes more to the war in the way of the spread of the spirit of the game than it does to ten or twenty years of development in the period before the war."[5] Equally significant, one of the greatest shocks war brought to educational leaders was the discovery that as a nation we were physically deficient. During the war, patriotic articles in such magazines as *American Boy* declared that the American system of school athletics trained young men in discipline, courage, teamwork, endurance, and other qualities necessary to soldiers.[6] Following the armistice, however, General Leonard Wood reported that half the American men drafted had been unfit for service. An avalanche of calls followed for mandatory physical education and for intramural and interscholastic athletic programs. Historians point to this "preparedness crisis" as an important context for the renewed emphasis on rugged sports as Americans returned to peacetime pursuits. Concern over the country's physical health, at the same time the economy was booming, leisure time was expanding, and the marketing of a new consumption ethic went into high gear, helped generate the sporting explosion of the 1920s.[7]

King Football picks up the story at this point. His majesty's reign began in the years between the two World Wars, when football underwent tremendous growth at all levels. In 1920, both a National Federation of State High School Athletic Associations and the organization that became the National Football League were formed. In that year, just 16.8 percent of Americans finished high school, but as that figure increased to nearly 50 percent by 1940, football became a basic part of high school life.[8] By 1923, 91 percent of high schools in one survey had football teams, and in forty-five of forty-eight states the teams belonged to the statewide interscholastic leagues and athletic associations that have continued to this day.[9] Newspaper coverage of high school football grew as well. Weekly column-inches of interscholastic sport coverage in the *New York Times* increased from about 200 at the turn

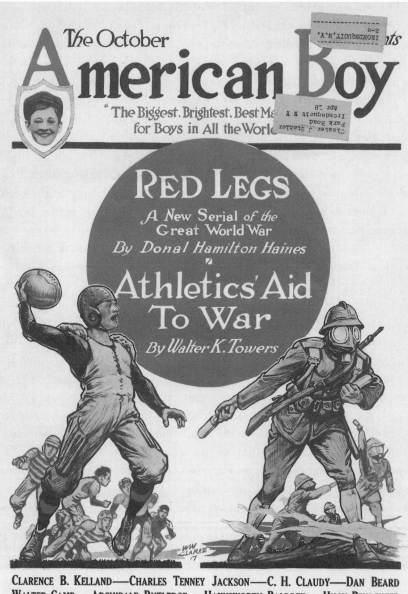

FIGURE I-1. Football as preparation for war: cover of *American Boy*, October 1917.

of the century to almost 1,000 by the First World War, then shot up to nearly 3,200 by 1926; that expansion played out in other newspapers as well. By the early 1930s, high school coaches were torn between the welcome impact and adverse effects of newspaper publicity: while it helped to boost attendance and gate receipts, the added attention could also negatively affect the impressionable boys who played the game.[10] The largest crowds for scholastic football watched the Catholic vs. Public league championships in Chicago and Philadelphia, and benefit games such as the PTA Milk Fund Carnival in Los Angeles, but the fiercest passions were likely aroused by the more routine contests played by the teams from rival towns all over the country. By the end of the 1930s, even the smallest rural high schools could field teams, through the invention of six-man football by a high school teacher in Hebron, Nebraska.[11]

The National Football League was born, as the now well-told story has it, in the office of an auto agency in Canton, Ohio, when the representatives from a handful of midwestern professional clubs formed the American Professional Football Conference.[12] What became the NFL in 1922 was strictly an industrial and milltown league, with transient teams and transient players, scorn from amateur purists, and indifference from the larger public. Apathy briefly turned to fascination in 1925, when Red Grange joined the Chicago Bears immediately following his final college game for the University of Illinois. Crowds instantly swelled to see the most famous football player in the land—the Galloping Ghost, the Wheaton Ice Man—but even Grange could not sustain interest in a football league to which most of the country felt no connection. The reorganization of the NFL in 1933 into its current structure of big-city clubs in two divisions, their leading teams playing for a national championship, launched professional football on its slow ascent to the pinnacle of American spectator sports.

Pro football paid poorly, attracting mostly collegians who could do no better in the depressed job market of the 1930s, but it was sufficiently profitable for owners to attract rival leagues. The NFL's first organized opposition was the American Football League, formed in 1926 by Grange and his agent, C. C. Pyle; it lasted but one year. A second and third incarnation of the AFL each survived two seasons, 1936–37 and 1940–41, again with negligible impact on the NFL.[13] The fourth rival league, the All-America Football Conference (1946–49), was considerably more consequential, temporarily escalating salaries and contributing three teams (the Cleveland Browns, San Francisco 49ers, and Baltimore Colts) to a restructured NFL. By this time, the New York Giants and Chicago Bears had become the principal football teams in the country's two largest cities, but it was not until the coming of television after World War II that the professional game could reach, and hold, a national audience.

Among the pros who became major stars with the coming of television in the postwar era, a disproportionate number were African American. This development followed what had been an unofficial but absolute ban on black players from 1934 through 1945, apparently demanded by the owner of the Boston (later Washington) Redskins, George Preston Marshall. Black stars of the 1930s such as Iowa's Oze Simmons and UCLA's Kenny Washington graduated from college football to minor professional leagues on the East or West Coast, not to the Giants or Bears. Reintegration was provoked by two factors in 1946: pressure on the Los Angeles Rams from local black leaders, who threatened to block the team's lease of the Los Angeles Coliseum; and the challenge of the All-America Football Conference, whose Cleveland Browns immediately signed two black future Hall of Famers, Bill Willis and Marion Motley, and dominated professional football over the next decade with conspicuously integrated teams.[14] NFL clubs gradually integrated over the late 1940s and 1950s, with the Washington Redskins holding out until 1962. By this time, professional football was a truly national sport, with a huge and growing TV audience; the sudden-death overtime championship game in 1958 is usually recognized as a turning point in the public's embrace of pro football through television.

However significant the expansion of high school football and the birth, then restructuring, of a major professional league, it was the growth of college football into a spectator sport to rival major league baseball that most importantly marks the years between the two world wars.[15] Given the relatively low percentage of Americans who attended college—8 percent of 18–21 year olds in 1920, increasing only to 12 percent in 1930, a little less than 16 percent in 1940 (still not quite 30 percent in 1950, despite the thousands attending on the GI Bill)—college football's broad appeal is remarkable.[16] Attendance at college football games increased 119 percent in the 1920s, exceeding 10 million by the end of the decade, slightly more than for major league baseball. Both as cause and effect of the tremendous new enthusiasm for football, a stadium-building boom in the 1920s planted huge concrete and brick bowls in landscapes throughout the Midwest, South, and Far West in the 1920s. By 1930 there were seventy-four concrete stadiums, fifty-five of them built since 1920, six of them with a seating capacity exceeding 70,000, including the Rose Bowl in Pasadena (1922), the Los Angeles Coliseum (1923), and Soldier Field in Chicago (1924). About 60 percent of the attendance at college football came from some forty institutions whose teams played in these massive structures.[17] Eight Big Ten universities built or expanded their football stadiums in the 1920s, including Illinois's 67,000-seat Memorial Stadium, whose formal dedication in 1924 was marked by Red Grange's astonishing six-touchdown performance against Michigan. That game became an instant legend because of the occasion, the size of the crowd, and the unusually large presence of the media—all the elements, that is, of football as media spectacle—now in place for the first time.

Before the age of television, football was fundamentally local—"our boys" against all others—and what college football offered fans that professional and high school football could not was a local team competing in a national arena. As football teams became public symbols of universities, communities, and entire regions in a hugely publicized national drama, intersectional games and postseason bowl games proliferated in the 1920s and 1930s. The upset of Harvard in 1921 by tiny Centre College made the unthinkable seem possible for every football team with ambitions; Notre Dame, an insignificant Catholic college transformed into a national phenomenon, became the model for university-building through the football team. Football power shifted westward in the 1920s and southward in the 1930s. Football regions became defined by major conferences: the Western (Big Ten), Pacific Coast, Southeastern, Southwest, and Big Six, more or less in that order of descending prestige. The East remained loosely confederated, with the Big Three of Harvard, Yale, and Princeton maintaining their preeminence as football's founders even as their football prowess waned. The Rose Bowl, which served as an unofficial East-West championship game in the 1920s, had to share New Year's Day with the Orange Bowl beginning in 1933, then the Sugar Bowl in 1935 and the Cotton Bowl in 1937. They were soon joined by dozens more as promoters throughout the Sun Belt sought to cash in, until the NCAA stepped in to regulate the bowl games in the 1950s.

The drama of each season played out in weekly episodes, as hundreds of teams battled for regional and national honors, and a new set of heroes held the public's attention for a few months; but each season was also attended by major or minor controversies deriving from that inextricable mixing of sport and promotion out of which big-time football was born. The Carnegie Foundation's report in 1929 on the widespread recruiting and subsidizing of athletes in a so-called amateur game undoubtedly provoked soul-searching in many university administrators, but its impact was blunted by indifference and outright resistance from the general public and the sportswriters whose columns they read. The elements of "professionalism" denounced by the Carnegie report eventually became standard practices, but not before three more decades of wrangling over the ethics of college football, with economics trumping ethics at each step along the way. Harvard, Yale, and Princeton, along with Penn, Cornell, Brown, Columbia, and Dartmouth, agreed in 1945 to a "deemphasized" brand of football, initially dropping scholarships, then in 1952 banning spring practice and bowl games as well, finally in 1956 officially becoming the Ivy League.[18] The Big Three, who taught the rest of America's colleges all the tricks of highly professionalized football, changed course, while King Football continued to rule elsewhere in the same old merry way.

Intercollegiate football endured the Depression more successfully than it did post–World War II prosperity. Attendance at college football games peaked in the late 1920s, dropped in the early years of the Depression, then crept back to 1920s levels just as the outbreak of war again put football on hold. Many schools suspended their programs, with wartime rations restricting travel for the rest. Colleges with military-training units walloped teams of seventeen- and eighteen-year-olds; service teams such as Iowa Pre-Flight and Great Lakes Naval Training Station were among the collegiate powerhouses; and Army—swelled by draft-avoiding transfers from other colleges—dominated all. After the armistice, as dozens of schools dropped football as too expensive, others threw themselves desperately into the pursuit of talented players, successful coaches, and the victories that both could bring. Concern over the ethics of big-time college football reached an unprecedented level, but not to the point that it forced radical reform. At the same time, attendance leapt immediately after the war, then dropped alarmingly and inched up slowly over the 1950s. A massive shift in American leisure habits was taking place, as a rejuvenated middle class moved to the suburbs and discovered new sources of amusement, but college officials were convinced that the enemy more simply was television. As the NFL embraced the new medium, the NCAA did everything in its power to keep football fans sitting in the stadium rather than in front of their TV sets, only in the 1960s recognizing the enormous revenues television could deliver.

Unlike the NFL, college football had never been totally segregated, but the postwar era likewise marked its more thorough, yet still incomplete, integration. The original elite game created by the Anglo-Saxon sons of Harvard, Yale, and Princeton was partially democratized in the 1920s and 1930s by a tremendous influx of Italian, Polish, Jewish, and other eastern and southern European immigrants, for whom football was a vehicle for achieving American success. While the ethnic transformation of college football caused uneasiness in some quarters, African Americans faced immeasurably greater resistance. Numerous schools outside the South—though by no means all—were minimally integrated as early as the 1890s, but no school anywhere in the country had more than a small handful of black players before the 1950s. Among the Big Three, for example, Harvard had a black player, William Henry Lewis, in 1892, but Princeton not until 1945 (Melvin Murcheson) and Yale until 1946 (Levi Jackson).

In general, northeastern universities integrated their football teams first. Integration (along with football power) moved westward in the first quarter of the twentieth century, centering most conspicuously in the Big Ten. By the 1930s, black football players could be found in every region of the country except the South, but most teams in any given year were all white—including, most conspicuously, Notre Dame and several other Catholic universities, along with Army and Navy.[19] Beginning in 1939, when Kenny Washington, Jackie Robinson, and Woody Strode starred at UCLA, along with a fourth black teammate, a few universities began to exceed the minimal tokenism of the period, while the Pacific Coast Conference joined the Big Ten in recruiting record numbers of black players. World War II fostered integration by creating a need to replace players departed for the armed services, and after the "war to save democracy," denying opportunities to returning black vets, and to all black citizens, seemed more hypocritical than ever. By 1955 there were sixty-three black players in the Big Ten, thirteen of them at Indiana, eleven at both Illinois and Michigan.[20] The Rose Bowl game that season between UCLA and Michigan State featured five blacks in the starting lineups, and four African Americans made the *Look* All-America team.

The significance of the accelerated integration of college football in the late 1940s and early 1950s, together with the reintegration of professional football (and baseball more conspicuously), must be recognized in the context of the civil rights movement: the postwar period marks a rare moment when sport did not follow but led a major transformation of American society. But the process was slow. The Big Six conference was integrated in 1947 and the Missouri Valley Conference in 1950, but the three major southern conferences remained entirely segregated until 1963, when Maryland took the lead in the Atlantic Coast Conference, the northernmost of the three. Integration by conference and within conferences proceeded north to south. The ACC was followed by the Southwest Conference in 1966, with all its schools integrated by 1970 when Texas and Arkansas fielded teams with black players. The Southeastern Conference integrated last, beginning with Kentucky in 1967 and Tennessee in 1968, ending with Mississippi, LSU, and Georgia in 1972.[21] There was no Jackie Robinson in football. There were William Henry Lewis, Fritz Pollard, Paul Robeson, Duke Slater, Joe Lillard, Oze Simmons, Kenny Washington, Buddy Young, Marion Motley, Levi Jackson, J. C. Caroline, Jim Brown, Bobby Mitchell—a collective "Jackie Robinson" who broke through the color line not in a single burst but a step at a time.

Over the long reign of Jim Crow in college football, all-black colleges created a separate but unequal football world beginning in 1892.[22] The black colleges had their own conferences, their own traditional rivalries, their own postseason bowl games and All-America teams, their own dynasties and star players and school mascots and bands, even their own controversies in the black press over corruption and reform. Most teams operated on meager budgets, with poor equipment, facilities, and, until the 1930s, coaching. Played before crowds typically of five thousand or fewer, black college football games never came close to rivaling Negro League baseball and the championship bouts of Joe Louis and Henry Armstrong in importance, but Homecoming and Thanksgiving Day contests among the top schools were major events on black America's social calendar in the fall. A sociologist at Howard University in 1927 described the annual Howard-Lincoln Thanksgiving football classic as a magnet drawing ten thousand black Americans for a week of parties, dances, and other entertainment preceding the football game.[23] In addition to Howard-Lincoln, annual contests between Tuskegee and Atlanta, Morgan and Hampton, Wiley and Prairie View were the Harvard-Yale, Army-Navy, and Army–Notre Dame of black-college football. With most of these schools located in the South, far from the black metropolises, promoters sometimes scheduled black-college classics for Soldier Field in Chicago, Municipal Stadium in Philadelphia, and the Polo Grounds in New York. Even here, crowds rarely exceeded 20,000 in stadiums seating three, four, and five times that many. This was football for an enthusiastic minority, not the majority, but that minority had its own fully formed football world. The black press celebrated "Jazz" Byrd of Lincoln University in the 1920s as the "Black Red Grange." Tuskegee's Ben Stevenson, Kentucky State's "Tarzan" Kendall, and Morris Brown's "Big Train" Moody filled the roles of Bronko Nagurski, Sammy Baugh, and Tom Harmon in a pantheon of black-college football heroes. But such players and their teams were virtually unknown in the larger world of college football, until Grambling in the 1960s became one of the NFL's major sources of star players.

FOOTBALL, THE MEDIA, AND AMERICAN CULTURE

The history of football just outlined is inextricably tied to the history of the media, each developing very differently if not for the other. The daily press had been present at the birth of American football and was chiefly responsible for transforming it into a national sport by the end of the nineteenth century. As the 1920s opened, sports coverage in the typical daily newspaper was relatively meager and subdued, but it doubled over the decade, as the mammoth sports sections with which we are now familiar developed. The newspaper remained the primary source of information about football for the serious football fan, but other media had greater impact in the 1930s in broadening the audience of casual observers. The 1920s has been known virtually since the decade ended as the Golden Age of Sports, but the 1930s was more truly the Golden Age of Football. College football had been a phenomenon in the 1920s; in the 1930s, it was utterly familiar, and that media-created familiarity is the point. Commercial radio began in 1920 and football broadcasts soon after, but it was not until the end of the decade that three networks and local radio stations everywhere were broadcasting games each week, to the point that in many communities in the 1930s football was just about the only thing to be found on the radio dial on Saturday afternoons.

Newsreels had brought images of football games into movie theaters since the beginning of the century and continued to do so through the 1920s, but two major newsreels became five by the end of the decade, and with the addition of sound beginning in 1927 they achieved their full power. Over the 1930s football in the fall (and other sports throughout the rest of the year) eventually accounted for 20 to 25 percent of newsreel footage. Everyone went to the movies in the 1930s, and if you came to watch a movie you saw a newsreel as well. Of those movies themselves, 48 in the 1930s were full-length football films, 40 percent of the 120 football movies that appeared between 1920 and 1960 (94, or nearly 80 percent, were made between 1925, Red Grange's senior season, and 1942). In an additional 28 nonfootball films in the 1930s, the heroes were introduced as football stars or former stars—football simply as shorthand to establish their heroic masculine character—or football figured in some other incidental way.[24] Four of these were westerns—*Arizona* (1931), *Fighting Through* (1934), *The Gay Caballero* (1934), and *Six-Gun Rhythm* (1939)—wedding football to the most powerful heroic narrative outside the world of sports. (In the same vein, NFL quarterback Sammy Baugh starred in a twelve-episode serial, *King of the Texas Rangers,* in 1941, as an All-American football star who joins the Rangers to avenge his father's death and save the Texas oil fields from foreign saboteurs.)

The *Saturday Evening Post* became an American institution in the 1920s, but not until the end of the decade did it begin routinely to publish articles on football. In the 1930s, both the *Post* and *Collier's,* its chief rival among the general-interest weeklies, carried an article on football virtually every week during the season. In addition, the two magazines together published forty-two football stories and six serials in the 1930s, by far the greatest concentration for any decade. The football story's basic plot became so formulaic that *Look* magazine in 1937 could serialize it as a photoplay with just brief captions to develop the narrative: the hero's rival frames him for poor sportsmanship, getting him kicked off the team and in conflict with his girl, but he is exonerated, wins the big game, and wins back his sweetheart.[25] Not every subscriber read the football fiction and journalism in the *Post* and *Collier's,* but all saw the football covers, 46 of which appeared in the 1930s, out of a total of 113 for the entire period. It was in this decade, in short, that all of the major media became saturated with football during the fall months. Football was on the page, on the screen, and on the airwaves wherever one turned from October into January. While the autumn season was ruled by King Football, there was little choice but to be a willing or unwilling subject.

The period of my study ends in 1960, a date that approximates the full arrival of television to transform the sport once more. Newspapers continued as the primary source for the daily unfolding of football's drama, but television usurped the roles of the other media. Radio became again what it had started out to be, a medium for covering the local football team, as network television became the primary medium of the national sport. Television newscasts also took over the role of newsreels, as the five major producers of the ten-minute shorts dropped out between 1956 and 1967. After its founding in 1954, *Sports Illustrated* struggled to find its voice and its audience in the 1950s but thrived in the new world of televised football, becoming a sporting institution in the 1960s under the inspired editorship of André Laguerre.[26] The general interest magazines, however, all but disappeared: *Liberty* folded in 1951 and *Collier's* in 1957, while the *Saturday Evening Post* lasted until 1968, *Look* until 1971, and *Life* until 1972. Photographs completely replaced artwork on football covers, and real games on television almost totally usurped the storytelling role of football fiction in both magazines and movies (football films made a comeback beginning in the 1970s).

After 1960, whatever football meant to its growing numbers of fans was increasingly shaped by television.

The world of football constructed by the pre-television media is the subject of the following chapters. What football contributed to American culture during this period lies in the myriad details from newspapers and magazines, newsreels and radio broadcasts and movies, but the details also point to some general assessments of football's place in American life. Commentators who pondered the relative popularity of baseball and football early in this period frequently concluded that baseball was Americans' national pastime but football our greatest spectacle.[27] Writing in 1928 in the staid *North American Review,* a journal more typically inclined to take a dim view of university-sponsored mass entertainment, Samuel Grafton not only declared football the nation's most colorful spectacle, he insisted that "repressed" Americans — this was the decade of the revolt against "puritanism" and the embrace of Freud — needed football because they were "afraid of color and display. . . . We are incorrigibly fearful of any vicarious vent for our cave man impulses. Instead of regarding football, as we should, as a gloriously recurring pageant of strength and skill and loyalty, we look upon it as a blight, a brilliant one, perhaps, but, none the less, a blight. Instead of seeing in football an authentic folk expression as real and definite as the jousts of the Middle Ages or the games of the Greeks, we look upon it as an enormous fungoid growth."[28]

Grafton overstated the opposition to football — it was more characteristic of readers of the *North American Review* than of the American public at large — but he couched his rebuttal in revealing terms. The pageantry and spectacle of football were what Eric Hobsbawm has called "invented traditions" rather than "an authentic folk expression," as Grafton would have it, but they were no less powerful for being modern and manufactured.[29] As a sport, football meant heroic males, their masculinity exaggerated by padded uniforms, engaged in struggles of almost primitive physical combat but governed by the most modern forms of discipline and strategy. As spectacle, football meant wild enthusiasm generated by "college spirit" and the pageantry that accompanied every big game. Bands and cheers (led by male students) had been a part of the game long before the 1920s; in that decade, card sections, mascots, and female cheerleaders were added to college football's pageantry. Bonfires and pep rallies on the eve of the game, fraternity and sorority decorations for Homecoming weekend, Homecoming queens and drum majorettes, garlanded floats in the Tournament of Roses parade, all came to be identified with college football in the public mind.

In April 1952, a writer named Ralph Cooper Hutchison in the non-denominational religious journal, *Christian Century,* attempted to explain what all this had come to mean. Writing in the midst of college football's gravest ethical crisis since 1905, Hutchison did not wish to heap more scorn on the colleges' scandalous behavior and hypocrisy, but to urge readers to understand what was at stake:

> Through no design or deliberation on the part of any man or group of men, football has become the emotionally integrating force of the American college. . . . It is the symbol about which are gathered the loyalties of students, faculty, alumni and friends of the college. These loyalties are to the college, to the culture for which it stands, to the ideas it embodies and the service it renders. These loyalties are, to some degree, to the very spiritual and Christian character of the college. Football is merely the integrating symbol about which such loyalties are rallied and through which they are integrated.

Against the fragmentation of the modern curriculum and the expansion of enrollments, through football "all elements of college society enjoy a common experience—athlete and nonathlete, student and professor, town and gown, men, women and children. Thus," reasoned Hutchison, "football grew beyond a spectacle and became a symbol of the great intangibles. Then and only then did it develop its excesses, its flamboyant extravagances, its deceptions and dishonesties." [30]

Hutchison overstated the breadth and depth of football's hold on the college community, and he ignored the "excesses" and "dishonesties" that also plagued the earliest years of the game, but his account of the role that football had come to play in college life, and American life more generally, was remarkably acute. At a time when sentimentality and cynicism governed public debate—football as character-building, football as corruption—Hutchison demanded recognition of football's subtler power as an "integrating symbol." The problem with intercollegiate football, according to Hutchison, was not that it was a great public spectacle, subsidized by misguided institutions of higher learning, but that it sacrificed academic integrity in producing that spectacle. The spectacle itself was a crucial part of football's value; it constituted the "symbol" beyond the game itself, making football valuable to the entire community, not just to a few dozen varsity players.

A few years later, the sociologist Max Lerner seemed to cast football and other spectator sports very differently. "The psychic basis of American mass sports," wrote Lerner in 1957, "is tribal and feudal."[31] This tribal nature was manifest superficially in teams' totem symbols (Dodgers, Pirates, Braves, and so on) and more deeply in the fan's attachment to a single team, perhaps a single player, who became a "god" or an "immortal" in a pantheon of heroes. Baseball provided most of Lerner's examples, but he included football in his analysis. In emphasizing football's exclusive rather than inclusive tendencies, Lerner did not contradict Hutchison but viewed sporting partisanship differently. Football aroused fierce loyalty to the school's or town's or region's team, "integrating" the community, as Hutchison argued, but on an exclusionary "tribal" basis. It was also tribal in some ways that Lerner did not have in mind. Football fans identified with their favorite teams not only through geography but also by race, religion, and ethnicity. During the years when Hutchison and Lerner wrote, while the multi-ethnic makeup of football lineups became unremarkable, the racial integration of football was still two decades from even token achievement.

Magazines such as *Life* and *Look, Collier's* and the *Post,* symbolically "integrated" football in several other ways over the period of this study. Since the 1890s, the popular image of the football hero had shared space in the mass media with such icons as the adoring female fan and the cheering throngs, but the mass-circulation general-interest magazines in the 1920s, 1930s, and 1940s expanded football's popular iconography. Much more often than football heroes, the covers of the *Post* and *Collier's* featured lovely coeds, cheerleaders, and perky drum majorettes, college bandsmen, campus revelers, dirt-smeared boys (sometimes with disapproving mothers)—the full range of football's domestic and social universe. *Look* and particularly *Life* in the 1940s and 1950s specialized in photo-essays on the college football weekend and on football in small-town America where the entire community rallied round the high school team. By the 1950s, everyone was invited into King Football's domain, though sometimes on terms that most Americans today would consider unacceptable. Women now are no longer relegated to the sidelines of sport; black athletes have transformed the games to which they once sought admission. Football in this earlier period was simultaneously integrative and exclusive. It represented the racial, class, gender, regional, and religious values and prejudices of a diverse people, while at the same time providing a common interest where those people came together, their prejudices in tow.

Football was both "integrative" and "tribal," then, and in their broadest implications these terms can serve as touchstones for the chapters that follow, in which I attempt, quite simply, to reconstruct the world of football experienced through the media during the period from 1920 to 1960. As cultural history, *King Football* is not primarily the story of the great players, coaches, and teams of the era, nor of the powerful individuals and institutions—team owners, universities, media corporations, the National Collegiate Athletic Association, the National Football League—who shaped the sport to their interests. Rather, it is the story of the game encountered through the media by the fans, both casual and committed, as well as the larger public. A full scholarly history of college football finally appeared as I was putting the final touches to my own book. Making full use of university archives, John Watterson's *College Football* is a history of who did what, not on the field but in the board room and the president's office, as the game developed into the highly professionalized commercial spectacle we have come to know. My book, in contrast, is an attempt to understand what the public thought about football as it developed, and where it got its information.

As the creators of our football culture, "the media" signify faceless corporations wielding enormous power on a national scale, but "the media" are also the specific sportswriters, magazine journalists and cover artists, broadcasters, newsreel photographers, and filmmakers who produced the words and images that shaped this football world within the constraints of corporate power. A handful of figures—not only the well-remembered Grantland Rice but also mostly forgotten men like Graham McNamee, Francis Wallace, J. C. Leyendecker, and William Fay—contributed disproportionately to the ways that Americans thought and fantasized about football during this period. McNamee developed the radio broadcaster's style that set excitement and entertainment above simple accuracy. Wallace wrote both magazine journalism and fictional serials (from which several feature films were made) that taught millions of readers and viewers to think about football as a semi-sordid business ruled by boosters in which good nonetheless triumphed. Through magazine covers and clothing ads, J. C. Leyendecker virtually invented the still-familiar visual image of the football hero, as well as the once ubiquitous but now long-forgotten football-playing ragamuffin kid. William Fay's short stories in the *Post* and *Collier's* in the 1940s created an enduring portrait of professional football players as heroic yet childlike, irresponsible but lovable bums. *King Football* examines the contributions of these individuals, but it is also an account of the conventional, formulaic narratives and images produced by dozens of seemingly interchangeable writers, broadcasters, and artists responsible for what today would be called the "product" of the period's most powerful communications media.

Unfortunately, this book cannot be a history of what football meant to its actual fans—that would be my wish—but only of the media universe within which they lived. Newspapers, magazines, radio, newsreels, and movies can reveal the ideas and images in widest currency, but they cannot finally tell us how their audiences understood them. For my earlier book *Reading Football*, I could claim with some confidence that most Americans learned what football meant in the 1880s and 1890s through their daily newspapers, because they overwhelmingly encountered the game in the press before seeing a contest actually played. For the period 1920–60, the media were collectively more pervasive and powerful, yet no single medium commanded the influence of the daily press in the 1890s; and, moreover, football fans experienced the game directly and developed their own informal football cultures outside the oversight of the media. My claims about what football meant during this period must therefore be tentative, and the hearts and minds of actual fans must remain elusive. Nonetheless, I have those audiences always in mind as I recount the ways that different media represented the game.

All of the media during the period of this study shared a common need to please the most and offend the fewest, in order to sell the largest possible audience to advertisers. The following chapters thus trace not a history of football and American "popular" culture but of football and American "middle-class" culture—a middle class, of course, with which a broad range of Americans identified themselves. This was no monolithic "mass culture" but a diverse, often self-contradictory one, and I attempt to illuminate it further through perspectives from outside the mainstream, such as those provided by black and immigrant newspapers and the Communist Party's *Daily Worker*. For the mainstream itself, I hope to capture its range and complexity through the comprehensiveness of my materials. Newspapers shared common material from the major wire services but also spoke to their own communities; *Life* and *Look* specialized in different kinds of articles from those in the *Saturday Evening Post* and *Collier's;* newsreels and radio broadcasts bring neglected sources to the reconstruction of football's cultural history. Most unconventionally, I also move freely between fact and fiction: between the local newspaper's account of last Saturday's game, a magazine profile of a prominent coach, the magazine's cover painting of a lovely lady ministering to her wounded football hero, and a short story or film about the son of a coal miner subsidized to play football at Ivy College or State U. Fiction has less been neglected than rejected as a resource for historians, but if the goal is to understand how people thought about football, the fantasies concocted by magazine covers and short stories were clearly important. I try to be properly attentive to the nature of the material, and to the ways that viewers or readers engaged it, while recognizing that audiences do not always consciously sort out the myriad images and narratives with which the media saturate the culture. Football's cultural power derived from this saturation rather than from distinct, uniquely powerful ideas.

How to organize my material posed a major challenge. Not just football itself, in each of its major forms—professional, intercollegiate, high school, even youth league—but also each of the media through which the game was represented has its own rich history. Every community and region has its own football history as well. A straightforward chronological account, interweaving all these histories season by season, or even decade by decade, seemed less likely to yield a coherent narrative than one more thematically focused. My cultural history of football is thus not a once-, nor a twice-, but a many-times-told tale, each chapter, after the opening one that surveys the media, exploring a particular issue or theme. Part 1 begins with an overview of each of the major media through which football was experienced (Chapter 1), then addresses the fundamental issues of local partisanship (Chapter 2) and reform (Chapter 3) at the heart of the reporting on intercollegiate football during this period. The next three chapters explore aspects of the larger world of football: first the construction of coaches and players as different kinds of football heroes (Chapter 4); then the various elements of football spectacle and its broader social world (Chapter 5); finally the transformation of professional football from an ignored, even despised, perversion of sport in the 1920s to the sport on the verge of becoming the country's favorite as the 1950s ended (Chapter 6). Part 2 then steps back to survey the underlying issues of class (Chapter 7), ethnicity (Chapter 8), race (Chapter 9), and masculinity (Chapter 10) through which football dramatized some of the most fundamental issues of personal and collective identity.

The large claims that I make in this book emerge from the details:

- that football was locally rooted during this period, serving as a powerful source of community identity and pride;
- that the contradiction at the heart of a great commercial spectacle sponsored by institutions of higher learning produced irresolvable ethical dilemmas, and for reasons both structural and personal the media were a powerful force working against reform;
- that the football hero was no monolithic figure but a construct of conflicting values and deep ambivalence;

- that the peculiarly American emphasis on coaches as football's true heroes grew from both the pragmatic necessities of the sports-media business and the broader cultural issues of male authority;
- that football defined not just an arena for male striving but an entire social and domestic world, idealizing a certain model of American middle-class life;
- that professional football gained a national audience through television, but it derived its initial hold on that audience from Cold War anxieties and concerns over the domestication and affluence of middle-class American life;
- that football was an agent of "Americanization" for immigrant groups but more tenaciously maintained its barriers to racial integration and equality;
- that this "democratizing" of the game was entangled with the "corruption" and "hypocrisy" of college football, as well as with anxieties and uncertainties about class and status;
- that in virtually every aspect football was tied to ideas about masculinity;
- and underlying all of these, that the mass media in ways specific to each medium were the most powerful forces in constructing a football culture on these several terms.

Most readers, I suspect, would readily assent to most of these propositions—some have become truisms in our thinking about sport—but in every case I believe that the interest lies in the details.

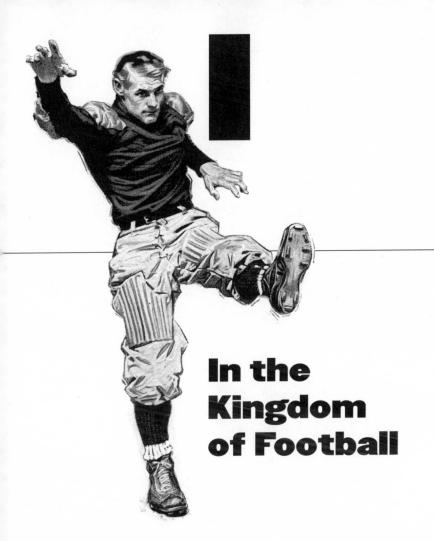

In the
Kingdom
of Football

Reading, Watching, & Listening to Football

On a typical fall weekend in 1939, newspapers, magazines, the radio airwaves, even movie theaters were full of football. For serious football fans, most of the news concerned their local teams, but the rest of the populace could hardly escape exposure to at least some of football's local or national coverage. On 18 November, Atlantans awakened to some final comments in their morning *Constitution* on the Georgia Tech–Alabama contest, with the game itself broadcast later in the day by station WSB. In Los Angeles, the *Times* and KHJ featured UCLA–Santa Clara; in Omaha, the *World-Herald* and KFAB had Nebraska-Pitt; newspapers and radio stations elsewhere carried their own local teams. All these newspapers also ran wire-service stories about the day's most important regional or national games, and NBC's Red and Blue networks, along with CBS and Mutual, broadcast two top regional match-ups, Dartmouth-Cornell and Missouri-Oklahoma, and an intersectional contest between Columbia and Tulane, through affiliates around the country. The *Saturday Evening Post* that week had a football cover: three young male cheerleaders slumping despondently after an obvious loss. Inside, sportswriter Tom Meany explained the peculiar passions of southern football players and their fans. *Collier's* likewise had a football cover, one of four that fall—this one a humorous portrait of a roly-poly player signing an autograph for a lovely fan as he lumbers down the field—along with a profile of St. Mary's coach Slip Madigan. *Life* ran Bill Stern's All-America team

that week; *Look* had a piece on southwestern football. Some local movie theaters showed Joe E. Brown's and Martha Raye's *$1000 a Touchdown* or Bert
Wheeler's *Cowboy Quarterback,* though neither of them was faring well with
either reviewers or the public.[1] Movie theaters everywhere ran a newsreel
before the feature film, with highlights of the previous weekend's Princeton-
Dartmouth and Notre Dame–Iowa contests, along with a few other top college games.

All this coverage cumulatively cast football as a great national sport, pageant, and spectacle, with countless local variants and several different faces
—all of them white, non-ethnic, and seemingly classless. Other publications
challenged this uniformity. *Nowy Swiat* and *Dziennik Chicagoski* reported exclusively on Polish American football players, *L'Italia* and *Corriere d'America*
on Italian Americans, and other papers on the Jewish-, Lithuanian-, Greek-,
Slovak-, and other "hyphenated" Americans in big-time football. Diocesan
and independent Catholic newspapers in most large cities offered readers a
syndicated weekly column by Marquette coach Paddy Driscoll on the football teams at Catholic colleges. A thriving black press, led by the *Chicago
Defender* and the *Pittsburgh Courier,* provided news of the football played at all-
black colleges and by the handful of African Americans playing in "mixed
football" in the North and West. Even the Communist Party's *Daily Worker*
had a sports page full of football, as part of an effort to reach out to American workers not drawn to radical politics. The national story in 1939, told by
the wire services and the popular magazines, was the rise of southern football, but local sports columnists clung to more partisan judgments.[2] For the
black press and the *Daily Worker,* 1939 was the season of Kenny Washington,
Jackie Robinson, and Woody Strode at UCLA, an unprecedented concentration of black prowess in big-time football. Langston, not Texas A&M, was
national champion in the *Chicago Defender.* Immigrant and Catholic papers
selected All-Polish, All-Italian, All-Jewish, and All-Catholic teams.[3] Little of
the football in any of these newspapers, or on radio or in newsreels and
popular magazines, concerned the professional game, except in the eight
cities with franchises in the National Football League. Big-time college football reigned supreme in 1939 and saturated all the mass media; it was more
difficult to remain oblivious to the sport than to encounter it somewhere.

THE MODERN SPORTS SECTION

The subject of this chapter is the specific contribution of each important
mass medium to the developing culture of football. Football in the United
States has always been experienced primarily through the media. Over the

last quarter of the nineteenth century, at a time when few Americans attended college, the extracurricular sport of young men at Harvard, Yale, and Princeton became a huge spectacle with an enormous popular following through the agency of Joseph Pulitzer and his rivals in New York daily journalism. Wire services brought the Harvard-Yale and Princeton-Yale games to every corner of the country, and the accounts provided models for provincial sportswriters covering their own local teams. By the turn of the century, most urban newspapers had at least a Sunday sports section of several pages, plus a page or two of daily sports coverage, all of which were filled with football in October and November.[4]

Sports coverage increased by 50 percent over the first two decades of the new century, then more than doubled in the 1920s as it became a major reason for men to buy newspapers.[5] Both the demand for more sports and the resultant growth of the sports section caused uneasiness among managing editors. Newspapers were supposedly for news, yet readers (and thus circulation and marketing departments) seemed more interested in sports. A 1929 survey revealed that one in four readers bought the newspaper for the sports section (in later surveys, 80 percent of male readers before World War II and 75 percent afterward read the sports section). Males from all occupational groups ranked sports just behind the front page in interest (while women ranked sports last among seven categories of news). Just as television advertisers would later pay the highest rates in the industry for appearing on the telecast of the Super Bowl, in the 1920s several New York newspapers charged premiums for ads in the sports section, and on three of these dailies the premium was the highest in the paper.[6]

The expanded coverage of sport came from many sources. Since even metropolitan dailies with large sports staffs could cover only a handful of local games, much of the copy in newspapers large and small came from the major wire services—the Associated Press, United Press, and International News Service—and from nearly 200 news, photo, and feature syndicates.[7] The wire services provided much of the basic football news read throughout the country: previews of upcoming games, reports of the past weekend's contests, rankings of teams, attendance reports, and news of rule changes and actions by the major conferences. Syndicated football material ranged from the news services of some of the major dailies (the *New York Herald Tribune* and the *Chicago Tribune*, for example) to the columns of Grantland Rice and well-known football coaches sold by the Christy Walsh Syndicate, John Wheeler's Bell Syndicate, and the North American Newspaper Alliance (NANA); to the photographs of big games and football stars provided by AP Wirephoto, Wide World Photo, and NEA-Acme Telephoto; to football cartoons sold by King Features and its competitors; to Sunday magazines (*American Weekly, This Week,* and later *Parade*) with football features.[8] Collectively, this material produced a degree of uniformity in newspapers throughout the country.

The look of football coverage was determined in part by a new kind of newspaper that appeared in the 1920s: the tabloid. The debut in New York of the *Illustrated Daily News* in 1919 caused no immediate ripples in New York journalism, but by 1921 the *Daily News* was second in circulation only to Hearst's *Evening Journal* and by 1926, when circulation first hit one million, it was number one in the country and remained there into the 1970s. One million copies meant 2.5 million readers, nearly 40 percent of New York's 6.5 million residents. The tabloid was simply a half-page newspaper, more convenient than the standard size for subway riders and railway commuters, and the brevity of the articles better accommodated the pace of modern urban life. But "the tabloids" quickly became notorious for sensationalism, for pictorial excess, for abandoning news in favor of crass entertainment, for exploiting the ill-educated masses—for pandering, in other words, to the worst instincts of the least literate. Contrary to the assumption of elitist critics that the tabloids appealed only to the unwashed masses, however, they were the papers that all classes read. A much higher percentage of the *New York Times*'s readership, for example, came from the upper classes, but a greater number of upper-class readers actually read the *Daily News.* By the mid-1930s there were forty-nine tabloids in small towns as well as large cities, read by millions of "average Americans."[9]

Sports figured importantly in the tabloid formula. An analysis of the three New York tabloids' content for October 1926 claimed 50 to 60 percent of their news space was given to "stories of crime, divorce, scandal, vice and sports." A later historian described the tabloid formula in similar terms: "sex, sports, and sentiment, with healthy doses of crime news thrown in."[10] Sport, no doubt, was the least objectionable part of this formula: only frivolous, not scandalous. Whether sports sold as many copies as the marital secrets of middle-aged "Daddy" Browning and his fifteen-year-old bride "Peaches" is doubtful, but sports coverage—including the back page of sport photos that became standard in tabloids—was crucial to the success of the *Daily News.*[11] The *News,* in turn, taught the rest of the newspaper world the value of graphic material, bold headlines, and lively, personalized writing in the sports section. These were the same lessons taught by Pulitzer and Hearst in the "yellow" 1890s, and before that by the first cheap papers in the 1830s. Over the first quarter of the twentieth century the sensationalism of the 1890s Pulitzer-Hearst duel for circulations subsided, but over the 1920s extravagant sports coverage returned and became more general. The "tabloidization" of the sports section was just one more episode in the development of the modern newspaper.

The sports section that we know today thus became uniform over the 1920s and 1930s. Whether in New York or Nacodoches, Texas, it was composed of both locally written and nationally distributed news and features, making it both distinctive to its own place and similar to other sports sections around the country. Most papers, large and small, ran a wire-service preview of the day's major college games on Saturdays and a recap of those games on Mondays, together with any number of syndicated features throughout the week. Alongside this wire-service and syndicated material, each paper's staff writers covered the local teams and games, usually with daily reports. And against the national and more or less impartial voice of the wire service or syndicated writer, the local sports editor/columnist wrote from the partisan perspective of the paper's own readers. Grantland Rice was by far the most famous sportswriter of the era, and several more became widely known through syndication (Damon Runyon in the many Hearst newspapers, Walter Eckersall and Westbrook Pegler through the Chicago Tribune News Service, a handful of others). But the voice most religiously read, attended to, and quarreled with was that of the local columnist.[12]

Though most of these men were read nowhere else, in Atlanta, H. C. Hamilton, Dick Hawkins, Ed Danforth, Ralph McGill, Jack Troy, John Bradberry, Furman Bisher, and Jesse Outlar were successively the primary voices of football in the *Constitution*. In Portland, the *Oregonian's* L. H. Gregory remained sports editor and columnist throughout the entire period, a single and thus singularly powerful voice for local football in one urban community. In the *Dallas Morning News, Omaha World-Herald,* and *Los Angeles Times,* not just the sports editor but several reporters were regular columnists. In Dallas, the longest-serving sports editors, George White and Bill Rives, were the principal voices; in Omaha, Frederick Ware, Floyd Olds, and Wally Provost had this role. In Los Angeles, over the 1930s, seemingly everyone on the sports staff was a columnist, from sports editors Bill Henry and Paul Zimmerman in the left-hand column on page one of sports, to Braven Dyer, Dick Hyland, and others throughout the section. Of all the papers under discussion here, only the *Chicago Tribune* lacked a truly distinctive voice despite having probably the most famous sports editor outside New York. Arch Ward, as his biographer puts it, was "a promoter, not a poet," the man responsible for the

College All-Star Game (as well as major league baseball's All-Star Game) and the All-America Football Conference. Many of his "In the Wake of the News" columns—more often just tidbits of sports gossip than sustained commentary—were ghostwritten by other *Tribune* staff writers, one of whom later commented, "Arch didn't put too much of a premium on writing." [13]

The names of these writers' columns, and of hundreds of others in papers large and small, were both their authors' signatures and their personal greetings to faithful readers each day. Ed Danforth's "Mawnin'!" column in the *Atlanta Constitution* in 1929 and 1930 announced that fact most explicitly. Distinctive typefaces for the titles served as their authors' own handwriting. Columns sometimes took the form of personal correspondence with (male) readers—just 5 percent of women paid attention to local sports columns (only 2 percent read syndicated ones)—with the column serving as the literary equivalent of the corner bar. Newspapers collectively were a mass medium, but individually they were the voices of specific communities, and the sports column—like the society column, which was women's favorite section after the front page—was highly personal. [14] Even in New York, the columnists for the major dailies—John Kieran and Arthur Daley of the *New York Times*, Paul Gallico and Jimmy Powers of the *Daily News*, Joe Williams in the *World-Telegram*, and so on—wrote about football from a distinctly local perspective for their own papers' readers. Columnists from the hinterlands often took their cues from their more famous, nationally syndicated peers, but they nonetheless gave each community its own characteristic voice.

Generalizations about sportswriting tend to focus on a few large cities: Chicago, perhaps Boston and Philadelphia, above all New York. Following Stanley Walker's already-commonplace distinction in 1934, it has become customary to speak of the "Gee Whiz" and the "Aw Nuts" schools of sportswriting: the florid mythmakers, led by Grantland Rice, and the wry debunkers such as Ring Lardner, Westbrook Pegler, Damon Runyon, and W. O. McGeehan. Perhaps touched by nostalgia as he reflected on his half-century in the business, Rice himself claimed a change with the First World War, after which a "lightheartedness" went out of sportswriting, never to return. Viewing the history of his profession somewhat differently, *New York Post* sports columnist Stanley Frank distinguished between the Golden Age of the 1920s, when "the temper of the expansive times called for garish embellishment and the boys laid on the superlatives and breathless adjectives with a trowel," and the Age of Reason of the 1930s, when "a sense of the fitness of things tempered the writing." Stanley Woodward, sports editor of the *New York Herald Tribune* from 1938 to 1948, declared in 1949 that the sportswriting of the day now belonged to what he termed an "On-the-Button" school, that drew on the strengths of both earlier ones and was best represented by the *Herald Tribune*'s own Red Smith.[15]

Frank and Woodward wrote as if modern sportswriting began in the 1920s, ignoring the generations of the 1890s (for football) and earlier (for baseball and boxing) that actually founded the profession and its styles. Because sport was not regarded as serious news, sportswriters on most newspapers had far greater license than other journalists. Three-quarters of the 125 papers surveyed in 1926 reported that the sports department edited its own copy, "independent of the checks that have been put upon the management of copy in most well-regulated newspapers offices for many years." The "complete liberty in typography, general style, and use of English" that resulted was among the many problems in the world of college sports criticized by the Carnegie report of 1929.[16] However objectionable to language purists, this imaginative freedom contributed enormously to the rendering of football as something on the order of pop mythology, rather than news or even entertainment. Instead of the usual distinction between "Gee Whiz" and "Aw Nuts" sportswriting, I would note shifts in football writing from an "epic" style in the 1890s, to a "heroic" style in the 1920s, then to a "realistic" style in the late 1930s and after, though at no time did a single mode obliterate all others. The signature of the epic style was the overblown classical allusion: football players as gladiators, the stadium as a Circus Maximus, contending teams as Greek and Persian legions.[17] The heroic style remained highly embellished but found its metaphors closer to home, in the nicknames of the teams, styles of play, even weather conditions. Writers elaborated imaginatively on USC's "Thundering Herd," Georgia Tech's "Golden Tornado," SMU's "aerial circus," and so on (Grantland Rice's Four Horseman lead in 1924, the most famous lines ever written about football, was a throwback to the epic mode). Though generations of realistic sportswriters would later disparage it, the heroic style of the 1920s was often lively and imaginative.

In a typical instance, when Georgia Tech beat Notre Dame for the first time ever, in 1928, the *Atlanta Constitution*'s Dick Hawkins tried to find prose to match the occasion: "The colors atop the golden dome of Notre Dame are hanging at half-mast tonight, and the Gold and White of Georgia Tech is riding high with the breath of a real Golden Tornado whipping at the mast. It was a real tornado that swept the great Irish from the field a defeated team. Like the untamable tornado in nature's storehouse of trouble, the forward wall of Tech's gridiron tornado swept on and on like the hand of doom."[18] Later that season, after Pittsburgh held Nebraska to a scoreless tie, the first blot on an unblemished season, the *Omaha World-Herald*'s Frederick Ware opened his account this way: "A merry gang of uppity, inconsiderate young men from Pittsburgh Saturday afternoon dredged up huge gobs of mud from the squashy floor of Nebraska's football playground and heaved them at the proud Cornhusker battleshield until the latter half of the 'unde-feated and untied' slogan had been completely obliterated."[19] Ware's touch was light compared to Hawkins's heavy strokes, but the writers shared a gen-eral sense during the interwar years that sportswriting was to be imagina-tively heightened.

Years later, one of the sharpest critics of the Grantland Rice school, Robert Lipsyte, acknowledged that "clever writers produced some amusing, even self-mocking, metaphorical stories in the twenties and thirties," but by the 1950s "it was pretty much a hack's technique." Lipsyte also pointed out that metaphorical inflation, particularly as employed by Rice's inferior imitators, ironically "dehumanized the contests and made objects of the ath-letes." To describe a football player's performance accurately, whether to criticize or praise him, respected what he did. "But the writer who likens a ballplayer to Hercules or Grendel's mother is displaying the ultimate con-tempt—the ballplayer no longer exists as a person or a performer, but as an object, a piece of matter to be used, in this case, for the furtherance of the sportswriter's career by pandering to the emotional titillation of the reader/fan."[20] Just so, but such extravagant sportswriting also had a cultural impact. Football players in the United States have never been regarded pri-marily as workers at a craft, whether paid or unpaid; they have served as figments of personal and collective fantasy. In football particularly, the sport in which craft is most obscured by spectacle, performance has always been mystified. Great American athletes have been simultaneously deified and dehumanized in the media, for the sake of the profits that come from satis-fying fans' emotional desires.

As accuracy replaced narrative drama, and as sports departments were subjected to the same journalistic standards that governed the rest of the paper, not all was gain. At its best, the overwritten prose of the 1920s and 1930s was lively and imaginative; at its worst, the professionalized sports-writing of later decades was pedestrian and dull. It is also important to recognize that, although sportswriters everywhere were influenced by the stars of syndication in New York journalism, different standards governed the metropolis and the provinces. The sort of "facetious cynicism" that *New*

York Daily Mirror columnist and sports editor Dan Parker characterized in 1942 as "the favorite pose of the profession" was a big-city stance, unimaginable for the local paper even in cities the size of Atlanta, Omaha, and Dallas.[21] Outside the major metropolitan areas, the local sports columnist and sportswriter had a more intimate relationship with both his readers and the local team than those in the big city, which led typically to heartfelt partisanship and precluded criticism almost entirely. The Carnegie report quoted one "veteran newspaperman" who noted that "a small college town paper would not be able to exist if it gave impartial accounts of home-team games."[22] Impartiality was required of news. No professional standards governed what small-town sportswriters actually produced: neither simply news nor entertainment, but bonds between teams and their fans. Sportswriters' unchecked boosterism had its costs—as we will see in a later chapter, it contributed hugely to the ethical quagmire in which colleges were hopelessly stuck—but it also contributed to a sense of community.

Red Smith led post–World War II sportswriters, as Grantland Rice led the interwar generation, but without establishing a new school. As Robert Lipsyte has explained, Smith's "talent was too large and special for his style to be successfully imitated. However, the mere presence of that talent on sports pages throughout America lifted the level of sportswriting."[23] This assessment is borne out by virtually any of Smith's columns for the *New York Herald Tribune.* In a wholly typical one in 1953, Smith described a game between Illinois and Wisconsin in which the Illini's speedster, J. C. Caroline, was stymied by the Wisconsin defense. Here is Smith's account of one play, fourth down and four from the Wisconsin twelve-yard line: "Ordinarily Caroline's speed will take him that far before the defense can intercept him. This time, though, he flashed around the sideline, tried to turn and encountered Ron Locklin, the Wisconsin end. J. C. was like a fat lady in the shopping rush hurrying around a corner with her arms full of Christmas packages. They picked up his initials all over the field."[24] The crispness, absence of cliché, then wonderfully incongruous simile marked a style that could be admired but not imitated. Three days later, Smith described Jimmy Conzelman's banquet-circuit account of coaching at Washington University in St. Louis, where he had few skilled athletes but much fun: "Conzelman pictures his Washington players as eager tots who scampered about the practice field rolling hoops, flying kites and begging sweetmeats from the coach. They were in fact kids who'd played on the third string in high school, if at all—tall, skinny, ungainly specters, awkward fat boys, scrawny little waifs."[25]

The rhythm of the sentences and the quaintly Victorian vocabulary were undoubtedly Smith's, not Conzelman's, a great raconteur improved by a greater writer.

Sportswriters of the 1960s and beyond charged the generations of both Grantland Rice and Red Smith with taking sport both too seriously and too lightly: on the one hand, making heroes of athletes; on the other, pretending that sports were only games.[26] The new breed would increasingly probe the economic, racial, and political dimensions of a powerful institution. Without discounting this assessment, I would emphasize the intimacy and visual quality of the sports pages in the period of this study. Sportswriting from the 1920s through the 1950s assumed a common enthusiasm between writer and reader for the local teams, players, and coaches. And whether floridly metaphorical or bitingly ironic, sportswriting before the age of television had to help readers see the games and players. The sportswriting we read today is written for fans who already know the scores and probably saw the highlights on *SportsCenter*. Sportswriting has become an adjunct to television, its primary role now to find the story behind the story, not to recreate sporting events for fans who could not attend them. The highly descriptive sportswriting of the earlier period was the primary medium of sporting news, its fundamental purpose to recreate the experience of the games for those who had to stay home.

ALTERNATIVE VOICES

Readers of the mainstream press were primarily interested in "our boys," whether the local team or local athletes playing elsewhere. For some Americans, however, "our boys" did not mean the nearby high school or college squad but the Polish or Italian or Catholic or black youths who played on it, or on teams throughout the country. Having originated at elite colleges in the Northeast, college football was radically democratized over the 1920s and 1930s, as the sons of eastern and southern European immigrants, a great percentage of them Catholic, increasingly made the game their own. Democratization remained incomplete, as African Americans were largely limited to their own black-college teams, while big-time football remained marginally integrated in the North and West, and totally segregated in the South. Oriented toward promotion and shy of controversy, sportswriting in the mainstream press all but ignored the social transformation of football and the continued exclusions, but a vital alternative press filled in the blanks.

A thriving foreign-language press had been part of the immigrant experience from the beginning, and in the late 1930s, even after a period of decline, more than a thousand dailies and weeklies in thirty-eight languages continued to be published.[27] The National Origins Act passed by Congress in 1924 ended the flood of so-called new immigrants from southern and eastern Europe at the very time their sons were beginning to transform college football. With fewer newcomers arriving who spoke and read only their native languages, foreign-language newspapers increasingly added English sections to hold the interest of the American-born second generation that by the early 1930s numbered 26 million. At that point, according to one calculation, 50 percent of Czech papers, 25 percent of Italian papers, 20 percent of Norwegian papers, 17 percent of Polish papers, and 79 percent of Jewish periodicals were printed in English, in whole or in part. By the end of the decade "several hundred" of the thousand immigrant papers had English sections. The fact that the leading topic in many of these English sections, particularly in the Slavic and Italian papers, was sport in itself tells us much about the role of sport in the immigrant experience. In an assessment of the foreign-language press in early 1933, Albert Parry noted that immigrant newspapers addressed "two contradictory tasks: to promote the Americanization of its readers, and to preserve their feeling of being different from Americans."[28] Accounts of football stars such as Benny Friedman, Bronko Nagurski, and Frank Carideo most conspicuously celebrated their Americanization.

The sports coverage in more than a thousand immigrant newspapers is beyond full accounting here, but certainly a great number ignored sport altogether. The newspapers published by old immigrant groups were generally less concerned with the athletic prowess of their own in big-time American sport. Among the German papers surveyed, the *Tägliche Omaha Tribune* and *Die Welt-Post*, also of Omaha, ignored sports, while the *Westliche Post* of St. Louis and the *New Yorker Staats-Zeitung und Herold* of New York mirrored mainstream sports sections in covering both local and national sport, with but the slightest German emphasis.[29] The weekly Norwegian *Skandinaven* in Chicago focused chiefly on the activities of the local Norwegian American sports club, while the Swedish *Omaha-Posten* included an occasional photo of a football player simply as part of the American scene. Of the two major Irish weeklies in New York, the *Gaelic American* in the 1920s and 1930s covered only Irish sports—chiefly hurling and Irish football, played both in Dublin and at Celtic Park in New York—while the *Irish World and American Industrial Liberator* included notes on the football teams of Notre Dame and other Catholic colleges. Missing from both papers was an emphasis on Irish athletes themselves in big-time American sport. After dominating first prize-fighting, then baseball, in the nineteenth century, Irish American athletes by the 1930s were so much a part of the American sporting scene that they needed no particular notice in their own press.[30] The balance of sporting news during the fall months in the immigrant press generally was toward the group's own local club sports—in Chicago's Polish newspapers, for example, bowling was the chief sport in the fall—and to professional boxing and wrestling, the national sports of greatest interest to the papers' predominantly working-class readers.

A significant portion of the new-immigrant press, however, found in big-time American football an important narrative of group achievement. Examples ranging from the Hungarian *Szabadsag* (published in Cleveland, New York, Chicago, Pittsburgh, Detroit, and St. Louis), the Lithuanian *Draugas* (Chicago) and *Amerikos Lietuvis* (Worcester, Mass.), the Greek *Helenikos Typos* (Chicago), *Ethnikos Keryx,* and *Atlantis* (both New York), the Slovak *Jednota* (Middleton, Pa.), and the Czech *Denni Hlasatel* and *Svornost* (both Chicago) gave readers at least occasional ethnic football heroes with whom they could identify as American successes. The most thorough and sustained coverage appeared in Italian, Jewish, and Polish newspapers. Italian dailies such as *Il Progresso Italo-Americano* and *Corriere d'America* in New York, and weeklies in many cities included columns—usually in Italian, sometimes in English—celebrating the exploits of such stars as Notre Dame's Joe Savoldi and Frank Carideo.[31] Although Yiddish dailies such as *Vorvärts* (the *Jewish Daily Forward*) ignored sports, the Jewish papers published in English celebrated the triumphs of Jewish football players as signs of the group's successful assimilation and the larger society's tolerance. A news service, the Jewish Telegraphic Agency, offered columns by a series of sports editors and, beginning in 1926 with George Joel's selections, an annual Jewish All-America team.[32] Joel was followed by Morris Weiner, while Harry Conzel and Irv Kupcinet wrote columns and selected Jewish All-Americans for the Seven Arts Feature Syndicate. Several sports editors—including Jule Zied and Barney Glazer for the *B'nai B'rith Messenger* (Los Angeles), Danny Erwin for the *Jewish Times* (Philadelphia), and Henry Levy for the *American Hebrew* (New York)—also named All-Jewish teams on occasion.[33] What the Jewish press did intermittently, the Polish press did regularly and more expansively.[34] Sports editors such as John T. Czech of *Dziennik Zjednoczenia* in Chicago and Henry Archacki of *Nowy Swiat* in New York gave readers weekly accounts of the forty-three or sixty-eight or whatever number of Polish football players whose names they found in mainstream papers over the weekend—a relatively easy task, given the number of second-generation Polish immigrants who became football stars at Notre Dame, Fordham, Pitt, and other universities. Having named his own Polish All-America team since 1930, Czech in 1934 organized the selection of a consensus team by sportswriters from Polish newspapers in nine cities in the Northeast and upper Midwest, which continued until his death in the 1940s.[35]

The Jewish press found its football heroes throughout the world of college football (the closest thing to a Jewish "home team" was at City College in New York, coached for a time by Benny Friedman and fielding predominantly Jewish players, but CCNY was undermanned, underfunded, and unknown outside New York). The rest of the immigrant press looked mostly to the same cluster of teams: Fordham and St. Mary's, Marquette and Holy Cross, Santa Clara and Villanova, and above all Notre Dame. Later Notre Dame teams would lord over the entire intercollegiate football world, but in the 1920s and 1930s the "Fighting Irish"—with their Poles, Italians, Lithuanians, and even Jews[36]—were in a special way immigrant America's team. Steel-town nonsectarian universities such as Pittsburgh and Carnegie Tech also had conspicuously Polish lineups in the 1930s, but "immigrant" and "Catholic" were nearly synonymous in this period. Ninety percent of Poles and 80 percent of Bohemians and Slovaks, as well as virtually all Italians, were at least nominally Roman Catholic, their lives in the United States centered around their Catholic parishes.[37] While many immigrant newspapers were affiliated with specific Catholic organizations, Catholic dioceses had their own newspapers as well, in which Catholic football was a regular feature.[38] The approach was the same as in Polish or Jewish or Italian newspapers—reports on "our" players—but with more than two dozen specific teams to follow rather than players scattered around the country. In his biography of Vince Lombardi, David Maraniss claims an intimate connection between football and Catholicism; the discipline and demand for perfection taught by the Jesuits at Fordham formed the bedrock of Lombardi's philosophy as a highly successful coach.[39] Likely for more pragmatic reasons—university-building on the Notre Dame model—Fordham, St. Mary's, Boston College, Holy Cross, Marquette, Villanova, Georgetown, Santa Clara, and a dozen others made the 1930s an era of big-time Catholic football.

The news service of the National Catholic Welfare Conference (NCWC) started a syndicated weekly football column in 1929, first written by Villanova coach Harry Stuhldreher, ex-Horseman of Notre Dame, then by Marquette coach Frank Murray for one season (1936) after Stuhldreher left for the University of Wisconsin, then by Paddy Driscoll, who succeeded Murray at Marquette. Weekly columns during the football season culminated in a Top 10 or Top 20 list of Catholic teams and an All-Catholic All-America squad. Of the two great chains of Catholic newspapers, the *Register* ignored sports, but beginning in 1935 *Our Sunday Visitor* published a regular football column, initially by the NCWC coach-columnist.[40] Among the independent Catholic weeklies, not all included sports pages in the 1930s, but it appears that most of those in large cities did, usually with the NCWC columnist to complement their own staff coverage of the local Catholic high schools and colleges.[41] Chicago's *New World,* for example, ran the columns of Stuhldreher and his successors alongside more thorough coverage of the Catholic high school league, whose champion carried the Church's banner against the best from the public high schools at Soldier Field before as many as 120,000 fans.[42]

The hallmark of all these papers, religious or ethnic, was fierce partisanship: tribal football for those who felt excluded from the mainstream American tribe. For all the sports columnists' attention to ethnic or religious identity, success in football served primarily to validate outsiders' claims to being fully American. Radical newspapers such as the Communist Party's *Daily Worker* likewise embraced football as an expression of "Americanism," though with quite different motives. Football, and sports more generally, had a minimal role in the broader labor and radical press. Among the small handful of labor dailies, the *Seattle Union Record* (1918–28) and the *Milwaukee Leader* (1911–38) had substantial sports pages, but they were distinguishable from the mainstream press only in their attention to workers' sports leagues, alongside the coverage of big-time college and professional football. Whether organized by companies or unions, bowling and baseball rather than football were the chief industrial-league sports, as the high costs and risk of injury associated with football made it unappealing.[43] In covering these or any sports, the *Seattle Union Record* and *Milwaukee Leader* were exceptions among labor newspapers. More typically, the four- or eight-page weekly, published either by a workers' political party or a local labor council, had little or no space for sports. With limited resources, these papers had more urgent issues; for sports, the local daily sufficed.[44]

Much of the radical press likewise ignored sport, but the various Communist Party publications eventually gave it considerable attention.[45] Initially, the various factions of the Socialist and Communist parties valued sport only for recruitment of new members or as workers' recreation organized by the Labor Sports Union, while castigating both intercollegiate and professional football as exploitative "bosses' sports."[46] Something akin to an unofficial

Communist Party position on big-time American sport emerged in publications such as the *Daily Worker, Western Worker, Young Worker, Young Communist Review,* and *New Masses* in the late 1920s and early 1930s: the view, in Mark Naison's words, that "all 'bourgeois' sports organizations, whether amateur or professional, represented conscious efforts to insure working class loyalty to capitalism and to inspire individualist and escapist fantasies that prevented workers from dealing with their problems."[47] Naison has identified a shift in 1933, when the *Young Worker,* published by the Young Communist League, inaugurated a regular sports column to forge "limited alliances with trade unions and socialist groups." The second shift came in 1935, as a byproduct of the antifascist Popular Front mandated by the Seventh World Congress of the Communist International.[48] Many radical publications continued to waste no space on sport, and some continued to be highly critical, but the Communist Party's youth publications—the *Young Worker, Young Communist Review,* and their successors—and more importantly the *Daily Worker,* reached out to workers in part by embracing their enthusiasm for spectator sports.[49]

Founded in Chicago in 1924, then based in New York from 1927, the *Daily Worker* had the best and most complete sports coverage of any of these papers.[50] With a circulation of approximately 30,000, climbing perhaps as high as 48,000 in 1940 before declining sharply during the war and ultimately ceasing daily publication in 1958, the *Worker* never succeeded in reaching a large readership—it always spoke for American workers more than to them—but its highly literate and opinionated sports columnists gained the attention not just of like-minded intellectuals but also of other New York sportswriters, if only as their whipping boy.[51] In its early years the *Daily Worker* was uniformly antagonistic to "capitalist sport," particularly as practiced by college football teams.[52] Beginning in 1936, however, as party leaders attempted to recast Communism as "twentieth-century Americanism," the *Daily Worker*'s sports page provided a capsule of the day's sports, from a partisan New Yorker's angle but also with a passionately democratic social conscience. Baseball was more truly the people's game, but football commanded attention in season. Sports editor Lester Rodney preferred professional to college football, but at both levels he emphasized football as labor performed by highly skilled but underpaid workers. In adopting this stance, the *Daily Worker* did not stand beyond the pale of mainstream sports journalism; rather, it emphatically and consistently took a position that mainstream sportswriters more cautiously and fitfully expressed. Thus, while celebrating the thrilling victories and brilliant performances, the traditions and the pageantry, that marked college football's appeal throughout the land, the paper also routinely addressed the unresolved contradiction at the heart of a million-dollar popular spectacle sponsored by institutions of higher learning.

When it integrated its own sports staff in the 1940s and 1950s, the *Daily Worker* acted consistently with its long campaign for racial justice in football, as virtually the only ally of the black press in this effort.[53] In the early 1920s, more than 250 black newspapers were published in all but ten states, all of them weeklies except for two one-page daily broadsheets. The leader among these was the *Chicago Defender,* whose circulation of 230,000 in 1920 (150,000 outside Chicago through its national edition) was read by five or six times that number, reaching about 10 percent of the black population. Three dailies appeared in the 1920s and 1930s, and in the late 1940s six nationally distributed weeklies had circulations over 100,000, led now by the *Pittsburgh Courier,* whose 300,000 surpassed even the *Defender.*[54] A wire service—the Associated Negro Press, founded by Claude Barnett in 1919—along with a newsreel, *All-American News,* and eventually the magazines *Ebony* and *Jet,* supplemented the black weeklies in reporting on the "other" side of segregated America. The black press even had its own sports cartoonists, such as the extraordinarily talented George Lee, whose finely detailed drawings rendered black football stars as distinct individuals rather than minstrel caricatures.[55] The black media, in short, were a fully formed "separate but equal" source of news for black America.

Robert Abbott, the publisher of the *Chicago Defender,* was "the pioneer for the Negro press as Hearst was for the white metropolitan press."[56] Like Hearst, Abbott in the 1920s dressed his paper in tabloid-style sensationalism, sometimes offending middle-class readers but making his paper a virtual Bible among the African American masses.[57] Sport was a crucial part of the black press's appeal to its readers, a continuing drama of triumph and injustice enacted by black prizefighters, Negro League baseball players, and football stars both in the black colleges and at predominantly white institutions. Data is scarce, but one survey of the *Chicago Defender'*s readers in the early 1940s suggested that sport may have been more important to black readers than to the population at large.[58] Explanations come readily to mind. Americans' worship of athletes raised the stakes for black achievement in sport and conferred great symbolic power on black triumphs over white competitors. The most celebrated black sports heroes were Joe Louis, Henry Armstrong, and other great boxing champions, while the most important sporting cause was the integration of major league baseball. Because few black Americans had the opportunity to attend college in these years,[59] football could not have the importance for the general black population that professional boxing and baseball did; but for the aspiring black middle class, college football resonated with the deepest hopes for the race, and for all readers of the black press the racial dramas of sport during the fall months took place mostly on football fields.

Though football in the black press was predominantly the game played by all-black colleges in the shadow of the big-time sport, the *Chicago Defender, Pittsburgh Courier,* and other black newspapers also provided an alternative perspective on African Americans in the predominantly white game. The football world of Lincoln and Howard, "Jazz" Byrd and Ben Stevenson, was unknown outside black communities, but the mainstream press also downplayed the racial dimensions of NCAA and NFL football. The black press recorded the racial indignities ignored by mainstream sportswriters—the sluggings, exclusions, and benchings of black players for southern opponents—while also highlighting the triumphs of black football stars such as Joe Lillard, Oze Simmons, Brud Holland, and Kenny Washington in the 1930s, Buddy Young, Levi Jackson, and Marion Motley in the 1940s, and J. C. Caroline, Ollie Matson, and Jim Brown in the 1950s. As black players proliferated in the postwar years, numbers rather than lone heroes became the story, epitomized in the weekly "Football Roundup" in the *Baltimore Afro-American* and the *Pittsburgh Courier* in the mid-1950s that alerted readers to dozens of black players.[60] As these men became an unavoidable presence in mainstream media as well, accelerating integration ironically rendered a black sporting press less necessary.

RADIO AND NEWSREELS

Although the wire services and feature syndicates gave newspaper football a national dimension, the daily press was primarily a local medium. Ethnic, racial, and religious newspapers were "local," too, only on terms other than geographical. Radio, newsreels, movies, and the periodical press were more truly national media, though to varying degrees. Radio balanced the national and the local in network broadcasts and coverage of the home team and its conference. Newsreel companies distributed the same reels to theaters around the country but sometimes included highlights of local games in selected cities. Only the nationally distributed periodical press and the films shown in movie theaters throughout the land were exclusively national media. All these media experienced something of a "golden age" during this period, and all were filled with football in the fall months. Col-

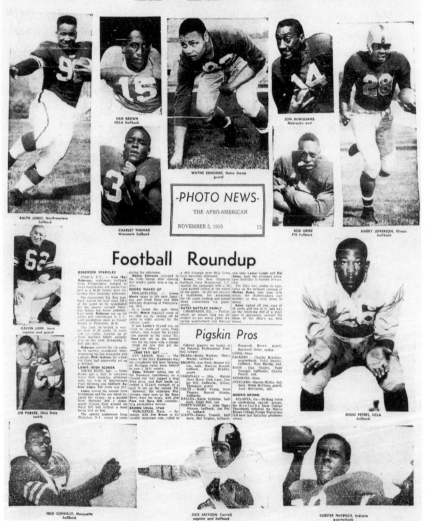

FIGURE 1-1. "Although tan faces on major college elevens have been plentiful in previous years, integration has undoubtedly increased the number now active." Thus the *Baltimore Afro-American* tracked racial progress in "mixed football" on 5 November 1955. (By permission of the *Baltimore Afro-American*)

lectively, they constructed a common football culture. Separately, each contributed to this common culture in distinctive ways.

New media have always embraced sport, both for its abundance of programmable events and for its appeal to the potential audience. Station KDKA in Pittsburgh began broadcasting on 2 November 1920 and presented its first football game, Pittsburgh–West Virginia, the following season.[61] Football was not radio's first priority. The Jack Dempsey–Georges Carpentier heavyweight title fight and baseball's World Series, both broadcast in 1921, are considered commercial radio's groundbreaking experiments with sport, and Thomas Allen Greenfield explains that while "boxing and then football proved to be programming staples as well, it was baseball that taught the radio stations, both major and minor, how to broadcast sports, how to cultivate sports broadcasters, how to compete with the newspaper sports pages, how to turn sports broadcasting into a lucrative part of station programming."[62] No football contest, not even the Army-Navy game or the Rose Bowl, ever matched the World Series as a broadcasting event, but radio nonetheless was a major factor in football's tremendous growth in the 1920s and 1930s, and football a factor in the growth of radio.

Radio did not exist before 1920 except as an experiment; by 1930 it was a national institution. From 60,000 households with radio sets in 1922, the number grew to 12 million by 1930, more than a third of American homes, then more than doubled again by 1940.[63] Over the 1920s, stations appeared in every city of any size, several of them owned by the newspapers surveyed here, such as WGN (for "World's Greatest Newspaper") by the *Chicago Tribune,* WFAA by the *Dallas Morning News,* KFAB by the *Omaha World-Herald,* KHJ by the *Los Angeles Times,* and KGW by the *Portland Oregonian.* The first networks, NBC's Red and Blue, were formed in 1926, followed by CBS in 1927, Mutual in 1934, and ABC in 1943, when the FCC forced NBC to sell one of its networks.[64]

Football games immediately followed the appearance of stations and networks. In the pre-network era, games were broadcast "on a regular basis" in New York by 1922. That season also saw the first long-distance broadcast, the Princeton-Chicago game carried over telephone lines from Chicago to New York. Chicago, Atlanta, Dallas, Omaha, Los Angeles, and Portland all began broadcasting local games between 1923 and 1928. As one measure of radio's immediate impact on football, and football's on radio, ads for radio sets explicitly for tuning in Saturday's football game began appearing in national magazines such as the *Saturday Evening Post* as early as 1923. As soon as the first radio network was created, it broadcast the Rose Bowl, on 1 January

1927; a year later, the radio audience for the Rose Bowl was 25 million. In 1930, the Army-Navy game was broadcast in Europe and Asia for the first time. By 1938, according to *Life,* 13 million sets were tuned in to football games each Saturday, with an audience up to three times that number.[65]

The 1920s and 1930s marked a period of discovery and innovation on all fronts: in technology, in broadcasting logistics and style, in federal regulation, in economics. Using telephone lines to bring radio signals to distant parts of the country made the networks possible. Determining the placement of microphones within the stadium and a mode for adapting the style of newspaper reporting to a new medium produced a broadcasting formula for football games. Working out the ownership rights to football broadcasts among universities, radio stations, advertisers, and federal regulators created an immensely profitable industry. Initially, university officials did not imagine that broadcasting rights could be a source of revenue; once sponsorship became an option, they still worried about radio's impact on attendance and gate receipts. By the late 1930s, however, most big-time football programs, Notre Dame conspicuously excepted, were earning income from radio.[66]

How listeners experienced football games over radio was determined by the pioneer broadcasters. Beginning his career in 1923, Graham McNamee (on NBC) dominated sportscasting over its first decade before yielding pre-eminence to Ted Husing (on CBS), who in turn was supplanted by Bill Stern (on NBC) in the 1940s.[67] Each of radio's first three football broadcasting stars had a distinctive style but a common essential quality, an ability to re-create the excitement at the stadium for the listeners at home. This was the primary goal during football broadcasting's founding era. With surviving football broadcasts dating only from 1935, what we know of the styles of the earliest broadcasters depends on contemporary comments.[68] McNamee was notorious for confusing what actually happened on the field, but his "breezy and colorful delivery" and "his vivid and breathtaking accounts" endeared him to fans and made him "the father of the now unshakable fast talk, fast-paced, entertainment style of sports casting."[69] McNamee was so popular by 1927 that *Time* put him on its cover, noting that although "sports experts grumble that he does not know the sport he is describing," his bosses "answer that neither do most of the listeners; that colorful, general reports are more satisfying to the masses than accurate technical descriptions." This is what McNamee offered, working himself into a frenzied state before each game, then pouring his emotion into the microphone from the opening kickoff. As late as 1936, on a surviving broadcast of the New York Giants play-

FIGURE 1-2. Advertisements such as this one from 8 November 1924, marketing radio sets specifically to pick up football games, began appearing in the *Saturday Evening Post* in 1923 (see also the issues of 27 October 1923, 2 October 1926, 8 October 1927, 15 October 1927, 3 November 1928, and 9 November 1929).

ing the College All-Stars, McNamee constantly fumbled for words, gave few details, and made outright mistakes (at one point calling a blocked punt into the end zone a touchdown, then correcting himself to say it was a safety), but his earliest fans had not cared.[70]

By this time fans expected greater accuracy with their thrills, and Ted Husing delivered it weekly for CBS. Husing was known for his conciseness, precise enunciation, and staccato speech. In contrast to McNamee, he refrained from creating what he called "false climaxes," relying instead on the game's inherent drama. "I get excited, but only on a ninety-yard run or a one-yard goal stand," he told the *New York Times* in 1945. Husing's forte was unadorned accuracy, the broadcaster's equivalent of Hemingway's prose: describe just what you see and the listener will feel the emotions.[71] In a broadcast of the 1949 Gator Bowl near the end of his career, Husing's cultured inflection and elevated diction (using words such as "panoply" and "protagonists," and referring to the "wily tutelage" of Missouri coach Don Faurot) make him sound detached and scripted rather than spontaneous, particularly in contrast to Bill Stern, the reigning king of the football broadcasters by that time.[72]

Stern followed the McNamee rather than the Husing model. Though more knowledgeable than McNamee, he adopted his predecessor's principle that listeners most of all wanted excitement. Stern was known for a "tendency toward exaggeration and overdramatization," for putting entertainment above truth, qualities that brought disdain from peers but made him popular with his audience. A broadcaster of the next generation, Marty Glickman, called Stern "the great fabricator" and remembered his "penchant for coming up with lateral passes after he had called the wrong man running for a touchdown." Stern became preeminent among the sportscasters of his generation, not in spite of putting entertainment above accuracy, but because of it.[73] In the dozens of Stern broadcasts at the Library of Congress, he alone of the three giants from the early period sounds like both an enthusiastic and a knowledgeable fan.

Outside New York, local radio stations developed their own broadcasting stars, just as the local papers featured their own columnists: Hal Totten and Quin Ryan in Chicago, Bill Munday in Atlanta, Kern Tipps in Dallas, Gayle ("Gloomy Gus") Grubb in Omaha, Don Wilson in Los Angeles, Dick Haller in Portland. As with the columnists, local broadcasters modeled their deliveries after the national figures, but—again as with the local columnists—their partisanship was local, as perhaps were their accents. I say "perhaps," because radio was a powerful force for standardizing spoken English, and no non-network early football broadcasts have survived. When NBC paired Bill Munday of WSB in Atlanta with Graham McNamee to broadcast the 1929 Rose Bowl between Georgia Tech and California, "Munday's exaggerated drawl and Southern charm soon made him a national favorite."[74] On the other hand, in a surviving broadcast of the 1935 Rice-TCU game, neither Kern Tipps nor his partner, Cy Leland, betrays a Texas accent. Football's tribalism would have competed with professional standards, and in other locales or with other broadcasters the case may have been different. An accent would have subtly reinforced local tribalism; standard English would have subtly reinforced a national norm. Exactly what role radio broadcasts of football games played in this regard remains uncertain.

Whatever the accent, the broadcaster's role in the 1920s and 1930s was different from what we expect today. Detailed expert analysis from both radio and television announcers became the standard after our period ended. Early radio broadcasters assumed a different function: more simply, to re-create for listeners the experience of being at the game. Much more so than baseball, college football games were staged in settings that mattered as much as the games themselves. The crowds, the bands, the card sections, the cheerleaders—the endlessly noted "spirit" of college football—were crucial to football's appeal, and thus to the announcers who tried to capture it. The technical handling of football games was crude at first, but the very crudity is revealing. The earliest football games were usually broadcast with two microphones: one for the announcer, stationed somewhere high in the stadium or in the press box if the stadium had one; the other closer to the field and nearer the cheering fans. The deploying of greater resources simply expanded this basic arrangement. The *New York Times* reported in 1924 that the Yale Bowl and Harvard Stadium had been wired for microphones "scattered about the cheering sections so that by throwing a switch the different microphones can be placed in the circuit by the announcer." The 1926 Harvard-Yale game broadcast by Graham McNamee and Phillips Carlin employed three microphones to pick up crowd noises and one for McNamee to relay the information fed him by Carlin, who followed the game through binoculars. In the late 1940s Bill Stern was still paying nearly as much attention to the swing bands from SMU and TCU as to their football teams battling on the field.[75]

Football posed unique challenges for the early broadcasters, most fundamentally the problem of simply following what happened on the field. Football announcers were far from the play, and players' numerals were small and not boldly set off from the colors of the jerseys. The greatest handicap, however, was the game itself, which was as confusing for the first broadcasters as it was for most fans. Writing at the dawn of network radio, Graham McNamee noted, "Anyone who has ever attended a gridiron game and tried to pick out football, play, and player from an entangled mass of twenty-two young men, who are trying to mask their maneuvers, can realize something of the problem presented. That we have been able to broadcast each step of the big games has seemed to some of our correspondents almost miraculous." McNamee and Phillips Carlin devised the first system of paired announcers. A few years later, Ted Husing added to this arrangement a homemade contraption he called his "annunciator": a box with twenty-two slots for the twenty-two players, behind each a light bulb controlled by a twenty-two-button keyboard. Husing's partner, Les Quailey, followed the game through high-powered binoculars in his right hand and worked the annunciator with his left. Amazingly, Husing himself did not follow the action on the field but kept his eyes on the annunciator, from which he reported the action. Husing also claimed to have prompted referees to devise signals for penalties, for the sake of the radio announcers on their high perch. These signals proved so helpful to everyone else at the game that the rules committee made them mandatory.[76]

Simply following the ball and identifying the players correctly were achievements for the first football broadcasters. Re-creating some of the spectacle and excitement for listeners was their other primary task. Despite the absence of surviving broadcasts, clues to what these first football games sounded like are available. While radio was still a novelty, newspapers occasionally published complete broadcast transcripts of major sporting events.[77] A stenographic transcription in the *Oregonian* of the inaugural football game in Portland's Civic Stadium, between Oregon and Washington on 9 October 1926, allows us to listen in with an early radio audience. Here is how Dick Haller's broadcast over KGW (and KFOA, Seattle) from the stadium roof began:

> Washington cheer leaders are now working out the Washington section of the stands. Oregon is still silent, waiting for the Oregon team to get on the grounds.
>
> The Washington team is about the most colorful spot in the stadium today. The crowds came to be prepared for rain; the predominating color in the bleachers is yellow—yellow chrysanthemums and yellow slickers.
>
> Here comes the green and yellow sweaters. The Oregon team is coming on the field. The crowd is giving them a tremendous ovation. The bands

are getting to their feet. Here they come—green sweaters and yellow trimmings, trotting the length of the field, passing the ball back and forth.

Six minutes to go until the game starts.

Haller announced the starting lineups, with no comment on the players' abilities or performances to date. He described the warm-ups: "The Washington team is still passing and kicking. The Oregon team is gathered in a little knot over on the side of the field." What's missing is most striking: no "expert" analysis, no prediction; no comment on who's favored, what the teams' records are, what the game means in the standings. Haller described exactly what he saw on the field, and no more.

The game began and proceeded without dramatic heightening on Haller's part: someone kicked, someone received, one team ran or passed, the other tackled and defended. Haller's descriptions were flat and literal. Oregon "made two successive passes now and has advanced the ball about 30 yards." Washington "held Jones when he bucked through center." The past tense is itself revealing: no attempt to make sense of the play as it unfolds, only terse descriptions of what has just happened. Midway through the first quarter, Haller did offer a bit of analysis: "The Oregon team seems very nervous and highstrung—they are dancing around pretty much." This was no "expert" speaking but an ordinary fan, sitting in for the fans at home. At halftime, Haller puzzled over the students' carryings-on down on the field, then he described the second half as he had the first, progressing (with no dramatic buildup) to the final play, then the pistol shot, and these closing remarks: "There's the end of the game. Washington beats Oregon by a score of 23 to 9." No postgame commentary or summing up. The game ended; the people left the stadium; the listeners turned off the radio.[78]

Dick Haller was considerably less experienced than Graham McNamee and the top broadcasters in New York and Chicago, and he seems to have lacked altogether what made McNamee a national celebrity—his ability to generate excitement—but the fundamentally descriptive, as opposed to analytical, manner of broadcasting remained the standard through the 1940s. A handful of games from 1935 preserved at the Library of Congress illustrate a basic formula: the announcement of certain narrative lines in pregame introductions (missing from Haller's broadcast in 1926); play-by-play description interspersed with nonexpert commentary; halftime discussion and interviews; and a brief postgame wrap-up. The Notre Dame–Northwestern game on 9 November 1935, for instance, opened with Tom Manning's pregame comments, then Ford Bond and Manning doing play-by-play in alternate quarters. As Manning set up the game, faint sounds of the crowd could be heard in the background. Periodically Manning stopped to pick up cheers from the stands and the playing of the band, either switching to an on-field microphone or turning up its volume. Having announced the lineups, related other scores, and described the coin toss, Manning told the listener, "You figuratively are sitting on the south side of the field," as the game itself began. The ensuing play-by-play was not very skillful or precise.

That simple sentence, "You figuratively are sitting on the south side of the field," sums up radio's fundamental role at football games: not to educate the listener in the fine points of football but simply to place him, "figuratively," in the stadium. The Harvard-Yale game two weeks later, on 23 November, with Ed Herlihy and Jack Englesaul, was distinguished by the almost British crispness of Herlihy's polished diction and greater precision in the play-by-play descriptions, but otherwise followed the format of the Notre Dame–Northwestern game. Another contest, on 23 November, between Rice and TCU from Fort Worth, with Kern Tipps announcing, was indistinguishable from the others. In this case, sectional partisanship emerged in comments on Sammy Baugh as the best passer in "a section of the country long known for that open style of play," and in a halftime interview with Texas's lieutenant governor—a pitch to the rest of the country for Southwest Conference football and the state of Texas—but otherwise the game from Forth Worth sounded like the games from South Bend and Cambridge.

Radio thus helped standardize football as part of a national sporting culture, but it also reinforced local partisanship, as is clear from the distribution of games in various cities. Newspaper listings of local broadcasts are not wholly reliable for the earliest years, and part of radio's initial appeal lay in its power to bring in distant stations, what aficionados called DX.[79] (Radio's transformation from technological experiment to medium of mass entertainment is reflected in the fact that the Sunday edition of the *Dallas Morning News* listed radio programs in the automobile section in 1927, then in "Amusements" in 1928.) Broadcast listings in newspapers nonetheless indicate when radio football became an established institution within different communities: in New York in 1922; in Chicago in 1923; in Portland in 1925; in Dallas, Omaha, and Los Angeles in 1926 (a full slate of games in Omaha not until 1929); in Atlanta in 1928.[80] Local games took precedence over network contests in every city, those network games heavily oriented toward the East, Midwest (Big Ten), and South, in that order, with Notre Dame far and away the single most frequently broadcast team. (West Coast teams were slighted due to time-zone constraints: a 1:30 game in the East could be broadcast in the West before the local contests, but western games started too late for eastern audiences.) High school games were regularly broadcast in Dallas, but this was not the norm among the cities surveyed here. Radio also had a negligible impact on professional football outside the cities with NFL franchises. Regular broadcasts of pro games began in Chicago in 1926 and New York in 1928, but not even the NFL championship was carried on network radio until 1940. Outside the NFL circuit, weekly radio broadcasts barely beat television into town.[81]

As football on radio became a Saturday afternoon institution by the 1930s, it also had a small place in prime-time broadcasting during radio's golden age. Grantland Rice had a weekly interview show on NBC in the 1920s and 1930s, and from October 1939 through June 1951 *The Colgate Sports Newsreel* brought Bill Stern's melodramatic renderings of thrilling or poignant moments in sport to millions of eager listeners. In fifteen-minute weekly segments, Stern told three or four brief stories, some true, some fanciful, the difference between the two not always evident. As with his broadcasts of live sporting events, Stern "never let the facts get in the way of a good story."[82] For outright fiction, Grantland Rice's *Sports Stories* dramatized tales previously published in popular magazines,[83] and youngsters could tune into *The Adventures of Frank Merriwell* (for a few months in 1934, then from October 1946 to June 1949) and *The Adventures of Dick Cole* (briefly in 1942). The greatest of the juvenile serials was the long-running *Jack Armstrong, The All-American Boy,* that from 1933 to 1950 re-created the athletic exploits of Jack and his chums at Hudson High, as well as their more exotic adventures battling cattle rustlers in Arizona, pirates in Zanzibar, or Nazi spies in Morocco. Developed expressly to market General Mills's new cereal, *Jack Armstrong* sold Wheaties "by the trainload" and made its boxtops the currency of choice for boys around the country who could mail them in for rings, medallions, bombsights, pedometers, and other paraphernalia of Jack's adventures.[84] All these programs simply transferred the conventions of magazine journalism and fiction to the new medium, saturating the airwaves with football in the fall.

Newsreels, too, were full of football. News films appeared with the beginning of motion pictures in the 1890s, but the American newsreel proper—the "ten-minute potpourri of motion picture news footage, released twice a week to motion picture theaters throughout the country"—was introduced in 1911 with *Pathé's Weekly.* In the words of the newsreel's major chronicler, Raymond Fielding, "from 1911 to 1967, it survived intact and unchanged, during which time it was as predictably a part of every theater's program as the Walt Disney cartoon and the Fitzpatrick travelogue." By the mid-1920s, newsreels were shown weekly in 85 to 90 percent of the 18,000 movie theaters in the country. *Fox News* introduced sound in 1927 and became *Movietone News* (1927–63). *American Pathé News* (1915–56, after 1947 as *Warner-Pathé News*) and the three other major newsreels—*Paramount News* (1927–56), *Universal News* (1929–67), and Hearst's variously named reels (*International News*, 1919–29; *Metrotone News*, 1929–36; and *News of the Day*, 1936–67)—first appeared or added sound between 1927 and 1929. By the mid-1930s, weekly attendance of 108 million at the movies meant a comparable audience for newsreels, with each reel seen by an estimated 20 million. Thirty-six theaters showed nothing but newsreels. Then came the steep decline; with the spread of television in the 1950s the newsreels all but disappeared.[85]

The earliest news films were of prizefights, and major football games (Army-Navy, Harvard-Penn, Yale-Princeton) were filmed as early as 1902. With the emergence of spectator sport as a popular passion at the turn of the century, major sporting events were simply newsworthy, but it was the inherent nature of these events—competitive, dramatic, "highly visual and filled with action and movement"—that made them ideal subjects for the motion-picture camera. Frequent, abundant, and scheduled in advance, they also minimized the logistical problems of the new medium. In its initial year, 1915, *American Pathé News* included football regularly in its programs, from preseason training at the University of Chicago and Central High School in Pittsburgh to games between Pitt and Penn, Syracuse and Colgate, Yale and Princeton, Nebraska and Kansas, Michigan and Penn, Chicago and Illinois, and Army and Navy. In the 1920s, Pathé increased both the number and frequency of games, as each twice-a-week release typically included one or more contests. By the early 1930s, the single most striking fact about all the newsreels was their attention to sport: 14 percent of the items in one newsreel from mid-1931 to mid-1932, 30 percent of another, the highest among the twenty-six categories surveyed. By the late 1930s, sport made up about a quarter of all newsreel footage, diminishing during World War II, then returning to prewar levels in the late 1940s. In a survey of movie audiences in 1949, sport was their favorite newsreel subject (followed by fashion and human interest). To critics, sport was the lightweight material tacked onto the end, along with the bathing beauties and trained monkeys, that undermined the newsreel's potential importance as a news medium. But the newsreel's most significant impact on American culture may have been its contribution to the quasi-mythic power of football and baseball, and to a national self-image in which sport had a central place.[86]

Newsreel football was the early ancestor of ESPN's *SportsCenter:* highlights in which every game is a big game, every play a great play, every crowd wildly cheering. With limited footage to shoot, newsreel photographers had to be lucky to capture the game's crucial plays along with the bands, cheerleaders, card sections, and cheering crowds. As one newsreel photographer explained in 1949: "Before the game we generally take [a camera] down field to make a few cut-ins such as the rooting section going berserk as in a touchdown, the teams running out on the field, the various mascots and any celebrities that might have saved enough dough to buy a box seat."[87] The calculated heightening of dramatic spectacle—to the extent of filming "berserk" fans cheering touchdowns before the game even began—was as important as the action on the field. Whatever the photographer shot became the big plays for the audience in the theater, and in a cruder way and a simpler time the producers of newsreels achieved the same effect as today's more extravagantly financed and technically advanced highlight films. Exclaiming over the long passes, thrilling runs, and leaping cheerleaders, announcers such as Ed Thorgerson (Fox *Movietone News*), Clem McCarthy (Pathé), Graham McNamee (Universal), Bill Stern (*News of the Day*), and Ted Husing (Paramount)—note the crossover of radio announcers into newsreels—heightened the drama and excitement of football in ways possible through no other medium of the day.

Three teams most conspicuously represented national football in the newsreels: Army, Navy, and preeminently Notre Dame. In the 1930s, Army appeared forty-four times in the Hearst newsreels, Navy forty-six and Notre Dame sixty-one. By the late 1920s, Notre Dame was the premier team in intercollegiate football in all media. Army and Navy, on the other hand, were featured in the newsreels far more prominently than in the print media until after World War II. The Army-Navy rivalry was just another big game for much of the country in the 1930s, on a level with Harvard-Yale, Michigan–Ohio State, and California-Stanford, but for the newsreels the usual 1,500–2,000 feet of footage was increased to 8,000–10,000 for Army-Navy, and the segments shown in theaters were roughly twice as long as ordinary games.[88] More than the game itself it was the spectacle of the service battle—the goat and the mule, the dignitaries in attendance, the rows upon rows of uniformed cadets and midshipmen marching before the game and cheering in unison throughout the contest, the enormous crowds at Soldier Field in Chicago or Municipal Stadium in Philadelphia—that was ideally

suited to the visual power of the medium. The accompanying spectacle likewise made postseason bowl games ideal subjects for newsreels, and newsreels
a major factor in establishing the bowl games as midwinter festivals in the
public consciousness. "Rose Carnival's great parade of flowers and bathing
beauties share spotlight with college heroes," announced *Metrotone News*'s
typical coverage of the Rose Bowl in 1933. The sunny January weather in
Pasadena, Miami, New Orleans, and Dallas made the bowl games look more
exotic to shivering easterners and northerners. Not everyone was a football
fan, but virtually all Americans went to the movies. Football fan or not, anyone who went to the movies the week after the Army-Navy game, the Thanksgiving Day contests, or the bowls on New Year's Day came to understand
football's role in the calendar of national rituals.

The portrait of national football in the newsreels roughly mirrored network radio's—a predominance of eastern, midwestern, and southern teams
—but West Coast football was featured more prominently in the newsreels,
for whom time-zone considerations were not a constraint. USC's emergence
as a premier national team owed much to its rivalry with Notre Dame and its
frequent trips to the Rose Bowl, but also to the power of the newsreels. The
Trojans appeared thirty-five times nationally in the Hearst newsreels in the
1930s (including four Rose Bowl games), in addition to nine local releases.
The sunny skies, pretty girls in the stands, and Hollywood celebrities in the
neighborhood, capped by the Rose Tournament parades at the end of the
season, stamped West Coast football with a distinctive image.

Big-time college football, accompanied by hyper-excited narration, was
the dominant form of newsreel football, but most seasons also had moments
of human interest or believe-it-or-not curiosity: Sing-Sing prison's opening
contest; a Midget Football Championship in Germantown, Pennsylvania; a
burlesque of football, "'Gay Nineties' Style," in Gainesville, Florida; a "powder bowl" between rival sororities; a game won by Boys' Town with Bing
Crosby and other Hollywood stars in attendance.[89] The newsreels barely
noticed pro football in the 1930s, but in the postwar years they recorded,
and contributed to, its growing popularity as the national version of the
sport.[90] Television killed the newsreels in the 1950s and 1960s. Television
simply offered everything newsreels provided, but more of it with less delay.

MAGAZINES AND MOVIES

Though reaching a smaller audience than either radio or newsreels, the
periodical press played a key role in embedding football in middle-class
American life. The great general-interest magazines in particular enjoyed a

golden age from the end of the First World War to the dawn of the age of television, as the circulations of weeklies such as the *Saturday Evening Post* and *Life* attained levels exceeding 4 and 5 million.[91] By the conventional calculation that each copy was read by four people, the *Post* and *Life* reached as many as 20 million readers in every part of the country. Various surveys reported that 15 percent of the American population read *Life,* 18 percent read either *Collier's* or the *Saturday Evening Post,* and 31 percent read one or more of these three magazines. A fourth general-interest magazine, *Look,* had a circulation greater than that of *Collier's* and nearly equal to the *Post's.*[92]

Together with *Reader's Digest* and the great women's and family magazines — *Ladies' Home Journal, Woman's Home Companion, McCall's, Good Housekeeping* — the general-interest magazines led a thriving periodical press that also included the newsweeklies *Time* and *Newsweek,* journals of opinion ranging from the staid nineteenth-century monthlies of the cultural elite (*Harper's, Scribner's,* and the *Atlantic*) to feisty, left-leaning weeklies such as the *Nation* and the *New Republic,* and eventually a specialized sporting press. Of the small handful of significant sports magazines, *Outing* died in 1923, while *Sport* and *Sports Illustrated* did not appear until after World War II. Published since 1882, most notably under the editorship of Caspar Whitney (1900–1909), *Outing* had been the magazine of the age of amateurism in its final struggle against creeping commercialism, though with little impact on American sport in its last years. A magazine called *All-Sports* had a brief run in the 1920s, then *Sport* appeared in 1946 and *Sports Illustrated* in 1954, but the latter did not became the country's leading sporting journal until the 1960s. With its sights initially on an upscale male readership, *Sports Illustrated* resisted becoming a magazine of mass spectator sports (as *Sport* magazine was doing) and did not find its true voice until the arrival of André Laguerre and a cadre of wisecracking Texan journalists.[93] From the 1920s through the 1950s it was the general-interest magazines that contributed most to a national football culture.

Henry Luce created the modern news magazine with *Time* in 1923, to compete directly with the *Literary Digest,* which was then at the peak of its popularity with a circulation of 1.5 million.[94] With a regular "Sports and Athletics" department, the *Digest* had long been reprinting comments on college football from the major New York newspapers and other sources. Initially, *Time* also filled its "Sport" columns with material rewritten from newspapers, especially from the *New York Times,* but in the 1930s it began to cover the news with its own staff and bureaus in unsigned articles. *Time* acquired head-to-head competition in 1933 when *News-Week* first appeared (becoming

Newsweek in October 1937), but the rival ran a weak second to *Time* through the 1950s, its 1960 circulation slightly more than half of *Time*'s.[95] *Newsweek* had a more distinctive voice in its sports department, however: a weekly column by John Lardner ran from 1939 until Lardner's sudden death in March 1960. Lardner was a wryly cynical columnist in the tradition of W. O. McGeehan, Westbrook Pegler, and his own father, Ring Lardner. Because Lardner was not particularly interested in football, however, it received less attention in his columns during the fall than boxing or horse racing.

The contribution of the newsweeklies to the national football culture was simply to confirm the "major" football stories that appeared in daily newspapers throughout the week. Initially, the magazines that set agendas for public debate were the "journals of opinion," a term that includes weeklies such as the *Outlook* and the *Independent* (combined in 1928 to hang on for four more years), both of which began as religious papers; secular liberal weeklies such as the *Nation* and the *New Republic;* as well as the prestigious monthlies—*Harper's, Scribner's,* the *Atlantic,* and a newcomer in the 1920s, the iconoclastic *American Mercury,* first edited by H. L. Mencken and George Jean Nathan. The journals of opinion had the smallest circulations of the major periodicals, ranging in 1930, for example, from 12,000 for the *New Republic* to 133,000 for the *Atlantic.* The aggregate for the seven just named was about 555,000, or slightly more than one-fifth of the *Saturday Evening Post*'s nearly 3 million. But these magazines contributed disproportionately to national debates over football through their status among the intellectual and cultural elites. An article on football in *Harper's* or the *Atlantic* was itself football news, provoking commentary in the daily press and more popular magazines. The principal contribution of the journals of opinion in the 1920s and 1930s was to register intellectuals' disdain for college football's commercial spectacle and its violations of the amateur spirit.

The prestige of the intellectual journals notwithstanding, it was the great general-interest weeklies that most shaped the larger football culture. *Collier's* had been a football booster since long before the 1920s and never abandoned that basic stance. As the decade began, *Collier's* was running regular columns by Walter Camp, already known as the "father of American football," then by Grantland Rice after Camp died in 1925, with Rice's stint continuing through 1932. Rice also took over Camp's All-America team, a feature in *Collier's* since 1891, and he continued in this role until 1948 when he moved to *Look.* These columns by the sport's foremost journalistic boosters were supplemented by numerous articles by other writers; by the 1930s virtually every issue of *Collier's* during the season included at least one article on football. The *Saturday Evening Post* was slower to embrace football, in part because its all-powerful editor, George Horace Lorimer, personally despised sports.[96] Pleasing readers took precedence, however, and following sporadic articles beginning in 1925, the *Post* began regular coverage of football in 1931. By the mid-1930s sport was dominating the magazine's nonfiction and became even more conspicuous after Ben Hibbs became editor in 1942.[97]

The articles in the *Post* and *Collier's* overwhelmingly took one of two forms: "inside dope" (the difficulties of line play, the intricacies of offensive systems, the keys to last season's Rose Bowl victory), usually explained by a coach; or celebrity profiles of coaches and players. When the great photojournals, *Life* and *Look* (the latter a bimonthly), hit the newsstands in 1936 and 1937, respectively, sport was part of their appeal to readers from the outset. Their most significant contribution to American football culture came from their photographic celebrations of football's pageantry and spectacle, and of the larger social and domestic worlds within which football was situated. Photo-essays on peewee, youth, and high school as well as college teams; on the cheerleaders, bands, and thrilled fans at the stadium; on small towns whose collective life centered on the high school football team; on collegiate homecoming weekends complete with queens, old grads, and decorated sorority houses—these defined a role for everyone in the kingdom of football and placed the sport at the center of an idealized, white, middle-class American social world.

While *Life* and *Look* published only nonfiction, a typical issue of the *Post* or *Collier's* by the 1930s also offered readers a football story, perhaps an installment of a serialized novel, along with a cartoon or two and several ads with football motifs, the entire contents often lying behind a football painting on the cover. The football story might have provided the screenplay for a feature film as well. While all this material, both textual and visual, stood apart from the football journalism—fiction, as opposed to fact—the boundaries between the two were never clearly drawn. Football "fact" always tended toward exaggeration: stalwart athletes and their savvy coaches were routinely idealized by sportswriters, columnists, and broadcasters. For their part, fictional narratives and images insinuated themselves into readers' views of reality in subtle ways. The chief figures in formulaic football films and stories—the hero, the heroine, the coach, the rival, the ethnic teammate, the booster—became absorbed into the public consciousness, to become part of the context when readers contemplated the "real" game.

Short stories and serialized novels were "the backbone of mass circulations"[98] during the golden age of the general-interest weekly magazines, with four to six short stories along with an installment of a serial appearing in each issue of the *Post* and *Collier's* in the 1920s and 1930s.[99] The football story never rivaled the popularity of westerns, mysteries, and romances, but its most prolific writers—James Hopper, Jonathan Brooks, Lawrence Perry, Lucian Cary, Frederick Hazlitt Brennan, George Brooks, Francis Wallace—though long forgotten, undoubtedly had many fans. Football fiction first appeared in popular magazines in the 1890s, as soon as college football first attracted national attention, and virtually all of the popular magazines with a male or general readership published an occasional football story in the 1900s and 1910s. By the 1920s, about three football stories were appearing each year between the *Post* and *Collier's,* that number increasing to five in the 1930s, until the Second World War all but stopped the flow (with real war in Europe and the Pacific, vicarious masculine adventure lost its importance). Football stories returned in 1946 and continued at about four a year in the *Post* and *Collier's* through 1955, after which they fell off to a trickle, television altering the media landscape here as well.

The 123 short stories and ten serials in the *Post* and *Collier's* from 1920 to 1960 defined the center of a much wider print world. A rich tradition of juvenile fiction had begun with the occasional football story in the great nineteenth-century children's magazines, *St. Nicholas* and *Youth's Companion,* then fully emerged in 1896 with the start of the seventeen-year run of the Frank and Dick Merriwell stories in *Tip Top Weekly.* Over the next half-century juvenile football fiction became a staple in magazines such as *Boys' Life* (the Boy Scouts' monthly) and *American Boy,* feeding a steady diet of heroic and didactic football narratives to young males. The first general-fiction pulp magazines also published occasional football stories over the first two decades of the century. Then, beginning in 1923, Street & Smith's *Sport Story Magazine* established sports fiction as a distinct pulp genre, continuing (as a bi-monthly through 1938, then a monthly) until 1943, by which time six specialized football pulps—*Football Stories* (1937–53), *All-American Football Magazine* (1938–53), *Football Action* (1939–53), *Thrilling Football* (1939–50), *Popular Football* (1941–50), and *Exciting Football* (1941–51)—along with a couple of short-lived ones (*Best Football Novels* and *All Football Stories*) and more than two dozen general sports pulps with football stories in season worked endless variations off a handful of formulas.[100] The print runs of these magazines were a fraction of those of the *Post* or *Collier's,* but cumulatively they reached a significant readership of highly impressionable male sports fans.[101]

Though few were big hits, football movies reached the largest audiences of all. Football films settled into a handful of formulas in the 1920s, the master narrative concerning a hero who overcomes some obstacle to win the big game in the final minutes.[102] This plot could serve serious drama, farce, and musical comedy equally well (or badly). Football farce—the preposterous triumph of the unlikely hero—debuted spectacularly with Harold Lloyd's *The Freshman* in 1925 and was frequently repeated, but, with the notable exception of the Marx Brothers' 1932 masterpiece *Horse Feathers,* rarely with any of Lloyd's comic genius.[103] (*The Freshman* did not satirize a film formula—one was just beginning to emerge—but rather the innumerable boys' stories written by the pseudonymous Burt L. Standish, Ralph Henry Barbour, and others.) With the advent of sound came *So This Is College, Sweetie,* and *The Time, the Place, and the Girl* in 1929, creating the college football musical that flourished in the 1930s.[104] Together, these two genres punctured the high seriousness and epic grandeur with which college football was invested by sportswriters and radio broadcasters, and played counterpoint to the era's military-academy dramas, hagiographic biopics (beginning with *Knute Rockne—All-American* in 1940), and melodramas set against the backdrop of recruiting and subsidization in big-time football.[105] The single person most responsible for this last type was Francis Wallace. In addition to writing the annual "Pigskin Preview" for the *Saturday Evening Post* beginning in 1937, Wallace wrote seven football novels in the 1930s, three of them serialized in the *Post* or *Collier's,* five of them adapted by Hollywood.[106] The novels had only modest sales, but the serials in the *Post* and *Collier's* and the movies reached millions over several football seasons, making Wallace one of the most influential shapers of the ways Americans thought, and fantasized, about football in the 1930s.

Finally, the most easily forgotten piece in the football mosaic was the magazines' artwork in its various forms. Cartoons mocked virtually every aspect of big-time football, providing readers an outlet for their ambivalence over making heroes of boys playing a game. Advertisements connected football to images of middle-class consumption and reciprocally connected the advertised product or company to the football ethos of teamwork and competitive success. The earliest ads with football themes were for items with some functional relationship to the sport: Quaker Oats or Cream of Wheat, say, to give the young athlete energy to play.[107] By the 1920s, such ads more likely promoted products with no direct relation to the actual game—automobiles, stylish clothes, fine watches—marketed now not for their use by football players but for their association with the ethos or social

FIGURE 1-3. In the Marx Brothers' football farce, *Horse Feathers* (1932), Harpo assists Chico on the field, while back in the president's office Groucho schemes to save the college with these two supposed ringers he has recruited.

world associated with college football. The most powerful visual representations of football appeared on the covers of the magazines. Together with the newsreel shown before the feature film at the movie theater, the magazine cover was the unavoidable advertisement for football, sitting on coffee tables everywhere and requiring no more effort than a casual glance. Their power was subtle because they interpreted football without seeming to do so. Readers who readily quarreled with sports columnists' opinions would not assume a magazine cover was trying to persuade them of anything at all.

Magazine cover illustration in general developed out of the poster art of the 1890s, then shifted in the 1930s toward scenic realism, then yielded all but totally to photography by the end of our period.[108] *Collier's* clung longer to the poster style—a figure or grouping against a blank background—and switched early to photographs (fifteen of nineteen football covers after 1941). Compared to photography, paintings afforded more artistic and editorial control of the image and "could more easily achieve fantastic, romantic, monumental, heroic, and other hyper-realistic or stylized effects."[109] The premier artist of the poster type, J. C. Leyendecker, was also the father of football illustration, his football heroes and ragamuffin kids providing the major influence on the poster-style football cover. Norman Rockwell, of course, was the genius of scenic realism, but it was his style rather than his actual football covers—he painted only three before 1960—that influenced the football scenes painted for the *Post* by artists such as Stevan Dohanos, George Hughes, John Falter, John Clymer, Dick Sargent, and Ben Prins. The 113 football covers on the two magazines between 1920 and 1960 (52 on the *Post*, 61 on *Collier's*), along with dozens more on the *Literary Digest, Liberty, American Magazine, Country Gentleman,* and other large-circulation weeklies and monthlies (as well as the juvenile magazines), created indelible images of the handsome hero, his lovely admirer, the strong-willed coach, the beleaguered referee, the leaping cheerleader, the strutting drum majorette, the festive bonfire, the shivering or cheering fan, and the winsome kids—lots and lots of kids—mimicking every aspect of this big-time football world. Pulp magazine artwork, in contrast, offered almost nothing but heroic football stars and furious, violent action.

The "smart" magazines—the *New Yorker, Vanity Fair,* the humor magazines *Life* (pre–Henry Luce) and *Judge*—featured different kinds of football covers. Those painted by top illustrators such as John Held, Jr., Russell Patterson, and Vernon Grant for *Life* and *Judge*, and about half of the *New Yorkers,* were brilliantly satiric.[110] The rest of the *New Yorkers,* along with *Vanity Fair's* sole football cover and several football programs painted in the late 1920s and early 1930s for Harvard, Yale, Penn, and Army, and for a number of West Coast universities, rendered the colors and geometries of football spectacle in the art nouveau styles for which magazines such as *Vogue, Vanity Fair, Harper's Bazaar,* and *Fortune* were known in these years.[111] Football programs became more uniform and generic in the late 1930s, when 80 percent of them were produced by the Don Spencer Agency in New York.[112] Over their brief life, the wit and sophistication of this small portion of the earlier programs marked a high point in an unwritten history of American sports art. Their audiences, of course, were limited to the spectators in the stadiums at a few universities and to the educated, relatively well-to-do, mostly urban readers who subscribed to *Vanity Fair* and the *New Yorker.* The football art seen by the great American middle class appeared on the covers of the *Saturday Evening Post, Collier's,* and the other large-circulation magazines. Heroism, human interest, and gentle humor ruled here.

Whether booster or fierce critic, avid fan or casual observer, Americans came to understand football within the culture shaped by these magazines,

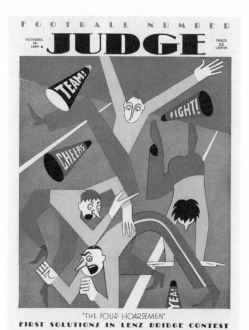

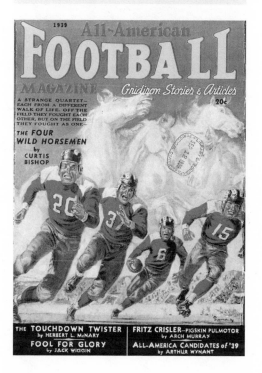

FIGURE 1-4. Football on magazine covers: *American Boy,* October 1920 (painted by W. W. Clarke); *Life,* 15 November 1923 (by Ellison Hoover); *Judge,* 19 October 1929 (unsigned); and *All-American Football Magazine,* Fall 1939 (by Norm Saunders).

FIGURE 1-5. The November 1930 *Vanity Fair* cover painted by emigré artist Constantin Aladjálov (later spelled Alajálov) suggests the influence of Russian Constructivism. The range of styles appropriated from modern art is also suggested by Robert Foster's art deco cover for the Penn–Ohio State football program, 11 November 1933 (he painted several others in this style for Army and Ivy League teams in the early 1930s), the Italian Futurist rendering of football for the St. Mary's–Oregon game on 27 November 1930, and Richard Stephens's collagelike use of the shapes and colors of football for the program of the Washington-Idaho contest on 29 September 1934. (Magazine cover copyright © *Vanity Fair,* Condé Nast Publications, Inc.; program covers reprinted by permission of the Collections of the University of Pennsylvania Archives and Records Center, College Archives Collection of St. Mary's College of California, and MSCUA, University of Washington Libraries)

movies, newsreels, radio broadcasts, and newspapers. For obvious reasons, the representation of football in the mass media was overwhelmingly benign. Two basic principles operated here: the broader the audience or the more dependent on advertising, the greater was the need to avoid controversy. Local newspapers could express local prejudices, but the national media—magazines, network radio, newsreels, movies, even wire-service and syndicated newspaper material—had to be inoffensive, which generally meant silence on such matters as race, ethnicity, and reform. Likewise, while the intellectual journals with little advertising (and small circulations) could be more outspoken, the media dependent on advertising—newspapers, magazines, and radio—could not risk offending their sponsors' potential customers. With these fundamental realities in mind, a racist caricature in a 1931 newsreel or a national magazine's attack in 1951 on corruption in college football becomes more telling: it represents, if not the common or dominant view, at least a view inoffensive to the great majority. No single master plot ran through all the facts and fictions, narratives and images of football from the 1920s through the 1950s, but the following chapters trace some of the most significant themes to which they constantly returned.

Local
Football

The 1920s and 1930s marked the age of intersectional football, when distinct football regions emerged, and competitions between their representatives each season mapped a shifting geographical balance of power. Newcomers to football in the Midwest, South, and Far West had long before World War I sought to test themselves against the eastern establishment, but it was in the 1920s that sectional comparisons and intersectional games became the primary theme in national football reporting. Football power shifted westward from the Northeast in the 1920s, then southward in the 1930s, with the Midwest and the Big Ten emerging as the premier football region and conference, the Pacific Coast just behind (except in the minds of its own sportswriters), and the South periodically upsetting the accustomed order. As the 1920s opened, college football was divided along an East-West axis with leading football powers from the two sections meeting in the Rose Bowl at the end of each season. Alabama consequently went to the 1926 Rose Bowl as the "eastern" representative, but over the course of their stay in southern California the boys from Tuscaloosa impressed local sportswriters as a distinctly southern team. Upsetting the University of Washington that year, then tying Stanford in the 1927 Rose Bowl, Alabama established the South as a true football region. The Southwest remained part of "the South" until the 1930s, when Southern Methodist brought its razzle-dazzle "aerial circus" to New York, South Bend (and thus Chicago), Boston, and

San Francisco, giving Texas and the Southwest a distinct image in the public consciousness. The lower Midwest of Nebraska, Kansas, and Oklahoma (the Big Six Conference in the 1930s) struggled for its own identity in the shadow of the Big Ten. A Rocky Mountain region emerged near the end of the decade due only to Whizzer White's Heisman Trophy season at Colorado, then dropped off the football map again. The Northwest was a distinct region only for internal Pacific Coast Conference affairs.

The creation and consolidation of conferences created traditional rivalries and fierce intraregional partisanship. Intersectional games thrust the home team onto the national stage, where the stakes were higher but more abstract. Some intersectional contests in the 1930s were the Big Game for the competing schools—Army–Notre Dame, USC–Notre Dame, St. Mary's–Fordham most notably—but the more intimate rivalries of neighboring communities or states usually loomed larger for the schools' most ardent supporters. Local columnists treated the home team's contests with distant rivals as crusades to prove the athletic prowess of the community and region, but games against nearby rivals usually drew larger crowds. The Big Game each season for Atlanta was not Georgia Tech–Notre Dame but Georgia Tech–Georgia; for Dallas, not SMU against the world but SMU against TCU. Whether SMU won or lost at West Point or South Bend determined the Mustangs' standing in the national polls but had less palpable consequences for daily life in Dallas and Fort Worth.

Wire-service football was a running commentary on the shifting balance of regional power. Saturday reports on the day's big games and Monday accounts of the weekend results featured intersectional contests. The Associated Press did not begin its weekly poll listing the top twenty teams until 1936, but it kept a weekly intersectional scorecard as early as 1925: rankings of an imaginary national conference comprised initially of the East, Middle West, South, and Far West, with the Southwest added later. Each week, the results from intersectional games—whether Notre Dame–Army or Oglethorpe-Xavier—were added to the running tally, with the top region proclaimed at the end of the season.[1] The announcement of All-America teams always noted the number of players from each region. When the AP named five midwestern players to its 1926 team, against four from the East and one each from the South and Far West—the first time the East had been outnumbered—it declared a shift in football power. But the same story was read differently around the country. In Atlanta, the *Constitution* announced, "Winslett, Alabama, on Composite All-American." In Omaha, the *World-Herald*'s headline read, "Midwest Places Most Men on Coaches' All-

American; 3 Huskers Are Mentioned." In Los Angeles, the *Times* declared, "West Awarded Most Honors."[2] Each of these papers also gave considerably more coverage each season to its own all-conference or all-region team. Whether the context was local or national, most football fans cared almost exclusively about "our boys," and every community was the center of its own football universe.

FOOTBALL AND COMMUNITY

From the initial discovery, in the 1880s and 1890s, that college football games could attract thousands of spectators with no direct connection to the competing universities, football served disparate interests. For many university officials, building a big-time football program meant a Faustian bargain: prestige and growth in return for surrendering control of the sport to the demands of popular entertainment. For local business and political leaders, a successful football team was unambiguously a major community asset, its packed stadiums on Saturday afternoons generating valuable revenues, its acclaim in the national media boosting the city's standing in the region or even the nation. For loyal alumni, the football team was a source of more intimate pride, but the general population on triumphant occasions could also feel powerfully connected to the team, and through the team to the community. In their most fundamental nature, football teams before the age of television were locally rooted, and that local-rootedness had both material and symbolic dimensions.

Football emerged as a spectator sport during a period of tremendous dislocation in American life. The period of football's most spectacular growth, the two decades after World War I, have been described by one historian of the regionalist movement as "a critical juncture in the centuries-long transformation of this country from a rural, frontier, decentralized, producerist, farm and village society—the older America—into the modern commercialized, consumerist, and mechanized mass society of the metropolis."[3] A nation whose citizens were accustomed to a profound sense of place came to seem a placeless arrangement of generic factories, department stores, and Main Streets. A people whose traditional mythos was rooted in rugged individualism and closeness to nature became a "mass" society of city dwellers.

The city meant both promise and disenchantment. Business and civic leaders competed to attract new capital, new industry, and new workers. Workers came eagerly, with hopes that often turned to disillusionment when higher and steadier wages proved insufficient for the American dream. Artists and intellectuals as diverse as the social visionary Lewis Mumford, the folklorist B. A. Botkin, the sociologist Howard Odum, and the poets of the Southern Agrarian movement became preoccupied with regionalism, envisioning authentic regional cultures as a utopian antidote to homogenizing, urban-industrial modernity.[4] Like-minded men founded journals with titles such as *Southwest Review* (1915), *Midland* (1915), *Frontier* (1920), and *Southern Review* (1935) to celebrate sectional distinctiveness. For ordinary citizens, cities meant the many attractions of modernity—the biggest and brightest and newest—but also the loss of traditional values; and modernity reached into the smallest towns and even farms through radio, popular magazines, Sears catalogues, and the like.

The increasing dominance of American life and national identity by the growing metropolis meant a concomitant marginalizing of small towns and rural communities. In the 1920s, consciousness of a gulf between two cultures—one urban and sophisticated, the other small-town or rural and old-fashioned—made bestsellers of novels such as Sinclair Lewis's *Main Street* and *Babbitt,* the novels in turn deepening public consciousness of the divide. The gulf opened along more than one fault line. The urban "smart set" scorned the banality of small towns, whose citizens countered with a loathing for the corruption of cities. Nativists despised and feared foreign immigrants, who came to the United States with their own "old-fashioned values" but also a desire to become "American," which meant modern. "Modernists" and "traditionalists" cut across both urban and small-town societies: self-professed modernists included a small cultural avant-garde and an army of up-to-date Babbitts, while traditionalists included both those with old money and those with old-time religion.

In this social context, one of football's deepest functions was to provide millions of Americans with moments of an emotionally satisfying reconciliation of their conflicting desires for local connection and a place in the modern world. Sport has long been understood, in the words of sociologist Gregory Stone, as "a collective representation passionately (if at times irrationally and irresponsibly) embraced by community members," serving as "a unifying force" through both "inter-community conflict" and "the intra-community communication network it establishes."[5] More simply, citizens bonded over games against teams from rival towns and through talking and reading about the home team. Sport historians have richly documented the role of mass sport in the development of the modern city and the role of the city in the development of modern sport.[6] Here I want to explore more specifically the emotional bonds between citizens and their football teams. More than any other sport, football embraced the competing values of the modern and the antimodern. On the one hand, it was the most complex, sophisticated, and even technological of sports; on the other, it was nearly as atavistic as boxing. The precision of a well-tuned "machine" and ferocious defensive play "in the shadow of the goal posts" were sportswriters' clichés that expressed equal parts of the game's attraction, appealing in very different ways to fans not conscious they represented "modern" and "old-fashioned" values. The modern and the antimodern have been continually redefined in football over the decades, but in some form the tension between them has been a constant throughout the sport's history.

Given its nearly instantaneous embrace in the 1880s and 1890s, football would have became a hugely popular spectator sport with or without the specific demographic shifts of the twentieth century. The role it came to play in communities throughout the land, however, seems incontrovertibly tied to the relocation of both people and the national mythos from the countryside to the city. For a mobile urban population football provided a sense of belonging to an identifiable community; for a rural and small-town population it provided a source of identity and defiant pride in the face of marginalization. Football did not uniquely serve this function, of course; organized baseball prepared communities to identify with their football teams. Football's relationship to its community had distinctive features, however. Whether major or minor league, the baseball team belonged to the entire community in a way that the college football team did not. Only a small minority attended colleges of any kind; private colleges such as SMU and USC did not represent the citizenry in the way that state universities did. At the colleges themselves, football was the focus of campus life dominated by fraternities and sororities, whose members went on to become the rabid alumni filling the stadiums and hounding the football coaches and athletic directors. Outsiders from the Greek system in college typically felt estranged from the schools' athletic teams as well.[7]

Football thus had differentiated publics, which were differently organized than baseball's. A writer in the *Nation* in 1920 distinguished the audiences for baseball and football as akin to those for "vaudeville or melodrama" on the one hand and "higher comedy" on the other. While the former sees only what happens on the diamond or stage, the latter grasps "the coherence and solidarity of an entire undertaking." Football's college-formed crowds were thus quite different from baseball's "heterogeneous ones."[8] Such elitism clung to college football as the 1920s opened and never entirely dissipated. Economics mattered, too. In emerging metropolises such as Atlanta, Dallas, and Los Angeles, football appealed most strongly to the civic and business boosters, who embraced the local team as a symbol of the city's energy and achievement. Yet when the team did well, it galvanized the entire community and could temporarily blur the boundaries between the elites and ordinary citizens, professionals and laborers. On these occasions, football could offer everyone a sense of belonging, and of somehow counting in the larger scheme of things.

Detailed studies of the impact of football on communities have unfortunately focused on the recent professional game, chiefly in regards to the financial terms on which franchises are sustained.[9] The professional football franchise, of course, is first and foremost an economic entity, its impact measurable in the profits it earns, the costs to taxpayers who perhaps finance a stadium, and the income it generates within the community. But whether all citizens gain financially from the presence of an NFL (or National Basketball Association or major league baseball) franchise, the familiar argument goes, everyone benefits from the enhancement to civic pride. American cities become "major league" by virtue of their multiple professional sports franchises, as recent sports columnists in the *Portland Oregonian,* for example, have periodically reminded the local politicians and business leaders who failed to pursue an NFL or major league baseball franchise with sufficient zeal. Indianapolis has the Colts and Pacers, the reasoning goes, Portland only the Trailblazers; ergo, Indianapolis by a certain sporting calculus is twice the city Portland is.

A different sporting calculus operated in the first half of the twentieth century. Football's local importance tended to be inversely proportional to the community's size and status. Major state universities were mostly founded in towns and small cities, rather than metropolises, and in many of these places—with no opera or symphony or skyscraping monuments—the football team became the chief source of local pride. An article in the *Saturday Evening Post* about the University of Nebraska's football coach in 1951 commented that "football commands much more than the average amount of interest in Nebraska. In this prairie state of great open stretches and small communities, where the average town is only 375 people, the university's football team is one of the strongest common bonds." Historian Benjamin Rader, himself a professor at Nebraska, has stated the more general case: "Citizens in states without a conspicuously significant history, great civic monuments, or remarkable physical scenery often formed strong emotional bonds to their state university football team."[10]

The most powerful bonds were often to high school football teams in towns without a university. As many as 120,000 Chicagoans turned out in the 1930s to see the Catholic-Public championship game at Soldier Field, and for Chicago's second-generation ethnic immigrants—in a city with more Poles, Slovaks, and Czechs than any other in the world, and the third largest numbers of Italians, Irish, Swedes, and Jews—high school football and other sports in the 1920s and 1930s provided what historian Gerald Gems has termed "communal pride" and "associational ties" to replace their parents' nationalism.[11] But it was in places like Canton and Massillon, Ohio, and throughout the state of Texas that high school football became legendary for consuming the entire community.[12] Newspapers from a handful of small towns around the country suggest varying degrees of football passion. In Hays, Kansas, the *Daily News* paid little attention to football of any kind, including the games played by the local high school. In Nacodoches, Texas, coverage of the local high school and of Stephen F. Austin College in the *Daily Sentinel* was meager in the 1920s, somewhat greater in the 1930s, and extensive after World War II. In Biloxi and Gulfport, Mississippi, major coverage of high school football began earlier. In 1925, what little sports coverage there was in the *Daily Herald* focused on the local high schools. By 1935, a full page of daily sports emphasized both Mississippi State and the high schools, with the schoolboy game clearly more important, occasionally warranting front-page coverage.[13]

The importance of high school football in Muncie, Indiana, fell somewhere between Hays and Biloxi. Robert and Helen Lynd conducted their initial study of "Middletown" in 1924–25, then returned ten years later to assess the changes.[14] The Lynds said nothing about football in their original study, and on their return they noted only that the number of boys from the tenth through twelfth grades playing football had increased from thirty-three in 1931 to seventy-seven in 1935.[15] For the 1924–25 study they reported that organized sports, nearly nonexistent in 1890, had become conspicuous, in YMCA, YWCA, factory, and high school teams, and on both municipal and country-club golf courses. Only the communitywide passion for high school basketball warranted specific mention, however.[16] High school football, then, came in second place, at best, to Muncie's "Hoosier hysteria" over basketball, but examination of the *Muncie Morning Star* helps place football in the larger contexts that these studies set up.

In their follow-up study, the Lynds noted a marked struggle among Muncie's citizens "between the old pride in localism, in being Middletown, and the opposed pride in being *en rapport* with the 'newest,' the 'smartest,' the 'most approved by the right people in the big outside world.'"[17] Though unnoted by the Lynds, football played a role in this modern/antimodern and local/cosmopolitan dialectic. In 1924, the typical twelve-page *Morning Star* included a page of sports (two on Sundays), in which the Central High Bearcats shared space with big-time college football, whose coverage was split between the state's major universities (Indiana, Purdue, and Notre Dame) and the national leaders. Red Grange was news in the *Muncie Morning Star* in 1924, as in newspapers everywhere. The local Normal college (not yet renamed Ball State) received much less coverage than the high school Bearcats, whose Saturday games commanded the largest headlines and were covered by the *Star*'s one staff sportswriter. The out-of-town Sunday papers from Chicago and Indianapolis, however, were full of Big Ten football, and nothing in the coverage of Bearcat football by the *Morning Star* points to intense local passions.

The crucial difference in 1935 challenges the greater cosmopolitanism that the Lynds found elsewhere in Muncie. In 1924, the *Morning Star* had no local sports columnist but ran Grantland Rice's syndicated "Sportlight" column once or twice a week. In 1935, against the expansion of syndicated material elsewhere in its pages, the paper no longer had a national sports columnist but now had one of its own, and in Bob Barnet's "Punts and Passes" column one can clearly see the role played by high school and local small-college football in the "Middletowns" of America. Appearing once or twice a week, "Punts and Passes" addressed only the Ball State Cardinals and the Central High Bearcats. Ball State's games with such nearby colleges as Danville, Valparaiso, Franklin, and DePauw, before crowds of a few thousand, did not register at all on the national football map; but Ball State was Muncie's team, and Barnet's columns took readers into the locker room and the coach's office for the sort of "inside" story of the Cardinals' season that readers expected of sportswriters. Barnet was upbeat, even when the team lost, and he always supported the coach. In a 1935 season marked by few victories, Barnet insisted that as long as the boys had fun, winning did not matter greatly.[18]

With the high school Bearcats, Barnet in both his columns and his game reports adopted a different tone, somewhere between a community voice and that of a loud, opinionated neighbor or an overinvolved uncle. Bearcat football emerges from these columns as a tribal affair, of interest to no one beyond the city limits perhaps, but a matter of giddy pride, extravagant hopes, bitter disappointment, and stern rebuke among the locals. The Bearcat players, of course, were the readers' children and neighbors. Columns full of their names (including four sets of brothers, two of them pairs of twins) read a bit like letters to grandma, describing what the kids are up to. What the boys did on the field was but part of the story. One column had some good-natured fun over the drum major's dropping his baton during the halftime show; two others described the comic adventures of Bill the albino goat mascot, who ran away, was captured and impounded, and ultimately raffled to an official "goat manager."[19] In another column, Barnet indulged in a bit of fancy writing of a type that had largely disappeared from metropolitan dailies, applying to high school football the overwritten grand manner developed at the end of the previous century for the college game. An early-season win over the Anderson Indians provoked this opening:

> Driven by an icy wind from the eastward, the surly Bearcat of Muncie came tonight to this shivering city. Upon an illuminated athletic field he met the red Indian of Anderson high school, taunting him, barring his way to the warmth of the victory he sought.
>
> For a time he pawed clumsily at his adversary, half-heartedly, he sought to drive him from his pathway. The red man brought forth courage, and his long arrows arched through the night sky and shivered in the Bearcat flanks. And the Bearcat awakened. Twice he struck with the swiftness of the lightning. Twice he struck in his wrath, and the Indian sank down in defeat.[20]

In the echoed rhythms of Longfellow's "Hiawatha" one hears the enduring appeal of Edgar Guest and James Whitcomb Riley, the homespun newspaper poets popular in the Middletowns of America.

Tribal resentments and allegiances, equally meaningless to outsiders, also were voiced in Barnet's columns. In one he expressed the townspeople's kinship with their neighbors from Newcastle, despite the Trojans' upsetting the local boys in a game that cost Central High the conference championship. "It is always a pleasure to meet Newcastle on gridiron or basketball court or track," wrote Barnet following the game. "The boys and the coaches, and even the sportswriters, are real gentlemen. They will ever be welcome in Muncie." The same good feelings were not extended to Arnel-Technical high in the big city, Indianapolis, however. After a 20–0 licking by the Techsters, Barnet noted that the Bearcat coach "doesn't like to lose to Tech, a feeling shared by many."[21]

Families have squabbles, too, and Bob Barnet stirred one up when he accused the boys of overconfidence in the loss to Newcastle. There must have followed a deluge of complaints, because the following Tuesday's column addressed the charge that Barnet's own pregame prediction of victory had created the Bearcats' overconfidence. Barnet accepted "a certain share of the responsibility"—"Our shoulders are broad, and not without saddle-boils," he confessed—but he declined the whole load: "But to say that the boys depend so greatly upon the written word that their game was wrecked completely by our lack of respect for Newcastle, that is too much. To say that we caused the boys to forget everything they ever knew about football and lose to a team which they should have beaten by three touchdowns, that is flattery of a brand too rich for our miserable blood. Gentlemen, you flatter us!"[22] This column, beyond all others in 1935, reveals the intrafamilial element of the small-town high school football team's relations to its followers and its local newspaper.

The citizens of Muncie received large doses of big-time college football from their out-of-town Sunday newspapers, from the newsreels at their thriving movie houses, and from their radios through which they could pick up CBS and two NBC networks, as well as the more powerful stations out of Indianapolis, Chicago, and probably Cincinnati, Cleveland, and other cities. Although the Lynds reported that Middletown had its own local radio station by 1935, radio listings in the *Muncie Morning News* reveal no local programming. Neither Ball State nor Central High football games were broadcast over the local station (nor were Bearcat basketball games that winter, "Hoosier hysteria" notwithstanding). But in the local newspaper the home team was the one that mattered in Muncie in 1935, as was the case in Middletowns everywhere. Neither Indiana nor Purdue fared well in the Big Ten that season; it took a championship, bowl-bound team to generate intense enthusiasm throughout a state or region. Notre Dame knocked off Ohio State in the 1935 season's "Game of the Century" and was touted for the Rose Bowl, only to lose to Northwestern the following week and slip back in the national rankings. But Notre Dame was an Indiana team only by accident of geography, and in predominantly native-born, Protestant Muncie, the school's symbolic appeal would not have been particularly strong.

As the case of Middletown/Muncie confirms, football was locally rooted —and the local newspaper was the primary public forum for local emotions —but the sport's local power depended on its broader resonance. Townspeople in Muncie could take their own Bearcat football team seriously because Harvard and Yale, Army and Navy, Notre Dame and Southern Cal, Ohio State and Michigan made football important to the country at large. However removed from the heights of big-time football, the Central High Bearcats derived their importance within the community by replicating big-time football on a local scale.

FOOTBALL, UNIVERSITY BUILDING, AND URBAN BOOSTERISM

What college football offered that high school football could not was a local representative competing for prestige in a national arena. Harvard's upset by the "Praying Colonels" of Centre College in 1921, after the Kentucky team's gallant loss in 1920, was the decisive event in launching the age of intersectionalism. The roads to football prestige lay through the Northeast, where the Big Three, Harvard, Yale, and Princeton, ruled the entire football world, and the most influential sportswriters covered the games, but not just anyone could travel those roads. Francis Wallace explained to readers of the *Saturday Evening Post* in 1929 that college football teams were divided into three classes: the "aristocrats" of the Northeast, a "middle group" comprised of the leaders from each section, and the "climbers" everywhere. Aristocrats scheduled whomever they wanted on whatever terms they preferred, conferring on their opponents prestige rather than dollars. The middle group "wants entry into the upper circle" and would accept the aristocrats' conditions. Climbers settled for the best deal they could get with any team above them.[23] The Big Three smiled favorably on southern schools such as Georgia and Virginia in the 1920s but were much less willing to take on Notre Dame, Nebraska, and the Big Ten powerhouses. Nebraska, in turn, declined a home-and-home agreement with NYU for 1928 and 1929, when the New York school was still a "climber," but "leaped on the opportunity to play Army" in 1928, as Francis Wallace noted. Shunned by the Big Ten, Notre Dame filled its schedule with teams from every corner of the country, becoming a national football team by desperation rather than design, then capitalizing on the unsought opportunity to build a truly national university through football.[24]

Intersectional ambition, constrained by these institutional realities, arose at different times in different places, always accompanied by enormous coverage in local newspapers, always as a campaign for local prestige. Georgia and Georgia Tech led the South in scheduling intersectional games in the 1920s, with the result usually a moral victory claimed after a hard-fought loss. Moral victories, too, were all that SMU and Nebraska won when both schools made their first assaults on the eastern football establishment in 1928, in both cases to play Army at West Point. George White, sports editor of the *Dallas Morning News*, proudly (and defensively) declared SMU's performance in a 14–13 defeat an exhibition of "the brand of football played in the Southwest" that "convinced the skeptics beyond all doubt 'that it will stand a solid test.'" White's counterpart at the *Omaha World-Herald*, Frederick Ware, was more disconsolate over Nebraska's 13–3 defeat by the Cadets. Ware termed the Cornhuskers' victory over Kansas State five days later to win the initial Big Six conference title "some consoling bits of provincial success from the sorrowful wreckage of their once promising dreams of national prestige."[25]

That simple phrase "provincial success" points to the larger stakes in intersectional contests, but whether national prestige was as important to all Cornhusker fans as it was to Frederick Ware is uncertain. The competing claims of national prestige and local bragging rights occasionally spilled into local sports columns. Criticism of Georgia Tech's campaigns outside the region provoked a response from the *Atlanta Constitution*'s Paul Warwick in 1923, after Tech lost games at Penn State and Notre Dame. "Each year," Warwick admitted, "there goes up a chant at the tail end of the football season, 'Stop these eastern and western invasions: they don't getcha anywhere. Whaddya win if you happen to beat an eastern team? Go up there and lose year after year—what's it worth?'" Warwick's answer: "In the opinion of this writer, it's worth a lot—for Tech, Georgia, Auburn and others of their sister institutions to make these eastern sallies. Football is a game for glory and sportsmanship, fundamentally and ideally, for that's the sincere supporter's and the player's attitude, and if there isn't glory and achievement in going back year after year, nothing daunted by defeat, making each time a deeper and more incisive impression on the great 'unbeatables'—then I'm willing to let them think that the south fears eastern and western gridiron prowess and is content in its own back yard." Tech's invasions of Indiana and Pennsylvania in 1923 had won great respect, Warwick insisted. Tech proved itself "the outfightingest gang that the Tornado has put on the field in some time," and "this correspondent likes to feel the warm glow that comes in realizing that people outside of this state's boundary lines know about it."[26]

Warwick, of course, was present in the foreign stadiums to feel the warm glow; back home, the respect Tech won was just a rumor. Warwick also belonged to a national sportswriters' fraternity, whose broader outlook shaped his provincial loyalties. And his newspaper, "the primary organ of the New South agenda," had early on recognized in football an agent for promoting a vigorous and modern South to the rest of the country. The *Constitution* had embraced football from the outset, even sponsoring the first intercollegiate game played in the state of Georgia, between Georgia and Alabama A&M (Auburn) in Atlanta in 1892.[27] For many Tech supports in Atlanta, however, local rivalries mattered more. Bad feelings suspended the Georgia–Georgia Tech rivalry between 1917 and 1924, during which time Tech's game with

Auburn became the season-ending traditional battle. In 1922, Notre Dame's visit to Atlanta drew 20,000 to Grant Field, while the Tech-Auburn game drew 25,000 (the largest crowd in the South to that point). In 1925, only 12,752 turned out for Rockne's men (in the rain), compared to 32,200 for Tech's renewal with Georgia (again the largest crowd in the South). Georgia Tech's home games that season with Alabama (17,000), Florida (17,000), and Auburn (16,000) also outdrew Notre Dame. Only the game with Notre Dame attracted national attention, but a greater number of Atlantans clearly cared more about Tech's standing within the region.

The competing claims of national recognition and local bragging rights played out in Dallas in similar ways. Following the loss to Army in 1928, SMU, unlike Nebraska, failed to win its own conference title, and George White took up the problem addressed by Paul Warwick. After Grantland Rice's All-America team appeared, with but two Southwest Conference players barely mentioned, White read the lesson that "only players who participated with teams that played a number of hard, testing games were considered. This is practically equivalent to saying that a team is out of the race if it does not meet a Notre Dame, Army, Navy, Yale, Harvard, Princeton, Dartmouth, New York U., Carnegie Tech or a strong team in the Big Ten, Southern Conference or Pacific Coast circuit and it is preferable that at least two or three of these teams be on the program." Teams from the Southwest must meet "an assortment of the recognized best. That, to Eastern critics, who have undeniable control of the situation, means elevens in their sector."

If playing top-rated elevens from other regions was the only way to win national prestige, however, there was a downside as well. "During recent weeks (since their defeat in the conference), considerable complaint has been heard about these contests among supporters of the Southern Methodists. The argument has been offered that the Army game took so much out of the Mustangs that they were 'shot' by the time they reached the halfway mark of their conference schedule." White offered alternative explanations, and with some defensiveness insisted that SMU's season must be considered a success: "What they did at West Point was enough in itself to stamp 1928 as a big year. It did more for Southwestern football than anything that ever has taken place." However much SMU's near-upset of Army did for Texas and the Southwest in the estimation of the broader football public, clearly within the region winning the conference championship was more important to many local fans. Two years later, SMU opened the season with another one-point loss in a big intersectional game, this one to Notre Dame, then again lost the conference championship. The following season, after the Mustangs did win the title, George White wrote: "The fact that S.M.U. sacrificed its chances in the conference to throw a scare into Army and Notre Dame is soon forgotten. The fact that they won championships in 1923, 1926 and 1931 is long remembered." [28]

Intersectional games were important, then, but to whom and for what reasons? Sportswriters like Paul Warwick and George White inevitably embraced the opportunities that intersectional games uniquely offered for standing in the national football arena. The newspapers in this study were uniform in casting big intersectional contests as major events of the season, but this was a view not shared equally by all their readers. As a group, football fans were wealthier and better educated than baseball fans. The game appealed initially to alumni of the competing colleges, then expanded to include the full range of classes, but still in the late 1950s a Gallup poll revealed that 36 percent of football fans were college-educated, compared to 21 percent of baseball fans. Even at the high school level, the students in A. B. Hollingshead's study of "Elmtown" were more likely to attend games if they came from the middle and upper classes.[29] Alumni who notoriously paid talented youngsters to play football for alma mater had to be sufficiently wealthy to indulge in this expensive hobby.[30] The civic and business leaders who most aggressively supported the local football team were in positions to capitalize on the economic benefits of large crowds and favorable publicity.

Newspapers offered occasional glimpses of the fans most committed to winning intersectional recognition. The *Dallas Morning News* reported that four special trains, taking 750 fans, accompanied SMU in 1928 to West Point. In 1930, 125 fans, along with the university's sixty-piece band, traveled to South Bend for the Notre Dame game; and 400–500 took five special trains to Baltimore for the Navy contest. Who these fans were, or at least what class they belonged to, can be easily deduced from ads in the *Morning News* in 1931 for excursions to Baltimore for the Navy game and to San Francisco for St. Mary's. Those who could afford $125 for the first and $150 for the second were surely from Dallas's business and social elites (the average weekly wage for manufacturing jobs in 1930 was $23.25). The next season, $126.99 was the advertised lower-berth fare for an excursion to Syracuse with the team. Football fans able and willing to pay such prices in the depths of the Depression viewed themselves and their city in national contexts.[31]

Such football boosterism was a national phenomenon in localized forms. Certain college presidents openly sought to build their institutions through the publicity won by a successful football team. John Thelin has described the "booster campuses" at state universities such as Georgia and LSU, but football had an even greater impact in elevating a few small private schools into major institutions of higher education through football.[32] One of William Rainey Harper's first acts as president of the new University of Chicago in 1890 was to hire Amos Alonzo Stagg at a full professor's salary, to help promote his university through a successful football team.[33] The Notre Dame case is even more striking: the small, undistinguished Catholic college in Indiana became a national university through the spectacularly publicized triumphs of Knute Rockne and his teams in the 1920s. Other denominational universities, such as Northwestern, USC, and SMU, followed a similar course, becoming large institutions in major conferences, rather than remaining tiny church-based schools, through the agency of their football teams.[34] As John Watterson has fleshed out the story, famously "tiny" Centre College briefly moved in this direction, then retreated. The romanticized "Praying Colonels" from Danville, Kentucky, were in fact more like "predatory Colonels," beating up on the local competition by scores like 95–0 and 120–0 before looking around for bigger prey and finding it in Cambridge, Mass. Led by Bo McMillan, a "talented pool hustler and quarterback" who had not managed to graduate from high school, the Colonels became the darlings of college football with their upset of Harvard in 1921, which also earned McMillan a coaching position at Centenary College of Shreveport, Louisiana, after leaving school (many credits short of graduating). At Centenary, McMillan's successful football teams increased enrollments but nearly got the college expelled from its conference "because of its lax athletic policies." Trustees at Centre were prepared to offer McMillan a salary greater than the president's to return as coach, but the distorted pay would have jeopardized the school's accreditation, and the president persuaded the board to reconsider. "As a result, the football program quickly withered on the vine." (Not Bo McMillan, however, who went on to coach at Geneva College, Kansas State, and Indiana, before moving on to the NFL.)[35]

University-building through football clearly did not come without risks, but several presidents were willing to take them. Under the leadership of Rufus von KleinSchmid, the University of Southern California emphasized football in the 1920s as part of its effort to gain financial stability. The University Junior College, created by von KleinSchmid to admit students not meeting state requirements, became "a haven for the football squad" (the Junior College was not abolished until von KleinSchmid retired in 1947). Southern Cal became known as a "football school" during the Howard Jones coaching regime in the late 1920s and 1930s, and its reputation as an undistinguished university with low entrance requirements clung through the 1950s.[36] Less ambiguously, USC football served the interests of the power elite in Los Angeles in the 1920s, who, as Steven Riess has written, "decided to utilize sport to advance their city's reputation for the purposes of encouraging the expansion of tourism, commerce, and migration." The key to their campaign was the building of the Los Angeles Coliseum, in which USC football generated 86 percent of the gate receipts by 1928. Harry Chandler, publisher of the *Los Angeles Times,* led the campaign to build the Coliseum, and the paper's sports staff championed USC football as a symbol of Los Angeles and southern California. A booster president, a booster urban leadership, and a booster press found their common interest in college football.[37]

Southern Cal's campaign "to become a sort of western Notre Dame" depended on intersectional contests, most notably with the Fighting Irish themselves, but nowhere was intrasectional rivalry more brutal than in Los Angeles. While East-West intersectional competition brought national recognition, North-South rivalries were more urgent and bitter, as part of the intercity war between arriviste Los Angeles and snooty San Francisco. Cal and Stanford scorned USC for its low academic standards. In return, Trojan victories over the Bay Area schools, according to two historians of USC, "gave vent to the Southland's sectional frustration and humiliation."[38] Southern Cal's East-West and North-South rivalries were further complicated when all four California schools in the Pacific Coast Conference found themselves at odds with the northern five or six (Oregon, Oregon State, Washington, Washington State, and Idaho, along with Montana until 1949).[39] To at least some in the L.A. press, the Northwesterners were the bumpkins of the league, as when Ed Hughes wrote after the Trojans beat Oregon Agricultural College (later Oregon State) in 1926, "The Oregon Farmers can now attend to their milking and other chores and forget all about winning the Coast Conference championship and representing the West against the East at Pasadena on New Year's Day."[40] (Enduring such condescension was the dues the small northwestern schools had to pay for competing in the PCC, a fact that periodically rankled L. H. Gregory, the sports editor of the *Portland Oregonian* throughout the entire period.)[41] Playing in Corvallis, Eugene, Pullman, or even Portland, instead of the 100,000-seat Los Angeles Coliseum, was always a nuisance and a financial sacrifice to USC, and later to UCLA after it rose to equal power in the 1940s and 1950s. The northern schools regularly lobbied at conference meetings for round-robin play—home-and-home arrangements, with each team playing all others in the conference (established in 1936, abandoned in 1947, resumed in 1956)—while the southern schools wanted more freedom to schedule big-payday inter-sectional contests and make fewer trips to the boondocks. Resentment esca-lated in the mid-1950s, when the smaller northwestern schools, along with Stanford, formed the majority that meted out fines and probation to USC, UCLA, and Cal (plus the University of Washington) for slush funds handled by booster clubs, thus infuriating their big-football rivals and leading to the dissolution of the Pacific Coast Conference in 1959.[42]

The booster clubs operating these slush funds—the Greater Washington Advertising Fund (for UW), the Southern Seas, East Bay Grid Club, and San Francisco Grid Club (for Cal), the Southern California Educational Foun-dation (for USC), and the Bruin Bench and the Young Men's Club of West-wood (for UCLA)—were given names and faces in the daily and periodical press as the PCC scandals unfolded in the 1950s, but usually such groups operated in college football's shadowy back rooms. While the Big Booster became a stereotypical figure in 1930s magazine fiction and movies,[43] local and even national sportswriters tacitly endorsed the boosters' role in run-ning the local football program by not exposing and criticizing it. Historians have brought some of these stories to light, however, notably the story of Dallas and Southern Methodist University. The details are particular to the school and its city, but comparable scenarios played out elsewhere.

After a few quiet years following its founding in 1915, SMU's second presi-dent, Hiram Boaz (1920–22), and his long-serving successor, Charles Selec-man (1923–1938), consciously promoted the university through its football team, in partnership with key figures from the Dallas business community.[44] Boaz hired Ray Morrison as coach in 1920 and assigned the university's vice president to aid him in recruiting a class that came to be known as the "Im-mortal Ten." The result was SMU's first rise to football prominence, as well as its first brush with football scandal: the conference charged after the "Ten's" sophomore season that SMU had violated rules on eligibility, recruiting, and subsidization. Some of the young men happened to be "adult specials" who lacked required credits and were remembered as "roughhewn giants driving down from Oklahoma to play in the game and then driving back home." Jobs that paid up to $1.75 an hour but entailed no work and loans that required no signature were the chief inducements.[45]

SMU's own vote prevented suspension from the conference, but an inter-nal faculty investigation corroborated the accusations and set the faculty against the athletic department, the administration, and the trustees. The most vocal of the trustees, a Dallas wholesale jeweler named H. R. Shuttles, resigned in outrage from the board, declaring "that SMU should be run and officered by business men while faculty of the university [believe] that the affairs of the school should be handled by churchmen and the faculty." Control of athletics was thus part of the larger issue of control of the university; the faculty won this battle but lost the war. The new president, Charles Selecman, built a stadium on the campus in 1926 for $190,000, delaying a library until 1939. Eighty-five thousand dollars were still owed on Ownby Stadium in 1935, when a most timely Rose Bowl bid brought $90,000 to the university to retire the debt. Selecman was not always so lucky, as he clashed with local businessmen in 1931 over his firing of R. N. Blackwell, the business manager of athletics, ostensibly for drinking but apparently for other causes never publicly acknowledged. Led by H. R. Shuttles again, now chairman of the board of trustees, "the Dallasites who backed the football team" attempted to force Selecman to resign, circulating a petition on Blackwell's behalf that also affirmed their loyalty to the university and their appreciation that "its record in athletics has brought great advertisement to and been worth much in a business way to Texas and especially the city of Dallas." As the Mustang football team dazzled New York sportswriters and fans with its "aerial circus" passing attack over the early 1930s, ultimately claiming the top ranking in 1935 and a trip to the Rose Bowl, faculty salaries dropped while the football coach's rose to several times that of a full professor.[46]

All this played out more or less privately, as the local sports pages simply celebrated the successes of the SMU football team and its promotion of Dallas. The Mustangs reflected glory on the entire Southwest, but a reputation for first-class football and first-class support by fans paid the greatest dividends to those who would benefit directly from growth and tourism. An expanded stadium (46,200 seats) at State Fair Park in 1930, as George White noted, promised to be "an asset to the city, too, for it may be the means of landing some big dishes that may bring thousands more visitors here, make this city a central attraction on the national gridiron map and further advertise the Southwest to the rest of the world." The serendipitous timing of a New Year's doubleheader on 1 January 1936—SMU in the Rose Bowl, TCU in the Sugar Bowl—created extraordinary opportunities to publicize the Texas Centennial Exposition planned for the following summer and fall, an event generally regarded as a turning point in the history of Dallas.[47] In the weeks before the Rose Bowl, the *Dallas Morning News* noted that the Mustang Centennial Specials carrying thousands of Texans to southern California were "spreading favorable publicity and building good will for this city, State and the Texas Centennial." The *Morning News* reported proudly that the invasion of eight thousand Texans would be a Rose Bowl record, easily surpassing the eight hundred Alabamans who went the previous year and dwarfing the mere sixty and seventy-five who accompanied Columbia in 1934 and Pittsburgh in 1933.[48] Champion fans, to match their champion football team, enhanced the image of Dallas as a go-getting city. A full-page ad placed by Dallas Power & Light in a special Rose Bowl Edition of the *Morning News* and *Los Angeles Times* on New Year's Day invited the world to the Texas Centennial Exposition, proclaiming, "Come to Dallas—You'll Want to Stay."

The two bowl games "launched the final phase of the Centennial publicity push and set the pattern for the ensuing campaign." Sending his lieutenant governor to New Orleans for the Sugar Bowl, Governor James V. Allred accompanied SMU to Pasadena, where he commissioned actress Ginger Rogers as an admiral in the Texas Navy. Centennial press director Dale Miller persuaded Jack Benny to do a Texas skit on his hugely popular radio program, and members of the Texas delegation presented a ten-gallon hat to every movie star and politician in sight. For the first time in Rose Bowl history, the visiting team was allotted part of the halftime show: a performance by SMU's famous swing band, followed by Governor Allred's invitation to NBC's nationwide audience to attend the Texas Centennial (the lieutenant governor offered the same invitation over network radio at the Sugar Bowl). Thanks to the two bowl games, according to one member of the Centennial advertising board, "People in the North and East who weren't fully acquainted with Texas are having their eyes and interests sharpened."[49] Football was by no means the only, or even primary, entertainment over the months of the Centennial Exposition the following summer and fall, but two of the three intersectional football games at Fair Park contributed to the fourth and sixth highest daily attendance. The conjunction of the Rose Bowl with the Texas Centennial created a unique opportunity for civic promotion through football, a high point in an ongoing relationship between SMU football and the Dallas business community.

Similar relationships played out in other cities. Every community, every big-time college football team, had its powerful football boosters and booster groups, deeply invested—whether financially or emotionally—in the fate of the local team. Some boosters were profit-minded promoters, such as the individuals and groups that sponsored bowl games. One radio announcer, by 1941 already weary of reading "bowl-game releases with sidelights about the glories of this or that section of the country," proposed that bowl promoters might more honestly stage "a bungalow or a lot-selling contest" rather than a football game. "The rivalry frequently seems to be more of a real-estate than a gridiron one," he complained.[50] The proliferation of bowl games as commercial promotions of scant financial benefit to the competing schools finally prompted NCAA regulation in the 1950s. The more routine, ongoing football boosterism usually entangled financial interests with less material motives. Many boosters were members of the business and civic elites who made up the urban "regimes" of large cities and the social, political, and economic leadership in smaller ones.[51] Others, of course, were alumni whose pride lay in the football fortunes of alma mater, but many others were ordinary citizens with no direct connection to the university who simply longed to feel part of something grand. For all of these, and to varying degrees, a winning local college football team helped make one's own city seem special, not soulless.

The machinations of powerful boosters usually played out behind the scenes, but occasionally they forced themselves onto the local sports pages. Antagonism hinted at in several of Frederick Ware's columns in the *Omaha World-Herald* in the 1930s, between amateur purists and boosters who demanded victories, erupted in 1945, when the university's athletic board decided that Biff Jones would not be invited back as coach when his military service ended. The meddling in Nebraska football by a group of Lincoln boosters—variously called the "O Street Gang," the "downtown interference," and "Holy Lincoln's downtown quarterbacks" by *World-Herald* reporters—escalated into a war between the principal newspapers of rival cities as well. The *World-Herald*'s bluntly worded attacks were answered by Cy Sherman, sports editor of the *Lincoln Star* for nearly half a century, who hurled blame back on an "obnoxious newspaper clique at Omaha" that "has been striving to confuse and confound the coaching situation with meddling misrepresentation of the good faith and purposes of university heads." Decades of rivalry and resentment lay behind the exchange of editorial missiles: the state's largest city and its leading newspaper on one side, the state's capital and home to the university on the other.[52]

This dark moment in Nebraska football history has its representative aspects. The tangled interplay of forces—university officials, local businessmen, statewide alumni, sports editors and newspapers, and the thousands of fans without direct power but representing the financial lifeblood of the program—that appeared in the airing of this highly public mess was part of college football generally. The *World-Herald* claimed to speak for "the vast majority of Nebraskans," whose wishes ran contrary to the methods of the regents and the "downtown Lincoln clique,"[53] but the *World-Herald* also spoke more narrowly for the university's alumni in Omaha, who resented their exclusion from direct involvement by alumni in Lincoln, and more narrowly yet for its own standing as the authoritative, independent voice of football in the state. At the heart of the Biff Jones affair was the question of who "owned" Cornhusker football, a question that since the 1890s, when universities first embraced the sport for its promotional and advertising power, had had no simple answer. When the team was successful, everyone felt proprietary in an uncomplicated way, and no one resented the claims of others. Losing seasons brought to the surface the complications and contradictions at the heart of a game that was at once a university activity, an economic resource, and the focus of community pride.

Recognizing the role of self-interested boosters can keep us from romanticizing college football as some sort of organic folk expression of local communities. But attention to the economic motives of the elites should not blind us to the larger role the game played for the general citizenry at the same time. For a broad cross-section of the entire South in the 1920s, for example, the triumphs of southern football teams validated the region against the scorn of outsiders. Historian Andrew Doyle has documented how Alabama's upset victory over the University of Washington in the 1926 Rose Bowl was widely celebrated as a vindication of the "benighted South." While middle- and upper-class citizens of Montgomery listened to a recreation of the game from wire transmission in the city's Municipal Auditorium (this was one year before the new NBC network first broadcast the Rose Bowl to millions), thousands of others stood two hours in the cold outside the local newspaper's offices to hear reports of the game. In Tuscaloosa, class antagonisms "temporarily evaporated as merchants, professionals, labourers and farmers on muleback joined Governor Brandon and other state political leaders in paying homage to the Tide." Alabama's Rose Bowl visits—including a second in 1927 and a third in 1931—had an economic impact: they gave the state, as one newspaper put it, "advertising that is of incalculable value," to be used by Governor Bibb Graves "in the never-ending crusade to attract outside capital to Alabama." But these Alabama victories were also symbolically meaningful throughout the South, as were other major intersectional triumphs such as Georgia Tech's victory in the 1929 Rose Bowl and Georgia's defeat of Yale in 1929 to inaugurate its new stadium.[54]

For the larger public drawn to the great popular spectacle, enthusiasm rose and fell with the teams' fortunes and with the comings and goings of key players. Fan interest in SMU's Mustangs reached unprecedented heights in the late 1940s due to the charismatic appeal of a single player, Doak Walker. The Cotton Bowl was enlarged from 45,000 to 67,000 seats for SMU's bowl game with Penn State following Walker's sophomore season of 1947, then to

75,000 in 1949, when Walker was a senior. The Mustangs moved all but one of their home games from 23,000-seat Ownby Stadium on the SMU campus to the expanded Cotton Bowl, which became "The House That Doak Built," and the years from 1945 through 1949 "The Doak Walker Era" in SMU and Southwest Conference football history.[55] Brilliant stars and spectacularly triumphal seasons rallied entire communities, states, and even regions. The Carnegie investigators' claim in 1929—that the general public regarded college football "solely from the point of view of popular amusement"—missed its often deeper meanings.[56] Football teams also focused local identity and pride, but as college officials attempting to manage the beast of big-time football were never allowed to forget, the locals identified more readily with winners.

FOOTBALL MYTHOGRAPHY

Every community had its own football culture, shaped by its own and its region's history, its resources, its civic aspirations, and countless other factors; and the daily newspaper was its principal public voice. Three regions developed distinctive images in the national football consciousness as well: the Midwest for rock-'em, sock-'em power football, the Southwest for wide-open passing, and the South for fierce combativeness. Football experts sometimes made comments on regional styles, as when Vanderbilt coach Ray Morrison offered a typical assessment for the Associated Press in 1935, crediting the Southwest with playing "the fastest and most advanced football in the country," calling the South "defense minded," and saying that the Midwest and Far West "go in mostly for power and have the best running attacks." Grantland Rice that season contrasted the "defense- and run-oriented style" of the Midwest and East to the crowd-pleasing gambling style of the Southwest. A writer in the *Portland Oregonian* in 1937 echoed this distinction while declaring the pass-happy Texas style closer to basketball than proper football.[57]

There was an element of truth in these popular images, particularly in the Southwest's emphasis on passing, but college football was also uniform, or rather multiform, without attention to regional boundaries; and coaching systems were portable. When Ray Morrison himself moved from SMU to Vanderbilt in 1935, he brought his supposedly southwestern passing game with him. About the same time, TCU's Francis Schmidt imported razzle-dazzle laterals to Ohio State, in Big Ten power-football country. More generally, in the 1920s and 1930s the great majority of teams played a version of either Knute Rockne's Notre Dame box or Pop Warner's single- and double-wing. Rockne's former players and assistant coaches installed the Notre Dame system at schools ranging from Fordham (Jim Crowley) and Boston College (Frank Leahy) in the East to Georgia ((Harry Mehre) and Alabama (Frank Thomas) in the South, to Texas (Jack Chevigny briefly) in the Southwest, to St. Mary's (Slip Madigan) and Washington (Jim Phelan) on the West Coast, to Wisconsin (Harry Stuhldreher), Iowa (Eddie Anderson), and Purdue (Noble Kizer) in the Midwest—and this is an abbreviated list. Whether Alabama won the 1935 Rose Bowl with "southern football" or the "Notre Dame system" was decided in the press box, not on the field. After rule changes limited the effectiveness of Rockne's backfield shift, and particularly after the spectacular reintroduction of the T-formation by Stanford in 1940 (and by the Chicago Bears in the NFL), teams either switched to the "T" or stayed with the single-wing through the 1940s and 1950s.

Climate and geography did affect football styles, however. Wet, cold weather in the Midwest put a premium on sure-footed power. The development of the passing game by Ray Morrison at SMU in the 1920s, and then throughout the Southwest Conference in the 1930s, owed something both to the dry weather that made passing possible and to the lack of brawny players that made a run-oriented offense difficult.[58] Dominating teams also tended, then as now, to play conservatively; upstarts took more chances. During the period of the East's preeminence, eastern football was known for conservative power, western football for innovation and wide-open attacks. The Midwest's association with power football occurred simultaneously with its ascendance to the pinnacle of the football world.

But the most distinctive regional styles in the popular mind owed more to sportswriters' inventiveness and the public's interest in a sort of football mythography than to such mundane facts. When the SMU Mustangs came to town, sportswriters in New York and San Francisco enjoyed casting their passing display as a Wild West shoot-out. Southerners likely competed with no more intensity than players elsewhere, but sportswriters both within and outside the region preferred to set them apart, and to attribute their fervor to the undying spirit of the Old South. In part, this regional myth-making simply resulted from sportswriters' need for catchy leads—and the nicknames of some Southwest Conference teams (Mustangs and Longhorns, Horned Frogs and Razorbacks) offered ready-made ones—but in part it also reflected a widely shared desire for regional distinctiveness in the face of an increasingly homogeneous American culture.

The principal football styles celebrated by sports journalists were southern and southwestern; one could be impressed by midwestern rock-'em, sock-'em football but not love it. The images of both southern and southwestern football were rooted in the regions' preexisting mythologies, but the South's myth went deeper. Wild West football derived from pop-western stereotypes that urban Texans at least half-wished to escape. Football as the spirit of the Old South derived from a historical reality transformed into popular myth that southerners clung to and northerners embraced. Consequently, the image of Wild West football remained on the surface of football journalism, while the image of southern football became embedded in the way many fans genuinely thought about the game as played in places like Georgia and Alabama. One measure of this difference is the fact that several short stories in the football pulp magazines took up the theme of Dixie-Yankee conflicts on fictional southern football teams, while southwestern football did not register in this fiction at all.

As the most self-scrutinizing of regions, the South had brought unusual sectional consciousness to football from its beginnings in the 1890s. Historians Andrew Doyle and Patrick Miller have documented how southern progressives embraced football as an emblem of their region's transformation into a New South, while conservatives, particularly evangelical ministers, reviled the game on essentially the same grounds. But southerners also dressed up modern Yankee football in the regalia of the Confederacy. Confederate flags, rebel yells, and bands playing "Dixie" gave typical football pageantry a distinctive southern flavor by the turn of the century. Female "sponsors" of the competing teams acted the role of the fair lady at a medieval tournament for whom the knights jousted. The University of Virginia originally adopted silver gray and cardinal red for its team colors, "to represent the glory of the Confederacy, dyed in the blood of the fallen." Louisiana State University took the name "Fighting Tigers" to commemorate the Louisiana Tigers, "among the state's most distinguished fighting units during the Civil War." Football may have been a "scientific" sport, taught initially to southern youths by Yankee coaches, but as early as 1892 the *Montgomery Advertiser* also likened Auburn's attack to Stonewall Jackson's flanking tactics.[59]

Although sectional consciousness was already old, then, it was over the course of the 1920s and 1930s that the South emerged as a distinct football region to the rest of the country. Every intersectional contest pitting the South against the East or Midwest became a small chapter in the developing narrative of southern football. Along the way, intersectional contests pitting the South against "the East" and "Midwest" came to an end, becoming instead the South versus the North in reenactments of the Civil War. "The

North" did not exist in college football's geography before the 1920s, when it was invented as the antagonist of the South for the sake of Civil War allusions. The identification of Dixie running backs with DeForest's raiders or Pickett's cavalry at Gettysburg began with southern sportswriters but was embraced even more enthusiastically by their Yankee colleagues, as part of the entire nation's romance with the legendary Old South and Lost Cause. Southern sportswriters began it out of a defensive need to assert southern worth; the national media embraced it to feed the longing for regional identities in the face of a rapidly expanding "mass" culture.

Alabama's successes in the 1926 and 1927 Rose Bowls were the first volleys against the popular stereotype of the "benighted South"; Georgia Tech's victory over Cal in the 1929 Rose Bowl was another, though this one was tainted by the famously freakish play by "Wrong-Way Riegels" that determined the outcome.[60] At least in Atlanta, however, the efflorescence of Civil War metaphors appears to have started with the Georgia-Yale game in 1929. With a Yale man as its founding president and the same colors and mascot, the University of Georgia enjoyed a special kinship with the New Englanders that had earned it a place on Yale's schedule since 1923. The games were always played in New Haven—kings don't visit commoners, commoners come to kings—until Yale condescended to travel to Athens in 1929 for the inauguration of Georgia's Sanford Stadium. A special "Georgia-Yale Section" of the *Atlanta Constitution* on the day of the game saluted the event as a tremendous "civic aid" to sleepy Athens; afterward, Georgia's unexpected victory made it another symbolic victory for the entire South as well.[61] "The war is over," Ralph McGill wrote in his account of the game:

> It has been for some 60 years. But the people left in the south are a peculiar people who haven't learned to make a vulgar noise when someone mentions ideals and fighting for a cause. And so when Harry Mehre, who thought the Mason-Dixon line was a railroad until he came down to coach Georgia's football teams, made a talk to the Georgia team before the game, he mentioned ideals and fighting for Georgia and doing one's best for all the Georgians out there. He mentioned something about making the state proud of them.
>
> And then Saturday the Yale band played Dixie.
>
> It ignited something. It touched a spark somewhere. The Georgians might have been charging up the slope at Gettysburg again. They might have been dressed in the butternut charging with Pickett. Certainly no man of that gallant death's crew flung himself at the enemy any more val-

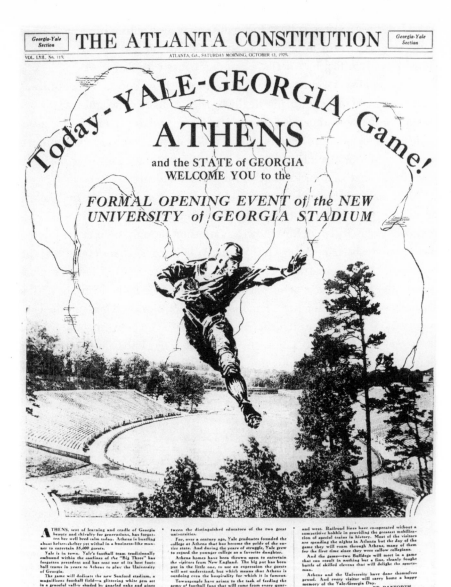

FIGURE 2-1. Yale's visit to Athens, Georgia, to inaugurate the home team's new football stadium on 12 October 1929 was just another intersectional game to most of the country but a major event in the rise of southern football for Georgians. (Reprinted with permission from the *Atlanta Journal* and the *Atlanta Constitution*)

iantly and desperately than did the Georgia football team when it met and repulsed the big blue team from Yale.[62]

Mehre, the Yankee from Notre Dame, mentioned state pride; McGill, the sportswriter from Georgia, mentioned Gettysburg and Pickett. Another Yankee, Dan McGugin, became famous as coach at Vanderbilt for taking his players to a cemetery for the Confederate dead before a game against Michigan and telling them, "Their grandfathers did that to your grandfathers!"[63] But it was sportswriters retelling these stories who made the metaphorical link of southern football to southern myth stereotypical. Ralph McGill attributed the tendency to northerners, noting before the Georgia-Holy Cross game in Boston in 1937 that "one of the gentlemen writing here says that Georgia, having left the union during the Civil War, has been trying to get even ever since by beating Yankee football teams." *New York Post* columnist Stanley Frank saw the matter differently, complaining in 1935 that southern football fans, not northern sportswriters, insisted on viewing every intersectional football game as an attempt to revise the outcome of the Civil War.[64] Who was most responsible for what Frank called "war ballyhoo" may be in doubt, but the ballyhoo itself was incontrovertible. Linking southern football to the myths of the Old South and the Lost Cause began in Dixie, and Ralph McGill's own paper indulged in Civil War metaphors as readily as any other, but it was taken up everywhere.[65]

The Lost Cause was not the only southern myth that became attached to the region's football teams. The *Constitution*'s Ed Danforth described Alabama's 1931 Rose Bowl champions after demolishing Washington State this way: "The giants who slaughtered the champion eleven of the Pacific coast with such a dazzling, merciless display of offensive power, and bottled up their foes with such a stout defense, are a strangely innocent sort. They are just a lot of country boys today, voicing homely philosophy and laughing immoderately over their own conception of the humorous features of the game. To them it was a lark, just a lark."[66] The self-image as country boys was a shrewdly assumed pose that southerners could strike to disarm outsiders (as southern politicians such as North Carolina's Sam Ervin still understood in the 1970s). When the Georgia Bulldogs arrived in Los Angeles for the 1943 Rose Bowl, their coach, Wally Butts, stepped off the train to tell waiting reporters that he wanted to cooperate with them but not be distracted from his primary responsibilities to his team. The *Los Angeles Times*'s Paul Zimmerman reported Butts's telling him, "But I also want youall to be my friends. I don't want to make anyone mad at me. I'm just a country boy in the big town for the first time and I want to do the right thing—just so I get a chance to coach my football team."[67] Like many southern coaches and players who preceded him in Pasadena, Butts came to town, charmed the socks off the sophisticated locals, then beat the pants off their team.

Applying southern myth to southern football was not a Yankee invention, then, but Ralph McGill was certainly correct in feeling that northern sportswriters embraced it extravagantly in the late 1920s and 1930s. Braven Dyer in the *Los Angeles Times* had found the spirit of southern chivalry in the Alabama football team at the 1926 Rose Bowl, and George Trevor in the *New York Sun* had celebrated Dixie grit after Georgia beat Yale in 1929. Writing in the *Outlook and Independent* the following season, Trevor declared that a kind of "primitive fury" was "the distinguishing mark of football in Dixie, a heritage from the powder blackened days when the ancestors of these boys, clad in butternut and tattered gray, raised the rebel yell at Antietam, Chancellorsville, and Gettysburg." This conceit, or versions of it, became a commonplace over the 1930s. Paul Gallico puzzled over the female "sponsors" at football games in the South, who linked "modern football and the tilting tourneys of the days when knighthood was in flower." Damon Runyon applied his characteristic irony to the Fordham-Georgia game in 1936: "Yes, Suh, folks, the perfume of the sweet magnolia blossoms wafting up out of the dear old Southland today is too much for our stalwart Fordham boys, more accustomed to the fragrances of Bronx byways." By 1935, radio broadcasters were so well known for declaring southern football an expression of the Confederate spirit that they could be parodied in a national magazine.[68]

The institution of the Blue-Gray All-Star Game in Montgomery, Alabama, in 1938 made at least casual Yankee-versus-Rebel analogies virtually inescapable, but it was the 1939 season that marked their full flowering, provoked by the startling string of southern victories in intersectional games to open the season, and perhaps by anticipation of the premiere of *Gone With the Wind* at the season's end. The New York press in October was full of references to the Civil War, Bull Run, Ford Sumter, "damn Yankees," and rebel yells, as NYU, Fordham, and other northern teams took their lickings. In December, as Rhett and Scarlet dueled on movie screens from Atlanta to Los Angeles, even the normally restrained Associated Press—in the account of the Blue-Gray game read in most of the country—joined in: "The South regained in measure today prestige lost in the 1860's to Yankee cannon and muskets at Gettysburg when a squad of picked Dixie college stars routed Northern football masters, 33–20, in Montgomery's second Blue-Gray gridiron classic." The South's alternative "country boy" image was evoked by the *New York Daily News,* a few days before Tennessee took on USC in the Rose Bowl, when Bob Bumbry reported that "the trusting and guileless young bumpkins from the Tennessee hills were lured to a typical Hollywood party." One's own cherished stereotypes, when used by outsiders, could come out less flattering. When Tennessee was defeated a few days later by a more powerful USC team (Tennessee's undefeated season notwithstanding, southern teams were always underdogs in mythical North-South battles), Grantland Rice reported to his vast audience in syndication, "It was a magnificent charge in a lost cause. It was Pickett at Gettysburg. It was an outclassed team, physically, giving everything it had."[69] Such metaphorical extravagance abated as sportswriting became more restrained in the 1940s and 1950s, but the South remained a distinctive football region in the public consciousness well into the 1970s.

"The South" as a football region had begun to be more narrowly identified with the Southeast in the early 1930s, as the Southwest emerged as a distinct region with its own colorful image in the national football consciousness. Southwestern football was Wild West, shoot-'em-up, gunslinging football: the air filled with balls thrown from everywhere on the field at any time during the game. While most teams used the forward pass sparingly for the element of surprise, and would not risk throwing from deep in their own territory or close to the opponent's goal line (until 1938, an incomplete pass in the end zone meant losing the ball), Southwest Conference teams became legendary for pass-happy, crowd-pleasing offenses. With coach Ray Morrison's "aerial circus" at SMU leading the way in the 1920s, Morrison's style was adopted throughout the conference over the following decade. Out of the Southwest Conference came Sammy Baugh, Davey O'Brien, Bobby Layne, Fred Benners, Don Meredith, and several lesser stars. Southwestern passing was a fact on which sportswriters extravagantly elaborated.

Unlike the southern football myth, which developed from within as well as outside the South, Wild West football was primarily an outsider's creation on which the insiders capitalized for promotional purposes (Texas schools and their followers would sometimes show up in boots and cowboy hats for big intersectional games). Southwest Conference team nicknames provoked a few colorful leads in the *Dallas Morning News* in the 1920s,[70] but it was writers outside Texas who seized on the possibilities in Longhorns and Mustangs and blew them up into a full-scale Wild West Show. SMU's dazzling offensive displays at West Point in 1928 and South Bend in 1930 impressed the locals without unleashing Wild West metaphors,[71] but Boston and New York writers went wild over the Texas-Harvard game in Cambridge in 1931. The AP preview of the game—the one read throughout the country—called the Longhorns "a hard-hitting bunch of range riders, born to the leather"; while in New York, the columnist for even the sober *Times,* John Kieran, predicted, "Doubtless the Texans will put on a real rodeo and fight hard for the honor of the Lone Star State."[72]

In Boston, the *Herald* and the *Evening Transcript* were relatively restrained in their pregame buildup and accounts of the game—a disappointingly easy 35–7 victory for Harvard—but the *Herald*'s colorful commentary accompanying the more sober game report was one long riff on Wild West motifs. Under a headline celebrating Harvard's star of the game, "Crickard Writes New Alamo for Longhorns to Remember," with a subhead that read, "Riding Herd on Texas Border no Cinch When Cowboys Tackle as if Wrestling Steers," the writer described the "Yippee's" and "Yahoo's" from the Texas rooters, and the holes in the Texas line "big enough to run a herd of steers through," much of the running done by a wriggling "broncho" named Jack Crickard. The *Boston Post*'s Bill Cunningham, the most flamboyant stylist of the era, squeezed the Longhorn metaphor even harder: "John Harvard ain't (I said 'ain't') had himself much experience around a cattle outfit. He probably wouldn't know a dogie from the rowel of a spur. He couldn't rope the horns of a mounted moose and the lazy lope of a pie-bald cayuse would probably fill him with panic. But yesterday in the big Allston corral, he sho' enough branded himself a big Texas Steer, when he burned a 35 to 7 trademark into the flank of a lean and lunging Longhorn and then let him up and loose to run." The "Special" report on the game sent from Boston to the *Dallas Morning News* was equally overblown.[73]

In San Francisco, sportswriters greeted SMU in 1931 and TCU in 1935 with much of the same. Will Stevens, Jr., in the *San Francisco Chronicle,* described the Mustangs' arrival for their contest with St. Mary's in 1931 this way: "Up from the far-flung ranges of Texas today and into San Francisco move the Mustangs of Southern Methodist, believing that no football team in the country can lay 'em down, hogtie 'em and make 'em like it in a big way." When TCU and Sammy Baugh arrived in 1935 to play Santa Clara, the *Chronicle*'s Prescott Sullivan got more carried away:

Samuel ("Buckshot") Baugh, a gentleman from Sweetwater, Texas, who they say, can pick a groundhog off a rock at 50 paces slicker 'n a whistle, arrives in town today.

He is reputed to be the greatest marksman since Dead Eye Dick or Annie Oakley, but being a real he-man, he spurns a rifle and does everything with his bare hands.

Give him a football, a tin of tobacco and box of matches and he can live off the country for years.

I am told he once killed a buffalo with a single pitch of a football, but that was a long time ago and the story is a little hard to believe, since Buckshot Baugh has just turned 20.

Remarkably, with such buildup, the games themselves did not disappoint, as SMU passed thirty-three times (while running the ball only twenty-nine) in losing to St. Mary's, and Baugh drew raves for a 76-yard punt as well as his passing in the Horned Frogs' victory over Santa Clara. In New York, the SMU-Fordham game in 1934 received similar treatment.[74]

Nineteen-thirty-five was the year that the general football public discovered southwestern football. The meeting of SMU and TCU on 30 November 1935, with a national championship and the Southwest Conference's first bid to the Rose Bowl at stake, was the first game from the region to receive full national coverage. Some of the nation's foremost syndicated sportswriters traveled to Texas for the first time: Grantland Rice praised the Southwest's gambling style of play; the New York World-Telegram's Joe Williams called it "flashy"; Paul Gallico of the New York Daily News declared that "for pure, sustained, sixty-minute suspense, fine running, passes, thrills and excitement, I have never seen it equaled." The Boston Post's Bill Cunningham likened the accuracy of Sammy Baugh's passes to shooting a fly off a fence at fifty yards. A "Special" to the New York Times characterized the winners as "a stampeding band of wild Mustangs." None of these accounts went hog-wild on Wild West metaphors—no shoot-outs at the OK Corral—but they contributed to the broader recognition of a distinctive Texan football identity. More important, the truly national media, including network radio and newsreels, for the first time brought southwestern football into homes and theaters throughout the country.[75]

The Rose Bowl game a month later, pitting SMU against Stanford, was given the full Wild West treatment by the Los Angeles Times. Because the Mustangs lost, most of the heroic western metaphors were shifted to Stanford, but it was obviously SMU's presence that elicited them. Braven Dyer praised Stanford's line for "fighting with all the fury of a herd of buffaloes," as they defeated SMU "before 85,000 yipping grid fans." Jack Singer described the happy Stanford players singing cowboy songs in the locker room afterward, and Dick Hyland lost his bearings completely in working out a tortured analogy to a "New Alamo." Grantland Rice's account appeared alongside these others, and the man known for his high-blown metaphors ironically injected a note of dispassionate realism. What Rice saw was "a drab ordinary football game that had few thrills for 85,000 spectators who waited in vain for the color and action that never came to light." According to Rice, SMU was defeated not by a smothering Santa Ana, as Hyland suggested, but more prosaically by "a bad case of jitters."[76]

The metaphors were running loose, however, and sportswriters dragged them in again and again over the next several years.[77] Hollywood capitalized on SMU's 1935 championship season with *Pigskin Parade* in 1936, one of the more popular football films of the decade. It is memorable in film history as the debut of Judy Garland, but notable here for its Wild West twist on the well-worn formula of the college-football musical comedy. In the film, Yale inadvertently schedules backwater Texas State University instead of the University of Texas, only to lose to the plucky underdogs in the grand finale, after which Judy and the cast—costumed in Stetsons, chaps, fringed cowboy shirts, and boots—march about the field, singing, "A Texas tornado is coming your way." A connection between the buckskinned musicians in *Pigskin Parade* and a distinctive style of football in Texas would be hard to find, but in linking Texas football to cowboy trappings the film nonetheless both acknowledged and contributed to the growing appeal of a popular stereotype. When Hardin-Simmons traveled to Los Angeles to play Loyola in 1939, the small-time Texas football school attempted to cash in on big-time Texas football's image by providing the local press with photos of players in full cowboy regalia.

As TCU and Texas A&M followed SMU to the top of the football polls in coming years, while TCU's Sammy Baugh and Davey O'Brien led a parade of Texas quarterbacks into the NFL (midway through the 1941 season, half of the top sixteen passers in the NFL had played high school or college ball in Texas),[78] national magazines fell in love with the image of the cowboy footballer. Henry McLemore in *Look* in 1939 described Southwest Conference football as "a game that combines the best features of a buffalo stampede, a three-ring circus, a hundred rolls of the wheel at Monte Carlo, and a running

FIGURE 2-2. The Hardin-Simmons Cowboys of Abilene, Texas, made a pitch for recognition in 1939 with publicity shots of the players in chaps and ten-gallon hats. This photo of the Cowboys' star, future NFL Hall of Famer Bulldog Turner, appeared in the *Los Angeles Times* on 27 October (along with similar photos on 22 and 26 October) as part of the coverage leading up to the Loyola game. (AP/Wide World Photos)

gun fight between cowboys and rustlers." *Life* the following season offered readers beefcake photos of "rugged, rangy and rough" Texas A&M football players—"storybook Texans"—at their summer jobs. For most sportswriters Wild West football became a cliché to be avoided, but where Southwest Conference teams were still a novelty the cliché would not die. After SMU upset Ohio State in Columbus in 1950, *Morning News* sports editor Bill Rives quoted a Chicago writer's comments about leathery plainsmen and cowhands, then commented, "It looks like the Easterner's cockeyed view of Texas never can be straightened. Well, anyway, it's good advertising for Texas." When the Dallas Texans joined the NFL, *Collier's* greeted the team with an article titled, "It's Hard-Ridin', Two-Gun Football, Pardner!" As late as 1958, it was virtually inevitable that some sportswriter would call Mustang quarterback Don Meredith "SMU's Davy Crockett."[79]

The provincial football outlook was compounded of pride and defensiveness, and it included a hypersensitivity to comments from outside the region. For readers around the country, Wild West football contributed in a small way to football's staging of a great national drama with distinctive local actors. Back in Texas, insofar as it denoted a unique style of play, it was welcomed when it reflected favorably on the region and deeply resented when it seemed merely mocking. That football could be a source of community shame as well as pride for those who deeply invested themselves is startlingly evident in the *Morning News*'s coverage of the Dallas Texans' one woeful season in the National Football League in 1952. After fourteen local millionaires purchased the New York Yanks and moved the team to Texas, Dallas had a chance to become a major-league sports city. Instead, as the poorly managed club lost game after game, before ever-diminishing crowds, the *Morning News* worried aloud that Dallas was becoming a national joke. After the Texans lost to the New York Giants to open the regular season, Bill Rives wrote in his daily column, "Football writers over the nation, who have heard for years about the tremendous enthusiasm for football down here, must have been shocked when they read that the Dallas Texans' league-opening game drew only approximately 17,000 fans." By the end of October, as losses mounted and crowds shrank, Rives was reporting that the team owners had sought financial assistance from Dallas's all-powerful Citizens Council, and he endorsed the effort for reasons beyond economics. "At the moment," Rives wrote, "Dallas has a solid standing as a sports center and this standing would be vastly increased with a successful professional football team. Dallas' reputation is sagging, however, because of the financial emergency of the Dallas Texans. In newspapers from San Francisco to New York, Dallas has recently been described in such biting terms as 'overrated' and 'bush league.' If the Texans fail to survive, Dallas will be the laughing stock of the sports world. The damage will be severe and it will take a long time to repair it." [80]

As the situation worsened, the newspaper's staff took to direct pleading. "It's up to you, in a great measure," Charles Burton told readers two weeks later when the Los Angeles Rams came to town, "as to whether Dallas continues in professional football. And this could be the day of decision." Burton acknowledged that the owners should have anticipated financial losses, but he insisted that they were not alone responsible for the current crisis. "Maybe everybody is a little bit to blame for the shameful news that is being bandied about in the nation's newspapers, and carried to our armed forces overseas—Dallas isn't a big-league town after all." The Dallas public was unswayed, as 10,000 showed up in the rain and cold to watch the Texans lose once more, and that week the NFL took over ownership of the team for its last five games on the road. While the resolution of the Texans' ownership was still in doubt, Bill Rives ruefully quoted one Los Angeles sportswriter: "If only all good citizens had chipped in with a few loose nickels, Texas could have been spared this shocking stigma. . . . One would think Texas would bust a saddle girth getting behind their Dallas football team, else Texas is going to lose a lot of prestige. It'll get so bad that when the bands play 'Eyes of Texas' they'll have to keep their hats on and their moufs shet." [81] That a city could be shamed for not supporting a bad team illustrates more clearly than the euphoria over Alabama's Rose Bowl winners in 1926 and SMU's national champions in 1935 the stakes that some invested in local football. The Texans' failure obviously mattered much more to local sportswriters (and likely to the business elites) than to the populace at large, who ignored a team that won but a single game all season.

The era of rip-snorting Wild West football passed with the taming of sportswriters' excesses, but Texas and southwestern football thrived more than ever in the 1960s. More than the Southwest generally, Texas in particular became a distinct region in the national football consciousness, less for the Dallas Cowboys (born in 1960) and the Southwest Conference than for the hundreds of high school teams and their rabid followers throughout the state. Television struck a blow at football's local-rootedness more generally, as it made every team a potential "home team" for football fans everywhere, enabling the National Football League to transcend geography. But a sense of regional distinctiveness did not altogether disappear. Southern speed and northern power defined broad differences in the 1960s, and both the South and Texas became known more than ever for their fanatical intensity. As the South supplanted the Midwest as the dominant football section in the 1980s, and Florida displaced Pennsylvania and Ohio in popular perception as the breeding ground of football players, football continued to be mapped by regions, though whether those regions were in any way distinctive became increasingly unclear.

Who Cares about Reform?

The South and the Southwest differed from the rest of the football world in more basic ways in the 1940s and 1950s: their teams remained segregated, they openly offered athletic scholarships, and they placed no restrictions on member institutions' participation in bowl games. The racial dimensions of football are the subject of a later chapter; here I want to explore the media's responses to controversies over scholarships, bowl games, and other ethical issues that haunted college football since the 1890s, when college authorities first realized the promotional benefits to be gained from staging football as a public spectacle. As an extracurricular activity, football meant healthy exercise for the players and amusement (or distraction from more dangerous vices) for the other students. As a popular spectacle, the big-time college sport was a commercial enterprise with a demanding public. The resulting dilemma for college authorities can be expressed in a variety of ways, but they all came down to the same thing: the need to recruit top athletes, irrespective of their academic soundness, all the while maintaining a fundamental fiction that college football players were student amateurs, despite their participation in a multimillion-dollar business. The fiction could not withstand close scrutiny, and the contradiction at the heart of big-time college football inevitably erupted into periodic "crises" and fitful attempts at reform.[1]

The ethical lapses in college football did not register at all on radio or in newsreels. Radio's role was to boost football in order to hold its audience; for newsreels, football and other sports were the thrilling and lighthearted counterweight to the serious news at the beginning of the reels. A new formula emerged in the 1930s in football fiction and film, in which the shady ethics of subsidization served as the backdrop for conventional romance, but these fictional narratives invariably blunted their critical edge for the sake of happy endings. Until the multiple crises following the end of World War II, the daily press likewise shied away from college football's moral and ethical dilemmas, leaving serious criticism to the periodical press. From the 1920s through the war years, reformers' attacks on football were duly noted in newspapers everywhere, then disappeared by the following weekend, as writers returned to covering the important local games. Would-be reformers lacked both a sustained voice within the mass media and a broad base of popular support. Whatever the convictions of individual sportswriters and editors, the media in general had a major vested interest in college football, as newspapers, radio, and magazines to varying degrees held much of their audience in the fall months with college football news. For its part, the football public in general and college boosters in particular cared considerably less about the ethics of the sport than about winning on Saturday.

The result was a constant suspicion of abuses in college football but lack of sufficient will or power to do anything about them. Problems under the general heading of "professionalism" were nearly as old as the game itself. "Ringers" and "tramp athletes" began appearing on college campuses in the 1880s, often staying only through the football season before returning to whatever employment occupied them the rest of the year. By the 1920s, established football programs had largely eliminated the problem of outright tramp athletes, but more subtle methods continued to provide good athletes who were not necessarily serious students. The "purity" of college football was also sullied by another practice common in the 1910s: the moonlighting by college players (and coaches) on professional teams, to pick up a few bucks on Sunday after Saturday's struggle for alma mater. The organization of professional football in 1920 into what became the National Football League was actually the first step toward eliminating such practices, but the need to insist that football somehow in its very nature depended on amateur purity and college spirit led to annual denunciations of pro football by college spokesmen.[2] As college football entered its golden era, then, its problems were not new but the ones unresolved since its beginnings.

The first of college football's two great crises of the 1920s came in 1925, when its most famous player, Red Grange, turned pro immediately following his last college game, at a time when professional football was about as respectable as professional wrestling and considerably less popular. Under the guidance of pro football's first sports agent, Charlie "Cash-and-Carry" Pyle, Grange left Illinois without graduating and debuted with the Chicago Bears on 26 November 1925 against the crosstown rival Cardinals, before an NFL-record crowd of 36,000. Grange and the Bears played nine more games in eight cities over the next sixteen days, including a contest with the New York Giants at the Polo Grounds before an astounding 65,000 (in a year when league-wide attendance averaged about 5,000). The Bears then embarked on a 7,000-mile trip through the South and West, a schedule-as-you-go barnstorming tour taking them to Coral Cables, Tampa, and Jacksonville in Florida, then on to New Orleans, before arriving on the West Coast for games in Los Angeles, San Diego, San Francisco, Portland, and Seattle through the month of January. (Apparently there were no takers for a game in Texas; possible contests in Houston, San Antonio, and Dallas, as well as Atlanta and Birmingham, were announced in the press on 19 December but did not materialize.) The opponents were locally assembled former collegians, led by a prominent national star such as an aging Jim Thorpe (in Tampa) or Stanford All-American Ernie Nevers (in Jacksonville), or by a local football hero (Tulane's Lester Lautenschlager in New Orleans, the University of Washington's George Wilson for all the West Coast games). Crowds ranged from 3,200 in Coral Gables to nearly 70,000 in Los Angeles, with most of the games drawing between 5,000 and 10,000. Newspaper coverage over the entire three months virtually erased any boundary between news and promotion.[3]

Grange's pro debut and barnstorming tour forced sportswriters and football fans everywhere to dwell at least briefly on the college game's peculiar status as a semi-professional amateur sport. Harvard's and Yale's campus dailies, Grange's own coach at Illinois, Robert Zuppke, and many others throughout the intercollegiate world accused Red of betraying his alma mater and befouling sacred amateurism. Grange's decision to turn pro before graduating led the Big Ten, Southern Conference, and Missouri Valley Conference to take stands against professionalism, provoking responses from local sports columnists. In Atlanta, the *Constitution*'s H. C. Hamilton found the anti-Grange hysteria overheated; professional football could go its own way, Hamilton insisted, posing no threat to the college game. In Dallas, on the other hand, the *Morning News*'s Chauncey Brown was deeply critical of Grange for appropriating fame that more properly belonged to his university, and he praised Andy "Swede" Oberlander of Dartmouth, who had refused professional offers and "thus will end a great career gloriously." Brown proved not a very good prophet when he added, "It is probable that the memory of Oberlander will remain fresh long after that of Grange has passed into the limbo of articles which looked like gold but turned out to be partially of inferior metal."[4]

What most engaged the press, however, and presumably its readers, was not the question of whether Red Grange had soiled himself with professionalism, but fascination over the amounts of money that he earned in just a few weeks as a pro. Whether in New York or Omaha or Seattle, this was the story that mattered most, the figures often inflated outrageously. Headlines proclaimed: "Red Grange Gets $82,000 in Eleven Days; $16,000 a Game Is His Average as a Pro," and "Grange's Profits Since Leaving University of Illinois Total Nearly $500,000." A cartoon cast Grange running alongside Father Time (reminder of fleeting fame) with a bag of gold under his own arm representing "The Million He's Out to Make."[5] A feature article in the Hearst chain's Sunday magazine, *American Weekly,* described the "Beggers [*sic*], Fakers, Get-Rich-Quick Schemers, Charity Workers, Designing Women, and the Income Tax Foxes" who were "Tormenting the Famous Football Star." Not just Grange's share of the gate for the football games, but also his endorsements and a movie contract (erroneously inflated to $300,000) received a full accounting: "$1,000 for admitting that a cigarette smelled all right, though he does not smoke; $10,000 for wearing a sweater and agreeing that it was warm; $5,000 for putting his swift feet in a pair of somebody's shoes; $2,000 for enjoying a ride in a certain automobile; $10,000 for permitting his name to be attached to a red-headed football doll; $10,000 more for his expert judgement that a certain firm's football felt as snug in his arm as any he had ever carried over a goal line, etc., etc." The writer was not critical of these extravagant giveaways but sympathetic to their beneficiary, who had become a target for the truly undeserving: tax collectors, pitchmen for various charities, "vamps of all kinds, with love on their lips and dollar signs in their eyes," even a supposed "welfare organization that worked to uplift the East Side poor of New York," but whose uplift turned out to consist of "Communist propaganda, which he does not care for. 'Red' Grange is not 'red' and does not think a football team could be run on Soviet lines." For those unmoved by pleas for amateur purity, Red Grange could be cast as a red-blooded, anti-Red, American son of the prairies or as a hero for the emerging age of consumption.[6]

The Hearst magazine's laissez-faire philosophy was shared by most of the daily press. An editorial in the *New York Times* insisted that the renowned Wheaton Ice Man "has that one talent which it is death to hide" and "enormously profitable to exploit," and memorably added that "there is no reason in morals or esthetics why the rewards should be withheld from the most famous name in the American ice industry since Eliza [in *Uncle Tom's Cabin*] crossed the Ohio in front of the bloodhounds."[7] Several games and endorsement contracts later, even worldly New York sportswriters were having second thoughts. After Grange remarked in a radio interview following his exhibition before 65,000 in the Polo Grounds that football's "rewards are spiritual rather than material," the *New York Daily News*'s Paul Gallico snorted, "That assays about 18 karat tommyrot," coming from someone "who has just collected $35,000 for three periods of football play." Gallico refocused his disgust overnight, his column the next day distinguishing between the earned wealth of a remarkable athlete and the unearned wealth of a celebrity managed by an agent: "The sight of the redhead thundering down the striped field, leaving a wake of fallen, chagrined bodies, is thrilling. It is worth any amount of money that people are willing to give to see it. The view of Grange sitting in a ballroom—so as to be able to accommodate all of those desiring to trade cash for his name—and with his manager, whom the cynical sport writers have named cash-and-carry Pyle, pulling in money, hand over fist and giving in return not one whit honest effort, to me is disgusting."[8]

Grange hysteria subsided but left two legacies: the slow advance of professional football in those cities with franchises, and recurring eruptions of controversy over professionalism in intercollegiate football. The college game's next great crisis arrived just a few years later, in 1929, when the Carnegie Foundation issued its blandly titled *Bulletin Number Twenty-Three*, an anything-but-bland attack on the pervasive "professionalism" in the so-called amateur sport. Commissioned by the NCAA in January 1926, following Grange's defection to the NFL, the Carnegie Report was wide-ranging in its criticism (including a chapter on the excesses of the press that was ignored by sportswriters). The AP account that was read in most of the country, however, focused on what Howard J. Savage, the report's principal author, called "'the deepest shadow that darkens American colleges and school athletics'—the widespread practice of recruiting and subsidizing athletes." Of 112 institutions that cooperated with the foundation, only twenty-eight were found guiltless. The rest were "the Fagins of American sport and American higher education," who "tempt young men to barter their honesty for the supposed advantage of a college course, dishonestly achieved." Unethical practices uncovered by the Carnegie investigators ranged from "rare and casual contacts made or directed by an individual in the athletic organization of the institution" to "an intensely organized, sometimes subtle, system that may utilize or coordinate numbers of agents on or off the campus"—in other words, recruiting. Also: payments to athletes in the forms of "athletic scholarships," campus jobs, and "slush funds"—that is, financial aid for athletic rather than academic ability. The corrupting "professionalism" of college football in the 1920s became the basis of the sport that we know today.[9]

The general response to *Bulletin Number Twenty-Three* was a collective shrug—so what's new? In a fairly typical response, Westbrook Pegler declared the Carnegie report a waste of time, "substantiating conditions which have been commonly known to exist." The problem in college football was not subsidization but "the pretense and concealment, couched in resolutions and agreements of the most elaborate amateur piety." A month later, Pegler proposed openly putting college players on the payroll, for the sake of honesty.[10] In papers around the country the AP account was typically accompanied by headlines and sidebars highlighting the report's assessment of the local institution. Pegler's view generally prevailed among provincial sportswriters, often coupled with local partisanship. In Omaha, the *World-Herald*'s Frederick Ware declared the findings old news, though he was pleased to note that Nebraska was listed among the few colleges found to be clean. In Dallas, *Morning News* sports editor George White simply defended SMU against the charges made by a "one-sided" report. In Atlanta, the *Constitution*'s Ed Danforth dismissed the study as a waste of "millions of dollars and three and a half years of work to find out what everybody knows," though he also mocked the idea that schools such as Tulane were any cleaner than Georgia and Georgia Tech. Danforth's colleague, Ralph McGill, was similarly bemused by "a ubiquitous organization which each year promulgates ponderous fulminations." In Chicago, an editorial in the *Tribune* called the revelations "an open secret" of little consequence. "We cannot become terribly indignant when some boy is helped through college," declared the writer. "We cannot see why it is more heinous to reward an athlete with his tuition than to reward with tuition members of the band which play before and between the halves." In Los Angeles, the timing of the report was most unfortunate, with USC playing its chief rival, Stanford, that weekend and several Trojan players appearing with Douglas Fairbanks, Jr., and Loretta Young in *The Forward Pass* at the RKO theater—more consequential matters. Although the AP account of the foundation's accusations appeared on the front page of the *Los Angeles Times* under sensationalized headlines, it was ignored altogether in the sports section.[11]

These responses highlight most clearly the dilemma of college authorities, caught between the demands of a major entertainment business and the ethical standards of higher education, with the local sportswriters who most directly influenced the public generally indifferent to reform. As John Watterson argues, the Carnegie investigators' insistence on athletic purity, instead of proposing a "realistic system" for managing a commercial enterprise, blunted its impact.[12] Over the 1930s, several universities and their presidents did, in fact, attempt to purify their football programs, but they could do so only by sacrificing the promotional benefits of a big-time football team. Newspapers in Atlanta, Omaha, Dallas, and Los Angeles illustrate how little interest in reforming college football was publicly expressed in places where the game was most firmly rooted. In the wake of the Carnegie report, virtually every season was marked by denunciations of corruption and hypocrisy in journals of opinion and eventually even the most popular magazines, but local newspapers continued to ignore, or contemptuously oppose, calls for reform. As Ed Danforth wrote in the *Atlanta Constitution*, although the Carnegie Foundation proved that athletes were subsidized,

> as long as the practice did not lead to the production in our colleges of thugs, gunmen, bandits, thieves, and the like we did not mind. The colleges seem to be turning out pretty good citizens right along; the tramp athlete and the out-and-out professional long since have been legislated out of athletic fields of institutions belonging to organized bodies of control. In fact the layman cannot see why it is destructive to the morals of a boy who can play football to help him through school. Ten to one he will go out into the world and become more of a credit to the institution than a pale flower with a 32-inch chest and an aptitude for Greek verbs and botany.[13]

The concluding anti-intellectualism was somewhat less typical, but Danforth's laissez-faire attitude toward subsidization was the rule in college-town newspapers. The exception among the papers surveyed here was the *Omaha World-Herald*, which over the 1930s repeatedly cited Nebraska football purity as compensation for the Cornhuskers' falling just short of the football pinnacle. The Cornhuskers' adoption of athletic scholarships in the late 1940s met no resistance in the *World-Herald,* however. Whatever the local football program wanted was right.

THE PERIODICAL PRESS AND FOOTBALL REFORM

Criticism of the abuses in college football was never wanting, but it came from a different source: journals of opinion and the intellectual monthlies and quarterlies, with their relatively small audiences limited to the cultural and intellectual elites. Prominent figures among the patrician reformers of the Progressive Era—men such as Theodore Roosevelt, Henry Cabot Lodge, and their chief spokesman in the sporting press, Caspar Whitney—had originally embraced football as an invigorating tonic for the nation in general and their own class in particular. The intellectuals of the new generation, both liberal and conservative, were overwhelmingly antifootball. Red Grange's decision at the end of November 1925 to play professional football followed by just a couple of weeks an article in the *Independent* by George Owen, a former Harvard All-American who claimed that most collegians did not even enjoy playing football, because of "the terrific grind necessary to keep in the running." College football was not a sport "but rather a stern and relentless business," the equivalent of Roman gladiatorial games. Owen's indictment stirred up furious comment and was cited for years afterward.[14]

Grange's turning pro a few weeks later, then his sudden transformation into a greater commercial commodity than even Babe Ruth, might logically have seemed reassuring to those upset by Owen's claims. If college football was indeed a grinding business, at least Red Grange had made it profitable for himself. A version of this view would eventually prevail among college football's critics, but not until after World War II. In 1925, the critics were not yet ready to concede the intercollegiate sport's commercial nature as a permanent condition. In contrast to the sportswriters in the daily press, writers in the journals of opinion clung to the amateur ideal. The *New Republic* satirized the commercialism that Grange's actions highlighted in a supposedly amateur sport. The *Outlook* more earnestly called Grange an ironic "blessing" on these same grounds, for turning "the glaring sunlight on the gross commercialism of college football." The *Outlook* also found hope in the possibility that openly professional football might draw the thrill-seeking public away from the college game, which could then return to its purely amateur roots.[15] Neither of these magazines adopted the pragmatic position taken by most sportswriters: that Grange had a unique talent he was perfectly entitled to exploit, and professional football posed no threat to the colleges.

The overheated controversies whipped up by George Owen and Red Grange cooled in the next few years, but they never went away. A debate in the *Forum* in 1926 with the title, "Shall We Abolish Intercollegiate Football?" pitted a scathing Upton Sinclair against a calm defender of the sport. In 1927, the president of Dartmouth, Ernest Martin Hopkins, provoked a flurry of responses with some rather quixotic proposals: to limit football eligibility to the sophomore and junior years, to have separate teams for home and away games, and to have all coaching done by undergraduates. Football still had a few intellectual defenders. In the most staid of the quarterlies, the *North American Review,* Samuel Grafton in 1928 acknowledged the rampant professionalism, then asked, "What of it?" and ended up arguing for college football as a healthy tonic for "a nation burdened with dull gray repressions." The Carnegie Foundation's report in 1929 put an end to such frivolity, however, as the intellectual journals unequivocally endorsed it.[16] Through the early 1930s the weeklies took up the issues of the moment—the annual death toll from football, which reached crisis state in 1931; Yale's proposals for deemphasis in 1932; excessive ballyhoo by sportswriters and radio broadcasters—but after mid-decade they virtually ignored football, whether out of resignation or disgust.[17]

The monthly journals still weighed in occasionally. "Commercialism," or rather the fundamental contradiction at the heart of big-time college football between commercialism and amateurism, in itself troubled many critics, but it also led colleges down two more specific dangerous paths: toward open "professionalism," by which was meant recruiting and subsidizing players, and emphasizing victory over every other consideration; or toward "hypocrisy," which meant doing these same things while protesting that college football, at one's own institution anyway, was truly an amateur sport. As colleges staked out a position for either "jobs" or "scholarships" as the proper form of subsidization—employment in often trivial or nonexistent work, or outright payment by alumni boosters—"purity" could be hypocritical while "professionalism" might be honest, and who held the moral high ground was not at all obvious.

There were two potential cures for hypocrisy, short of dropping big-time football altogether, as the University of Chicago famously did in 1939. The first was to eliminate professionalism and restore the game to some pure state it supposedly occupied in the past; the second was to frankly acknowledge that college football was a business requiring skilled performers who deserved appropriate pay. Several proposals to pay-the-boys-what-they're-worth were offered in the late 1920s in both the weekly and the monthly journals of opinion, but the demand for purity ruled the 1930s.[18] In this, the elite magazines and the intellectuals who read them revealed their ultimate detachment from the American public. Princeton dean Christian Gauss wrote a widely cited attack on professionalism in *Scribner's* in 1931, which was echoed in the *Atlantic* in 1932 by Henry Pritchett of the Carnegie Foundation, as well as by "Left Wing" in the *Nation* in 1935 — amateur purity could attract strange bedfellows — but the single writer whose voice was loudest and most persistent on the issue of professionalism was John R. Tunis. The Great Scold of college football was primarily a tennis and golf journalist (and later the author of boys' baseball novels), but he also wrote about football for numerous magazines, always with the same basic theme. Tunis's first major polemic, "The Great God Football," appeared in *Harper's* in 1928: a wide-ranging attack on commercialism and the making of football into "almost our national religion." This and other writings formed the basis of a book that same year, *$port$ Heroics and Hysterics,* in which Tunis laid out his full indictment of "The Great Sports Myth."[19]

Variations on his central theme appeared in *Harper's* and the *Atlantic* over the next several years, always in generalized or hypothetical terms. Then in articles for the *American Mercury* in 1936 and 1939, Tunis stripped away the cover to name names, assigning the major football-playing colleges to three categories: Amateurs, Semi-Pros, and Professionals.[20] The Amateurs were mostly small liberal arts colleges, the Professionals the big-time football powers, but each list held some surprises, provoking responses from college presidents, athletic directors, and local sportswriters, as the Carnegie Report had done. Letters to the *American Mercury* in 1939 expressed approval from the supposed amateurs and mostly derision from sportswriters, one of whom called Tunis "the literary nudist who has earned many a penny by authoring sport exposés for the magazines." Another exclaimed, "If it isn't John R. Tunis again! Yes, it's old Johnno stirring up another dish of trouble." In *Newsweek,* John Lardner yawned, "The evils of college football have been exposed officially, with names and numbers, for the eighteenth time in the last ten years, by John R. Tunis. . . . The new revelations . . . have left America stagnant with excitement."[21]

These letters and Lardner's sarcasm exemplify the powerful resistance facing the amateur purists. In laissez-faire democratic America, particularly during the hard times of the Depression, the values of sporting gentlemen were an impossibly hard sell. Tunis never could bring himself to the position that openly compensating college athletes was a practicable solution to the game's hypocrisy. This became the prevailing view, but it came from elsewhere.

FRANCIS WALLACE AND THE CASE FOR OPEN PROFESSIONALISM

The most consistent spokesman for the alternative position, the anti-Tunis of college football, was Francis Wallace, whose principal forum was the "Pigskin Previews" he wrote for the *Saturday Evening Post* from 1937 through 1948 (excepting the war years, 1943–45), then for *Collier's* from 1949 through 1956. Articles on football reform never displaced the celebrity profile as the dominant form of football journalism in the great general-interest magazines, but the *Post* and *Collier's*, together with *Life* and *Look*, eventually made the corruption of college football a general problem, not just an intellectuals' complaint. Wallace prefaced each "Pigskin Preview" with a sort of State of the Game address, in which he repeatedly criticized college authorities for not facing squarely the commercial nature of their sport. Wallace was an enemy of hypocrisy, not professionalism. As the football preview became a magazine staple—Fred Russell took over the *Post*'s after Wallace departed for *Collier's*, Grantland Rice and then Tim Cohane wrote *Look*'s—Francis Wallace alone put some bite in the conventional puffery for preseason All-Americans and the top teams from each region. But the editorial stances of the general-interest weeklies eventually shifted in his direction.

Wallace had been Knute Rockne's student press agent in the early 1920s, then a sportswriter in New York for the *Evening Post*, the *Daily News*, and the *Daily Mirror*, before becoming a regular freelance contributor of both fiction and nonfiction to the *Post*, *Collier's*, and other magazines. In his fiction in the 1930s, Wallace established the subsidized football player and his sponsoring booster as conventional figures, but only as the background against which the older conventions of heroic adventure and romance played out. In his nonfiction he took a much clearer stand on the ethics of college football. A year before Tunis's first call for reform of college football, Wallace wrote "The Hypocrisy of Football Reform" for *Scribner's*. The problem with reformers, Wallace wrote, was "that they have not the courage to admit" that football had already become "a semi-professional sport." College presidents spoke in "tremendous platitudes," and conferences such as the Big Ten prescribed "a sugar pill" for the abuses of recruiting. The players, meanwhile, received "a four-year course in deception and the coach learns to shout mightily at the faculty revival meetings." "Football is commercial," Wallace declared. "Who cares? Who made it so? Who collects the profits?" This last question was the incisive one, and the answer was clearly the colleges. Given that reality, there was nothing wrong with alumni paying "the expenses of a boy through college as long as that boy is a legitimate student." And nothing wrong, as well, for that boy to earn his living in professional football after graduation, "using exactly the same talents for his own benefit which he used so prodigally to enrich his alma mater for three seasons." College authorities could acknowledge these simple truths, or they could "continue to wade in mud of their own mixing while prating in generalities of an outworn ideal; to preach against bootlegging while collecting the profits; and to shout at athletic revival meetings while living in sin."[22]

The title of that first article might have appeared on each succeeding one. In "This Football Business" in 1929 and "I Am a Football Fixer" in 1936, as well as his "Pigskin Previews" beginning in 1937, Wallace simply wrote variations on the position he first staked out in 1927. Like Tunis, Wallace classified colleges by their systems of subsidization. Unlike Tunis, he found subsidizing acceptable and applauded the schools that did it openly but with restraint. As Wallace laid out the situation, alternatives to the legal scholarship administered by the athletic department included advocates of alumni scholarships, "tacit consenters" ("the great majority quietly practices subsidization and achieves the same net result as either of the first two; but does not openly admit subsidization"), reformers, and "cuties" ("who still try to eat their cake and have it too. Some are hypocrites, some are ostriches and some are merely struggling with the academic conscience"). Wallace identified these four classes in his 1936 article, then six in his 1937 "Preview" and five in 1938, but the terms varied little. He did not name the schools in each category, however. Unlike Tunis, who wanted offending schools to abandon shady practices, Wallace wanted to expose no one but urge all schools to practice openly what reformers like Tunis mistakenly condemned. Wallace did not advocate sky's-the-limit subsidies but properly administered, reasonable, and honest grants. In his first "Pigskin Preview" he used a phrase that he would repeat over the next several years: "All college officials know by now that the stork doesn't bring football players." Knowing and admitting were two different things, however, and a consensus about athletic scholarships was still in football's distant future.[23]

In 1938 and 1939, the *Saturday Evening Post* offered readers the University of Chicago and the University of Pittsburgh as Exhibits A of purity and professionalism, and Francis Wallace was the reporter on the Pitt situation. Chicago president Robert M. Hutchins made the case for purity in the *Post* in 1938, then the following season he convinced the university's trustees to drop football altogether, after nearly a decade of "deemphasis."[24] As the University of Chicago became the model of rectitude for football's harshest critics, the *Chicago Tribune*'s coverage of the once-proud Maroons' woeful final season as a long-running farce suggests that many in the football public viewed the matter differently. In a typical sally, after Harvard thrashed Chicago 61–0 in mid-October, the *Tribune*'s Charles Bartlett ladled out heavy irony:

> College days being reckoned among the happiest in a young man's life, the 1939 Harvard university football players can now add to all the pleasant hours of their undergraduate careers the dandy afternoon they enjoyed yesterday at Stagg field. They played 60 minutes of football. There were four honest-to-goodness officials. Before the game and between halves, a number of beauteous majorettes twirled batons. The weather was ideal. And after the timer's impolite gun had put an end to the sport, the score board on the wall of Bartlett gym read:
>
> Harvard, 61; Chicago, 0.
>
> 'Twas a grand afternoon, indeed—for the Harvards. The Maroons? Well, those hard working lads at least obliged by filling out the other eleven places required in a gridiron competition.

Succeeding losses to Michigan, Virginia, and Ohio State, by a combined score of 169–0, were accompanied by acerbic headlines ("Maroons Hold Michigan and Harmon, 85–0," "Maroons Hold Ohio 12 Minutes, Then Lose, 61–0"). After Chicago beat tiny Oberlin, 25–0, the *Tribune* still showed no mercy, announcing the following week's game with the headline, "Those Illinois Players Better Watch Maroons; Oberlin Massacre Spurs Our Boys Today." Illinois entered the game having scored 29 points that season while giving up 74, but won the contest 46–0 ("Illinois Finds Par Against the Maroons Is 46"), leaving Chicago's point totals for the season 37 for, 308 against—"one of the most disastrous seasons in the gridiron history of a major institution." When President Hutchins announced in December that the university was dropping football, the *Tribune* viewed the act as a mercy-killing. United Press sports editor Henry McLemore spoke out for the amateur purists when he named the entire Chicago lineup to *Look*'s All-America team for 1939, but purity was a nice idea that few football people truly wanted put into practice.[25]

The Pitt case was more complicated, and more representative of the struggles that university authorities either engaged in or ducked during this period. In a two-part article in the *Post* in 1939, Francis Wallace provided names and faces and concrete details, in place of the vague suspicions always swirling around college football. For close observers, the football program at Pitt had long epitomized the professionalism of big-time college football. Reports in 1935 that Ohio State players were on the state payroll as legislative pages caused a brief stir, but Pitt's was the only program to be thoroughly scrutinized, though only after it had been "purified."[26] The questions now were whether purity was fair and if it could work. As Wallace recounted the events, the athletic side and the academic side had coexisted uneasily at Pitt since the early 1920s, as the athletic program was allowed to operate more or less independently. A well-organized system of subsidies for football players had been in place at least since 1928, when recruited football players earned $500 per year, plus tuition and books. The stipend increased to $650 in 1929, then dropped to $400 in 1933 before being stabilized at $480 in 1934. In December 1937, Pitt players made explicit their status as paid workers when they voted not to accept an invitation to play in the Rose Bowl unless three demands were met: inclusion of the entire squad in the travel party (the previous year, only thirty-three from the roster of sixty-five had made the trip); adequate spending money (for the last Rose Bowl each player had received just $7.50 from the coach, while the university made $100,000); and a two-week vacation immediately afterward. When the athletic director, Don Harrison, refused the spending money, coach Jock Sutherland sided with the players and their dispute led to Harrison's resignation. In the aftermath of this embarrassing incident, Pitt's academic-minded chancellor, John Gabbert Bowman, initiated mild reforms that aroused resistance within the athletic community and its alumni supporters. All-out reform, the Code Bowman, followed a year later: football players would have to work not only for their living expenses but for their tuition as well.[27]

Trouble erupted in November 1938, when freshmen on the football team were confronted with tuition bills that they assumed were to be waived. The players also claimed that they had been promised they would have to work only fifteen to twenty minutes a day for their board and room; instead, they were now required to do full work for the same pay offered other students.[28] As events played out—the threatened revolt of the freshman in November and December, Sutherland's resignation in March 1939, a strike by some students on behalf of Sutherland, additional reforms the following season, and Bowman's repeated assertions that Pitt would continue to play top-flight football but on a strictly amateur basis—the press presented them as a conflict between academics and athletics, and between amateurism and professionalism, pitting Chancellor Bowman and his new athletic director against the players and the alumni. As a journalist, Wallace could not assert his own position on these events, though he treated Sutherland sympathetically in his *Post* articles. Wallace simply offered Pitt as a test case, whose success or failure in reforming without destroying football would be learned over the coming seasons. (Pitt would abandon "deemphasis" in 1949 after a decade of football mediocrity.)

How the *Post*'s large audience read Wallace's account of the mess at Pitt cannot be known, but there was certainly no groundswell of support for similar reforms elsewhere, and where Wallace's own sympathies lay was obvious from his annual "Pigskin Previews." "The field of subsidization" became one of the topics—along with the new rules, the dominant offensive and defensive strategies, and the top teams and players—to be reviewed at the beginning of each season. Despite endorsing scholarships, such as the Southeastern Conference had begun offering in 1935, Wallace was wary of southern excesses, particularly when alumni paid for the players. Reacting to the SEC, the Southern Conference had tried athletic purity for one year before abandoning it, then, in 1937, approved athletic scholarships but only if provided by non-university sources (that is, alumni and boosters paying athletes was considered by some in this unsettled period to be more ethical than athletic departments paying them). In his 1939 "Preview," Wallace noted a trend "definitely away from excess, except in the South." In 1940, the story was much the same: "The South has the boys because the South is paying for them." By 1942, recent signs of restraint were disappearing: with football talent at a premium due to the military draft, "the pursuit has been intense. And there's more fat on the pigskin for the wily young shopper than ever before." [29] In each of these "Pigskin Previews," having offered such criticisms, Wallace proceeded to celebrate the great players, coaches, and teams returning for another glorious football season; after all, this was the preview's primary function. The formula of criticism-plus-celebration tended to naturalize the corruption and hypocrisy in college football, to foster mild cynicism without any consequences. And the fat on the pigskin grew inches thick after the war.

THE TRIUMPH OF PROFESSIONALISM

Francis Wallace might be viewed as college football's best friend or worst enemy: as the voice of honesty amidst hypocrisy, and of reason amidst insanity, or as a champion of amoral expediency. Either way, his view won out, as sportswriters generally shifted from antiprofessionalism to a plea for open professionalism as the only way to preserve college football's minimal integrity. Except for Wallace's writings in the *Saturday Evening Post,* the popular weeklies largely avoided controversy until after World War II, when the *Post* took the lead in exposing the financial machinations in big-time football. An article in 1937 about the "angel" behind the football program at the University of Texas had portrayed him as a selfless public benefactor. Now, in 1945, a report on the suddenly successful program at the University of Tulsa—four bowls in four years in the early 1940s—provided more troubling details. The author, Bob Broeg, offered no judgment, but he named the wealthy oilmen who lured top athletes to the school, reported that thirty of Tulsa's top forty players came from outside Oklahoma (some as transfers from Missouri, Texas, Fordham, Georgetown, Baylor, and other schools), and noted that Tulsa's president, one of the football coach's "most ardent admirers," was "a businessman, not an educator."[30] Such facts had not found their way into magazines such as the *Post* in the 1930s.

The end of the war released thousands of veterans with football experience to resume college or pro football. The availability of ex-soldiers well into their twenties had the effect of offering college football coaches three or four recruiting classes in a single year, and the scramble to land the best of the returning players became a no-holds-barred affair. Schools that suspended football during the war resumed the sport, as more than three times as many colleges fielded teams in 1946 as the year before. Professional clubs competed with the colleges for the same players and often lost out to a higher bid. The "boys" on the team were sometimes twenty-five-year-old men, married and with children, less inclined than rosy-cheeked freshmen to give their all for alma mater but pragmatic about the need to support their families. With 2.2 million veterans going to college on the GI Bill and "completely dominat[ing] higher education between 1945 and 1950," these men made up over 50 percent of the players in college football, as much as 85 and 90 percent on some teams.[31]

The feeding frenzy of these years—the extravagant offers of cars, apartments, promises of postgraduate employment, and large cash payments to recruited players—was documented in major magazines. Journalists were required to remain neutral, but the stories themselves spoke volumes. In 1946, Francis Wallace dryly noted in his "Pigskin Preview" that "there has been no small amount of strictly mercenary grid-naping" over the past several months. Later that season, in "Football's Black Market," he provided detailed stories of Shorty McWilliams's offer of $15,000 from an unnamed school, along with the use of a car, a $300-a-month vacation job, and employment after graduation at the same starting salary; and of recruiters pursuing Bill De Correvont, Buddy Young, and others with similar deals. In the *Post* and *Collier's*, similar details were included in celebrity profiles of Young and Charlie Trippi, highly successful recruiters such as Wake Forest coach Peahead Walker and Kentucky coach Bear Bryant, and booster presidents such as Maryland's Curly Byrd and Michigan State's John Hannah. The journalists offered no criticism, and seemed implicitly to approve, yet the details themselves revealed a sport awash in chicanery and booster dollars.[32] Whether indignant or indifferent, readers of these articles had to grow more cynical about the ethics of college football.

By the late 1940s, recruiting and subsidizing in some form had been accepted in most of the football world, but how and to what degree became the irresolvable questions. On recruiting, questions of whether coaches or alumni should be involved, whether recruiting should be kept in-state, and whether some sort of contract should be required (what we now know as the "letter of intent") found no common answers. On subsidization, the Big Nine (becoming the Big Ten again in 1949 with the admission of Michigan State) and the Pacific Coast Conference, along with much of the East, lined up on the side of on-campus employment (or "jobs" of the clock-winding variety, as their critics derisively insisted). The three major southern conferences—the Southern, Southeastern, and Southwest—came down on the side of athletic scholarships. Narrower issues such as the curtailment of spring practice and the elimination of bowl games, along with debates over television and substitution rules (permitting or restricting two-platoon football), pitted colleges and conferences against each other and blocks of colleges against the NCAA in a wild free-for-all that generated journalistic disgust, and ultimately resigned silence.[33]

The crucial events of the postwar crisis were the adoption, then abandonment, of the so-called Sanity Code; then a pair of major scandals in 1951, first the exposures of point-fixing in college basketball in the winter and spring (which reflected indirectly on football as well), then the dismissal of nearly the entire Army football team in August for "cribbing" on exams. The Sanity Code, pushed through the NCAA convention in January 1948 by the Big Nine and PCC, required that financial aid be determined by need and administered by the institution only; be limited to tuition, incidental fees, and a single meal during the season; and be earned by work "commensurate with the services rendered." Opposition, led by the major southern conferences, erupted most openly in a bitter fight at the 1950 convention over seven universities accused of violations; then its opponents succeeded in overturning the code at the 1951 convention. The gutting of the code, followed over the next several months by the point-fixing and cribbing scandals, prompted formation of a presidents' panel by the American Council on Education (ACE). The council was headed by Michigan State's John Hannah, a "bogus reformer," as John Watterson calls him, "who had engaged in the same practices that the ACE hoped to eliminate." Due in part to Hannah's machinations, the committee's recommendations for reform were ultimately rejected or watered down by the NCAA.[34]

In his "Pigskin Previews" throughout this tumultuous period, Francis Wallace sided with what he called the "legal-athletic-scholarship plan, chiefly identified with Southern institutions." These he called the "Semipros," as opposed to the "Hypocrites," who were the "job-plan bloc" led by the Big Nine/Big Ten and Pacific Coast Conference. After the hypocrites prevailed at the NCAA convention in January 1948 by establishing the job plan as the basis of the Sanity Code, Wallace noted that fall that "the football black market seems to be operating about as usual." After the semipros succeeded in watering down, then dumping the code altogether, Wallace was optimistic that the "well-intentioned" majority would at last conduct the business of college football on a sound basis.[35]

The events of 1951 exploded that illusion. Both the daily and the periodical press generally held Army coach Red Blaik blameless in the West Point cribbing scandal, typically treating the incident as an embarrassment to be ignored, but the incident itself spoke loudly.[36] The point-fixing scandals in college basketball were potentially more disturbing. The threat of actual gamblers, always a stigma attached to professional football, had long hovered vaguely over the college game as well.[37] Student gambling had provoked concern as an issue of campus morals as early as the 1880s; professional gamblers more seriously threatened the integrity of the sport to which universities had attached their public image.[38] The gambler kidnapping the hero or attempting to fix the big game had been a staple in magazine fiction since the days of Frank Merriwell in *Tip Top Weekly,* and he was a familiar figure in 1930s football movies.[39] Though fictional, these characters likely fed suspicions in the public mind. Bookmakers began offering odds on college games in 1931, and by 1935, according to *Time,* betting on college football had become a national mania. John R. Tunis claimed in 1936 that games had in fact been thrown. "Everybody knows it and admits it," he insisted, "except a few sports writing ostriches, adolescent alumni, or those who stamp Graduate Manager of Athletics [the term for an athletic director] beneath their signatures."[40] Such charges were never substantiated, how-ever, as nothing like the attempt to fix the 1946 NFL championship ever hit college football.[41] Not counting one in 1935 that proved a hoax, just three attempted bribes—one in 1952, of three players at the University of Mary-land, and two in 1960, of players at the University of Florida and University of Oregon—were ever reported in the press, and none of them succeeded.[42]

Francis Wallace commented briefly on gambling in his 1946, 1947, and 1948 "Pigskin Previews," and in the aftermath of the basketball scandals Stanley Woodward warned readers of *Look* that college football was next for gamblers' fixes.[43] In the absence of confirming incidents, however, games fixed by gamblers remained a vague rumor, while the exposés of routine but questionable recruiting practices most tainted college football in the 1950s. Wallace's position was the one he had held consistently since 1927, that college football's problems stemmed from its "deep-rooted schizophrenia: the insistence on amateur standards in a profit-making business." As always, Wallace was less troubled by excessive subsidies and uncontrolled recruiting than by hypocrisy. In 1956, *Collier's'* final football season, he took one last shot (before taking his "Football Preview" to Hugh Hefner's *Playboy*). In that year, players at USC and UCLA were ineligible, and both schools, along with Cal, the University of Washington, and Ohio State, were banned from the Rose Bowl; in addition, Texas A&M, Auburn, and Florida were also on pro-bation. Wallace declared that the players were merely pawns, "whose grid-iron labor is sold by the college at a tremendous profit," while the coach was "a captive of the system." Responsibility for the mess belonged entirely to "well-meaning college administrations which demand both big-time profits and 'classic amateurism.'"[44]

Such criticism of college football became a major theme in the general-interest magazines in the 1950s. In 1951, the *Post* ran consecutive articles by the president of Georgetown University, whose school had just dropped football, and a former coach at the University of Texas who had quit the game. A high school coach's explanation for resigning in disgust over the abuses at even that level, a fired college coach's case against "The Hypoc-risy of College Football," and another fired coach's account of the sensible life at a small college after brutal years in big-time football followed over the next few years.[45] Portraits of football in the Ivy League or at small col-leges elsewhere became a minor genre, pointedly offering an alternative to the no-holds-barred big-time game.[46] *Life* and *Look* turned from their con-sistently "soft" coverage of football to some of the hardest-hitting attacks on the game's abuses. With the basketball point-fixing and West Point cribbing scandals fresh, it was presumably *Life*'s new sports editor, Marshall Smith, in 1951 who wrote "Football Is a Farce," an editorial contemptuous of the "annual fraud" of college football, whose "silly season" had now commenced, overseen by college presidents who acted more like prizefight promoters than guides to culture and morality.[47] *Look* sports editor Tim Cohane was a virtual clone of Francis Wallace. Both Cohane's own articles and those by other writers in the magazine took a consistent position: that frank, open subsidization of athletes at a level that could support them was the only reasonable way to manage college football. Players and coaches were blameless (players underpaid, coaches overpressured), while alumni—the villains in many such scenarios—were merely contributing financial aid that university authorities were too blind or hypocritical to provide. Guilt belonged almost entirely to myopic university presidents and faculty athletic representatives.[48] Even *Sport,* a publication for avid fans, regularly exposed college football's corruption and hypocrisy in the 1950s.[49]

When collected in this manner, these stories convey a sense of moral outrage that would seemingly have overwhelmed the public. The articles, however, were spaced over several years, or sometimes concentrated in a particular season but even then appearing weekly (or bimonthly in the case of *Look*); the daily newspaper with its focus on the home team's business as usual remained the dominant source of football news. And all the while, the same popular magazines continued to celebrate football heroics, coaching genius, and the exhilarating pageantry of big-time college football. According to the journalists in the periodical as well as the daily press, the game had problems, but those problems lay in misguided principles rather than ethical laxity. Schools such as Michigan State, Ohio State, and Auburn that spent time on probation in the 1950s were guilty only of getting caught doing what everyone did, or of violating ridiculous rules.[50] As far back as 1929, *New York Times* columnist John Kieran, writing in *American Magazine,* had termed the balance between wild enthusiasm and wild reform "the budget in imbecility" in college football.[51] Much was added to both sides of the ledger over the following decades, but the budget somehow always seemed to balance.

REFORM AND THE DAILY PRESS ONCE MORE

Even in college football's darkest years, the early 1950s, newspapers continued to place expediency above reform. Within the NCAA, slumping attendance was the issue that all members could agree was serious. Attendance surged immediately following the war, but after peaking in 1949 it declined each season through 1953 and then recovered at a creeping pace, not top-ping 1949's total until 1960. Television was chiefly blamed, and while the NFL built its audience through exploiting the new medium, the NCAA did everything possible to keep fans from becoming hooked on watching foot-ball at home.[52] In this double crisis, for economic survival and for ethical integrity, the position of the daily press was overwhelmingly on the side of preserving big-time football against excessive reform.

Responses to the crises and the reform movements they spawned varied by writer and locale, but the common pattern for local sports columnists was to stand by the home team first and its conference second, treating the opposing sides with scorn. In Chicago, the *Tribune's* Arch Ward generally endorsed the position of the Big Ten (or Big Nine in some of these years) for "purity" through job-based and need-based financial aid, as well as its oppo-sition to nationally controlled television broadcasts; and he stood by Notre Dame above all others.[53] Ward weighed in most heavily in September 1951, when he made several rather bizarre proposals for reform, the strangest one a suggestion that coaches rotate among the schools in the conference, so as to eliminate the incentive to hold spring practices and recruit top players. Ward congratulated himself for his brilliance in subsequent columns, and the following January he claimed credit for starting the entire reform move-ment since taken up by the presidents' committee of the American Council on Education. Always the promoter, Ward was his own principal cause.[54] In Omaha, the *World-Herald* more modestly endorsed the positions taken by the University of Nebraska and its Big Seven Conference, but also worried about the Cornhuskers' ability to compete with Oklahoma and its power-ful recruiting. The *Atlanta Constitution, Atlanta Journal,* and *Dallas Morning News* stood with their local schools' conferences in support of open athletic scholarships against the hypocrisy of the self-righteous Big Ten and Pacific Coast Conference. Local sportswriters everywhere stood up for "clean and honest" college football, but cleanliness and honesty were defined locally.[55]

Commenting on the 1953 NCAA meeting, *Dallas Morning News* sports edi-tor Bill Rives reported, "The general feeling in the pressroom seemed to be: 'Oh, these professors. What do they know about football?'"[56] Such anti-academic sentiment had popped up intermittently since the beginnings of football, but its fullest flowering came in the *Los Angeles Times* in the 1950s. The Pacific Coast Conference in that decade offers the most thoroughly documented case of college presidents in conflict with their own athletic departments and alumni boosters; the entire sports staff of the *Los Ange-les Times* stood emphatically on the side of the latter.[57] The PCC and the

Big Nine/Big Ten had the most stringent rules among major conferences and were the most self-scrutinizing and self-policing organizations, but what looked like noble principles to some appeared merely hypocritical pretension to others. The PCC and Big Nine were the chief sponsors of the Sanity Code, but instead of endorsing it, too, in the usual alignment of sportswriters with their home teams and conferences, the *Times* ridiculed it from the outset because it was so at odds with the athletic interests and actual practices at USC and UCLA. In June 1949, after the conference levied fines on member schools ranging from $120 to $5500 for violations of the Sanity Code, the *Times*'s Dick Hyland declared that "the dear, dull dillies who control the Pacific Coast Conference" had proven themselves once again either hypocritical or "so stupidly ineffective that it verges on the ludicrous to place them in position of power and authority." In Hyland's view, the Sanity Code was as ill-conceived as Prohibition in the 1920s, and for the same reason: no one wanted it. What Paul Zimmerman during the 1950 NCAA convention called the "insanity code" devised by the "big shots" of "the great and august NCAA"—the "rah rah bigwigs" to Braven Dyer—found support from no one at the *Times*. Zimmerman, Dyer, and Hyland all insisted that reasonable subsidization of college athletes was a principle that, in Hyland's words, even "the moldiest of narrow minded professors" should be able to accept.[58]

The Pacific Coast Conference was unique in vesting nominal athletic power in its faculty representatives, and Hyland's attacks on "the dear, dull dillies" and "narrow minded professors" were just a taste of what would come. At various times, Hyland and his colleagues offered calm criticism of PCC proposals to eliminate bowl games and spring practices, and even endorsed the action at the PCC meeting in December 1951 that turned enforcement of the conference code over to the university presidents. Following the PCC meeting the next year, sports editor Zimmerman went so far as to praise faculty representatives' efforts to grapple with difficult issues while keeping the welfare of the athletes in mind.[59]

These measured responses came before the presidents and faculty reps responded to the slush-fund scandals that broke over the first half of 1956. The fund operated by the Greater Washington Advertising Fund in Seattle was the first to be uncovered, at the end of January; then over the next few months boosters at Cal, USC, and UCLA exposed similar groups at rival schools. "Slush fund" meant outright payments to athletes, made in secret rather than openly, but conference coaches and sportswriters defended these operations as unfortunately necessary, because conference officials refused to acknowledge that the $75 monthly limit that athletes could earn at campus jobs might cover expenses in Corvallis or Pullman but not in Los Angeles or San Francisco. The majority of faculty representatives—from the schools in Corvallis, Pullman, Eugene, and Moscow, along with Stanford— were unmoved by such rationales. On 6 May, they placed the University of Washington on probation for two years, and two weeks later handed a three-year probation to UCLA, along with a year of ineligibility for all beneficiaries of the Bruins' slush fund. On 8 July, USC received a two-year probation and a year of ineligibility for forty-two football players, and Cal was fined $25,000.[60]

The *Los Angeles Times* exploded. Over the 1956 and 1957 seasons, as USC and UCLA played without their ineligible athletes while Oregon State and Oregon won conference championships, Braven Dyer and Paul Zimmerman, but particularly Dick Hyland and new columnist Ned Cronin, sniped repeatedly at the tyranny of the smaller schools in the Northwest which, along with Stanford, self-righteously punished the others for engaging in common practices, motivated by sheer resentment, particularly of Red Sanders and his too-successful UCLA teams. The dean of the law school at the University of Oregon, Orlando Hollis, who chaired the faculty committee, became the personal target of much of the *Times*'s amazing vitriol. Ned Cronin—the former sports editor of the *Los Angeles Daily News,* who joined the *Times* in 1954 to become the sports department's humorist—harped on "the Foundering Fathers of the PCC" and seemingly stayed up nights inventing ever more inventive insults for Dean Hollis: "Orlando Hollis, Avenging Angel and well-known inventor of unworkable athletic codes," the "Fifth Horseman of the Apocalypse," "Orlando Hollis and his gay group of vestal virgins from the University of Oregon." When Oregon played UCLA in 1956, Cronin referred to the Ducks derisively as "the Hollis varsity" and "the University of Hollis."[61]

Red Sanders's shocking death from a heart attack in a Los Angeles hotel room in August 1958 put an end to UCLA's reign as a major football power, but not to the *Times*'s campaign against the PCC and its northwestern tyranny. (In a manner unthinkable by today's journalistic standards, the paper also tried to protect Sanders's reputation by omitting any mention of his companion in the hotel room, described discretely in the AP report as "a blonde, about 30, who said she had just been introduced to Sanders.")[62] The *Times* continued to push for USC and UCLA to withdraw from the conference—not out of spite, the writers insisted, but so as to compete only with academic and athletic equals—and it welcomed the dissolution of the PCC when it finally came in 1959. Professed ideals, at both the southern and northern ends of the conference, overlay the competitive imbalance and conflicting economic interests between small-market and large-market teams. The columnists for the *Times* were no less "principled" than their colleagues elsewhere. Throughout their attacks on "the Foundering Fathers" they defended the players as victims and faulted an unworkable code rather than those who violated it. Like sportswriters everywhere, they defended the honor—and coincidentally the competitive interests—of the local teams.

Between 1945 and 1960, college football assumed its modern form, and for all the turmoil of the early 1950s, it emerged from the decade on the verge of "a period of unprecedented prosperity."[63] In the 1930s, following the report of the Carnegie Foundation, many universities had struggled openly against the contradiction at the heart of the game. Having embarked on big-time football in the late 1920s, Columbia and NYU retreated in the 1930s. After pulling off the greatest upset in Rose Bowl history by beating Stanford in 1934, Columbia coach Lou Little went on to lose more games than he won over the next twenty-three seasons, famously becoming the highly paid coach (perhaps the highest paid of all) who did not have to win.[64] Chancellor Bowman of the University of Pittsburgh put an end to the most open system of subsidization in college football, with the result that Pitt teams fell from the pinnacle of football power to mediocrity before reform was abandoned a decade later. The president of the University of North Carolina devised the "Graham Plan," briefly adopted by the Southern Conference, which permitted no subsidization of athletes, but then quickly discarded it when the schools realized their competitive disadvantage. And after a decade of deemphasis, the president of the University of Chicago made the most drastic move of all, dropping football altogether in 1939.

In the supercharged atmosphere of college football after World War II, universities faced the decision to get out or go along. Dozens of schools dropped football for financial reasons, and Georgetown's president undoubtedly spoke for many of his colleagues when he expressed relief at no longer having to maintain the charade of amateurism.[65] Georgetown was but one of many Catholic universities that dropped football at this time, including one-time major powers such as Fordham, St. Mary's, and Santa Clara. The Ivy League showed the way to opt out of big-time football while maintaining the sport at a highly charged lower level. Penn tried to be both big-time and Ivy League but was forced to choose and went with the Ivies. Most colleges that stayed had to accept the new order of recruiting and subsidization. Pitt retreated from purity, while several schools seemingly abandoned ethics altogether. As a consequence of the scandals in the Pacific Coast Conference, the NCAA at its 1957 convention approved non-need-based athletic scholarships, at last making "professionalism" the very basis of the system that continues today. Having met the threats of both television and reformers, the organization grew stronger over the 1950s, as its infractions committee meted out penalties for breaking its rules.[66] Rogue programs such as those at Maryland and Auburn nonetheless taught a lesson not lost on their competitors: do whatever it takes to build a winning team, accept your wrist-slapping by the NCAA if you get caught, then enjoy the fruits of championship football. Men such as Bear Bryant developed the corollary for coaches: do whatever it takes to win at one school in order to move on to the next, should the first be caught cheating.

Radio and newsreels were silent on these issues. Popular magazines played a schizophrenic role: an exposé one week, celebrity puffery the next. The stance of the daily press in the emergence of this new order cannot be reduced to a simple consensus, but in general, sportswriters and columnists supported their local coaches and football programs on whatever terms prevailed locally. The degree to which local newspapers shaped or merely reflected popular sentiment cannot easily be determined, but their support for business as usual, whatever the nature of the business, guaranteed that no groundswell for radical reform ever gathered force. Fifty-three percent of respondents to a Gallup poll in 1951 said that scholarships and other remuneration for football players should be disallowed; only 27 percent were in favor of them. Fifty-six percent of those polled (75 percent among the college-educated) thought that colleges and universities placed too much emphasis on athletics.[67] How many of those would-be reformers were passionate fans, or believed their own team guiltless of the general distortions, or would feel the same way when their team was undefeated as when it was struggling near the bottom of the conference, is unknown. In the absence of any popular reform effort, what that poll most plausibly suggests is widespread mild cynicism but insufficient outrage to demand change; a belief that, yes, college football had problems, but that they existed everywhere except at home.

Players' or Coaches'— Whose Game Is It?

Among the sports heroes from the so-called Golden Age of Sport—Babe Ruth, Jack Dempsey, Bill Tilden, Bobby Jones—two figures from the world of football stood out: Harold (Red) Grange and Knute Rockne. There had been celebrated football stars before Grange—Tillie Lamar, Pudge Heffelfinger, the Poes of Princeton, Jim Thorpe, Eddie Mahan, and dozens more—but Grange became football's first true celebrity through the full resources of a media machine that only emerged in the 1920s. Grange actually performed the feats that dazzled football fans in the mid-1920s and drew the media to him, but the "Galloping Ghost" and "Wheaton Ice Man" were in turn creations of the media. Following his spectacular six-touchdown performance against Michigan on 18 October 1924, Grange received unprecedented wire-service and syndicated newspaper attention over the rest of his junior and senior seasons, including a serialized biography written by James Braden of the *Chicago Daily News* that ran in October and November 1925 in many papers. Henry Luce's new *Time* magazine placed Grange on its 5 October 1925 cover, and every other magazine that featured sports documented his exploits. Grange's signing with the Chicago Bears immediately following his final college game provoked newspaper commentary by seemingly every syndicated and local sports columnist; and his subsequent games with the Bears, including his exhibition tour throughout the South and West over the winter of 1925–26, were headline news wherever he appeared.

Grange's collegiate career ended a year before the first radio network was created, but several of his games in 1924 and 1925 were broadcast by WGN in Chicago and accessible outside the region to listeners whose sets could pick up distant stations.[1] With their unique, and uniquely powerful, capacity to let the vast moviegoing public actually see their heroes in action, newsreels brought images of Grange to theaters in every state in the union. Hearst's *International News* captured his spectacular showing against Michigan in 1924. With Grange already an All-American, the photographer positioned himself behind the Michigan goal for the opening kickoff and aimed his camera at #77. After Grange ran the kick back for a touchdown, the photographer kept his camera focused on him and caught the rest of his touchdown runs as well.[2] *International News* also covered Grange's final collegiate game (against Ohio State), his appearance with the Bears against the Giants in New York, and his game against a local club in Washington, D.C., a few days later. *Pathé News* covered Grange's college games in 1925 with Nebraska, Penn, and Ohio State, and his pro contests against the Giants and the team assembled for the first stop on his southern tour, in Miami. (Pathé also filmed Grange meeting the famous horticulturist Luther Burbank while on his football tour in California, then showed him hauling ice blocks back home in Wheaton, Illinois, that summer, then again in September in training camp with his newly formed New York Yankees.)[3]

The Penn game in Philadelphia was particularly significant outside Chicago: in his first and only appearance in the East, Grange gained 363 yards on thirty-six carries, scoring three times (once from fifty-five yards out, once from forty), in a 24–2 upset of the heavily favored easterners (Illinois entered the game 1–3, Pennsylvania 5–0). Grantland Rice, Damon Runyon, and other top eastern sportswriters attended the game and gushed over Grange in their syndicated reports, while newsreels brought Grange in action, larger than life on screen, to fans everywhere. In Chicago, the week following the game, ads for Harold Lloyd's new football film, *The Freshman*, announced that newsreel footage of Illinois-Penn was included on the program. In what must be the earliest cross-marketing of football and cinema, ads in Chicago newspapers invited moviegoers to "Compare the two Super Harolds," and the image of Lloyd was the identical pose of Grange in one of his most reprinted photographs (except that Grange held the ball in his left arm, Lloyd in his right).[4] Harold Grange drew customers to see Harold Lloyd, not the other way around.

All of this today would seem the typical handling of top athletes by the media; we simply must recognize that Red Grange was the first football star to receive the full treatment possible within a dramatically expanded media culture. We must also recognize that sports heroes helped shape that media culture, even as their celebrity was created by it. As the first football player with his own agent, Grange broke new ground with the range of his product endorsements: a fact, as we saw in the last chapter, that fascinated his public and troubled some sportswriters. In 1926, Grange made a football feature film, *One Minute to Play* (in a performance praised by reviewers), and in 1931 a football cliffhanger serial, *The Galloping Ghost*, both of which were also made into boys' books.[5] Other football stars, including leading men such as Johnny Mack Brown and Herman Brix, followed Grange to Hollywood. (John Wayne was just a USC scrub before leaving school for a film career.) It cannot be wholly coincidental that the season following the Grange hysteria marked the beginning of major football coverage in the country's favorite magazine, the *Saturday Evening Post*. Having used just two football covers earlier in the decade (one in 1923 and the other, by Norman Rockwell, in 1925), the *Post* ran three in 1926, along with Amos Alonzo Stagg's eight-part autobiography, its first serious editorial attention to the game. Football films suddenly proliferated in Hollywood: after just one each in 1922 and 1924, and three in 1925, eight were released in 1926 and twenty-two more over the next three years. Grange, of course, had nothing to do with the creation of the first radio network in 1926, but according to Chicago broadcasting pioneer Quin Ryan, Grange's popularity persuaded NBC to schedule weekly college football games that first season.[6] In the early 1930s, although injuries reduced Grange's effectiveness as a professional for the Chicago Bears, he remained the most widely known football player in the land. *The Galloping Ghost* appeared in twelve installments in movie theaters in 1931, Grange "wrote" (coauthored with George Dunscomb) a half-dozen articles for the *Saturday Evening Post* between 1932 and 1935, and the magazine *College Humor* serialized Dunscomb's *"77,"* a fictionalized novel of Grange's career, in 1932–33.[7] Upon his retirement, Grange moved into radio broadcasting and, in the 1950s, television. In short, although Red Grange was obviously not alone responsible for the tremendous expansion in media attention to football, his personal role was crucial, and through the media his name continued to be identified with football for decades after he quit playing.

Knute Rockne did not burst so suddenly and spectacularly as Grange into the public consciousness, but his celebrity became broader and survived even longer.[8] There were famous coaches before him—men like Fielding Yost, Amos Alonzo Stagg, and Percy Haughton—but Rockne was football's first celebrity coach. As Murray Sperber has shown, Rockne initially had to work hard to win attention for his teams, cultivating sportswriters by giving them blocks of tickets and arranging for them to speak at postseason banquets and to referee Notre Dame games. The *Chicago Tribune*'s Walter Eckersall, the most influential sportswriter in the Midwest and West during the 1920s, was a particular beneficiary of Rockne's favors, and "Eck" reciprocated with unstinting celebration of Rockne's teams in the *Tribune*'s pages and generous treatment in his annual All-Western selections.[9] Rockne's efforts to promote the Notre Dame–Army series with New York sportswriters paid off finally in 1924, when Grantland Rice (who penned his immortal "Four Horsemen" lines for the *New York Herald Tribune*), Heywood Broun (*World*), Damon Runyon (*American*), Paul Gallico (*Daily News*), Joe Vila (*Sun*), and Allison Danzig (*Times*)—each paper's top writer—certified Notre Dame's stature as the nation's premier football team.

Rockne also pioneered the use of press agents, initially student assistants who fed stories to midwestern sports editors. Both Francis Wallace and Arch Ward served in this role before going on to distinguished sportswriting careers, during which they continued to promote Notre Dame football. Besides covering the 1924 Notre Dame–Army game for the Associated Press, Wallace helped popularize the name "Fighting Irish" in the *Daily News* in 1927 (Notre Dame had been the "Ramblers" or "Nomads" for their cross-country intersectional schedules) and first reported the "Win one for the Gipper" halftime speech after the Notre Dame–Army game in 1928. Ward made the *Chicago Tribune* a conduit for the Notre Dame line on every football issue that arose. A third student press assistant at Notre Dame, George Strickler, who later followed Ward to a long career at the *Tribune,* arranged the famous photo of the Four Horsemen that became one of the monumental images of college football.[10]

The newsreels missed the Notre Dame–Army game in 1924 (the same day as Grange's six-touchdown performance against Michigan), but *Pathé News* covered Notre Dame–Stanford in the 1925 Rose Bowl and was full of Rockne and Notre Dame beginning in 1926, as were Hearst's and the other newsreels once they appeared. Network radio likewise embraced Rockne and his football teams from its first season. Rockne wrote (or had ghostwritten) weekly newspaper columns for the Christy Walsh Syndicate and, with Pop Warner and Fielding Yost, composed Walsh's first All-American Board of Football for selecting one of the many All-America teams, a role he continued until his death. Rockne's off-season banquet-circuit speeches and coaching clinics always won favorable reviews in local newspapers, and he became a spokesman for American business as well as an endorser of its products (the coach died too soon to see Studebaker's six-cylinder "Rockne" model hit the market in the fall of 1931). Rockne followed Red Grange onto the cover of *Time* on 7 November 1927. *Collier's* published Rockne's serialized memoirs in 1930, just months before his death in a Kansas cornfield prompted an outpouring of national mourning and tributes from the president of the United States and the king of Norway, among countless others. By the end of that year, no fewer than five biographies in addition to Rockne's own autobiography were published, collectively transforming Rockne from a shrewd and charismatic football coach into the mythic spirit of college football itself.[11] Over the rest of the decade no one could write about great coaches without invoking Rockne. His many former players coaching at colleges throughout the country kept his name constantly in newspapers and magazines, and rival coaches all claimed a special kinship with the beloved Rock, even if they had once resented him. Rockne's ultimate deification, of course, came in the Pat O'Brien–Ronald Reagan movie *Knute Rockne—All American* in 1940, which added nothing new to the Rockne mystique but preserved it for future generations.[12]

SPORTSWRITERS AND COACHES

Rockne along with Grange as a football hero: what's wrong with this picture? Nothing, but only because he belonged to *American* football. We have grown so accustomed to superstar coaches that we likely are unaware how odd the concept is. Albert Einstein's favorite math teacher was not *Time's* Man of the Century. None of Mariah Carey's music teachers ever won a Grammy. The public has no idea who taught Bobby Fischer to play chess. More to the point, in the football (soccer) played in most of the world, the coach is little more than a spectator on the sidelines once the game begins. Not the American football coach. Everything that transpires on the field is understood to be the execution of the coach's game plan, perhaps devised by an offensive coordinator or "assistant head coach" in today's highly specialized times, but ultimately deriving from the top man himself. Coaches as well as players are elected to the American football halls of fame.

Under the guidance of Walter Camp, football developed in crucial ways as a coaches' game from the very beginning: a sport structured much like a corporation, with the coach as both tactician and manager.[13] Initially, the players themselves developed the rules and strategies of play, and as football took root at Harvard, Yale, and Princeton, Yale led the way in developing a system of old grads returning to prepare the current students. As the game spread to the South and West, the hiring of paid coaches, typically

Yale graduates, became inevitable. Where the game was utterly new, some-one from the outside had to teach its fine points. While Harvard, Yale, and Princeton agonized over the ethics of "professional" coaches for themselves, the rest of the growing football world hired them as a matter of course. This was not an inconsequential matter, however. If football was to be understood as training for future leaders, decision-making by a coach had to seem a con-straint on the players' self-reliance. For decades, rule-makers attempted to prevent "sideline coaching"; in 1917, for example, a new rule forbade any substitute to communicate with his teammates until after one play. Over the 1920s and 1930s, referees hovered about the huddle to make certain no in-structions were sneaked in by the coach. Even after substitution rules were repeatedly liberalized, and two-platoon football came, went, and returned, sideline coaching was not officially sanctioned until 1967.

Such rules were ineffective, however, and over the 1920s and 1930s foot-ball critics periodically protested what some called a "coach-ridden" game, and they praised those coaches who fostered players' self-reliance. Rockne was admired not only as a strategist and motivator, but also as a teacher who instructed his pupils thoroughly, then let them play the game themselves on Saturdays. Walter Camp, the man unwittingly most responsible for turn-ing football over to coaches, praised Rockne in 1923 for developing "men who make their own decisions and then carry them out on their own ini-tiative." For Camp, football was primarily valuable as a preparation for life, and Rockne's style served this purpose: "When those boys leave Rockne to hurl themselves against the massed and tricky formations with which life will oppose them, they will be splendidly equipped for that most impor-tant of all battles." Yet by singling out Rockne, rather than those young men he turned loose once the game began, Camp contributed to the popular identification of college teams with their coaches (this was one of the minor complaints in the Carnegie Foundation report in 1929), and Rockne's meth-ods were not universally approved. One critic insisted that eliminating shift plays—of which Rockne's Notre Dame shift was the most prominent—was needed in order to give the game back to the players, and John R. Tunis included Rockne among the "petty czars" who made football a "contest be-tween coaches." "Hand Back the Game to the Boys," demanded an article in the *Forum* in 1926. "Whose Game Is It?" asked Tunis in his polemic.[14]

Opposition was thus never lacking, but coaches gained more, rather than less, control over the game as it developed decade by decade. Players, of course, came and went, while coaches remained, but other less necessary factors also contributed. Institutional structures ceded power to coaches early on, though not without pockets of resistance. The football coach at Notre Dame reported directly to the university vice president and president, and as late as 1947 students at the University of California retained the power to hire and fire coaches (an arrangement, in the words of a disapproving journalist, that made Cal a "coaches' graveyard"). Most athletic departments, however, operated more or less independently by the 1930s, their football coaches more accountable to powerful alumni and financial boosters than to university presidents. The most widely publicized example was the University of Texas, where the "archangel" behind the football program convinced the Board of Regents in 1937 to hire Dana Bible away from Nebraska with a ten-year contract at $15,000 a year (and rumors of a $40,000 or $50,000 annuity as well). When some objected that the football coach would earn nearly twice what was paid the university president, and three times the salary of the highest-paid professor, the state legislature devised a solution: raise the president's salary to $17,500 and hire Bible.[15]

On the field, coaches' control over the play of the game was constrained by substitution rules through the 1930s. More or less unlimited substitution was first approved in 1941, due to the wartime manpower shortage, but not fully exploited until after the war, when Fritz Crisler at Michigan and Red Blaik at Army developed true two-platoon football. The deployment of separate offensive and defensive teams was controversial in the postwar years for several unrelated reasons—it replaced all-around players with specialists (as the pros had long been doing) and gave a tremendous advantage to the big football powers that could stockpile good players—but also because it put more control of the game in coaches' hands. Traditionalists succeeded in rescinding open substitution in 1953, but it returned to stay in 1965, after which the long evolution toward today's level of specialization became virtually inevitable.[16]

Coaches' control of football thus resulted from numerous specific factors within the game itself and its regulation. The increasing pressure on coaches to win, particularly during the frenzied period following the Second World War, also made them less inclined to let the boys win or lose on their own. But the early identification of teams with their coaches also derived from football's deep entanglements with the media and from the intimate relationships that developed between coaches and sportswriters, as exemplified above by Knute Rockne. Rockne initially had to cultivate the press because a small private school in Indiana had no obvious claims on the attention of writers in New York or even Chicago. With teams conspicuous for their immigrant-rich Catholic lineups, Rockne was also confronted by the anti-

Catholic, anti-immigrant hysteria of the early 1920s. Rockne won over the press with his charm, his favors, and his wonderful teams. The more typical relationships between coaches and local sportswriters had no such barriers to overcome.

As Murray Sperber notes, sportswriters most simply "needed the coaches for team schedules, rosters, free rides to and from games, press box and locker room passes, game information, [and] quotes." Sportswriters did not begin interviewing players in the locker room until after World War II; coaches alone provided the "inside" perspective essential to the sports-writer's job. Numerous other factors drew sportswriters to coaches or made sportswriters dependent on them. While football was not prone to the out-right payoffs and slightly more subtle bribes from boxing promoters that produced what Paul Gallico called "the ancient scandal that adheres to the sports-writer," the arrangements that coaches like Rockne made with sports-writers like Walter Eckersall came close. The value of the favors on both sides was considerable. Sportswriters working as officials earned $50 to $75 a game, figures which Sperber points out were equal to "the monthly pay range for most sportswriters at the time." For handling publicity in Chicago for a Notre Dame game in 1927, Rockne paid Eckersall $250, "the price of a new Dodge coupe," as Sperber puts it. A survey of 125 newspapers in 1926 revealed that forty to fifty of them permitted their sportswriters to accept positions as referees, scorers, timekeepers, and other officials.[17] Coaches re-ceived much more in return. The free publicity that favorable sportswriting provided for universities had a literally incalculable value, while the result-ing celebrity of coaches meant more easily measured rewards. Long before Dana Bible, coaches' salaries routinely exceeded those of full professors.

Between the coach and the sportswriter stood the coach's press agent (today's sports information director), who became a fixture in every athletic department by the 1930s. "College praise men," as John R. Tunis dispar-agingly called them, were responsible for much of the puffery and "inside dope" that were the staples of sports reporting. By the mid-1930s, virtually every college football program had what *New York World-Telegram* sports col-umnist Joe Williams described as "a press department, which, in personnel, equipment, and efficiency, will match anything Mr. Mike Jacobs, the czar of the prize-fight industry, has to offer." One college press agent, writing in *Liberty* in 1935, described his job as a "sweet racket" but a "gentle" one, since it gave pleasure to "gullible fans." Press agents puffed star players and cam-paigned for their schools' All-America candidates, but from day to day they primarily managed the flow of information from coaches to sportswriters and monitored the public images of the coaches they served. Daily coverage of the football team was thus inevitably a joint production of sportswriter, coach, and press agent.[18]

Deeper than the dependence of sportswriters on coaches' press agents, their personal relationships with the coaches themselves greatly affected the football journalism in this period. From the sportswriter's perspective, the college coach was the "adult" representative of the team, his players just "boys." If he was at all successful, the coach remained at the university, in a long-term relationship with local sportswriters. Out of these professional contacts friendships grew. Like major league baseball writers, the men who covered college football traveled with the team, drank and talked with the coach in his hotel room the night before the game, and celebrated or commiserated with him afterward. In his memoirs, Grantland Rice noted that his friends among football coaches were too numerous for him to name the fifteen or twenty dearest without hurting many feelings. The football reminiscences of Fred Russell are full of the coaches at Vanderbilt, Tennessee, and throughout the South with whom he worked. Nationally prominent sportswriters such as Russell and Francis Wallace acknowledged that they steered promising high school athletes to their favored coaches' schools. Sportswriters routinely collaborated with coaches in writing articles for the *Saturday Evening Post, Collier's,* and other popular magazines. As sports editor of *Look* after World War II, Tim Cohane spent a week before each season in idyllic masculine retreat with Army coach Red Blaik and his inner circle. Unsurprisingly, Cohane praised and defended Blaik unstintingly in his journalism, then cowrote Blaik's memoirs for *Look* after he retired from West Point.[19] Small-town sportswriters were more limited in their coaching friendships, but their relationships with the local college coaches could grow particularly deep. In college towns, those smallish communities dominated by a major university, negative comments on the coach in the local newspaper were rare. Fired coaches might receive some backhand criticism the following season, but only to reinforce how much better things were under his successor.

INSIDE DOPE AND CELEBRITY PROFILES

A number of factors, then, lay behind football journalism's long history of setting coaches above players. The journalism itself suggests the consequences. Through the mid-1920s, the football nonfiction in the *Post* and *Collier's* had no particular emphasis on coaches, but by the end of the decade the celebrity coach had fully emerged. In *Collier's,* an interview with Knute Rockne in 1927, then long-time coach John Heisman's eight-part memoir in 1928, followed by three more anecdotal articles by Heisman in 1929, then Rockne's autobiography in eight parts in 1930 and Pop Warner's reminiscences in six parts in 1931, placed coaches at the center of the college game.[20] The *Saturday Evening Post* embraced football belatedly, but when it did, in 1926, it started with University of Chicago coach Amos Alonzo Stagg's eight-part autobiography.[21] Sustained coverage in the *Post* did not begin until 1931, first with a referee's reminiscences in three parts (the beginning of what became its own journalistic genre),[22] then almost weekly articles, most of them for the first two years by or about star players rather than coaches. Nineteen thirty-three marked a dramatic shift, as the *Post*'s football journalism became overwhelmingly coach-oriented. Except for three articles written "by" Red Grange, every football article for three years was by or about a coach. At the same time, after a 1932 season marked by articles by former athletes, *Collier's* from 1933 through 1937 published twenty-four articles about coaches and one—just one!—about a player. Columbia's Lou Little wrote six of these in 1934, immediately following his team's startling upset of Stanford in the Rose Bowl. Alabama's Frank Thomas contributed two articles the following season, after his team's Rose Bowl victory over Stanford. Stanford's Tiny Thornhill earned his own turn—three articles in 1936—after Stanford finally won at Pasadena, beating SMU. For Little, Thomas, Thornhill, and dozens more coaches in the 1930s, writing for the popular magazines offered a lucrative addition to their salaries (and to those of the sportswriters and press agents, who often wrote the articles). For their readers, each article reinforced a basic principle that coaches determined the outcomes of games.

Collier's took another turn in 1938, toward greater balance between coaches and players, and toward a new form of sports journalism: the celebrity profile. Football journalism until this time meant primarily "inside dope": the story behind the story, known only to insiders. Articles by coaches (or their collaborators or ghostwriters) and by football "experts" such as Walter Camp and Grantland Rice explained what was happening within the swirling masses and behind the scenes. The coaches who wrote for the *Post* and *Collier's* gained celebrity by doing so, but the true celebrity profile was a different kind of football article that emerged in *Collier's* in 1938. In a story about a 230-pound quarterback at Rice University and another about Rhodes Scholar and Pittsburgh Steeler rookie Whizzer White, freelance journalist Kyle Crichton shifted attention from football's behind-the-scenes mysteries to the subject's own life and personality.[23]

Whether Crichton should be personally credited with inventing the genre is uncertain, but he introduced it to *Collier's* with a distinctive style that spread to the *Post*. Astonishingly, writing as "Robert Forsythe," Crichton had written scathing articles for the radical *New Masses* in 1934, 1935, and 1936, denouncing college football as commercial exploitation and a "national opiate," at the same time he was celebrating football for *Collier's* under his own name.[24] Whether from a pragmatic career adjustment or a true conversion, Crichton dropped "Robert Forsythe" after 1936 and began contributing regularly to *Collier's* a kind of football article about as far removed from these radical polemics as they could be. Shifting the focus from the inside story to his subjects' personality and life experiences, Crichton wrote this new kind of essay in a breezy, irreverent style. The *Post* resisted such hero-worshipping of football celebrities until 1941, when it published a profile of Stanford's Frankie Albert, then after Ben Hibbs became editor in 1942, the new style became central to the *Post*'s formula as well.[25]

The emergence of celebrity football profiles was part of the more general shift in magazine nonfiction in the 1920s and 1930s that Leo Lowenthal has described in a well-known essay. Portraits of political, business, and professional leaders, that provided "genuine information" about the powerful figures shaping the readers' real world, gave way in this period to personal biographies of popular entertainers. Lowenthal termed the new heroes of magazine biography "idols of consumption," in contrast to the "idols of production" of the earlier type. Within the world of football, Amos Alonzo Stagg, John Heisman, Knute Rockne, and Pop Warner would qualify as "idols of production." Though spiced with entertaining anecdotes, the inside dope they shared with readers was akin to what Lowenthal termed the "technical requirements and accomplishments" of various professions in the articles about statesmen and financiers. The celebrity profiles of both coaches and players that began appearing in the late 1930s were versions of the new type of biography identified by Lowenthal: adulatory rather than instructive, their purpose to construct not a blueprint for better understanding the real world but "a dream world of the masses." In Warren Susman's equally well known formulation, as American consumer culture expanded in the 1920s and 1930s, personality replaced character as the key to advancement and personal fulfillment. The coach's personality had always been part of the inside dope offered by magazines—a key to his "psychology" in handling players, for example—and the behind-the-scenes side of football remained part of the celebrity profile, but the two types can nonetheless be distinguished, and the shift toward personality and celebrity marks an important stage in the evolution from "sport" to "entertainment" that has become increasingly conspicuous in our own time.[26] Over the 1940s and 1950s, more than half of the articles in the *Post* and *Collier's* were celebrity profiles.

This recasting of football on more personal terms seems less a distortion of sport by powerful media than a belated response to public desires. Despite the extraordinary attention to Red Grange in 1924 and 1925, and more briefly to stars such as Yale's Albie Booth and Harvard's Barry Wood over the following years, the great popular magazines had held back from routinely conferring celebrity status on individual college football players. Football shed its sheen of amateurism reluctantly. College players were *boys;* individuals were less important than the *team;* the coach could represent the entire team in ways the individual player could not. These were among football's fundamental principles, more powerful for being largely unspoken. To make a celebrity of a college football player was to worship someone not yet an adult, to elevate him above his teammates, and to transport an amateur sportsman to the realm inhabited by paid entertainers. Professional football players were suitable for celebrity worship—prizefighters and major league baseball players had long received such attention—but professional football had no hold yet on the American imagination. College football was supposed to be training in character and life skills.

Football fans, however, had always wanted heroes. Walter Camp initially agonized over the unseemliness of singling out the eleven top players of the year as a violation of football's essential team spirit, but football fans loved the idea of "All-Americans," and by the 1920s not just *Collier's* but virtually every wire service, feature syndicate, and major metropolitan daily was selecting an All-America team. Celebrity profiles served the same desires. There were no moral lessons in these portraits, most of which simply described their subject's personality and the circumstances of his success. No single temperament trumped all others. A football star could be a cocky, fun-loving quarterback like Frankie Albert, who performed masterfully when the situation demanded, or a temperamental Yankee running back like Frankie Sinkwich, who won over the locals to become the most popular student on the University of Georgia campus.[27] What seemingly interested readers was simply a sense of intimacy with their football heroes through knowing what they were "really" like.

Most of these profiles, however, were not of players but of coaches. From 1946 through 1949, the magazine most oriented to the business classes— the *Saturday Evening Post*—profiled eighteen coaches and just two players; then forty-four coaches and sixteen players in the 1950s. Players slightly outnumbered coaches, twenty-three to nineteen, in the more populist *Collier's* during this period, but these players increasingly were pros, not collegians. In the two magazines together, eighteen of thirty-one profiles of football players in the 1950s were of professionals, men with adult struggles and accomplishments, not boys molded by powerful adults. In college football, coaches continued to rule.

HEROES AND DUMB JOCKS

Numbers alone cannot tell the whole story, and other cultural indicators suggest that fans were not simply won over to a coach-centered view of the game. The media forms with the broadest audiences—radio, newsreels, and movies—were dominated by star players. Radio and newsreels recorded the football played on the field, not devised on the sidelines and behind the scenes. *Knute Rockne—All-American* may have been the most popular football movie of the era, but the heroes of the more routine football films were overwhelmingly players rather than coaches. Dashing Hollywood leading men who played football stars in the 1920s and 1930s, conferring their own glamour on the role that they played, included Francis X. Bushman (*Brown of Harvard* and *Eyes Right*), Douglas Fairbanks, Jr. (*The Forward Pass*), Ramon Navarro (*Huddle*), Joel McCrea (*The Sport Parade*), Dick Powell (*College Coach*), Robert Young (*Saturday's Millions* and *The Band Plays On*), Van Heflin (*Saturday's Heroes*), and numerous others less well remembered.

Magazine covers are particularly revealing. Of the 113 football covers on the *Saturday Evening Post* and *Collier's* between 1920 and 1960, just 3 featured coaches. On a 1921 *Collier's,* an intense older man grips the shoulders of his young player and fills him with earnest instructions. The same configuration, only with the player now of college age, appeared on a *Collier's* cover in 1939. And on a 1940 *Post,* the players on the bench look anxiously toward their elderly coach, the emphasis here on his calm confidence rather than inspiring intensity. All these images emphasized the dependence of players on the commanding power of the coach, yet these were just 3 covers out of 113, over a period of forty years. The remaining 110 covers did not all feature heroic players—magazine covers' primary attention to football's social aspects will be discussed in the following chapter—but star players outnumbered coaches many times over.

Although the heroic visual image of the football player had no single creator, J. C. Leyendecker had the greatest influence. The foremost cover artist for the *Saturday Evening Post* before Rockwell, and unrivaled as a commercial artist in his day, Leyendecker painted football covers for *Century* and

Popular Magazine (a pulp) in 1909, in addition to two for *Collier's* and six for the *Post*, four of them between 1908 and 1914, when the major elements of football's popular iconography were emerging.[28] Leyendecker's early covers portrayed the football hero in action, his body defined by straight lines and sharp angles, rendering him as the physical embodiment of the machine-age dynamo. Leyendecker's brother Frank had painted the very first football cover for the *Post* in 1899 (a pair of linked figures, the scholar and the athlete, that J. C. later adapted for a 1928 cover), and the brothers Leyendecker used the same sharply angled style for the cover and interior illustrations in the 1909 *Century*. But it was J. C. who made the deepest imprint on football iconography. His earliest football heroes were strikingly handsome, but then in 1916 he painted for *Collier's* a new version: a rugged figure embodying raw physical power. The jersey torn off one shoulder, exposing both shoulder pad and the bare skin underneath, introduced what became a Leyendecker signature, a strangely erotic image of masculine power. Finally, Leyendecker blended his handsome hero and powerful brute into a single titanic figure in the 1920s and early 1930s, both for *Post* covers and for Kuppenheimer ads. Leyendecker's football heroes were not just iconic but monumental, appearing as if chiseled from granite for a gridiron Mt. Rushmore.[29]

Leyendecker's football hero was essentially his Arrow Collar Man in shoulder pads: the broad-shouldered, supremely confident male with shining skin, chiseled features, and steely eyes gazing away from the viewer. (He painted the same figure for products ranging from Ivory soap and Chesterfield cigarettes to Pierce Arrow automobiles, Interwoven socks, and Kuppenheimer and Hart Schaffner & Marx suits and overcoats.) Leyendecker's Arrow Collar Man became the very "symbol of fashionable American manhood" for an entire era, his models for these ads receiving as many as 17,000 fan letters in a single month in the early 1920s, more than even Rudolph Valentino at the peak of his fame.[30] Leyendecker's football hero was a less familiar presence in popular magazines, but he was a virtual clone who represented the same masculine ideal, and he powerfully influenced other artists' renderings. Heroic figures from other sports appeared on magazine covers, of course, but it was football alone that routinely conjured up the image of the supremely handsome, almost overwhelmingly masculine athletic ideal. (A baseball player Leyendecker painted for a *Collier's* cover just a month before his football "brute" in 1916 was decidedly less handsome and virile than his football heroes.)[31] The great irony in Leyendecker's influence on the popular image of the football hero is that the artist's usual model was his partner and lover, and historians of homosexuality

FIGURE 4-1. The football hero as painted by J. C. Leyendecker for the covers of popular magazines (*Saturday Evening Post,* 14 November 1908, *Popular Magazine,* November 1909, and *Collier's,* 18 November 1916) and in an ad for Kuppenheimer clothes, 1921.

FIGURE 4-2. Leyendecker's ultimate football hero, for the *Saturday Evening Post*, 24 November 1928. (Copyright © 1928 The Curtis Publishing Co.)

in the United States have located in Leyendecker's artwork coded expressions of homoerotic desire.[32] Readers of the *Post* and *Collier's* certainly had no clue that the most potent visual image of the football hero as heterosexual ideal was a gay man's creation.

The Leyendecker signature—the torn jersey exposing the bare upper arm and shoulder of his football hero—in his covers for *Collier's* in 1916, the *Post* in 1928, and a Kuppenheimer ad in 1927 was appropriated by other cover artists such as E. M. Jackson and Herbert Paus, who softened the eroticism of his portraits to suggest boy-next-door wholesomeness. These football heroes on magazine covers of the late 1920s and early 1930s were boyish but regal, literally enthroned in several images, bestriding the four points of the compass in another, embodying the spirit of winged victory in yet another.[33] This was the Big Man not just on Campus but on the planet. The football hero nearly disappeared from the cover art of the *Post* and *Collier's* after Leyendecker's last, in 1933, but the figure still appeared in the interior illustrations accompanying every football short story, and he returned to magazine covers in the photographs of actual stars in the 1940s. The most widely known football heroes in the 1940s and 1950s were the players—including Michigan's Tom Harmon, Army's Glenn Davis and Doc Blanchard, Notre Dame's Johnny Lujack and John Lattner, and preeminently SMU's Doak Walker—who made the covers of *Collier's*, *Life*, *Look*, and *Time* (Walker appeared on nearly fifty magazine covers in 1948 and 1949).[34] After *Collier's* largely shifted from artwork to photographs in the 1940s, not one of the sixteen cover photos was of a coach. Of the fifty-nine football covers on *Time*, *Life*, and *Look*, just seven had coaches: six on *Time*, none on *Life*, and one (Notre Dame's Frank Leahy) on *Look*. Thirty-two covers for these three magazines were photos of individual players.

If the magazine covers suggest a popular love affair with football heroes, the fiction inside tells a more ambivalent story about these athletes. To be sure, the dominant mode was heroic, though no single type predominated. The fictional football hero could be a paragon of physical prowess or a little man who triumphed through determination and savvy, a timid freshman who proved his worth to the mighty seniors or a senior captain who sacrificed his own All-America prospects for the good of the team, an arrogant star who learned to value others or an unsung scrub or blocking back who finally won the recognition he deserved. All these figures confirmed what the sports pages told readers daily: that football was genuinely heroic, and that football players embodied many of the culture's most cherished masculine virtues.

FIGURE 4-3. Leyendecker-influenced football hero painted by E. M. Jackson for the *Saturday Evening Post*, 21 November 1931. The torn-shoulder motif also appeared on another Jackson cover for *Collier's* on 18 October 1930 and one by Herbert Paus for *Collier's*, 5 December 1931, as well as covers by V. E. Pyles for *American Legion Magazine*, 28 November 1924, the program for the 1932 St. Mary's–Oregon game, and an interior illustration by Albin Henry for a football story in the *Post*, 21 November 1931. (*Post* cover copyright © 1931 The Curtis Publishing Co.)

Flawless football heroes were indeed ubiquitous, then, but so, too, were players characterized primarily by their flaws. In many ways the most revealing stereotypical figure in football fiction was the "dumb jock," in whom we can most clearly recognize the public's ambivalence about making heroes of "mere" athletes. The actual "tramp" athletes of the 1890s first raised issues of academic chicanery at supposed institutions of higher learning, but the popular stereotype of the dumb football player seems to have originated in the Siwash stories of George Fitch in the *Saturday Evening Post*. Fitch introduced Ole Skjarsen in 1909 as a strapping lumberjack from the northern woods who proves on his arrival at Siwash to be hard as flint and fast as a jackrabbit but equally muscular between the ears. After his acid-tongued coach explodes at him never to stop once he gets the ball, literal-minded Ole in the very next game runs over the entire Muggledorfer team, through the end zone, out of the stadium, and down the highway nine miles before the exasperated coach can catch up with him.[35] Ole's offspring did not pop up everywhere until the Catholic and state university teams of the Midwest, manned by the sons of millworkers and farmers rather than bankers and bond brokers, supplanted Harvard, Yale, and Princeton atop the college football world. At that point, humorous tales of the dumb jock quickly became a part of both the literary conventions and the folklore of the game.

Fitch's Ole Skjarsen was reincarnated as Sam Hellman's Plug Mehaffy and Beef Branahan, as well as Horatio Winslow's Ivory Ivorson, in stories in the *Post* between 1925 and 1930, and he reappeared in a handful of stories in *Collier's* in the late 1930s and early 1940s.[36] Ole's cousins particularly abounded in 1930s football films, seemingly half of them played by Andy Devine, the character actor who later became Roy Rogers's sidekick in a long-running series of western movies. In *The All-American* (1932), *Saturday's Millions* (1933), *The Big Game* (1936), and *Swing That Cheer* (1938), Devine's genial oaf defined the type for millions of moviegoers. The supreme version was played by Jack Oakie, another fixture in 1930s football movies, in the 1941 film *Rise and Shine,* based on a James Thurber story. Thurber's fictional account of his undergraduate years at Ohio State included a deadpan portrait of the brontosaurean football player Boley Bolenciecwcz, struggling to master economics with sympathetic help from Professor Bassum. In the story's finest scene, Boley is asked in class to name one means of transportation. Our hero sits mute, despite Bassum's gentle prodding, until the professor tries a new tack. "'Choo-choo-choo,' he said, in a low voice, and turned instantly scarlet. He glanced appealingly around the room. All of us, of course, shared Mr. Bassum's desire that Bolenciecwcz should stay abreast of the class in economics, for the Illinois game, one of the hardest and most important of the season, was only a week off. 'Toot, toot, too-tooooooot!' some student with a deep voice moaned, and we all looked encouragingly at Bolenciecwcz." When further sound effects bring no response, Mr. Bassum tries another line of inquiry:

"How did you come to college this year, Mr. Bolenciecwcz?" asked the professor. "*Chuffa* chuffa, *chuffa* chuffa."
"M'father sent me," said the football player.
"What on?" asked Bassum.
"I git a 'lowance," said the tackle, in a low, husky voice, obviously embarrassed.
"No, no," said Bassum. "Name a means of transportation. What did you *ride* here on?"
"Train," said Bolenciecwcz.
"Quite right," said the professor. "Now, Mr. Nugent, will you tell us—"[37]

In the film, this scene becomes the exam Boley must pass to remain eligible for the Big Game. As word of Boley's academic triumph reaches the breathlessly waiting students outside the building, the entire campus erupts into song and dance to celebrate the good news. The dumb jock would seem to mock mere physical prowess and universities' distorted priorities. As a comic figure, however, he evoked bemusement rather than outrage, while contributing to a schizoid popular view of football players as both heroes and oafs.

"POP" AND "BIFF"

For coaches, too, it is necessary to probe football fiction as well as journalism to fully recognize their cultural power. Had football initially developed like baseball, as a professional rather than a college sport, its cultural import would have differed in crucial ways. Because football players were culturally defined as boys—as adolescents, to be more precise, during the period when psychologists such as G. Stanley Hall were "discovering" adolescence as a distinct and decisive stage along the path toward adulthood—coaches and players quickly came to be understood not just as teachers and students but as surrogate fathers and sons.[38] A remarkable article written by a former Harvard player for *Harper's Weekly* in 1892 suggests that football was already being understood as a rite of passage for a society that had lost touch with its primitive roots. It describes a "new boy's" initiation into the sport's sacred

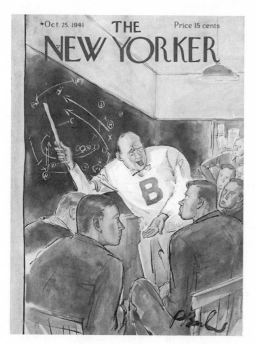

FIGURE 4-4. The figure of the dumb jock was satirized on covers of the *New Yorker,* here on 25 October 1941, and, more subtly, in a series of covers painted for *Collier's* by Arthur Crouch, one each season from 1933 through 1940. Crouch's roly-poly football players were the physical representation of what the public recognized as the dumb football player. (*New Yorker* drawing by Perry Barlow, courtesy The New Yorker Magazine, Inc., Condé Nast Publications, Inc.; reprinted by permission; all rights reserved)

rituals and mysteries by team elders, the veteran players and old grads returning to help out with the team, and, presiding over all of them, the aloof and almighty coach.[39] An equally remarkable scene in Owen Johnson's classic football tale, *Stover at Yale*, serialized in *McClure's* magazine in 1911–12 and then published as a novel in 1912, makes even more explicit the coach's role as the powerful father figure whose respect the young athlete must earn. As a 160-pound freshman, Dink Stover is a natural end, already one of the best in the land, but late in the season he is forced to play fullback due to injuries and an unusually weak Yale team. The rules and reigning style of play in this period made football a kicking game, with victory depending on a fullback who could punt great distances (often on third, second, or even first down from deep in one's own territory) and ends who could cover the punts downfield. Dink is a weak punter—as an end, he had no need for the skill—but unfortunately Yale has no one better. In the season-ending contest against a superior Princeton team, Dink gets off punt after punt in the face of a ferocious Princeton rush, but as the game wears on and Dink wears down, each punt is shorter than the last. When Princeton finally scores, the margin of victory is much closer than any Yale fan should have expected, but the uncomprehending ones in the stands think that Dink cost Yale the game. In the locker room afterward, as Dink slumps exhausted, "Two or three coaches came up to him, gripping him with silent grips, patting him on the back." Within the inner sanctum of the locker room Dink's gallant effort is fully understood, and in a powerful ritual of silent male bonding the fathers salute the son who has just proven himself a man.[40]

Versions of this story were common over the first quarter of the century. At a time when anxiety about a decline in American virility was acute, football's role as a vital masculine tonic was expressed over and over in popular magazines, as coach-fathers made men out of player-sons by driving them to their limits, then affirming their physical courage. James Hopper, for example, wrote several versions of this story for the *Saturday Evening Post*. Besides playing football for Cal in the 1890s, Hopper had been a grade-school classmate of Jack London and was later a loyal member of "The Crowd" that gathered around London when he reigned as the country's most famous writer.[41] Although London published several boxing stories, he wrote none about football, but Hopper gave football the London treatment. His stories such as "The Strength of the Weak: The Story of the Full-back Who Got Used to It"—the title tells the tale—were steeped in London's romantic primitivism and celebration of Anglo-Saxon toughness. The coaches in these stories were hard-driving taskmasters whose role was to make men out of boys through relentless toughening.[42]

Beginning in the 1920s, the fictional figure of the football coach bifurcated into this familiar tyrant and an altogether new type: the kindly, nurturing father. More than a change in coaching styles on the field, this development in football fiction seems to have reflected changing ideals of fatherhood and masculinity in the larger culture that were projected onto the game. According to historian Robert Griswold, the older "breadwinner" model of fatherhood was undermined by a new ideal of "masculine domesticity" during this period. Fathers were told by experts in *Parents' Magazine* and other periodicals "to become pals to their offspring" and to defend the family against the disruptive forces of modern life. This new ideal did not simply supplant the old, however, but in turn provoked a "crisis in masculinity" and a demand "for a retoughening of American boyhood."[43] The men most susceptible to the competing demands of this "New Fatherhood" were the middle-class males who also followed college football and read the football fiction in magazines like the *Post* and *Collier's*.

The contradictory requirements that fathers be both nurturing and demanding were reflected in the radically different models of the fictional football coach that began appearing in the popular weeklies in the 1920s. Within the world of actual football, these figures were related to the two "theories" of coaching explained by Penn coach Lou Young in the *Post* in 1929: the "romantic" (followed by "coaches who directed their teams with alternate outbursts of blistering invective and impassioned rhetoric") and the "accurate" (practiced by coaches who were "calm and sympathetic leaders, teaching candidates the game slowly from its fundamentals up, and watching their health, their morale and their academic standing with the solicitude of devoted parents").[44] Within the world of football fiction, these coaching styles were translated into archetypes of tyrannical and nurturing fathers in what any pop-Freudian of the day would have recognized as football-as-family-romance.

We can name these figures "Pop" and "Biff." Appealing to adolescent readers, the pulp magazine *Sport Story* was full of characters literally named Pop or Biff, as well as variations such as "the Old Man,"[45] but the fiction in the *Post* and *Collier's* was only slightly more subtle. Sometimes the two types were rivals in the same story: James Logan and "Locomotive" Watkins, Ol' Man Thomas and Mike Tyrone, "Pop" Hensley and Bingo Crock.[46] Francis Wallace's serialized novel "Razzle-Dazzle" developed the opposing types most fully. A small-college team, coached by conservative old "Pop" Hensley and led by a bunch of spirited boys (with names like Duke and Blackie and Larry), defeats the big-time football school, coached by ex-pro Bingo Crock with his "razzle-dazzle" (that is, both modern and corrupt) system, manned by subsidized goons with names like "Tarzan" Miller. In other words, everything good in college football is embodied in Pop Hensley, everything tawdry or corrupt in Bingo Crock. Francis Wallace, the tough-minded journalist who called on college authorities to pay players what they were worth, was a conventional sentimentalist in writing his fiction. Wallace's hero, Larry Todd, is an orphan whose dying father sent him to Pop. In beating Bingo Crock's big-time razzle-dazzlers, Larry both restores life to the dying father—he saves Pop's job—and proves himself a worthy son.

Not every story was quite so schematic, but many of them defined the figures of "Pop" and "Biff" in comparable ways. In the absence of literal Pops and Biffs, equally unambiguous names such as the Skipper and Dad Benton, or "No Alibi" Nelson and Hack Merne, sometimes announced the coach's fundamental character.[47] Sometimes a trainer or doctor played the role of Pop, as in Jonathan Brooks's tales of Big Bill and Little Bill Brown for *Collier's* in the early 1920s that were narrated by a Pop-like trainer who eventually took over the team from a hardboiled Biff.[48] William Brent's "Yesterday's Heroes" (a *Collier's* serial in 1939, a film in 1940) set a fatherly doctor against a ruthless coach, "Cleats" Slater. In all these cases, Pop always represented the ideal of male authority, Biff its debasement.

The actual "Biffs" in college football in the 1920s and 1930s—profane, hard-driving coaches such as Princeton's Bill Roper, Fordham's Frank Cavanaugh, and Pittsburgh's Jock Sutherland—were treated quite differently in the press, where they were celebrated as masters of discipline or shrewd psychologists. The popular discovery of psychology as the key to success and personal fulfillment provided a context in which the coach served as a model for businessmen as well as fathers, as a motivator of others to overreach themselves. The serialized autobiographies of Amos Alonzo Stagg, John Heisman, and Knute Rockne in the *Post* and *Collier's* inevitably included one installment on coaching psychology, and the halftime pep talk became a topic of particular fascination.[49] "The Coach's Tongue-Lashing That Sometimes Wins the Game," in the *Literary Digest* in 1926, singled out Princeton's Roper as the master of halftime inspiration, while noting that Knute Rockne rarely resorted to the tactic. Two years later, in "Lashing a Team to Do or Die," the *Digest* included Rockne with Roper, along with Pop Warner, Amos Alonzo Stagg, Tad Jones, Howard Jones, Gil Dobie, Doc Spears, and several others—most of the prominent coaches of the day—as masters of locker-room psychology. Rockne became the most famous halftime orator of all after Francis Wallace reported his "win one for the Gipper" speech in the *New York Daily News* after the 1928 Army game. Pep talks and coaching psychology fell in and out of fashion over the 1930s, with Rockne's performance becoming a permanent part of football lore thanks to the Pat O'Brien–Ronald Reagan movie of 1940.[50]

Real-world Biffs notwithstanding, in football stories and movies Pop reigned supreme. In the films *Maker of Men* (1931) and *Touchdown* (1931), ruthless coaches come to realize that their players are more important than mere victories. In *The Band Plays On* (1934), a fatherly coach rescues four tough ethnic kids from the streets and makes men of them on the football field, through teamwork rather than toughness. On the screen, real coaches, too, were transformed into Pops. The Knute Rockne of the 1940 biopic is cast as the father his wild star, George Gipp, never had. *Harmon of Michigan* (1941), an entirely fictionalized rendering of Tom Harmon's postgraduate football career, has the hero clashing with a coaching Biff, then becoming one himself, then finally learning from his mentor, Pop Branch, the proper way to handle his players. The 1943 biopic of Frank Cavanaugh, *The Iron Major*, transformed a famously brutal and profane Biff into a saintly Pop: the father of six sons and a daughter who followed him to war, and a fatherly mentor to hundreds of young football players at Boston College and Fordham. *Jim Thorpe—All-American* (1951) worked a similar metamorphosis on the ironically named Pop Warner. In life, Warner had been dismissed from Carlisle in 1914 after complaints from players about his profanity and abusive treatment.[51] In the movie, Pop is a surrogate father who nurtures Thorpe at Carlisle, then rescues him years later from alcoholism and despair. The figure of "Pop" was the product of a sentimental popular culture, not of the violent world of real football.

Baseball in recent years has been sentimentalized as the game of fathers and sons: playing catch in the backyard or in a magical ballpark built in an Iowa cornfield. Football has a longer claim, but in a violent rather than pastoral setting that points to a grittier, more anguished relationship. In numerous magazine stories sons reconcile with their fathers, usually in one of two basic plots: redeeming a failed father or proving himself to a demanding one, in both cases through triumphs on the football field.[52] The plot of sons proving themselves to their fathers was usually handled with no reservation or irony whatsoever, the father's right to demand that his son prove his courage on the football field unquestioned. A few stories challenged such assumptions. In one, a son simply repeats the great mistake his father made twenty years before. In another, a father who had been too small to "take it" succeeds in producing a son who proves he can, only to see his boy ruined by addiction to the "heady wine" of football fame.[53] Though they are fiction—make-believe—these stories, like the ones with "Pop" and "Biff," had to influence the way readers understood actual football, and they contributed to the tremendous cultural authority conferred on coaches. Beyond the game, the profound ambivalence that emerges from the entire body of football fiction and journalism, in the competing demands for absolute authority and benevolent paternalism, illuminates the conflicted state of American masculinity in the twentieth century.

POSTWAR REVISIONS

The relationships between coaches and players, in both reality and fantasy, was altered by the Second World War and the upheavals in college football that followed. Returning veterans were not "boys" but war-toughened, often married men, for whom football was no game but serious business. The frantic recruiting and extravagant bribing of football players that convulsed the world of college football registered in journalism and fiction in different ways. With the return of football fiction after the war came the familiar old stories with their dumb jocks, fathers and sons, and the hero winning the girl through proving his toughness, but football in general was treated less seriously.[54] The distinctive new voice was found in lightweight comic tales by writers like Willard Temple and William Scott, and new heroes emerged: the married ex-GI who must balance football with family responsibilities; the ordinary guy—a substitute, or lineman, or blocking back—who envies the campus football hero but gets his own chance to do something grand and win the girl; the coach who is neither a tyrant nor a fatherly mentor but a decent ordinary man, himself a husband or a father, trying to survive honorably in a tough business.[55] The coaches in such films as *Father Was a Fullback* (1947) and *Yes, Sir, That's My Baby* (1949) were like the fathers in television sitcoms of the 1950s, simply trying to do their jobs and keep peace amidst domestic chaos. In *Trouble Along the Way* (1953), John Wayne played a divorced and disgraced former coach given a reprieve by the desperate president of a small Catholic college. The only way to rescue the nearly bankrupt school in the supercharged world of big-time football is to buy players and stage football spectacles at Yankee Stadium—practices that the school fathers finally cannot permit—but Wayne's character wins over his pixyish priestly boss (Charles Coburn) and, with the help of a shy but lovely social worker (Donna

Reed), keeps his spunky daughter (Sherry Jackson) out of the clutches of her ruthlessly selfish mother. Such films, and the postwar magazine stories as well, humanized and sympathized with beleaguered coaches, absolving them of any selfish motive, at a time when recruiting scandals and revelations about slush funds were mocking the integrity of the college game.

The married GI's in *Yes, Sir, That's My Baby* were just befuddled husbands trying to escape babysitting duties in order to play football. *Trouble Along the Way* portrayed the buying of football talent but only in a good cause, and the one genuinely critical postwar football film, *Saturday's Hero,* cast a Big Booster in the villain's role. Coaches remained blameless, as they did in football journalism. Articles about coaches beleaguered by rabid alumni, and about Wisconsin and Cal as "coaches' graveyards," cast them as victims of a system over which they had no control.[56] Articles that described recruiting tactics or a booster group's fund for athletic scholarships typically adopted a neutral tone that implied that such actions were simply the way things were done, by coaches who were personally honorable. Southern coaches, prone to criticism for open "professionalism" and pursuit of victory at any cost, were sometimes cast in the national (that is, northern) magazines as the good ol' boys northerners loved to romanticize. A coach named "Peahead" might be a mild embarrassment to a university's faculty, but Wake Forest's "Peahead" Walker in the *Saturday Evening Post*'s 1947 profile was a cornpone humorist out of the Will Rogers school. Portraits in the *Post* and *Life* of West Virginia's Art "Pappy" Lewis, another legendary recruiter, cast him as a sweet-talking hillbilly who could visit a Polish tackle's home and seem as Slavic as Mom and Dad. Herman Hickman, a jovial 300-pound Tennesseean much loved by sportswriters when he coached at Army and Yale, related his "hilarious adventures hunting athletes while on safari into football country." Yet another fabled recruiter, Paul "Bear" Bryant, left a trail of reprimands and probations as he moved from Maryland to Kentucky, Texas A&M, and then finally Alabama, but he was celebrated in *Collier's* for his recruiting prowess as "Dixie's No. 1 Gridnaper" and in the *Post* as "Football's Jittery Genius." The story of Bryant's first football team at Maryland—he arrived the week of the opening game with fourteen just-discharged servicemen, whom he paraded through the admissions office on the way to the football field—was told not as a case of academic laxity but as an amusing anecdote about an enterprising young man who already knew where he was going.[57]

Unlike the coaches in football fiction, the men profiled in the popular magazines were anything but befuddled. More explicitly than since the

FIGURE 4-5. The comeuppance of the dumb jock. This *Post* cover by Dick Sargent from 17 October 1959 proclaimed that, in the post-Sputnik world of higher education, the football player was no longer the campus hero. An article in *Life* by Marshall Smith, titled "Sad News from the Campus: Nobody Loves the Football Hero Now," said the same thing in 1957. (Copyright © 1959 The Curtis Publishing Co.)

FIGURE 4-6. In *Yes, Sir, That's My Baby* (1949), Donald O'Connor and his fellow married teammates must balance football with their domestic responsibilities, while their harried coach, Charles Coburn, helps them manage their demanding wives.

game's earliest years, the coach became a model of executive leadership in the post–World War II era—a combination "executive, whip-cracking taskmaster, strategist, field general, actor, director, spellbinder and talent scout," as *Sports Illustrated* grandiosely characterized him in 1958.[58] The single postwar short story with a tyrannical coach, Joel Reeve's "The Pigskin Heart," published in *Collier's* in 1947, portrayed him as a monster brought down by his abused players.[59] Actual Biff-type coaches such as Bear Bryant, Bill Glassford of Nebraska, Wallace Butts of Georgia, Woody Hayes of Ohio State, and Jim Tatum of Maryland and North Carolina were celebrated more openly than ever for their relentless driving of their players. In Cold War America, under what seemed the looming threat of the Soviet Union, and in a society newly affluent after the deprivations of the Depression and World War II, sportswriters and magazine journalists rediscovered physical toughness as football's primary contribution to the nation, and celebrated the coach for producing it. A profile of Butts in the *Saturday Evening Post* termed him an "exacting drillmaster" who earned the respect as well as the fear of his players, one of whom recalled his first training camp at Georgia, during which half the squad quit. "That session darn near killed me," the former player admitted, "but, as trite or silly as it may sound now, it made a man out of me." Writers in both the *Post* and *Collier's* similarly praised Bryant for his "tough-guy approach," which broke down a "long tradition" of pampering Kentucky players by "the horsy set."[60]

The new Biff was part demanding father, part masterful executive, while players were just the material shaped by the coach into his vision of what a football team should be. The case of Bill Glassford at Nebraska is particularly revealing of the players' place in a college football world ruled by the all-powerful coach. After earning a bid to the Rose Bowl in 1940, the Cornhuskers suffered through season after season of misery, never winning more than four games in a season between 1941 and 1949. The ugly battle in 1945 over replacing Biff Jones (another figurative as well as literal Biff), as described in Chapter 2, led to the hiring of Bernie Masterson, who won just five games in two years. His contract was then bought out for $20,000 by members of the ever-meddling "O Street Gang."[61] After Nebraska's athletic director, Potsy Clark, stepped in to coach for one season, Bill Glassford brought modest improvement in 1949, then seemed the Cornhuskers' true savior in 1950. With sophomore running back Bob Reynolds rushing for more than 1,300 yards and leading the nation in scoring, Nebraska won six games, lost two, and tied one, compiling the team's first winning season since 1940. Suddenly a miracle worker, Glassford was courted by other schools, until the athletic board stepped in with a new five-year contract and an option—his, not theirs—for five more.

Bill Glassford was thus a hot young coach as the 1951 season opened, suitable for a profile in the *Saturday Evening Post*. In "The Hungry Young Coach of Nebraska," Harry T. Paxton and B. F. Sylvester described Glassford as a boyish-looking thirty-seven-year-old who had been known as the Baby-Faced Assassin when he played under Jock Sutherland at Pitt in the 1930s. Sutherland had been the quintessential Biff, an aloof and "exacting taskmaster." According to Paxton and Sylvester, Glassford "adopted many of Sutherland's precepts—his iron discipline, his refusal to settle for anything less than top performance"—but unlike his mentor, Glassford "doesn't keep at arms length from his players. He steps right in and chews them out himself." The authors described Glassford as "merciless with any player he thinks is falling short of his potentialities," yet "no undiluted slave driver. Basically gay and companionable, with a puckish sense of humor, he takes an all-round interest in his boys." "In essence," the authors summed up, "Bill Glassford is a typical high-powered young executive who happens to be applying his energies to football."[62]

The *Post*'s profile of Glassford conflated three distinct images of the postwar coach. Besides the familiar Biff, the "gay and . . . puckish" humorist was related to Wake Forest's Peahead Walker, Georgia Tech's Bobby Dodd, Clemson's Frank Howard, and Michigan State's Biggie Munn and Duffy Daugherty—college football's Laughing Coaches, who made football fun.[63] The "high-powered executive" was Walter Camp's original ideal, retooled for the 1950s corporate "rat race." What the *Post* called "the brisk new young-executive breed" also appeared in profiles of Bud Wilkinson, Ivy Williamson, and Terry Brennan.[64] Whether puckish or perfectionist, all of these men were models of successful leadership; they only differed in the ways they motivated their employee-players. Some coaches, like Navy's Eddie Erdelatz and Stanford's Chuck Taylor, were loved by their players, according to magazine profiles; others, like Georgia's Wallace Butts and UCLA's Red Sanders, were more feared and respected.[65] The Laughing Coach and the Executive Coach addressed the two sides of the dilemma posed by postwar prosperity for the expanding white-collar class: the need to be a winner in the "rat race" and the longing for personal fulfillment that pursuit of success seemed to nullify. The profiles of coaches, that is, were companion pieces to the influential works of popular sociology by David Riesman, C. Wright Mills, and William Whyte, and to popular novels and films like *Cash McCall* and *The Man in the Gray Flannel Suit*. A meticulously organized executive who had fun at his job represented corporate America's elusive ideal.

Whatever the coach's temperament and manner, the players were implicitly just raw material to be molded into a successful team. As an example of Bill Glassford's methods for controlling his players, the authors described his grading system: assigning a score from zero to three to each individual on every play, with three the highest score. The study of game film and grading of players were becoming the norm in the more intensely professionalized world of big-time college football in the 1950s, and Glassford was an up-to-date coach. As a telling anecdote, the authors offered one game in 1950, when Nebraska faced fourth and one on Missouri's thirty-five-yard line, and Bob Reynolds, the brilliant sophomore running back, took the ball off-tackle, as the play was designed, but changed his direction when he found no room to run. Paxton and Sylvester described what happened next: "He was cornered and chased all the way back to his own thirty-five-yard line. There he picked up some blockers and ran back for a touchdown. His grade? Zero. In Glassford's view, this exhibition was like that of a batter who, when ordered to bunt, swings away and hits a home run. Reynolds should have gone for the yard."

Here is a crystalline moment when a player's creativity meets a coach's control, and although the authors offered no comment, the tone of their profile clearly endorsed Glassford's judgment. In a related incident reported by Paxton and Sylvester, Glassford dismissed from the team a star tackle who tried to compete on the track team in conflict with spring football practice; the player was then given one more chance "on about the twentieth appeal." Glassford told his assistants, "But he goes on the B squad," to which "one of Glassford's saltiest assistants" knowingly responded, "Put him on the B squad during the week. But start him on Saturdays." The all-powerful executive who manipulated players for the success of the team was also one lesson in the profile of Wisconsin's Ivy Williamson in 1953. Cast as an "unpretentious" and "gentlemanly" coach, Williamson was also a master of "thorough and efficient planning." After his All-American running back, Alan "The Horse" Ameche, asked Williamson to consider playing one of his friends at quarterback, "Ameche found himself shagging balls for the place kickers" in practice, and sitting next to his friend on the bench when the game started on Saturday. "Ivy let Ameche sweat it out for several minutes, then turned him loose. There was no holding The Horse that day." [66] But there was obviously one man holding the reins on The Horse.

What the football executive could do that his counterparts in business could not was drive his players brutally, to make men out of boys, as the survivor of Wallace Butts's first training camp put it. The *Post*'s writers noted that sixteen out of seventy boys did not survive Bill Glassford's initial training camp at Nebraska, and the chancellor of the university worried that his new man "was being too rough," but the team's success in 1950 clearly vindicated his methods, and the fifty-four who did survive presumably became "men." Relentless driving and brutal tongue-lashings did not end with training camp, however. Among the *Post*'s usual photographs of coach and players in action was one less common: "the boys" entering a strangely elevated locker room at the end of an exhausting practice by pulling themselves hand over hand up a suspended ladder, enduring their "final agony."

This piece appeared in October, written after Bob Reynolds had separated his shoulder in practice and Nebraska had lost its opening game (training camp–hardened "men" were no less prone to injuries than "boys"). The Huskers lost four of their next five, on their way to a 2–8 record, and Glassford was no longer a hot young coach. After the team improved to 5–4–1 in 1952, with Reynolds still hobbled by injuries (who mattered more to Nebraska's success in 1950, the team's fans might have asked, Glassford or a healthy Reynolds?), then slipped to 3–6–1 in 1953, thirty-five squad members signed a petition at the end of the season demanding Glassford's removal. The players complained not that Glassford was a "taskmaster" or "slave driver" but that he ridiculed and embarrassed them, ignored their injuries, and kept them fearful of losing their scholarships.[67] After the athletic board and the board of regents in January requested the coach's resignation, Glassford wavered but then demanded his contractual rights and was retained.

Of greatest interest here is the treatment of the disgruntled players by the *Omaha World-Herald* and its long-time sportswriter, Gregg McBride. The paper sided with Glassford, as it had with Biff Jones in 1945, but this time the implications were quite different. In a long and surprisingly direct attack on the players following their initial rebellion, McBride mocked the idea of 230-pounders quivering "in great fear of being ridiculed and embarrassed" and wondered "how this band of Cornhuskers managed to win a single game last fall."[68] After Glassford forced the university to honor his contract, the *World-Herald* printed in full the players' complaint against the paper's coverage of their campaign. The opening paragraph, reprinted here as it appeared in the paper, read: "We are very depressed on (sic) the way the World Hearld (sic) has handled our statements. The World Hearld (sic) has turned many of these statements to mean the direct opposite." The rest of the piece continued in this vein, amounting to character assassination through lack of copyediting. The editors might have contacted the students and suggested corrections. Instead, the occasional "(sic)" highlighted the players' apparent intellectual shortcomings, evident also in their poorly worded testimony. In the same issue the paper likewise printed the complete statements against Glassford submitted by six players, under a misleading headline, "Smith Says Players Hurt 'Physically and Financially.'" The actual complaints concerned Glassford's ridiculing of injured players, his refusing them treatment, and his disregard for their education. In fact, no fewer than four assistant coaches had resigned since Glassford took over because they disapproved of his methods.[69]

As always, the extreme case has its representative aspects. Debates in the early 1950s over two-platoon and one-platoon football posed the same question of coaches' control in less heated terms. Critics of unlimited substitution disliked its emphasis on specialization and the loss of "iron men" from the game, but they also regretted the greater control it gave coaches.

As Walter Byers, the long-time executive director of the NCAA, configured the struggle, "aggressive, ambitious younger coaches" preferred two platoons, while a minority of "senior coaches," who still believed "that the game was for the players," lobbied for one-platoon football.[70] Coaches advocating open substitution claimed to represent the fans' and players' interests, but when the NCAA abandoned two-platoon football in 1953, Fred Russell happily told readers of his "Pigskin Preview" in the *Saturday Evening Post,* "Imagination blooms again in the huddle. . . . Under the new rules there will be less coaching from the bench." In his "Football Preview" for *Collier's,* Francis Wallace concurred: "The game will undoubtedly be less smooth-running in the professional sense, but it also will be less like something turned out by a coaching mimeograph machine." The following season, *Collier's* sports editor Bill Fay explained how Notre Dame quarterback Ralph Guglielmi had three seconds to decide which of 200 plays to call each time he came to the huddle. Here was football run by players being trained for life after football.[71]

The abandonment of two-platoon football from 1953 to 1965 proved a brief rearguard action against the expansion of coaches' control, and as the colleges followed the pros back to unlimited substitution, the pros followed the colleges in taking play-calling away from the quarterbacks. These developments would come later, but already in the 1950s the outcome was obvious. Some journalists might welcome the return to one-platoon football, but the foundations of the coach's cultural power were too deep and too solid to be undermined so easily. Bill Glassford's fundamental problem at Nebraska was that, unlike other coaches of the iron-fisted school such as Woody Hayes at Ohio State or Bear Bryant at Texas A&M, he won too few games. Not even Gregg McBride defended simple abusiveness; he insisted that the players did not measure up to Glassford's appropriate standards of toughness. Closer to the scene in the Nebraska case, Cy Sherman's successor as sports editor of the *Lincoln Star,* Norris Anderson, defended the players without altogether abandoning the local sportswriter's usual allegiance to the coach. Anderson expressed sympathy for Glassford as a working man just like his readers, with a mortgage and a family, but he also publicly reminded Glassford "that football players are human beings with a heart, a mind and sensitivity. They must be dealt with squarely and, unlike the old Jock Sutherland school, they must represent more than the numbers on a jersey." Anderson expressed relief that Glassford's former assistants had kept quiet ("We've heard their stories and they don't make agreeable reading"), and he reported that of seven players he had contacted from Glassford's brief glory years (the 1949–50 seasons), not one would speak up for their old coach.[72]

In the different responses of Gregg McBride and Norris Anderson one sees the dilemma posed by the all-controlling coach. If football was a rite of passage, one might fairly ask after reading about Bill Glassford, what was it a passage to? That 1892 article in *Harper's Weekly* portrayed a freshman initiated into the tribe of upper classmen. Owen Johnson's fictional Dink Stover was trained in practice to withstand the brutal pounding in Yales' big game against Princeton. By mastering the demands of football, both Dink and the freshman were presumed to be better prepared to meet the challenges with which life would surely confront them. Bill Glassford's brutal training camp prepared his players for brutal practices and humiliations throughout the season, each practice concluding in the "final agony" of dragging themselves hand over hand up a ladder into the locker room. Glassford was unusually harsh, but one might ask what the players were trained for if the coach never surrendered control.

The fundamental relationship between coach and player would not be widely challenged until the late 1960s, when a youth movement permeating the entire culture would defy adult authority, and young black men in a more integrated sport would lead the way in declaring themselves "boys" no longer. Coaching styles would be forced to change, but not so radically as to undermine coaches' control of the sport.

Gridiron, U.S.A.

The 7 November 1955 issue of *Life* set this scene for a photo-essay, "Football Takes Over All Over":

> Date: The Last October Weekend for 1955
> Time: Afternoon
> Place: Gridiron, U.S.A.

What followed were ten pages of images from the world of high school and intercollegiate football, the settings ranging from College Park, Maryland, to Seattle, Washington; from "Big-Time Games" between Cal and UCLA, Maryland and South Carolina, Navy and Notre Dame, and Michigan and Iowa, to high school battles in Massillon, Ohio, and Seattle. The scenes themselves included a marching band on the streets of Massillon; picnickers at Princeton and on a hill above the University of Arkansas stadium; gamblers in Las Vegas; homecoming queens at UCLA; social-register partygoers at the Piedmont Driving Club in Atlanta; a torchlight parade in Fayetteville; an open-air hop at UCLA; sorority girls at Maryland putting the finishing touches on a floral display; Michigan fans carousing on a special train to Ann Arbor; and fraternities at Purdue, Arkansas, and Georgia Tech decorated for the football weekend. And more: spectators in stadiums at Michigan, Illinois, and Minnesota cheering the home team; the falcon mascot of the Air Force Academy; "bewildered Bolsheviks" (Russian visitors) at the

Maryland–South Carolina game; a bearded player at Missouri, where the team had vowed not to shave until they won; and last but certainly not least, a full-page photo of a "starry-eyed" cheerleader from Roosevelt High in Seattle, embracing the team's tackle after the game, conferring the "victor's reward." "Football is everything that America is," intoned the brief text, "—fast, young, colorful, complex, efficient, aggressive. Sitting in the stadium, watching the pretty coeds, singing the stirring old fight songs and yelling themselves hoarse (sometimes softening the chill of the air with a quick nip), the spectators could only agree the whole spectacle furnished a fine reason for being alive." Here was an entire social world centered around the spectacle of a football game.[1] Football's cultural power lay not just in the clash of teams on the field but also in the many ways it contributed to an ideal of middle-class American life.

FOOTBALL AS SPECTACLE AND SOCIAL EVENT

Football became our greatest sporting spectacle in three distinct senses: as the game on the field, with its swirling chaos of bodies and often incomprehensible, yet "spectacular," action; as a pageant of bands, cheerleaders, card sections, mascots, and cheering multitudes—the surrounding "spectacle" as necessary to the football experience as the coaches and players; and as a sport fundamentally defined by the act of spectating itself, the viewers understood to be active participants. From nearly the beginning, college football, unlike baseball, was a game more for watching than playing. When in 1880 the season-ending Thanksgiving Day game between the two leading teams among the Big Three was moved from college grounds to New York, it quickly became an event on the social calendar of the city's fashionable elite. By the end of the century the Thanksgiving Day game in New York became the model for "Big Games" played everywhere. Woodcuts and line drawings of football games in the newspapers and magazines of the 1880s and 1890s regularly framed the image with well-dressed, cheering spectators in the foreground, the players themselves dimly visible in the distance. Visually, the game was made to seem less important than watching it or being seen watching it. Newspaper accounts of Harvard-Yale and Yale-Princeton games settled into a formula that split attention between the action on the field and the socially notable citizens in the stands. The social elite, who a generation earlier would have been appalled by public notoriety of any kind, were paid homage by being named in the pages of the *World* or *Herald,* their presence in turn confirming for readers the social importance of the new sport.[2] As the game spread southward and westward, the original importance of the act of spectatorship continued to be attached to it. All this—football's status as a social event and the media's coverage of the spectacle and the spectating as well as the game itself—was well in place by the 1920s.

As football's appeal spread from the Ivy elite to state universities and Catholic colleges, it retained its power as spectacle and social event, but now with an ever-broadening audience. By the 1920s, a sports journalist's commonplace was beginning to distinguish baseball as our national pastime from football as our greatest sporting spectacle. The *Literary Digest* in 1922 pointed to the erection of huge stadiums, covering more ground and accommodating greater crowds than the Roman Colosseum, as the clearest evidence for "Football as Our Greatest Popular Spectacle." The accompanying photograph was typical: like the woodcuts of the 1880s, it was shot from behind the "serried masses of humanity" at the Harvard-Yale game, the spectators filling most of the frame, the field but a small wedge cut into the portion of the packed stadium captured by the photographer. Other events could be staged in these great structures, the writer acknowledged, "but it is admitted that, without the 'pomp and pageantry'—and thrill—of football, the money would never have been forthcoming to build these huge bowls."[3]

Time in 1930, then again in 1935, placed on its cover not a currently famous coach or player but "Football's Public" as the sport's true hero. "Once the crowd was one-quarter its present size," *Time* reported in 1930. "It was composed of undergraduates, parents, alumni, their wives, sweethearts, cousins. For years it has been growing until it has come to include every element in the country." *Time* rattled off the midseason numbers—450 college teams, 15,000 players, 1,400 games, 3 million tickets sold, and $10 million in gate receipts (surprisingly low estimates)—to make the point that "the public, taking possession of a game which was once the private property of the colleges, has changed it almost unrecognizably." Just a year earlier, the Carnegie Foundation had detailed the troubling consequences of a college sport possessed by its fans. Here, *Time* noted that fact only with satisfaction.[4] Membership in "Football's Public" had become a mark of upwardly mobile middle-class status, not by initiation into the game's subtle mysteries but by responding to and becoming part of the spectacle.

To value football for its spectacle was altogether different from celebrating it as a training ground for leadership and success. A writer in *Outlook* in 1923 who saluted the "guiding intelligence" of quarterback, captain, and coach in devising a strenuous and intricately chesslike sport explicitly contrasted this side of football to the ordinary fan's interest in mere spectacle.[5] Spectatorship was controversial in the 1920s, one of the growing pains of the

FIGURE 5-1. As had been the case at the turn of the century, the game in the 1920s continued to be framed to emphasize spectating, as in this cover from the *Literary Digest*, 13 November 1920.

new consumer culture, but controversy was overwhelmed by the demands of a vast public hungry for the spectacles made possible by the stadium-building boom.[6] Football's intricacies, in any event, were lost on even knowledgeable sportswriters. Paul Gallico, sports editor of the *New York Daily News,* declared football, among the sports he covered, "the biggest mess and the most difficult to write accurately," and admitted that he could write his reports as well from home, sitting by his radio, as at the stadium. At the end of a fifty-year career Grantland Rice likewise confessed that "after centering much of my life around football, much of the game still leaves me bewildered." Magazines continued to publish articles on how to watch football into the 1950s. One magazine writer in *Esquire* in 1941 facetiously remarked that sports fans welcomed the football season in part because it reduced sportswriters to their level of incomprehension.[7]

Failure to understand football meant no inability to enjoy it as America's grandest spectacle. If Paul Gallico found football difficult to describe with technical accuracy, he had no reservations about its power to move those who watched it. After the 1928 Notre Dame–Army game, he wrote of football's capacity to transport spectators, if only temporarily and occasionally, into a realm of almost unbearably intense emotional experience. "When football becomes a near-tragic race against time," Gallico wrote, "there is nothing like it for thrill or excitement or suspense. The game exerts its magic and you forget that it is just football. . . . In the fading minutes of a great game, with a losing team fighting to hold off defeat, nothing seems to matter but the successful conclusion of the human endeavor on the field." Two years later the Army-Navy game, which was played in cold and rain before an enormous audience at Soldier Field in Chicago, made Gallico wonder about "the amazing grip that football has, to bring 125,000 people out of their warm homes in suicidal weather to sit unsheltered and unwarmed for three hours! You explain it; I don't think even baseball could do it. It is an ever astonishing social phenomenon."[8]

As noted in Chapter 1, the formulas for radio and newsreel coverage of football games from the very beginning paid more or less equal attention to sport and spectacle: microphones were placed not just in the press box but also around the stadium to pick up the bands and cheers, and footage of cheering throngs and football pageantry were edited into the game action. Bands and organized cheering appeared long before the 1920s; in that decade, card sections, mascots, and eventually female cheerleaders were added to college football's pageantry. The game on Saturday afternoon became the focal point for festivities often extending over several days. Bonfires and pep rallies on the eve of the game, fraternity and sorority decorations for homecoming weekend, homecoming queens and drum majorettes, garlanded floats in the Tournament of Roses parade, all became increasingly identified with college football in the public mind. Radio, newsreels, and magazine covers made football games inextricable from these accompanying elements of football spectacle. Radio and newsreels had a particular impact on making the season's major football spectacles—the Army-Navy and bowl games, whose pageantry far exceeded that of ordinary games—national events. The vast audience reached by college football was not made up primarily of serious analysts of the game, but of the millions who responded to it as a gaudy festival of virile action and youthful enthusiasm, and for whom spectatorship meant active participation in that enchanting world.

The staged events in enormous stadiums dotting the landscape drew on the new cultural power of a transformed collegiate world. The pep rallies and bonfires, pregame teas and postgame dances, were important not only to the participants—they provided much of the "campus life" that was prized above classroom education—but also to the larger public, for whom they expressed youthful pleasures that were quintessentially American. The historians of college life, Paula Fass and Helen Lefkowitz Horowitz, have described the central role of football in the social organization of student communities. As Horowitz notes, "The Saturday-afternoon game became the symbolic event that bound together all students, past and present." Football was the centerpiece of the larger social world governed by fraternities, which also dominated the proms, student theatricals, and hazing rituals at American colleges from the 1920s through the 1950s. Between a quarter and a third of all students belonged to fraternities and sororities during this period, and at many private colleges they comprised a majority of the students. Standing for hedonism and anti-intellectualism, extracurricular activities and school loyalty, fraternities courted football players to become members, and sometimes policed the rest of the student body to assure attendance at pep rallies and games. As Fass explains, football's primary role in college life lay in fostering "school spirit." "While an athletic victory certainly expressed the urge to competition on the campus," she writes, "it was above all the symbol of group cohesion and thus first among peer activities." [9]

Fass and Horowitz also have much to say about the non-Greek collegiate world—the independents or "barbs" (for "barbarians") and rebels who were excluded from the fraternities and sororities and did not share their passion

BEGINNING **THE WILSONS** by ELEANOR WILSON McADOO

FIGURE 5-2. Here, in this 14 November 1936 cover from the *Saturday Evening Post*, a college couple on their way to the pregame bonfire illustrates one of the many images of the spectacle and social world of college football. (Copyright © 1936 The Curtis Publishing Co.)

for sports—but the college spirit popularized in the media rarely hinted at such conflict. "College spirit" had differentiated football from prizefighting in the 1890s, when the game was so brutal it almost did not survive its infancy. According to the game's apologists, however violent it was, a college football player was a gentleman battling for the glory of alma mater, not a bowery tough slugging it out for a few bucks. In the 1920s and 1930s, this same spirit was endlessly invoked as the crucial distinction between college football and the newly threatening professional version of the sport. Grantland Rice offered a typical comment in 1926, when he acknowledged that "professional football may overshadow the college game in skills but cannot match it in spirit and tradition." That "spirit" required no definition. It was epitomized by the immortal cry of "Pop" Grant, "I'd die for dear old Rutgers," as he was carried from the field with a broken leg during football's earliest years. An instant cliché, Pop's youthful outburst became both the motto and a parody of college spirit. As one magazine journalist insisted in 1936, that phrase "has become a source of derision, but in fact that spirit is what makes college football superior to the professional game."[10]

Derided by skeptical sportswriters or not, the appeal of college spirit permeated the culture. College spirit not only meant sportsmanship toward opponents and self-sacrifice for the team, it also meant vast throngs of the young and the would-be-young engaged in joyous celebration of a glorious game. In the context of 1920s hedonism, college spirit meant innocent pleasure. In the context of 1930s unemployment and poverty, it meant relief from such dispiriting conditions. All the media contributed. Magazine features on the football weekend became more common in the 1940s and 1950s, but from early on, the sports pages of daily newspapers routinely printed panoramic shots of filled stadiums, photos of cheering coeds, and portraits of civic and social leaders in the stands. Special games—postseason bowls, traditional rivalries, the dedication of a new stadium—meant additional articles to capture the full range of festivities that accompanied the main event. Red Grange's astonishing performance against Michigan in 1924 was not the only story in the *Chicago Tribune* the next day. A female reporter was assigned to cover the sidelights of the inaugural game in Illinois's new stadium: the marching bands and cheerleaders and annual "hobo parade" put on by Illinois students before Grange took the field. A typical "Rose Tournament Pictorial Section" of the *Los Angeles Times* in 1925 had three pages on the parade, one on the game. In Sunday newspapers everywhere the society pages chronicled the social life of the football season. The resumption of the Georgia–Georgia Tech rivalry in 1925, after a feud of several years, meant a "gay social whirl" of luncheons and dances in Atlanta— every detail, along with photographs of four "Pretty Members of the College Set," described for readers of the *Constitution*. Writers on fashion advised young women on how to dress for "warmth and swagger" at the big game.[11]

As football movies in the 1920s settled into a small handful of plots and settings, those included the ivy-covered buildings on campus grounds evocative of English country estates, the boisterous camaraderie of fraternity brothers, the pageantry and wild enthusiasm of the big game, the deep satisfaction at the victory dance afterward where the campus beauty rewards the football hero with her undying love. To be young, in college, and playing football or cheering from the stands was to have the best of what up-to-date America offered. Youth was a widely discussed and analyzed "problem" in the 1920s—its seduction by the new morality, or rather immorality, of the Jazz Age—but at the same time youth was celebrated, and envied, as never before. A few college football films in the 1920s focused on erring youth. Hugh Carver in *The Plastic Age* (1925), from Percy Marks's novel, falls under the influence of the sorority vamp but regains his bearings to salvage his football career (and win the chastened vamp as well). Light-hearted, light-headed Tom Brown in *Brown of Harvard* (1926) slips into dissipation but redeems himself in time to win the big game. Even when their heroes stumbled, these films let viewers glimpse the joys of being young and beautiful and athletic in a place where those qualities were all that mattered. The world of college football became one of those scenes in popular fantasy where privileged youth played out their culture's desires. For all their foolishness, the college football musical comedies of the 1930s sustained this fantasy in the midst of a crushing depression, projecting a carefree world in which everyone danced and cheered and sang silly songs as the boys won the big game on Saturday.

The typical ten-minute newsreel, divided into a half-dozen segments with the football game coming last, epitomizes football's place in the larger cultural landscape. In the 1930s newsreel, after the stories about unemployment lines or the kidnapping of the Lindbergh baby, the assassination of King Alexander I of Yugoslavia or Mussolini's invasion of Ethiopia, came the football game between Notre Dame and Army or Illinois and Michigan. Against the grim news of the times, football would have seemed a quintessentially American celebration of triumph and innocent pleasure, not just the game itself but also the surrounding pageantry of bands, card sections, mascots, and above all the collective enthusiasm of stalwart athletes, youthful cheerleaders, and the great American public represented by the crowd. Other, more troubling ideas about college football competed with this one in the media, to be sure—the complaints about "professionalism" and hypocrisy explored in Chapter 3—but the game continued to project youth and energy, tradition and public ritual, an expression of the triumphant American spirit amidst the confusions of modern life. Warren Susman has described how, during the Depression, as the social and economic order seemed rapidly disintegrating, "the sharing of common experience" or search for an "American Way of Life" became a preoccupation.[12] The narrative of football as one part of this American Way of Life was powerfully implicit in all the media.

CUTE KIDS AND CHEESECAKE

Everyone had a role in this football world represented in the media—everyone, that is, who was white and broadly middle class. The faces of football on magazine covers included ragamuffin kids acting out the roles of their heroes, lovely coeds posing prettily or admiring their battered beaus after a hard-fought victory, cheerleaders and bandsmen doing their part to bring glory to alma mater, and wholesome couples on their way to the pep rally or bonfire before the big game. As noted in Chapter 4, football heroes themselves were surprisingly rare on the covers of the *Saturday Evening Post* and *Collier's*, where the most striking feature was the number of ragged but winsome kids. J. C. Leyendecker, who contributed more than any other artist to the visual image of the virile football hero, had an equal influence on the popularization of a figure we might call the "football rascal." Leyendecker's urchin on a 1914 cover for the *Saturday Evening Post*—with bandaged head and eye, the football cradled in his arm nearly half the size of his small body, and a preposterously self-assured stance—was Tom Sawyer in football togs, the Good Bad Boy (always in trouble but with a tender heart) named by literary critic Leslie Fiedler as one of the country's favorite self-images.[13]

Cute kids of all kinds, not just in football suits, were favorites on virtually every popular magazine pitched to families. Versions of Leyendecker's football rascal appeared on five of the *Saturday Evening Post*'s six football covers in the 1920s (the sixth was of a slightly older boy, a cheerleader rather than a player) and three of the first seven football covers on *Collier's*. In general, the illustrations of football kids grew more sentimentalized over time, the Leyendecker-inspired rough-and-tumble rascals of the 1920s becoming icons of pure sweetness. *Good Housekeeping* had just two football covers in the 1930s, both portraying darling tots playing "grown up" in their football

FIGURE 5-3. J. C. Leyendecker's "football rascal," from the *Saturday Evening Post*, 21 November 1914.

uniforms or cleated shoes. *Country Gentleman* gave readers a young boy and his dog: the boy sitting on the bench with all the determination of a two-hundred-pound All-American to get in the game, his dog more intent on getting a cool drink from the water bucket. *Liberty* offered a determined tot in lineman's stance, his sweetly innocent face sporting a black eye. As the *Post*'s covers shifted from simple iconography to storytelling in the 1930s, they portrayed boys hoisted on the shoulders of admiring adults, anxiously watching grandma blow up the football, waiting glumly for the violin lesson to end before football practice, sitting sullenly and begrimed in the bathtub afterward, changing shoes at the insistence of a stern mother.[14] In each case, the sentimental, the heroic, and the parodic are equally present.

Whether the kids' mimicry of the actions and poses of grown-up football players gently mocked or endorsed football heroism was not obvious. The football articles and stories read by boys themselves—in magazines such as *Boys' Life, American Boy, Youth's Companion, St. Nicholas,* and *Open Road for Boys* —left no doubt that playing football was the best possible character training. The football fiction in *Boys' Life* was but one tale after another of either the unsung hero winning his due or the selfish hero learning the values of teamwork, two versions of a single didactic tale of sportsmanship and self-lessness, sugar-coated with football heroics. The attitudes toward kids' football in adult-oriented media were more ambivalent, both more sentimental and more troubled. The cute kids on magazine covers appeared also in news-reels, whose "human interest" stories in the 1930s included the "shoeless wonders" of an orphanage team in Lynchburg, Virginia; a "midget" football championship in Germantown, Pennsylvania; and a "grid thriller" staged by "tiny tots" in Hell's Kitchen.[15] In startling contrast, a number of articles in women's magazines viewed kids' football with almost hysterical alarm. The most stunning collision of cover with contents was the September 1936 issue of *Good Housekeeping,* whose cover had an adorable toddler putting on his big brother's oversized football shoes, while inside readers found Bob Considine's chilling article, "Death on the Gridiron," with its warning to parents that crippling injury and even death constantly stalked the football field. Imagine a reader poring over the cover illustration, then turning to the melodramatic scenario with which Considine opened: "Your son or mine" catching a kicked ball, then taking "the last few steps of his life."

> Somewhere between the point at which he caught the ball and the goal which the rules of the game command him to attain, he will be bru-tally hit by one or more tacklers and thrown heavily upon the unyield-

FIGURE 5-4. The disjunction between cover and inside article of this September 1936 issue of *Good Housekeeping* is the most dramatic reminder that football was governed by no single master narrative.

ing ground. The crash may crush the very framework of his body, or in the ensuing pile-on he may be kicked in the temple or the spine. If the accident happens in a little town, he will be rushed in some bouncing, honking automobile to a hospital cot, there to die in a little while in a haven ill-equipped to combat such unique visits of death. If he is mortally wounded in a great game, as was Cadet Richard Sheridan in the Army-Yale game a few years ago, the full forces of medical science will be summoned to his aid. He will be placed in a grim steel box called an artificial lung, whose wheezes and puffs are dreadful enough in their own right. But soon the mechanized sighs will flutter and be no more, and he, too, will have added his name to the long list of youths of America who have given up their lives in a game long romanticized beyond its intrinsic value.[16]

In less extreme forms football fans were constantly bombarded by competing, often contradictory narratives and images. Parents, of course, wished both to protect their children and to raise them to become strong adults. Football, they were told, was the ideal training ground, but not without risk. Considine's article was one of two he wrote for *Good Housekeeping*, the other with an equally discomforting title, "No Holiday for Death." The physical risks of sandlot and high school football became a major issue in the early 1930s, after the Army cadet mentioned by Considine and forty-eight other players at all levels died in 1931, and 100,000 more were seriously injured. Articles in *Ladies' Home Journal, Woman's Home Companion, McCall's,* and *Parents'* magazine had less melodramatic titles than *Good Housekeeping*'s —something closer to "Making Football Safe" or "Should Your Boy Play Football?"—but all carried the same warning. The answer to the latter question was always, yes, but only if the boy had regular medical attention, adequate equipment and facilities, sound coaching, and healthy habits. This reassurance came only after the writer had scared the bejeezus out of mothers with tales and statistics of fatalities and maimings.[17] The physical risks of football were worth taking, the authors of these articles ultimately declared, because football was invaluable in helping boys become self-assured adults. The magazine covers with cute little boys more simply indulged in popular sentimentalism without contemplating the consequences.

Girls and young women were assigned a different role, about which there was no uncertainty whatever. "Pretty girls" were a major feature on the football covers not just of *Collier's* and the *Saturday Evening Post* but of all the popular magazines, including more than half the football covers of the humor magazine *Life,* several for *Judge* and *Liberty,* and four of the five for *American Magazine. Ladies' Home Journal* had two football covers: one of a lovely fan in November 1927, the other, in November 1930, of a beauty with rival male admirers (reversing the conventional trope of the pretty girl adoring the football hero). As the 1933 hit song put it, "You gotta be a football hero / To get along with the beautiful girls." The romance or love pulps contributed several covers to this sexual fantasy: the handsomest of football heroes and the loveliest of coeds wrapped in each other's arms and rapt in love.[18]

The *Saturday Evening Post* kept the handsome hero and his lovely admirer on separate covers—due, most likely, to editor George Horace Lorimer's notorious prudishness—but *Collier's* brought them together, more frankly to acknowledge their sexual attraction.[19] The wounded hero with his adoring or ministering companion was a particular favorite, the supreme example of which, in 1939, showed a battered and bandaged but supremely satisfied young hero with a dark-haired, sleekly sheathed beauty at the victory dance. He: no Ivy League sophisticate but a broad-shouldered hero of State U, a representative of the common people; dressed in tuxedo but with barely tamed hair threatening to erupt into a dozen cowlicks; out of his element yet smugly at ease after a lopsided victory. She: dark, exotic, seductive in her purple dress and bracelet bangles; the aggressor in the mating dance, a woman of the world with a bumpkin beau, yet somehow also the supplicant to the lordly hero. He and she appear to come from different worlds; she could dazzle a prince in distant lands, while he would feel lost anywhere the buildings have more than two stories. But leaning into our champion, with gaze fixed on his blackened eye and self-satisfied grin, she has clearly chosen to bestow her considerable charms on the bumpkin hero, while he still smugly weighs the offer. A little bit erotic, a little bit heroic, a little bit satiric, this cover compressed several narratives of football, sex, and gender into a single image.

Pretty girls on magazine covers were more than objects of sexual attraction. Attention to the women at football games had been part of the reporting in daily newspapers from the outset, both to signify college football's standing as social event and to render the brutal game more "civilized."[20] Girls wearing blue chrysanthemums for Yale or orange for Princeton were as necessary as the battling teams themselves to the spectacle of the great Thanksgiving Day game in the 1890s, and female spectatorship remained important to the reporting on all big games. "College Co-eds Cheer Gridiron Teams When Season Opens in Portland," ran a typical headline

THE FOOTBALL NUMBER

Life

Her Tackling Dummy

FIGURE 5-5. The great illustrator John Held, Jr., cast his well-known flapper in the role of tender admirer with her wounded football hero on this 13 November 1924 cover of the humor magazine *Life*. Held also painted another football cover for *Life*, 19 November 1925 (another flapper), and covers for Yale games with Princeton in 1927, Harvard in 1928, and Army in 1929.

December 2, 1939

5¢ A COPY

FIGURE 5-6. This cover from *Collier's*, 2 December 1939, followed a long tradition of wounded football heroes with adoring beauties.

in the *Oregonian* on a full page of photographs—typical also of newspapers throughout the country and throughout the period.[21] As the quintessential spectator, the cheering coed better represented the ordinary newspaper reader than did the triumphant stars of the game. Cheering males in the stands might seem pale reflections of those playing; pretty coeds were reveling in their proper role. As noted in Chapter 2, the most formalized and ritu-alized female spectatorship developed in parts of the South, where "spon-sors" represented each team in big games, in the manner of medieval ladies for whom knights jousted in tourneys.[22] The *Atlanta Constitution* continued to recognize these female sponsors at least through the 1940s, as the tradition spread, not outward into other regions but downward into other age groups. In 1940 and 1941, the *Constitution* gave full coverage to an annual football tournament for nine- and ten-year-olds staged by the Fritz Orr Club, com-plete with photos of the tiny sponsors sitting decorously, and decoratively, on the sidelines, just like their big sisters. Prepubescent sponsors were still part of the annual event in 1949.[23]

By this time newspaper attention to women in football tended more to cheesecake than to little-girl innocence. Half-clad females had been a staple of the raciest American journalism at least since the *National Police-Gazette* in the nineteenth century, and in the 1920s, the cheesiest of the tabloids led the way. A typical rotogravure section in Bernarr McFadden's *New York Evening Graphic,* for example, "contained about eighteen pictures of which fifteen were females in undress."[24] As in other aspects of the modern news-paper, the tabloids charted the course that mainstream papers followed more cautiously. Bathing beauties and seductively posed Hollywood starlets were part of the "news" in respectable papers everywhere, and sometimes a sports editor got lucky, as when a Chicago White Sox pitcher married a burlesque queen and her half-clad body could be shown in the sports sec-tion.[25] More typically, as Paul Gallico explained in the chapter titled "S.A." (for "sex appeal") of his *Farewell to Sport,* swimmers, divers, and figure skaters served a similar function. "The newspaper editor and publisher for many years has been aware of the value of s.a. in his pages as a sales stimulus," Gallico explained.

> Incoming cuties and movie actresses on transatlantic liners cross their legs for the camera man. Follies girls and fan dancers make elegant page lay-outs. Society girls sunning themselves at the social beaches, bathing beauties on parade, the female figure in any form of exposure, sell papers.
>
> But there is a definite limitation imposed upon the editor. The use of these figures and exposures must be legitimate, otherwise it will prove a boomerang and cost him more in sales and class advertising than it will win for him. He cannot afford to turn his paper into a form of *Police Gazette,* with nudity displayed merely for the sake of nudity, or he will offend the solid-citizen background of his circulation, the "family."

For the news editor, the crossed legs of attractive women were "legitimate news" only when they "belong[ed] to prominent people," as were "the full-length portraits of scantily clad professional beauties, actresses and night-club cuties . . . when they have pistoled a husband or lover or sued for divorce or are blackmailing for alimony of promise." The sports editor, however, had superior resources: "But semi-legitimate as are these uses, nothing of late years has been able to approach in sweet innocence, coupled with undeniable sex-appeal, photographs of handsome young girls in revealing bathing-suits lined up on the edge of a pool, waiting for the starting gun, or poised on the end of a spring board or diving-tower, or caught in mid-air in full flight. It is news—sports, decent, completely privileged, in good taste and at the same time arresting and stimulating as all get-out." [26] Gallico wrote this just as female cheerleaders and drum majorettes were becoming more common on college gridirons, and as bowl games with beauty queens were popping up in Sunbelt cities. Opportunities for getting sex appeal onto the sports pages during football season were proliferating exponentially.

Exactly where and when young women made inroads into the male domain of college cheerleading has not been recorded, but they began appearing sometime in the 1920s, initially at southern universities. As Chicago sportswriter Hugh Fullerton explained in *Liberty* in 1924, the young men who led the cheers were campus celebrities who became leaders in business and public life after graduation. Fullerton also mentioned that girls had taken over this role at some Ohio high schools, but for Chicagoans this was only rumor.[27] Just a year later, Tulane arrived to play Northwestern with Miss Marion Draper, "former Follies beauty," leading the cheers; and a few days later, the *Chicago Herald and Examiner* reported that the novelty in Chicago was old news in New York, where Evander Childs High School football teams were cheered on by not one, but three young women, shown in a photograph leaping like "a trio of 'Little Evas' ascending to Heaven, as little Evas used to do in the 'Uncle Tom' shows."[28] Such to-do over female cheerleaders was replayed in other locales whenever they appeared for the first time. *Collier's* first recognized female cheerleaders in 1928: two leaping young women in modest bloomers and long-sleeved sweaters, one of ten images of activity on the sidelines of a big game. Male cheerleaders appeared on covers of the *Saturday Evening Post* in 1926, 1930, and 1939; the first females not until 1940. Over the 1940s, female cheerleaders became more common. The University of Georgia's first female cheerleaders took the field in 1940, SMU's in 1945. (Cal held out until 1953, Michigan State until 1954, Michigan and Wisconsin even longer.) The *Atlanta Constitution* welcomed the "Debut of

'Da Beauts'" with a front-page photograph. The caption for the photo in the *Dallas Morning News* of Mary Martha Mitcham, "the first girl cheer leader in Southern Methodist University history," described a pedigree very different from the football hero's: "She was one of the SMU Rotunda beauties last year, is a member of the Zeta Tau Alpha sorority, the Y and COGS clubs and the Arden Work Shop." Here was the campus beauty's resumé, to set alongside the football star's rushing or passing yardage and all-league honors.[29]

Although cheerleaders appeared in pinup art as early as 1930,[30] the young women on the sidelines, initially in long skirts and loose sweaters, were not widely recognized as sex symbols until after World War II. In the 1930s, that role belonged to the strutting drum majorette. From SMU's Betty Bailey in 1935 to Purdue's "Golden Girl" in 1958, some of them became minor celebrities. With its program of swing music rather than Sousa marches, SMU's band was the razzle-dazzle accompaniment for the team's aerial-circus offense, and Betty Bailey received a share of the Mustangs' acclaim in their championship season of 1935. After SMU's first visit to Los Angeles, where they beat UCLA late in the season, the *Times*'s sports editor, Bill Henry, was utterly smitten by "blond Betty Bailey, the struttin'est Betty Co-ed you ever saw, who quickstepped all over the field on the arm of the band-leader." After SMU received the Rose Bowl bid, Henry anticipated Betty's return, to "raise the temperature in our town about seven degrees." When the Mustangs next came to Los Angeles, to play UCLA in 1937, she was still remembered as "Miss Betty Bailey, who intrigued Los Angeles football fans when she was sweetheart of the band in 1935." Betty was now "Mrs. Bobby Wilson, wife of the famous Bobby Wilson of Rose Bowl fame," undoubtedly the perfect conclusion to her story for readers of the *Times*. Wilson and his teammates had lost the Rose Bowl to Stanford, but Betty Bailey had won her own major prize, the team's star quarterback, in the arena in which young women were expected to compete.[31]

The proliferation of bowl games seems to have had the greatest impact on the eroticizing of football. The football game was the lesser event in the Tournament of Roses for which the parade was the centerpiece. Beauty queens waving from flower-bedecked floats were brought to millions outside southern California by newsreel cameras, to become an indelible part of the region's image. Hearst's *News of the Day* described the 1934 Rose Bowl as equal parts football and beauty— "Rose Carnival's great parade of flowers and bathing beauties share spotlight with college heroes" — and all the newsreels followed this formula in their coverage of the major bowls.[32] Print coverage in the *Los Angeles Times* did the same: writers assigned to the floats, to the queen and her court, to the bands, and to the spectators—and beginning in 1940, a writer assigned to the drum majorettes.

Among the "beauties and cuties" celebrated at the 1940 Rose Bowl were the "high-stepping drum majorettes in white boots, bare legs, white satin short pleated costumes." The caption to a photo the following year described the Long Beach Junior College majorettes as "the pick of the crop in a city which majors in majorettes."[33] War moved the 1942 Rose Bowl to Durham, North Carolina (for fear of a Japanese attack on the West Coast) and canceled the parade in 1944 and 1945, but with peace returned the annual tribute to the short skirts and bare legs of high-stepping beauties in each Rose Parade. "Majorettes Add Dash and Color to Gay Pageant," declared a headline in 1946 ("Prancing, dancing their way along the crowd-banked streets, the white-satin uniformed teenaged cuties traveled more miles afoot than the motor-propelled floats did on wheels"). "Dancing Girls Twirl Batons," "Cavorting Majorettes Feature 17 of 19 Bands," "Music Dispels Chills for Jaunty Majorettes," read headlines the next three years. A story on the 1951 parade described the wolf calls from onlookers and the "snappy reply" from one "shapely young bathing beauty" to a request for her telephone number. These majorettes were high school or junior-college students, not Hollywood starlets, but over the 1950s the *Times* increasingly acknowledged that what was on parade was sex appeal.[34]

By the late 1950s, the obligatory story about majorettes became more self-conscious. These pieces were always unsigned, but reading them consecutively, one senses the same writer returning each season, grown older as the prancing twirlers have not, feeling his mortality ever more sharply. In 1957, he indulged in a remarkable elegiac tribute to beauty and youth, his own youth seemingly passed, the lovely majorette embodying dreams no longer possible. His ideal majorette was "as always, young and lithe and lovely and she was parading—as were all her counterparts—with a kind of joy that pervaded the throngs of onlookers and made them share her joy." Her sparkling eyes, "the gyrating rhythm of her teen-age body," and her "cunning costume" conveyed a "kind of glory in her passing as the crowds caught from her the whole philosophy of the Rose Parade." She may be a Helen or a Marilyn or an Elizabeth, but "Whatever her name, she is youth eternal under the Pasadena sun every New Year's Day. As she marches with the parade in her hour of glory, she is more than youth. She is hope."[35]

To the guys shouting out for telephone numbers and offering their tribute in wolf whistles rather than poetic musings, the bare-legged majorette was no Platonic ideal, and through the 1950s the *Times*'s own writer did not fail to note the "bodies sinuous" and the "skimpy costumes" of the young women he saluted as the spirit of the Rose Parade.[36] By this time, sex appeal was bluntly promoted at dozens of bowl games in ways that would stun our own more permissive but also more gender-conscious time. Other cities had long envied the promotional power of the Tournament of Roses, and as promoters in New Orleans, Miami, and Dallas developed their rival bowls in the 1930s, they competed with Los Angeles in more than football. All the bowls had queens and courts, but the Orange Bowl promoters led the rest in selling sex appeal. Whether the Orange Bowl's organizers were indeed more shameless exploiters, or wire-service photographers were simply drawn to Miami, sports editors around the country could count on an annual shipment of cheesecake from Florida each December.

Cheerleaders and drum majorettes at least were part of the football world. From Miami each winter came photographs of bathing beauties on the beach whose connection to football existed only in male fantasy. Orange Bowl queens were photographed in bathing suits for wire services at least as early as 1936,[37] but it was in the postwar era that bowl games seemed promoted by Hollywood press agents rather than local businessmen or football conferences. Sports editors initially may have been perplexed by what came over the photo wire. A photograph of a bathing beauty between two football players was accompanied by this caption in the *Atlanta Constitution* in 1947: "It's the Miami influence, you know—that's the only reason we could figure out for putting this obviously non-football picture in the middle of two of the football battlers who will clash in the Orange Bowl on Jan. 1. Anyway, she is Boots Byrd, who will be on hand to help make the visiting gladiators feel at home in South Florida."[38] Mildly ironic captions on similar images suggest continuing editorial self-consciousness, but not enough to leave them off the sports pages. An AP wirephoto from the Orange Bowl in 1949 showed a young woman in shorts and T-shirt bent over the ball in the center's position, another mounted behind her as the quarterback, her hands under the "center's" bottom. Another photo the same month showed a candidate for Orange Bowl queen in a bathing suit picking out oranges at the market, her breasts hovering over the display as if two more fruits to be picked out. A bathing-suited Orange Bowl "greeter" sits on the knee of a giant Baylor end over a caption, "Big Bear and a Little Miami Cutie." And much more of the same.[39] The male role at the Orange Bowl was to battle for the championship; the female role was to titillate male fans.

These are images from one bowl game in one newspaper (the *Omaha World-Herald*), but all newspapers sprinkled their football coverage with bowl-season cheesecake, and promoters of all the bowls exploited female sexuality in varying degrees. The most preposterously posed photographs— that "center" and "quarterback" from Miami in 1949; bathing-suited Bakersfield coeds using a Geiger counter to find the top junior-college teams for the 1954 Potato Bowl; a leggy coed sitting on the goalpost before the Junior Rose Bowl in 1958; a Miss Junior Rose Bowl jump-passing in short-shorts and high heels in 1959[40]—sold only more openly and clumsily what all these photographs were selling. The Kilgore Rangerettes, a junior-college drill team from East Texas, became a national phenomenon in the 1950s as the Radio City Music Hall Rockettes of the gridiron, undoubtedly appreciated by male onlookers more for their short skirts and long legs than for the precision with which they kicked them. Founded in 1940 by Gussie Nell Davis, the Rangerettes first gained national fame performing at halftime of the 1946 Junior Rose Bowl, then went on to appear at the Sugar Bowl and the College All-Star game, on Ed Sullivan's television show and a George Murphy TV special, and in the 1950s they became the star attraction each year at the Cotton Bowl. The line of forty-eight long-legged Texas lovelies, in short skirts and cowboy hats, were a photographer's dream, and they were featured in *Life* and *American Weekly* (the Hearst chain's Sunday magazine), as well as the *Dallas Morning News* and the wire services.[41] Utterly wholesome yet provocative, the Kilgore Rangerettes epitomized the girl-next-door sexuality of football pageantry. In a 1974 profile, after twenty-four seasons of Cotton Bowl appearances, Gussie Nell was "dismayed" by the suggestion "that sex has anything to do with the Rangerettes' appeal." "Sex is a word I have never used with my girls," she insisted, adding, "Sure, I tell them that when they're out on that field I want them to forget they're mama's little girls and *project*! After the game they're mama's little girls again." The "prancing, glamorized dolls who do high kicks in red panties," as the obviously unpersuaded writer put it, were famously expert at "projecting."[42]

The postwar years also saw the apotheosis of the cheerleader as sex symbol. A 1947 *Esquire* cover with a cartoonishly buxom cheerleader distracting the players, and even more so the pinups on the cover or inside *Look* in 1942, *Play* in 1944, *Cartoon Humor* in 1948, and *Esquire* in 1949, eroticized the cheerleader as never before,[43] but slightly subtler versions appeared in ads and on the covers of the family-oriented magazines as well. In her history of beauty in America, Lois Banner has identified two ideals from the 1950s: the innocent, childlike beauty and the voluptuous, sensual one, both embodied in the single figure of Marilyn Monroe, the sex goddess of the decade. Both were also embodied in the newly designed cheerleader, a pose Monroe her-

FIGURE 5-7. The front page of the *Dallas Morning News* on the day of the Cotton Bowl, here on 1 January 1955 and again in 1956, featured the Kilgore Rangerettes, not the teams competing that afternoon. (Reprinted with permission of the *Dallas Morning News*)

self adopted for a *Look* cover in 1952. Magazine covers and ads featured perky, sweater-popping cheerleaders, with skirts flying teasingly above the knee, perfect blends of sexual fantasy and girl-next-door wholesomeness. The new *Playboy*'s October 1954 and October 1956 covers confirmed the cheerleader's role as the object of a collective male sexual fantasy.[44]

That sex appeal was not peripheral but integral to football's cultural role is no more apparent than in *Sports Illustrated,* a magazine targeted, after all, to serious sports fans, that paid as much attention to the girls of football as did magazines such as *Life* and *Look*. The influence of *Life, SI*'s sibling publication, is apparent in such photo-essays as "Football's Girls" and "Beauty and the Bowl." The cover for a story in 1959, "The Happy Moods of Football," showed a University of Texas player and his pretty wife, arm in arm after a

FIGURE 5-8. This Texaco ad from 1955 captures the 1950s version of the cheerleader, voluptuous yet wholesome.

victory, as "symbols of modern U.S. college campus society." The magazine's "Football Issue" in 1957 included a photo-essay on "Saturday's Moods," one of which was "Beauty," as represented by the "bright young bodies" of a drill team. The "Football Issue" for 1960 featured a cheerleader on the cover and a story, "Babes, Brutes and Ole Miss," about the University of Mississippi's tradition of turning out both "successful football and dazzling Miss Americas."[45] "Babes" and "brutes" were but other names for the twin icons who had presided over the football world for more than half a century.

All of these "babes" of football were wholesome—emblems of youth and beauty, not sex—but Paul Gallico had spilled the sports editor's little secret back in 1938, and postwar pinups shouted it out (though for undisguised ogling it would take the Dallas Cowboy Cheerleaders in the 1970s to put sex openly on the football field). Sex in the 1950s remained furtive, not just in football but throughout American culture. Skirt lengths for cheerleaders and drill teams rose with changing fashions, a few inches above street-wear length, a couple inches below showgirls' costumes, always crowding an invisible boundary between the wholesome and the frankly sexual. No college authority would have admitted to purveying sex appeal, but the public knew. A brief history of cheerleading in the family-oriented *American Magazine* in 1956 understood what the coeds on the sidelines were about: "Pretty young things in vestigial skirts, amply-filled sweaters and wearing baby shakos, they've burbled and twirled many a Saturday afternoon away to the intense enjoyment of those fans easily distracted from the male carnage at midfield by a few well-placed curves."[46] Male carnage and female curves were a potent mix.

Dozens of Gussie Nell Davises policed that boundary between the wholesome and the erotic, though occasionally their vigilance slipped. In 1939, wire-service reporters had great fun when the dean of women at the University of Nevada decreed that majorette Elsie Crabtree's skirt showed too much of her "dimpled knees."[47] In 1958, Purdue's "Golden Girl," a gold-spangled freshman majorette named Adelaide Darling, "wiggled too much in doing her hula dance last weekend at the Purdue–Notre Dame game," as the AP story explained, and after complaints from Purdue coeds she had to be de-wiggled for the Illinois contest. The resulting crush of photographers the following Saturday forced officials to ask sweet Adelaide to move away from the Purdue bench before the game. Such stories invariably indulged in at least one cheap pun, in this case the comment that "the blonde freshman from Manteca, Cal., went thru her halftime show without any backfield-in-motion penalties being called." *Sports Illustrated* rhapsodized over Miss Darling's "fetching, skin-tight, gold lamé whatchamacallit" and, in the same piece, reported that "a great in-sucking of alumni breath was to be heard in the stands" when Anne Lane, Vanderbilt's first female baton twirler since the early 1940s, took the field. "The following week Anne was out of work, and a revered heritage was preserved."[48] To imagine college authorities calculating how much feminine skin to show in their halftime shows, much as they had to calculate how much corruption to tolerate in recruiting, creates an odd picture of higher education.

DOMESTICATED FOOTBALL

Life and *Look* made early contributions to eroticizing the females of football: *Life* in a 1938 cover of two drum majorettes, the photograph shot from ground level, directing the reader's gaze up the long sleek legs of the young women; *Look* in a 1939 cover featuring Hollywood starlet Lana Turner attired as a drum majorette for the film *Dancing Co-ed*. For the accompanying story, "Sex Appeal in Sports," Henry McLemore introduced photos of cheerleaders, drum majorettes, and other football beauties with a paean to "Girls on the Gridiron. Pulchritude and pigskins. Beauties and the beasts. The girls are getting into football in a big way. Hundreds of gals like the one on the cover are marching and cheering for old alma mammies all over the country as the football season gets under way in a blaze, as we say, of beauty."[49]

Such football cheesecake was simply part of the two magazines' initial emphasis on photographic sensationalism, but both *Life* and *Look* became family-friendly magazines in the 1940s. In doing so they contributed importantly to rooting football in the American Way of Life described by Warren Susman, not by inventing football traditions, of course, but by validating them as the common American experience. Of the photographs on *Life's* first six football covers, from 1937 through 1940, half were of football heroes (USC captain Chuck Williams, Columbia's Sid Luckman, and Michigan's Tom Harmon), the other three of drum majorettes, a ten-year-old in football helmet and dental braces, and a female fan wearing chrysanthemums in her team's color. Magazines such as *Life* and *Look* reached their broad audience by appealing to all its segments, while at the same time constructing what Wendy Kozol has termed an "ideal of a consensus society of middle-class, white, nuclear families" as "the foundations of a national identity."[50] Football was just one aspect of this idealized America, and only some of the football coverage conjured it up, but even during the years when *Life* and *Look,* as well as the *Saturday Evening Post,* were most critical of football hypocrisy, they were representing it elsewhere in the magazine as a corner-stone of American life.

What *Life* and *Look* did most conspicuously—and to a greater extent than *Collier's* and the *Saturday Evening Post*—was to situate football within a web of domestic relations. Players and coaches were routinely portrayed as sons and fathers or with their girlfriends and wives. The All-America team picked by radio announcer Bill Stern for *Life* in 1939 pictured each player with his girlfriend (except for Cornell tackle Nick Drahos, who "has no time for girls").[51] *Look's* covers of football stars regularly featured the hero with a lovely companion: Michigan's Bob Chappuis in 1947, SMU's Doak Walker in 1948, Vanderbilt's Bill Wade with not one but two young women in 1949, Notre Dame's Bob Williams with four in 1950, Minnesota's Paul Giel in 1953, and Maryland's Dick Bielski in 1954. (*Collier's* similarly surrounded Stanford's Frankie Albert in 1941 and Bill McColl in 1951 with a bevy of admiring females.)[52] Doak Walker's girlfriend, Norma Peterson, was undoubtedly the most famous coed in America in 1948 and 1949, after appearing with her handsome football hero on the covers of both *Look* and *Collier's* (they later married, then divorced). The fantasy that the hero basked in the admiration of these young women was strained for Notre Dame's Williams, whose all-male school lacked a crucial ingredient. If the star's girlfriend did not have the desired look, the magazine could find a substitute: sharing *Look's* 1953 cover with Paul Giel was a young woman identified as Margaret Ellefson, the "Sweetheart of Sigma Chi" at Minnesota, with the explanation that she was not Giel's girlfriend. The photographer merely wanted to contrast her "blond beauty" to "Giel's brawn" for effect. What ultimately awaited the football hero and his lovely admirer was captured on the October 1953 cover of *American Magazine:* the two of them arm in arm, pushing Junior in his baby stroller, all three attired in matching letter sweaters.

The mating of beauty and brawn was but part of football's more thorough domestication in the periodical press over the 1940s and 1950s. *Look's* profiles routinely emphasized the social and domestic world within which the football hero moved. An altogether typical case was the portrait of Indiana's Billy Hillenbrand in 1942. The text was only four short paragraphs, identifying Hillenbrand as the Big Ten's top star that season, a triple-threat back and law student, "mild-mannered, industrious and unchanged by fame," who "graduated with honors from high school, ranks in the top tenth of his class at Indiana and was one of only 53 boys accepted as advanced students in the University ROTC unit." Hillenbrand was simply another Frank Merriwell in the flesh. But his fuller story was told in ten photographs and their

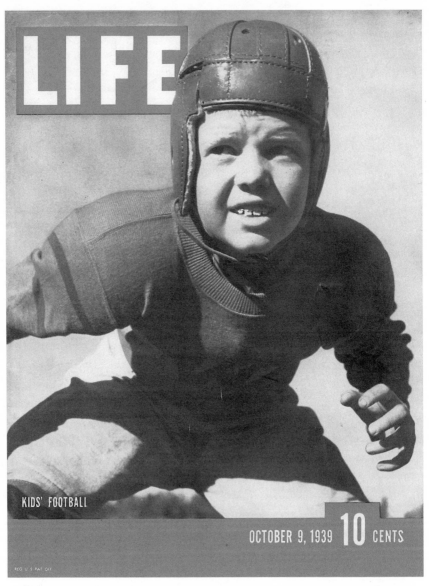

FIGURE 5-9. With a photograph by Alfred Eisenstaedt of eight-year-old Billy Gregory on the cover, "*Life* Goes to a Kids' Football Game" (9 October 1939) described the Young America League in Denver, where 550 boys promised at their initiation ceremony "to be a good student and not to bully the girls" and "to remember that what matters most is courage; that it is no disgrace to be beaten; but that the great disgrace is to turn yellow." (Alfred Eisenstaedt/TimePix)

Collier's

15c

December 10, 1949

The <u>60th</u> All-America...

FIGURE 5-10. The All-American couple, Doak Walker and Norma Peterson, on the cover of *Collier's*, 10 December 1949.

captions, only three of which portrayed him in action as a football player. Others showed him in his ROTC uniform instructing a younger student; in the training room having his ankles taped; at his fraternity house working for his board and room; at a park roasting marshmallows with friends; on the campus lawn studying with his pretty girlfriend (obviously studying each other more intently than their books); at the fraternity hazing pledges; and at home receiving a heap of mashed potatoes from his widowed mother, who raised ten children while running a grocery store. Friends, lovers, admirers, mothers—all were part of the football hero's world. The caption for the photo at the fraternity house—"Muscles ripple as Hillenbrand makes beds neatly"—most explicitly distilled the fusion of heroic masculinity and domesticity. What ABC television would later label the "Up Close and Personal" portrait of the athlete had the effect of removing football from the stadium to embed it in the day-to-day life of the family and nation.

Coaches occasionally received similar treatment. The next issue of *Look* included a portrait of the Chicago Cardinals' Jimmy Conzelman, "a football coach who can play a piano, compose a song, panic a banquet or deliver a commencement address." And be a husband and father as well. Conzelman was shown not just at work but also at a bar with sportswriter cronies, at a party playing the piano for friends, at his trucking business, at home with his wife, and—in the largest photo—at his small son's bedside, where "wide-eyed and intent, young Jimmy listens to his father's bedtime stories."[53]

Articles by coaches' wives and ones about "bantam" or "midget" football placed the sport at the center of the American family.[54] Photo-essays on the pageantry of football—on cheerleaders, drum majorettes, marching bands, card-section stunts, and homecoming queens—placed football at the center of an entire social world.[55] All these also appeared in the *Saturday Evening Post* and *Collier's*, but they were most conspicuous in *Life* and *Look*. All four magazines also collaborated in creating a distinct genre that was probably the most powerful for confirming football as a foundational part of the American Way of Life. This was the story about "Football Town," a small community in which the local team (usually the high school's) was the center of community life. *Collier's* introduced the genre in 1937 with a piece about Green Bay, Wisconsin, "a typical American community which has great pride in itself," much of it centered on their NFL champion Packers, owned by no wealthy sportsman but by the town's citizens.[56] More than a dozen stories over the following two decades located Football Town in Canton and Massillon, Ohio; in Whitehall and White Plains, New York; in Weymouth and Everett, Massachusetts; in Atchison and Lawrence, Kansas; in Amarillo and throughout Texas; in Alhambra, California, Menominee, Minnesota, Marinette, Wisconsin, and Donora, Pennsylvania.

Jimmy Breslin's probing study of Donora captured the desperation that drove boys to football to escape their fathers' fate in the local zinc and iron works. More typically, Football Town USA was an uncomplicated place.

Massillon ("Football Town") and Canton ("Football City") had been ancient rivals since the early days of professional football, but their "football dementia" was now focused on their Washington and McKinley High teams, producing crowds topped in Ohio only by Ohio State University. In Whitehall ("a football town indeed"), a community of 5,000 where 100 of 160 boys in the high school turned out for football, Main Street was deserted during games as crowds of 10,000 filled the stadium. In Amarillo ("a football-mad town"), children "grow up with a football in their hands, are scouted even before they reach one of the city's junior high schools." In White Plains ("The Whole Town Made the Team"), "Fathers, brothers and uncles pounce upon chubby youngsters almost as soon as they can walk, and school them in the intricacies of a jolting stiff arm and how to toss a bullet or floater pass." In Atchison ("Football Crazy Town"), every boy between the ages of nine and twelve and a half could receive a full football suit for free, through the fund-raising of a former high school coach frustrated with his once-woeful team. In Weymouth, (where "football permeates the town" and a high school game "is a civic and social must"), the city raised $13,000 one season to send the team to Jacksonville, Florida, for a schoolboy Gator Bowl.[57]

There was never a hint of trouble in Football Town. No hint, for example, of the physical risks of high school football, addressed sometimes sensationally in women's magazines. No hint, either, of subtler dangers, of what we might call (after the title of a more recent book) the Friday Night Lights Syndrome: the constriction of adult lives and the pressure on mere children when the pride, ambitions, frustrations, and resentments of an entire adult community are borne on the shoulders of adolescent boys each time they trot onto the field. Nor was any connection hinted between stories about Football Town and the stories about high-powered recruiting and hypocrisy in college football. The occasional celebrity profile of a high school football star never mentioned outrageous offers by recruiters or alumni.[58] Only after his life spiraled out of control in college was Ohio schoolboy and Ohio State All-American Vic Janowicz singled out for a particularly poignant cautionary tale. It was told first, in 1951, as a story about a high school star who became a college football hero but who, as a "weak-willed boy," was "unsettled" by the corrupt system; then it was told again, in 1958, as an account of the former star, with no college degree, his professional career having ended abruptly in an auto accident, now looking for jobs on loading docks in Columbus. Accounts of Football Town offered no hint of these other football worlds, nor of high school coaches who quit because of the exploitation, overemphasis, and commercialization at even the schoolboy level.[59]

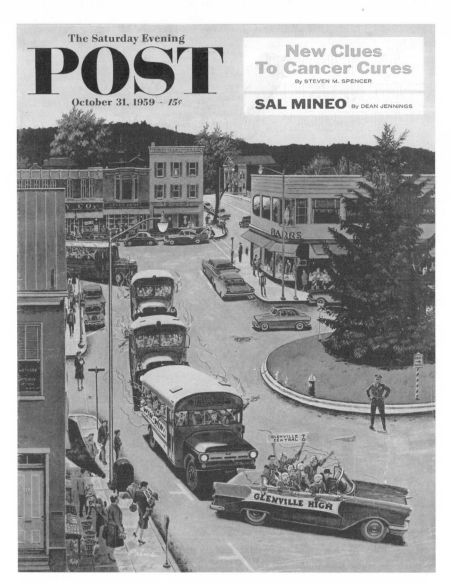

FIGURE 5-11. Football Town was a Norman Rockwell cover come to life—actually, a Ben Prins cover from the *Saturday Evening Post*, 31 October 1959. (Copyright © 1959 The Curtis Publishing Co.)

Football Town was related to a different side of college football, increasingly celebrated in the popular weeklies in the 1940s and 1950s: to the social whirl of the football weekend, when old grads and current students gathered to reenact ancient rituals of college life. This was *Life's* particular specialty, from "Life Goes to a Football Game" in Knoxville, Tennessee, in 1939, to "It

Spells the Big Campus Weekend" in 1959. Football Town and the Football Weekend met most conspicuously in the *Life* feature in 1955 that headed the present chapter. A more localized version appeared the following year, in a photo-essay on Texas football, where on each weekend 902 high schools played on Friday nights, seventeen junior colleges on Saturday nights, and the major colleges on Saturday afternoons. Among other magazines' contributions, in "How to Behave Yourself on Your First Football Weekend," *Cosmopolitan* in 1950 explained to young women the basic rules for enjoying "the most exciting date of all." [60]

Football in the periodical press by the 1950s was not simply American but America itself. A new theme appeared on covers by John Falter and John Clymer for the *Saturday Evening Post* that we might call "Autumn pastoral": scenes of boys at play outside a country schoolhouse, on a hilly field, and on a tree-lined street. Football in these settings evoked none of the violence, modern innovations, or ethical controversies of organized football, but rather a vision of innocence in small-town or rural America, the young boys at play barely intruding on pristine nature. This image of football harking back to an edenic past was required by the times, a longing for virtuous simplicity in the face of the turmoil of big-time football, as well as of the country's headlong rush into a materialistic and competitive future.

In this same spirit the *Post* inaugurated a feature in 1955 called "The Face of America," a two-page photographic mirror held up to the nation each week. "The Face of America" included four football scenes in the late 1950s. "Twirlers Are Made, Not Born" caught majorettes learning their art at a pep camp at Pepperdine University. "The Artful Blockers" showed kids playing football—at play, not in training for their fathers' "rat race." The other two were more portentously titled, capturing two sides of America's premier autumn ritual. The formal "Rites of Autumn" were enacted in enormous stadiums, such as the one in Ann Arbor, Michigan, where 84,000 gathered for the Minnesota-Michigan game in 1957. "Early Autumn," in contrast, was quietly celebrated on village greens everywhere, by boys who needed only a ball and a cleared space, with no witnesses (except for the *Post*'s camera, and thus all of America).

All these images and narratives of football's social dimensions contributed to the powerful domestic ideology that emerged in the postwar United States.[61] In the 1950s, the convulsions of a recent war, the threat of nuclear holocaust, the final march toward racial integration, and the sudden expansion of material prosperity were profoundly unsettling. In myriad ways, Americans were told to go home, have kids, buy a tract house in the suburbs

FIGURE 5-12. This "Autumn pastoral" by John Clymer for the *Saturday Evening Post,* 8 October 1955, was also evoked by *Post* covers painted by John Falter in 1953 and 1956 and by a *New Yorker* cover painted by Ilonka Karasz, 4 October 1952. (Copyright © 1955 The Curtis Publishing Co.)

Rites of
Autumn

Of the millions of small boys who take up the virile American sport of football, a few grow proficient enough to perform for these large colleges which stage the game as one of the greatest outdoor spectacles on earth. The swift and rugged competition on the field, the colorful supporting activity of bands and cheering sections, bring out multitudes of spectators each autumn. Nowhere are these gatherings larger than at the University of Michigan in Ann Arbor, national attendance leader for the past two years, where the turnouts sometimes strain the 101,001-seat capacity of the biggest college-owned stadium in the land. When this sweeping picture was taken last October twenty-seventh with a special wide-angle Japanese camera, 84,620 people were on hand to watch Michigan battle Minnesota for the traditional Little Brown Jug. At this point during a pleasant Saturday afternoon, home fans were enjoying the intermission band show and a 5-0 half-time lead. But Minnesota came back to carry off the Jug, 40-2—a defeat that was to cost Michigan the Big Ten championship and a trip to the Rose Bowl. — Photographs by Mac Shaffer

EARLY AUTUMN

Who knows? That hotshot quarterback or that lanky linebacker may be an All-American ten years hence. But now they're schoolboys playing touch football during lunch-hour recess, on the beautiful green of a New England village, Norwich, Vermont — originally Norwhich, before Vermont became a state—lies on the New Hampshire border and has a population of 1,037. Like most village greens, this one serves many purposes. In spring the green functions as a Little League baseball field. In July the Congregational Church, at left, where an original Paul Revere bell hangs in the steeple, holds its annual fair here. In winter the Norwich Lions Club obligingly floods the green, and there some boys may be found ice skating on it. And so goes the years on a green where fun knows no season.

— Photograph by Hanson Carroll

FIGURE 5-13. These two "Faces of America" represented sharply contrasting images of football in the 1950s—public spectacle on one hand, pastoral innocence on the other. (*Saturday Evening Post*, 21 September 1957 and 3 October 1959; copyright © 1957 and 1959 The Curtis Publishing Co.)

as an escape from, and reward for, competing in the corporate rat race. At the same time, they were told to be vigilant against Communists at home and abroad, to prepare for nuclear attack, and to counter the dangerously softening tendencies of peacetime prosperity. Football embodied both imperatives. Football stood not just for winning through sacrifice and physical toughness but also for youthful energy, for a social world in which "everyone" had a role, for community cohesion, for unambiguous gender roles, and for the family.

In the following chapter I will return to the resurgence of physical and mental toughness as a very different ideal in the 1950s, the one that has continued more conspicuously into our own time. But representations of football's domestic side were equally potent in this earlier period. *Life* in 1956 found the model football family for the 1950s in the Majors clan: a father coaching two of his sons in high school, where his one daughter was a cheerleader; two other sons playing for Tennessee and Florida State; and a wife/mother who was the "biggest booster" of her football-obsessed brood.[62] At a time when Americans were torn between nostalgia for a simpler, pastoral, small-town past and the heady excitement of a razzle-dazzle future, the Majors family perfectly represented one side of a bifurcated football world.

Sanctioning Savagery

In 1939, two articles in the *New York Times Magazine* heralded the beginning of a new football season. The first, by L. H. Robbins on 8 October, welcomed the college game as the annual renewal of a particularly American form of ritual and mass excitement. Barely acknowledging the teams on the field, Robbins recreated the sport's more important elements: the atmosphere and spectacle experienced even by fans "who miss the fine points of the game":

> The cheer leaders turning cartwheels on the turf. The mascot mules, lion cubs, bulldogs and what not. The sideline benches with their coaches, blanketed reserves and team captains of bygone days. The water-wagon squads, the bands and the banners. The scoreboard scouts flashing their signal cards. The mysterious hut atop the west stand where the fourth estate writes and broadcasts. The brewery-sponsored plane circling overhead.
>
> Then the spectator throng. Beauty in fox and mink, and chivalry in coonskin. Whiskered old grads and whiskied young grads. Sub-freshman and sub-debs. People eating sandwiches. People in other people's seats. People imploring other people, "Please sit down!" . . . And below, on the white-striped green, the half-dozen officials who risk their middle-aged lives and limbs to run the game, and the twenty-two lusty lads who play

it. Here's a whole lot of watching to be done all in a couple of hours of a pleasant Autumn afternoon.

For some, wrote Robbins, football was an exhibition of intricately designed, precise teamwork; for most, it was a grand show. Mrs. Oldboy and Mrs. Blivens chat about their grandchildren while their husbands complain about the decline of the game since they played. Surrounding these old grads, the great majority of the 50,000 cheer madly for the player who makes the spectacular run, while the Mr. Killjoys scattered throughout the stadium growl that credit really belongs to the ten blockers, a fact utterly lost on the noisy, uncomprehending masses. Robbins was ultimately for the common fan, not the expert, for innocent enjoyment rather than self-flattering expertise. "All over the peaceful land on Autumn days the whistles blow, the booted leather rises, and untold thousands of Americans settle down to watch football games. We pay a price for it over and above the price of our tickets. We pay in hope and fear, in ecstasy and despondency, in the elation of triumph and the heartache of defeat. We come away as near to exhaustion as the players; we, too, have given our all for dear old Whoosis."[1]

A week later, the *Times Magazine* welcomed football a second time, but a different football now. Most fans, Robert Kelley acknowledged, "will continue to associate football with college colors, undergraduate drum majors, pretty girls with chrysanthemums and a generous number of assertive old grads," but "there is another kind of football scene today and another kind of audience." Kelley's topic was professional football, once "the ambiguous and faintly disreputable offshot [*sic*] of the college game," but today "a major sport in its own right—healthy and still growing." If the contest on the field was secondary for many spectators at college games, for pro fans it was all that mattered. These purists "proclaim that what they see is football played for football's sake. They say they approve, rather than deplore, the absence of such colorful but irrelevant trimmings as college pennants and cheer leaders." The two games differed "not only in atmosphere but in rules and in style and spirit of play." Kelley approved the pros' more open, more spectacular offenses. Compared to collegians, professional football players were more experienced and technically more expert; they had "better football judgment" and played with smoother "polish." As for college spirit, "The professional also knows that wasted effort means wasted strength. He has a scornful term—'old college try'—for the gallant but futile gesture which the more emotional college player will make in behalf of an obviously lost cause." As for the pro's fans:

His audience approaches the game in a similar spirit. There are no eager little family groups out to see Son or Brother make his letter. Instead of the family parties there are groups of heavy-set men as quiet and absorbed as doctors watching an operation. These are college coaches and officials, regular attendants at the games in the league cities. . . .

The crowd as a whole behaves like a crowd at a professional baseball game. The spectators know football and they know how they want it played. Uninhibited, they are free with advice to their favorites and merciless toward the player who bungles. The crowds in the college stadia have their organized cheering. The crowds at the professional games have the raucous and derogatory Bronx cheer—a noise that the college crowds would consider unsporting.

Kelley conceded that the majority of football fans still preferred the college game, but the professional version was well established and growing stronger every season.[2]

BECOMING AN NFL CITY

Robert Kelley's contrast of professional to college football in 1939 could have been made in 1925 as well, with but two differences: the pros had few fans of any kind, and what Kelley described among the distinctive pleasures of pro football—the absence of distracting "color" and overwrought emotion on behalf of alma mater—would have counted strongly against it. What was new in 1939 was Kelley's suggestion that the pro game was worthy to stand alongside the college one, "a dignified and honored member of the American athletic family," as Arthur Daley proclaimed in the *New York Times* in 1938.[3] Although this was by no means the general feeling among football fans in the country, a quasi-official declaration by the sober *Times* that the game played by the New York Giants was as legitimate as the one played by Columbia, Fordham, and NYU reconfigured the world of football in a crucial way. The Giants averaged 39,000 fans per game in 1939, while the NFL as a whole averaged over 23,000, yet outside the NFL circuit interest remained slight. Newspaper coverage in the rest of the country was meager, except when there was some reason for local interest. In Dallas, insofar as wire-service reports permitted, readers of the *Morning News* followed the Washington Redskins' Sammy Baugh and the Philadelphia Eagles' Davey O'Brien, recently graduated quarterbacks from nearby TCU who had thrust Southwest Conference football into national prominence. In Los Angeles, the continuing efforts of local promoters to win an NFL franchise brought regular attention to NFL games. But in cities without a local team or local boy making good in the big time, the NFL was barely an afterthought on Mondays.

The newsreels began covering the College All-Star Game and the NFL championship in the 1930s, but regular season games were ignored until nearly after World War II, and not until 1949 did they begin to cover the pros on a weekly basis.[4] Network radio did not cover even the NFL title game until 1940. NFL teams had played postseason exhibitions in California and throughout the South since Red Grange's extravagantly hyped tour in the winter of 1926, but those games rarely attracted sizable crowds, and network radio provided the first opportunity for curious football fans west of Chicago and south of Washington to experience pro football at its best. The serendipitous timing of the Chicago Bears' 73–0 rout of the Washington Redskins in that first network game guaranteed that many new fans turned off their radio sets appreciating what the pros could do. As Arthur Daley's lead the next day in the *New York Times* declared, "The weather was perfect. So were the Bears."[5] Perfection was about the last thing pro football would have represented for most of the previous twenty years.

In the years leading up to World War II, professional football was not yet every boy's—or even every football player's—dream. None of the first five Heisman Trophy winners pursued careers in pro football. Jay Berwanger (1935), from the University of Chicago, passed up the NFL altogether for business and part-time coaching at his alma mater. Larry Kelley (1936), from Yale, played one year in the short-lived American Football League before becoming a history teacher and coach at a New England prep school. Kelley's teammate, Clint Frank (1937), went into advertising. Davey O'Brien (1938), the tiny passing whiz from TCU, played two years with the Philadelphia Eagles, then quit to join the FBI. And Nile Kinnick (1939) went directly from Iowa to law school (and later to an early death in the war). The collective rejection of professional football by these early Heisman winners suggests the pro game was still the choice only for football players without better options. Over the 1940s and 1950s that situation gradually changed. The Heisman winners from 1940–44 saw their pro careers delayed or interrupted by the war, but all played in the NFL at least three years. And after the war, only the Heisman winners from the military academies (Doc Blanchard and Pete Dawkins) and Princeton's Dick Kazmeier did not try pro football.

Few Americans thought about pro football at all until 1925, when Red Grange joined the Chicago Bears a day after his final college football game. Pro teams in industrial towns in Ohio, Pennsylvania, and a few other places had their followers, but the football law of local-rootedness ruled absolutely. While the *Evening Repository* in Canton, Ohio, provided daily reports on the local Bulldogs of the NFL, with double-column articles and banner headlines for games, newspapers in cities such as Atlanta, Dallas, Omaha, Los Angeles, and Portland barely registered the existence of a national professional league.[6] About the only pro football news worth reporting was provided by official denunciations or scandals. Attacks on the NFL were as old as the league itself. In 1920, the Western Conference (Big Ten) ruled that undergraduates would lose their varsity letters if they participated in a professional game, and that officials who worked for professional leagues would be banned from the college game. In December 1921, the American Football Coaches' Association endorsed these rules and unanimously declared professional football "detrimental to the best interests of American football and American youth." The following January and February, eight Notre Dame players and nine from Illinois were suspended after playing a game for rival Illinois towns, on which each side had bet $50,000. As the investigation unfolded, twenty-two players were eventually banned from college football. The last major pro football news before the debut of Red Grange was Amos Alonzo Stagg's excoriation in 1923 of the pro game as a "menace" to personal character and national health.[7]

It was in this climate that Grange shocked the collegiate world by turning pro without graduating. As we have seen, Grange's act forced sportswriters and football fans everywhere to dwell at least briefly on the relative merits of the semi-professional amateur sport and the outright professional version. Grange's ten games with the Bears in November and December, followed by his barnstorming swing through the South and West, brought unprecedented attention to professional football but could not sustain public interest. Grange himself on the field remained an attraction. The following season, Grange's New York Yankees, in the rival American Football League created by Grange and his agent, averaged crowds of about 19,000, while the NFL's Giants averaged about 12,000. The club the *New York Times* routinely called "Grange's team" or "the Grangers" dominated the coverage in the New York press and drew the largest crowds and greatest coverage on the road as well.[8] Grange's aura could not save the AFL, however, which folded after one season, leaving the Yankees to join the NFL in 1927. The Yankees themselves lasted but one more season, then an injury kept Grange out of football altogether in 1928. In 1929, he returned to the Chicago Bears, where he remained through 1934.

With Grange's departure, coverage of professional football shrank in both the *New York Times* and the *Daily News,* the establishment paper and the people's paper, then began steady growth in the 1930s as the Giants and the type of game they played became more deeply established on their own merits. One of pro football's appeals was strictly economic: tickets for college games were expensive and often hard to get. Commenting on the enormous crowd at the Polo Grounds for the Giants' game against Grange and the Bears in 1925, an impressed editorial writer for the *New York Times* suggested that professional football appealed primarily to local fans "who do not go to college football exhibitions, mainly because tickets are scarce and the cost prohibitive."[9] Most of those fans also had to work on Saturdays but were free on Sundays when the pros played. Thousands who could only dream of watching Army and Notre Dame could go to the Polo Grounds assured of a seat for the Giants' game. Once there, they found a team that they could claim as their own.

In Chicago, Grange's initial impact was at least as great as in New York, but, more so than in New York, interest in the hometown pros remained after he departed. Early in October 1925, while Grange was still at Illinois, the "Wake of the News" column in the *Chicago Tribune* declared pro football inferior to the college brand, not in skill but in spirit, "the difference between the patriot and the mercenary in warfare."[10] Once Grange joined the Bears, however, the *Tribune* embraced the NFL and never let go. Not all Chicago papers took up pro football with the same enthusiasm. In 1930, for example, the *Daily News* paid minimal attention to the NFL, but the *Herald and Examiner* provided about the same coverage as the *Tribune.* Big Ten football remained the number-one game in town, but by the end of the 1930s, the University of Chicago had dropped football, attendance at Bears' games periodically matched Northwestern's, and the *Tribune* had expanded its NFL coverage to daily articles and staff reporting even for road games.[11] The *Tribune* and its sports editor, Arch Ward, also created the College All-Star Game in 1934, pitting the previous year's NFL champion against the pick of collegiate All-Americans, a crucial step in breaking down barriers. A charitable cause justified extravagant promotion in the *Tribune,* an arrangement with many winners, not least of which was professional football itself.

By the 1940s the Bears, not the University of Chicago or Northwestern, were Chicago's Team. In 1941, an eight-part series by Edward Prell on "The Big Bad Bears" created a legendary history for a professional team of the sort the football world had long reserved for collegians. Promoting the *Tribune* as well as the Bears, Prell exaggerated his newspaper's embrace of pro football in its earliest years, when Stagg and the Big Ten were its harshest critics. In Prell's account Bears' coach George Halas was a combination of Tom Swift (gee whiz! why don't I start a pro football club!), a character out of a Horatio Alger novel (carrying copy to newspaper offices and begging for an inch or two of space), a zookeeper trying to contain his wild men, and a kindly patriarch. Foundation myths in sport typically have a strong antimodern element: the giants of the past have disappeared, leaving more ordinary mortals to carry on. College football of the 1890s, the age of Heffelfinger, Hinkey, and the Poes of Princeton, was regularly cast in these terms. Prell's account of the Bears had some of this, the wild characters of the past so different from the "frugal" professionals of 1941; but pro football lent itself more readily to narratives of progress. After a couple of installments filled with anecdotes of brawls and gang warfare in the early years, Prell focused most of his series on the game's economic and popular growth, and on Halas's success through superior organization. "The Story of the Big Bad Bears" was chiefly George Halas's. In another seven-part series in 1948, this one on the evolution of pro football generally, Prell focused as much attention on the (again inflated) contributions of the *Tribune*—Arch Ward launching the College All-Star Game in 1934, then conceiving a rival league, the All-America Football Conference during the war—as on the sport itself.[12]

In both 1934 and 1937, the growth of professional football was voted by the Associated Press as the year's major trend in sports, but that growth remained restricted to the cities that had their own teams.[13] Little can be learned about changing attitudes toward professional football in the newspapers of non-NFL cities, but in New York, as the principal newspaper of the professional and business classes, the *New York Times* can suggest how college football's natural audience came to shift at least some of its loyalties to the professional game. New Yorkers' embrace of professional football was made easier by the absence of a major college football power that belonged to the entire city. The great state universities and land-grant colleges in the United States were not established in major urban areas but in smaller cities and towns, while the National Football League, after its reorganization in 1933, was strictly a big-city league (with Green Bay the sole exception). Founded in 1925, the Giants were a latecomer to the NFL, but they became one of the league's dominant teams in the 1930s. At the same time Columbia and NYU slid into mediocrity, leaving Fordham, a Jesuit university in the Bronx, as the sole remaining local collegiate power before its decline began in the early 1940s. (Pro teams likewise had little competition from the colleges in Detroit, Cleveland, and Washington.) As Westbrook Pegler noted in a column in 1933, "In New York and Brooklyn there is only the narrowest interest in the football affairs of the local colleges and universities. . . . the popular interest is not very great compared to the potential interest which can be aroused by a couple of good local professional teams playing known opponents on an intelligible schedule."[14] Pegler spoke prematurely, since 1933 turned out for New Yorkers to be a miraculous collegiate season that ended with Columbia upsetting Stanford in the Rose Bowl. But of greater lasting impact on football in New York, 1933 was also the year that the modern NFL structure of two divisions, their winners meeting in a championship game, was established—the "intelligible schedule" Pegler called for— and the Giants, along with the Redskins, dominated the Eastern Division over the next fifteen years. In that 1933 season, while Notre Dame, USC, and Michigan were playing regularly before well over 50,000 rabid fans, twenty-nine college games in metropolitan New York (drawing on a population of more than 6 million) averaged 18,000. The New York Giants and Brooklyn Dodgers likewise drew 18,000 fans a game.[15]

In part due to the lack of a top-ranked football power of its own, by 1930 much of the city had adopted Knute Rockne's Notre Dame Ramblers, particularly on that Saturday each fall when Notre Dame and Army staged their memorable battles at Yankee Stadium. A charity game between the New York Giants and a team of Notre Dame all-stars at the end of the 1930 season thus shocked New York football fans, who assumed that professional football, while perhaps no menace, was simply inferior to the college game. It seems remarkable now that anyone would think that former college players assembled for just a few practices could beat an organized professional team, but such was the case in 1930. As Allison Danzig reported in the *New York Times*, "a splendid crowd of 50,000 spectators look[ed] on with bewilderment" as "Benny Friedman and his husky professional mates" licked Rockne's men, 22–0.[16] Over the course of the 1930s, the annual College All-Star Game, played in August before 75,000 to 100,000 at Soldier Field in Chicago—with no competition from other football games for coverage in newsreels and newspapers everywhere—gradually confirmed the quality of the professional game. From 1934 through 1939, the pro champions won two, lost two, and tied two, then won seven of ten in the 1940s and again in the 1950s. From our perspective, those ties and losses to the college boys are surprising; for football fans in the 1930s the victories of the pro teams were more notable.

It took more than quality, however, to win a broad following for professional football in the 1930s. Equally important as these meetings between collegians and pros was an event seemingly tangential to the history of the NFL: the 1929 report of the Carnegie Foundation on "professionalism," that perennial bugaboo of college sports. Although the Carnegie report failed to provoke a great public outcry, it did thrust into the open the issues of cheating and hypocrisy that formerly circulated chiefly by rumor. More important, for worldly, cynical metropolitan sportswriters with no intimate connection to a local college team and coach, it made subscribing to the necessary fiction of amateur purity seem more obviously the refuge of fools or scoundrels. In this climate, sportswriters in NFL cities more readily embraced professional football because it was openly professional and pretended to be nothing but what it was. The responses to the Carnegie report in the New York press were mixed. Columnist John Kieran in the *New York Times* reacted like most of his colleagues, expressing surprise only "that there should have been any surprise at the findings made public in the report," but adding that conditions in college football "are far better than they were in the same sports years ago." At least college athletes today were expected to be real students. Kieran, however, also welcomed the report for bringing "the problem out into the open." The *New York Herald Tribune* more openly sided with the Carnegie Foundation and other champions of "pure amateurism," while the two great tabloids were more openly contemptuous of all parties. The *Daily News* and *Daily Mirror* attacked with about equal verve the ponderous earnestness of the Carnegie Foundation, the corruption and hypocrisy of the colleges, and, most interestingly, the concept of "amateur purity" itself. Paul Gallico in the *Daily News* declared the report "not exactly unfamiliar material in the various editorial rooms throughout the country," yet nonetheless "a complete and dreadful commentary on the venery of our institutions of learning." Francis Wallace in the *Daily Mirror* noted that Chicago, Illinois, Cornell, Yale, and Army were among the "major institutions given a 'clean bill,'" then added, "and the question before the house is whether or not these would be willing to trade some of their lily whiteness for a running backfield or a few more victories than they have been scoring in recent years." The day after the report appeared, Wallace noted that, despite the Foundation's indictment, "the college football business is going on as ever today at the same old stands." Jimmy Powers in the *Daily News* pointed with bemusement to the upcoming games that weekend as contests between "the pure" and "the scarlet."[17] Metropolitan sportswriters embraced the pro game before the population at large, in part because they grew weary of the "amateurs'" charade.

While the absence of a major football power among the public universities in New York made it easier to scorn the hypocrisy of the collegians, the success of the NFL's Giants in the 1930s—making it to the title game in 1933, 1934, 1935, 1938, and 1939, winning twice—made it easier to embrace professional football. That the football coverage in the *Daily News* was relatively balanced between the colleges and the pros by the end of the 1930s is unsurprising, given the class sympathies of the paper. The embrace of the NFL by the *New York Times* is more revealing, considering the newspaper's natural ties to college football. Although John Kieran had covered the Giants' very first home opener, in 1925, for the *New York American* and declared the trial a success,[18] his primary allegiance after moving to the *Times* in 1927 as the paper's first sports columnist was to the collegiate game. Kieran's increasing attention to the Giants and their rivals in the 1930s thus chronicles professional football's emergence as a respectable sport in New York.

PRO FOOTBALL BUMS

After covering the Giants for the *Times* throughout the 1930s, Arthur Daley took over Kieran's "Sports of the Times" column in 1943 and brought even more emphasis to the professional game. The ascendance of professional football in New York newspapers, and likewise in Chicago's, was relative—far more column inches continued to go to the college game—but a decisive shift was underway in those cities that would not take place throughout the press more generally until the 1950s or later. Outside New York, Chicago, Detroit, Philadelphia, and a few other large cities, what people knew about professional football likely came less from their daily newspapers than from magazines such as *Collier's* and the *Saturday Evening Post,* where articles on the professional game began appearing in 1932. Pro football did not warrant a magazine cover on either the *Post* or *Collier's* until 1959: a referee calmly marching off a penalty, oblivious to the hulking players towering over him.[19] But the *Post* published six articles under the byline of Red Grange and George Dunscomb from 1932 through 1935, giving readers the sort of "inside dope" on pro football that was the essence of most sports journalism. In addition to explaining the intricacies lost on most spectators, Grange made an explicit pitch for professional football to skeptical fans. He acknowledged that college linemen tended to be better blockers, with ball carriers at both levels about equal, but he insisted that "in tackling and general defense the professionals are far superior; that in headwork and in cool sureness, in utilizing every ounce of immense brawn, the professionals have a marked advantage." Grange acknowledged that the absence of college spirit had always been held against the play-for-pay game, but the pros had compensated by opening up the passing game: "Football, collegiate or professional, is a branch of the show business. In the professional game, however, we've lacked the props—that is, bands, organized cheering, mass meetings and football girls—which make college football a pageant. Hence we've been striving to give the crowds a spectacular show—exciting, but without sham. We've simply opened up the game several extra notches, and I've no doubt some of the pioneers of push-and-tug football are spinning in their graves." Colleges would be playing the same way within a few years, Grange correctly predicted, to please the fans.[20]

The *Post* published another five articles on the pros in 1930s, two by or about George Halas, one by George Preston Marshall, owner of the Boston (later Washington) Redskins, and two by players (one of them highly critical).[21] This small handful—just eleven out of sixty articles on football, one of them reiterating the long-standing view that pro football was a detour from life's serious work—surely did little to increase interest in the professional game. Though publishing even fewer articles, *Collier's* perhaps built more good will for the NFL. Four of the magazine's eight pieces on professional football from 1932 through 1939 (out of almost seventy on the sport in general) explicitly made the case for pro football's superiority to the college game. Ex-Michigan and then NFL star Benny Friedman claimed in 1932 that the pros were bigger and more talented, while their "only inferiority" lay in the "business sense" that playing for pay instilled in them. Journalist Kyle Crichton and Brooklyn Dodgers player-owner John "Shipwreck" Kelly claimed otherwise, that the pros played with the same enthusiasm and intensity as the collegians: there was no "checkbook football" in the NFL, as Kelly put it. Friedman's second article was considerably less positive than his first, pointing out that today's glory was short-lived and that the football hero needed to find a real job.[22]

But *Collier's* also ran three pieces of a type not found in the *Saturday Evening Post,* with its pronounced preference for coaches and owners. Profiles of the Pittsburgh Pirates' Byron "Whizzer" White, the Washington Redskins' Sammy Baugh, and the New York Giants' Mel Hein were the sort of celebrity profiles that eventually became the staple of football journalism. White, the running back from Colorado, was the quintessential student athlete, signing a lucrative contract with the Pirates (later the Steelers), for whom he quickly became a star, without giving up his opportunity to study at Oxford on a Rhodes Scholarship. Baugh was the tall skinny kid from Texas who became the NFL's greatest passer; Hein, another young man from the sticks (Washington State College in Pullman) who became the best at his position. Whizzer White was Frank Merriwell in the flesh, Sammy Baugh and Mel Hein the country boys who made good in the big city. Such heroic narratives had long been formulaic, but attributing them to professional football was new.[23]

Over the 1940s and 1950s, attention to pro football increased in both the *Post* and *Collier's,* contributing in a small way to the embrace of the game by a national audience. At the same time, fictional portraits of professional players and their game registered continuing resistance. Over the 1920s and 1930s, as professional football slowly gained respect in the daily press, its image in short stories and films suggests how far the public was from accepting it. In one of Jonathan Brooks's stories for *Collier's,* in 1923, when Little Bill Brown accepts $500 to play with the Chicago Bruins in order to pay some debts, his fatherly college coach hurries to the rescue, knowing Little Bill's pro teammates are likely to be "a bunch of big hulkin' roughnecks that'd as soon kill a man as give him a cigarette." Newsreels and network radio simply ignored professional football for the most part; movies, like magazine fiction, cast it in a decidedly unglamorous light. In *The All-American* and *The Sport Parade,* both from 1932, the hero briefly tries pro ball to make a living after college, only to quit or be fired after refusing to throw a game. In *St. Louis Woman* (1934), the football is clean but the owner a corrupt gambler. In 1935, a story in the *Post* titled "End of Fanfare" endorsed professional football, but only as a "rather grim job" made necessary by the Depression. The most positive fictional portrait of pro football in the 1930s came in the 1939 film *Cowboy Quarterback,* but its conceited rube hero conferred little glamour on the professional game.[24]

Most significantly, William Fay's "Uptown Boy" in *Collier's* in 1938 introduced a new kind of pro football story, whose hero quickly defined a new type: the pro football bum. This new character was emphatically a charming bum, and always redeemable by a good woman—his redemption constituted the plot—but he was a far cry from the traditional Frank Merriwell hero or even the flawed heroes of the typical college football stories and films of the 1930s. This football bum was the hero of six of the seven pro football stories published in the *Saturday Evening Post* and *Collier's* between 1938 and 1941. William Fay (no relation to William Cullen "Bill" Fay, who became sports editor of *Collier's* in 1948) wrote four of them, ten altogether of the nineteen pro football stories published in the *Post* and *Collier's* through the 1950s. A prolific writer for the pulps as well, Fay brought a breezy, irreverent pulp style to these stories that defined for a generation the fictional image of the professional football player in the general-interest magazines. In Fay's "Uptown Boy," the hero is a former sandlotter who never went to college, now a beaten-up ten-year veteran of the NFL and pro wrestling, the two jobs nearly indistinguishable as he thinks of them: "legal and acceptable murder" on the one hand, "the grunt-and-endure-it circuit" on the other." In Ben Peter Freeman's "A Ball Game for Delia," published a year later in the *Post*, the bum is a hardened, beaten, heavy-drinking former All-American from the coal mines and a veteran of six brutal seasons of pro football. The other stories in these years offered more of the same:

- a washed-up thirty-three-year-old former star, now playing for a minor-league team in Jersey City;
- a thirty-two-year-old aging star, a "many-muscled bum" with no post-football prospects;
- a team whose players are "a crazy bunch who go out every Sunday and commit mayhem for too little money" but are redeemed from squalor by their sentimental bonding with their owner;
- another sandlot player who became an NFL star, now running a money-losing small-town bar and restaurant and haunted by his last game, which he lost for a local minor-league team;
- a five-year veteran lineman, "strong as an ox and no smarter" (the line lifted directly from James Thurber's "University Days"), unable to imagine his life beyond pro football until he wakes up to realize that the game is "grinding, demeaning labor." [25]

The grim circumstances were usually offset by a light-hearted tone; the pro football bum was not a tragic or even a pathetic figure, but a comic one. These stories likely influenced a 1941 profile of a real NFL player, the Washington Redskins' Wee Willie Wilkin, the 6'4", 265-pound "five-star screwball," who was "eccentric, reckless, happy-go-lucky, courageous, thoughtless and, like all of his ilk, never has learned the value of a dollar." [26] Whether portraying him accurately or not, the decision to feature such a player reflected the appeal of the new stereotype and the continuing uncertainty of whether professional football was a legitimate career, the players just overgrown children. Among these stories, in all but one the plot climaxes with a triumphant performance in one last pro game, after which the "bum" walks away from football to a real life, inspired by a good woman. In other words, in the manner of popular fiction generally, stories about pro football bums insisted on having it both ways: redemption comes from leaving football, but not before one last victory. The good woman points the hero in the direction of adult work and responsibilities, but the hero wins the woman through his prowess on the football field, not by majoring in accounting and getting a job after graduation. Unresolved ambivalence about professional football as both heroic and childish saturates these stories.

Of the two pro football stories written during the war years, Fay's "The Girl from Columbus" was yet another tale of an aging NFL star unable to envision life beyond football until a good woman shows him the way. The other, Fay's "Merry Widower," reversed the redeemed-bum plot to set a new pattern picked up in the postwar years. The hero remained a football junkie, but here he was set against an excessively prudent, responsible player who approached football as a business. Through the influence of the heroine— always the power of a good woman—the hero now found redemption in the joy of football rather than by leaving the game. The prewar stories of the bum redeemed turned on the hero's recognition that football was a game for emotional children and that his adult responsibilities lay beyond it. The postwar stories inverted that revelation: redemption lay not in accepting responsibility but in surrendering to the joy of childlike play. In both plots the professional football player was essentially a child, but in the postwar period his earlier shortcoming became his chief virtue.

Fay's "The Golden Arm," "Throw the Bum Out!" and "The Fainthearted Fullback," along with William Heuman's "I'm Back, Coach" and William Cox's "Playoff Game," cast football in these terms. All had fun-loving heroes pitted against colorless, businesslike rivals, or football bums who find redemption by returning to the game they love. In "Playoff Game," a rookie initially finds his teammates to be "weary, cynical old jerks" who conduct themselves in the locker room "like a meeting of the department heads of mercantile establishment." In the big game, however, they become little boys: "big scarred, craggy men . . . yelling like high-school kids" after a touchdown, "leaping like kids" after they win the game. Not every postwar pro football story registered this shift, but the dominant fictional image of the professional football player was decisively transformed. The new theme of redemption through the discovery of childlike joy and male bonding contributed to a new view of professional football as the epitome of intense masculine experience.[27]

CONTROLLED SAVAGERY

In John Kieran's columns in the *New York Times*, the pro game pointedly emerged as football for adults—not just the players but also those who watched them—in contrast to the prolonged adolescence of college football and its fans. The fiction by William Fay and others insisted otherwise, that professional football players were essentially children: in the prewar years, children who refused to grow up; in the postwar years, adults who had not forgotten how to play. Rather than claim a neat progression in these views, it would make more sense to see them as inherent in professional football's fundamentally ambiguous status—as a boys' game played by grown men for money—but articulated at different times and for different audiences in different ways.

The professional football player as adult returned, literally with a vengeance, in the 1950s. The childlike player in magazine fiction seems radically unlike a figure who dominated football journalism at the end of the decade, a pro football brute reimagined as hero; yet spontaneous joy and sanctioned savagery were complementary responses to the deadening conformity diagnosed in 1950s America. Because professional football's most dramatic popular growth came in the 1960s, the violent and cataclysmic events of that decade are sometimes invoked to explain pro football's new appeal. It was in fact in a very different cultural climate—the postwar, Cold War, newly affluent 1950s—that professional football began to seem a tonic for the age.

The differences between college and professional football explained in the *New York Times Magazine* in 1939 took on new coloration in the 1950s. As the pageantry and social dimensions of college football became grounded in the powerful domestic ideology that emerged after the war, professional football came to represent an equally powerful resistance to the domestication of American masculinity.[28] None of the "Faces of America" in the *Saturday Evening Post* belonged to professional football. A common domestic narrative linked bantam to high school to college football, each earlier stage a preparation for the next, each earlier stage also mirroring the fully developed social world of the college game. Pro football existed as if a different sport altogether, defined in isolation from anything akin to enthusiastic undergraduates, sentimental alumni, riotous boosters, or anyone else beyond the playing field.

The fundamental dialectic of football as brutal contest and football as social event, present from virtually the game's beginnings, became most sharply demarcated in the early Cold War era, and the great weekly magazines' most powerful influence in shaping a national football culture lay in articulating the competing fantasies. It is impossible to know, of course, the extent to which the *Post, Collier's, Life,* and *Look* altered the popular view of professional football or merely recorded the shift, but at the very least in validating a new understanding they gave it cultural authority. After their meager coverage of pro football in the 1930s, beginning in 1940, about 40 percent of the football articles in *Collier's* dealt with the pros, while the *Post* shifted more slowly: about one in six of its football articles in the 1940s, one of five in the early 1950s, nearly half from 1957 through 1960. The balance in *Life* and *Look* was roughly similar. The most striking difference between the articles on college and professional football in these years was the greater emphasis on players among the pros, particularly in *Collier's*. Pro football was represented by stars such as Sammy Baugh and Bronko Nagurski, Don Hutson and Steve Van Buren, Otto Graham and Johnny Unitas, to a much greater extent than by George Halas, George Preston Marshall, and Paul Brown. The balance was about even in the *Saturday Evening Post,* the magazine's overall business orientation reflected here as well, but even in the *Post* the pro football reporting was not nearly as coach-oriented as the college coverage. Professional football served up not lessons for life but fantasies of personal power.

There was also greater latitude in drawing the professional's portrait. The Frank Merriwell ideal always hovered over college football: the image of the handsome, boyish, clean-cut, immensely talented yet modest hero, as remarkable for his sportsmanship as for his football prowess. The original Merriwell stories had been written between 1896 and 1913, but regular reprintings, a cliffhanger movie serial in 1936, and a radio series in the 1930s and 1940s kept the Merriwell name in the public consciousness through the 1950s and made him a touchstone in the periodical press. In the celebrity profiles of college players, whether he was a Hungarian coal miner's son or a country boy from Alabama, he could not deviate far from the outline of Frank Merriwell. He might be a fun-loving guy, like Paul Christman or Frankie Albert, working-class Yankees like Frankie Sinkwich and Charlie Trippi recruited by a southern university, or Yale's first black player and captain, Levi Jackson, but he must have the core of Merriwellian values.[29] Pros, in contrast, were making a living at football rather than building their character. Initially, this difference put them at a seemingly insurmountable disadvantage in gaining public favor; they were no more suitable than professional wrestlers to be held up as ideals. In the 1950s, however, their separation from juvenile storybook values made them increasingly more compelling as cultural heroes for pro football's growing audience.

Pros could be bruising fullbacks like Bronko Nagurski and Steve van Buren; they could be "mountainous individuals, who would not shrink from throwing a block from a moving van," but who were so "childish" they needed a psychologist "to think for them, soft-soap 'em just as though they're your own kids." A pro could be "The Meanest Man in Football," or a "brat" who fought not only his opponents but his own coach as well, or a 350-pound lineman who "specializes in not moving. . . . He squats and waits." He could even be a hard-drinking, beer-bellied quarterback whose coach tolerated his carousing as long as he showed up on time and alert for practice. Few of the professionals profiled in the *Saturday Evening Post* and *Collier's* could be squeezed into the Frank Merriwell mold required for college athletes.[30]

No clear pattern emerges from these profiles, but a dramatic shift in representing pro football over the course of the 1950s is unmistakable, at the same time that the popularity of the game underwent remarkable growth. After surviving a four-year struggle with the All-America Football Conference from 1946 through 1949, the NFL saw average attendance increase 72 percent from 1950 to 1959, from 25,000 to 43,600 per game, at the same time that television was at last creating a truly nationwide audience. The sudden-death overtime championship game between the Baltimore Colts and New York Giants in 1958, viewed by 30 million on television, is commonly recognized as the crucial event. What exactly this dramatically expanded audience saw in professional football can be glimpsed in magazines such as the *Post* and *Life,* and most emphatically in *Esquire.* A major element of pro football's image both early and late was its brutality: a popular view against which the National Football League had struggled since the 1920s. No gradual evolution can be traced from one season to the next, but the difference between the portraits in the periodical press at the end of the 1950s and earlier ones is remarkable. In 1953, *Life* showed the game's decidedly unglamorous side in a piece on the Detroit Lions' preseason training camp, where 353-pound Les Bingaman struggled to lose thirty pounds. Bingaman in shorts and T-shirt on a scale in the locker room looked anything but athletic, his body itself an equivocal pro football text. Another piece two years later, "Savagery on Sunday," complemented Bingaman's inelegant bulk by highlighting the routine "dirty play" of pros who "get in their licks with knees and elbows down under the pile." (Controversy over dirty play in pro football ran hottest in 1956, following accusations made in the *Post* by the Cleveland Browns' Merriwellian quarterback, Otto Graham.) In 1957, "Hefty Pros Get Even Heftier" in *Life* returned to the theme of unglamorous bulk, though this time acknowledging linemen's brains as well as their brawn ("Like huge walking Univacs their minds are stuffed with intricate orders").[31]

In 1958, the gap-toothed smile of the Detroit Lions' Stan Campbell might have reminded some readers of a similar photograph, in 1952, of four Notre Dame players with their front teeth missing, in what would otherwise have seemed an innocuous preseason feature with a conventional title, "The Fighting Irish Look Tough Again." Notre Dame officials were outraged by the photo and *Life*'s clear implication that the Irish were a bunch of roughnecks—with no mention of the fact that the featured players had insignificant roles on the team and were the only ones missing teeth. The university demanded, and received, an official apology two issues later, along with new photos of the players in coats and ties, their dental work firmly in place.[32] No such response followed the photograph of Stan Campbell; it was no slander to imply that a professional football player was a roughneck. The visual texts of *Life*'s photo-essays were always more powerful than the accompanying words.

Then in 1959 and 1960—following, that is, the overtime championship game in December 1958 that marked the NFL's breakthrough to a nationwide television audience—*Life* suddenly embraced the pro game unequivocally, not despite its lack of glamour but because of it. Pro football did not become less "dirty" in just a couple of years; rather, the game's "savagery" was suddenly its chief virtue. A piece in 1959 on the New York Giants' linebackers had the title, "Greetings to Our Victims in Play-off," with a subhead, "Rough Trio Leads Giants' Savage, Successful Defense." The article played off the believe-it-or-not fact that Cliff Livingston, Harland Svare, and Sam Huff had girls' names in the Giants' defensive scheme. Photos of the three linebackers were signed, "Devotedly, Sara," "Faithfully, Wanda," and "Constantly, Meg," as if tokens for admirers; and the accompanying text explained that these "improbable autographs . . . are not playful terms of endearment but serious code names used for a rough purpose. . . . The girlishly named gang is the most effective trio of linebackers in pro football today and the nucleus of the most devastating defense in modern football." Knowledgeable fans might have known that "Sara," "Wanda," and "Meg" designated the strong-side, weak-side, and middle linebackers in the Giants' defensive alignment, but the incongruity of feminine names for hypermasculine football players was the real point. These Giants were the antithesis of the feminine. They were literally Giants, and *Life*'s first-ever cover story on the pros the following season extended this image to pro football generally. With no trace of irony or ambivalence *Life* now declared the pros' game to be as thrilling as a cliff-hanger serial, with a television audience now of 50 million each Sunday (a tremendous overstatement) and knowledgeable fans at the stadium whose "pro version of the old college spirit has a ferocious quality and runs the gamut from salty tears to apoplectic glee." The photograph of teams lined up for a kickoff on the magazine's cover was shot from ground level, from which the teed-up football (prominently labeled "The Duke") in the foreground looked as tall as a man. This was the pro game—now, after nearly forty years—larger than life, a "savage" game, yes, but for an audience eager to embrace savagery as heroic.[33]

After decades of slighting professional football, the rest of the major popular magazines openly celebrated it in similar ways at the end of the 1950s. The case for the pros since the early 1930s had always stressed their more spectacular style with their wide-open offenses, in contrast to the conservative play of the colleges. In the early 1950s the pass-oriented Los Angeles Rams epitomized this style, as when *Look* called them "Pro Football's Most Hectic Team." At the end of the decade, after a quarter-century of efforts to soup up the offenses, defensive savagery suddenly became the key to a great game. *Time* had celebrated pro football in an earlier cover story, in 1954, distinguishing the "high and violent art" of the pros to the "game" played by college boys, and reveling in the rough play of paunchy quarterback Bobby Layne and the rest of the burly, boozing, brawling, scarred, and toothless, yet also happy-go-lucky, players of the "man's game." These were William Fay's pro football bums in the flesh, without apology. "A Man's Game" is what *Time* titled its next cover story in 1959, with Sam Huff on the cover and commentary inside on both the "precise and powerful virtuosity" and the "awesome violence" of pro football, epitomized by Huff and rest of the New York Giants' defense. *Look* in 1960 took up the theme of "savage contact" as the key to pro football's hold on its audience of 25 million (a more modest claim than *Life*'s), and *Sports Illustrated* celebrated "The Violent Face of Pro Football" in a photo-essay. *Collier's* was gone by this time, but the *Saturday Evening Post* titled its profile of hard-living Bobby Layne, "This Is No Game for Kids." As if in response to those earlier photographs in *Life* of thick-bodied pros, the quarterback of the Detroit Lions admitted that sometimes "I've had trouble keeping my belly inside my belt," but in pro ball a little "puffiness around their waists" helped linemen hold up through a hard season, and quarterbacks could handle a bit of extra weight, too. "You have to be a man and be treated like one," Layne told the *Post*'s writer, and he was grateful to have a coach in Buddy Parker who understood that reality.[34]

Quarterbacks such as Layne and Baltimore's Johnny Unitas lacked the glamour typically associated with the position, as did the New York Giants' Charlie Conerly, featured in *Look* as an aging veteran.[35] Cleveland's Jim Brown was a fullback known for his fearsome power; the Giants' linebackers and the Colts' Big Daddy Lipscomb and Gino Marchetti were scary bruisers. The pros featured in the *Post, Life,* and *Look* in the late 1950s differed from the college heroes—still boys, not men—and differed, too, from Frank Gifford, a "Gridiron Glamour Boy," and Bob Waterfield (with his gorgeous wife, Jane Russell), professionals profiled earlier in more conventional ways. Bobby Layne was a boy, too, but a good ol' boy, a role later played most famously by Don Meredith. Magazine articles did not all tell the same story, of course; no cultural consensus was dictating a new orthodoxy. But a dramatic shift was nonetheless pronounced. When the *Post* ran a story in 1960 about pro football's "Fancy Dans," the league's top wide receivers, that name itself diminished them in contrast to the game's savage bruisers. Just the hands of the Colts' unimpressive-looking but astonishingly talented receiver, Ray Berry, were the subject of a photograph in *Life,* and the small finger on his left hand, swollen and bent at an odd angle, placed Berry in the company of Huff and Marchetti, not among the "fancy dans." Berry's damaged finger was yet another bodily text, this one illustrating that even wide receivers in the NFL were tough. None of these late-1950s profiles domesticated the pro football stars by posing them with their wives or mothers.[36]

While these magazines did not explicitly analyze professional football's new appeal, the terms of praise—a man's game, controlled savagery—and the photographic emphasis on fast, violent play by tough, oversized men pointed in obvious directions. *Esquire,* a magazine most concerned with defining the current state of American masculinity, did step back to speculate on what drew fans to pro football. By the 1950s, *Esquire* had drastically reduced its initial emphasis on sport, but its occasional football articles embraced the pros early. "The Gladiators" in 1950 celebrated the violence of professional football—by criticizing the trend away from run-oriented "muscle-backed combat" toward a pass-oriented "aerial folk dance"—at a time when the popular weeklies still waffled. This celebration of savagery became *Esquire*'s dominant theme at the end of the decade. In 1960, "The Brutal Art of Red-Dogging" profiled New York Giants' defensive coach Tom Landry—who directed Sam Huff, Harland Svare, and Cliff Livingston, the linebackers celebrated in *Life*—as the man who "revolutionized defense play into a cagey, crackling, tigerish spectacle that makes fans stamp their feet, yell their heads off, tear down goal posts and start riots." Two issues later, a look back at the "Highlights of a Golden Decade" in sport included the Colts' overtime victory over the Giants in 1958 among the great sporting events of the 1950s. Nine lines of verse by Roger Kahn (with echoes of early Carl Sandburg) accompanied a painting by Daniel Schwartz:

FIGURE 6-1. Daniel Schwartz's painting that accompanied Roger Kahn's poetic evocation of pro football in December 1960 was all blacks, blues, and greens, a pyramid of colliding bodies, pure antipastoral. (By permission of *Esquire* magazine, © Hearst Communications, Inc. *Esquire* is a trademark of Hearst Magazines Property, Inc. All rights reserved.)

The men at work were beef trusts.
Knots bulged behind their necks.
Their thighs seemed like the thighs of elephants.
Within the grotesque press of pads and helmets,
they surged and butted one another,
as mercenaries trained to an ordered rage,
and from their grossness this cool winter day
the beef trusts spun
almost a dance.[37]

The same spirit was captured in a more prosaic, but equally remarkable piece in *Esquire* the previous football season. In "The Wham in Pro Football," Thomas B. Morgan attempted to account for the game's remarkable growth in the 1950s. Citing an essay by Dan Wakefield in the liberal-left intellectual journal *Dissent* that chastised its readers for disdaining football—for not recognizing in the sport "the rituals that men so stubbornly conceive to graft an element of glory onto the deadly drudgery of everyday life"—Morgan articulated the sport's new role in American life that was emerging throughout the periodical press. It was not violence for its own sake that these magazines were promoting, but controlled violence as a necessary tonic for the age. The Bobby Layne who insisted that pro football was no game for kids was himself no hero for starry-eyed adolescents. Layne was a role model for middle-aged guys who punched the clock five days a week, whether at the factory or the office. Pro football was an antidote to an enervated society, not a symbol of its violent spirit.

Morgan tied pro football specifically to a "decline of exuberance in daily life." Twelve months earlier, *Esquire* had published "The Crisis of American Masculinity" by the historian Arthur Schlesinger, Jr., who had traced the problem to a loss of personal identity as male and female roles grew increasingly indistinguishable. The problem was not aggressive women, Schlesinger insisted—male supremacy, like white supremacy, "was the neurosis of an immature society"—but rather the "overpowering conspiracy of blandness" and conformity that were the consequences of democracy and modernization. As if in response to Schlesinger, Morgan saw in pro football a solution to the dilemma of blurred gender roles. Pro football tolerated women, he noted, but it neither encouraged nor welcomed them. The male-dominated atmosphere at a pro game—men outnumbering women four to one, according to Morgan—"is rather like that of an outdoor, stag poker game. Cigar smoke hangs in the autumn air. One feels a general air of well-being and relief, as though the boys are glad to get out of the house on Sunday afternoon. Club owners have wisely shunned ladies'-day promotions while injecting the short skirts and perky bosoms into the half-time festivities." The game itself was "harder, faster, meaner and more acute" than college football. The pros "move with speed, if not always grace, creating a kind of brutal rhythm on the field." They hit "with vengeance and sometimes style." The appeal of this preeminent contemporary sport was to a crowd that "lives its daily life in a tightly-civilized, humdrum community and pro football is, in contrast, a kind of sanctioned savagery." For the fans, "the pleasure in this savagery" is "an escape from or a substitute for the boredom of work, the dullness of reality." [38]

Morgan's portrait of the period is familiar: it was the view of David Riesman, William Whyte, C. Wright Mills, and other popular sociologists of the decade, who characterized life in the postwar era as a "rat race" run by "other-directed" conformists and "organizational men," who were more prosperous than Americans had ever been before, but at the cost of emotional and spiritual impoverishment. What later historians recognized as a powerful domestic ideology was also implicit in Morgan's analysis of the suffocating world from which professional football offered escape. Morgan's essay invites us to think about football in these familiar contexts, and the photographs in *Life* and the articles in all of the popular weeklies bear out Morgan's reading. Against the gee-whiz boys of college football, the pros were men, oversized and brutally toughened, engaged in a savage sport that they transformed into something like a dance. Since the 1880s and 1890s, a major part of football's appeal, expressed in a variety of ways, had been the intensity of experience—physical, emotional, psychological—that it offered players and fans alike. This intensity was invoked most powerfully in the 1920s and 1950s—periods of national prosperity, with their attendant concerns about prosperity's "spiritual" costs—and was least noted during World War II, when real life required no artificial or vicarious heightening. The "brutal rhythm" of professional football, its "vengeance and sometimes style"—or in Kahn's words, its "ordered rage" and almost-dance of "beef trusts"—were all attempts to capture in a single cryptic phrase the unique tension between brutality and artistry that satisfied a deep need at a particular historical moment. (*Look* came up with similar phrases, pro football's "brawny ballet," featuring the "rough grace" of the linemen.)[39] Morgan also noted how the ironic purity of professional football—football with neither ethical complications to the pursuit of victory nor the distractions of pageantry and the social whirl that enveloped the college game—helped make it men's choice for self-expression.

Historian Donald Mrozek has described "the cult and ritual of toughness," in which "combative games and sports became the special rites of a Cold War political culture that rested on the premise of struggle and competition." Anxiety over widespread physical decline led Dwight Eisenhower to establish the President's Council on Youth Fitness in 1956, and in the opening years of the next decade John Kennedy would make vigorous touch football one of the symbols of his administration. Kennedy diagnosed his country's problem in *Sports Illustrated* in 1960, where he argued that an "age of leisure and abundance" had created what he called in his title "The Soft American," unfit to meet the challenges of the Soviet Union as well as American responsibilities at home and around the world. As Robert Griswold has explained, Kennedy was but one of many for whom the "flabby American" became a metaphor for a morally corrupt and self-indulgent way of life.[40] The glorification of pro football as an antidote to bland conformity and softness addressed these same concerns, while also reacting against football's domestication celebrated elsewhere in the periodical press.

In describing the relative absence of women from professional football, Thomas Morgan noted, "The social reasons—the fraternity week end, the big prom—that usually attract women to college games do not exist for the pro games." Whether or not Morgan accurately accounted for women's presence in college stadiums, he identified a conspicuous distinction between the competing versions of football in the periodical press. Football had two sharply contrasting images at the end of the 1950s: the "Face of America" seen at kids' and high school and college games, and the "sanctioned savagery" of the professional sport. Physical toughness was also prized in college football, to be sure. As noted in Chapter 4, magazine profiles of coaching "Biffs" such as Bill Glassford and Bear Bryant celebrated their iron-fisted handling of players—making men out of boys justified all kinds of coaching brutality—while the "iron men" of old returned with the restoration of one-platoon football in 1953. The Midwest's "rock-'em, sock-'em" style set the standard—the sports editor of the *Dallas Morning News* worried that southwestern razzle-dazzle seemed "semisissy" in contrast—and "three yards and a cloud of dust" became the motto for the hard-nosed game of one-platoon football ruled by men like Woody Hayes.[41] Even reputedly "dirty" college football players, such as Michigan's Ron Kramer and USC's McKeever twins, were defended in the *Post, Life,* and *Collier's* in what one writer called "The Case for Rough Football."[42] This was but one theme, however, in the wider narrative universe of the college sport, domesticated as well as wild; for pro football it became the overriding theme. Competing ideas about football present since the game's beginning had settled into separate channels, and professional football was now redefined to meet a distinct set of psychological needs.

What We Think About When We Think about Football

Class?

Football's most fundamental development from the 1920s to the 1950s was its (incomplete) democratization, its transformation from a predominantly Anglo-Saxon "gentleman's sport" to a multi-ethnic, classless one. This democratization entailed both the spread of big-time college football from a handful of elite northeastern institutions to state universities, land-grant colleges, and immigrant-rich Catholic schools throughout the country, and the popular acceptance of professional football as a legitimate sport rather than an organized brawl staged by hired thugs. College football was democratized by the sons of Polish steel workers and Italian coal miners who transformed the faces, and the names, of football lineups. Football helped democratize American higher education more generally, less through the actual number of working-class and second-generation immigrant boys it brought to college than for its symbolizing a new American melting pot. Whether the well-publicized success of stars such as Bronko Nagurski, Frank Carideo, and Alex Wojciechowicz actually helped more second- and third-generation Ukrainians, Italians, and Poles understand that they, too, might go to college is impossible to know, but there is no question that their presence in the game led the American public to revise its views not just of college football but also of the institutions that sponsored it. Democratization remained incomplete at the end of the period, chiefly because opportunities for African Americans were still limited, but even here the process of integration was irreversibly underway.

All this happened with little analysis in the media. Just as today, when after a full generation of thoroughly integrated football many of the major controversies surrounding college sports—those dealing with admission requirements, graduation rates, recruiting practices, appropriate compensation for athletes—are also racial issues despite our reluctance to address them as such, in this earlier period the comparable controversies were often issues of ethnicity or class, and we were as reluctant then as now to deal with them on such discomfiting terms. Both the early controversies over professional football and the varied, often confused responses to the new elements in the college game reveal the oft-noted reluctance of Americans to acknowledge the realities of class in our supposedly classless democracy. As the twentieth century opened, football alone among the country's major spectator sports was supposedly played by gentleman amateurs, but by the 1920s its "amateurs" were generating millions of dollars in profit from a major entertainment business. The sport opened doors to husky second-generation Polish and Italian immigrants at the very time Congress was closing doors to their countrymen; if all the subsidized athletes had been named Adams or Smith instead of Brovelli or Pulaski, the context of the debates would have been very different. In short, the narratives of football from the 1920s through the 1950s expressed the general confusion over issues that should not have mattered at all in democratic America but that mattered greatly indeed.

Underlying virtually every narrative of football was the most fundamental issue of all: what it meant to be a "man." While the expanding mass media drove the growth of football's audience, concerns about masculinity were a major factor in making that audience receptive to the game. Brawny and brainy football heroes represented contrasting models of masculinity. Black, Catholic, Jewish, Polish, and other immigrant football players challenged exclusionary definitions of these ideals. "Professionalism" in college football threatened received standards of social and moral manhood. Pride in the local football team was in part an assertion of the community's collective virility. Regional football styles—midwestern power, southwestern razzle-dazzle, hot-headed southern passion—also represented styles of masculinity. Debates over free substitution and two-platoon football in the 1950s concerned whether the ideal male was an "iron man" or a talented specialist. Coaching styles reflected different models of managerial manliness, while the fictional figures of "Pop" and "Biff" represented alternative modes of fatherhood and male authority. Whether or not masculinity has been "in crisis" at various times in the twentieth century is debated by historians of gender, but in either case masculinity has been constantly in flux. Consumerism in the 1920s, declining wages and unemployment in the 1930s, and the grinding routines of the "rat race" in the 1950s successively challenged the reigning assumptions about masculinity and expectations for men. Only during the Second World War were American males heroically engaged in an unambiguously "masculine" enterprise. Football's cultural importance was at its lowest during the war; throughout the rest of this period it provided an arena in which traditional ideas about masculinity were both affirmed and adapted to changing conditions.

FOOTBALL AND CLASS UNCONSCIOUSNESS

This chapter is a study of confusion and uncertainty. Football games by their nature are classless—victory is determined by performance, not birth or social position—yet football's roots in the American university entangled it in class issues that persisted for decades. By the 1950s, the opening up of higher education to returning GI's after World War II—at the same time that televised professional football began to win a broader following, and, more generally, the economy expanded, the civil rights of minorities began to gain legal and popular backing, and a belief in the United States as a classless or broadly middle-class society became the reigning ideology—established football within that common middle-class or classless American experience. But football's early years were more complicated.

In a history of what he calls "the conundrum of class," Martin Burke has described the pattern of assertion and denial of class distinctions and class conflict that has marked American public discourse since the eighteenth century. "Class," as Burke comments, "has been a mobile and unstable social category."[1] This mobility and instability were reflected in contradictory attitudes toward football, due to the fundamental conflict between a simply meritocratic game and its more complicated social grounding. Class feelings were rarely expressed openly, but in the disputes about amateurs and professionals, the debates over subsidization, and the relationships of owners, coaches, and players, football dramatized the struggles of groups competing for the spoils of American success.

The visual rendering of spectators was clearly marked by social class. The ruddy-faced fellow at a baseball game on a July 1912 cover of *Everybody's*—in shirt sleeves, suspenders, and straw boater tilted back, a cigar clenched in his left fist—appears to be a village shopkeeper sneaking off for an afternoon at the ballpark, a very different figure from the well-groomed football fans on magazine covers. The earliest football illustrations featured gentlemen in top hats. By 1920, the crowd was slightly more democratized, but the youth waving his cap in Figure 5-1 (see Chapter 5), as well as his companions, both male and female, still dressed more formally than their baseball counterparts. As baseball continued to be represented as the people's game, the attire of football fans on magazine covers continued to signify more than cool autumn weather.

Magazine ads, too, whose purpose was to sell their own products, indirectly sold college football as an ideal of upwardly mobile middle-class social life. Ads showing genteel fans driving to the stadium in stylish automobiles or sitting in the stands in fashionable overcoats—several particularly striking ones painted by J. C. Leyendecker—were examples of what Roland Marchand has termed "social tableaux," scenes seemingly drawn from life but actually "depicting settings at least 'a step up' from the social circumstances of the readers." Advertisers had discovered by the 1920s that "people did not usually want ads to reflect themselves, their immediate social relationships, or their broader society exactly." Ads were to project fantasy and wish fulfillment. Having examined 180,000 ads, Marchand noted that they rarely portrayed "sports fans enjoying a boxing match or baseball game."[2] The case was very different with football, a measure of the college sport's identification with an upscale social world and its ties to the middle-class consumers with disposable income whom advertisers wished to reach.

College football's class status was more convoluted than such simple icons and marketing images suggested, however. As we have seen in other contexts, football's birth at Harvard, Yale, and Princeton encumbered it with a definition of amateurism it was unable to shed for several decades. The reality of football from the beginning was a no-holds-barred pursuit of victory that meant both exploiting the rules to one's own advantage and attracting students often more adept on the field than in the classroom. Recruiting "ringers" began early and proceeded fitfully into the opening decades of the twentieth century, as one college team after another realized the need for a professional coach, who in turn developed methods for acquiring the best players. In his columns in *Harper's Weekly* and *Outing* in the 1890s and early 1900s, Caspar Whitney was outraged by the tramp athletes who occasionally showed up at New England prep schools and elite colleges, but he located the wholesale abuses of recruiting in the rising powers of the Midwest. David Riesman and Reuel Denney date systematic recruiting and subsidization from around 1915, about the time that football power

SUNDAY MAGAZINE
Of THE ROCKY MOUNTAIN and the Denver Times NEWS

DENVER, COL.   NOVEMBER 15, 1908 PART VI. 20 PAGES

The Diplomat

J. V. McFALL

FIGURE 7-1. The top hat of the 1890s became a bowler in this 1908 Sunday magazine, but the social class of the fans was unchanged. As such formal wear gave way to more casual attire in the 1920s, football's representative class became the prosperous middle rather than the more narrowly defined elite, but the upscale image was still pronounced. See, for example, the covers of the *Saturday Evening Post* for 16 November 1929, 15 November 1941, and 19 November 1960; and the covers of *Liberty* for 14 October 1933, 25 November 1933, 14 November 1936, and 20 November 1937.

FIGURE 7-2. Ads like these for Kuppenheimer men's wear in 1922 (by J. C. Leyendecker) and Ollendorf watches in 1929 cast college football as part of an American world of social aspiration, fantasy, and wish fulfillment, while at the same time rendering football more glamorous by association with emblems of conspicuous consumption.

shifted westward, and the two developments were of course related.[3] After the interruption of the First World War, the recruiting of top football players resumed with renewed emphasis in all regions.

Whether acknowledged as such, class issues were thus inextricably part of football's expansion and development, for the brawny stars luring fans to the massive new stadiums in the 1920s typically came from farming and working-class families outside the traditional collegiate world. In the popular press, the first two decades of the twentieth century were ruled by the class bias of the amateur sporting code. Complementing the columns of Caspar Whitney and likeminded spokesmen, the most distinctive fiction of this period cast football as the training ground for an American ruling class. The stories celebrating manly toughness by writers such as Jack London's old friend, James Hopper—with five stories and a three-part serial in the *Saturday Evening Post* between 1904 and 1916—implicitly endorsed the romantic Anglo-Saxon primitivism of the Progressive Era: the idea that the upperclass Anglo-Saxon owed his supremacy in the world to his barbarian ancestry, kept alive in these perilously soft modern times by activities such as the rugged new game of college football.[4] Endurance of physical pounding in these stories was thus joined to the other virtues of the aristocratic amateur: sacrificing oneself for the team; playing the game for its own sake, not for material gain; losing oneself in school spirit. In the 1900s and 1910s, the hero who embodied or learned these values was typically an upper-class youth whose triumph proved that the old elite, contrary to that class's fear of displacement by the new plutocracy of self-made men, remained the most fit to rule the modern industrial and financial worlds. The epitome of this story, "The Exquisite Thug" by Rupert Hughes in 1909, featured a hero who was "a living refutation of the ancient fallacy that easy life makes a weak man." A patrician of distinguished lineage, Cornelius Evertsen approaches the responsibilities of his football captaincy "with an energy that would have made him a captain of industry." In the big game Evertsen remains disdainfully aristocratic as he humiliates the lower-class ringer on the rival team.[5]

The democratization of football by state universities and Catholic colleges rendered such plots irrelevant and introduced a new theme and new class hero: the working-class youth who overcomes prejudice, or perhaps his own shame, to prove his right to pursue a college education and the rewards it makes possible. Class consciousness was a major issue in the few football films of the early 1920s. In *Ashamed of Parents* (1921), the son of a shoemaker becomes a football star and falls in love with a society girl, but has to overcome his own shame over his upbringing. In *The Snob* and *Two*

Minutes to Go (both 1921), a working-class boy and the son of a bankrupted father, respectively, struggle with their social status as they work their way through college while starring on the football team. The treatment of class in these movies was part of a shift in the film industry noted by labor historian Steven Ross, who points out that, although "class was a central theme in silent films," in the 1920s class conflict on the screen gave way to "far more conservative films that emphasized fantasies of love and harmony among the classes."[6] These few football films played a minuscule role in that development, but by dramatizing the idea that the class consciousness of the poor, not class or poverty itself, was the chief obstacle to success, they also contributed to a comparable shift in representing football throughout the media. Several stories in *Collier's* during the 1920s had similar plots in which poverty was no obstacle to the determined hero. The over-the-top version was Wadsworth Camp's "The Guarded Heights," serialized in *Collier's* over eighteen weeks in 1920, then published as a novel in 1921, then serialized again in newspapers the following year. The hero of Camp's tale could have come from an Ayn Rand novel twenty-five years later. Beginning as a lowly groom to an imperious heiress, George Morton proves himself initially as a football star at Princeton, then rises to become a ruthlessly powerful Wall Street financier, only to discover that service to others is more rewarding; finally he marries the woman who once scorned him as a stable boy even as she fought her attraction to him.[7]

These stories that seem saturated in class consciousness and conflict actually denied the importance of class. George Morton was not trapped in a servant's lowly station but, with football at an elite institution as his vehicle, rose to the very pinnacle of wealth, power, and social position. Class barriers were not the problem in movies such as *Ashamed of Parents* and *Two Minutes to Go* but rather the hero's initial misguided belief that economic or social status mattered (in *The Snob* it is the wealthy heroine who must learn that the hero's having to work his way through college is not shameful). In accordance with the great American faith in opportunity and mobility, these narratives acknowledged differences in wealth and social position only to demonstrate that such disparities were irrelevant to an enterprising youth.

Since Werner Sombart first attributed "American exceptionalism" to the greater buying power of American workers, social scientists have struggled to account for the absence of class consciousness in the United States despite the obvious reality of social and economic classes. Particularly in the 1920s and 1950s, times of conspicuously expanding production and consumption, the definitions of "middle class" became blurred and expansive.

Steven Ross points to the 1920s as the decisive period, when the booming consumer economy "created great confusion over modern class identities." White-collar workers identified with the expanding "middle class," against the blue-collar working class that often earned higher wages. In a much-cited survey conducted by *Fortune* in 1940, 79 percent of Americans identified themselves as "middle class," and even in what turned out to be the waning years of the Depression, a majority believed they would be more prosperous than their fathers. *Fortune*'s results were challenged by Richard Centers in 1949, in whose own survey 51 percent identified themselves as working class, compared to 43 percent as middle class. More recently, Reeve Vanneman and Lynn Weber Cannon have disputed the long tradition of denying class consciousness in the United States with studies that point to a highly conscious but weak working class comprising 70 percent of Americans.[8] Representations of football in the media cannot resolve this larger debate. On the one hand, as one of the conspicuous amusements of the prosperous middle class, football was embraced, both in fact and in media-made fantasies, by a broad audience. On the other hand, the occasions when class consciousness does break through the mainstream media's usual silence on class issues point to feelings likely held by many Americans.

The general confusion, or inconsistency, on these issues is no better illustrated than by the print and film versions of Lucian Cary's "White Flannels." In the magazine story published in the *Saturday Evening Post* in 1925, a working-class tennis star rises to the top of his sport, then confesses his background to the woman he loves, expecting her to recoil, only to discover that she comes from a similar family and, like him, merely seems to belong to the upper-class world. With no obstacle to their love, they can live unapologetically in the world of wealth and privilege that has accepted them. The 1927 film not only made the hero a football star, it also completely inverted the plot: when the hero's supposed friends learn of his working-class background, they turn against him, and he leaves college to return to his own people and the girl he left behind. In the *Post*, the hero can live in his new social world without conflict or shame; in the film, he is made painfully aware that he is an outsider. Both versions sympathize with the talented working-class striver confronting class barriers, but in one the barriers are illusory and in the other they are real, and insuperable. The magazine version was more typical. Football narratives, even when steeped in class prejudice, tended to insist that, ultimately, class did not matter. The film's opposing viewpoint suggests that many Americans knew better, and film was more fully a "popular" medium than were middle-class magazines.

Class feelings often took forms that obscured their origin. Underlying the revulsion against professional football in the 1920s, for example, apart from colleges' simpler objection to an economic rival in the entertainment business, was essentially a class bias no critic openly acknowledged. Antagonism toward professional football was akin to the view of hunting held by patrician sportsmen such as Theodore Roosevelt in the late nineteenth century. Roosevelt celebrated hunting for sport—for the challenge of the kill and for the head or horns as trophy—as the best of all recreations for a virile ruling class, while denouncing those who killed for subsistence as mere "game butchers" and "pothunters."[9] If the higher morality of killing for sport rather than survival is not at all self-evident, nor is the superiority of football played for school spirit rather than to make a living. When Red Grange turned pro at the end of his senior season, the resulting furor was largely couched in terms of loyalty versus betrayal, college spirit versus "professionalism." In the press's most common reading of Grange's college career to that point, the "Wheaton Ice Man" had been cast as a great democratic hero: a son of the American heartland who made himself a football star as he earned his college tuition by hauling blocks of ice at his summer job. His story could have been written by Horatio Alger himself.[10] Yet cashing in on his prowess rankled his critics, to whom Grange seemed to be trading social distinction for tawdry wealth, and some of the more tough-minded sportswriters recognized the underlying class bias in these complaints. Writing in the tabloid *New York Daily News,* Paul Gallico bluntly declared that Grange's critics simply objected to "all this gorgeous jack falling into the hands of socially inferior persons who were in the thing only for gain, and didn't even pretend that they were doing it because they loved it."[11]

Bill Cunningham elaborated on this point in a syndicated story. No one complained about the money earned by Jack Dempsey or Babe Ruth, Cunningham pointed out, but that was because Dempsey was "an alumnus of the brake beam and fellow of the handout," Ruth "the most famous alumnus of a Baltimore orphanage and a magna cum graduate of the National Sand Lots." For them, playing for pay violated no sacred principle. Grange's turning pro, on the other hand, in Cunningham's lively analogy, was greeted "as if Mary, the minister's pretty daughter, who sang in the little church choir, had snapped her hymn book shut and stepped out of her gingham and signed on with some tawdry burlesque troop to chirp shoddy ditties and kick toward the rafters a shamelessly unclothed limb." Looking back on six weeks of Grange hysteria, Cunningham characterized the debate over Grange's actions as "Groceries Vs. Ideals," seemingly to mock Grange's critics, yet despite some obvious ambivalence he sided finally with the ideal-ists. He sympathized with Grange's coach at Illinois, Robert Zuppke, who in a public speech immediately following Grange's defection to the Bears had declared that "Grange has no right to capitalize upon his athletic fame; his fame belongs to Illinois, not to him." Or to one individual at Illinois in particular: Cunningham noted that Zuppke "considers Grange his master-piece." Cunningham likened the Illinois coach to "an architect who had cre-ated a majestic building—a consummate masterpiece he felt would secure his fame through all the years to come, only to have it fall by some twist of fate into the money-hungry hands of some greasy alien, who forthwith turned it into a livery stable." Cunningham's summation: "Red Grange may make his millions and the world may vote him wise, but he's lost his campus precinct in the process and the blessings of the man who originally chartered his path to glory—and escorted him there." [12]

This piece is extraordinarily revealing on several counts, not least of which is its own ethnocentrism and class bias. Cunningham mocked the im-plicit class prejudice of pro football's critics, who denounced Red Grange while making heroes of Babe Ruth and Jack Dempsey, yet Cunningham was seemingly blind to his own assumptions. Although his "greasy alien" was just a metaphor, it was a metaphor that resonated powerfully not only with the era's anti-immigrant ugliness, but also with football's peculiar relationship to "professionalism." Cunningham wrote as "greasy aliens" matriculating from steel mills and coal mines instead of Andover and Exeter were increasingly showing up on college football teams. In attributing Grange's stardom to Zuppke's coaching rather than his own hard work and talent, Cunningham also subscribed to that peculiarly American view of coaches that implicitly valued the "bosses" over the "workers." Cunningham's piece illustrates how class feelings could creep into discussions even when the writer was con-sciously denying them. Likewise, ten days before ridiculing the class bias of Grange's critics, Paul Gallico himself, as we saw in Chapter 3, had expressed disgust at Grange's peddling his name to anyone willing to pay for it. The most openly class-conscious sportswriters could themselves be highly incon-sistent on matters of class.

Despite the fact that the players were overwhelmingly college educated, at a time when higher education was the privilege of a minority, profes-sional football remained for another two decades a sport for "the masses" rather than "the classes," as an editorial in *Sport Story* characterized it in 1926; meanwhile, college football became an arena in which Americans' am-bivalence about class and classlessness continued to play out. [13] In the late

1920s, the *New York Daily News* usually managed to give its readers at least one democratic football hero each season. In 1926, after Notre Dame beat Army 7–0 on Christy Flanagan's sixty-five-yard touchdown run, the *Daily News* declared Flanagan the "First Gift of Stevedoring to Grid." Having grown up in Port Arthur, Texas, where he worked on the oil docks, Christy "learned to scoot up reeling masts, swing jibsails, and carry oil kegs and lumber on his shoulders." Flanagan did not quite qualify as a working-class hero, however, since his father and uncle happened to own the oil company. Rather, he was the heir to privilege who declined to accept it, with a father and uncle who "could have left in his mouth the silver spoon he was born with" but instead "chose to replace that with a hempen line." [14] The man of wealth and position who clung to the values of hard-working common people was as much a democratic hero as the man born in poverty who proved himself the equal of anyone.

Bruce Caldwell in 1927 and Albie Booth in 1929 came from this other side of the economic divide. Caldwell was a Yale halfback hailed in the East as a star of the season, until he was declared ineligible just before the Princeton game. Someone leaked information that Caldwell had played briefly at Brown as a freshman before transferring to Yale and had thus used up his eligibility. The Big Three had long been notorious for their squabbling over issues of eligibility, but Paul Gallico conjectured that in this case the complaint was provoked by "jealousy of the publicity that was coming to a young man who was not considered the social equal of others." An editorial in the *Daily News* also saw the controversy as symptomatic of a more general prejudice. "The Caldwell mess arose from the colleges' increasing tendency to make fine distinctions between amateur and professional players," the paper declared. "In England, this distinction is so sharp that an amateur in any sport is a 'gentleman' and draws a Mister before his name when he lands in the papers, while a professional is viewed as almost a menial. It seems to us that the colleges in this country, at least the high-toned eastern colleges, show a tendency toward the same sort of snobbishness." The writer then turned from Caldwell to Red Grange and professional football, declaring, "And speaking of democracy, giving every man a chance—professional sport qualifies." [15]

Yale's Albie Booth became a national sensation two seasons later, when as a sophomore running back he defeated Army single-handedly. Although he would never rise so high again, newspapers and magazines could not get enough of Booth for several weeks after the Army game, and interest in him continued intermittently over the next two seasons. The lessons of Booth's story varied in the telling. Grantland Rice likened Albie to great little men of the past—Frank Hinkey, Little Bill Johnston, Joe Sternaman, Arthur Poe, Jerry Travers—who taught the important lesson that innate advantages can prove a handicap to effort, while overcoming obstacles through "the heart and the brain" can lead to greater success. This had been a bedrock assumption of the success ethic endlessly popularized since the Gilded Age of the late nineteenth century and was easily transferable to football. The *Daily News*, however, characteristically emphasized Booth's working-class background. In a syndicated three-part series, Noel Busch made much of little Albie's growing up in New Haven, the son of a foreman in the Winchester Arms factory. Having worked since grammar school at the munitions plant, on a vegetable wagon, for a dairy, and in a meat-packing plant, Booth developed "complete physical control" as well as extraordinary self-assurance that served him on the football field and would serve him equally well in pursuing success after college. Westbrook Pegler told a similar story, adding that "the Booths are of the aggressively independent New England Nordic working class, who do not consider themselves poor and cannot be patronized by any one." (Within Pegler's celebration of working-class virtue, that single word "Nordic" spoke volumes on a different subject.)[16]

From his columnist's chair at the *Daily News*, Paul Gallico followed the Booth phenomenon with some bemusement, seeing reporters "all aflutter with the importance of their assignments to make a life study of Albert J. Booth, Jr." Gallico noted that "Yale always manages to have a football hero sprung from poor but honest parents who is working his way through college"—he mentioned Bruce Caldwell as a recent case—"and some day I would like, just for a change, to print the story of an Eli fullback or quarterback who comes from a family of socially prominent millionaires, never did a lick of work in his life beyond the labors in the tackling pit, and hopes to keep his record clear in after years." Gallico mocked the cliché of the democratic hero, yet his own paper conspicuously invoked it. Christy Flanagan had been born to privilege but refused to slide by on his prerogatives; Albie Booth (like Bruce Caldwell) had been born poor but refused to accept poverty as his destiny. Both figures were heroes in the master narrative of American democratic classlessness, and both were regularly represented in football journalism. Celebrity profiles in the *Saturday Evening Post* and *Collier's* featured many more Booths than Flanagans, because the oft-noted reality was that poor boys were more likely to make the sacrifices necessary for football stardom and its rewards.

Gallico's comment that Yale regularly gave the football world a Bruce

Caldwell or an Albie Booth points to the special role that the Big Three of Harvard, Yale, and Princeton played in American feelings about football and class. Gallico himself, a Columbia graduate but also the son of an Italian-immigrant concert pianist and composer—Ivy League culture with an Ellis Island background—was obsessed with the exclusiveness of Big Three football.[17] In 1926, after Harvard lost to Brown for the fourth straight time, Gallico noted, "The Brown victory over Harvard will be most enjoyed by those citizens who like to see the high hat booted around in the dust a little, or for that matter, a great deal. I number myself among these, and was particularly charmed with what, from the accounts, appeared to be the ease of the Providence victory." A week later, Gallico covered the Harvard-Yale game himself and reported afterward at length on the "social aspect" of the game, which was "generally a great deal more interesting than the actual football."

> The football, as exhibited by two expertly trained teams, was abominable, but society, in panorama, closeup and cross-section, was more than fascinating. By their own admission the blood that pulses in the veins of the spectators when Yale and Harvard play football is several shades bluer than the life fluid represented at other meetings of great institutions of learning. You have only to stand in the lobby of the Taft hotel in New Haven on big-game day to see the offspring of what passes for aristocracy, mostly a combination of family and money and sometimes simply money. . . .
>
> Most of them are thin-lipped, with scornful eyes and fine patrician noses, aquiline faces, far from high-colored, and set off by their magnificent coats and rakish hats. The two great universities have given them polish and manners. They speak in the softest of voices, and their English is the English of culture. They wear the finest clothing manufactured. They have down to a fine art the wearing of the air of knowing who they are and what they are about. They are also delightfully wholesome as they move gracefully through the crush with some of the most beautiful girls in the world on their arms. . . .
>
> It is their celebration and they seem to conspire by their freshness, their feeling of being so alert and living the happy moment, to make you feel old and unwanted, unless you belong to the moment yourself.[18]

This extraordinary mix of longing and resentment, fascination and self-pity, turned to simple disgust as Gallico went on to describe "the white-faced boys and the gorgeous girls" falling-down drunk on "bad whisky and worse gin" after the game, the football weekend at Yale becoming an object lesson on the destructiveness of prohibition. But the earlier evocation of well-bred youth at play, addressed to a readership that spanned New York's social and economic classes, evoked the conflicted feelings of "the masses" for "the classes" in the context of college football. Writing about an early-season Yale-Georgia game in 1928, Westbrook Pegler echoed the more mocking tone of Gallico's 1926 piece on Harvard and Brown. Pegler described the uncharacteristically informal atmosphere when the southerners came to New Haven—so different from that surrounding a late-season Harvard or Princeton game—as "something like meeting one of the Astor girls on wash day." With admission lowered from $5 to $1, the locals could actually attend the game, including a "knothole gang" of kids in one end zone. "I never knew Yale knew there were common kids in New Haven who might be interested in seeing the Yale team play football," Pegler observed. "It was my idea that they all sold parking space in their front yards or peddled feathers, balloons, chrysanthemums, sandwiches, or programs, and, because they were one way or another barred from the stadium, hoped Yale would not lose by any trivial margin." The Yale Bowl sat "within an iron shot of the town dumps of New Haven," where the junked cars, baby carriages, and wash boilers announced that the townsfolk "drive flivvers and have babies and women get their arms into the suds in New Haven, and the Yale people know and don't mind. What do you think of that?" Pegler confessed that "the hospitality to the townies and the knothole gang during the Georgia game" had challenged his belief that Yale people spent all their time "holding their chins so high and being rich, refined and exclusive." He warned readers that "if you like to feel that way about Yale keep away from there early in the season or you'll find yourself liking them."[19]

Pegler and Gallico must have spoken for class antagonisms that extended well beyond the press box. Gallico also wrote simpler paeans to Big Three football, as when he described the "life, the color and the beauty of Princeton . . . at nightfall long after the tired teams have trotted from the stadium and victory is with the Tiger," and on another occasion "the football parade of pretty ones and their swains en route to the spectacle" of the Harvard-Yale game. In contrast to such patrician beauty, Gallico reported seeing at the 1932 Notre Dame–Army game "the darnedest set of beezers, schnozzles, mugs and pans I have ever seen on a ball field," when he trained his binoculars on the Notre Dame players. Gallico was an extravagant admirer of the Fighting Irish in their stirring annual struggles with the Cadets, but it seemed to Gallico that, although several Army players had that indefinable "It" that "might cause a feminine heart to flutter," the Notre Damers "all looked like prize-fighters. This is not a vital matter and I don't know why I bring it up. It's just something I noticed." [20] Gallico brought it up because, as his columns repeatedly made clear, he loved the beauty of football—the spectacle and the flowering youth in attendance as well as the game itself— but he also, perhaps unconsciously, recorded the tangled feelings about class (and ethnicity) that football evoked in the 1930s, sometimes in the very faces of the players. The unlovely mugs for Notre Dame, of course, belonged to working-class Poles, Italians, and other new immigrants. In Gallico's columns he identified with the outsiders, longed to be one of the Harvard or Yale insiders, loathed his own longing, and resented their arousing it. There, in a neatly complicated package, he expressed more widely held American feelings about class.

Democratic football heroes and Paul Gallico's ambivalent relationship with the Big Three appeared in the pages of the *Daily News* alongside the ongoing controversies over professionalism in college football. Amidst the general indifference to the Carnegie Foundation's 1929 report in the daily press, at least a few sportswriters recognized that subsidization was inherently a class issue. In New York's other great tabloid, *Daily Mirror* sports editor and columnist Dan Parker dismissed the entire business of reform with the sarcastic observation, "After all, since the quest for knowledge is one of the noblest motives in life, the college coaches who go out into the highways and byways and rescue stout peasants from a career behind the plough and yank young huskies right out of the maws of the police force, and put them in the way of acquiring even a modicum of higher learning so that they may become successful bond salesmen in later life—these magnanimous coaches, I say, are performing a noble mission in life."

An editorial in the *Daily News* responded more seriously, in the same spirit in which it commented on the Bruce Caldwell affair. Noting that American football ethics were derived from the English, for whom "an amateur sportsman is a 'gentleman,' while a professional is only a 'player,'" the editorial declared: "That is right in England. We have long believed that it is not suited to the United States. There is little class distinction here, and there should be none in American sport, between the man who earns his living and the man who lives on the income from inherited wealth. If a man can play football, he should not be denied the right to earn an education with the talent that he has. He should not be encouraged to stay away from college because he has a quick mind and a powerful body but little money. Many college authorities seem to feel that football playing should be confined to the rich.

They are wrong." The *New York Herald Tribune* explicitly defended both the Carnegie Foundation and other champions of "pure amateurism" against such charges of snobbishness and class bias, but the tabloids highlighted most clearly the antidemocratic consequences of athletic "purity."[21]

Neither journalists nor writers of fiction consistently confronted the realities of class, however. The debate over subsidization waged by writers such as John R. Tunis and Francis Wallace cast the issue in moral and ethical terms (professionalism vs. hypocrisy) or claimed a pragmatic position, but rarely addressed it as an issue of class. Where class consciousness broke through the surface, it often appears inadvertent, a betrayal of the writer's better nature. In his memoirs for *Collier's* in 1931, Pop Warner characterized the typical tramp athlete of long ago as a "husky gent with a half-inch brow" and noted that the "number of miners, blacksmiths and plumber's helpers taking art courses was a standing joke" in those years. Agonizing over repeated Nebraska failures in its annual intersectional contest with Pitt, the *Omaha World-Herald*'s Frederick Ware wrote in 1936, "It is only necessary to read the names of the Pitt players and take a look at their faces to conclude that the bearers of both are not in college for an education." Warner was defending the modern game against a supposedly more tawdry past, Ware worrying over the ability of Nebraska farmboys to compete with the subsidized sons of Pennsylvania miners and millworkers, but in conjuring an image to illustrate football's dark side both men resorted to what amounted to simple class and ethnic stereotypes.

Earlier in 1936, in a rare foray into verse, Ware's "Ballad of the Lost" included stanzas about the fullback who had worked on the waterfront until he was twenty-three, the tackle from the steel mill, the end who had been a truck driver, and the center from the coal mines. Each ended in the refrain, "Where the hell do I go from here?" and the poem concluded with these lines: "Of strong-backs football makes in college / The Fall-time gods of the hemisphere. / But strong-backs often lack in knowledge — / Pray tell us where do they go from here."[22] The poem seems sympathetic to the football-playing sons of the working class, whose promise of upward mobility proves illusory as unemployment haunts even college graduates during the Depression, but it also questions their right to be in college at all. A logic derived from stereotypes operates in the poem: manual labor produces strong-backs for football, but strong-backed youth lack the intelligence needed by students. Big-time college football exploits these muscular but unintelligent young men, while the young men in turn degrade the colleges.

The stories of subsidized football players by Francis Wallace and other writers in the 1930s most fully expressed the tangle of class consciousness and denial of class. In one sense Wallace's fiction and nonfiction were consistent: they refused to declare subsidization corrupting. But whereas in his journalism Wallace consistently argued that football players were categorically entitled to reasonable pay for their services, in his fiction he distinguished between worthy and unworthy recipients of subsidies. In many ways, the football fiction from this period is more revealing than the journalism, because it sometimes expressed unexamined feelings rather than consciously constructed arguments. At a time when American capitalism was receiving its most searching criticism and the American labor movement was gaining real power, in Wallace's stories there were no classes in America, only individuals in differing material circumstances who responded well or poorly to the opportunities and challenges presented them. This, of course, was the fundamental American creed, routinely challenged but never finally undermined. We can imagine a quintessential 1930s football story, its plot centering on two pairs of characters: two sons of the working class, both of them subsidized (on the "gravy train") but one virtuous and the other corrupt; and two sons of the elite, one conscientious and the other merely spoiled. The hero, of course, must be the poor but worthy young man for whom a college education means access to a noble profession and perhaps relief for a widowed mother. Initially the two poor boys are pals and rivals to the rich kids, who both seem snobs, but as the story unfolds the pal reveals his cynicism while one of the rich kids turns out not to be pampered and arrogant after all. As the worthy son of the working class proves that he belongs in college, the worthy son of the upper class proves that he accepts his position as a responsibility, not a privilege. Albie Booth meets Christy Flanagan.

Wallace wrote this quintessential 1930s story in "The Double Ride," serialized in the *Saturday Evening Post* in 1936, then published as the novel *Autumn Madness*. (Wallace's "The Odds against Honor," serialized in *Collier's* in 1935, then adapted by Hollywood as *The Big Game*, dealt with only the first pair of characters.) Working-class John Barton and Peck Fox are set against upper-class teammates, Taylor Lane and Carter Rossman, and the team in general is split between the "muscles" and the "cuties." With John's sister, Anne, involved with Taylor Lane and John himself with Lane's cousin Sally, a fraternity system ruled by the "cuties," and a big-time football program overseen by an aloof gentlemanly head coach and a tough-guy assistant, a dizzying array of plot complications are saturated in class-consciousness and conflict.

As in "The Odds against Honor" as well, the setting is not a state college but an elite university, this one named Colonial, where social class matters more. John and Anne Barton attend Colonial on a "double ride," scholarships for both in order to lure John to the school. John is courted yet scorned, as the campus community complains of imported "coal miners and bricklayers" and of "legitimate Colonial men forced to compete against a crowd of professionals for the honor of representing their school." Overhearing this derision, Anne Barton thinks in response, "No point in telling them . . . that these professionals were brought in because the legitimate students like themselves were too soft." Thus, Wallace seemingly sets up college football as the place where a vigorous but brutish working class usurps the role of an emasculated gentry through the agency of the athletic subsidy. Such turns out not to be the case, of course. John Barton's fellow "muscle man," Peck Fox, indeed proves himself corrupted, while Taylor Lane's fellow "cutie," Carter Rossman, is indeed soft and weak, but John and Taylor themselves meet as equals on the football field in the climactic big game. Earlier in the season the two demonstrated the distinctive styles and shortcomings of their social classes. The pampered son of a disappointed father, Lane plays with "dash" but is physically overpowered on a key play. Barton plays with brute force and fury, but in losing his temper he costs Colonial a victory. In the climactic game, however, Taylor replaces Peck and plays for the first time like a "muscle man," while Barton plays selflessly in the timeless manner of the gentleman. Despite serious injuries, the two team up to win the game in the closing seconds, then end up in beds in the same hospital room where the final reconciliations take place. The stunning moment in this final scene occurs when Sally's father offers John a job in his construction company. "Can you imagine an agitator telling this guy where to get off?" he says to Taylor's father. A story that begins with sympathy for bricklayers' sons taking advantage of the system ends with the former working-class brute about to join the plutocrats in controlling the workers.[23]

Stories such as "The Double Ride" (and "The Odds against Honor," too) raised class issues only to evade or ultimately deny them. In David Garth's "The Boy Who Sold Himself," a noble son of the working class is set against a foul-mouthed, dirty-playing, and decidedly ethnic teammate (Tony Mazzotti), both of them subsidized but only one of them corrupted. In George Brooks's "The Pie Slinger," the hero has no dark twin. He blocks for the glory boys and becomes an engineering honor student while working his way through college at the diner where the "rich men's sons" eat.[24] The pulp magazine *Sport Story* gave readers numerous stories and serials in the 1930s in which a working-class hero, usually contemptuous of spoiled college boys, becomes one of them as he learns sportsmanship and teamwork in a big-game victory.[25] Films such as *Touchdown, That's My Boy, The Band Plays On,* and *The Big Game* likewise featured working-class heroes who ascended the social ladder through the meritocratic college game. These stories and films were anti-elitist and sympathetic to the hard-working poor, but they were unwilling to face the hard issues raised by academically ill-prepared coal miners' sons on football scholarships at American colleges. Appeals to personal virtue ignored the realities of economic hardship which, in fact, motivated working-class young men to withstand the rigors of football, and made scholarships necessary. These stories offered no solution to the debates over subsidization in actual college football, but rather contributed to the confusion. Rules governing subsidization had to treat football players as a group; football stories viewed them only as individuals, some deserving, others not. The narratives of football thus neatly mirrored the larger cultural resistance to class analysis. In democratic, ultimately classless America, worth was measured only by performance and personal virtue. As David Garth put it in "Battling Sixteen," "Football and men are the same everywhere."

FOOTBALL AS WORK

As Reeve Vanneman and Lynn Weber Cannon have argued, status has substituted for class in the long tradition of "American exceptionalism": doctors and company presidents have higher social status than electricians and plumbers, but they supposedly do not belong to separate classes.[26] Football players occupy a particularly anomalous position in the status hierarchy, arising ultimately, perhaps, from their sport's uncertain position between work and play. The amateur code insisted that football was play—serious play, because it trained boys and young men for success in the adult world, but play nonetheless. Professionalism, however, from the hiring of coaches to the subsidizing of players, implicitly recast football as a form of work. Outright professional football players, of course, were paid workers, and this alone made them objectionable to the champions of amateurism. But even pro football's defenders downplayed the athletes' status as workers, incessantly claiming that playing-for-pay did not eliminate the collegiate sport's fundamental spirit that made football an uplifting game rather than grinding labor. At neither the collegiate nor the professional level was football understood to be fundamentally work. Casting coaches and players as fathers and sons on the one hand, and as managerial geniuses and the instruments of that genius on the other, only added to the confusion.

As we saw in Chapter 3, in the controversies over subsidization many sportswriters eventually came to recognize the players as producers of huge profits for universities but little or nothing for themselves. And from the insistence that football should be fun (and dismay over the claims of players such as George Owen in 1925 that it was not), to the eventual consensus that players should be properly subsidized, sportswriters and journalists regularly sympathized with the players. As noted in Chapter 4, on the other hand, for a variety of reasons many of these same writers implicitly endorsed coaches' absolute power over the players. Play requires freedom; work within the structure of the team entails submission to authority. Sportswriters' competing loyalties to players and coaches coexisted until conflicts arose, when they had to choose one side or the other. At the extreme, some sportswriters regarded players, including professionals, as essentially children whose best interests should be determined by their wiser elders; but even when Francis Wallace and others insisted on proper subsidization, they stopped short of viewing players explicitly as workers with rights.

In this climate of ambivalence and ambiguity, the Communist Party's *Daily Worker*, beginning in the Popular Front era, was virtually alone in consistently regarding football players as workers without hedging on the consequences. It is important to recognize that in taking that stance the *Worker* offered not a radical assault on the football establishment but an unswerving voice at the outer limits of mainstream sports journalism. That is, the *Daily Worker* at times sounds like Paul Gallico in the *Daily News* or Francis Wallace in his "Pigskin Previews" or Tim Cohane in *Look* in the 1950s, but the *Daily Worker* alone maintained this stance without equivocating and followed it through to its logical conclusions.

Informing the paper's coverage of football at all levels was a workers' viewpoint that located a proletarian element wherever it could be found. Among local colleges, the *Daily Worker* embraced CCNY more than Columbia, NYU, and Fordham. "The C.C.N.Y. gridders are an unusual outfit in these days of big business football," Ted Benson wrote in 1936. "Nearly all of them the sons of workers and members of working class families, none of them ever attended a classy prep school."[27] Among the national intercollegiate powerhouses the *Daily Worker*'s "home teams" at different times were the University of Minnesota, fondly termed "the huskies from the progressive campus of the Farmer-Labor state," and the "UCLA Proletarians."[28] And in the debates over "professionalism" and "purity," the *Daily Worker* saw only the underlying issue of workers' rights. "Professionalism," as Bill Newton noted in 1940, "often means decent treatment for the hard-working players—as long as the mortgage on the stadium has to be met. After that? Ah, 'purity.'" Against those critics who viewed the husky miner's son as the embodiment of colleges' hypocrisy, the columnists in the *Daily Worker* viewed him as a symbol of democracy, a working-class kid given a chance to go to college. Subsidized players were not corrupted amateurs but underpaid workers. At the end of the 1936 season, Ted Benson ridiculed the Carnegie Foundation for "hold[ing] up its collective palsied hands in horror at the thought that Joe Zilch, son of a miner, receives all of fifteen simoleons a week during the football season plus his room and some plain unfrilled chow." Players at Michigan were "going hungry because they were underpaid," Benson reported. His solution: a union. "Our suggestion is for the boys who tote the leather for dear old Alma Mammy to get wise to themselves and form the American Federation of Football Players and Substitutes under the banner of the C.I.O."[29]

The endorsement of the CIO was a clear signal of the paper's reconsideration of big-time football under the banner of the Popular Front. Over the following years, in response to a series of incidents that went nearly unreported in the mainstream press, the *Daily Worker* developed a consistent analysis of football as an institution that did not stand apart from economic and political life in the United States but was deeply embedded in it. In 1936, the *Worker* seems to have been alone, outside the black press, in covering a strike by football players at Howard University over inadequate equipment, medical treatment, and food. Supported by a one-day walk-out in which 85 percent of the student body participated, the players forced the cancellation of Howard's game against Virginia Union and the annual Thanksgiving Day classic against Lincoln. The *Daily Worker* sided entirely with the players.[30] In December 1937, the Associated Press reported that University of Michigan coach Harry Kipke had been fired, due to "alumni dissatisfaction" over the team's recent failure "to cope with Minnesota and Ohio State successfully." The *Daily Worker* reported Kipke's firing as well, but claimed a different cause. Three weeks earlier the *Worker* had informed its readers that Kipke was cooperating with "union-busting thugs" at a Ford plant near Ann Arbor, where several Michigan football players had summer jobs. The players, reportedly, were expected to spy on fellow employees, though "none of them exert themselves in the 'co-operating,' as they have a sense of fair play." (The *Worker* absolved players and blamed coaches as readily as the mainstream press did the opposite.) The *Worker* added that progressive students at the university were going to fight "to do away with this 'big business finger' in the state-supported school." When Kipke was fired the following month, while the wire services spoke of unhappy alumni and too many losses, the *Worker* (much less plausibly) credited the efforts of the progressive students.[31]

The same month that Kipke was fired, when players at the University of Pittsburgh voted not to accept an invitation to play in the Rose Bowl, the *Daily Worker* elaborated on the details found in the wire-service reports. As the situation at Pitt played out over the next two years, the *Worker* consistently sided with the players against an administration it saw as set on exploiting them. Under the headline, "Pitt Double Crosses Frosh Grid Stars on Subsidies," the *Worker* in November 1938 presented the students' side: that working at their jobs, "combined with the thoroughgoing practice schedule at Pitt, takes up all their time, and leaves them barely enough time for their studies." "Under the guise of 'purity'" the university was simply trying "to get rid of Sutherland or keep their football labor 'cheap.'" The following season, after Francis Wallace's two-part account appeared in the *Saturday Evening Post*, the *Daily Worker* gave Jock Sutherland a forum to respond. Neither a "Biff" nor a win-at-all-costs coach in the *Daily Worker*, Sutherland was the benevolent employer who recognized the worth of his workers. He had resigned, Sutherland explained, not in defense of athletics against academics, but in support of "the boys who are so vitally necessary" to the football program that the university claimed to want. What the public abhorred as "subsidization" Sutherland insisted was for the player "nothing more than a bona fide chance to help himself." Unmoved by Pitt's appeals to amateurism, the *Daily Worker* endorsed Sutherland's view.[32]

Jock Sutherland was undoubtedly not so high-minded as the *Daily Worker* portrayed him, but the *Worker*'s advocacy for the players was consistent for twenty years. In 1938, the paper reported on three more incidents: two players at Auburn quit the team after their demand for better pay was refused, the Board of Regents at the University of Nevada canceled the season after the football team asked for the resignation of the coaching staff, and a player at LSU was dropped from the team after "he dared to 'agitate for a union' of the players." Summing up these cases, the *Worker* welcomed "the developing awareness among football players which eventually will make the subsidy an honest and open inducement instead of a hypocritical and low paid device to snare star athletes." The *Worker* fully supported the players again in two incidents in the 1940s when they complained about lost holiday wages due to postseason bowl games. In 1940, the Stanford football team successfully lobbied for up to $50 each for playing in the Rose Bowl, but Arizona's players were rebuffed in 1948 when they demanded $175.[33]

The players received little sympathy in the mainstream press. When the two young men at Auburn quit in 1938, the *Birmingham News* and *Birmingham Post* offered only the coach's explanation: that one of the players quit because the coach accused him of "loafing" in the game against Rice, and the other, his roommate, quit out of sympathy. After the Stanford players demanded pay for the 1940 Rose Bowl, *Los Angeles Times* columnist Paul Zimmerman briefly alluded to the incident without taking sides.[34]

Unsurprisingly, the writers for the *Daily Worker* also declared their preference for professional football from the beginning of its revamped coverage in 1936,[35] but the paper also refused to acknowledge any absolute boundary between the pro and college games. Football in the *Daily Worker,* whether collegiate or professional, was a sport played by worker-athletes for the pleasure of worker-fans. As one consequence of this position, an unusual respect for the players as ordinary men ran consistently through the coverage, in contrast to both the hyping of heroes and the occasional debunking of dumb jocks in the mainstream press. Sports editor Lester Rodney, for example, pointedly objected to the slanders of football movies. "Either you see the pathetically feebleminded comic rah rah boy of the Oakie kind," Rodney complained after the release of Jack Oakie's *Rise and Shine* in 1941, "or you get an 'angle' which shows the whole game to be a sinister, crooked racket." A third plot—the halfback winning both the blond and the game with a touchdown in the last minute—was just as bad. Rodney proposed an alternative screenplay:

> Why not a picture about, let's say, a youngster from the Pennsylvania mining region, a good high school running guard who accepts the offer of a college to pay his tuition and expenses in return for playing ball on the team because he wants a college education and couldn't get it otherwise? A boy who takes the bumps and bruises of the almost year round practice sessions, takes on odd jobs around the campus in addition to studying and practicing so that he can send a little money home. He has a conflict. He doesn't get headlines and much glory, he doesn't get as much time to study as he'd like, he doesn't particularly care for some of the snobbery of the "old grad" bunch and those who look upon him as a hired hand. But then like all good players he really likes the game, likes the team camaraderie, in which boys of all types and derivations work together purposefully with high spirit, likes the learning and putting into practice of the subtleties of play, the development of himself and the team, the excitement of winning the big game, the appreciation of teammates, coaches,

real fans and opponents for his hard and skillfully done anonymous work up front on the line, where more games are won and lost than in the back-field.[36]

The *Daily Worker*'s own attempts at football fiction in its Sunday edition were notably inept—clumsy romances about football heroes won over to progressive politics by (ideologically) good women—but no worse than the strange anti-Red film, *Fighting Youth* (1935), whose none-too-bright hero is rescued from the scheming Reds by a good woman on the other side of the ideological divide.[37]

The *Daily Worker*'s socialist realism worked more effectively in Lester Rodney's columns. In stark contrast to later Marxist and neo-Marxist critiques, Rodney found football not corporate but cooperative, not inherently capitalist but socialist, "American" in an honorific, not pejorative, sense. Returning from the war in 1946 to resume his duties as sports editor, Rodney reaffirmed his enthusiasm for a "rough and tough but well devised and peculiarly American" game. He regretted that college football was "somewhat loused up by" by Chambers of Commerce and "alcoholic old grads," and by "the humiliation often visited upon the hard-playing working class boys" made to feel shabby for accepting scholarships. "But it's still a good game. Because it's PLAYED by the boys, not the bankrolls, and that means it's played hard and honestly and with high team spirit and amateur verve. Rough and bruising, it also happens to be a democratic game that above the Bilbo-Rankin line has little patience with those who would judge a man by the color of his skin or anything else but his ability to play good football. . . . That's college football. Professional football starts in technique where college football leaves off." Several days later, at his first pro game in five years, Rodney rediscovered why he preferred it to college football: "Especially, from the technical point of view as opposed to the rah rah college stuff, is professional football an enthralling spectacle. . . . *And* the players get a salary, which still could be a little more commensurate with the box office receipts, but still an honest salary without the subtle degradation of some colleges' subsidizations." [38] The work of pro football became a regular theme in the postwar years. Columns in 1947 described "the average working routine of the play for pay performer" and a typical day of "hard, detailed work, correction of error, and practice, endless practice." In 1948, as the "suicidal" consequences of the rivalry between the upstart All-America Football Conference and the NFL began to show up in attendance figures, the *Daily Worker* joined the mainstream press in calling for "some kind of regularization," but insisted that the new arrangement "need not (MUST not) result in any salary cuts."[39]

The *Daily Worker* spoke not from the radical fringe but from the most progressive position occasionally staked out in the mainstream press. Three incidents—a one-day strike by San Francisco '49er players in 1949 for playoff pay, the merger of the NFL and AAFC one week later, and the struggle by NFL players in 1956 and 1957 to win recognition for their union—place the *Worker*'s view that professional football players were workers with rights within the larger context of football journalism. On the eve of their playoff game against the Cleveland Browns in December 1949, the '49ers objected to a rule stipulating that players would receive no pay for conference playoff games but shares of the gate from the league championship. Their "strike" lasted less than a day, ending with the players' total capitulation, and it received surprisingly little comment, even in NFL cities, but it did jolt a few writers into revealing responses.[40] The *Daily Worker*, of course, supported the players unconditionally and welcomed "the overall growing union tide among professional athletes." While most of the mainstream sports columnists in New York and Chicago ignored the incident, Arthur Daley in the *New York Times* sided as completely with the owners and the league as the *Daily Worker* did with the players, praising '49er boss Tony Morabito for "the courage of his convictions" and AAFC commissioner O. O. Kessing for "adhering to principle."[41] In San Francisco, the *Examiner*'s acerbic Prescott Sullivan and the *Chronicle*'s Bill Leiser staked out rival views that they would continue to hold in the subsequent incidents. After the strike was announced, Sullivan facetiously declared himself disillusioned to discover that the '49ers played for financial gain rather than glory, and mockingly reported that "Owner Morabito" was "wracked with sobs" at the news of his players' rebellion, gulping, "Why—why they were like sons to me." More seriously, Morabito threatened reprisals, not "to let a bunch of irresponsible kids drive me out of the business." Sullivan viewed the players as professionals, not kids, and he noted that after playing three preseason games without pay (another policy imposed by the league), they now "were being required to make another gift of their services." The title of Bill Leiser's column in the *Chronicle*, "Pro Grid Owners Deserve a Break," could not have made its opposing viewpoint any clearer. It was the owners, in Leiser's view, who "gambled millions on the AAFC," while "the players risked nothing" and "gained heavily."[42]

Just one week later, the costly four-year war between the NFL and the All-America Football Conference finally ended, when Cleveland, San Francisco, and Baltimore were accepted into the NFL, and the rest of the AAFC's players

FIGURE 7-3. This is a typical sports page of the *Daily Worker* (from 17 November 1948), with Lester Rodney's column, a story on the possibility of a merger between the NFL and the AAFC, and Rodney's editorial note insisting that player salaries be protected in any such merger.

were disbursed among NFL clubs. Aside from the disbanded AAFC teams that had been losing great sums of money anyway, the clear losers in the merger were the players, who no longer would benefit from the bidding war for their services. After top players had earned between $3,000 and $6,000 in the 1930s, the four-year rivalry of the AAFC had driven the average NFL salary up to $8,000 by 1949, with top stars earning $25,000.[43] The merger was far more momentous than the '49ers brief strike, and it provoked considerably more comment. Everyone agreed that the interleague war had been foolish, but attitudes varied on the consequences of the peace. In the *New York Times,* Arthur Daley took his customary stand with the owners, noting that the players "no longer will be able to command astronomical and out-of-proportion salaries," and Bill Corum in the *Journal-American* also took a mildly pro-owner view. Joe Williams in the *World-Telegram* and Dan Parker in the *Daily Mirror,* on the other hand, mourned the damage to players. "Pro footballers were shamelessly under-salaried before the challengers came along," Williams wrote. "They've been crazily overpaid ever since and my philosophy in this respect happens to be that the hired hands are worth all they can get." Parker sadly announced that the "bull market for players and customers is now over. With no competition, the magnates can resume their sly tricks with tickets and will get together as soon as possible to lower the ceiling on players' salaries. It was a foolish war while it lasted but for years it gave the fans and the players a break they won't get again for a long time to come."[44] Columnists in Chicago, San Francisco, and Los Angeles staked out positions similar to either Daley's or Parker's, with Prescott Sullivan and Bill Leiser in San Francisco again standing poles apart, most of the writers taking the side of the owners.[45]

Joe Williams, Jimmy Powers, and Prescott Sullivan in varying degrees joined Dan Parker in thinking about professional football players as "hired hands" deserving whatever they could get, but while no columnist echoed Tony Morabito in calling professional football players "irresponsible kids," many of them seemed to believe in, or long for, benevolent paternalism as the proper way to run pro football. The men who owned football teams were, in fact, throwbacks to the paternalistic mill and factory owners of the nineteenth century, long since displaced by corporate ownership with its very different labor relations.[46] The continuing acceptance of paternalism in professional football must have owed something to the cultural construction of coaches as father figures. Owners, too, were sometimes cast as kindly fathers, as in a few of William Fay's stories of pro football bums and in Edward Prell's history of "Papa Bear" George Halas and his club.[47] Whether dispelling the illusion of benevolent paternalism or challenging patriarchal authority, players' demands for their rights as workers cast their relations with owners on altogether different terms.

In December 1956, NFL players first attempted to form a union. They were refused recognition in early February 1957, then won commissioner Bert Bell's approval the following December (Bell, worried about pending antitrust legislation, forced the union on the owners). Once again, sports columnists on the NFL beat were apparently reluctant to recognize the players as working professionals: this decisive event in pro football's labor relations received surprisingly little attention. Arthur Daley was conspicuously silent, as were most of the columnists in the discussion. With the exception of the *San Francisco Chronicle*'s Bill Leiser, those who did speak out were pro-union, but one wonders if the silent majority was uncomfortable with the idea of unionized football players. After the owners refused to recognize the union in early February, Leiser and Prescott Sullivan took characteristically opposing views on the legal question. Leiser thought the NFL likely to win congressional exemption, like major league baseball, from the Taft-Hartley law against monopolies; Sullivan declared the owners "pop-headed" for thinking they could continue to violate antitrust law. Joe Williams took his customary stand with the players, as did Dan Parker even more vehemently. Parker was appalled by the union leadership's agreeing to maintain the college draft, which made players "the exclusive property of the drafting team" in clear defiance of the U.S. Constitution.[48] Commissioner Bert Bell's recognition of the union in December was reported everywhere via wire service but with almost no comment. The *Daily Worker*'s Lester Rodney, of course, welcomed the union but mourned that it had won only minimal benefits for the highly skilled professionals of the NFL. Outlining the terms of the first contract—a minimum salary of $5,000, preseason pay of $50 a game (an increase from zero), and an injury clause that for the first time guaranteed medical treatment and the player's salary if the injury was reported within thirty-six hours—Rodney dryly noted: "What a commentary on past practices that this elementary obligation must be spelled out."[49]

The silence of so many columnists throughout this struggle for a union reveals either blindness to the most momentous change in professional football (next to integration and television), or profound uneasiness over the idea of football players as unionized workers. Vanneman and Cannon can help us recognize football players' anomalous status that perhaps lay behind this uneasiness. In distinguishing class divisions from status hierarchies, they point to the importance of power, as opposed to prestige, identifying three elements that separate the middle class from the working class: owner-ship of productive property, supervisory authority, and mental labor.[50] Foot-ball players enjoyed enormous prestige, but coaches and owners held all three kinds of power. Players' attempt to claim some of that power for them-selves threatened to disrupt a long-standing order.

While the *Daily Worker* consistently sided with the players in what it openly regarded as class conflict, class feelings erupted only intermittently in the mainstream media; but when conflicts arose between players and coaches, or players and management, sportswriters were forced to take sides in what suddenly seemed uncomfortably like class warfare. The columnists in NFL cities were the hard-headed realists of the profession. If they were reluc-tant to recognize football players as skilled workers with rights, sportswriters in college towns, where most of the players were not old enough to vote, could not come close to such a perspective. As noted in Chapter 4, rebellious Nebraska players after the 1953 season received no support from Gregg McBride and his colleagues at the *Omaha World-Herald,* and the *Portland Ore-gonian*'s L. H. Gregory responded in a similar manner to the firing of Uni-versity of Washington coach John Cherberg in 1956 following complaints by players.[51] Neither college nor professional football players were traditional workers, but nor were they traditional amateurs (nor typical entertainers, for that matter). Fans grew comfortable with the confusion and uncertainty about their status, granting the players a certain privileged powerlessness, until a new crisis in college football or a labor dispute in the NFL forced them to confront the ambiguity. The longing for benevolent paternalism that often emerged on these occasions would haunt both the black rebel-lions in college football in the 1960s and the NFL's labor troubles when they returned in the 1970s.

Ethnicity

Class and ethnicity were linked. Not all working-class football players were new immigrants, but new-immigrant football players in the 1920s and 1930s were overwhelmingly from the working classes. The second-generation Jews, Italians, and Poles who became football stars came from the tenements rather than the mansions of New York, from the mines and mills rather than the office suites of western Pennsylvania and Ohio. The ethnic transformation of college football raised its own set of issues, however. Most important, it contributed to the redefinition of "whiteness."

In 1922, a nationally prominent physical educator at the University of Michigan described "Racial Traits in Athletics" in a series of three issues for the *American Physical Education Review*. Drawing on his own experience as a coach and what had been reported to him by others, Elmer Mitchell classified the sporting behaviors of "races" such as the Negro, the Oriental, and the Indian, but also the American, the English, the Polish, and the Jewish—no fewer than fifteen different "racial" groups. Outwardly dispassionate and fair, Mitchell's analysis arrived at unsurprising conclusions, given the temper of the times. The disciplined northern European races such as the German and Scandinavian produced better athletes than the emotional southern Europeans and the Slavs, but not as good as the English; and by incorporating the superior traits of many races (though none of the deficiencies), American athletes were superior to all.[1]

Mitchell's specificity is startling today. The Irishman, for example, had an aptitude for individual sports but was deficient in team play, "owing to his weakness in self-discipline, coupled with the lack of steadfastness that has not been given the Celtic peoples by nature." Notre Dame football in 1922 was not yet an unavoidable phenomenon in American sport, but Mitchell cited the "well-known strength of Notre Dame, Holy Cross, and other Irish denominational schools in baseball" as an illustration of the Irishman's "fighting spirit" but also his failings in teamwork, discipline, and steadfastness. The new immigrants who were arousing the deepest anxieties at the moment fared less well in Mitchell's racial taxonomy. Like other Latins such as the French and the Spanish, the Italian was "better fitted for games of quickness, dexterity, and skill, rather than of rugged strength." He lacked self-discipline and was "too fiery and impulsive of feeling" for contact sports. Compared to American athletes, Italians' "tendency to the extreme of elation, or to the opposite extreme of despondency," made them "fearless, daring, and reckless" but also "more easily stampeded into a rout if beaten." In stark contrast, as a cross between a Slav and a German, the Poles were "eager, attentive, and grateful learners," and thus "very good at team work," but they lacked initiative and were "too dependent upon a rigid leadership." As for Jews, they demonstrated remarkable "racial vitality," despite lacking "the physical strength of other races." The same traits the Jew showed in business and urban strife he demonstrated on athletic fields: "his subtlety in applying social or individual weakness to his own benefit," "his lack of moral sensitiveness," and his "strong self-assertiveness and love of display." In short: the pushy Jew. His "tendency to favor a sport because of its opportunity to disport before the public" led him to professional ones such as boxing "rather than the game which is played solely for the joy of participating." In other words: the showy Jew. And finally, Jews were "quick thinkers, alert to grasp the strategy of the game, both of their own teams and of their opponents." The clever Jew.[2]

Mitchell offered similar portraits of other "races," with the Russian faring worst of all, a Big Red scare in the world of sport. To a reader today, the sources of Mitchell's "scientific" analysis appear obvious: popular literary and theatrical stereotypes, the current arrangement of dominant and subject nations, the political and social interests of the United States at the moment. Football and other sports simply provided a stage onto which prejudices could be projected. Mitchell attributed these athletic traits to both nature and nurture. The Irish, for example, were "Celtic by heredity, and Saxon by environment," while Poles were "Slavic by blood, but German by environment." Used in this manner, "environment" simply meant the influence of a different heredity: biological Saxons and Germans created the environments that helped shape the behavior of biological Irishmen and Poles. Mitchell concluded that environment, as he conceived it, was ultimately "a more potent factor than heredity in the playing of athletic games." While heredity determined "the capacity or bent for certain types of exercise" and "the emotional reaction to them," environment governed "the extent of opportunity, and hereditary instincts seem to be modified to a large extent by this."[3]

Here lay the fundamental basis of Americans' athletic superiority, more so than their melding of races. The social environments of other countries led "decadent nations" (Spain and Italy, say) to enjoy bullfights, cockfighting, and professional wrestling, while autocratic nations (such as Germany) were drawn to "disciplined, machinelike, and systematic gymnastics." Democratic nations, in contrast to both, preferred amateur team sports. "All through history, democracy has been accompanied by an interest in amateur sports," Mitchell claimed, pointing to Greece in its Golden Age and Rome in its Republican period (misled by the era's self-serving British histories of Greek sport that ignored its thorough professionalism). For all their supposed amateur purity, however, the Greeks and Romans did not have real democracy and so lacked team play. "Team games and democracy are inseparable," Mitchell explained, "the one goes with the other as a training for free citizenship." Football and baseball were thus quintessentially democratic and American.[4]

FROM "RACE" TO "ETHNICITY"

We can take Mitchell's series of articles as a rough index to the climate within which Jewish-, Polish-, Italian-, and other hyphenated American athletes took to football fields in the 1920s. Although Mitchell's articles appeared in a publication for specialists in physical education, his analysis represented a more sweeping viewpoint. Mitchell's bibliography included works such as Joseph Deniker's *The Races of Man* and Daniel Brinton's *Races and Peoples,* and titles such as "Inferior and Superior Races" (*North American Review*), "Anglo-Saxon Stock" (*Review of Reviews*), "Teuton vs. Slav" (*Independent*), "Emotional Races" (*Nation*), "The Italian Temperament" (*Fortnightly Review*), and "The Russian Character" (*Fortnightly Review*)—in other words, a rich sampling of the current thinking about "race" and nationality in some of the most influential intellectual journals. Mitchell saw on playing fields what he had been reading by "experts" on "race."

The tremendous growth of football in the 1920s came at the end of the great migration of Europeans to the New World. Beginning in the 1890s, a renewed anti-Catholic, anti-radical, Anglo-Saxon nativism had arisen, in response to the waves of immigrants who now tended to come not from the British Isles, Scandinavia, and Germany, but from darker, less "Nordic" nations in southern and eastern Europe. The manifestations of this prejudice ranged from the racist jeremiads of Madison Grant and Lothrop Stoddard to A. Mitchell Palmer's raids on foreign-born anarchists and communists following the Great War, the rebirth of the Ku Klux Klan in 1915 and its dramatic expansion from 1920 to 1924, and ultimately—as the expressed will of the old-stock American establishment—severely restrictive immigration laws.[5] In 1917, Congress established a literacy test for entrance into the country. In 1921, it established the first quotas: immigration limited to 3 percent of each group's representation in the 1910 census. Finally, in 1924, Congress passed the National Origins Act—alternately known as the Johnson-Reed Act or Immigration Act or Immigration Restriction Act—reducing the quota to 2 percent and tying it to the census of 1890, when there were few immigrants from southern and eastern Europe. The annual Polish quota, for example, dropped from 31,000 to 6,000; the Italian from 42,000 to 4,000; the Greek from 3,000 to 100.[6]

The National Origins Act curtailed the influx of the "Alpine" and "Mediterranean" "races." Madison Grant's *Passing of the Great Race,* first published in 1916 and reissued in 1918 and throughout the 1920s, popularized the idea (derived from Joseph Deniker and William Ripley) that Europeans comprised three races: the Nordic, the Alpine, and the Mediterranean, in descending order of development and desirability as immigrants. Both the original colonists and the immigrants who came to the United States over its first century as a nation were overwhelmingly "Nordic." (Celts from Ireland initially were despised as inferior to Anglo-Saxons, but their political and economic successes eventually won them standing as quasi-Nordics.) By the end of the nineteenth century a dramatic shift in immigration patterns was taking place. Between 1899 and 1924, 3.8 million Italians, 1.8 million Jews, nearly 1.5 million Poles, and hundreds of thousands of Hungarians, Greeks, Bohemians, Slovaks, and others from the same part of the world came to the United States for a piece of American prosperity.[7] Many viewed these "hordes" of "Alpines" and "Mediterraneans" as a threat to the traditional American gene pool.

Not just Nordics, Alpines, and Mediterraneans, but also Germans, Irish, Italians, Poles, Greeks, Lithuanians, and Jews were separate "races" in the terminology of the times. A congressional commission in 1911 identified forty-five distinct "races or peoples," thirty-six of them from Europe, each with its characteristic temperaments and traits. A "Racial Adaptability" chart used by some employers in the 1920s profiled thirty-six races.[8] With "race" understood as virtually equivalent to nationality, the "Italian race" referred to the customs and manners, as much as the physical characteristics, of the people who were born and lived in Italy and Sicily. In a crucial turn for the relationship of the old-stock American majority to its new immigrant minorities, by classifying the peoples of northern, central, and southern Europe as Nordics, Alpines, and Mediterraneans, Madison Grant and his followers recast this cultural and geographical sense of "race" into narrowly biological terms. It became widely believed that the old immigrants, including the Germans and Irish who came in great numbers in the 1840s and 1850s, easily assimilated their new American culture because they shared a common racial stock. The new immigrants from Italy, Galicia, Hungary, Bohemia, Greece, and Russia, on the other hand, would remain alien, unassimilated, because they were not just culturally or socially but biologically different.

The triumph of revitalized nativism marks the immediate background for the ethnic transformation of college football in the 1920s, a dramatic development that received remarkably little comment. In general, sportswriters and journalists in all media ignored the "race" of football players in the 1920s, increasingly mentioned their ancestry over the 1930s but without elaboration, then after World War II routinely celebrated football's ethnic mix as proof and symbol of the glorious American melting pot. Two distinct but related processes were at work here: the "Americanization" of these immigrant groups and the transformation of different "races" into "ethnic" Americans. When the new immigrants were viewed as alien "races," their presence in football lineups would have seemed an invasion of the unwanted, had football not been regarded as a potent force for Americanization. But belief in the Americanizing power of football depended on viewing these new immigrants as assimilable, as ethnic groups rather than racial outsiders.

For the immigrants themselves, sports had been a powerful agent of Americanization for decades before they embraced football. In his classic study, *The Uprooted*, Oscar Handlin wrote that, after 1880, "Increasingly the thoughts of the children were preoccupied with the events of the world of sport within which were played out the vivid dramas of American success and failure." Handlin noted that gangs and professional sport offered the shortest two roads to status and success in the strange new land; sport did not pay as well, but it had the advantage of being legitimate. Sport historians who have dealt with the immigrant experience have elaborated on Handlin's claim. Whereas early immigrant groups such as the Germans and Irish brought their own sporting traditions to the New World, the newcomers typically did not. First-generation new immigrants were generally antagonistic to sport, viewing it as a waste of time, but their offspring embraced athletics as a key part of their new American culture and identity. Sport meant one of two things within immigrant communities: the neighborhood and local sports clubs—Czech sokols, Polish falcons, neighborhood bowling leagues, parish baseball or basketball teams—that both preserved ethnic identities and fostered assimilation into mainstream American culture, and the school and professional sports that meant distinctly American success and more thorough absorption into the mainstream. To play football, whether at the local high school or on a college or professional team, was to be thoroughly American.[9]

Football was not part of an open campaign by the guardians of the nation to Americanize the immigrants, nor by the immigrants to be Americanized. Polish and Italian youths were simply drawn to football in high school as a vehicle for achieving status. College coaches grabbed them not as aliens to be Americanized but as rugged and hungry football players. Seeing them succeed, their communities celebrated such achievements highly prized in their new country, and more youngsters saw an opportunity to make it in America by following this example. Through this more "natural" process football contributed to the new immigrants' acculturation over time far more powerfully than such concerted efforts as the Americanization movement during the First World War.[10]

Football had been racially marked by its elite beginnings. In the late nineteenth century, several of the leading spokesmen for the new racial thinking—Henry Cabot Lodge, Nathaniel S. Shaler, Francis A. Walker—had also been outspoken champions of the new sport of intercollegiate football. These men, along with sportswriters such as Caspar Whitney who shared their views, embraced football as an expression of the Anglo-Saxon racial character.[11] Over the game's formative years, up to the First World War, the idea that football expressed some unique Anglo-Saxon genius clung to it as it spread throughout the country, along with a competing idea, however, that football was fundamentally democratic. Those outside the Anglo-Saxon world could thus prove that they merited its respect, if not inclusion, by playing football according to the highest standards. The football teams of the Indian vocational school at Carlisle, Pennsylvania, from the 1890s to the First World War most conspicuously represented this possibility. As Notre Dame and the state universities in the Midwest subsequently challenged eastern football supremacy, and as the game consequently became more fully democratized, its increasingly non-Anglo-Saxon cast of players more openly challenged the belief in football's Anglo-Saxon character. A writer in the *American Hebrew* cast this development in explicitly racial terms in 1929. The conspicuous success of Jews in football, wrote Franklin Gordon, has led Americans "to wonder whether the predilection for sports as a particularly Anglo-Saxon trait was, after all, confined only to Anglo-Saxons."[12]

Americanization of new immigrants meant, in part, the loss of their distinctive "racial" identities. Changing responses to football in the 1930s confirm Matthew Frye Jacobson's analysis of the shift from race (biologically defined) to ethnicity (culturally defined) in American thinking about European immigrant groups.[13] After 1924, as anxieties about inassimilable "racial" aliens receded, acceptance of "ethnic" Italian and Jewish and Polish football players became easier. Prejudice by no means disappeared completely—the anti-immigrant editorials of George Horace Lorimer in the *Saturday Evening Post* in the 1930s confirm its persistence[14]—but the football prowess of Bronko Nagurski, Frank Carideo, Alex Wojciechowicz, and hundreds of others became a potent force in naturalizing the new immigrants in the public consciousness. The performances of powerful Italians like Joe Savoldi and sturdy Jewish linemen like Fred Sington belied the earlier generation's racial stereotypes. As the media in the 1930s belatedly acknowledged what had been happening in the world of football, the dominant story became not an invasion of alien races but a collision of cultures between Old World parents and their football-playing New World sons.

FOOTBALL AND "AMERICANIZATION"

In an article in *Harper's* in 1928, John R. Tunis quoted a publicity release from the football program at the University of Minnesota: "Returning letterman are Nagurski, Kabel, Hovde, Lekeseles, Brookmeier, Westphal, Pulbrabek, and Teeter. Emlein and Ukkelberg will supplant Apman and Angevik; and Norgaard and Burquist will provide promising material to guard the flanks." Tunis was concerned here with the overheated publicity machines run by supposed educational institutions, but the racial or ethnic makeup of the team was certainly conspicuous. Readers could have sorted out the mix of "old" and "new" immigrant stocks only by lingering over the list of names, but the general foreignness of Minnesota's lineup, in the absence of Smiths or Johnsons or Adamses, would have struck readers immediately. And Tunis promptly added, "No, this is not, as you might imagine, a list of future citizens of these United States who have passed or are about to pass the rigid requirements of the Quota; but simply a sample of up-to-date football publicity sent out last summer by one of our large Middle Western state universities."[15]

Tunis's mild joke about the Quota might seem to suggest that football lineups made up of immigrants' sons were uncontroversial by 1928, but certainly this was not the case everywhere. The national media in the 1920s largely ignored the "racial" transformation of college football, most likely for fear of offending some part of the audience, but newspapers were less constrained in speaking for their own local communities. References to Notre Dame teams in the 1920s, for example, sometimes betrayed how alien they appeared in some parts of the country. Dick Hawkins's reference in the *Atlanta Constitution* to the "1927 edition of Rockne's Irish, Swedes and Poles" was not openly derogatory, yet it implied an invasion of foreigners, not just a rival football team, when Notre Dame came to town. The "Fighting Irish" nickname itself, which in the 1920s gradually supplanted "Nomads" and "Ramblers"—both signifying nothing more than the cross-country schedules that made Rockne's teams unique—was initially resisted by the Notre Dame administration as a racial slur, until it became clear that the teams' continuing excellence had made the name honorific. Newspapers regularly called Notre Dame teams "the Catholics," or even "Papists," "Horrible Hibernians," "Dumb Micks," or "Dirty Irish." Nebraska students' halftime skit in 1925 depicting Notre Dame students as hod-carriers, and a headline in the *Dallas Morning News* in 1928—"Lumpkin, Former Leopard Ace, Stars as Georgia Tech Beats Micks"—suggest why school officials were defensive about "Fighting Irish." As late as 1931, following a loss to Southern Cal, a West Coast sportswriter attributed USC's victory to the superiority of its "native American stock" over Notre Dame's multi-ethnic mix.[16]

Fierce partisanship from both sides attended Notre Dame's games. If Rockne's teams aroused anti-immigrant and anti-Catholic feelings in places such as Lincoln, Nebraska, when they came to New York for their annual struggle with Army in Yankee Stadium, they were overwhelmed by admirers among the immigrant groups represented by the team. While school authorities were being inundated by requests for tickets, Army officials grew increasingly disgruntled over the home-team support Notre Dame received in Army's own backyard. With an Irishman (Jimmy Walker) and later an Italian (Fiorella LaGuardia) as mayor, and its teeming ethnic and Catholic neighborhoods, New York indeed offered Notre Dame a home away from home, and the Notre Dame–Army game rivaled the World Series as an athletic event (with the Fordham–St. Mary's game next in importance). Obtaining tickets might require political or university connections, but hundreds of thousands of "subway alumni" could follow their beloved Fighting Irish through the abundant coverage in the local newspapers.[17]

The comment in 1931 about USC's superior "native American stock" prompted a response from Notre Dame president Charles O'Donnell at the team's postseason banquet in South Bend. With its players' names invoking the legacy of Lafayette, Kosciuszko, and Von Stueben, declared Father O'Donnell, Notre Dame was "an American university in the full and the best sense of the term," and Notre Dame football was "an American game" played by Americans.[18] This was the bedrock claim that underlay the football coverage throughout the immigrant press as well. The most despised immigrant groups, Italians and Jews, had potentially the most to gain from success in football. For Italians, Notre Dame's Joe Savoldi and Frank Carideo, along with Macaluso, Siano, Brovelli, Dell' Isola, Maniaci, Daddio, Bottari, Principe, and dozens more throughout the 1930s proved the triumphant Americanism of a people smarting from the stereotypes of Sicilian gangsters. It was in this spirit that John Billi in *Il Progresso Italo-Americano* declared that the Italian stars at Notre Dame, Fordham, and other eastern colleges in 1930 were "the sturdy descendants of those formidable Legionaires who carried the Roman Eagle to the ends of the world."[19]

Italian war heroes and Jewish athletes became figures in that ethnic joke about the world's shortest books, but contrary to the joke, Jews were a major presence in football as well as other sports in the interwar period. Unlike the German Jews who preceded them, the 2 million Eastern European Jews who arrived between 1882 and 1914 brought no sporting traditions from the Old World. Against the resistance of their elders, the second generation of Russian, Polish, Galician, and Rumanian Jews embraced American sports both as an escape from poverty and as an emblem of Americanization, attracted primarily to sports that paid off in jobs, in a college education, and in local fame.[20] Jews dominated prizefighting for a time in the 1920s, succeeding the Irish and preceding the Italians, and their preeminence in basketball in the 1930s and 1940s was nearly unchallenged. Jews did not have a comparable impact on football, but Benny Friedman, Sid Luckman, Marshall Goldberg, and hundreds of lesser figures in the 1920s and 1930s gave Jews an honored place in the sport.

Jewish football stars conspicuously challenged specific racial stereotypes dating in some cases from the Middle Ages. In addition to the greedy Shylock, the Jew in the American imagination in the 1920s was pushy, vulgar, ostentatious, and physically weak. One Anglo-Saxon alarmist in 1914 expressed a common view when he characterized Jewish immigrants as "the polar opposite of our pioneer breed. Not only are they undersized and weak-muscled, but they shun bodily activity and are extremely sensitive to pain."[21] Who could better counter such stereotypes than a rugged, modest, team-oriented but also individually brilliant football star? As historian Steven Riess has summed up football's power, "Jewish participation in college athletics, especially football, the most important college sport, generated community pride, demonstrated that they were not too scholarly or unfit, and provided them with an opportunity to gain greater acceptance in the broader society." Jews began playing college football from its beginnings in the 1870s, and the 1920s opened with Arnold Horween elected as Harvard's first Jewish captain, but the first football star to be fully lionized in the Jewish press was Benny Friedman. The son of a Russian-immigrant tailor, Friedman was the University of Michigan's All-American quarterback in 1926 and later the first great passer in the National Football League. Friedman was followed a few years later, first at Michigan and then in the NFL, by Harry Newman; then, in 1936–38, Columbia's Sid Luckman and Pittsburgh's Marshall Goldberg (the "Hebrew Hillbilly" from West Virginia) presided over a brief golden era of Jewish football. In 1936, twenty-five Jewish Americans, almost a quarter of the 111 who would play in the National Football League before 1950, were on the rosters of NFL clubs.[22]

The columns of the *American Hebrew* are particularly revealing of what football could mean to Jews anxious to dispel derogatory stereotypes and prove their capacity to be fully Americanized citizens. Against the "pushy" Jew the *American Hebrew* offered Semitic Frank Merriwells: Benny Friedman in 1925 (who never gave himself the ball when the team was in scoring position, and who kept a scrapbook "for his own satisfaction and not for display") and Wisconsin's Sammy Behr in 1928 (known for his "reserved demeanor and modesty"). Notoriously cocky Harry Newman less easily fit into this mold, but columnist Henry Levy insisted that the Michigan quarterback was "misunderstood" and was, in fact, "a 'good egg,' a thoroughly likable and genial pal"—language right out of the Merriwell tradition. Against the cowardly Jew the *American Hebrew* offered not individual stars but the hundreds of football-playing Jews en masse. In either the special "Who's Who" issue or the "College Number," both published each December, the *American Hebrew* gave readers long lists of Jewish football players throughout the nation's colleges. "The evidence of the past few years," wrote Franklin Gordon in 1929, "seems to give the lie to those who had been accustomed to shout . . . that Jews were 'yellow' and could not 'stand the gaff' of the punishment involved in a season's play of football." Levy estimated that season that "at least five hundred Jewish youths served their respective alma maters this fall on the gridiron," the same number he claimed in 1938. "Year after year," Levy wrote in 1931, "it becomes more difficult to comprehensively survey the Jewish intercollegiate sport scene." While every Jewish football player rebutted the stereotype of physical deficiency, for a "people of the book" the other extreme would have been equally troubling. Benny Friedman's "football brain," Albert Cornsweet's Rhodes Scholarship in 1928, Sammy Behr's standing as "an excellent student" the same year—all these examples pointed to the special importance of the scholar-athlete ideal for assimilationist Jews.[23]

Modesty, selflessness, and the mix of brawn and brain were aspects of the larger cultural ideal that had been attached to football since the game's beginnings. The *American Hebrew* claimed no unique Jewish contribution to American football but rather the exemplary Americanization of Jews who played the game. At a time when elite American universities were establishing quotas on Jewish admissions, the *American Hebrew* also saw in college football hopeful signs "of equality, of assimilation, and of tolerance." Peter Levine reminds us of the discrimination and prejudice Jewish athletes experienced on college campuses, but he also notes that the athletic field was the place where Jews were treated most fairly. The *American Hebrew* called particular attention to Jewish football captains—Friedman at Michigan in 1926, Cornsweet at Brown and five others in 1928, "a liberal sprinkling of captaincies" in 1932—because even more than All-Americans, who were selected primarily for their prowess, captains signified the respect and acceptance of teammates.[24]

Poles were not subjected to the specific stereotyping inflicted on Jews and Italians; in the words of John Higham they were just "foreigners par excellence: uncivilized, unruly, and dangerous."[25] A Polish American, Stanley Tomoszewski, played at Boston College as early as 1893, but it was not until the late 1920s that Poles became a conspicuous presence in big-time college football.[26] Their foreignness was most conspicuous in their tongue-twisting names, a major obstacle to radio broadcasters and a periodic joke to mainstream sportswriters.[27] In 1933, for his *New Yorker* story "University Days," when James Thurber wished to poke fun at the collision between athletics and academics in higher education, he fished a very Polish-sounding name from the immigrant melting pot, Boley Bolenciecwcz. Initially, the Polish press was bitterly defensive about such mockery. In 1929, a King Features Syndicate cartoon titled "Try and Pronounce 'Em!" poked fun at "gridiron jawbreakers" such as Pieculewicz, Hojnacki, Truskowski, Uansa, Lubratowicz, and Oosterbaan. A columnist in *Dziennik Zjednoczenia* in Chicago angrily responded that "if names like Truskowski or Hojnacki are such jaw breakers for the 'Angles,' howinell's an average fellow, not an Anglo-Saxon, going to pronounce names like Hughes, Kavanaugh, McGillicuddy, Marlborough, McGeorghean, Keough, etc. etc. . . ?"[28]

As this outburst makes clear, even in the absence of commentary in the mainstream media, the names of football players were potent in themselves. With or without comment by sportswriters, the sibilant or multisyllabic, consonant-rich names of a lineup at Notre Dame or Minnesota or Pitt declared an unmistakable transformation in college football. For the immigrant groups, the presence of those names in the nation's newspapers and on the airwaves was itself evidence of achievement, with the result that there was something important at stake in claiming those names. Columns in the immigrant press in the early 1930s often wrestled with such questions as whether Notre Dame's Vic Wojciechowski was a Pole or a Rumanian, or whether the team's running back, Marty Brill, was a Jew. Both Italian and Polish papers claimed Fordham's Tony Siano as one of their own in 1930.[29] Anglicized names posed particular challenges. Readers of the Italian press had to be reminded that Columbia coach Lou Little was born Luigi Piccolo. Northwestern's Steve Toth (Tóth István) was the Magyar football star of the mid-1930s, Andy Pilney (Pilneyho) the Bohemian hero of Notre Dame's victory over Ohio State in 1935, Charley Klem (Klemaszewski) another Polish star for Creighton in 1935 — but only because sportswriters in the immigrant press uncovered their ancestry.

In the most protracted case of ethnic misidentification, the Polish press lost Bronko Nagurski after years of celebrating him as its brightest star. An All-American at the University of Minnesota at both tackle and fullback before going on to professional careers in football and wrestling, Nagurski was a figure out of football folklore. In an oft-repeated story, Minnesota coach Doc Spears had found Bronko on a recruiting trip in rural Minnesota, when Spears asked a strapping young farmer for directions to a nearby town. When the lad pointed southward—with his plow—the coach knew he had a prospect. Nagurski in this tale was a husky northwoods farm boy; for the Polish press, he was emphatically a Polish American football star, the greatest of them all. In 1935, however, after several years recounting every Nagurski triumph on the football field (and the wrestling mat), the sports editor of *Nowy Swiat,* Henry Archacki, reported receiving a letter stating that Nagurski was not Polish at all, but Bohemian. Two years later, John T. Czech finally got it right: Nagurski was Ukrainian.[30] His loss was mourned, but such concessions no longer hurt as they once would have. By 1936, *Dziennik Polski* could joke about sportswriters calling Alex Wojciechowicz, Fordham's All-American center, the "thirty-letter man" (for the number of letters in Alexander Franklin Wojciechowicz); and in 1938 *Nowy Swiat* could suggest that a Slav-laden All-American team, selected by the Typographical Union "on the basis of the amount of typesetting" required, "should draw a smile from the Polish sports fans."[31]

By the late 1930s and early 1940s, Polish football stars had become so numerous that an air of retrospective complacency settled over the Polish press. Reviewing the history of Polish American football in a series of articles in *Nowy Swiat* in 1942, Henry Archacki reminded readers that both Knute Rockne and former Fordham coach Frank Cavanaugh had declared years ago that Poles were the greatest football players, and the achievements of Ed Danowski, Alex Wojciechowicz, Bill Osmanski, and dozens of others had seemingly borne out their claims.[32] Archacki offered his readers a full-blown myth of Polish athletic superiority, coupled with American patriotism. Archacki wondered how the typical Polish parents, "a small rotund mother and a medium-sized mustached father," could produce the "wiry long-sinewed young man weighing anywhere between 175 to 220 pounds," who starred on so many college and professional teams:

> To find the answer, we must dig back further than just one generation. Centuries of toil amidst Poland's rolling fields, where the average peasant gripped with one hand the handle of a plowshare and with the other on a gun in defense of that very land have developed a medium-sized race of men who inch for inch and pound for pound outrival any other race. Migrating to America the sturdy Pole found an unheard of liberty and his off-spring grew up unfettered and untrammeled. It was like planting a hardy perennial in fertile soil. The results were amazing. The girls turned out to be good-looking sensible lassies and the boys—the answers to every football coach's prayer![33]

Archacki could have been describing Thomas Jefferson's ideal hardy yeoman rather than a transplanted eastern European. A few years earlier, Archacki mused about the "singular" achievements of Ed Danowski for Fordham and the New York Giants "that typifies the Polish character." Da-

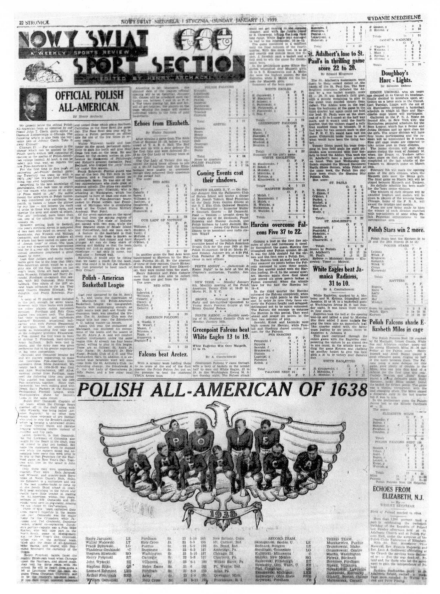

FIGURE 8-1. A typical sports page from *Nowy Swiat*, 15 January 1939, with Henry Archacki's weekly column; also special because it announces the consensus Polish All-America team for 1938.

nowski was "an athlete who played the game for all it was worth. Never vain, he did not choose to grab the spotlight."[34] Dating to the 1890s with Frank Merriwell, such qualities were about as unsingular and non-Polish as they could be. When Archacki, or Henry Levy in the *American Hebrew*, attempted to describe distinctive Polish or Jewish contributions to American football, he simply appropriated the conventional language of sportsmanship and teamwork, modesty and prowess, that had been attached to the game since its beginnings. A Jewish or a Polish Frank Merriwell was just another Frank Merriwell with a Jewish or Polish name. There was no distinctively Jewish or Polish—or Italian or Hungarian or Lithuanian or Ukrainian—contribution to American football. Bronko Nagurski was a latter-day Pudge Heffelfinger. There was nothing Jewish about the passing of Benny Friedman or Sid Luckman that distinguished it from the passing of Sammy Baugh; nothing Polish about the line play of Alex Wojciechowicz that distinguished it from Mel Hein's. A tremendous irony appears in the classic study of second-generation Italian Americans published in 1943: those who most resisted acculturation expressed the greatest interest in famous athletes of Italian descent, yet that athletic success itself became a powerful agent of acculturation.[35] Thousands of Jews, Poles, Italians, and other new immigrants became more American by playing or following football. They made the game theirs as much as it had belonged to the Anglo-Saxons who predominated at Harvard, Yale, and Princeton at the turn of the century; but theirs as Americans, without hyphens.

IMMIGRANT SAGAS

Triumphant complacency in the immigrant press by the late 1930s was made possible by the growing acceptance of ethnic football players in the mainstream media. Although it was still unusual to mention the foreign ancestry of football stars, the year 1930 saw the publication of football's first great immigrant saga.[36] Knute Rockne was the subject, his autobiography serialized in *Collier's* with the title, "From Norway to Notre Dame." Rockne (or his ghostwriter) attributed his drive for excellence to that "traditional venturesomeness of the Norsemen, aided by infiltrations of Irish blood acquired when the earlier and hardier Vikings invaded Ireland looking for trouble and returned to Norway with colleens for wives."[37] Rockne described growing up in Irish and Swedish neighborhoods in Chicago (where all Scandinavians were "Swedes"), playing no-holds-barred street football against Irish kids before graduating to better-regulated games in high school and college. Rockne called his life "a typical American story," and in various versions it was told at the height of his fame, retold frequently after his death in 1931, then memorialized fully in the hagiographic biopic, *Knute Rockne— All-American*, in 1940.[38]

The film opens in Voss, Norway, a quaint Old World village where Lars Rockne, a carriage maker, tells his friends he is going to America, "a new country, full of opportunity for working men like me." As a ship steams across the Atlantic, the anthem of America, land of promise, scrolls down the screen: "Among millions like themselves, simple hard-working people from the old countries following the new road of equality and opportunity which led to America, the Rockne family settled in Chicago." Next we see young Knute introduced to football by a group of older kids (including one black boy—a startling image, given Rockne's later penchant for racist anecdotes and the absence of black players at Notre Dame until the 1950s). After earning the respect of the older, bigger boys, Knute arrives late and bloodied to dinner one evening, to be scolded in Norwegian by his father. The boy insists that football is "the most wonderful game in the world," then asks his father to, please, speak American. "We're all Americans now," declares young Knute. This American from Norway then begins his ascent to the pinnacle of football fame in the New World.

What this "typical" story typified was the heroic saga of the *old* immigrant. Americans in the 1930s could more easily embrace a Scandinavian immigrant saga than an Italian or Jewish or Polish one. In no way was Knute Rockne's story in the 1930s read as Frank Carideo's or Alex Wojciechowicz's or Sid Luckman's. It was the story of Willa Cather's Swedes on the Nebraska prairies, of Ole Rölvaag's Norwegian "Giants in the Earth" in South Dakota, but not of the eastern and southern Europeans whose invasion triggered the anti-immigrant hysteria of the 1910s and early 1920s. In a sympathetic account in *Collier's* in 1933 of Chick Meehan's rise and fall as coach at NYU, Bill Cunningham used revealing language to describe the school's predicament before Meehan took over the football program in 1925: "Being located in New York so close to the foreign-born element and drawing its undergraduates almost exclusively from the great metropolitan sector, the school seriously needed outside undergraduate blood to combat the throttling evils of city psychology, the vile germs of Communism and other continental curses that came in with the New York City trade."[39] The "foreign-born" whom Cunningham casually associated with urban "evils" and the "vile germs" of imported ideas were the Jews, Italians, and Poles whose sons played for Fordham, Columbia, and even NYU in the 1930s—none of whom he mentioned, of course—not the Norsemen who ventured on the ship with Knute Rockne and his parents.

Over the 1930s, the ethnicity of college football players was less consistently avoided than in the 1920s, but it was never celebrated in the great popular magazines. Toward the end of the decade (as Hitler's aggression in Europe increased American sympathy for the threatened nations), *Life* identified Columbia's Sid Luckman as Jewish and Tennessee's George Cafego as Hungarian, and noted the ethnic makeup of Pitt's "dream backfield" in 1938—an Italian (Richard Cassiano), a Jew (Marshall Goldberg), and a Rumanian (John Chickerneo). Profiles in *Look* and *Collier's* also mentioned the ethnicity of Goldberg and the Chicago Bears' George Halas.[40] In each case, facts of ancestry were noted without elaboration. Silences are difficult to document and interpret, but Benny Friedman wrote six articles for *Collier's* between 1932 and 1942, and not one of them told the story of his childhood and youth as the son of a Russian-immigrant Jewish tailor in Cleveland. *Life* told readers only that Luckman, Cafego, Goldberg, and his Pitt teammates were poor, came to college on scholarships to play football, and proved their ability—the conventional American success story. How one should feel about an Italian, a Jew, and a Rumanian in the Pitt backfield, or a Jew at Columbia and a Hungarian at Tennessee, was left entirely to the reader. Throughout the thirties, the striking new look of All-America teams went unnoted in Grantland Rice's annual articles in *Collier's*. Rice's first, second, and third teams in 1933, for example, included Petoskey, Dell' Isola, Volok, Danowski, Cewppi, Vuchinich, Matal, and Mikulak—without comment. Rice's only ethnic reference came in 1936, and it was oblique: repeating the quip about Wojciechowicz as "Fordham's 'thirty-letter man'" and calling him "the Menacing Pole."[41] Fordham's coach, Jim Crowley, joked with an AP reporter before the 1936 season, "I feel at home with this squad because they're big and I can't pronounce their names." Wojciechowicz in particular was "the great unpronounceable," but there was no story here, just a good-natured joke.[42] Fordham's line that season, celebrated as the Seven Blocks of Granite, was made up of Paquin, Franco, Pierce, Wojciechowicz, Lombardi, Babarsky, and Druze (how did Pierce make that team?). Such multi-ethnic lineups had been common at Fordham, as well as Notre Dame and other Catholic colleges, for several years, but not a single article appeared in a major magazine about them.

Less constrained than the large-circulation weeklies (whose first requirement, for the sake of selling space to mass-market advertisers, was to offend or disturb no one), and more likely read by working-class second-generation immigrants themselves, the pulp magazine *Sport Story* openly acknowledged the ethnic transformation of college football. Though primarily publishing fiction, the magazine included articles on the current football scene, and here readers found in 1930 a feature on Carnegie Tech, whose coach, Walter Steffen, described his team as "a sort of League of Nations squad . . . boys who are American by birth, but German, Italian, Scotch, Irish, Swedish, Slovakian, Polish or French by immediate descent." In the 1950s, such a lineup would be widely celebrated as a symbol of the American melting pot. In the 1930s, it had to be defended: "I've never found that race or nationality matter on the gridiron," Steffen insisted. The previous season, an editorial made the same claim for college football generally. "Nothing is better proof of how much football has changed in the last twenty-five years or so," the writer declared, "or better proof of the present-day game's really national appeal, than the names of the boys who are playing it." He then documented the shift from English and Irish names to Oosterbaan, Bueschsenschuss, Kazmerchak, Ujhelyi, Erf, Wiragos, and so on.

> All of which means that football has ceased to be a game of the classes, and has become a game of all the people. A few years ago a prominent coach — I think that it was Bob Zuppke of Illinois — remarked that it was the poor boys who were playing college football, while the sons of well-to-do parents were sitting in the stands comfortable in coon-skin coats. Partly true, no doubt, although there is many a rich man's son going through the hammering grind of the gridiron season, and making no heavier weather of it than is the laborer's son who is playing next to him. The reason for these new names in football is not that the sons of our "old line" families have stopped playing it, but that it has become a truly democratic sport, open to boys who come from all social levels. Rich man's son and poor man's son — on the football field they are equal until one can prove that he's a better man than the other.[43]

Sport Story addressed openly what the more "respectable" press evaded. It is not likely that enlightened sportswriters considered ethnicity irrelevant (many sportswriters were themselves second-generation new immigrants), but that ethnicity and class still raised uncomfortable issues for some readers. Anti-immigrant feelings slackened in the 1930s, but tensions within immigrant communities between ethnic identity and acculturation and between these communities and the American mainstream were far from resolved. In football, moreover, the ethnic transformation of the college game was entangled with the controversies over recruitment and subsidization. In an article in the *American Mercury* in 1936, John R. Tunis invented the name "Slats Miskowitch, the Power House of East Dakota," as the prototype for the subsidized college football player who was debasing the amateur game. Poles from Chicago playing for the University of Washington might be a source of pride in the Polish American press but evidence of professionalism in an article in *Collier's*.[44]

The deeper feelings prompted by the ethnic transformation of football are found in the fiction of the period. As noted earlier, an ethnic name like "Slats Miskowitch" in itself, conjuring up Old World ghettoes and New World slums, could serve as a simple marker for disruptions in both football and American society. Joel Sayre played with readers' uneasiness in "Rackety Rax," his extravagant burlesque of big-time college football, in which the professional wrestlers hired for one team include Nick Tossilitis; Hazos, the Horrible Hun; Baliban, the Neckless Wonder; and three former collegians from Notre Dame, Dartmouth, and Nebraska. (In life, Bronko Nagurski and Joe Savoldi were the most prominent of many ethnic football stars who went on to careers in pro wrestling.) As the chief "recruiter" in Sayre's story tells his boss, there is no need to change their names. "I pointed out that football players all over the United States have the goofiest names ever heard of anyway, and nobody would think Switz, Radeswicz and Woola anything out of the ordinary." Calling names "goofy" would not have obscured their ethnicity for contemporary readers. In movies, too, names such as Dubrowski (*Saturday's Heroes*, 1937), Wagurski (*Hold That Coed*, 1938), and of course Bolenciecwcz (*Rise and Shine*, 1941) were attached to large-bodied, not-very-bright football players on the gravy train.

Sport Story, too, indulged in such stereotyping on occasion—in T. W. Ford's "The Pinch Kicker" (1933), the leader of the opponents' ringers, "a veritable bull with short, thick neck," is named Crodak, recalling Edgar Rice Burroughs's use of Slavic names for the most brutal apes in his Tarzan books—but in general, the pulp magazine celebrated the football melting pot a decade before the more respectable "slick" magazines picked up the theme.[45] The new immigrant's football story emerged in the 1930s in two basic plots—Americanization through football or the family tensions wrought by Americanization—but the first was more common. *Sport Story* offered several versions of this tale. In "Panski of the Irish," the son of parents who "spoke in English but thought in Polish" bonds with Irish and German teammates in the Notre Dame melting pot. In "Latin from Manhattan," an Italian-American "fresh punk" from New York wins over the "Nordic, Scandinavian and plain old Middlewestern American types" among the veterans on the professional Chicago Americans. Other stories worked similar variations off this theme.[46]

What happens in these stories is not the ethnic transformation of football but the more reassuring Americanization of ethnic football players. A 1929 story neatly illustrates the distinction. A multi-ethnic scrub team—manned by the likes of Cornelius Aloysius O'Brien, Tony Dondero, "Swede" Nelson, Johnny Jones, Dave Epstein, and Heinie Schwartz—whips the "Blood-and-money Ring" led by J. Gifford Leffingwell and Courtlandt van Courtlandt. Yet the scrubs are led by an Anglo quarterback, "Brainy" Tyler, who demonstrates "an ability to lead and instruct and inspire his material."[47] This configuration of Anglo brains and immigrant "material" also played out in a series of tales about the "Three Musketeers" written for *Sport Story* by Jackson Scholz, whose three heroes include a "dizzy little wop" and the son of a Swedish farmer who are led by a Kansan "of good old American stock."[48] Remarkably few feature films made ethnicity an issue, but those that did offered similar reassurances.[49] In *Huddle* (1932), from Francis Wallace's novel, an Italian-American steelworker becomes an American gentleman through playing football at Yale. In *The Band Plays On* (1934), a street gang of Italian, Jewish, and Irish kids is saved from delinquency by a football coach who teaches them proper values and later mentors them through their college football careers. Roman Novarro was a credible Italian in *Huddle,* but as Tony Ferrara, the leader of the gang in *The Band Plays On,* Robert Young was about as authentic as the white actors playing Indians in western movies of the period. Movies could mute cultural and ethnic differences simply by casting performers who betrayed no visible ethnicity, then plug the immigrant football player into the familiar formulas of American success.

The quintessential story of Americanization in the 1930s centered on a conflict between the first and second generations, in which the uncomprehending or resistant parents are won over by the son who loves the American game. (This was also the plot of the baseball biopic of Lou Gehrig, *The Pride of the Yankees.*) This formula appealed not only to outsiders: in one of his columns in *Nowy Swiat,* Henry Archacki cast the football career of Alex Wojciechowicz at Fordham in exactly these terms.[50] Stories from *Collier's* in 1930 and *Sport Story* in 1939 with almost identical plot details illustrate two very different perspectives on this generational conflict. In the first, Frederick Hazlitt Brennan's "This Football," an Italian Mamma who longs for a son with "the gift" of genius in the arts watches with dismay as her Lennie instead becomes the Big Ten's high-scoring halfback, celebrated in the newspapers as "the Dazzling Duce from Little Italy" and "the Big Stiletto." In the later story, "Pappa Morelli's Boy," Pappa replaces Mamma as the anxious parent; otherwise the stories are nearly identical, yet the similar endings are viewed very differently. Both young men are rewarded for their football heroics with jobs in a steel mill after graduation. While Pappa is relieved to see that the wealthy alumni have not merely exploited his boy after all, Mamma is crushed by the thought of her Lennie spending his life working with "peeg iron." "It ees not beautiful," she cries in the final scene. "It ees not beautiful." [51]

In "This Football," Brennan left the consequences of assimilation through football unsettled. Whether Mamma is a foolish old woman trapped in backward Old World beliefs or the only one able to see the trash behind the tinsel in big-time football is left to the reader. "Pappa Morelli's Boy" more simply celebrated the absorption of its ethnic football hero into the American mainstream, as did a 1933 story in *Country Gentleman* with the telling title, "All-Americanized." A job in a steel mill became an issue in yet another football story, this one a serial in *Sport Story* that began in the same issue as "Pappa Morelli's Boy." Although it eventually lost its way in a tortuous plot, "The Climax Game" initially offered the most realistic portrait of the subsidized working-class ethnic player in this period. Tony Feduccia makes no apologies for being on the "gravy train" at upscale Bolton University, and he vows he will not end up like a former Bolton star, Steve Yard: recruited out of a steel mill and made into a football hero, now back in the steel mill, completing the "cycle," because he "didn't know that he could be *in* a great college without being *of* it." As cynical Tony tells the naïve hero, Tom Brooks, "I'm not one of those guys born to be a college graduate. There's no more tradition behind me than the lamp in my old man's miner's hat—my old man, who never even got as far as short division! But I'm not going to wind up like Steve Yard, back in the steel mill. And I don't want to see you heading that way, either." Tony's plan is to make a name for himself in football, then open up a saloon back home in "Checkohungary, Pennsylvania." [52] This scene, unfortunately, appears in the first installment of a three-part serial that unravels into multiple plots involving virtually every convention in football fiction, while the issues of ethnicity and class simply disappear. Such evasions were also conventional in the football fiction of the 1930s.

THE POSTWAR MELTING POT

This quintessential Depression-era story was not pushed to its logical conclusion until 1951, with *Saturday's Hero,* a film made from Millard Lampell's

1949 novel, *The Hero* (the radical Lampell was a blacklisted screenwriter in the 1950s). As the film opens, Steve Novak is a high school football star in a close-knit working-class Polish family and community in New Jersey, who is "adopted" by a wealthy alumnus of an elite southern college that does not officially offer scholarships. (This was the arrangement by which stars such as Frankie Sinkwich and Charlie Trippi emigrated from Pennsylvania coal country to the University of Georgia and other southern institutions in the 1940s.) Eddie, the local sportswriter, warns Steve that he won't belong at upper-class Jackson, but Steve is drawn to the school's glamour and sets off to play football and study engineering. His teammates are an ethnic mix of rich and poor, coached by Biff-like "Preacher" Tennant but ruled by Steve's benefactor, T. C. McCabe, whose niece Melissa becomes Steve's love interest over her uncle's objections. Both the cast and the situation were right out of the conventions of 1930s fiction, the stories Francis Wallace wrote for the *Post* and *Collier's*, but *Saturday's Hero* worked through the conflicts rather than just pushing them aside. Steve initially becomes a conscientious student, winning the respect of his skeptical English professor, but in time he begins neglecting his studies as he gets caught up in football stardom. Eddie, the honest but cynical sportswriter, becomes a dishonest and cynical publicity man for McCabe and the football team. One of Steve's honest and hard-working but subsidized teammates is kicked out of school when he jeopardizes Jackson's pristine reputation. In his junior year Steve himself is forced to play with a seriously injured shoulder because, as McCabe tells him, football is now all he has. His grades have been fixed for the past two years, and he can no longer compete academically with the men who have been studying all along. As these events have unfolded at Jackson, Steve has grown estranged from his father and brother back home in New Jersey.

Saturday's Hero gave viewers the requisite happy ending for a Hollywood film, though not on football terms. Steve defiantly quits Jackson, but just too late — his father dies before he can return home — then asks his brother to help him find a job while he finishes college at night school. The movie ends with a telegram from Melissa, saying that she's on her way to join him. Despite the upbeat ending, *Saturday's Hero* left intact the radical difference between Steve Novak's honest and nurturing working-class ethnic home and the ruthless, corrupt, and hypocritical world of big-time football at Jackson. Nearly as damning were a pair of magazine articles about Ohio State All-American Vic Janowicz. In a 1951 portrait by Stanley Frank for the *Saturday Evening Post*, Janowicz, the son of "poor Polish immigrants," had been "unsettled" by a corrupt system of subsidization by Ohio State's alumni "angels" but still had a promising future. In Tim Cohane's portrait in *Look* seven years later, Janowicz's was a more poignant story, *Saturday's Hero* without the happy ending. Raised "to respect church, education, money, and work," Janowicz had become "a striking example of the small-town boy exposed to the lunatic adoration of big-time football." "Easily sidetracked" from his studies, he flunked out of Ohio State in his senior year, after his football eligibility had expired. He tried professional baseball, unsuccessfully, then found a new beginning in pro football, only to have an auto accident following a party (he was with a young woman not his wife) end his career. Now, out of work and with no college degree, a daughter at home with cerebral palsy and his marriage shaky, Janowicz was back in Columbus, hoping for a job on a loading dock or for the state highway department.[53]

The cautionary tales of Steve Novak and Vic Janowicz, the fictional character and the actual player, were exceptions in the postwar years. More typical than *Saturday's Hero* was *All-American* two years later, with Tony Curtis cast as Nick Bonelli in a tale of athletic and social triumph in which all obstacles faced by the working-class Italian outsider simply disappear from both the football field and the elite fraternity. This period saw both the darkest and the sunniest views of ethnic acculturation through football, but sunshine predominated. With millions of offspring of once-suspect new immigrants fighting in Europe and the Pacific, the Second World War permanently altered the popular view of the American melting pot, and football contributed to the reimagining of that old idea. As Murray Sperber has shown, the multi-ethnic football teams of the 1930s provided a model for the multi-ethnic platoons in such war films as *Appointment in Tokyo, Guadalcanal Diary, Bataan,* and *Air Force,* which in turn influenced the casting of multi-ethnic football teams in the postwar era as the very embodiment of American democracy.[54]

A strange story in the *Saturday Evening Post* in 1950 made this point with the simplicity of allegory. In "One-Play Oscar," with the big game looming, a neighborhood sandlot team called the All-Americans—whose players include Camiglia, Wang, Nunez, Blucher, Miecislaus, Novikov, Morimoto, Olson, and so on—nearly breaks up over Cold War politics. The father of Frank Adamic, a Yugoslav, tells his son he cannot play with Tony Campiglia until the Italians get out of Trieste. Frenchy Dorais has to quit because Blucher, the German, is on the team; Polish Mike Miecislaus is not allowed to play with the Russian Novikov; Wang can't play with Morimoto. "Everybody was fighting except Joe Nunez and Swede Olson," until police officer Oscar Lewis talks to the fathers of the kids and wins permission for them to play. In the big game against the Japanese Settlement team, the opponent's gigantic star, Irish Hagaromo (thirty-five years old and 225 pounds) scores every time he touches the ball, leaving the All-Americans trailing 49–0 at the half. After the kids talk Officer Oscar into playing in the second half, a horrendous collision—the "one play" of the title—leaves Oscar woozy but knocks Hagaromo out of the game. The All-Americans then run up a 62–49 lead before Irish returns, but now they are no longer afraid, and by ganging up on him they stop him from scoring and win the game. What to make of "Irish Hagaromo" as the name for the monstrous antagonist is uncertain, but the story's main theme is simple enough: multi-ethnic America can overcome any obstacle once it sets aside Old World hatreds.[55]

Saturday's Hero and the plight of Vic Janowicz notwithstanding, "One-Play Oscar" epitomized a postwar consensus about multi-ethnic football. A "football town" feature in *Look* magazine in 1945 centered on four players on the local high school team in Everett, Massachusetts: left guard Richard (Brud) Ringdahl, whose Swedish-born father was a painter; Louis (Chick) Romboli, son of an Italian-born iron-works fireman; Edward Connolly, son of a bus driver who came from Ireland; and Amando (Mundo) Mazzone, whose father was a foreman at the iron works and the son of a machinist who arrived from Italy in 1913. In the typical photo-essay manner, four small pictures told the story of each of these young men at work, at home, and at play, while two statements in bold type declared the theme of their composite portrait: "Studies, family, jobs, fun are important to Everett High School's football players," and "Everett players are sturdy, unspoiled, come from modest homes, hard-working parents." Four larger photos showed the boys in action on the football field, with the last caption clinching the main point: "Everett typifies American high-school football at its spirited best." This was also the American melting pot at its best. Two Italians, a Swede, and an Irishman were simply American boys, doing all the things that American boys did. The Swede had an Italian girlfriend; one of the Italians had an Irish one. With seven teammates presumably just like themselves, the four boys constituted a "team" such as the one that had just saved the world from fascism.[56]

The multi-ethnic team appeared in juvenile football fiction in the postwar years. In *Touchdown Pass* (1948), the first football novel in Clair Bee's Chip Hilton series, Chip's teammates at Valley Falls High include Red Schwartz, Biggie Cohen, Fats Ohlsen, Nick Trullo, and Lou Mazotta, along with Anglo and old-immigrant types like Tuffy Collins, Tippy Taylor, and Speed Morris. When Chip graduates from Valley Falls to State U in *Freshman Quarterback*

(1952), Schwartz and Cohen accompany him, where they join up with Kornowitz, Maxim, and George "Bebop" Leopoulos, among predominantly old-stock teammates. In both novels, dissension within the team is unrelated to this ethnic diversity, yet the coming together of the feuding players to win the state championship or the big Thanksgiving Day game implicitly affirmed the new ideal of the football melting pot. As Murray Sperber summarizes the entire Chip Hilton series, "Like the combat crews of World War II movies," Chip's teammates "represent diverse races and ethnic groups, and they usually overcome internal strife and external prejudice on their way to athletic victory, with teamwork solving all character and plot problems." *Boys' Life* adjusted more cautiously to this new postwar paradigm: a team's starting lineup in an atypical 1951 serial included Meyer, Alboni, Brott, and Klotz, but ethnic names remained scarce through the 1950s. (Both *Touchdown Pass* and the *Boys' Life* serial are also notable for racially integrating the world of boys' football fiction. In *Touchdown Pass*, a black opponent is both "smart" and a "deadly tackler," in direct contrast to the racial stereotyping to be explored in the following chapter.)[57]

In the general-interest magazines over the postwar years, the new immigrant's story was told fully now, always as the perennial American story of humble beginnings, hard work, obstacles overcome, and final success—young Ben Franklin arriving in Philadelphia with one Dutch dollar and a copper shilling in his pocket, by the end of his life charming European aristocrats in Paris—only the hero now had an Italian or Polish father. Once ignored or noted in passing, ethnic ancestry now became an essential part of his story. When a profile in *Collier's* in 1942 of Notre Dame quarterback Angelo Bertelli mentioned his "nice smile, blue eyes, brown hair, surprisingly Nordic features," it seemingly cautioned readers not to judge Bertelli on the basis of his Italian name. After the war such reassurance was no longer necessary. An article in *American Magazine* in 1946 called Notre Dame lineman Ziggy Czarobski a "tough Polish giant" and Frank Kositkowski a "strapping Pole." A cover story on Frank Leahy in *Time* the same season referred to Notre Dame's star quarterback, Johnny Lujack, as "a brown-eyed, brown-haired Polish 21 year-old." Such language seems unremarkable, and that is just the point. The ethnicity of college football players was largely unremarked in the early 1930s but unremarkable after the war. Marchy Schwartz's parentage—Jewish father, Irish mother—that had been ignored during his playing days, and provoked speculation in the Jewish press, was finally clarified in a profile of him as coach at Stanford. Other magazine profiles of Georgia's Charlie Trippi, Virginia's John Polzer, and Pitt coach John

Michelson likewise stressed their ethnic backgrounds, but never as obstacles to acceptance or success.[58]

The fullest telling of the new-immigrant saga was Stanley Frank's 1953 profile of Yale coach Jordan Olivar, an Italian immigrant's son who became a coach in the aristocratic Ivy League. The son of Kid Blackie, "a third-rate preliminary fighter" who quit the ring to become a waiter in a Brooklyn chophouse after his son was born, was the least likely man to coach at Ivy-draped Yale, and Frank pounded on that theme. "You say this is a snobbish, patronizing attitude to take toward the career of a football man?" he asked rhetorically after describing the family background. "Consider these facts. Jordan Olivar, who never played football in high school and was lost in the shuffle of grubby sand-lot competition, hustled towels and tips in small gyms catering to fat businessmen for three and a half years after graduation from high school. He had no prospect of going to college until a professional wrestler, intrigued by his prowess in handball, got him a football scholarship to Villanova." From this sporting netherworld came "The Man Who Saved the Day for Yale," as Frank's piece was titled. That scholarship at Villanova had meant "professionalism" in the 1930s, and the football lineup at Villanova in those years, like those at Notre Dame, Fordham, Holy Cross, St. Mary's, and other Catholic colleges, was too close to Ellis Island for the comfort of many Americans. Yet this son of an Italian pug became the football coach at Walter Camp's alma mater, where scholarships were forbidden and the gentleman amateur spirit was enshrined. If it could happen at Yale, Stanley Frank implied, it could happen anywhere.[59]

Football was tailor-made for this immigrant story, the star player and the team perfectly exemplifying individual success and national unity. Stories of immigrant football success ranged from *Look*'s simple celebration of the boys at Everett High to Jimmy Breslin's more probing and poignant version of a "Football Town" that "manufactured" athletes as well as steel. Breslin found a virtual allegory in the lives of the second- and third-generation Slavic immigrants in Donora, Pennsylvania. From the high school that sat atop a hill wound down two roads: one to a dreary life in the zinc and iron works owned by U.S. Steel, the other to college and what lay beyond. The school principal told Breslin that in an average graduating class of 125, 17 would go to college on athletic scholarships, compared to just 2 or 3 with academic grants; not an ideal situation, he acknowledged, "but that's the way things are." At least those 17 won a chance to escape life in the mill. Breslin concluded that "everything good and bad in high-pressure school-boy football seems to be wrapped up in the Donora situation."[60]

The more typically unrestrained celebration of Americanization through football in magazine profiles and Tony Curtis's *All-American* came at a time when ethnicity had become uncontroversial within the larger culture. In the broad history of ethnicity in the United States, the 1950s is viewed as a period when ethnic consciousness declined, until the African American activism of the 1960s triggered an ethnic revival among other groups.[61] In football, non-Anglo names were no longer exotic, not even a joke, but simply the norm. By 1949 fully a third of the players in the National Football League were the sons of immigrants.[62] Even in the most critical story of football and ethnicity in the 1950s, *Saturday's Hero,* although Steve Novak is not Americanized by football, he is thoroughly American. Everything his family stands for—honesty, loyalty, love, forgiveness—is right out of the domestic ideology ruling postwar America. The ethnic family in *Saturday's Hero* ironically becomes the repository of traditional American values endangered by the corruption of the big-time college racket.

Just one group was conspicuously missing from the postwar melting pot. After the 1956 Sugar Bowl was integrated by a single black player, Pittsburgh's Bobby Grier—though not before the governor of Georgia had provoked a major civil rights confrontation by initially forbidding Georgia Tech to participate in the game—the sports editor of Atlanta's black *Daily World* saw a hopeful sign. "Note well," wrote Marion Jackson about the players in the game, "Corny Salvaterre, Lou Cimarolli, Fred Glatz, Ralph Jelie, Pete Neft, John Paluck, Joe Walton, Ray DiPasquale, and Bob Grier in the Sugar Bowl." "The Negro," Jackson noted, "was but one ingredient" in the "melting pot of the races that had tongue-twisting names that identified them with Italy, Portugal, Austria, Germany, Poland, Sweden, Czechoslovakia, Bulgaria, Yugoslavia." Jackson pointed out that Georgia Tech currently embraced "every minority . . . but the Negro." What difference would one more make?[63] Jackson's hope was premature—Georgia Tech would not have a black football player on its squad until 1970—but he also more fundamentally misread what had happened to the "melting pot." The grandfathers of Salvaterre, Glatz, Paluck, and the rest had belonged to alien "races" in the 1920s, but as Matthew Frye Jacobson explains in *Whiteness of a Different Color,* in becoming "ethnic" Americans they had also become "white." The period of mass European immigration had seen "a fracturing of whiteness into a hierarchy of plural and scientifically determined white races," but after the establishment of quotas in 1924, whiteness was "reconsolidated" in response to the northern migration of African Americans from the South. In the 1930s and 1940s, the new immigrants became Caucasian in both popular thought and official designation, as race in the United States was redefined as a matter of black and white. The assimilation of new immigrants was thus "inseparable from the cultural story of racial alchemy" by which all Europeans "became Caucasians." [64]

Football was one of the crucibles in which that alchemical reaction took place. By the 1950s, the sons and grandsons of European immigrants, new as well as old, were just more white football players and a symbol of American inclusiveness, as the game confronted its final struggle over race.

Race

Elmer Mitchell's survey of "Racial Traits in Athletics" included the Indian and the Negro. The Indian had "a tall, well-knit structure" but also a basic psychological failing: "he is not at home outside his own environment." Mitchell granted that Jim Thorpe was "probably the greatest all-around athlete of all times," but football stars such as Thorpe and Joe Guyon of Carlisle and Georgia Tech were "not truly representative" of their race. Coaches observing typical players on All-Indian teams agreed that "the Indian cannot stand reverses; that he will play sensationally while winning, but give in easily before setbacks; also that the Indian teams do not do well away from home"—surprising news to former Carlisle athletes who played nearly all their games on the road. "Indian teams lack persistent effort," Mitchell added, "and training or practice quickly become irksome if not relieved by novel methods." Playing with his own kind, "the Indian shows the traditional red man's traits. He is stoical in enduring pain. He is crafty, with the sense acutely developed. He nurses a wrong. He is cruel." But he is also strong and brave, "ready to repay a kind deed," and unselfish with his own race.[1]

The Negro, according to Mitchell, was "quiet and unassuming," and, unlike the Indian, content with an inferior status on white teams. His good humor enabled him to accept teammates' "pranks" and "to meet intentional rough play and jibes of his opponents with a grin." On teams entirely of his own race, "he is an inferior athlete," because he undermines his own "natural skill" with a "tendency to be theatrical or to play to the grandstand, a trait which the presence of white team mates suppresses." Mitchell also offered a strange defense against the common charge by coaches "that the negro is 'yellow'" and unstable, that he "fails in a crisis" and thus "cannot be relied upon for the big games":

> Personally, while I think that there is truth in the charge of instability, I do not think that the negro lacks the fighting bravery of the white. The reason for what seems to be an apparent failure to play up to his normal standard in the heat of a big game seems to me not that the negro is failing to give his best, but that the white is playing above par. This peculiarity of the white to excel and outdo himself, in critical strife, and to force himself when tired, is explained by the surplus of nervous energy with which nature has endowed him. The negro, lacking this nervous make-up which often makes a weakling white seem strong, seems to be lagging behind men whose efforts normally he could equal or surpass. But all the while the negro, making allowance for his trait of instability, is really giving as much as should be expected of him. This explanation seems plausible on the ground that medical studies have shown the black race to have blunted nervous sensibilities as compared with the white.

The difference, then, lay not in Negro inferiority but in white superiority, not of body but of character. Other lesser traits of the Negro included a "shuffling gait," an inclination to laziness, and a handful of others tossed off in the final sentence: "his susceptibility to superstition, his capability for self-devotion or hatred, his imitativeness, his love of frankness and especially his love of praise." [2]

Any reader of such words today immediately recognizes familiar stereotypes: the stoical red man as both savage and noble savage; the lazy, grinning, excitable darky of plantation myth and vaudeville stage. The football field served as one terminal for the circulation of racial stereotypes: images projected onto Indian and black players were circulated back into the larger culture from which they originated. But the salute to Jim Thorpe also reminds us of the power of the exceptional minority athlete to disrupt the circuit. The transformation of football discussed in the previous two chapters from an upper-class Anglo-Saxon sport to a more democratic, multi-ethnic one was a major development in the game during the period of this study. Its further transformation to a multiracial, ultimately black-dominated sport was only beginning by the end of the 1950s, but these later developments make the earlier history of football and race crucial for understanding the game.[3]

VANISHING ALL-AMERICANS

When Haskell Institute of Lawrence, Kansas, dropped intercollegiate football in 1938, two decades after Carlisle closed its doors, the once-conspicuous Indian presence in the intercollegiate game ended. From 1895 through 1917, teams representing the Industrial School at Carlisle, Pennsylvania, had become renowned throughout the football world both for their victories over the best teams of the day and for their exemplary sportsmanship.[4] Later, they became known for their love of trick plays as well. Their sportsmanship was real. Students at Carlisle had won approval to play big-time football only by promising their superintendent that they would comport themselves as true gentlemen on the field, to counter the popular view of Indian "savagery." Indians' love of trick plays as their second distinguishing mark owed more to the claims of writers such as Pop Warner, Carlisle's coach during its glory years.[5] Playing for pleasure in trickery—rather than for pride in their own prowess or retaliation against whites—made the Indians unthreateningly childlike. Playing both as gentlemen and as children made them "noble savages" in a long tradition rooted more in the projected desires of whites than in any truth about Indian manners and beliefs.[6]

Jim Thorpe played professional football through 1929, but since pro football mattered to no one outside the midwestern towns that fielded teams, he was not a continuing presence for most football fans. One of the pro teams for which Thorpe played, along with other Carlisle and Haskell graduates, was the Oorang Indians of LaRue, Ohio, a team owned by a breeder of Airedale puppies who staged mini–Wild West shows before games and at halftime. Thorpe and his teammates "played Indian" for the amusement of white spectators (a strategy of racial self-parody later adopted more successfully by Abe Saperstein with his Harlem Globetrotters basketball team): shooting at targets that were retrieved by the owner's Airdales; performing "Indian dances, fancy tomahawk work, knife and lariat throwing." Indian activist Philip Deloria has described these performances as an opportunity for the Indian players to "make some money and to have some fun." As one of the players recalled, "White people thought we were all wild men . . . even though almost all of us had been to college and were generally more civilized than they were. It was a dandy excuse to raise hell and get away with it."[7] Playing "wild men" could be personally liberating, but it also fed into stereotypes.

The closing of Carlisle in 1918 left only Haskell Institute to represent Indians on the football field.[8] Haskell achieved a degree of renown in the 1920s, but although playing teams such as Notre Dame and Minnesota in those years, and appearing in Pathé newsreels in 1925, 1926, and 1927, the team never achieved the fame of the Carlisle squads that had challenged Harvard, Yale, and Penn for supremacy of the football world. Haskell's schedule each season was made up of small colleges in Kansas and adjoining states, together with distant road games, but the usual intersectional competition came from the likes of St. Xavier in Cincinnati and Gonzaga in Spokane rather than Harvard and Yale. John Levi made Walter Eckersall's All-America team, and Knute Rockne placed Louis Weller on his All-Western squad, but calling each player "another Jim Thorpe" could not capture the magic of the original. Haskell's contests were not covered as major games by the wire services, but the Indians' visits to Minneapolis (to play Minnesota), Detroit (University of Detroit), Boston (Boston College), Philadelphia (Temple), New Orleans (Loyola), and other cities received special attention in the local press, less for the football itself, however, than for the encounter with the exotic.

Like Thorpe's Oorang Indians, Haskell teams sometimes "played Indian" for the locals. Arriving in Minneapolis or Philadelphia, Haskell players would pose in full headdress or later be photographed sitting on the bench wrapped in colorful Indian blankets.[9] Games in Minneapolis and Detroit were occasions for reunions of Carlisle and Haskell graduates or a gathering of nearby tribes, whose members arriving in full regalia made the conventional football pageantry more exotic.[10] All this display of Indian culture was highlighted by local sportswriters and routinely photographed for the newspapers. In simply being who they were—Indians in traditional dress—they also became what whites thought them to be—wild Indians such as the ones they read about in pulp magazines and saw in movies. John Levi and a few of his teammates sometimes performed physical feats for the public before games,[11] and the local schools often built up the gate by promoting the Indians' exoticism. When Haskell played Loyola University in New Orleans in 1928, the Loyola athletic department sponsored a contest in which "kiddies in Indian suits" were admitted to the game free, and the Haskell captain, Eugene Fritz, selected the boy with the best costume.[12]

A small handful of movies and magazine stories from this period cast the Indian football star as a doomed noble savage. Three silent films of the 1920s—*The Great Alone* (1922), *Braveheart* (1925), and *Red Clay* (1927)—each with a self-sacrificing Indian hero whose love for a white woman was

Little Rabbit to Strut Here

FIGURE 9-1. When Haskell Institute played Texas Tech in Dallas in 1931, this photograph of Louis (Little Rabbit) Weller appeared in the *Dallas Morning News* on 11 October. Such images in the local newspaper were typical when Haskell came to town. (Reprinted with permission of the *Dallas Morning News*)

doomed, were football versions of the 1925 film *The Vanishing American*.[13] The pulp magazine *Sport Story* imagined the ultimate self-sacrifice: an Indian rescuing his football rival's father, the very man who led the slaughter at Wounded Knee in which the hero's own mother died. These tales of heroic renunciation harked back to Cooper, Longfellow, and Lydia Maria Child, who, in the words of historian Robert Berkhofer, "romanticize[d] the safely dead Indian." Football functioned in these films to establish the Indian's nobility, whose privileges he then heroically renounced, leaving the field to whites.[14]

The local coverage of Haskell's road games around the country was likewise informed by the enduring stereotypes of the savage and the noble savage. Much of the coverage was straight football reporting, but the impulse to view these games as allegories of manifest destiny, as was done with the earliest Carlisle teams, remained strong. As Sam Greene wrote of the players when Haskell visited Detroit in 1927, "The simple fact that they are Indians lends a romantic touch to their appearance. . . . Any game in which they take part carries a suggestion of the ancient struggle for supremacy in America between the white man and the red man."[15] The writing about Haskell was governed by a set of adjectives not commonly found in the sports section: its teams and players were "romantic," "colorful," and "picturesque," as well as "wily," "crafty," and "tricky."[16] The names of Haskell players—Swift Antelope, Good Soldier, Jumping Bull, No Belly, Kicks His Wife—fascinated urban writers, who saw these young men as relics of the Wild West stalking the paved sidewalks of modern America.[17] Sportswriters played up this collision of cultures. The appearance of "aborigines" was a "strange sight," reported one writer in the *Philadelphia Record* in 1931: "Startled palefaces . . . watched a haughty chief, dressed in the head feathers and moccasins of a Cherokee chieftain, walk out of the tepee known as the Ritz. His long buckskin suit, his feathers nodding beautifully in the October zephyrs and his handsome face caused many a feminine heart to flutter." Writing for the *Boston Herald* in 1924, Stanley Woodward (the future sports editor of the *New York Herald Tribune*) decided that John Levi was "one of the few perfect Indian types in the line-up," as shown by his "powerful body set on long rather small legs, high cheek bones and the long slightly hooked nose so commonly seen in illustrations of King Phillip's war." Woodward seemed to regret that "typical Indians are few and far between on the Haskell squad, though most of the players have the features of the noble redskin." In general, they looked "exactly like any other college football player."[18] The overriding question when Haskell came to town seemed always the same: how "Indian" would these Indian players prove to be?

The rare writer understood that the Haskell players might be playing a role. After opening his 1926 piece with the litany of Indian names noted above, the *Boston Herald*'s W. E. Mullins then commented:

> All this Injun junk about Roaring Bull, Takes a Gun and Wrinkle Meat, hands them quite a laugh. It's quite true that they occasionally burst out with shrieks of blood curdling war whoops, but that's only to give the razzberry to some of the folks around who fall for the romantic blah about pipes of peace, tomahawks and moccasins. As a matter of fact, it's a typical squad of football players. They dress quite as nattily as those highly polished gents in the haberdashery ads. This Theodore Roebuck, for instance, he's the tackle who played through last year's game at Braves Field without a head guard, is a dude. He is a big handsome buck who wears

his black hair plastered down on both sides with slickem, and his natty siders half way down his cheeks in the most approved shiek style.

Mullins may have been too shrewd to buy the Wild West bunk, but he was obviously blind in different ways. Traditional names were much more than "Injun junk" to those on whom they were conferred, and if the Haskell lads indulged in a few war whoops to razz the locals, the accoutrements of "romantic" Indian life dismissed by the worldly sportswriter had a real place in their history. Though coifed in the latest style, moreover, the Indian shiek was to Mullins a "buck." The Haskell players seem to have had but two possible public roles: to be "a typical squad of football players," or to be Injuns in accordance with popular stereotypes; to either have no identity of their own or to have a pop-Indian identity created for them. What football actually meant to these young men—uprooted from their homes to live at a boarding school whose purpose was as much to erase their traditional cultures as to immerse them in a new one—had to be extraordinarily complicated. But to appear in the popular press as real Indians, whatever that might mean, was not an option.

By the 1920s, most metropolitan sportswriters had abandoned the rhetorical sensationalism of the 1890s when Carlisle first burst on the public scene. More often than not, the reporting on the game was straight football, though sportswriters had no control over the headlines concocted by copy editors. "Massacres," "braves," "scalps," "tomahawks," and "warpath" were liberally sprinkled in headlines and the captions for cartoons and photographs.[19] Calling the Haskell teams "Vanishing Americans" in Los Angeles papers in 1925 simply appropriated a more specific stereotype, but a writer in New Orleans elaborated on this term in a quietly chilling way in 1928. "History tells us that the Indian race is slowly but surely becoming extinct," Gene Thatcher wrote in the *Times-Picayune* before the Haskell-Loyola game, "and the Loyola Wolves hope to hurry along this process by vanquishing the Haskell Institute football team this afternoon."[20]

Some writers could not resist dipping into the bag of pulp-western imagery for a colorful lead. The *Omaha World-Herald* in 1923: "The Haskell Indians, pride of western tepeeland, will do their famous gridiron war dance against Creighton university's football camp at Creighton field this afternoon." The *Detroit Free Press* in 1927: "Much after the fashion that the early settlers beat back the Redskins to claim valuable territory, University of Detroit repulsed the Haskell Indian eleven yesterday afternoon at Dinan field and made a complete job of it in winning, 38 to 7." The *Philadelphia*

Record in 1932: "The traditional Indian war-whoop was missing, and the tomahawk strangely absent when 24 red-skinned Braves from the Haskell reservation arrived in town yesterday. Tonight on the gridiron of Temple University these same Indians will scorn the scalps of the white men and seek instead a football triumph over the heretofore undefeated Temple eleven."[21] As John Bloom has noted, Haskell's grand homecoming in 1926 to inaugurate its new football stadium was covered by local papers in similar ways.[22]

Occasionally a writer went for full immersion. The *New Orleans Times-Picayune* and *Philadelphia Record* in particular found the visiting Indians as exotic as the natives that first greeted Columbus. In New Orleans, the motive was clearly promotional, and the effort succeeded as 8,000 fans made up the largest Loyola crowd ever. In addition to the contest for kiddies in Indian costume, readers of the *Times-Picayune* were treated to a full week of stories about "real, live Indians" who "know how to play football as well as give the old blood-curdling war whoop that made the white men shiver in years gone by"; about "Redskins, who like football and play it almost by instinct"; about Indian players who are "fast and tricky, delighting in fooling the white man." The writer of most of these articles, Gene Thatcher, covered the game itself as straight football, but an accompanying piece made up for his restraint. "They fought with touchdowns instead of tomahawks," wrote Gwen Bristow, "and Loyola scalped the Indians Saturday to the bloody score of 20 to 0 and got revenge for their last year's knifing" on Haskell's home field. "The substitutes, wrapped in bright Indian blankets, sat on the sidelines like braves itching to go on the warpath, and thousands of beautiful women with lots of war-paint on shouted to their heroes to bring in the scalps."[23] In Philadelphia in 1931, the *Record*'s Gordon Mackay treated readers to a similar smorgasbord of picturesque redskins and racial warfare.[24] In the cities Haskell visited, the Indians gave an exotic touch to the color and pageantry of college football while putting an entertaining twist on familiar pop-western stereotypes, but they also seem to have embodied a complex of unarticulated ideas about football and American life. Their "natural" or "instinctual" skill invested the game with the Indians' own romantic savagery, heightening football's potency as an antidote to the softening tendencies of modern civilization. White players, of course, were the chief beneficiaries of this heightening, and no one tried to penetrate the mask of the wild Indian to see what football actually meant to the young men.

After the Bureau of Indian Affairs decided that big-time football had little value in preparing Haskell students for life in modern America—the school deemphasized the sport in the early 1930s before dropping it altogether in 1938—images of Indian football lost all connection to actual players. The lone Indian football star to retain a hold on the popular imagination was Jim Thorpe. By the late 1920s Thorpe had become just another aging, washed-up football player, but a four-part series by Charley Paddock in *Collier's* in 1929 and Pop Warner's three articles for the same magazine two years later began Thorpe's canonization as the greatest athlete of all time. A character named Big Jack Thorpe, cast as a former Indian football hero in the 1934 Western movie *Fighting Through,* was clearly meant to evoke the ex-Carlisle star; and articles by Grantland Rice in 1939 and Kyle Crichton in 1942 confirmed Thorpe's standing as a giant of the past. Thorpe's final anointing came in 1950, when *Collier's* placed him on its "Midcentury All-America" team, and two separate AP polls named him the greatest football player and the best male athlete of the first half of the twentieth century. The enduring image of Jim Thorpe came a year later, from Burt Lancaster's portrayal in *Jim Thorpe—All-American,* which cast Thorpe as the once proud but now pitiable fallen hero, rescued from his misery by Pop Warner: a superb natural athlete with a flawed character, saved by a Great White Father.[25]

Aside from Thorpe, Indian football in the 1930s and 1940s became merely a set of images out of Wild West pageantry, like the mascots for colleges such as Stanford and Dartmouth. When George Preston Marshall, the pro football owner most obsessed with showmanship, purchased an NFL franchise for Boston in 1932, he named it the Braves after the local baseball team, then rechristened it the Redskins the following season, hiring Haskell's Lone Star Dietz as coach and outfitting the players in feathers and warpaint before the first game.[26] (When he moved the team to Washington in 1937, Marshall retained the Redskins name.) The noble savage sentimentalized in 1920s silent films became a comic figure in the Ritz Brothers' *Life Begins in College* (1937); and in one last football story, published in *Collier's* in 1946, a woman in Birmingham, Alabama, bracing for the visit of wild Indians from Haskell, discovers that they are true gentlemen, while her husband and his neighbor are the ones who get rip-roaring drunk.[27] Carlisle and Haskell had disappeared from the sports pages, but the noble savage of the gridiron lived on.

SAMBO ON THE GRIDIRON

Though far from numerous, these stories and films on Indians were considerably more than those dealing with black football. While Indians disappeared from big-time college football but lingered in popular memory, African Americans made slow but steady gains on football fields, yet remained nearly invisible in popular representations of the game. Of the 113 football covers of the *Saturday Evening Post* and *Collier's* between 1920 and 1960, not one showed a black face. Of the 120 full-length football films, just one had a black star: *While Thousands Cheer* (1940), a conventional melodrama of gamblers, kidnappings, and last-minute heroics, but with an all-black cast led by former UCLA star Kenny Washington. Just two others cast black football players in minor roles: Washington, with a small speaking part as an injured player in the 1949 pro football film *Easy Living;* and four black Los Angeles Rams in *Crazylegs,* the 1953 biopic of Elroy "Crazylegs" Hirsch. Tank Younger spoke a few lines in *Crazylegs,* and in one remarkable scene, unimaginable before the 1950s, "Deacon Dan" Towler leads the team in prayer before a key game. Of the 122 stories and ten serials in the *Post* and *Collier's* in our period, not until the 1950s did any deal seriously with race.[28]

Among the hundreds of covers, stories, and movies from the 1920s through the 1950s, in just these few was football integrated. Except for the three films mentioned, black characters in football movies were limited to porters, waiters, servants, and trainers or "rubbers," exceedingly minor characters who helped fill in the background against which the drama or comedy of (white) football played out.[29] (To this scant record of black representation should be added the 1929 musical *Sweetie,* in which first Jack Oakie, then the entire student section, sings "Alma Mammy" in blackface before the big game.) Several teams apparently did employ black water boys and "rubbers" (masseurs), who occasionally provided journalists with amusing sidelights on the main story. An article in *Collier's* in 1941 mentioned the "gorilla-chested old East Texas Negro" who was the unofficial mascot and trainer for an orphanage team. A portrait of Georgia coach Wally Butts by his daughter for *Collier's* in 1954—a hard-driving Biff on the field shown to be daddy at home—waxed sentimental over "the leading symbol of undying loyalty at Georgia," described as "a flap-jawed Negro waterboy-trainer named Clegg Stark, who doesn't know his own age or how long he has been there." In appreciation for the old black man's long service the Georgia players recently raised money to buy him a house. The following season, the Associated Press reported on Mississippi students' salute to their favorite black man, old Blind Jim, who had rooted for Ole Miss for sixty years.[30] The motif was familiar to anyone who knew *Gone With the Wind* or countless other southern romances: the "undying loyalty" of the plantation darky for Ol' Massa and his family, evoked here in the 1950s even as bus boycotts and court-ordered desegregation were beginning to throw the Jim Crow South into turmoil.

A generation earlier, figures such as Clegg Stark provoked humor rather than nostalgia. In his 1928 memoir in *Collier's*, veteran coach John Heisman illustrated the complications of football signals with a story about a "negro rubber" named Bob Sponsor, who worked for him at Alabama Poly (Auburn) in the 1890s. "To Bob the game was clear enough aside from signals," Heisman explained in setting up his tale. One day the black man came to him for help:

> "Mistuh Boss Coach Heisman," whined Bob, "please, suh, tell me about them signal nummers. I aim to learn somethin'."
>
> And then Bob explained that his evenings were devoted to coaching a team of colored boys who were going to Tuskegee to do battle. Signals being a bit too much for him he had dispensed with them, but it had occurred to him that his team might do better if it had them. I explained at length.
>
> The next day I went with Bob to see his team operate. Bob was not only coach but captain, quarterback, field general and big boss. Drawing himself aside from his team he began shouting a long string of tremendous figures in a loud voice. Inasmuch as he had not informed his men that the team now had signals, there was much consternation.
>
> "Whut's all them nummers mean, boy?" demanded Bob's fullback.
>
> "Them," said Bob loftily, "is signals, nigger. Don't go botherin yo' fool haid bout them. I is havin' trouble enough. Jest do whut yo's told."
>
> So Bob began all over again:
>
> "Fo' million seben hun' an sixty thousand eighteen hund'ed an ninety-two plus e-leven. Pass me that yere ball, center-boy. Here, nigger, tek this-yeh ball and run around the right end, yo' fool."
>
> The fullback took the ball and not only ran around the right end of the opposing team but gained at least ten yards.
>
> "There," said Bob, "there, nigger. Does yo' see now whut good them nummer signals is? Boy, we gets us some more does I get time to think up some."[31]

This was typical of the humor in the enormously popular radio program *Amos 'n' Andy* and in Octavus Roy Cohen's stories about Florian Slappey that appeared regularly in the *Saturday Evening Post* in the 1930s. Amos Alonzo Stagg told a slightly different version in his autobiography serialized for the

Saturday Evening Post in 1926, attributing the story to both Knute Rockne and former Princeton star "Big Bill" Edwards, who in turn had reported hearing it from a southern football official. Rockne himself related a similar story in his own autobiography for *Collier's* in 1930. In this one, two black teams devised signals based on favorite foods: "Pork chops meant a smash through right tackle, pigs' feet a run around right end, fried chicken a split buck, and so on." After one team had marched to the one-yard line, the quarterback screamed the "final challenge: 'Now, boys, over that line with the whole blame dining-car!'"[32]

The "joke" was simply that blacks could not possibly understand a game so complex as football, a theme that can also be traced through cartoons from the 1890s into the 1920s. The "coon" jokes and cartoons that were a staple of the humor magazines *Life* and *Judge* at the turn of the century occasionally had a football setting. The joke was always the same—depictions of "Coontown" or "Blackville" football teams in *Judge* in the 1890s ridiculed the very idea of blacks engaging in the premier intercollegiate sport—and this theme was carried into the new century.[33] By the 1920s, such openly racist football material had largely disappeared from the mainstream press, but the anecdotes told by Heisman, Stagg, and Rockne, as well as a couple of cartoons in *Life,* confirm that a great many Americans were not yet offended by racist caricatures.

It was in this cultural climate that a few dozen black football players competed in the big-time college game in the 1920s and 1930s. Aside from the occasional joke or racist anecdote, the popular magazines of the interwar years all but ignored them. How much attention radio broadcasters paid to the race of the black stars on integrated teams is uncertain. No games with black players from the 1930s survive, and Bill Stern enthused over Buddy Young against Pitt in 1946 and against UCLA in the 1947 Rose Bowl without mentioning his race.[34] This silence was most likely typical of network broadcasts in the 1930s as well, in order not to offend those in the audience opposed to integration, but on at least one occasion Mutual's announcer made so much of race that he irritated the sports editor of the *Chicago Defender.* When Northwestern with Bernie Jefferson played Purdue in 1937, Fay Young found the repeated references to "that colored player, Jefferson," insulting. "Suppose they said 'that Irish fellow,' 'that Jewish player,' 'that Greek player,' 'that Italian player,' and so forth," Young wrote in his column that week, "giving the nationality or color behind each individual? . . . Perhaps the gentleman at the mike wanted to give the race credit for Mr. Jefferson's

FIGURE 9-2. This football program for the game between San Jose State and the College of the Pacific in 1935 was one of a series done for West Coast universities by John W. Haynes. (The same cover was used for the Washington State–USC game in 1935, and a similar one for Loyola-USC in 1932; there were undoubtedly others.) The cover suggests a casual assumption about the "proper" role of black Americans in the world of big-time college football. (Reprinted with permission of the University of the Pacific Archives)

"AMID THE CHEERS OF THE SPECTATORS THE ELEVEN TOOK THE FIELD."

FIGURE 9-3. This cartoon in the 19 November 1925 "Football Number" of *Life* suggested that shooting craps, not football, was the big-time black sport. A cartoon with a similar theme appeared in *Life* on 11 November 1926.

playing. Most of the fans can't believe it that way. They don't like it and all morning Monday, our telephones were busy calling our attention to it." [35]

The implications of racial consciousness and unconsciousness in the mainstream media are not simple and obvious. Ignoring their race rendered black players both individual and invisible. Newsreel coverage of big-time college football followed the pattern of the other national media: in the 1930s, there was occasional identification of "the flashy Negro back" (Bernie Jefferson in 1938) or "sensational Negro back" (Kenny Washington in 1939), but by the 1940s any comment on race had become rare.[36] The startling exceptions to this restraint appeared in a handful of pieces on all-black football in the 1930s. In November 1931, *Hearst Metrotone News* filmed a football game between Booker T. Washington and St. Joseph's high schools in Norfolk, Virginia, distributed to theaters with the title, "Colored Gals Get Football Fever." With introductory music more appropriate for a Busby Berkeley musical than for a serious football game, the narrator announced that "until you've seen Afro-American football, you ain't seen nothin'." As the film shifted back and forth from the "dark shadows" playing on the field to the cheerleaders and female fans in the stands, the action was accompanied by commentary such as this: "The Booker T. boys have developed a shift that's better than pork chops, and every time the captain calls the magic signal, 'Come seven, eleven,' they plow through the St. Joseph's bunch like they were on a coon hunt." The cheerleaders and fans of overmatched St. Joseph's were described this way: "The losers have a red hot mama that keeps the crowd a-sizzling, and every time her man makes a couple of downs, she starts a ragtime chorus." One player "gets the football in a watermelon clinch," then "off he goes as if the farmer was after him." Another is downed "on the chicken yard line with a drumstick tackle." The contest ends on this note: "The St. Joseph's team forgot its rabbit's feet, so it didn't have a chance. The game might be going on yet, only the referee had such a hard time telling the players apart that he called the game on account of darkness." Win or lose, "the girls of High Yaller High" lost none of their enthusiasm.[37]

This was football in minstrel blackface, football as buffoonery, football played by Amos 'n' Andy, yet nothing in the images on the screen suggests anything but a conventional game. Though less polished than Rockne's Four Horsemen, the teams apparently played a version of the Notre Dame shift used by half the football world. The "red hot mama" leading the cheers is dressed in a white collared blouse, cardigan sweater, and long skirt—a typical high school girl of the period. This newsreel was seen and heard in movie theaters throughout the country, along with four others produced by Hearst's company in the early 1930s. The only other one that survives, from 1936, did not indulge in the specific stereotypes of dice-rolling, coon-hunting, watermelon- and fried-chicken-eating, ragtime-singing, sexually uninhibited, superstitious darkies—a virtual encyclopedia of stereotypes in two minutes of narration—but it did present the football game as decidedly less interesting than the commotion in the stands. "If you want to hear football rootin' that *is* rootin'," the narrator opens, "hear this," as the camera zooms in on the cheerleaders and the crowd. The opponents again were Booker T. Washington and St. Joseph's, but the stars were "those happy fans" shown gyrating and chanting in the bleachers.[38] The emphasis in both newsreels on the "colored gals" on the sidelines is particularly striking. At a time when female cheerleaders were not yet the norm, black football was sexualized in these newsreels far more overtly than was permissible with "white" football. While the football hero and his lovely admirer had been pop-culture icons since the turn of the century, their relation to each other, their sexual relation, remained barely implicit. The "colored gals" at the Booker T. Washington–St. Joseph's games were exuberant and expressive, but nothing in the newsreel footage warranted the suggestion that the female cheerleader was a "red hot mama" cooking up something for "her man."[39]

One more item, from 1938, shown by three of the five major newsreels, likewise suggests a broad tolerance for racial mockery. A preseason practice session at LSU, obviously staged for the newsreel cameras, included what Paramount's announcer called "a brand new stunt for forward pass training." As the quarterbacks toss a ball through a hole in a canvas stretched over a frame, suddenly the hole is filled by the helmeted black head of what Universal's release sheet called a Negro "dodger" and Hearst's described as a "live jungle mascot," who jerks his head about as he attempts to avoid being hit by the ball.[40] Throwing a baseball at the head of a "darky" poked through a screen had been an amusement at county fairs at the turn of the century.[41] That such a demonstration was staged in Baton Rouge, Louisiana, in 1938 is less astonishing than that it could still be considered comical for national distribution by the major newsreels.

This "jungle mascot" was dodging footballs at the same time that Brud Holland was earning All-America honors at end for Cornell, and Kenny Washington was dazzling football crowds up and down the West Coast. Over the 1930s, sportswriters in the mainstream press were increasingly exposed to black football prowess, and scattered details in newspaper coverage, particularly early in the decade, reveal the resistance black players had to overcome.[42] Joe Lillard was regularly called "Happy Joe" and "Shufflin' Joe" in the *Portland Oregonian* in 1931, when he briefly starred at the University of Oregon. About this same time, the *Los Angeles Times* ran a photo of UCLA guard "Sad Sam" Storey with arms upraised to break up a pass—a typical football play—with a caption declaring that "it looks as though the theme song should be 'All God's Chillun Got Wings.'"[43] And the *Chicago Tribune* in the early 1930s more explicitly transformed a big black end at Indiana University, Fitzhugh Lyons, into a figure from the minstrel and vaudeville stage. In the *Tribune*'s account of the Indiana-Chicago game in 1931, when Lyons caught a touchdown pass, he "didn't seem to realize that he had scored, but attempted to dodge a couple of belated Maroon tacklers" (why it was Lyons, not the "belated Maroon tacklers," who did not know he had scored is unclear). To describe the black end, at the customarily heroic moment of scoring a touchdown, as comically unaware of his own feat cast Lyons as the dim-witted darky in a slapstick vaudeville routine. The following season, after Lyons scored on a fifty-yard pass in a losing effort against Chicago, the *Tribune* deflated his achievement with another mildly slapstick touch: Lyons "slid the remaining distance with half the Maroon team aboard him."[44] In the other Chicago papers these touchdowns were ordinary football plays.[45] A *Tribune* writer also referred to Lyons and black teammate Jesse Babb in 1932 as "the two able 'ho-de-hi' boys," misstating Cab Calloway's signature refrain.[46] Among the major Chicago dailies, the *Tribune* (notoriously reactionary in its news coverage and editorials) stood out for subtly but routinely evoking racial stereotypes.

Such portraiture suggests both the ready availability of racial stereotypes and the audience's tolerance, if not enthusiastic acceptance, of them. "Shufflin' Joe" Lillard was cast in a Steppin Fetchit role on the gridiron, Sam

Storey as the childlike primitive, Fitzhugh Lyons as the broad-backed but dim-witted field hand. All were versions of what Joseph Boskin has identified as the "Sambo" figure in American culture, the black American jester who, from the plantation darkies of 1850s novels to the chauffeurs of 1930s movies, was found "in every nook and cranny of popular culture." Racial and racist stereotypes, in other words, existed everywhere in American culture in the 1930s, and therefore nowhere in particular. Football was no special repository of such stereotypes but was embedded in a web of racial representations so familiar that regular explicit connections were unnecessary to keep them alive. Sambo starred in *Amos 'n' Andy;* he appeared as Uncle Tom in *The Littlest Rebel* (featuring Bojangles Robinson alongside Shirley Temple) and as the brutal savage in *Tarzan's* many sequels.[47] Casting black football players as Sambo reaffirmed white superiority, as blacks were making slow inroads in the sport where American masculinity was most conspicuously on display.

FOOTBALL IN BLACK AND WHITE

Somewhere behind the Sambo masks superimposed by a racist culture were the actual young black athletes. Among the 1,500 black students on marginally integrated campuses in the 1920s and 1930s, all of whom were "essentially pariahs,"[48] those who played football suffered additional indignities. Every star player was a marked man on the field; black players were marked by their race as well. The most brutal incident occurred in 1923, when the first black athlete to play for Iowa State, Jack Trice, died from injuries suffered in a game against Minnesota. The most widely publicized incident occurred nearly thirty years later, in 1951, when Drake's Johnny Bright was slugged by an Oklahoma A&M player, and the evidence was captured by a photographer for the *Des Moines Register* and distributed over the AP wire. After Drake issued a formal complaint, the Missouri Valley Conference dithered, then refused to punish the player or his school, prompting Drake to resign from the conference. But the widespread publication of the damning photos provoked editorials and condemnations by sports columnists throughout the country, guaranteeing that the act would not be simply ignored and quickly forgotten.

Other incidents were subtler, and nearly invisible to the football public. A startling moment in Notre Dame's upset of Minnesota in 1937, for example, almost went unreported. After Minnesota coach Bernie Bierman sent "negro guard" Horace Bell onto the field to kick the extra point after a Gopher touchdown, Bell "left the field without attempting it. The Minne-

FIGURE 9-4. The slugging of Johnny Bright was captured by a photographer for the *Des Moines Register* and distributed by the Associated Press, then picked up by *Life* on 5 November. The sequence of photos also won a Pulitzer Prize the following spring. As the NCAA leader in total offense, Bright was a marked man for his talent, as well as his race. (Photo by John Robinson and Don Ultang, copyright © 1951, the *Des Moines Register* and Tribune Company; reprinted with permission)

sota players apparently preferred George Faust, substitute quarterback, to make the attempt." This was the account reported by the United Press. The more widely distributed Associated Press coverage did not mention Bell at all, nor did either the (white) *Chicago Tribune* or the (black) *Chicago Defender.* Closer to home, one of Minneapolis's black weeklies, the *Twin-City Herald,* likewise reported nothing, while another, the *Minneapolis Spokesman,* as well as the *Minneapolis Tribune,* quoted Bierman's explanation that Bell had been injured earlier in the game. Closest of all to the events, the University of Minnesota's campus paper, the *Minnesota Daily,* also said nothing initially but four days later mentioned Bell among the injured Gopher players trying to recover in time for the next game. His injury? A strained shoulder ligament. Reconstructing this event more than a half-century later, we cannot be certain that the "negro guard" was rebuffed by teammates, as the UP writer implied, but it is at least possible that the Minnesota–Notre Dame game was one episode in the undocumented history of racial slights in football that is many times greater than the documented one.[49]

The reticence of the *Chicago Defender* and the black weeklies in Minneapolis was due, of course, not to a conspiracy of silence but to a shortage of staff and thus dependence on outside sources. The *Defender* and the rest of the black press, in fact, waged a continuous struggle for racial justice and black dignity in football. The most blatant acts of discrimination, the ones that provoked the deepest passions in the black press, were the periodic benchings of black players to placate southern opponents.[50] Initially, northern schools refused to accommodate southern prejudices, but as intersectional ambitions grew, principle gave way to expediency. Rutgers in 1917 had refused to hold Paul Robeson out of a game with West Virginia, and Washington and Jefferson likewise refused to bench Charlie West for the Washington and Lee game in 1923, but in 1925 Northwestern agreed to hold out Fred Moore against Tulane. Four years later, when New York University coach Chick Meehan agreed to keep his black quarterback, Dave Myers, out of NYU's games against West Virginia Wesleyan and Georgia, a new shameful era in college football fully began. Such benchings became increasingly common in the 1930s, as more major football schools in the North integrated their teams, and as universities from all regions scheduled intersectional contests in quest of national prominence. Ohio State's Bill Bell was benched for games against Navy in 1930 and Vanderbilt in 1931, Iowa's Windy Wallace and Borce Dickerson against George Washington in 1932, Michigan's Willis Ward against Georgia Tech in 1934, Minnesota's Dwight Reed against Tulane in 1935, Reed again with teammate Horace Bell (Bill's brother) against Texas in 1936, and Syracuse's Wilmeth Sidat-Singh against Maryland in 1937. Sidat-Singh's case is most revealing: he was an acceptable opponent when mistaken for a Hindu, but not as an African American.[51] In 1939, Boston College running back Lou Montgomery was benched three times in one season—for Florida, Auburn, and finally Clemson in the Cotton Bowl—but it was NYU's benching of Leonard Bates against Missouri in 1940 that provoked the greatest outrage: a full-scale campus protest that continued for months, with a "Bates Must Play" committee of students and faculty aligned against the athletic department and the more moderate Student Council.[52]

Northern schools sometimes deferred to southern segregationists even when playing on their home fields. NYU's contests against Georgia and West Virginia Wesleyan in 1929, for example, were played in New York; Michigan's game with Georgia Tech, in 1934, in Ann Arbor. Patrick Miller has identified the NYU–North Carolina game in 1936 as the breakthrough event. Although North Carolina's president, Frank Porter Graham, did not publicly proclaim his stand, he privately arranged with NYU officials for their star black running back, Ed Williams, to play in the game at the Polo Grounds.[53] Following this contest, the typical arrangement between North and South was to observe the traditions of the host team: integrated contests in northern cities, segregated ones in the South. Syracuse's Sidat-Singh, held out of the Maryland game in Baltimore in 1937, played against both Maryland and Duke in 1938, but at home. UCLA, with black athletes, played SMU in 1937 and TCU in 1939, on both occasions in Los Angeles, at a time when integrated games in Dallas or Fort Worth were unthinkable. Left home when the team traveled to Missouri in 1940, Len Bates played against Texas A&M, Tulane, and Georgetown in New York that season, and would have played at home against Missouri in 1941 had he not been injured. There were exceptions to this home-field rule: the Auburn game for which Boston College agreed to bench Lou Montgomery in 1939, for example, was played in Boston. There were no exceptions on the other side for several years, however: no integrated team played in the South until Harvard's Chester Pierce was welcomed to Charlottesville by the University of Virginia in 1947. (The Cavaliers' hospitality had its limits, as they walloped Harvard 47–0.)

With the benchings of black players usually ignored by the national wire services and sometimes barely acknowledged by local newspapers, the *Chicago Defender, Pittsburgh Courier,* and rest of the black press were nearly alone, joined only by the Communist Party's *Daily Worker,* in denouncing the expediency of the northern schools and sometimes the complicity of the black players who quietly accepted their humiliation. The black press made no attempt to shame the southern "Cracker" schools—their racism and segregationist policies were simply taken for granted—but blasted the hypocrisy of northern institutions purportedly committed to democratic principles. There is no clear evidence that the black press had a major impact on the increasing integration of football, as it did in the case of major league baseball, but newspapers such as the *Defender* and *Courier* at least guaranteed that such decisions would not go completely unnoticed.

The broader campaign for black dignity was a more difficult struggle, because the opposing targets were more elusive, a general climate of racism rather than specific racist acts. A minstrel clown in the *Chicago Tribune,* Fitzhugh Lyons was a "race star" in the *Chicago Defender,* and a series of black football heroes followed Lyons in the *Defender*'s pages: in 1932 and 1933, the Chicago Cardinals' Joe Lillard, the last black man to play in the NFL before reintegration in 1946; Iowa's Oze Simmons in 1934, 1935, and 1936; Northwestern's Bernie Jefferson in 1937 and 1938; UCLA's "Sepia trio" of Kenny Washington, Jackie Robinson, and Woody Strode in 1939. Washington seems to have been the greatest of these players, the limitations on his awards and opportunities the most egregious injustice due to race, but for the ecstasy and anguish of his career at Iowa, Oze Simmons was the quintessential black football player of the 1930s: immensely talented and hugely celebrated initially in both the mainstream and the black press, but confronted by constant racial obstacles that ultimately blighted his once-glorious career.

A Texan who came to Iowa for the opportunity to play integrated big-time football, Simmons startled the sporting world in his first conference game as a sophomore in 1934 by scoring on a 49-yard run and gaining 166 yards as Iowa upset Northwestern, 20–7. Wilfrid Smith in the *Chicago Tribune* was as effusive as David Kellum in the *Chicago Defender*. Smith described Simmons in breathlessly mixed metaphors as "the torpedo of the Hawkeye attack" who "had the Wildcats fumbling at his twinkling heels most of the afternoon, clutching at empty spaces," as the crowd of 25,000 "acclaimed his superiority." Kellum inflated the size of the crowd and cast its response to Simmons in terms of race relations, but otherwise sounded the same note: "A remarkable demonstration of interracial goodwill and sportsmanship and one almost without precedent in grid history was witnessed here today when 35,000 spectators of all races and nationalities arose from their seats as one, and proclaimed Oze Simmons, Iowa's slippery, elusive and sensational new football thunderbolt, for his dazzling individual exhibition against a stubborn Northwestern university team." Harry MacNamara, the chief football writer for the *Chicago Herald and Examiner,* described the crowd's tribute to Simmons in the same way.[54] At least some later commentators, pondering what went wrong in Simmons's career at Iowa, concluded that his spectacular debut raised fans' expectations impossibly high and fostered resentment among his own teammates over his headlines and newspaper copy. Whether this instant publicity was more dangerous for a sophomore or for a black player is the question that hovered over Oze Simmons's career.

By his second game Simmons had already become in the *Chicago Tribune* "the Negro boy who made himself famous a week ago against Northwestern." He provided most of the offense but also a costly fumble in a one-point loss to Nebraska, then the following week fumbled twice and was completely held in check as Iowa lost to Iowa State, 31–6. For the fourth game, against powerful Minnesota, Simmons was still expected to give the crowd "a few thrills, such as he provided against Northwestern three weeks ago." Instead, Simmons was knocked out of the game twice as Minnesota won 48–12. Next came a scoreless tie with Indiana, in which "the highly touted Oze Simmons, Iowa Negro half back, was not in form." And so it went.[55]

The *Chicago Defender* had more at stake in Simmons's rise, then fall, from opening-day grace. Two weeks after reporting on Simmons's spectacular debut, the *Defender* fleshed out for readers a black Horatio Alger hero: a young man who left Texas with his brother Don, coming to Iowa because of Ossie Solem's reputation as a coach and Iowa's reputation as a place where "Race boys had succeeded as members of Hawkeye teams." Simmons took a job in a carwash to pay his own way; he remained in Iowa over the summer and "doggedly made up work to become eligible." Quiet and modest, Simmons was a black Frank Merriwell. Unwilling to surrender the hopes raised by Simmons's spectacular debut, the *Defender* even downplayed the debacle against Minnesota. On the fact that Simmons was knocked out three times (the *Tribune* mentioned only two), the second incident bringing a roughness penalty and ejection of the Minnesota player, David Kellum wrote, "Your correspondent hardly thinks that the fact that Simmons was a member of the Race was responsible for his unusually rough treatment. It just happens that he was the best man on Iowa's team and it is the policy of the Gophers to get the best man." Red Grange had been treated the same way. As to the disastrous outcome of the game: with Minnesota so much better, Simmons had no chance. But at season's end a disquieting note appeared in the *Defender*'s pages: rumors that Simmons would transfer to Northwestern because of "lack of cooperation from the rest of the team and the coaches."[56]

By the start of the 1935 season all seemed well again, as Simmons shared the Iowa spotlight with backfield mate and team captain Dick Crayne, the two of them playing out in the *Chicago Tribune*, the *Herald and Examiner*, and other dailies what would become the familiar roles of steady white and spectacular black players. The opening South Dakota game saw Simmons's "apparent return to last season's early form," as he scored on punt returns of 71 and 51 yards. Against Colgate the next Saturday Oze was "brilliant" (while Crayne was "dependable"). Two weeks later fans watched Simmons "dazzle" Illinois with 192 yards rushing on sixteen attempts, including another 71-yard touchdown run (here, Simmons was "elusive," Crayne "smashing"). A 58-yard touchdown by "the black jackrabbit of the prairie states" that salvaged a 6–6 tie with Indiana marked another premature end to Simmons's and Iowa's glory for the year. In the final three games Oze "gave the Gophers many anxious minutes" in a narrow loss to Minnesota, then threw an interception that keyed a Purdue victory and was bottled up by Northwestern in a season-ending scoreless tie. Crayne "had to come to the rescue of the colored star" in this finale.[57]

A star of erratic or frustrated brilliance in the *Chicago Tribune* (as well as the *Daily News* and *Herald and Examiner*), Oze Simmons was a once-in-alifetime genius in the *Chicago Defender*, as the University of Iowa in 1935 emphatically became black Chicago's home team and Oze Simmons the black messiah of college football. A full page of Simmons in the *Chicago Defender* on 2 November proclaimed Oze "The Joe Louis of Football" and, after darting 71 yards for a touchdown against Illinois, a black Red Grange as well. In one column the *Defender's* Al Monroe strove to separate Oze from the run-of-the-mill football heroes created each year by newspaper hype. "A star is a product of circumstance, ability and training," Monroe wrote, "a combination which is found at intervals that not even the great Dr. Albert Einstein, famed for his abstruse theory of relativity, could reduce to mathematical certainty." True stars, "like poets, are not made. They are born. . . . they come unheralded, once in a generation."[58]

Iowa's games in 1935 became pilgrimages for black America. Under the headline, "Hundreds Go To Iowa For Grid Games," on 16 November, the *Defender* named the most famous of the 350 black football fans—including Roy Wilkins, editor of the *Crisis,* and Duke Slater, a Chicago judge and former NFL star and All-American at Iowa—who for one day swelled Iowa City's "Race population of nine families." Minnesota won the game but by a narrow margin, and "the Brown Shadow of the gridiron" amply rewarded his followers. Dan Burley slipped into the epic mode of 1890s football journalism, invoking classical history rather than black folklore (John Henry with his hammer would have fit) to describe Iowa's valiant resistance to a superior foe: "Like Leonidas and the Spartans at the Pass of Thermopylae, the courageous Hawkeye crew withstood the thunderbolt assaults of the Norsemen until the third period when the murkiness of the darkening skies besmeared a wet field with shadows admitting that defeat was inevitable." As the disappointments of 1934 were repeated, however, Oze Simmons appeared less a Leonidas among Spartan teammates than a king deserted by his men. "The Lad Who Ran Alone" is what Al Monroe termed him in an end-of-the-season column; more prosaically, a brilliant running back whose teammates would not block for him.[59]

The 1935 season ended on a sour note, with Iowa deciding not to elect a captain for the following year, an unprecedented move aimed obviously at Oze Simmons, the only real candidate for the position. And the 1936 season played out in bitterness and recrimination, with race and racism seemingly the causes. By 1936 Simmons had acquired an astonishing array of alliterative and allusive nicknames from sportswriters, the most elaborate ones coming from the black press: the Ebony Eel, the Texas Tornado, the Sepia Sprite, the Wizard of Oze, the Hula-Hipped Hawkeye Hog Hide

Handler. That season Simmons broke loose against South Dakota and Indiana, and he had his moments against Carleton, Northwestern, Illinois, and Minnesota, but as the season wore on it repeated his sophomore- and junior-year frustration. The *Tribune* noted that in the Northwestern game "his own teammates failed to block or to interfere or to produce the holes through which he might have sped," but otherwise credited the opponents' defenses. The *Defender* made uncooperative teammates its major theme. In Iowa's loss to Northwestern on 3 October, Oze received "little or no support" from his teammates, who "play[ed] stupid football." Two weeks later, "buzzing tongues were wagging plenty around the campus this week as the result of a direct charge that members of the varsity were refusing to 'take out' and block for Oze Simmons whenever the famous back carried the ball." Al Monroe also raised the issue again in his column. When it was reported that the revered Duke Slater had been hired to coach the Iowa linemen, perceptive readers likely wondered if his unannounced charge was to teach racial cooperation. If so, his efforts failed.[60]

The ugly situation soon came to a head and Oze Simmons's career to a conclusion as painful as its beginning was delirious. In the days following the brutal 52–0 defeat by Minnesota on 7 November, Simmons, stung by coach Ossie Solem's criticism while watching game film, retorted (as the press recreated the scene), "Okay, okay, I lost the game 52 to 0." Solem told him to "shut up" and to leave the dressing room. Simmons missed practice on Tuesday, then reported the next day, but when he refused to apologize Solem ordered him off the field. After Solem and a faculty member visited the running back in his room that night and worked out a reconciliation, Simmons returned to practice, then played in Iowa's final two games, against Purdue and Temple. The *Chicago Tribune* followed these events with daily reports blaming neither Solem nor Simmons, but without editorial comment. The coach tried to maintain discipline on a disintegrating team; the star player could not be held responsible for his teammates' failings. And the *Tribune* did print Simmons's own view of the dispute: his anger over being accused of "laying down" against Minnesota when he in fact played with an injured leg. Simmons sounded like anything but a prima donna when he declared, "I came to get an education and I want to finish as soon as possible and get a job that will help me take care of my mother." The *Chicago Daily News* also gave the controversy full and even-handed treatment, sympathetic to Simmons, critical of his teammates.[61]

As a weekly, the *Chicago Defender* could only report the incident after its resolution, and it quoted from the statements published previously in the *Tribune, Daily News,* and other Chicago papers. The *Defender* probed the underlying causes: blockers' "opening the switch" on Simmons—letting their men through to smear him, a common practice in professional football but sometimes, as in this case, race-related—and the racist stereotype underlying Solem's claim that Oze "couldn't take it." The *Defender* also reprinted a telegram sent to Ossie Solem by one Iowa supporter: "Heartily approve your Simmons action although three years late. Let's develop Iowa talent now." "Iowa talent" meant white talent, as local talent did for most of the state universities in the North where football most thrived. During football's tribal era, African Americans were mostly outside the tribe. The *Defender* did not take Simmons's side entirely. Al Monroe contributed a column highly critical of Oze's brother Don, a reserve end on the football team, who it now appeared had been Oze's spokesman throughout his career at Iowa. According to Monroe, had Don known "the essentials of keeping quiet when the importance of a grid career and a free education was at stake," Oze would have been "the greatest football player the western conference has ever seen."[62]

As Oze's star dimmed, then was extinguished, the sense of great loss can still be felt when reading the pages of the *Defender* today. There was more sadness than outrage in the reporting of Oze Simmons's final month as a Hawkeye. In the same issue that reported on the blow-up with Solem, another story proclaimed Northwestern sophomore Bernard Jefferson "among the great backs of Big Ten history," a combination of Grange and Simmons, designated to fill the void left by Oze before Oze had even left it. When junior end Homer Harris, Simmons's black teammate, was named Iowa's MVP by the *Chicago Tribune,* then captain by his teammates (who had bypassed Oze the year before), the *Defender* was torn between pride in the first black player so honored and bitterness over yet another indirect slight to Simmons. The *Chicago Daily Times* reported at the end of the season that Simmons would play pro football the following year, but the reporter was apparently not privy to the NFL owners' "gentlemen's agreement."[63] Instead, Simmons stayed on the margins of football for several years after leaving college, playing on minor-league and semi-professional teams such as Paterson (New Jersey) in the American Association and the all-black Chicago Panthers, and reappearing in the *Defender*'s pages for an occasional all-star game. The *Chicago Defender,* and the black community to which it spoke, invested heavily in black football stars like Oze Simmons. When those investments did not pay off, whether through black failure or white obstruction, the loss was equally heavy.

Northwestern's Bernie Jefferson was in the wings to assume Simmons's role on the college football scene, as were Brud Holland at Cornell, Ed Williams at NYU, and Wilmeth Sidat-Singh at Syracuse; in 1939, UCLA became black America's team, with Kenny Washington, Jackie Robinson, and Woody Strode (particularly in this, his junior season, Robinson was more renowned as a running back at UCLA than as a baseball player). Washington was as celebrated in the *Los Angeles Times* as in the black weeklies, but he remained a West Coast football hero who went on to star not in the NFL but for the Hollywood Bears and the San Francisco Clippers in the Pacific Coast League and the American Professional Football League. It was not until 1946 that an NFL team, the Los Angeles Rams, signed him, but by then, six years after graduation, his battered knees had reduced him to an ordinary player. Over the late 1940s and 1950s, no single Oze Simmons or Kenny Washington represented "mixed football" in the black press; rather, the increasingly numerous black players in the Big Ten and Pacific Coast Conferences, and in the All-America Football Conference and the newly reintegrated NFL, evoked pride in numbers instead of lone heroes.

The presence of Buddy Young, J. C. Caroline, Jim Brown, and dozens more black stars in big-time college football in the postwar years made the increasing integration of football an unavoidable fact, even for southerners whose own football was still segregated but whose newspapers reflected the reality elsewhere. The South's last stand for racial purity took place before the 1956 Sugar Bowl, the first major battle over segregation to be a truly national event. The attempt by Georgia's governor, Marvin Griffin, to prevent Georgia Tech from playing against Pittsburgh and its one black player, running back Bobby Grier, caused a small riot by some 2,000 Georgia Tech students, who stormed the capitol and burned the governor in effigy, and provoked a subsequent debate in which sports columnists and editorial writers throughout the country weighed in.[64] Griffin had initially, but privately, approved Bobby Dodd's decision to play Pitt, following the custom for Georgia Tech and Georgia to play integrated teams away from home.[65] When the issue became public, however, and thus politicized, Griffin seized the occasion to promote white Georgians' "massive resistance" to desegregation. "The South stands at Armageddon," declared Griffin's telegram to the Board of Regents. "The battle is joined. We cannot make the slightest concession to the enemy in this dark and lamentable hour of struggle. There is no more difference in compromising the integrity of race on the playing field than in doing so in the classrooms. One break in the dike and the relentless seas will rush in and destroy us."[66] Called to an emergency meeting, the Board of Regents after considerable debate (reported in detail in wire-service accounts) endorsed Tech's contractual obligation to the Sugar Bowl but also reaffirmed the state of Georgia's commitment to segregation. The Regents' ruling was a short-term victory for integration but cast doubt on all future intersectional games, including bowl games, for the state's two major universities.

Newspapers everywhere carried the same wire-service accounts, some as the lead story on the front page, others in the sports section. The distinction mattered—implying whether it was a story about civil rights or about sports—given the current upheavals over school integration, bus boycotts, and other desegregation efforts targeting the South. Sports columnists and editorial writers expressed each paper's own voice more directly; the sentiment was overwhelmingly anti-Griffin but on revealingly varied terms. In the North, the *Philadelphia Inquirer, New York Daily News,* and *Boston Record* launched attacks on the segregationists (the *Record* called Griffin "a boob of . . . limited intellectual capacity"), while the *Portland Oregonian* saluted the rioting students at Georgia Tech as civil rights activists. The *Newark News* translated the incident into a Cold War story: Griffin's wrongheaded action providing fodder for Soviet propagandists to cast the United States as "an enemy of the colored peoples of the world." To the *New York Post,* the gridiron seemed an inappropriate arena for promoting segregation (the entire affair smacked of "a deadly note of burlesque"), but the *Christian Science Monitor* quite differently predicted that this seemingly "trivial" objection to integrating a mere football game "will have repercussions extending far beyond a college campus." The *New York Times* agreed in seeing sport as an ideal arena for demonstrating the unreasonableness of racial prejudice.[67] The northern press in general subscribed to a view that integration in sports was not a political issue, a redistribution of power by legal means, but an issue of fair play and sportsmanship: the right of blacks to demonstrate their worth in open competition.

Many southern editors and sports columnists were critical of Governor Griffin as well, more often, however, on grounds of contractual or sporting honor rather than racial justice. They took Griffin to task not for being racist but for embarrassing the South or jeopardizing football in the state of Georgia, or for damaging the cause of segregation itself. At least one southern newspaper, the *Louisville Courier-Journal,* did openly champion racial and social equality. In an editorial on 6 December the paper praised the "highly articulate" students at Georgia Tech for creating a true "social phenomenon" out of an athletic issue, and denounced Griffin for his "unreason" and his white supremacist ideas. If the *Washington Post* can be considered a southern newspaper, it, too, should be noted for its pro-integration stand. Other newspapers in the border states tended to take more moderate positions. The *Nashville Banner* and *Raleigh News and Observer* worried along with *Atlanta Journal* sports editor Ed Danforth that if Griffin prevailed, "both Tech and the U of Georgia will be wrecked athletically." In Atlanta the *Constitution* and the *Journal* subscribed to the view that a football game, not the future of the South, was at stake, seemingly a tactical decision by progressive editors with a long-term agenda of unforced, gradual integration.[68]

Moderate Atlantans and editors in the border states by no means spoke for the entire region. Deeper south, at least one newspaper, the *Jackson Daily News,* sided entirely with Griffin from the outset and didn't give a damn about the opinion of any outsider. The *Daily News* and its editor, Frederick Sullens, were obsessed with segregation and integration in December 1955. The murder of Emmett Till, what David Halberstam has termed "the first great media event of the civil rights movement," had taken place just a few months earlier, in August, with the acquittal of his murderers in September.[69] Though itself not yet a national news story, the Montgomery bus boycott was also underway in December, and likely known to a newspaper editor in neighboring Mississippi. As the Grier episode unfolded, a kind of hysteria marked the two front-page editorials and two front-page columns by Sullens that raged against southern teams' participating in both the Sugar Bowl and the Junior Rose Bowl, where a Mississippi team, Jones County Junior College, was to meet a California team with eight black players. Sullens warned that Jones's participation in the Junior Rose Bowl would be tantamount to "acceptance of social equality" and would contribute to the "mongrelization of the white race," and he threatened Jones officials that the state legislature would remember this betrayal when the school's budget was considered at the next session. About the Sugar Bowl, he warned again against "the NAACP's mongrelization scheme." Although Pitt had just one black player, "being a little bit integrated is like being a little bit pregnant. A few short years ago only one Negro was in the National Baseball League!!"[70]

Sullens's racist rantings were atypical of editorials even in the deep South, most of which seem to have clung to segregation but feared that Governor Griffin had unwittingly set back the cause. The pro-segregationist *Augusta Chronicle* berated Griffin for "strain[ing] at gnats" at the risk of Tech's football program. Sports editor Naylor Stone expressed the same worry in the *Birmingham Post-Herald,* while editorials in the *Post-Herald,* the *Albany Herald*

(Georgia), and the *Charleston News and Courier* also worried that Griffin's extremism over a football game would undermine the larger cause of segregation in the South.[71] The most conspicuously silent of southern newspapers was the *New Orleans Times-Picayune*, likely to minimize the controversy for the sake of attendance at the local bowl game. Discussing the local coverage of the school integration crisis in Little Rock in 1957, David Halberstam has noted that most newspaper editors of the day tended to "put their own survival first and tried not to offend local sensibilities. Often, in moments of crisis, their instinct would be to protect the community against its critics, to soften accounts of its failings and, above all, to blame outsiders."[72] Coverage of the 1956 Sugar Bowl confirms this judgment.

With the mainstream press, even in the South, overwhelmingly critical of the Georgia governor and supportive of an integrated Sugar Bowl, however various the rationales and motives, the black press was no longer an isolated voice from the margins. But its voice remained distinctive. The more progressive southern editors saw the Grier episode as a single incident in what would have to be a gradual shift toward integration. Their more conservative colleagues saw it as a tactical retreat to preserve segregation where it mattered more. The black press challenged not only these positions but also the *New York Times*'s faith in a color-blind sporting world *now* where performance alone mattered. Black commentators entertained no illusions that Joe Louis, Jackie Robinson, and Roy Campanella—or, in football, Buddy Young, Marion Motley, and Ollie Matson—had ushered in a world in which race was no longer a handicap.

Above all, what the black press insisted was that the Grier affair was a racial matter, not a football matter. Writing in the *Atlanta Daily World,* Marion Jackson exulted that the controversy had done "a tremendous job of blasting wide open the sullen, smoldering bigotry which kept the area in social and economic slavery."[73] While the *Atlanta Constitution* and *Atlanta Journal* reassured white readers that the status quo had been preserved, the *Pittsburgh Courier* assured black readers that much was changing. Where the southern press particularly tried to minimize the peripheral social integration in New Orleans that would result from the game, the *Courier* proclaimed that "Bobby Grier, the 195-pound University of Pittsburgh varsity fullback, will travel, eat, sleep, practice and play, when his team goes to New Orleans for the Sugar Bowl game" (Grier and his white teammates in fact stayed together at Tulane University to avoid segregated hotels). Seating in the Pitt section would not be segregated, the *Courier* reported; the Pitt band, with a number of black members, would also attend. Grier himself was portrayed as popular with his teammates, not a loner who showed up for practice and then went his own way. When a secondary segregation issue arose over the postgame banquet—Grier could attend the dinner but would leave before the dancing began, so as not to offend whites in attendance—the president of a local black college publicly invited Grier to an alternative party. In response, the *Courier*'s Bill Nunn regretted squandering an opportunity for a symbolically powerful confrontation.[74] Within the general sense of qualified triumph in the pro-integration camp, Sam Lacy, the sports editor of the *Baltimore Afro-American,* stood out as a thorough skeptic. While his own paper shared in the exhilaration of defeating racism, Lacy saw likely shrewdness in the adversary: the possibility that what seemed to progressive folk to be Governor Griffin's mere buffoonery might play well with those who had elected him on a segregationist platform.[75]

The contest itself proved a fitting climax to the pregame controversy, when, as if by some prankster god's meddling, Grier became the central figure in a controversy that determined the outcome of the game. Tech won the contest 7–3, the lone touchdown following a pass interference penalty against, of all people, Bobby Grier. Not one but two stories thus emerged from the Sugar Bowl: the first on the game itself, the second, on Grier's tearful denial that he had pushed the Tech receiver. As if the game were not already sufficiently dramatic as racial theater, the official who called Grier for interference was one Frank Lowery, of Birmingham, Alabama, in the heart of the segregationist South. Neither the wire-service photographs nor the newsreel coverage of the controversial play was conclusive.[76]

The Atlanta press applauded the Sugar Bowl as proof "that in sports at least there is no place for racial discrimination or prejudice," finding fault only with "the elaborationists" of the northern press who tried to transform a "commonplace incident" into a "sociological crisis."[77] Marion Jackson took the some position in the *Atlanta Daily World,* even predicting, "In less than five years negroes are going to be playing on Tech's Grant Field and Georgia's Sanford Stadium or else both will be out of the football business."[78] History eventually bore out Marion Jackson's prophesy—though in more like fifteen years than five—but not before fully justifying Sam Lacy's skepticism. In the aftermath of the Sugar Bowl, Georgia had an official mandate to maintain athletic segregation within the state, but legislative attempts in 1956 and 1957 to lock this policy in statute failed, and Georgia schools continued to play integrated teams, though only on the opponents' fields. Outside Georgia, the presidents of Mississippi's thirteen junior colleges preempted legislation to ban all integrated sports by agreeing to ban it themselves (the four-year universities followed this unwritten law as well); and the Louisiana legislature passed an anti-integration statute for athletic events that precluded a second integrated Sugar Bowl until 1965, after the Supreme Court had struck down the law.[79] The Southeastern and Southwest Conferences, nonetheless, began integrating by the late 1960s, but the Georgia schools were among the last to do so, Georgia Tech in 1970 and Georgia in 1972. The most powerful force for integration was not high-minded principle but the need to win football games, and integration, as future generations would learn, could mean recruiting ill-prepared young athletes with slight prospects of graduating. Opportunity and exploitation became deeply entangled.[80] Football was a powerful force for racial justice, but powerfully limited as well.

GREAT SPEED, NO GUTS OR BRAINS

Outside the South, a crucial shift in the popular representation of black football players had taken place by the 1950s. The number of African Americans playing major college football increased dramatically in the 1930s, at the same time that black athletes in other sports, Jesse Owens and Joe Louis most conspicuously, were forcing the sporting public to respond to black athleticism as a general phenomenon. In a highly influential book in 1896, Frederick L. Hoffman had used statistical data to "prove" that blacks were physically inferior to whites: their mortality rates were higher; their physical strength, lung capacity, and resistance to disease lower.[81] But in the 1930s, as black sprinters won gold medals at the 1932 and 1936 Olympics, and Joe Louis reigned over the heavyweight division beginning in 1937, the possibility of black athletic superiority for the first time seemed a real possibility. If this were to be the case, however, a compensating black inferiority had to be found. The racial stereotypes that became widely familiar in later decades began to emerge at this time.

Mainstream press coverage of sprint champions Eddie Tolan and Ralph Metcalfe at the 1932 Olympic Games resorted to stereotypes of the primitive and the childlike Negro—the comforting figure of Sambo.[82] Four years later, however, as Jesse Owens triumphed over Aryan supremacy as well as the world's best sprinters and long-jumpers in Berlin, writers increasingly bandied about possible explanations of black athletic success. The pioneering black medical researcher Montague Cobb had conducted a series of anatomical studies of Owens in 1935 that debunked such racial theories, but his results warranted only a brief wire-service notice and were largely ignored.[83] Joe Louis, however, was the dominant black athlete of the era, and coverage of Louis in the popular press most conspicuously reveals the high cost of praise for black athleticism. Although Louis was a boxer, responses to his rise reflect the climate in which black football stars played as well. The virulent racism that swirled about the first black heavyweight champion, Jack Johnson, in the 1910s was not replayed at the same hysterical pitch in Louis's case, but from Louis's first major fight, against Primo Carnera in June 1935, until his victory over Max Schmeling in their rematch in June 1938, coverage in the mainstream press resorted incessantly to the stereotype of the jungle savage. For hyped accounts of Joe Louis's victories, the same imaginative impulse that cast football games as epic battles led not to Greece and Rome but to the jungles of Africa. Louis was routinely termed a "jungle killer," a stalking "panther," or a "savage tiger" by the most respected and widely syndicated writers of the 1930s, men such as Grantland Rice and Paul Gallico, as well as wire-service reporters.[84]

Simply as a prizefighter, irrespective of his race, Louis was susceptible to less-than-flattering portraiture. The *Philadelphia Evening Bulletin* in 1926 had described Jack Dempsey on the eve of his first fight with Gene Tunney as a "Neanderthal" with "the backward sloping brow of a man born to be a fighter."[85] Jesse Owens, on the other hand, as well as Oze Simmons and his fellow black football players, were college students, not bowery pugs. As Westbrook Pegler dryly noted about much of the commentary on Owens, "It is a doubtful compliment to a Negro athlete who is qualified to attend college to attempt to account for his proficiency on the field by suggesting that he is still so close to the primitive that whenever he runs a foot-race in a formal meet between schools his civilization vanishes and be becomes again for the moment an African savage in breechcloth and nose ring legging it through the jungle."[86] The same was true for black football stars. When Oze Simmons erupted on the Chicago football scene against Northwestern in 1934, Red Marberry in Chicago's tabloid *Daily Times* heard the beat of "jungle tomtoms."[87] Marberry was just a sportswriter, straining for a catchy lead; in 1935, when a psychology professor at the University of Iowa ran tests on Oze Simmons to determine the source of his "unusual perception and reaction," this scientific interest in itself spoke volumes about more serious racial assumptions.[88] Likewise in 1939, when *Los Angeles Times* sportswriter Dick Hyland set up a "miracle eye" camera to discover the secret of Jackie Robinson's elusiveness as a running back—merely human sight was inadequate—the elaborate procedure created a distinct sense that Robinson's body and instincts defied ordinary human limits. No one set up a miracle eye camera to demystify Tom Harmon's open-field running, or performed psychological tests on Sammy Baugh. Perhaps Simmons and Robinson were simply more wondrous to those who saw them. But perhaps the wonder they evoked derived from their race.[89]

There was no simple consensus on race and athleticism in the 1930s. As George M. Frederickson has laid out the time line, among white intellectuals in the North the biological racism that predominated in the nineteenth century, then the "paternalistic" racism of the Progressive Era, and the "romantic racialism" of the 1920s were in turn challenged by liberal environmentalism in the 1930s.[90] Racial stereotypes, however, do not come and go with intellectual fashion but persist as layered strata within the culture. Sambo thus coexisted with the great "natural" black athlete in the 1930s and survived into the 1950s. The first integrated Cotton Bowl, played by SMU and Penn State in 1948, ended when one of the northerners' two black players, Dennie Hoggard, dropped a pass in the end zone that would have won the game. George White, sports editor of the *Dallas Morning News,* described the play this way: "Dennie Hoggard, lanky Negro end, dropped a bullet touchdown peg into his breadbasket from Elwood Petchel. He was behind the goal line on his knees, closely crowded, but he could have won the game by holding the pigskin. . . . He rolled over in disgust for a moment, then leaped up grinning from ear to ear, grasped Doak Walker's hand and lauded him for his great performance." One must wonder at White's keen eyesight in reading the helmeted black man's facial expression from the distance of the press box. (The Associated Press reported nothing about this play, or about Hoggard—typical silence in the national press.) In 1954, another writer in the *Morning News* described a "huge, good-natured Negro" named Clarence Barnes, standing 6'3" and weighing 285 pounds, who showed up at the semi-pro Dallas Hornets' practice one day and announced, "Don't want no money. . . . I just want to play football."[91] It had long been a journalistic rule to clean up athletes' ungrammatical (or obscene) language for print. The Babe Ruths of the sporting world spoke like Sunday school teachers in their press interviews. Barnes's own words, if they were his, were obviously quoted for their racially comic effect.

Behind both accounts lies the figure of black Sambo, ever available for representing football players as well as film characters or pancake houses. Yet Dennie Hoggard was a model sportsman as well as a grinning Sambo, Clarence Barnes a black player on an integrated football team in the heart of segregated Texas. These examples reveal the persistence of the minstrel show stereotype even as segregation was being weakened. At the same time, new racial stereotypes were beginning to appear, in some cases to accommodate earlier generations' racial thinking, in others to turn it on its head. As Oze Simmons, Jackie Robinson, and Buddy Young led a parade of swift running backs into the increasingly integrated game, belief in Negro physical inferiority yielded to new assumptions about black speed. On the other hand, the physically talented but mentally or psychologically limited black football player adapted the figure of the jungle beast to a new environment, as did the belief in blacks' "natural" ability, as opposed to whites' hard work. Likewise, the idea that blacks "couldn't take it"—they were fast and elusive but could not withstand hard tackling—recast the lingering belief in black weakness, docility, and moral inadequacy. Fumbling, to the consternation of coaches everywhere at all times, is inevitably a part of football. When a black running back like Oze Simmons or Kenny Washington fumbled in the 1930s, it was potentially a sign of racial deficiency.[92]

Football coverage in black newspapers reveals writers aware that they must constantly counter racist stereotypes. In the 1920s, Fay Young felt called on to refute the claim that black players lacked the "guts" necessary for football. When the *Chicago Defender* praised Oze Simmons's "brain" and "courage," and his rare combination of "circumstance, ability, and training"; and when the *Pittsburgh Courier* quoted Simmons's coach as saying that Oze had "the stuff" without a touch of "yellow"; and when the *New York Amsterdam News* celebrated the "mechanical perfection" of Simmons's running and called him a "tough hombre" and a "fierce and relentless" tackler, the writers in every case were clearly conscious that they attributed to Oze Simmons qualities that black players were commonly assumed not to have. Whereas the treatment of race in mainstream press likely drew on unexamined assumptions, in the black press it was highly self-conscious.[93]

It is important not to oversimplify the representations of black football in the mainstream press throughout the Jim Crow era. The coverage of Kenny Washington by the *Los Angeles Times,* for example, was remarkable not just for avoiding but for shattering racial stereotypes. Washington and Jackie Robinson played familiar roles in a racially revisionary way in 1939: the dependable, all-around back and the elusive speedster were both black. The nickname "General" Washington not only named a black man after the Father of His Country but acknowledged his "generalship," the qualities of intelligence and leadership usually reserved, since Walter Camp's treatises during football's formative years, for small white quarterbacks. To stress not only Washington's leadership but also his all-around ability on both offense and defense, his consistency and dependability, reinforced his profoundly antistereotypical role. In Dallas, too, Sambo by no means prevailed, unchallenged, in the *Morning News*. The coverage of Jim Brown's play for Syracuse in the 1957 Cotton Bowl fully acknowledged his brilliance—and his race—in the annual football game that most touched Texas pride. More than anything else, according to sports editor Bill Rives, Brown was powerful and "indestructible," his indestructibility silently refuting the long-held belief that blacks "couldn't take it." In addition, Brown "learns fast, and can do almost anything." Rives even compared Brown favorably to one of the Southwest's own legendary running backs, Texas A&M's All-American John Kimbrough (a first-team All-American in 1939, when Kenny Washington was relegated to the second). In football-mad Texas this was the highest praise.[94]

By the 1950s, overt racist stereotyping was no longer permissible in the press, at least outside the South, and the example of the *Dallas Morning News* suggests the dangers of oversimplifying for even the sections that remained openly segregated. Likewise, the great popular magazines—*Life, Look, Collier's*, and the *Saturday Evening Post*—published profiles of black stars such as J. C. Caroline, Prentice Gautt, Jim Brown, and "Big Daddy" Lipscomb, that stressed their triumphs over poverty, as well as their decency and gentleness away from the field.[95] The magazines' rendering of all-conquering black men in a violent sport as "good Negroes" might have reassured readers uncomfortable with black prowess, but nothing in the texts or photographs cast these black players in derogatory stereotypical terms. They differed little from profiles in *Ebony* in the 1950s. *Esquire* even addressed directly the mayhem inflicted on black players simply because they were black.[96]

Nonetheless, subtle stereotypes hint at racial thinking that, though muted in public discourse, persisted in the larger culture. *Sports Illustrated*—launched in 1954, the year of *Brown v. Board of Education*, at the dawn of full integration—can provide a particularly telling example of the subtle racialization of football. The magazine's racial reporting in the 1950s was overtly progressive, singling out key black players along with whites in scouting reports and coverage of games. University of Iowa guard Calvin Jones, Chicago Cardinal running back Ollie Matson, and Cleveland Browns fullback Jim Brown were among the twenty football players to appear on *SI* covers from 1954 through 1960; Matson, Brown, the Colts' Lenny Moore, and the Bears' Willie Galimore among those featured in articles. Galimore was praised by his coach, George Halas, for his intelligence as well as his speed; Brown was given a forum to explain the subtle techniques and tricks of his fullback trade in one of a series of primers on playing different positions.[97] Black stars had not just speed and power, in other words, but also understanding and reflection.

But *SI*'s football coverage was also embedded in both football's cultural traditions and its larger social context. Coaches had been celebrated as the brains directing their players' brawn since Walter Camp began to promote the game in the 1880s. In the 1950s, because all the coaches outside the black college ranks were white, an article featuring Willie Galimore and his coach George Halas, or Jim Brown and his coach Paul Brown, inevitably cast the (white) coach in the role of genius tactician, the (black) player as his brilliantly used material. When the players were white, race was irrelevant in such articles. When the players were black, the articles could unintentionally reinforce racial thinking. The various skills demanded by football also had become color-coded by the 1950s. Natural talent and speed in particular had been delegated to blacks; toughness, intelligence, and teamwork to whites. In a more general way, blacks were recognized to excel on offense, where physical abilities were assumed to be preeminent; while defense, where qualities of will and character were deemed most important, remained a specialty of white players.

Within this cultural context, whether the evaluation of players was just or not, *SI*'s preview of the 1956 bowl games (to cite one particularly telling example) overwhelmingly reinforced these racial portraits. Two of the four major bowls, the Rose and Sugar, involved black players that year; in the case of the Sugar Bowl, only Pitt's Bobby Grier. Each player starting for the competing teams received two or three sentences in *SI*'s pregame scouting reports. Here are Grier's: "Unpopular with governor of Georgia [a signal of the magazine's progressive view on the racial controversy] but a good fullback. Strong runner, fast, elusive, hits hard up middle. Only fair blocker, weak defensively." For UCLA and Michigan State in the Rose Bowl, five of the twenty-two starters were black. For UCLA, fullback Sam Brown was one of three: "A great runner with speed, lots of deception, marvelous balance. Passes fair, good punter, kicks off deep. Good pass defender but does not like to tackle." Left guard Hardiman Cureton: "Made some All-Americas. Great on defense, hard charger. Pulls and leads plays on offense, a standout blocker, but has only fair speed." Right end Rommie Loudd: "No defensive giant, either, and may loaf at times, but a whale of an offensive end. Aggressive blocker, great receiver with speed." Michigan State's two black starters were halfback Clarence Peaks ("Very fine offensive back; runs with speed and is an outstanding pass receiver. Only average blocker, sub par on defense") and John Lewis ("Above-average end; reasonably good on defense and very good on offense. Packs real speed and is favorite pass receiver").[98]

Perhaps these were astute assessments, but the fact that the players' weaknesses echoed all-too-familiar racial stereotypes at the very least reminds us that preexisting stereotypes render objectivity difficult. Of the five black starters in the Rose Bowl, only Hardiman Cureton had "white" qualities: great blocking and defense (moreover, he lacked "black" speed). But even in the case of Cureton, the All-American left guard, his importance to the team was reduced by contrast to his (white) counterpart at right guard, Jim Brown: "Probably best of a great UCLA line. So consistently good, he never appears spectacular. Has speed, leads plays, blocks hard. Charges hard, great on defense." Perhaps Brown truly was better than Cureton, the black man's All-America selections notwithstanding. What is certainly true is that the terms of praise for Brown made him a quintessential "white" football star: unspectacular, steady, hard-working, great on defense. On the other hand, Rommie Loudd's loafing and the defensive weaknesses of Loudd, Peaks, and Lewis—as well as Bobby Grier—constructed a similarly quintessential collective "black" football player.

Whether or not *SI*'s experts viewed blacks stereotypically, their evaluations, accurate or not, would have been read in December 1955 in the context of familiar stereotypes and would have reinforced them for innumerable readers. In the face of stereotyping, mere human imperfection confirms racist beliefs. Racism in sport is perpetuated in subtle ways, and history always haunts the present.

BLACK STYLE?

Behind the scouting reports in *Sports Illustrated* lay assumptions about the proper way to play football that today would seem "white." Given the current consciousness of white and black sporting styles, one must wonder if an incipient black style emerged during the Jim Crow era. Oze Simmons, for one, carried the ball in a manner that provoked not just wild metaphors but also considered commentary. Writing in the *Saturday Evening Post* in 1935, Ohio State coach Francis Schmidt described how Simmons, when sweeping the end or sprinting downfield, would suddenly stop. "As the tackler advances," Schmidt explained, "Oze holds the ball right out in front of him in one hand, and then breaks to the right or left at incredible speed, or even pivots like a basketball player and turns his back to the tackler." When he pulled this move in the previous year's game against Ohio State, as the Buckeye tackler reached for the ball, "Oze grinned, flashed to the left and raced straight past him. This colored boy has raised shiftiness to a new level and he's probably the most dangerous punt receiver in America in the past ten or fifteen years." One newspaper sportswriter interrupted his own account of the Iowa-Colgate game in 1935 to declare, "And some space right here should be devoted to Ozzie's technique. He runs as if he were climbing stairs—golden stairs maybe—packs the ball in one hand, and when a tackler grabs at him he goes into a convulsion near the hip line which would do justice to Gilda Gray in her most supple moments." Writing in the *Chicago Defender* in 1935, Al Monroe characterized Simmons's style this way: "The lad often holds the ball in one huge hand. He waves it to the front and side, almost in the face of the tackler."[99]

In the 1960s, Simmons would have been denounced for "showboating." Today, he would be recognized simply as a black running back. Since the 1970s, football fans have increasingly encountered what seems, in the words of Nelson George, a "black athletic aesthetic," perhaps first explicitly associated with football in 1974, when a black journalist, Clayton Riley, wrote that while white football fans cared only about winning, black fans wanted to know, "Did O. J. dance?"[100] O. J. Simpson, the Buffalo Bills' great running back, was Riley's principal embodiment of a more general phenomenon. In addition, in 1971, Kansas City Chiefs wide receiver Elmo Wright performed the first end zone dance, a simple affair soon choreographed by a host of other black receivers and running backs into elaborate routines. As the NFL in the 1990s moved to ban "excessive celebration," several black journalists saw the rule as an attempt to mute black racial expression. The attempt, of course, was futile. Deion Sanders, high-stepping into the end zone at the end of a long punt return, along with high-flying basketball stars and slow-trotting home-run sluggers, have created a popular understanding of a distinctive black athletic style that numerous cultural critics have connected to a broader African American expressive culture.[101]

This racial transformation of football over the past three decades raises the question whether its sources lay in the black football played in the Jim Crow era. Suggestive hints come from a variety of sources. Recall that Elmer Mitchell criticized the players in all-black football for a "tendency to be theatrical or to play to the grandstand." More positively, in a column in the *Pittsburgh Courier* in 1932, William Nunn acknowledged that black-college football was "played without the precision and exactitude of detail of white college teams," but it compensated by being "every bit as hard-fought, more vicious, more daring and far more colorful." Color was the key: "Spectacular! Glamorous! Full of dash and pep! Natural showmen that they are, colored college grid stars play with an abandon and recklessness which is very seldom perceived in the average white college game. Not as well trained and conditioned and without the deception and finesse which plays executed by white college teams possess, they nevertheless make up for that lack by the way in which they enter into the spirit of play."[102]

Regarding not the players but the fans, historian Patrick Miller has called attention to the extemporaneous eruptions of the "rabbles" at black-college football games in the 1920s: students with musical instruments pouring from the stands before the game or at halftime for an improvised dance on the field. In contrast to the precision of marching bands in the Big Ten or Pacific Coast Conference, such performances injected a note of spontaneous hilarity into the more usual organized ritual. Miller quotes the *Howard University Record*'s account of the Howard-Lincoln Thanksgiving Day game in 1921: "The ending of the first half was the cue for 'rabble' exhibitions. . . . The rabbles of both schools pounced upon the field in spite of its mud-soaked condition and the continuous rain. The 'Blue and White' rabble, headed by its band, executed a wild snake dance while the Lincoln horde did its serpentine dance. The weather forbade society exhibitions . . . and kept the ladies in their seats, prohibiting the fur coat parade of last year."[103] In its account of the same game, the *Baltimore Afro-American* reported that Howard's ROTC band, or "rabble," had also paraded through the railway cars of incoming fans. In contrast to the students from Howard, "Lincoln rooters hired their band, which had on pretty uniforms and refused to get them wet by marching around the field during the intermission." The *Chicago Defender* commented on the "snake dances" performed by the fans of both teams.[104] Accounts of later Howard-Lincoln Thanksgiving Day games—*the* football game of the year for black America in the early 1920s (the *Defender*'s Fay Young called it in 1924 "the greatest social event as well as the greatest athletic event in the country")—described the Lincoln students' "war dance" in 1923, and in 1924 the "big march around the field amid drowning cheers from the grandstand," led by the schools' bands and "hundreds of followers." A 1927 sociological study of African American recreation and amusements in Washington, D.C., noted the "rabbles" as an essential element of the annual Howard-Lincoln contest. As late as 1928, the fans of the two schools were still referred to as "rabbles" in the *Afro-American*.[105]

Finally, a third source of perhaps an incipient black style in football: in the 1930s, the New York Brown Bombers delighted crowds with their "Trucking Shift": the players "trucking" to the line of scrimmage from the huddle. The contemporary record is particularly meager here, but the *New York Amsterdam News* reported on the Bombers' antics in one game in

1936: "White spectators could not keep from laughing at their amusing 'Trucking Shift.'" The Bombers' crowd-pleasing routine also included singing spirituals.[106]

Trucking, rabbles, and athletic showmanship. With so little information, how extensive and conspicuous they were in black football is uncertain. I have located no accounts of snake-dancing rabbles beyond those at the Howard-Lincoln games in the 1920s. Had they been more common and continued into the 1930s, the Hearst newsreels, which emphasized the crowds as much as the games themselves, would surely not have ignored them. The Brown Bombers survived only a few years in the mid-1930s and never attracted more than a few hundred fans. Whether black running backs consistently displayed a distinctive style is particularly unclear. The nicknames of Lincoln's "Jazz" Byrd in the early 1920s and Howard's "Showboat" Ware in the early 1930s suggest racial athletic showmanship, but "Big Train" Moody and "Tarzan" Kendall have different connotations altogether. The *Baltimore Afro-American*'s attempt to explain Byrd's spectacular performance in his last game, in 1924, pointed to his use of "his own resources and wit" rather than following "the rules" of conventional football. Instead of running into a mass of bodies simply because the play dictated that hole, Byrd "scoots for the nearest path" to the goal, having "the time of his young life laughing at the stupidity of the tacklers." In this same spirit, Byrd was remembered in 1928 as "flashy, brilliant and colorful at all times."[107] But the "stupid tacklers" were also black, as were the rule-governed backs to whom he was compared. Byrd was celebrated for being exceptional among black-college running backs, not typical.

Nonetheless, this scant evidence at least raises the question whether a distinctive black football style emerged in the 1920s and 1930s. The Brown Bombers' antics, apparently modeled on Abe Saperstein's Harlem Globetrotters, were likely calculated to please white audiences by casting black football players in the comic Sambo role ("playing Negro" as the NFL's Oorang Indians in the 1920s had "played Indian" for the amusement of Anglo spectators). Scholars such as Eric Sundquist on the cakewalk and W. T. Lhamon on blackface minstrelsy have emphasized how such performances could challenge or mock racial stereotypes at the same time they were enacting them.[108] While similar claims might be made for the Brown Bombers' trucking shift, Nelson George distinguishes such clowning—which, however clever, was demeaning for the clown—from the artistry of black athletes who over the years transformed basketball from a game of predetermined patterns and flat-footed set shots to the improvisational above-the-rim spectacle created by black superstars.[109]

Snake-dancing "rabbles" seem more directly grounded in black expressive culture, related to what William Piersen has identified as an "African-American festive style" in parading and dancing traditions, dating from the eighteenth and nineteenth centuries, that "typically featured a raucous improvised style of music and a back-and-forth interaction between spectators and parade performers." The same elements of spontaneity, improvisation, and interaction between performers and audiences can be found in the Jon Koonering celebrations in eighteenth-century Virginia and North Carolina, street dancing in New Orleans in the 1820s, and funeral processions in Georgia in the 1840s. As Piersen explains, these processional dances often satirized the more formal celebrations of the master class, as the "rabbles" can be seen to parody the precision marching bands of the big-time football universities. Piersen claims that the marching bands at historically black institutions in the 1990s still retained a "cake-walking heroic (and comedic) quality," very different from the style at, say, the University of Michigan or Ohio State.[110]

Accounts of "rabbles" disappeared from the *Chicago Defender* after the early 1920s, though its spirit may well have survived, unremarked, in the marching bands of black colleges. There is no evidence that the trucking shift outlasted the few years of the Brown Bombers' existence. Whether there was consciousness of a marked style in black running backs or other players is most difficult to determine. What is clear is that the black press did not consistently celebrate a distinctive black style, because it acknowledged but one right way to play football during the Jim Crow era, what in effect was the white way. When Al Monroe described Oze Simmons's habit of holding the ball out with one hand, he explained it not as style or "bravado" but as a technique "to retain his balance for the stops, starts, sways and sprints." One consequence was a tendency to fumble, as Simmons did in his second and third games following his spectacular debut as a sophomore. Coaches screaming, "Tuck it in!" to speedy black running backs holding the ball out for balance while making sharp cuts became a routine part of football with the coming of full integration. For Al Monroe in the 1930s, style never trumped efficiency. Whatever excitement Simmons aroused with his open-field running was secondary to his fundamental soundness as a football player. A fumble at the end of a long run was just a fumble.[111]

If there was indeed a black football style in the Jim Crow era, it persisted outside the notice of the media, whether black or white, until a critical mass of black athletes in a fully integrated game could give it full life. And if a black football style was struggling to breathe in the 1920s and 1930s, it received no assistance from the weekly and periodical black press. In his monthly articles on sports in the *Messenger* in the mid-1920s, Edwin B. Henderson, the first important black intellectual to take sport seriously, declared football and other sports to be "white men's games," which he urged young black men to master so as to learn the "principles [that] are used in the game of business, politics, or others" and thus gain "the respect or at least tolerance of thousands."[112] Henderson, as well as the black sportswriters who echoed him, stood squarely with a black middle class concerned with "uplift," respectability, and being "a credit to the race," that was consequently unreceptive to, even embarrassed by, black folk culture. In the recent celebration of African American expressive culture, this black bourgeoisie of the past is often cast as a collaborator with the white establishment. But the writings of Edwin Henderson and black sports journalists remind us that, in the absence of an alternative football or broader sporting tradition within black culture, there was only one standard, a "white" one, against which to assess black performance in football. These men were also writing within the context of the prevailing integrationist philosophy that guided black higher education (as it guided black political activism, too) during the Jim Crow era.[113] Insofar as college football was recognized as both the symbol of triumphant modern America and an agent for success within it, it is nearly unthinkable that black spokesmen in this era, whether college officials or sportswriters in the black press, would reject the standards of mainstream football for an alternative black expressiveness.

Black sportswriters struggled for recognition not of black distinctiveness in football but of racial equality. The immediate topic was usually the relative ability of all-black and white (or "mixed") football teams, and a consensus emerged in the black press: that the black colleges turned out individual stars to rival the best anywhere but were handicapped in producing teams of comparable quality, due to inadequate funding, facilities, and coaching staffs.[114] Direct comparisons were impossible in the absence of white opponents for black colleges or an integrated National Football League. A rare exhibition game in 1938 between the Chicago Bears and a team of Colored All-Stars, reportedly selected by three million readers from a poll by a hundred black newspapers, was thus a watershed event for at least some in the black press. For the Bears and their fans, the contest was merely the third exhibition for charity on the club's early-season schedule, its relative unimportance obvious from the coverage in the *Chicago Tribune* and *Chicago Herald and Examiner*.[115] For the black press, the contest was anticipated as a monumental opportunity that proved a debacle in every way, from the 51–0 score to the small crowd (6,000 instead of the anticipated 45,000), to the All-Stars' postgame wrangling over their promised pay. The *Pittsburgh Courier's* William Nunn called it "the most disappointing sports spectacle of the decade . . . a 'promotion' which will set Negro college football back years."[116]

It is remarkable that anyone could have expected a collection of hastily assembled all-stars to compete with a top NFL team, but in the aftermath of this disaster came the black press's most anguished reflections on the relative ability of black and white players. In 1939, Dan Burley posed a question in the *New York Amsterdam News*, "Do all-colored teams compare with top mixed units?" Answering his own question in the negative, Burley probed his nation's most offensive racial stereotyping for whatever underlying truth he might find:

> It used to be the habit of sports writers to credit spectacular athletes with mystic glands and hereditary powers drawn from jungle forebears when no other explanation was available in analyzing some superhuman effort or triumph which white athletes could not duplicate.
>
> That policy has now almost disappeared on the parts of the boys with the pens[,] and the supremacy of Negroes in certain sports is generally accepted at face value except in the case of the die-hards who insist Joe Louis is mostly Indian or Nordic and those who contend that most colored stars, in reality are savages beneath a thin coating of civilized veneer.
>
> However, statistics are at a loss to explain why in certain sports most all-colored teams are unable to match the teamwork and co-ordinated versatility of white opponents in football, and in rare instances baseball. In numerous cases, all-colored teams have faced white aggregations which didn't begin to compare individually with the Negro outfits, but which usually were on the long end of the score when results were checked out.
>
> Seriously, the subject gives rise to the question whether it is to the advantage of colored athletes to perform with white teammates instead of as all-negro units.

Why, Burley wondered, would the best black-college teams be pressed to tie even the top high school elevens in northern cities? An unnamed black star had once told him, "The urge to win and to look good while doing it is stronger in the white team as a unit than in an all-Negro team. The white player's mentality is such that everything is forgotten except the job at hand, beating the other fellow scientifically as well as physically." Too many black-college players, on the other hand, had "to learn the value of sacrifice of personal ambitions for the benefit of the whole." The problem was not race, then, but training. As one black coach put it, "Football isn't a game where everybody carries the ball at the same time." UCLA in 1939, with Washington, Robinson, and Strode in starring roles, "presented a classic example of Negroes integrating themselves into the thought-system of the white man in team sport."[117]

In the 1940s, after North Carolina A&T beat an all-white naval squad and Wilberforce beat Bergen College of New Jersey at the Polo Grounds, following several charity games between all-black and all-white service teams in New York, parity between black and white teams of comparable rank seemed more firmly grounded.[118] Yet as late as 1955, in the midst of the open confrontations and heady victories of the early civil rights era, apparent black football failure provoked another searching inquiry in the *Pittsburgh Courier*. With black players on NFL clubs in unprecedented numbers, Ric Roberts pondered why none of them were quarterbacks. In a piece titled, "Can We Build Thinker-Thrower?" Roberts surveyed the top twenty-five black quarterbacks of the past, wondering if any of them had "NFL proficiencies." He posed the problem: "Has the deficiency centered in finesse? Are the pro diagrams too intensive and extensive? Are the T-slot leadership patterns too steep? Will touted gridiron graduates from major colleges ever respect the intelligence of a minority college product? . . . Could [top black quarterbacks of the past] have taken the mauling dished by 240, 250 and 260 pound linemen and, at the same time, have managed a Ph.D. signal-calling job?" "Tarzan" Kendall, Roberts noted, "had stronger hands, longer arms, pegged much harder, much longer, than [Sammy] Baugh, for example; but did he have the Ph.D. capacity of a Sid Luckman?" Leaving his questions unanswered, Roberts concluded by asking his readers: "Look at the list of our QB's, herewith, and count those you remember. Who, in your opinion, had the animal and the brain qualifications for top pro?"[119]

If the withholding of answers was evasive, the questions were brutally direct. Ric Roberts's references to "animal" and "brain" qualifications, and Dan Burley's comments on "the thought-system of the white man" touched perilously close on racial stereotypes. The reader today can recognize that both the black press's usual celebration of black triumph and its occasional probings of black failure were framed by stereotypes at the heart of a continuing struggle over racial identity. A desire to find evidence of a distinctive black football style thus needs to be tempered by a careful consideration of the times. Although "white football" and "black football," however misrepresenting the more complex realities of race, can be fully imagined today as alternative possibilities, in Jim Crow America there was only one broadly sanctioned standard for football, from which any deviation was measured as failure. Whereas black athletes have reinvented football since the 1960s, as they have become the majority of players at the highest levels, in the earlier period they were too marginalized to have an impact on the dominant football culture. Football was created and developed by white collegians, institutionalized initially at overwhelmingly white universities, its purported values articulated and promoted in what were essentially white periodicals and newspapers. When young black men took up football in Jim Crow America, they took up a *white* college sport.

The story of African Americans over the first half of the twentieth century, as Ralph Ellison famously declared when the Jim Crow era was nearing its end, was neither a simple tragedy nor a simple comedy but the one infused with the other, as in the blues: "An autobiographical chronicle of personal catastrophe expressed lyrically."[120] A "football blues" can be read in the pages of the black press, a simultaneously painful and joyful chronicle of triumph-in-failure and failure-in-triumph in a sporting world shaped by segregation and prejudice. During the Jim Crow era, the black sportswriters who judged black football by white standards did not betray their race but acknowledged its plight, savoring its triumphs without minimizing its obstacles.

Masculinity 10

Upper or lower class, old stock or new immigrant, white or black, football players were male, and masculinity was fundamental to the game from its earliest beginnings. In 1936, Lewis Terman published his findings from a test of junior high students and other groups to measure degrees of masculinity and femininity in males and females. Better known for revising the Binet IQ test to measure intelligence, Terman also developed a model in his Masculinity-Femininity (M-F) test that was used by schools as late as the 1960s and became "the basis for virtually all studies of gender-role acquisition ever since, including some of the most widely used psychological tests in our nation's history."[1] Terman devised his test simply by determining the popular views of what were "masculine" and "feminine" traits, then developing questions to determine whether his subjects possessed them. He also polled both men and women to discover what occupations seemed most and least masculine to them. While the primary purpose of the M-F scale was to provide early warning of homosexual tendencies, both the polling and the testing coincidentally revealed something else: that college football players were ranked as the most masculine of all groups by both male and female judges, and that these athletes scored highest in masculinity among those tested. In short, Terman scientifically proved that football players were the most masculine males in America.[2]

What Terman actually "proved," of course, was the link between popular thinking about football and the current model of always-shifting standards of masculinity, and similar polls and tests at almost any time between 1920 and 1960 would likely have produced similar results. (As Allen Guttman points out, the Minnesota Multiphasic Personality Inventory continues to score "a male's dislike of sports as an indication of homosexual tendencies.")[3] The perception that football players were America's alpha males drew boys and adolescents to play the game and men and women to watch it. But exactly what constituted the ideal of "masculinity" was not as simple as Terman's m-f test implied, nor was masculinity definitively affirmed merely by playing football. Football in our period, as before and after, was an arena in which masculinity was at issue, not a settled matter. Football set a standard against which young males were tested. Unlike the following period, beginning in the 1960s, in which football masculinity was increasingly defined in racial terms—white masculinity versus black masculinity—in this earlier period it was defined more simply by sex and gender. The football player as ideal male was not-female and not-feminine, neither a girl nor a "sissy." The obsessiveness with which these claims were made suggests, if not masculinity in crisis, at least anxiety that it was at risk. Reassurance came not just from football players' performances but also from their idealized ultra-feminine counterpart: the lovely coed, the perky cheerleader, the lithesome majorette, who complemented and confirmed the football player's ultra-masculinity. These twin figures, the football hero and the beauty on the sidelines, presided over the world of football from the 1920s through the 1950s as seemingly indestructible icons, though one of them would remain intact just another decade before being challenged by the women's movement and Title IX.

In the 1890s, football's value as an antidote to an increasingly effete civilization was proclaimed by a wide range of journalists, professors, ministers, and politicians, as well as the creators of the game such as Walter Camp, but by the 1920s its status as a bastion of masculinity had become self-evident.[4] Constructions of gender were only a subtext in the discussions of professionalism, tactics, coaching styles, and so on—corollaries of an unstated assumption—but at times these gender issues broke through to the surface, and in those instances what was always at stake in football again became clear. This chapter will focus not on the routine narratives but on moments of excess when the gender stakes became most explicit.

NO GAME FOR SISSIES

In the fictional world of the pulp magazines there was no more damning insult than to be called a "sissy." If at the beginning of a story the protagonist was called a sissy, by the end he had heroically, thunderingly proved the accusation false. The word "sissy" today sounds both juvenile and old-fashioned: it's what kids called other kids when our parents or grandparents were young. The proclamation of "Old King Football" in the cartoon from the *Portland Oregonian* cited in the introduction commanded his subjects to "pay less attention to ping pong, jigsaw puzzles and such sissy games," now that the football season had arrived. The fact is, sportswriters and coaches used the term, too; not often, and not in this joking manner, but in contexts that emphatically declared what was most fundamentally at stake in football was the players' (and coaches') masculinity. The word sometimes appeared in seemingly casual, offhand comments. Describing Fritz Crisler's resurrection of the football program at Princeton in 1933, Bill Cunningham noted Crisler's radically different style from that of his predecessor, "hard-fisted and bass-talking" Bill Roper. Crisler, in stark contrast, "didn't roar. He didn't cuss. He didn't bulldoze his charges. He looked and talked more like a clergyman than a professor of blocking and tackling. Yet he certainly wasn't a sis." Say what? A description of a soft-spoken, moderate coaching style wanders precariously close to some dark forest, and the writer jerks back, to reassure readers that no boundary has been crossed. A similar abrupt turn marked a 1939 column by Dick Hyland in the *Los Angeles Times* on the need for sound officiating. Hyland's explanation of the importance of good officials became a celebration of the game in their care—as "a potent 'leveler' in our democracy that draws all classes and professions"—then, unexpectedly, an exhortation on the country's need for football as "about the one remaining virile interest of many sissy-pants who would be concerned only with getting dates for themselves if this football interest was lessened or destroyed. Football breeds men and no one can be sincerely interested in it unless he, too, is manly and respects manliness."[5] Whew!

"Sissy" seems to have been the insult of choice particularly in the 1930s. In 1934, as USC prepared to play at Pitt, Braven Dyer informed Los Angeles readers that the Trojans were "burned up" by local newspaper headlines in Pittsburgh. Sportswriters there were calling the players the "Toy Trojan team" and "Film cuties' pets"—bad enough—but the most galling headline declared, "Ex-gridiron terrors of Southern California now held sissies." The Pitt team that proceeded to whip the Trojans was coached by Jock Sutherland, who as a proponent of rock-'em, sock-'em power football was the football world's premier anti-sissy. In a 1935 piece in the *Saturday Evening Post* (actually written by his coauthor, no doubt), Sutherland explained that "Pitt is a sock-it-to-'em school," whose players prefer power football to the current vogue for lateral passes. His players "say that throwing laterals is an attempt to sissify a man's game and that there is no fun in getting over the ground that way." Sutherland insisted that power football was also a better character-builder. After all, "What kind of youths do colleges and universities want to graduate? Do they want to graduate youths who plan to succeed in life by being more a city slicker than the other fellow? I think not." It is hard to believe that Sutherland could have been serious about the connection between lateral passes and city slickers, but it is certainly the case that anti-sissy rhetoric followed his career. Marshall Goldberg, Sutherland's greatest player of the past three seasons, wrote a 1939 story in the *New York Journal-American* in which he described his teammates as "tough" but also "sentimental," bawling in the locker room after they upset Washington in the 1937 Rose Bowl and shouting, "A bunch of sissies, us!" The point was unclear—were they mocking their critics or themselves for crying?—but in either case their trouncing of the Huskies proved themselves anything but "sissies." In 1947, when Sutherland visited New York as coach of the NFL's Pittsburgh Steelers, *New York Times* columnist Arthur Daley described him as still glorying in "blood-and-thunder" and "rock 'em and sock 'em" football, still following the principle that "only sissies throw the ball."[6]

While the Midwest was the home of rock-'em, sock-'em football, regions such as the Southwest that relied more on passing "were regarded as semi-sissy," complained *Dallas Morning News* sports editor Bill Rives in 1952. Rives, like Daley in 1947, used the word "sissy" with a bit of self-conscious irony, but the word still had serious connotations in the 1950s. The following year, after writing that Southwest Conference teams lacked Notre Dame's "killer instinct" (following Notre Dame's 40–14 thrashing of SMU), Rives reported hearing criticism from both sides: "Notre Dame partisans thought I was accusing the Irish of being murderers," while "Southwest fans thought I was accusing teams from this area of playing 'sissy' football." By "killer instinct," Rives explained, he had intended to compliment the Irish for their "competitive spirit." To defenders of the Southwest he simply repeated his criticism that "teams down here don't play with the same ferocity as Notre Dame and other midwestern teams." Rives merely wanted the teams in the Southwest Conference to follow Notre Dame's example in maintaining their "fighting spirit" at the same high pitch throughout the season. Rives himself had not used the word "sissy," but just the implication was enough to provoke outrage.[7]

A "sissy" was an effeminate, an unmanly male, and football was valued as one place in modern life where no sissy could survive. In the 1920s, prominent spokesmen such as Grantland Rice, Bill Roper, and Knute Rockne reprised the theme of the 1890s that football was an antidote to an effete and feminizing culture. An explanation is easy: after the Great War tested American manhood (and the number of Americans unfit for duty raised alarms), the comforts and dramatically expanding consumerism of the 1920s reawakened old concerns. In his weekly columns in *Collier's* in 1925 and 1926, under titles such as "The Stuff Men Are Made Of," Rice celebrated football as one of the "main barriers" against the "striking tendency in many of our leading colleges to-day toward jazz music, tea dances and bootleg booze." Football instilled "iron in the soul and steel in the heart" at a time when "so much of the world [is] turning to softness or the comfortable ease that money can buy." Football developed "courage, brains, initiative, discipline, spirit, hardihood, fortitude and training, all essential qualities in the progress of the race, especially in an age given over so largely to luxury and soft living." Modern life was *soft*, in short; football was *hard*. Football was "one of the last masculine touches left in college life."[8]

Roper and Rockne reiterated these themes. Writing in the *New York Herald Tribune*'s Sunday magazine, Roper, the hard-driving coach at Princeton who was later replaced by Fritz Crisler, answered complaints about the "soft men" produced by "the refinements and comforts of a mechanical age." Roper offered the 250,000 young men playing football as evidence to refute such claims: "For when a game that requires the courage, the stamina, the combativeness, the virility—in a word, the 'hardness' that is demanded by football"—is so popular, "then it's going to be pretty hard to convince me that men are getting pallid and namby-pamby, that men are getting 'soft.'"[9] Rockne shared Rice's concern about colleges taken over by tea-sipping jazz babies. In an article for the *Chicago Herald and Examiner* in 1924 (likely syndicated as well), Rockne imagined the report on a Notre Dame–Nebraska game in about ten years if fraternities and social clubs were allowed to dominate college life: "Receiving at fullback for Nebraska was M. Bickerdyke Hicks III of the famous North Platte family. His team was gaily attired in scarlet and mauvette tunics and suspended from their necks were pendants on which was engraved 'Fight furiously, but fairly.' About the waist was a girdle with a Louis XIV buckle. The shoes were by Hoofus & Son, hosiery by Charlot. Their striking costumes were very much commented on by the spectators." And so on, for several more paragraphs, illustrated by two line drawings of players in lace and gaudy buckles, one calling an opponent, "Horrid thing," and another, more sportingly, whispering, "There's a run in your stocking." Assisted by Francis Wallace, Rockne had first presented this comic nightmare fantasy in handbills distributed on the Notre Dame campus in 1923; Murray Sperber reports that the Notre Dame coach "lengthened it to a twenty-minute presentation and narrated it hundreds of times." Rockne also arranged for Notre Dame students to act out a version of his little spoof at halftime of the 1927 Notre Dame–USC game at Soldier Field in Chicago before 120,000. Through such displays and his banquet-circuit jokes Rockne became well known for what Allison Danzig called in a 1929 profile in the *New York Times* his "scorn for a certain type of collegian whom he terms 'powder puff youths,' 'rumble seat cowboys' and 'mezzanine floor hurdlers.'" As Rockne insisted in the final installment of his autobiography in *Collier's* in 1930, football was a sturdy American bulwark against the "culture" represented by mustachioed, pomaded, and perfumed Frenchmen.[10]

The homegrown antitype of the football player was the sybaritic student or effete scholar, Rockne's "rumble seat cowboys" or the "pale flower with a 32-inch chest and an aptitude for Greek verbs and botany," as the *Atlanta Constitution*'s Ed Danforth caricatured him in 1929. Pop Warner expressed a similar sentiment in a 1931 article in *Collier's,* when he dismissed the complaint that newspapers "prefer articles from the football coach to a series of scholarly essays from the professor of dead languages." No sane person would assume otherwise, he implied. Danforth's comment came in his response to the Carnegie Foundation's report—the football player, he insisted, was "more of a credit to the institution" than this shriveled scholar—and reformers' attacks repeatedly provoked such responses from serious football men. Rockne thought of reformers as "effete easterners . . . trying to change the game of football from a he-man's sport into a silk stocking contest." The follow-up report by the Carnegie Foundation in 1931, in which Howard Savage predicted that touch football would eventually replace the game of tackle, led Haskell coach Lone Star Dietz to thunder, "They're trying to make a sissy game out of football."[11] Faculty attempts to take control of the crisis-ridden college game in the years following the Second World War were doomed in part by this popular tradition of contrasting the virile football player to the sissy scholar. Attempts at reform proposed by the NCAA and the American Council of Education were greeted by sportswriters in Atlanta as the foolishness of "stuffed academic gowns" and "a starry-eyed bunch of educators." The penalties meted out by faculty representatives in the Pacific Coast Conference in 1956 were attacked by Ned Cronin in the *Los Angeles Times* as the posturing of "intellectual giants who are suddenly feeling their muscles," as the acts of "egg-heads" who were "frustrated, thwarted and diabolically envious of the fame achieved by football coaches and players, since their own search for personal acclaim has proved futile." That these "Foundering Fathers" of the PCC, as Cronin repeatedly called them, were "sissies" was only implicit, but heavy-handedly so.[12] Resistance to reform derived in part from a kind of male hysteria.

These examples point to a paradox: the virility of football and football players was an unquestioned article of faith, yet football was easily threatened by an effeminate American culture. Intermittent concerns about violence in football invariably provoked more urgent anxieties about sissifying the sport. Celebrations of Jock Sutherland's rock-'em, sock-'em brand of football followed closely on the clamor over football fatalities in 1931–32.[13] A furor over the USC-California game in 1951—in which the Trojans' Pat Cannamela put Cal's Johnny Olszewski out with a twisted ankle the first time he carried the ball—played out in a pattern that had been fixed since the 1880s. Denunciations of Cannamela and more general concern about brutality—this incident occurred the same day as the more egregious slugging of Drake's black star, Johnny Bright, by an Oklahoma A&M player— were met by defenses of the Trojan player and of the necessary roughness of the sport. Cannamela was initially a hero in Los Angeles. Reporting on the game for the *Los Angeles Times,* Braven Dyer crowed that "murderous Pat," who "knocked Johnny Olszewski, Cal's famed back, clear out of the game the first time Johnny-O carried the ball," deserved equal credit for the victory with USC's own star running back, Frank Gifford. After Bay Area writers accused Cannamela of deliberately injuring Olszewski, Dyer and his colleagues at the *Times* had to fall back on the defensive. Paul Zimmerman noted the "interesting fact that some of the very same writers who are complaining were among those who have said one flaw in Pacific Coast football compared with that in the Big Ten has been failure of our players to block and tackle viciously."[14]

An inflammatory photo-essay in *Life* suddenly made the incident a national issue. "Rough Day in Berkeley" perfectly illustrates both the power of carefully selected photographs and *Life's* characteristic "use of innuendo" in its photo-essays.[15] *Life* described the contest as "the most brutally spectacular game of the 1951 season," and described Olszewski as "pounced upon by U.S.C.'s human gorilla, Pat Cannamela." One of the accompanying photographs showed a Cal player slugging a USC opponent, but the more damning one filled the final page of the story: "crippling linebacker Pat Cannamela" and Frank Gifford, USC's offensive star, in a victors' embrace. *Life*'s photographer captured the perfect image for assassination by innuendo—Cannamela's thick-lipped, fleshy face, in sharp contrast to the finely chiseled features of Hollywood-handsome Frank Gifford—using the homely mug with which Cannamela was born to indict him as a "human gorilla."[16] Braven Dyer declared the *Life* article mere "exaggeration and exhibitionism to keep up circulation," but it apparently had an impact. After the season Zimmerman quoted one West Coast coach who attributed USC's poor finish to "those condemning remarks in certain newspapers and magazines" that made Cannamela and his teammates play less aggressively, despite the fact that "no Trojan was doing anything but playing the game as it should be played."[17]

Concern about sissifying football was inevitably highest when American life seemed softest, in the 1920s and 1950s, not the 1930s and 1940s. As I noted in earlier chapters in other contexts, the violence of college and particularly professional football was celebrated in the 1950s more openly than ever before. Competing desires for danger and safety, violence and beauty— savagery and civilization in their many guises—informed responses to football from its beginnings, and this profound tension touched the very core of conflicting ideas about masculinity. This tension played out regularly in the competing claims that football players "in the old days" were giants and that the modern players were superior. Other sports share with football a capacity for creating rich histories almost instantaneously: the games, records, and players of seasons past that live in fans' memories and are annually recorded in books and magazine articles. The sports fan is always looking backward, measuring today's against yesterday's heroes. Football wed this common outlook to its own distinctive modern/antimodern dynamic, that measured progress or decline not just in prowess and technical efficiency, but also in a sort of national virility quotient: the country's collective VQ, as it were.

At any given time, "modern" and "antimodern" elements in football can be identified, though they are constantly changing. Modern football in the 1890s meant mass plays; antimodern football was the open game—end runs, laterals, players spread across the field—more closely tied to the original rugby from which American football evolved. After the introduction of the forward pass, modern football more often meant the current version of wide-open offense, the razzle-dazzle of SMU's "aerial circus" in the 1930s, for example, with Pitt's or Minnesota's power football as the antimodern alternative. Modern and antimodern could also signify professionalized and simon-pure football, with the country's morality rather than its virility at stake, or the new souped-up T-formation of the 1940s versus the Pop Warner single-wing and Notre Dame shift that had dominated the 1920s and 1930s. Professional football sometimes exemplified the modern, both in its thoroughly developed skills and in its emphasis on entertainment, with college football seeming antimodern in its ties to school spirit. At other times, pro football as the more violent game was antimodern, while college football with its sparkling pageantry played the modern. The term "antimodern" was never used in these discussions of football—it appeared as "traditional," "old-fashioned," "old-time," and the like—but the word "modern" was ubiquitous, and recognizing the difference between the modern and its antithesis was as simple for ordinary football fans as it is now for the cultural historian.

American masculinity was not always at stake in the competition between the modern and the antimodern, but often it was, whether openly or tacitly. Preference for midwestern power football over southwestern passing could be tactical conservatism, but it also could be a conviction that *real* football players—*real* men, like those on Jock Sutherland's Pitt teams—ran the ball down opponents' throats rather than tossed it over them. Articles comparing present to past players necessarily claimed either progress or decline. "Were the Old-Timers Best?" Grantland Rice asked in 1925, then in his diplomatic way concluded that the moderns in general were better but individual older stars were unrivaled. Periodic All-Time All-America teams canonized a pantheon of ancient heroes, among whom Jim Thorpe and Red Grange stood out most conspicuously. Grange himself declared in 1952 that modern players were so much better than those from his era that he could not even make the team today, but such self-effacement by former players was rare. More typical were Pudge Heffelfinger's articles for the *Saturday Evening Post* in 1938, in which the 1890s-vintage Yale All-American boasted that "nobody ever put me on my back." Players in his day were fundamentally more sound, according to Heffelfinger, and individuality had become lost in the modern game dominated by coaches. In "We Really Played Football in the Gay Nineties," another oldster, James Hopper (Jack London's former crony still writing about football after more than forty years), wrote in the *Post* in 1945 about a time when there were no substitutes, as teams would "hammer, hammer, hammer" without trick plays, keeping "a breathless pace" with no delays for incomplete passes. The players of Hopper's day ate raw beef at the training table and had no doctors to "overcoddle" them, only a trainer who "was usually an ex-pro wrestler who had turned masseur." In short: football players in the 1890s were men.[18]

Heffelfinger's and Hopper's common theme, that there were giants in the old days, was a continuous thread in both local and national sportswriting, but so, too, was the theme that football today is better than it has ever been. Until the 1940s, professional football could not afford the luxury of celebrating its past. Pro football over its first dozen years was a pretty tawdry affair, after all, and it needed to sell itself to the public by being ever different and better than it used to be. As Arthur Daley wrote in the *New York Times* in 1938, professional football was the "one sport where they never sigh for 'the good old days.'" By the 1950s Daley himself could indulge in such sighing. Aging sportswriters inevitably grew fond of aging former football stars and the game of their own youth. When Steve Owen stepped down after two decades as the New York Giants coach, Daley mourned the passing of the "personal touch" from pro football, a game today that had become "more a business for better-paid athletes, played on a business-like basis." Daley was not simply mired in the past but torn between past and present, the two-way vision that was fundamental to football reporting in general. In a 1955 column Daley could refer disparagingly to the "Neanderthal days of pro football" when linemen away from the play simply leaned on their opponents, unlike in today's faster, fiercer modern game in which "twenty-two bodies crash recklessly in all-out efforts." The following season, however, Daley bemoaned the invasion of high-tech gadgetry, and applauded the commissioner for his ban on the latest electronic communication systems by which coaches ran the game from the press box. He told stories of Bronko Nagurski, Don Hutson, and Sammy Baugh, who needed no assistance from modern technology. "These stars of the past employed a device that's beyond the power of man to invent," Daley wrote. "It's called 'football instinct.'" . . . After forays into the atomic age, pro football returns today to its old-fashioned ways of man against man instead of robot against robot, wig-wag signaling instead of electronic transistors."[19]

On one day in 1958 Daley could celebrate Jimmy Brown as a modern star "destined to rank with Jim Thorpe and Bronko Nagurski as a legendary figure," the next day spin tales of the "fantastic Johnny Blood," for fifteen years "the most colorful player in the league."[20] Even more than college football, the pro game acquired this dual personality: wild, larger-than-life men in the old days; technically superior, proficient, and more thoroughly coached athletes in the present (Brown was an exception, larger than life in his own time). Edward Prell's eight-part "Story of the Big Bad Bears" in the *Chicago Tribune* cast the Chicago Bears in these terms in 1941: wild brawling characters in the past, "frugal" professionals on a highly organized team in the present.[21] Arthur Daley cast pro football in the 1950s in the same way. Three decades later, those skilled, businesslike modern athletes of the 1950s were themselves transformed into the wild, larger-than-life legends of pro football's past, so different from the flashy moderns.[22] In football, we are always not the men that the giants of the past were, yet teams and players are always reaching new heights. These contradictory beliefs were (and are) pervasive not just in football but throughout American culture, but in football masculinity was implicitly at issue.

BEING MEN TOGETHER

Arguments whether football players in the old days were better than today's were conducted along the lines of barroom debates: loud and blustery but not very deep. The deeper anxieties over masculinity that football dramatized are more evident in fiction than in journalism. The license of make-believe gave the writer of fiction both freedom and invulnerability denied to the sportswriter: freedom to write about the fears and failures of invented characters, as the sportswriter could not write about real ones, and invulnerability from exposing one's own anxieties and desires. No sportswriter ever called a real football player "yellow," but numerous fictional ones struggled to overcome this shame. Teammates in the sports pages could be casual buddies or good friends, but nothing deeper. Only in fiction could more complicated male bonding be explored with safety. The centrality of these subjects in football fiction, particularly in the pulps, suggests that football served powerful emotional needs not registered in the factual reporting on the game.

In 1939, the *Saturday Evening Post* and *Collier's* both published stories about a football player's redemption. In Paul O'Neil's "Game Day," a hardboiled Navy man, Sailor Edwards, has come to college with grand dreams only to have them shattered when he accidentally breaks little Billy Cooper's leg in a football game and is booed and hounded and even kicked out of his fraternity. The next season his play deteriorates, until on the eve of the final game, with Billy Cooper again as opponent, he is afraid to play. After Billy provokes him into playing, Sailor comes to realize that Billy, too, is afraid but dealing with his fear. Sailor plays fiercely and brilliantly in leading his team to an upset victory, honoring Billy by not holding back. The story ends with Billy and Sailor meeting on the field at the end of the game to silently acknowledge their mutual respect.[23]

In Ben Peter Freeman's "Right of Conquest," the protagonist is Billy Cody, team captain and fourth in his family to make All-America, who hates his inherited role of football hero and those who make him play it. On the eve of the big game Billy selfishly trifles with his teammate Swanson's girlfriend, Margot, kissing her with "savage joy." Playing next day in his typical passionless manner, as his team falls behind 10–0 at halftime, Billy suddenly decides to try to win, to "show Margot he wasn't the ruthless, selfish egotist she feared he was." Enraged and defiant at last, Billy discovers for the first time the "sweet, fierce joy" of fighting alongside his teammates, those "wonderful men" with whom he had previously felt only mutual loathing. His teammates find Billy wonderful in return: "Cody was driving ten quietly frenzied men on ten ribbons, and he knew that they loved him. And it was someplace in those bitter, beautiful yards that he loved them back and acknowledged his captaincy." This powerful bond is a revelation to Billy: "This was what it was then: this fine, high pride of having earned his mates' respect and admiration. They didn't mistrust him any longer as an arrogant lone wolf. They didn't resent his ability as something he held cheaply and wasted. He had given himself for the first time to their cause, and in return they accepted him and gave him his gift of leadership." After the game, Billy quietly renounces Margot by asking Swanson to tell her goodbye. Margot, meanwhile, has fallen for Billy and is startled by his desertion, but Billy has found a truer love.[24]

Both "Game Day" and "Right of Conquest" were love stories, but the love celebrated was the kind possible within football among teammates and between opponents, not outside the game with women. The inarticulate meeting of Sailor Edwards and Billy Cooper at midfield after a fiercely fought contest, and the fierce joy of Billy Cody as he discovers his true self among his teammates, were versions of a masculine sentimentalism that had long been an important part of magazine football fiction (as of westerns and other popular male-adventure genres). By 1939, however, such stories were rare in the *Post* and *Collier's*, whose football fiction since the late 1920s had shifted predominantly to more conventional romance in which the game tested the hero's worthiness to claim the Good Woman as his own. Tales of male bonding might also be considered romances, but of an utterly different sort. It has long been a truism that sport provided opportunities for the expression of powerful male emotions that were banned from a society anxiously on guard against sexual "deviance." The male camaraderie that was wholly accepted and "normal" through most of the nineteenth century became tainted with suspicion of homosexuality by the century's end, the period when football first appeared on the scene. Students of sexuality might argue whether football simply provided a safe outlet for now-repressed emotions, or was a more complicated expression of what Eve Sedgwick has called "homosexual panic,"[25] or perhaps regulated male sexuality in some other way; but any interpretation would have to account for a remarkable body of fiction, more conspicuous in *Sport Story* and other football pulps than in the *Post* and *Collier's*.

Stories of proving one's toughness, its achievement recognized by the silent acknowledgment of other males, were prominent in the *Post, Collier's*, and other popular magazines over the first quarter of the twentieth century, but these became the distinguishing mark of *Sport Story* and its pulp offspring as the mainstream magazines shifted to other themes for a broader audience. With adolescent males as its primary readership, *Sport Story* in these tales addressed the males most vulnerable and anxious about their own masculinity. *Boys' Life* was also directed to young males, but as the official voice of the Boy Scouts of America it was governed by a genteel moralizing standard to which pulp magazines were immune. *Sport Story* constantly appealed to readers' desires for masculine power and their fears of failing to acquire it, much as action movies in the 1990s appealed to adolescent and pre-adolescent viewers by magnifying both the threats and the hero's capacity to overcome them. The sometimes cartoonishly violent prose of pulp fiction was the print equivalent of the seemingly endless collisions, explosions, beatings, and hairbreadth escapes in, say, numerous films in Arnold Schwarzenegger's oeuvre. Pulp football stories were about the readers, not the characters, about their longings and anxieties. More so than the fiction in the *Post, Collier's*, or *Boys' Life*, these stories were pure projection culminating in wish-fulfillment, but only after passing through nightmare.

Whether football stories ought to have girls in them was argued by readers writing to the "Locker Room" department of *Sport Story*, and the editors clearly determined that the majority would vote no.[26] Well under 10 percent of the stories could be designated romances. *Sport Story* focused overwhelmingly on a cluster of topics and themes: the triumph of the unlikely or unsung hero, the redemption of a shamed hero, the son proving himself to his father, the hero proving his physical toughness or his commanding "personality," the hero overcoming an "inferiority complex"—in every case, a hero wounded in one way or another who is made whole on the football field.

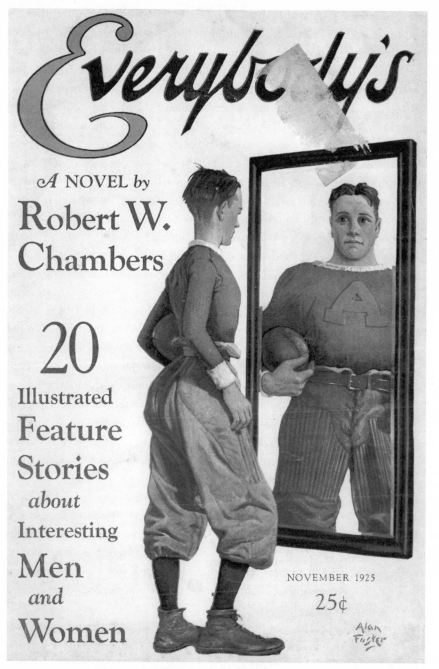

FIGURE 10-1. This November 1925 cover of *Everybody's*, painted by Alan Foster, though gently satiric, captures the appeal of football to young males longing to have their masculinity confirmed.

Terms such as "personality" and "inferiority complex" were lifted directly from popular self-help literature and fashionable psychological theories of the day, to be plugged into formulaic plots.[27] The shift described by Warren Susman from a "culture of character" to a "culture of personality," discussed in Chapter 4 in relation to the emergence of the celebrity profile, was also reflected in the commanding personality of the football coach or team captain in football fiction. Likewise, the hero who overcame an "inferiority complex," instead of an impoverished childhood or a tendency to fumble, dressed up an old football plot in new clothes. As a source of narratives about masculinity, football had always been adaptable to current fashion. Here, we see a conjunction of popularized Freudian and behavioral psychology, both of which thoroughly penetrated American culture in the 1920s.[28] The inferiority complex was an obstacle deep in the Freudian unconscious; playing football was thus a physical regeneration of the inner self.

Together with the numerous stories of the selfish star who discovers his place within the team, these tales of wounded heroes usually played out in an all-male environment, often with a climax marked by a highly self-conscious expression of male sentimentalism. What was at stake in the varied tellings of this single master narrative is most obvious in a surprising number of stories with similar gimmicks: the hero has an explicitly "feminine" trait that he must disprove through his actions on the football field. In "The End Run" (1924), the young hero is nicknamed "Lady" for his "effeminate features," falsetto voice, and genius for playing female roles in the school's dramatic productions. In "Angel Face" (1925), the hero is cursed with "large, mild-blue eyes, pink cheeks, slightly puffed, white teeth, a small nose—and all this crowned with curling, amber-colored hair." In "Graceful" (1926), the boy is mocked by that epithet and thought more fit for cheerleader than football player. In "Pigskin Feud" (1931), "Beauty" Cruger has "the delicate features and pink cheeks of a girl."[29] In each of these stories the young hero proves he is no "sissy" by an act of physical courage on the football field, and in several others an equally stark mark of effeminacy—physical beauty, musical or artistic talent, delicate mannerism—is exorcised in a ritual of football violence.[30]

One of these stories would seem an instance of pulp fiction at its most bizarre; more than a dozen constitute a formula. And this formula only expressed more crudely a theme that was pervasive in pulp football stories for three decades. The anonymous blocking back, the lowly scrub, and the undersized would-be quarterback were "wounded" males only in less obvious ways, and their triumphs validated their masculinity only less explicitly.

The emphasis on proving one's toughness and showing "fighting spirit" was greatest in the late 1920s and early 1930s, but it was a current or undercurrent throughout the run of *Sport Story* and the football pulps that succeeded it. As just one example, a particularly over-the-top tale of toughness but one that nonetheless represents dozens of more restrained ones, we might consider the only football story written for *Sport Story* by Max Brand (the pseudonym of Frederick Faust, the prolific author of pulp westerns). Brand's "Thunderbolt," serialized in *Sport Story* in 1932, tells the story of Joe Cochrane, "the Thunderbolt" of the title, a magnificent physical specimen with speed, brains, and strength but not the most important quality of all—"grit." Joe Cochrane seems "yellow" on the field, but one day the narrator of the story, the team's line coach, overhears a group of striking teamsters planning to beat up Cochrane, and learns that Joe works five or six hours a day as a drayman, around sleep, studies, and caring for his younger brother. (The anti-union sentiments were also typical of *Sport Story*.) How, Lew Marvin wonders, does Joe fit football into this schedule, particularly football played "yellow"? While pondering this mystery, Lew rushes to assist Joe against the strikers, only to see him transformed into a "madman," emitting a "whining sound of horrible joy" as he mangles the men who ambushed him. Afterward, Lew sees Joe at home with his kid brother, Tommy, who pleads with him to say he has not hurt anyone. And the next day at football practice, Joe asks Lew to forget what he saw last night. Lew is left baffled as the first installment ends, wondering why Joe "seemed to have everything that should be in a man, except too little gameness on a football field, and too much of it in a fist fight!"

Veteran pulp readers likely had no difficulty unraveling the heart of the mystery—Joe is anything but "yellow"—if not the specific explanation. In the second installment, Lew learns that Joe's and Tommy's father was "Fargo" Cochrane, a great prizefighter who killed a man with his fists, then later was shot and killed in a brawl. Lew realizes that Joe loves football but is afraid to lose control and go berserk, and so confirm his biological destiny. Joe's hands are "like the unsheathed claws of a wild beast," but—inspiration!—Lew realizes that an offensive lineman is not allowed to use his hands. He shifts Joe to this new position and sets about to teach him to play football while mastering his temper, keeping his "brute inheritance" under control. (Lew also warns Joe against developing an "inferiority complex"—pulp plots typically overrunneth with topical themes.) All comes to pass as it must in the big game. Joe is brilliant and inspires his teammates while mastering his own temper. When the great but frustrated opposing tackle takes a swing at him, Joe simply grabs his wrists and holds them like a child's. "Joe Cochrane had beaten his inheritance, and proved that a man's soul can be greater than the call of his birth."

In an earlier game, Joe left the field with blood pouring down his cheek and his torn uniform exposing "the great arch of his chest" and "the pantherlike ripple of muscles all the way up one leg" (the Leyendecker bare-shoulder motif hugely magnified, pulp-fashion). Then at halftime of his climactic game, Joe's teammates are inspired by "surveying his magnificent body." Back on the field, Joe again has his jersey "ripped from his back" as he scores the winning touchdown. Afterward, Joe claims the sorority beauty, Ruth Wainwright, as his trophy, though as Lew Marvin tells us, "After he found himself that day, he could have married any one he chose. He was a king among men, and the best women know that sort of a man when they see one!"

In its atavistic fascination with brute instincts and magnificent bodies, "Thunderbolt" might seem closer to Edgar Rice Burroughs's Tarzan novels and Robert E. Howard's Conan stories of this same period than to formulaic football fiction, but pulp football stories were in fact loaded with such stuff. Joe Cochrane's challenge was less to prove to others he was not "yellow"—the more typical plot—than to prove to himself that he was civilized, but the obsession with physical toughness and fighting spirit, and the fascination with the "magnificent" male body, were elements in dozens of stories. Tarzan and Conan were but the most blatant expressions of a cult of primitivism that had flourished since the opening decades of the twentieth century, in manifestations as diverse as the cowboy heroes of Owen Wister, Zane Grey, and a host of pulp writers led by Max Brand himself; the Tarzan tales beginning in 1912; the "Negro primitivism" of the 1920s that sent sophisticated whites uptown to Harlem jazz clubs, where the rhythms and sensuality seemed to emanate from the jungle; even the rediscovery of Herman Melville as a great American writer.[31] The primitive embodied what civilization had repressed, but in no instance was civilization abandoned altogether. Wister's Virginian tamed the violent frontier in order to marry the schoolmarm and become a western entrepreneur, Tarzan was Lord Greystoke as well as the King of the Apes, and those who walked on Harlem's wild side at night returned to the security of their downtown apartments by dawn.

I include the rediscovery of Melville in this account to convey the breadth of this cult of primitivism, engaging some of the era's foremost intellectuals as well as its consumers of pulp fiction. In 1928, still early in the Melville revival, the critic Lewis Mumford celebrated the author of *Moby-Dick* as a man who "embraced Life" rather than mere "living," and in doing so set himself against his age and his potential readership. By his death in 1891, Melville was all but forgotten, a writer of once-popular travelogues or romances of the South Seas who had lost his audience and his way. Melville's rediscovery in the 1920s came at a time when the very excesses of his Romantic imagination, coupled with the facts of his actual whaling experiences, made him seem to Mumford and other intellectuals a tonic for an anemic Philistine culture. Mumford ended his essay by proclaiming that "we who follow where his lonely courage led him, embrace [Life] too." [32]

I do not want to draw the relationship of football to *Moby-Dick* too fine, but the crudest of the fiction in *Sport Story* suggests how football in the 1920s, and throughout the period of my study, meant something similar: Life writ large, in the epic, heroic mold, as opposed to the pedestrian living of everyday American existence. A few years after his essay on *Moby-Dick*, Mumford himself declared the rise of spectator sports to be the response of a population "drilled and regimented and depressed to such an extent that it needs at least a vicarious participation in difficult feats of strength or skill or heroism in order to sustain its waning life-sense." [33]

Football was created and won a following in the last quarter of the nineteenth century when a collective sense of diminishment—of opportunity, of personal liberty and power, of "manliness"—was becoming acute among American males of the middle and upper classes. The longing for "real" experience and a reinvigorating "strenuous life" in the midst of an increasingly organized and bureaucratized society made even the brutality of early football not just tolerable but welcome to many. This longing for intense, authentic experience became less acute as the twentieth century wore on, but it persisted as a basic feature of the modern temperament (down to our own time). The atavistic tales in *Sport Story* suggest how college football captured something of this cautious longing for the "primitive," for direct physical experience, but made safe by the "civilized" structure of elite institutions. Football was embraced in the 1890s, despite its disturbing mayhem, by the same groups that were appalled by prizefighting, because football was played by college gentleman, not by lower-class thugs. A generation later, college football was set against professional football on similar terms. The horrified objections to professional football in the 1920s are difficult to comprehend today, in particular their appeal to an antidemocratic ideal of "amateurism" and an anticapitalist scorn for money. Most revealing was the charge that professionals lacked college "spirit." The absence of rah-rah spirit was not viewed as an aesthetic deficiency in professional football but as a moral one;

college spirit was the sign of civilization, if you will, that contained and legitimized football's primitivism. A college football player, in effect, was Lord Greystoke swinging through the jungle, but a professional football player was just a powerful ape. Professional football gained a following in the 1930s through an alternative sign of civilization, the excellence and technical superiority of the players, but the question of the pros' "spirit" continued to be addressed as if it somehow mattered most. The transformation of pro football's popular image in the late 1950s was yet another embrace of "the primitive" at a time when civilization seemed to sap American virility.

The football player always wore many faces in the popular imagination, but from the 1890s through the 1920s the most potent one—that of the indomitable rock-ribbed Titan, the master of a universe populated largely by pygmies—embodied what elsewhere in the culture was expressed as a longing for "Life" or the "primitive" or "real" experience. This figure appeared larger than life in the sports pages of William Randolph Hearst's *New York Journal* in the 1890s, and he adorned the cover of *Collier's* in 1916 in J. C. Leyendecker's "football brute." He also appeared in much of the distinctive football fiction of the period, in the *Saturday Evening Post* and *Collier's* as well as *Sport Story*, in pieces such as Rupert Hughes's "The Exquisite Thug" and the many stories of James Hopper noted in earlier chapters. By the late 1920s and 1930s, stories in the *Post* such as F. Scott Fitzgerald's "The Bowl" and J. P. Marquand's "Fourth Down" were portraying this figure on a more human scale. "The Bowl" opens by drawing on Fitzgerald's personal disappointment as a failed football player, then becomes the story of a Princeton football hero who so hates the sport he intentionally injures himself; but having grown bored with inactivity and the endless jabber of phony intellectuals, he finds his true self by playing on his damaged ankle in the big game against Yale. In deciding whether to play again, the hero must choose between football and his girl, and chooses football. In Marquand's "Fourth Down," cynical snobs at a college reunion are forced to realize that their classmate who had just one moment of football fame has carried it with him, while they have nothing to believe in. By the end of the 1930s, a more poignant version of this plot emerged in stories about the former football star for whom life becomes a long decline from early glory. The best of these, Irwin Shaw's "The Eighty-Yard Run," published in *Esquire* in 1941, would become a classic.[34]

"The Bowl" and "Fourth Down" would seem to have little in common with Darwinian fantasies like "Thunderbolt," but the longing for intense experience and heroic action in Fitzgerald's and Marquand's stories was simply magnified enormously in the pulps. Self-conscious Darwinism appeared primarily in the early years of *Sport Story*, in tales such as "The Wolf Man," whose hero suffers "spells" of wolflike behavior on the field (howling, growling, sinking his teeth into opponents' necks), due, he thinks, to a "wolf taint" in his blood inherited from sled dogs in his "remote ancestry." "The Wolf Man" certainly reads as parody today, but it is humorless and its theme appears in numerous stories. The rugged players in one are shown "amusing themselves in the rough-shod fashion belonging, of rights, only to Newfoundland pups and full-grown men who have been trained back several links in Mr. Darwin's pet chain." The winners in a freshman-sophomore class battle emit "the howl of a malemute gone back to his pristine state of wildness." [35] These stories were likely spawned by Jack London, their primitivism, atavism, and fascination with supermen bearing the marks of *The Call of the Wild*, *The Sea-Wolf*, and other London tales. Joe Cochrane's literary ancestry was well established by the time he appeared, and he embodied a widely and deeply felt longing.

In "Thunderbolt," the principal viewers of Joe's rippling muscles are his teammates and the football crowd at large, only incidentally Ruth Wainwright. In this, the pulp football hero was different from other hugely muscled pulp heroes such as Conan the Barbarian, to whom half-naked princesses were constantly clinging after he had rescued them from "the fate worse than death." In the football story, the male body was gazed on chiefly by admiring males, often teammates in the locker room, always the male readers. The undersized hero of one story lacks weight but has the "magnificent muscular development" of "one of those small-boned men with beautifully distributed, flat muscles—the type that must have posed for the old-time sculptors." Watching him from across the room, a "scrub's heart throbbed achingly as he gazed at the lithe, superb figure of the man standing near the scales beside the coach and Meehan, his loins towel-draped." The hero of another story "was beautifully built, his waist narrowing sharply between the deep, broad chest of a swimmer and the sinewy thighs of a practiced skater. Five-feet eight in height, he had not nearly his full growth yet; but his muscles were well-developed. His forearms and wrists were slight; but his biceps bulged when he raised his arms, and as he rolled his shoulders, little knobs of muscles sprang out on his back." In yet one more, the hero's body is defined by contrast to two others. The coach is "a square, ponderous person, built along the lines of a public library." His triple-threat fullback is large, too, "but he carried the suggestion of speed and power through his wedge-shaped body, narrow hips, and rangy legs." The hero,

Ivan Kuchinski, a dancer in the tradition of his Russian ancestors (this is another story of the seemingly effeminate hero who proves his manliness), is slighter but no less muscular, as the coach immediately recognizes. Ivan wears loose-fitting clothes that "hid the smooth symmetry of his muscles, but the coach had seen enough to arouse his curiosity."[36]

I have intentionally quoted passages that hint most loudly at homoerotic undertones. In numerous other stories the magnificent male body is described in less highly charged ways.[37] The scrub's aching heart throb and the "curiosity" of the coach aroused by a glimpse of symmetrical muscle seem to suggest that more is going on in these stories than simple admiration of a powerful football player. These stories might seem to hint at the same erotic attraction recent historians of closeted homosexuality have found in J. C. Leyendecker's illustrations. Allen Guttman's study of *The Erotic in Sports* offers a different perspective. Guttman notes that "the more or less unproblematic recognition of athletic eroticism by the pagan cultures of classical antiquity stands in sharp contrast to the hostile comments, the 'erasure,' and the confused obfuscation that have characterized most modern discussions of the phenomenon." Guttman also reminds us of the frank appreciation of muscular male bodies by nineteenth-century sportswriters, "who never had to tremble at accusations of 'latent homosexuality.'"[38] Pulp fiction was not carefully regulated, as were more respectable publications, and it thus could more openly address readers' deepest desires; but we must be cautious in psychoanalyzing the pulp readership, let alone an entire culture, through these stories. Presumably, the stories appealed less to uncertainly or openly homosexual readers than to young men convinced of their own heterosexuality, yet on guard not to compromise it, as their culture warned them. For them, the magnificent male body in this fiction would likely have figured as the literally embodied symbol of perfect masculinity. Stories of wounded heroes proving their heroic masculinity touched the longings of these readers for that same unambiguously masculine identity for themselves. The magnificent football body in this fiction served to impress male peers and surrogate fathers rather than potential female lovers. A woman might sometimes be one of the hero's rewards, but he proved his masculinity among other men.

The goal in these stories was less to vanquish all male rivals, whether teammates or opponents, than to prove one's worth among them. The most powerful emotions came from moments of silent acknowledgment: the male sentimentalism mentioned earlier that was no less powerful, and no less silly to an unsympathetic reader, than the female sentimentalism of gushing words and flowing tears that had been a major feature of popular women's fiction since the 1850s. The motif was established in *Sport Story*'s first year of publication in a story narrated by an older man about his four years as a lowly scrub—practicing faithfully but never getting into the games or winning his coveted letter, looked down upon by the arrogant varsity players and seemingly ignored by the coach, whose respect he desperately wants to earn. In the big game of his senior year, he watches as the team wears down the opponent's star ends, able to do so because he himself has prepared them so well by his relentless self-sacrifice in practice. When the team finally scores the winning touchdown, our scrub feels let down, knowing he's made the victory possible but knowing also that no one shares that understanding. He sees the coach running in his direction, apparently to congratulate someone else, but the coach stops. These are the story's final paragraphs: "He grabbed me by the shoulders and squeezed. Then he shook me, a bit roughly. He pushed me away from the others, and I saw there were tears in his eyes. He sort of choked for a second, and then in a funny sort of voice, said—Rats! I'm not going to tell what he said! Nobody else has ever known, and telling might spoil it even now! Anyhow, what I'm trying to get at is this: A letter, after all, amounts to nothing. Even playing on the varsity isn't much, compared to real things." [39]

This, too, is the silent meeting of Sailor Edwards and little Billy Cooper at the end of Paul O'Neil's "Game Day" in the *Saturday Evening Post* in 1939. Similar scenes played out in numerous issues of *Sport Story:* coach and player, feuding teammates, bitter rivals on opposing teams meeting silently at midfield or on the sidelines to express overwhelming emotions—respect, understanding, love—with gruff restraint or no words at all. The story of the scrub who never earned his letter insisted on silence in a highly self-conscious manner, but the motif of silent bonding quickly became routine. Feuding teammates who have learned to respect each other in the furious violence of the game grip hands "eagerly, and for several seconds the pair stood thus, captain and player, oblivious to the world, silently cementing an eternal friendship." At the end of another bitterly fought game one team's star salutes his rival: "Tie gripped hard. There never had been a feud." Rough joshing and affectionate cursing were permissible, as were halting, inarticulate efforts to say what could not be said, but often nothing more was needed than what *Sport Story*'s most prolific football writer, T. W. Ford, perfectly termed in one of his serials the "grip without words." [40]

Male silence—or "inexpressiveness," or "masculine reserve"—has been linked in gender studies to men's fear of intimacy and incapacity to feel emotion. Writing about the minimalist dialogue of popular westerns, the literary critic Jane Tompkins has argued that the western as a genre "is at heart anti-language."[41] In these football stories, too, silence was the language of male emotion because there were no socially sanctioned words to express the characters' feelings. The skepticism of modernist writers such as Hemingway toward the degraded language of a sentimental culture is well known. Here we have the same skepticism operating in the popular realm of football and football fiction. There were no words for coaches and players to utter, because the language of sentiment had become culturally marked as feminine; the bonds between men could be forged only in a few gruff syllables, or in silence. These stories expressed powerful emotions and the closest intimacy, but also the inadequacy of language or the suspicion of language to describe these feelings. One of the few sanctioned terms of endearment was "old man," as in this exchange between roommates after one has been in a fight and might get in trouble with school authorities: "'Beat it, Brick,' he said quietly, 'Get out quick, before you're caught here.' 'What sort of a skunk do you think I am?' Brick demanded angrily, 'I'm not that yellow!' 'I know that, old man,' Jack said calmly."[42]

This male sentimentalism clarifies one of football's fundamental roles in a changing culture. The separation of male and female activities, or "spheres," in the nineteenth century was continuously undermined in the twentieth, except in a handful of areas such as fraternal organizations and sports, among which football was by far the most visible and culturally powerful. As American society became more heterosocial, at the same time that anxiety over homosexual "deviance" verged on hysteria—what Michael Kimmel terms a "pansy craze" in the 1920s and 1930s—the emotional bonds of male friendship and camaraderie became highly constrained.[43] In this newly arranged social world, football could offer immunity from the anxieties caused by changing gender roles, but only to those who met its demands. Football could become an arena in which traditional standards of masculinity might be affirmed, at the same time that the emotions of male bonding could be expressed without arousing suspicions. But expressed only silently: masculine sentiment must reject feminine verbosity. And the license to forge powerful emotional bonds with other males would have been available only to those who proved themselves worthy. For readers of *Sport Story*, football provided fantasies in which the dilemmas and anxieties of their own lives were miraculously solved.

Sport Story addressed gender issues most openly, most crudely at times, but they were elements also in the fiction of the *Saturday Evening Post* and

Collier's. Fierce rivals in a *Post* story in 1925, who also fiercely love each other, speak—"when they speak at all—in terms truculent and bitter," but as the narrator comments, "The words of youth must be read with a glossary."[44] Proving one's manhood through physical toughness disappeared as a major theme in the mainstream magazines by the end of the 1920s, but by this time it was so firmly attached to football, it did not have to be constantly reiterated. By looking at the fiction in the *Post* and *Collier's* from the perspective of gender, one recognizes the ways that football could affirm traditional standards of masculinity while adapting them to the changing demands placed on American men. In the stories of the 1940s and 1950s, the "football bum" has already proven his masculinity as an All-Pro; now he has to prove his ability to take on the responsibilities of husband, father, and long-term breadwinner. The veteran returning from wartime duty has already proven his masculinity in battle and has proven it again by returning to football; now he must recover the joy and playfulness that war had crushed in him. In each case, the intense masculinity of football players is an unquestioned assumption. *Sport Story* and the football pulps addressed issues at the center of football's broad appeal, not on its lunatic fringe.

OFF SIDES

If the football hero was fundamentally nonfeminine, not a woman, his female counterpart had to be everything he was not: slim, not muscular; weak, not powerful; soft, not hard; gentle, not tough; decorative, not substantial. Almost all sports journalism was implicitly addressed to male readers, the chief exceptions being the occasional article in women's magazines about the risks of kids' football, the handful of articles in the *Post* and *Collier's* by coaches' wives (a genre to which the syndicated newspaper articles written by Perian Conerly, wife of the New York Giants quarterback, in 1960, also belonged), and the odd article or book about women's adjustment to men's passion for the strange game.[45] But as outsiders, women played a key role in defining the center. The cheerleaders, majorettes, and adoring female fans catalogued in Chapter 5 enhanced the masculinity of football players by contrast. While pairing the football hero with the lovely coed on magazine covers seemed to illustrate a basic law of natural selection, the numerous parodic, ironical, or humorous versions of these twin icons only reinforced the power of the images even as they mocked them. If the hero and his admirer were just kids, mimicking the poses and attitudes of adults, their image implied that sexual selection was a powerful force even for males and females unaware of sex. The female's role was to admire male prowess and confirm its importance beyond the football field. Playing football was what a man did to prove he was a man. Basking in the devotion of the campus beauty afterward was both his reward and the connection of his masculine achievement to the larger social world. *Her* reward was to win this paragon of masculinity.

In the 1930s, several covers of pulp and risqué movie magazines featured pinup girls in football poses: babes in skimpy outfits punting, passing, centering the ball, one sprawled over an invisible goal line with her blouse torn off not one shoulder, à la Leyendecker, but two. The joke lay in the incongruity of ultrafeminine cuties masquerading as ultramasculine football players. The world of babes and brutes was a well-ordered universe, in which men and women alike knew their proper roles. These covers were meant to seem far-fetched, but newspapers and magazines considerably more serious than *Paris Nights* or *Film Fun,* as well as newsreels, also did occasional stories about football games played by real girls or women. These "powder bowls," as they were frequently called, usually involved sororities at a university, or rival classes at a high school, playing a game of touch football for fun or to raise money for a local charity. As early as 1922, *American Pathé News* covered Wellesley coeds playing such a game, and in 1927 and 1928 Pathé did pieces on the young ladies at exclusive Woodberry School in Atlanta, who "Play Football Like Boys."[46] *Fox Movietone News* began filming similar pieces in the early 1930s, and Hearst, Universal, and Paramount added an occasional one. All told, at least a dozen such female football games were featured in newsreels—not a great number but enough to make "powder bowl" a familiar term.

Newspapers printed occasional short pieces of this sort as well, most of them appearing in the 1940s and 1950s. Hearst's Sunday magazine, the *American Weekly,* gave national exposure to a powder bowl at Carnegie Tech in 1938; and another at Western State College in Gunnison, Colorado, in 1939, received unusually broad distribution via wire service, finding its way even into the Polish newspaper *Nowiny Polski* in Milwaukee. *Sports Illustrated,* with its national audience, added stories on sorority powder bowls at Ohio University (the eighth annual) in 1954 and the University of Iowa in 1958. That sports editors considered these female faux football games newsworthy is the interesting point, understandable only in their relation to the "real" game played by boys and men. An AP story from Austin, Texas, in 1950 conveyed the typical tone and language. "Two football teams were probably never in better shape," the obviously male writer smirked, after their week of "squealing scrimmages" in preparation for the big game. The star of a

FIGURE 10-2. This November 1935 cover of *Film Fun* most directly parodied
E. M. Jackson's Leyendecker-inspired 1931 cover for the *Saturday Evening Post*
(see Figure 4-3). Similar pinup beauties in football poses were painted by Enoch
Bolles, George Quintana, and other artists for the covers of *Paris Nights*
(November 1930), *Snappy* (December 1931), *Film Fun* (November 1930, October
1932, November 1934, and November 1938), *Movie Humor* (November 1936,
December 1936, and November 1937), and *Real Screen Fun* (November 1937). The
gimmick had been used since the early 1920s for publicity photos of Hollywood
starlets. See, for example, Betty Compson on the cover of *Movie Weekly*,
12 November 1921, and Billy Dove on the cover of *The Flapper*, November 1922.
Covers of *All-Sports* (November 1924 and October 1925) and *Physical Culture*
(November 1926) also featured pretty women in football helmets or kicking a
football.

1959 game in Dallas "was voted prettiest halfback in Dallas high school foot-ball" afterward. Some of the stories included details of the larger spectacle: male cheerleaders, "powder boys" running onto the field with compacts and combs during timeouts, the girls primping before or after the game. At Western State, the coeds played tackle, not touch, wearing helmets and shoulder pads but also "trim shorts and tennis shoes."[47]

Headlines and captions sometimes teasingly suggested that these female footballers might represent a genuine social revolution. "Who Says They're the Weaker Sex?" asked one, "Girls Show Up Mere Men; Play Football In Shorts," declared another. *American Weekly* drew out the possibilities: "After all, women nowadays keep right on invading various precincts previously held exclusively by men. So why shouldn't fair co-eds don football togs and encroach upon the gridirons of the country?" The very next paragraph, however, all but assured readers that no such revolution was conceivable. Wondering how girls would play the game, the writer asked rhetorically: "Would they give in to one of those well-known and well nigh irresistible feminine instincts, and pull hair in a scrimmage. And what eager little con-fidences would they exchange with each other in a huddle, not overlooking a bit of down-right gossip? On the other hand, would they really discuss the strategy of the next formation, or would the huddle only be an occasion for playing 'powder puff, powder puff, who's got the powder puff'?" Females playing football would still be females, their vanity and love of gossip as im-mutable as their biology. Female football was a good-humored joke, a mas-querade, a game of make-believe.

The powder-puff football game at Carnegie Tech was indeed a joke, just a publicity stunt staged by the editor of the campus humor magazine. But powder bowls were always a joke to the sports editors who ran the stories and, seemingly, to the readers who read them. The games were not the sort of cross-dressing explored by Marjorie Garber that challenged binary thinking about gender construction, but a light-hearted playing with gender roles, just for fun.[48] Or were they? A long story in the Feature Section of the *Dallas Morning News* in 1924 described two women's football teams at Gustavus Adolphus College in Minnesota, organized by coeds who "went so far as to visualize the day when the winner of the series would challenge, meet, and defeat the boys' team of the college." The writer noted the battering and bruising, which would mar "lovely girlish features," but reported that the young women were nonetheless taking to football, "as they have entered al-most every other realm of sport where once man reigned supreme." Unfor-tunately, the women lost their "admiring coaches," members of the men's varsity, before they could complete a single season, when the men's coach exploded at his "fine bunch of cake-eaters" who "ought to be wearing white bloomers instead of football pants," and demanded that they be on time for their own practices. Although the rest of their season had to be cancelled, the women of Gustavus Adolphus were determined to try again the following year, and they were confident "that, seeing they have broken the ice and invaded the sphere of the pigskin, their sisters in other schools and colleges will follow and take up football with as much zeal as they have displayed." Dean J. Anna Norris, director of physical education at the University of Minnesota, was given the last word, however, and it was far less encouraging. Dean Norris "doesn't believe that football for girls ever will make much headway. She frankly admits that she was horror-stricken when she heard that members of her own sex at Gustavus Adolphus had taken up the game. 'I can't imagine nice girls playing a fighting game with success,' she said. 'Girls just aren't fighters.'"[49]

Dean Norris spoke for all of those physical educators in the 1920s who curtailed the growth of intercollegiate athletic competition for women, substituting "play days" as more appropriate.[50] Apparently, the women at Colorado Teachers College fielded a team in 1927, but how many other schools experimented with women's football remains unknown, and there is no reason to suspect that there were very many. The similarity between a showgirl's and a punter's high kicks made photos of young women in this pose irresistible to sports editors, but these served only for amusement or mild titillation.[51] If the pose seemed too serious, however, alarms went off. In 1933, the ultimate Amazon athlete of the era, Babe Didrickson, was filmed playing with SMU's football team for Grantland Rice's *Sportlight* films, and a photo of the Babe in punting form was reprinted as late as 1947 for a piece in *Life*. Didrickson was no Follies girl, however. As her biographer, Susan Cayleff, has shown, because Didrickson's genuine athleticism, along with her mannish appearance and behavior, made her seem too masculine for many sportswriters and sports fans, she had to adopt feminine manners and style to assure the public she was a proper woman. The 1947 photo in *Life* of Didrickson punting in an SMU uniform (along with others of her throwing the javelin, tossing a baseball, shooting a basketball, and posed for a dive) was accompanied by a story, "Babe Is a Lady Now," that described her love of feminine apparel, cosmetics, and cooking for her big bear of a husband. As part of this makeover, Babe repeatedly denied the persistent (and apparently true) stories about playing football while growing up with her brothers.[52]

The anonymous author of the story on football at Gustavus Adolphus was almost certainly female — otherwise, a man who wrote about women athletes with extraordinary sympathy — and her own enthusiasm for the serious efforts of the young women to play football disappeared from the popular press. The teasing, cloying tone of the story in *American Weekly* became the norm for reporting on the cutely aberrant powder bowls that occasionally provoked a wire-service story. The point of these stories was not to challenge but to affirm conventional gender roles. A basic formula emerged for presenting these cross-gendered football games: part of the story portrayed the young women as real football players; the other part reasserted their femininity in some obvious way. The players' outfits were described, or they were shown fixing their makeup or powdering their noses during a time-out. This was the formula for both newsreel and print. In a typical instance, a powder bowl between two sororities at the University of British Columbia in 1955, Hearst's *News of the Day* shows the young women putting on their makeup in the locker room and donning their helmets in front of a mirror before coming onto the field, then playing the game, urged on by male cheerleaders in drag.[53]

These pieces on powder-puff football did not take their subject seriously — female players and male cheerleaders good-humoredly mocked the gender conventions — yet their reassurance that the gender order was intact, in the scenes of powdering noses and putting on makeup, suggests at least some anxiety about its permanence. Powder bowls only teased their audiences, but two other kinds of stories were potentially more disruptive. Between 1935 and 1947 at least a half-dozen cases of girls or women playing football on male teams made it onto the newspaper wire. In 1935, "a pretty 14-year-old girl" named Esther Burnham played for the Middlefield (Connecticut) Air Cadets. In 1937, the faculty at American University in Washington, D.C., would not allow a co-ed kicker on the varsity team, despite an appeal from coach Gus Welch. That same season, the Associated Press reported that a coed at San Diego State, Helen Bilyeu, was "ready to kick the extra points after touchdowns" (the photo showed an attractive young woman, in shorts, her kicking form equally appropriate for football or the Rockettes). High school girls in North Wilksboro, North Carolina, in 1938, in Atmore, Alabama, in 1939 and 1940, and in Stinnett, Texas, in 1947 succeeded in getting into the boys' games and onto the nation's sports pages for doing so. The AP story about Luverne Wise, the kicker for her Alabama high school team in 1939 and 1940, followed the powder-bowl formula, noting how Atmore's "'oomph' girl" warmed up by "running prettily up and down the side lines and flexing her dimpled knees" before entering the game.[54]

The AP paid more honest attention to Frankie Grove's few minutes at tackle, not as place kicker, in Stinnett High's season-ending game against archrival Groom in 1947. At 5′4″ and 123 pounds, Frankie declared herself "serious about this business," not doing it for a "stunt." After she played eight downs as her team lost, 14–6, the male reporter offered the obligatory cute comment—"All this, fans, without ever smearing her lipstick or without losing her enthusiasm for the game"—but he also quoted Frankie herself. "It was great fun," she said simply. "I'm not hurt a bit, just got my face mashed in the mud is all." She also declared that she would "be out there with the team again next year," but on this point she proved to be mistaken. Two historians of high school football in Texas completed the story. Frankie had been discovered by Stinnett coach Truman Johnson, who was apparently impressed by her ruthless tackling, not by her potential to attract crowds. Whether he was giving a girl the opportunity she deserved or acting out some personal defiance, the coach went too far when he actually allowed her to play. After the game, Johnson was fired by the school board, and the state interscholastic association afterward ruled girls ineligible.[55]

As a dimple-kneed kicker in white satin, Luverne Wise was a sideshow attraction. As a hard-nosed tackler with her face mashed in the mud, Frankie Grove was a real football player, and putting her in the game got her coach fired and the rules changed. A responsible historian cannot make overmuch of two small-town incidents several years apart, but they virtually serve as allegories for American football culture throughout the period we are considering. Football derived much of its cultural power from being emphatically, unquestionably masculine, yet whenever its masculine exclusiveness was questioned, the gender police began scurrying. Football players were the most masculine American males because they played football, which was the most masculine American sport, because it was played by the most masculine males. By such circular logic cultural assumptions are impregnable, until the circuit is broken. What if "sissies" could play football? Or females? The edifice of football masculinity would be undermined at its foundation.

In addition to these sporadic intrusions of powder-puff and co-ed football into the strictly gendered world of sport, there were at least three attempts to organize serious semiprofessional football for women. In 1934, two women's teams scheduled games in Dayton and Toledo, Ohio; Newport, Kentucky; and Detroit. Although newspapers all but ignored them, they were filmed at practice by photographers for *Universal News* and at practice and in a game later in the season by Hearst's *News of the Day*. The Universal piece was shown in theaters on 17 September but has not been preserved; the Hearst material was apparently never shown but does survive (though without sound). The Hearst footage hints at why the teams likely failed to generate much interest. Though not edited for showing in theaters, the film contains the conventional images for the powder-bowl formula: shots of the women in action, shots of the women fixing their hair and applying makeup. In its unedited form the footage is particularly fascinating: decidedly unglamorous young women playing on a dusty field, then awkwardly attempting the gestures of female vanity required for the "feminine" segment of the story.[56] This was material that no film editor could make cute.

Until someone uncovers more information on this Ohio league in 1934, and on those in Los Angeles in 1939 and Chicago in 1941, we cannot know exactly why they failed, but the coverage in local newspapers suggests quite clearly why women's football had little chance to compete with boys' and men's: simply because it was played by women. Women successfully competed in professional baseball and rodeo—not without obstacles, to be sure—but efforts at football failed almost immediately.[57] The explanation could lie simply in inferior marketing and financial backing, but cultural resistance was also likely crucial. In all three sports, the female athletes were required to preserve their essential femininity—as cowgirls, for whom beauty and costume mattered, or by wearing short skirts on the diamond—but football was less easily feminized. The necessary padding for a contact sport flattered the male physique and mocked the female, but also the cultural marking of football as masculine was simply deeper. A female football player was potentially a true transgressor, challenging both the essential masculinity of football and the exclusive masculinity of males. Newspapers, magazines, and newsreels rendered professional women's football no more threatening than powder bowls.

In June 1941, Chicago papers reported the premiere of local women's professional football in an exhibition game between the Chicago Rockets and the Chicago Bombers, to be played at Spencer Coal Park. Neither the *Tribune* nor the *Times* reported the event, but the *Daily News* and the *Herald-American* printed stories and photographs. The *Herald-American* ran a promotional photo on Wednesday before the Saturday game: an obviously posed shot of one Lillian Napier leaping through a hole so wide she could have strolled. Under a heading, "Yea, Team! No Sissies Here," the caption read: "It may be mid-Summer to you, but not to these young women who make up the personnel of the Chicago Rockets, the feminine grid team which plans to play a schedule of games within the next few months. The squad worked out yesterday at Spencer Field, and this picture shows Lillian Napier coming through the line." The day before the game, the *Daily News* spread three photos across the top of a page under a headline, "A New Type of Football— but the Same Old Sort of Shiner." In the center, the smallest of the three photographs shows one of the women tackling another in what looks to be an actual scrimmage, but flanking this simple image of real women playing real football are two larger, more clearly staged ones. On the left, Bomber tackle Dorothy Brown "proudly displays the black eye suffered in practice." On the right, three players demonstrate that "a different technique exists on the bench than when football is played by men." While one is "cheering enthusiastically" and another "cools off with a dipper of water," the third "gives the setting an exclusive feminine touch by using her compact in the heat of battle." After the game, the *Herald-American* reported (in just another long caption to a photograph of the action), "Football proved a 'muddenly' sport for these young women (who, no doubt, made mud pies as little tots) when they engaged in their initial football combat last night at Spencer Field." After briefly describing the scene in the photograph of two women tackling a ballcarrier on the muddy field, the caption ended: "These athletic huskies will yield the powder puff and vanity bag to mere men anytime."[58]

The multiple readings of women's professional football offered by these Chicago papers are easy to recognize but impossible to sort into a coherent narrative. The woman with her compact, reverting to her accustomed femininity, reassured gender traditionalists that playing football was unnatural for her; the one with the black eye questioned what was, in fact, "natural" for women. The players in action on a muddy field appeared to usurp the male role, yet the caption held out the possibility that they were, in essence, making grown-up mud pies rather than playing football. Assigning the powder puff and vanity bag to "mere men" was done facetiously, yet it called into question whether these tools of feminine vanity belonged necessarily to women. Whatever these women were ultimately doing at Spencer Field, it was not what women typically did. Trying to conceive readers' responses, one can imagine admiration, disgust, uncertainty, hilarity, derision. The way this story was framed within the larger context of the newspaper helps to discover the editorial stance among these possibilities. The *Herald-American*'s photograph of the game appeared on page 3. On page 4 was a photo of a very attractive softball player in brief shorts, outstretched to catch a ball (the *Herald-American* covered women's softball throughout the summer). On

A New Type of Football—but the Same Old Sort of Shiner

"Hit her hard, hit her low," is Edna Ritter's slogan as she tackles Lillian Napier, Rocket fullback. Miss Ritter plays left end for the Bombers and hopes to do this sort of tackling in the premiere of this type of football Saturday night.
[BY A STAFF PHOTOGRAPHER]

A different technique exists on the bench than when football is played by the men. Here, although Fritzie Hechtman (right) is cheering enthusiastically, Sophie Aramian (center) gives the setting an exclusive feminine touch by using her compact in the heat of battle. Edna Ritter (left) cools off with a dipper of water.

It's hardly the same old game of football now that the gals have taken it up in earnest in preparation for the approaching girls' grid battle Saturday night at Spencer Coals Field between the Rockets and the Bombers. But Dorothy Brown, Bomber tackle, shows that the women play for keeps too as she proudly displays the black eye suffered in practice.

FIGURE 10-3. These three photos and their captions from the *Chicago Daily News,* 27 June 1941, capture the always-mixed messages that the media sent about women's professional football. On the one hand, just as the Oorang Indians "played Indian" and the Harlem Globetrotters "played black" for the amusement —and reassurance—of white fans, the Rockets and Bombers "played feminine." On the other, they were tough enough to play real football and endure real black eyes. (Reprinted with special permission from the Chicago Sun-Times, Inc., © 2000)

page 5 appeared six bathing-suited beauties from a water ballet, the sort of sports "news" with sex appeal that Paul Gallico described as a sports editor's delight. Women's professional football was not covered as news but as novelty, in the context of a highly gendered sports page on which women most conspicuously represented Sex and Beauty.

Two years earlier, one prominent sportswriter, Dick Hyland of the *Los Angeles Times,* openly declared his view of women playing football. While we cannot take Hyland's position to represent the culture at large, in a town where creating icons of perfect masculinity and femininity was a major industry, Hyland's hysterical response to the blurring of gender boundaries by football-playing females cannot be dismissed as merely idiosyncratic. In 1939, the Hollywood Stars and Los Angeles Amazons, otherwise known as the Chet Relph Stars and Marshall Clampett Amazons after their local sponsors, gained the widest publicity of all these forays into women's football, when *Life* joined the wire services and one of the major newsreels in carrying their story. Coverage in Los Angeles papers was mostly typical. A photo of one of the players, a somewhat stocky young woman named Bubbles Bressie, appeared in both the *Daily News* and the *Evening Herald and Express* wearing short shorts in the classic pose of the punter. The *Evening Herald and Express* also printed a story, obviously provided by the game's promoters, describing the two teams, their offensive systems (the short-punt formation for Amazons, the Notre Dame shift for the Stars), and the players. The emphasis was on heft: with the addition of 275-pound Dorothy Dunegan, to join 205-pound center Andy Fay, the Stars outweighed the Amazons "by a wide margin." [59] This is the point that Hyland seized on for his column.

The game was played about a month before Hyland's comments on officiating in which he broke suddenly into a defense of football as "the one remaining virile interest of many sissy-pants." Masculinity and femininity were clearly on his mind that fall, perhaps in part because of the Amazons and Stars. Commenting on what seems to have been the same promotional material used without comment in the *Herald and Express,* Hyland opened his column with apparent bemusement over a right guard named "Dopey" who prefers "Butch" and snarls to her coach to "just send that Doris Lynd over my position again and see what happens." Bemusement, however, shifted quickly to questions about the "physical ramifications of this idea of the ladies smashing the line, bucking off tackle, hitting the turf, being pounded from stem to stern by half a dozen or more sisters who eventually dump the poundee face downward and pile on." These questions, in turn, led to some fairly nasty personal comments about 205-pound center Andy Fay, who "does not shave, so they say," and a right end named "Mugs" Hyam, whose mother allowed her to play football growing up but not her brother, "which is no reflection upon the strength, size, and courage of the brother but rather a comment upon Mugs. (That's me at the head of the column, Muggs [sic], if you come after me. D. H.)" The columnist challenges the female football player to prove who's the better man! In his final lines Hyland dropped the heavy-handed irony and belligerent posturing to declare more simply, "What, WHAT is this world coming to? The loving, clinging vines now are 'smashing types and good hard blockers!' I don't know what all of this feminine activity is supposed to prove in the world of sports. In fact, I'm wondering if the report of it doesn't belong on the entertainment pages or over with the crime news." [60]

Dick Hyland's hysteria was an extreme personal response, and I have found nothing in any of the media to match it, but even in its excessiveness it still illuminates the issues football raised for the entire culture. The AP story about the powder bowl at Western State College in Gunnison, Colorado, appeared the day after Hyland's column. Here, the tackle weighed 115 pounds, not 205. Some of the coeds reported loving the game, but others, "nursing bruised muscles, were all for giving the sport back to mere men." Here, female football was a cute parody of the real thing. For Dick Hyland, the Stars and Amazons crossed a boundary and set off alarms. The era's insistence on clearly defined masculinity and femininity drove athletes such as Babe Didrickson to cultivate a properly feminine image. Dick Hyland's outrage was directed less at Amazon athletes than at their desecration of football as the pure essence of masculinity. The more typical coverage of the Stars and Amazons followed the formula that governed powder bowls and girls playing high school football. The *Los Angeles Times* printed just one more brief announcement of a game one afternoon, but the *Herald and Express* ran a half-dozen photos or short pieces in November, all of them of the conventional sort. One wirephoto of the Stars and Amazons inaugural game showed players in a "make-up huddle," fixing their hair and cosmetics. The pieces that made the wire services likewise yoked the "feminine" and "masculine" sides of female football.[61]

American Pathé News and *Life* magazine followed the same formula. Pathé reported the story as an "invasion" by the "mythical weaker sex," that "drops all pretense to put on a furious, fighting football game at Gilmore Stadium. Wearing chic pullovers and white striped off-the-face helmets, the Amazons hit the 180-pound-average line of the Chet Relphs for four quarters to hang up a new high for the gentler gender."[62] So, too, one page of the spread in *Life* had two photos of game action, while on another page appeared the counternarrative. Along with a shot of a smiling player with a bandage on her cheek and another of the women dousing each other with water during a timeout were two more of pure cheesecake: one of a long-legged center, wearing brief shorts and snapping the ball between her legs toward the camera; the other of a pretty blond, half-dressed, showing the pads placed over her breasts for protection.

Sandwiched between these two pages was a third, with one more photo and a three-paragraph text. The opening paragraph set the nursery-rhyme definition of little girls as "sugar and spice" against the "rude shock" of a tackle football game played by women in Gilmore Stadium before 3,000 "philogynous spectators." The second paragraph praised the women as real football players: "It was no powder-puff battle. The girls were rough and tough. They kicked each other in the stomach, dirtied each other's faces, tackled and blocked savagely, knocked four girls unconsciousness. And, strangely enough, they played good football, seldom fumbling or running away from their interference." After a few details about the score and the game's star, the third paragraph then abruptly challenged the implication that women might be as suitable as men for playing football: "When doctors heard about the game, most of them were horrified. Football, they said, is a dangerous sport for girls. A woman's body is not heavily muscled, cannot withstand knocks. A blow, either on the breasts or in the abdominal region, may result in cancer or internal injury. A woman's nervous system is also too delicate for such rough play. It would be better, they thought, for the girls to stick to swimming, tennis and softball."[63] Medical expertise here, if it was real and not made up by *Life*'s staff, was little less prejudicial than Dick Hyland's outrage. Both derived from cultural definitions of femininity and, by contrast, of masculinity.

None of these efforts to organize serious women's football received full, straightforward coverage in either the local press or the national media. No doubt these incidents, scattered over four decades of football reporting, barely registered on the public consciousness. But the rigidly formulaic manner of their presentation—the insistence on conventional femininity to counteract the unconventional behavior—and Dick Hyland's hysterical reaction to the threat of 200-pound female linepersons clarify football's role in maintaining unambiguous gender categories. At no time in this century has a simple consensus prevailed in thinking about gender (or about football). As indicated by these isolated instances of female intrusions on the male domain, even in extreme circumstances the media generated competing ideas rather than a single response. But the various narratives of gender prompted by women playing football, whether seriously or for fun, circulated around common assumptions that football was inherently masculine and that masculinity was unambiguously demonstrated in football. Such tautological reasoning went unchallenged until women put on pads and scheduled games. Then reason fled and emotions flared, but this did not happen often enough to disrupt the powerful link between playing or watching football and being a man.

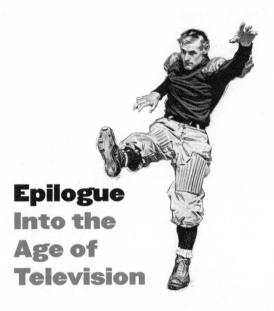

Epilogue
Into the
Age of
Television

It was the coin toss before a game between the Baltimore Colts and some forgotten opponent, and the Colts' All-Pro middle linebacker, Mike Curtis, was advancing to midfield to meet the officials and the opposing captains. This was a time, circa 1970, of awkwardness for white males: the well-intentioned white guy when meeting a black man was never sure whether to extend his hand with fingers forward for a traditional handshake, or fingers up, with thumb ready to hook the other's in what was known as a "soul shake." The trick was to keep your fingers loose, with your wrist as a pivot, so that you could rotate your hand in the necessary direction at first contact, with as little clumsiness as possible. Curtis was a throwback, a rugged linebacker of the old school, for whom American society in the late 1960s and early 1970s must have been changing too fast. As he arrived at midfield and extended his hand to his black opponent, he barked, "Regular, damn it, regular!"

I first heard this story from Kansas City Chief teammates in the early 1970s, and it was repeated several years later in *Sports Illustrated,* so it must be true. My response then was to laugh, the joke touching on my own awkwardness in like circumstances; today, I take that incident to mark a turning point in football history. The Washington Redskins became the last NFL team to integrate, when they signed Bobby Mitchell for the 1962 season. The American Football League expanded the opportunities for black collegians, as the

AAFC had done in the late 1940s, and my own Kansas City Chiefs were the first professional team to have a majority of black players. The last of the all-white major college football teams held out until 1972, around the time that racial turmoil, spilling onto the football field at many northern universities, was subsiding. In 1971, my rookie teammate on the Chiefs, a wide receiver from the University of Houston named Elmo Wright, caught his first NFL touchdown pass and did a little high-knee stutter-step in the end zone to celebrate, a carryover from his college days. Elmo's dance infuriated opponents raised on Frank Merriwellian sportsmanship, but that simple two-step escalated over the years into the "Ickey Shuffle," "Funky Chicken," "Electric Slide," "Highlight Zone," and countless other elaborately choreographed routines, trademarked by an array of black receivers and running backs. An indisputable black football style had arrived, and as football at both the college and professional levels grew increasingly black over the 1970s, 1980s, and 1990s, race supplanted gender as football's dominant marker. No one notices any more whether a white player has a Polish or Italian or Mayflower-stock British name, but everyone is conscious whether a player is white or black.

Football did not become any less masculine with this transformation, of course; football masculinity was reconfigured on racial terms. Despite the appearance of professional women's football leagues in 1965 (the Women's Professional Football League), 1974 (the National Women's Football League), and 1999 (the Women's Professional Football League), big-time football remained a male preserve in fact and in the public consciousness; but women's relegation to the periphery of the sports world changed dramatically with the women's movement and the passage of Title IX about the same time Mike Curtis made his plea for a "regular" handshake. At the very moment that the Dallas Cowboy cheerleaders elevated "projecting" to previously unimagined levels, young women were finding open to them a variety of ways to be athletic besides doing cartwheels at halftime of football games. The woman's movement also put an end to sports-section cheese-cake and tolerance for the more extreme gender stereotyping in the media, but the deep connection between football and American masculinity found new expression in such places as the brilliantly choreographed work of NFL Films—the testosterone tangos of slow-motion collisions, spiraling passes, and rough camaraderie, set to soaring musical scores—produced for high-light films and Super Bowl pregame shows. Football changes; football remains the same.

As I hope the preceding chapters have demonstrated, between 1920 and

1950, football became deeply embedded in American life, not just in our choice of amusements and in the rhythm of our sporting seasons but also in basic assumptions about ourselves and the world in which we live day to day. During these years, football became big business and mass entertainment; it became inextricably part of every new mass medium; it became not an adjunct to higher education but a fundamental aspect of it. But football also altered assumptions about race and ethnicity, while creating new ways to dream and fantasize about personal triumph.

Football was most dramatically transformed by two factors after 1950: by the increasing number of black players and by television. Each of the media explored in this book was fundamentally altered by the coming of television in the 1950s. Television killed the newsreels and the general interest magazines, as well as the pulps; it encroached on daily and weekly newspapers; it returned radio to its local roots; it temporarily sent movies into decline. *Monday Night Football* debuted in 1970, bringing professional football into prime time and accelerating pro football's rise to the most popular spectator sport in the United States. While NFL commissioners Bert Bell in the 1950s and Pete Rozelle in the 1960s and 1970s saw in television pro football's future as a national sport, the colleges fought television in the 1950s as the chief threat to gate receipts. Only in the early 1960s did the NCAA give up the battle and embrace television belatedly as the guarantor of its own financial well-being (only to be later challenged by the College Football Association's demand to allow teams and conferences to sell rights to their own games). With the marriage of football and television consummated at last, each of the many offspring of that union with which we have become thoroughly familiar arrived in due course: *Monday Night Football*, ESPN, Sunday and Thursday night football, several games a day instead of a Game of the Week, billion-dollar network contracts for the NFL and radically uneven distribution of television revenue among the colleges, teams of analysts in the studio and the broadcast booth, and seven-hour Super Bowl pregame, game, and postgame marathons.

At some point television's quantitative impact on expanding football's audience became also a qualitative impact on that audience's relation to the game. The most obvious shift in broadcasting style from radio and early television has been the triumph of expertise. From the sport not even sportswriters could follow, football has become a game about which every fan can feel expert. Color commentators became analysts (remember when Howard Cosell used to complain about former coaches and players replacing professional journalists in the broadcast booth?). Technological advances such as slow motion, instant replay, and diagrams scribbled over the televised image gave the new generation of analysts tools for teaching the rest of us football's fine points. Panels of experts in the studio established "story lines" for each game, providing the sort of "readings" of football attempted by cultural historians (such as yours truly) simply as part of their job. Through the 1960s and 1970s television continued to emphasize college football's pageantry, but as halftime analysis replaced marching bands, and replays filled much of the time once given to cameras looking for "honey shots" and cheering students, football pageantry became less important for fans not at the stadium. Television's control of football and other sports—from dictating schedules, starting times, and commercial time-outs to determining financial health at the most fundamental levels—has been much bemoaned, but its less easily measured impact on fans' relation to the game has been equally great.

Post-1950s football acquired some brand new meanings, as in the Vietnam era when the game was politicized as never before. A handful of sports-conscious leftist critics arrived at the bizarre notion that football was fundamentally a game of seizing territory (as if winners were determined by total yardage rather than the final score), countered on the political right by the equally bizarre notion that football, properly managed, could halt the chaos of the times by putting blacks back in their proper place and restoring coaches' paternal authority over their players.

Change within continuity has been more apparent than rupture with the past. The cult of coaching genius has grown most intense in college basketball (due in no small part to the dominance of former coaches as television commentators), but certainly in football, too, the identification of teams with their coaches has not slackened since the 1950s. By now, we have long ago abandoned the quaint notion that a successful football coach should make no more money than a mere college president. "Professionalism" disappeared as an issue when colleges embraced the athletic scholarship, but other issues, particularly ones related to academic standards for "student-athletes," have guaranteed that college football has seen few seasons without controversy. Football ethics now often intersect with race instead of class, as college authorities still profess a desire to maintain both academic integrity and educational opportunity, while never losing sight of the need to win football games.

Trade unionism has remained a hard sell in professional football for both the players and the fans (Mike Curtis was among those who crossed the picket lines during the first NFL players' strike, in 1974). In one of the great ironies of labor relations in sport, baseball players (in supposedly the most individualistic of team sports) have consistently stood united in labor disputes, from journeyman to superstar, while large numbers of football players (in the supposedly most team-oriented of sports), with some of the league's top quarterbacks conspicuous among them, have undermined their striking teammates by crossing picket lines. Baseball's owners, on the other hand, have clung to rugged individualism, to the great good fortune of the players, while football's owners have banded together as an invincible team. Only the courts, not the players' own union, have guaranteed that football players now receive a reasonable share of the enormous profits the NFL has generated over the past quarter-century.

Deserved or not, multimillion-dollar salaries have been hard on fans for whom football still exists in a netherworld between work, play, and entertainment, but other forces have also exerted pressure on the once-powerful bonds between fans and "their" teams. In the NFL, the Raiders belonged to Oakland, then Los Angeles, then Oakland, then who knows? The Baltimore Colts, whose overtime championship in 1958 inaugurated a new era of televised football, slipped out of town in the dark of night to reappear in Indianapolis. The Cleveland Browns, the team most responsible for redefining professional football in the postwar years, metamorphosed into the Baltimore Ravens, then were replaced by a new Cleveland Browns with no relationship, except for the name and colors, to the originals. And so on.

Football's local-rootedness has not disappeared entirely, but it has been powerfully countered by the homogenizing power of television, through which NFL teams belong to football fans everywhere and an unofficial de facto super conference of college teams has emerged among the dozen or two that dominate the national rankings and television listings. A sense of regional styles in college football has disappeared, as has the Southwest Conference itself, once a powerful source of local identity and outside fascination. Florida and the Southeast have supplanted western Pennsylvania, Ohio, and Texas as the primary breeding ground of football talent for the most successful teams, but without an accompanying myth or folklore. Only high school football in Texas—thanks in part to *Friday Night Lights*, H. G. Bissinger's saga of Odessa, Texas—has a distinctive image as the new century begins. It is not a pretty one, however—no idyllic "football town" here.

The commercialization of football has expanded so tremendously that, as with television, the sheer numbers fail to convey the impact. The Poulan Weed Eater Bowl and kindred arrangements have made it impossible to deny that big-time college football is fundamentally a commercial enterprise, while universities continue struggling to balance that commercial reality with educational ideals. In 1971, Tom Wolfe wrote a prescient story titled "The Commercial," in which a baseball player finally believes he has become a star only when he is signed to film a commercial for television. I doubt that Wolfe foresaw the day when endorsement contracts for superstars would top their salaries, or when athletes' personalities and identities would be fixed by Nike ads rather than magazine profiles, but "The Commercial" pointed in that direction. Television, plus the marketing of athletes, has virtually erased the boundary between heroes and celebrities. Corporations' rental of luxury boxes and sponsoring of bowl games have had a less profound influence on football's place in American life than the team-logo clothing worn by most of the boys (and a large portion of girls) in the country. When I was a kid in the 1950s, owning a T-shirt with "Property of WSC Football" or some such lettering meant you knew someone with connections. Today, it means you shop. The very act of dressing has become a daily declaration of allegiance to some team or other, usually one whose merchandise is stocked by the local Sears or Target. Kids can change "their" teams as easily as their T-shirts.

The countless pages of ads in the *Saturday Evening Post* seem naïve and clumsy compared to the million-dollar-a-minute spots that air with each Super Bowl. From whichever direction we come, it is television that has redefined everything about football as a cultural phenomenon. Hundreds, perhaps thousands of games are watched on television for every one seen in person. The first source of football news for hard-core fans is ESPN's *Sports-Center* rather than the daily newspaper. Newsweeklies now pay minimal attention to football or any sport; general-interest magazines have nearly vanished altogether. Even *Sports Illustrated,* which played a vital role in the 1960s and 1970s as the chief source of reflective analysis, to complement the daily-breaking stories in the newspapers, has seen that role usurped by the instant analysis provided each evening on *SportsCenter.* Popular football fiction has all but disappeared in print forms. Football movies (typically with underdog plots) made a comeback in the 1980s and 1990s; even they are more often viewed at home, on video, than at the theater. The football artwork of magazine covers has disappeared completely without any obvious replacement, while the photographs of football stars on *Life, Look,* and *Collier's* have become the myriad images that flicker on the TV screen.

These comments are simply from the memory of one who lived through these times. By every concrete measure football has grown in importance, yet whether it plays a more powerful role in American life today is less certain. As I make final revisions to this book in October 2000, two events in the news signal how much the world of football has changed since the 1950s. In the first case, a jury in Greensboro, North Carolina, awarded $2 million to a young woman named Heather Mercer, upholding her charge that Duke University cut her from the football team, as a place kicker, simply became she was female (the award was immediately appealed). In the second, a 314-pound backup offensive tackle at Georgia Tech, Dustin Vaitekunas, quit the team after his coach, George O'Leary, handed him the ball after he messed up in practice, then sent four defensive lineman after him to let him experience what the quarterback feels when his linemen fail to protect him. "He tried to kill my son," claimed the young man's mother, as she called for O'Leary's arrest. Here are two more egregious signs of American litigiousness, unsympathetic newspaper readers might insist, but they are also signs of changes in our football culture, one forced from without, the other from within. Title IX in 1972 forever stopped the exclusion of girls and women from school athletics, even in football; and coaches' absolute power was challenged by black players in the late 1960s and has not been reestablished. Whether football can repeatedly adjust to cultural shifts, or will at some point become irrelevant, is impossible to know.

The tremendously intensified commercialization of the game likewise raises questions about football's future. If those who run the game—NFL owners, NCAA executives, television networks, corporate sponsors—fully succeed in establishing football as a marketable commodity or entertainment, rather than something closer to that "integrating symbol" described by Ralph Cooper Hutchison back in 1951, one wonders about its fate in competition with every other commodity and entertainment in the marketplace. For now, at least, football retains a powerful hold on Americans' imaginations as well as their wallets. In any case, a full accounting of its evolution since 1960 would require its own book. This one's long enough.

Appendix A
Football Films, 1920–1960

The following list is compiled from *The American Film Institute Catalog of Motion Pictures Produced in the United States* (for 1920s and 1930s), and Zucker and Babich, *Sports Films* (for the 1940s and 1950s). An asterisk (*) indicates that the film was viewed for this book. The *Saturday Evening Post* is abbreviated as *SEP.*

Ashamed of Parents (1921). Melodrama.
Live Wires (1921). Melodrama.
The Snob (1921). Comedy-drama.
Two Minutes to Go (1921). Comedy-drama.
The Great Alone (1922). Melodrama.
The Dangerous Blonde (1924). Romantic comedy.
Braveheart (1925). Melodrama, remake of *Strongheart* (1914).
The Freshman (1925). Comedy-drama.
The Plastic Age (1925). Drama from the novel by Percy Marks.
Brown of Harvard (1926). Romantic drama from a 1909 play by Rida Johnson.
College Boob (1926). Comedy-drama.
College Days (1926). Romantic comedy-drama.
Collegiate (1926). Romantic comedy.
Eyes Right (1926). Melodrama.
The Kick-Off (1926). Melodrama.
One Minute to Play (1926). Drama (Red Grange's film debut).
The Quarterback (1926). Romantic comedy.
The College Hero (1927). Romantic comedy-drama.
The College Widow (1927). Romantic comedy, remake of 1915 film, from 1904 play by George Ade.
The Drop Kick (1927). Drama.
Quarantined Rivals (1927). Romantic comedy.
Red Clay (1927). Melodrama.
West Point (1927). Comedy-drama.
White Flannels (1927). Domestic melodrama, from a story by Lucian Cary in *SEP.*
Brotherly Love (1928). Comedy-drama from a story by Patterson Margoni in *Liberty.*
The Cheer Leader (1928). Romantic drama.
Harold Teen (1928). Comedy, based on a comic strip.
Hold 'Em Yale (1928). Farce, from a 1906 play by Owen Davis, *Life at Yale.*
Making the Varsity (1928). Drama.
Triple Pass (1928). No prints exist, nor is any information available.
Win that Girl (1928). Comedy, from a story by James Hopper, "Father and Son," in *SEP.*
College Love (1929). Comedy-drama.

Flight (1929). Adventure melodrama.

The Forward Pass (1929). Romantic drama, with songs.

Salute (1929). Drama.

*So This Is College (1929). Comedy-drama, with songs.

The Sophomore (1929). Comedy-drama.

*Sweetie (1929). Romantic musical comedy.

The Time, the Place, and the Girl (1929). Musical comedy-drama, from a 1907 play.

College Lovers (1930). Romantic comedy.

**Eleven Men and a Girl* (alternative title, *Maybe It's Love*) (1930). Romantic comedy.

The Girl Said No (1930). Farce.

Good News (1930). Musical comedy from a 1927 play.

Sunny Skies (1930). Musical comedy.

Maker of Men (1931). Drama.

The Spirit of Notre Dame (1931). Drama.

*Touchdown (1931). Drama, from the novel *Stadium* by Francis Wallace.

The All-American (1932). Drama.

**Hold 'Em Jail* (1932). Comedy.

*Horse Feathers (1932). Comedy.

*Huddle (1932). Drama, from the novel by Francis Wallace.

Rackety Rax (1932). Comedy, from 1932 story by Joel Sayre in *American Mercury*.

70,000 Witnesses (1932). Drama.

*The Sport Parade (1932). Drama.

That's My Boy (1932). Drama, from a novel by Francis Wallace.

*College Coach (1933). Drama.

*College Humor (1933). Musical comedy.

Saturday's Millions (1933). Comedy-drama, from a serial in *SEP* by Lucian Cary.

**The Band Plays On* (1934). Drama, from "The Gravy Game," by Harry Stuhldreher and W. Thornton Martin in *SEP*.

College Rhythm (1934). Musical comedy.

The Most Precious Thing in Life (1934). Melodrama.

St. Louis Woman (1934). Drama.

*Dinky (1935). Drama.

*Fighting Youth (1935). Drama.

*Gridiron Flash (1935). Drama.

**Hold 'Em Yale* (1935). Comedy, from a story by Damon Runyon in *Collier's*.

*The Big Game (1936). Drama, from Francis Wallace's serial, "The Odds against Honor," in *Collier's*.

*Pigskin Parade (1936). Musical comedy.

*Rose Bowl (1936). Comedy-drama, from *O'Reilly of Notre Dame* by Francis Wallace.

**We Went to College* (1936). Comedy.

**Hold 'Em, Navy!* (1937). Drama.

**Life Begins in College* (1937). Comedy.

**Navy Blue and Gold* (1937). Drama, from the novel by George Bruce.

Over the Goal (1937). Drama.

**Saturday's Heroes* (1937). Drama.

Two Minutes to Play (1937). Drama.
 Come On, Leathernecks (1938). Drama.
The Gladiator (1938). Romantic comedy.
Hold That Coed (1938). Comedy.
Mr. Doodle Kicks Off (1938). Comedy.
Start Cheering (1938). Musical comedy.
 Swing That Cheer (1938). Comedy-drama.
 Touchdown, Army (1938). Comedy-drama.
 Up the River (1938). Comedy-drama with songs.
Cowboy Quarterback (1939). Comedy.
 Hero for a Day (1939). Drama.
$1000 a Touchdown (1939). Comedy.
 High School (1940). Teen comedy.
Knute Rockne—All-American (1940). Biopic.
The Quarterback (1940). Comedy.
Too Many Girls (1940). Musical comedy.
 While Thousands Cheer (1940). Drama, rereleased in 1945 as *Crooked Money*.
Yesterday's Heroes (1940). Drama, from the serial by William Brent in *SEP*.
Harmon of Michigan (1941). Fictionalized biopic of Tom Harmon.
Rise and Shine (1941). Musical comedy, from James Thurber's "University Days."
 West Point Widow (1941). Drama.
Pardon My Stripes (1942). Comedy.
Smith of Minnesota (1942). Biopic of Bruce Smith.
The Spirit of Stanford (1942). Fictionalized biopic of Frankie Albert.
The Iron Major (1943). Biopic of Frank Cavanaugh.
High School Hero (1946). Musical comedy.
Good News (1947). Musical comedy, a remake of the 1930 film.
The Spirit of West Point (1947). Biopic of Glenn Davis and Doc Blanchard.
King of the Gamblers (1948). Drama.
 Triple Threat (1948). Drama.
Easy Living (1949). Drama.
Father Was a Fullback (1949). Comedy-drama.
Yes, Sir, That's My Baby (1949). Musical comedy.
Peggy (1950). Comedy.
The Guy Who Came Back (1951). Drama, from a story by William Fay in *SEP*.
Jim Thorpe—All-American (1951). Biopic.
Saturday's Hero (1951). Drama, from the novel *The Hero* by Millard Lampell.
That's My Boy (1951). Comedy.
Bonzo Goes to College (1952). Comedy.
Francis Goes to West Point (1952). Comedy.
Hold That Line (1952). Comedy.
 The Rose Bowl Story (1952). Drama.
All-American (1953). Drama.
Crazylegs (1953). Biopic of Elroy "Crazylegs" Hirsch.
Trouble Along the Way (1953). Comedy-drama.

Appendix B

Football Covers on the *Saturday Evening Post* and *Collier's*, 1920–1960

Saturday Evening Post

24 November 1923. E. M. Jackson. Boy hawking pennants.

21 November 1925. Norman Rockwell. Boy tackling another.

16 October 1926. Harrison McCreary. Boy blowing up football.

13 November 1926. Frederic Stanley. Boys in rough game.

20 November 1926. Alan Foster. Young male cheerleader.

12 November 1927. Alan Foster. Boy whispering into another's ear.

24 November 1928. J. C. Leyendecker. Handsome hero and Pilgrim.

16 November 1929. Alan Foster. Five coonskin-coated youths singing the Alma Mater.

18 October 1930. Sam Brown. Two young male cheerleaders leaping.

15 November 1930. Eugene Iverd. Three boys playing.

21 November 1931. E. M. Jackson. Handsome hero sprawled over goal line.

15 October 1932. J. F. Kernan. Players in action.

5 November 1932. Tempest Inman. Coed in stands.

19 November 1932. John E. Sheridan. Football hero seated, as if on throne.

4 November 1933. J. C. Leyendecker. Handsome hero in repose.

17 November 1934. Eugene Iverd. Boy carried on the shoulders of admiring parents.

12 October 1935 . M. L. Bower. Players in action.

10 October 1936. Revere F. Wistehuff. Young female trombone player.

14 November 1936. Monte Crews. College couple on way to bonfire.

23 October 1937. E. M. Jackson. Young punter.

27 November 1937. Frances Tipton Hunter. Boys at play.

1 October 1938. Wesley Neff. Lit football stadium at night.

22 October 1938. Lonie Bee. Player pleading with grim referee.

5 November 1938. Douglass Crockwell. Forlorn coed drenched by rain.

19 November 1938. Norman Rockwell. Cheerleader sewing numeral on player's jersey.

21 October 1939. Photograph. Female fan, with player reflected in her sunglasses.

18 November 1939. Lonie Bee. Three anxious male cheerleaders.

28 September 1940. Walt Otto. Pretty twin cheerleaders.

26 October 1940. Russell Sambrooke. Grandma blowing up boy's football.

23 November 1940. Emery Clarke. Five players on bench looking anxiously toward coach.

18 October 1941. Lonie Bee. Referee trying to retrieve ball from dog.

15 November 1941. Gene Pelham. Well-dressed male fan huddled in blanket.

10 October 1942. Al Moore. Soldier and girl with chrysanthemum.

14 November 1942. Lonie Bee. Boy in uniform glumly waiting for violin lesson.

13 November 1943. Kenneth Stuart. Boy running with ball, his pants falling down.

19 October 1946. Stevan Dohonos. Bandsmen, with football reflected in tuba.

1 November 1947. John Falter. Players running onto field, as male cheerleaders lead a cheer.

23 October 1948. Constantin Alajálov. Puzzled referee trying to find the ball in a pileup.

15 October 1949. Thornton Utz. Two platoons: fresh team coming onto field.

21 October 1950. Norman Rockwell. Coin toss with gangly players.

25 November 1950. Stevan Dohanos. Trainer tries to revive fallen referee.

17 November 1951. George Hughes. Small uniformed boy, looking fierce in the mirror.

15 November 1952. John Clymer. Filthy boy in bathtub, his uniform on the floor.

17 October 1953. John Falter. Country boys playing in a field by a school.

20 November 1954. Thornton Utz. Battered players leaving field at halftime.

8 October 1955. John Clymer. Boys playing football in country field.

17 October 1956. John Falter. Boys playing in small-town yard.

5 October 1957. Dick Sargent. Mother making son change shoes.

17 October 1959. Dick Sargent. Coeds hanging on engineer, spurning the football player.

31 October 1959. Ben Prins. High school football caravan through small town.

5 December 1959. Constantin Alajálov. Referee marches off penalty as huge players look on.

19 November 1960. George Hughes. Well-dressed fans cheering in stands.

Collier's

18 December 1920. Unidentified artist. Coin toss with handsome players.

1 October 1921. Charles H. Towne. Coach giving advice to young player.

5 November 1921. William Mead Prince. Boy preening in uniform before envious peers.

25 November 1922. Donald Gardner. Lovely coed gazing at handsome hero.

17 November 1923. George Brehn. Lovely coed tending to wounded hero.

25 October 1924. Paul Martin. Boys whispering a play.

12 November 1927. J. F. Kernan. "Little rascals" in rough play.

27 October 1928. Unidentified artist. Runner in action.

12 October 1929. E. M. Jackson. Handsome hero, as if on throne.

2 November 1929. Sam Brown. Boy practicing violin before football.

28 December 1929. E. M. Jackson. Lovely coed draped in coat of pennants.

18 October 1930. E. M. Jackson. Handsome hero in virile pose.

22 November 1930. C. C. Beall. Players in action.

17 October 1931. Ronald McLeod. A place kick.

24 October 1931. Lawson Wood. Monkey with football hurdling pig.

5 December 1931. Herbert Paus. Player as winged victory.

22 October 1932. Earl Oliver Hurst. Boy with two admiring girls.

5 November 1932. Scott Evans. Drum major.

7 October 1933. Gene Klebe. Dog in helmet.

21 October 1933. Arthur Crouch. Roly-polies in action.

4 November 1933. C. C. Beall. Cheering coed.

2 December 1933. Gerard C. Delano. Lovely coed, with handsome hero looking on.

13 October 1934. Arthur Crouch. Roly-polies rolling dice.

3 November 1934. Ronald McLeod. Players in action.

10 November 1934. Harry Beckhoff. Female cheerleader, with players behind her.

12 October 1935. Arthur Crouch. Roly-poly substitute for battered teammate.

9 November 1935. Robert O. Reid. Boy and girl as battered hero and lovely admirer.

17 October 1936. Arthur Crouch. Roly-polies score a touchdown.

7 November 1936. Ronald McLeod. Player in action.

9 October 1937. Arthur Crouch. Roly-poly with photographer.

30 October 1937. Jorji Harris. Battered hero and lovely coed.

15 October 1938. Guy Hoff. Lovely coed.

5 November 1938. Alan Foster. Water boy keeping up with running player.

3 December 1938. Arthur Crouch. Roly-polies squashing a referee.

4 November 1939. Henry Heier. Punt soaring into the air.

18 November 1939. Arthur Crouch. Roly-poly autographing ball for lovely woman.

2 December 1939. Martha Sawyer. Battered hero with lovely admirer.

16 December 1939. Ronald McLeod. Coach and player.

12 October 1940. Arthur Crouch. Roly-poly flattening radio announcer.

9 November 1940. El Gilchrist. Ball inscribed with "Hello, Babe" flying toward lovely coed.

15 November 1941. Walter Bomar. Ball carrier and blocker.

13 December 1941. Photograph. Frankie Albert with admiring coeds.

14 November 1942. Photograph. Referee.

12 October 1946. Photograph. Action in the line.

18 October 1947. Photograph. Pileup.

8 November 1947. Stanley Ekman. Dejected young fan alone in stands after game.

18 September 1948. Photograph. Leaping drum majorette.

23 October 1948. Photograph. Male and female leaping cheerleaders.

6 November 1948. Photograph. smu backfield.

11 December 1948. Photograph. Charlie Justice.

29 October 1949. Stanley and Janice Berenstain. Tiny kids' football game.

19 November 1949. Barney Tobey. Photographer ignores team to snap the lovely majorette.

10 December 1949. Photograph. Doak Walker and Norma Peterson.

15 September 1951. Photograph. Bobby Reynolds.

24 November 1951. Barney Tobey. Teenagers pushing jalopy to game.

15 December 1951. Photograph. Bill McColl and cheering coeds.

30 August 1952. Photograph. Jack Scarbath.
6 December 1952. Photograph. Dick McAuliffe.
10 December 1954. Photograph. Alan Ameche.
9 December 1955. Photograph. Helmets of players.
7 December 1956. Photograph. Profiles of three players.

Appendix C

Football Fiction in the *Saturday Evening Post* and *Collier's*, 1920–1960

Saturday Evening Post

11 September 1920. V. H. Cornell, "His Big Moment."

20 November 1920. Lawrence Perry, "Man to Man."

16 September 1922. Ralph E. Mooney, "Polysynthetic Football."

25 October 1924. James Hopper, "Father and Son."

31 October 1925. Sam Hellman, "Rough and Rah-Rah."

7 November 1925. Ben Ames Williams, "Scapegoat."

5 November 1927. Sam Hellman, "Soft and Sappy."

21 January 1928. F. Scott Fitzgerald, "The Bowl."

10 November 1928. Sam Hellman, "Offside."

15 December 1928. Charles Wertenbaker, "The Twelfth Gentleman."

30 November 1929. W. Thornton Martin, "Scrapbook."

7 December 1929. Frederick Hazlitt Brennan, "College Hero."

4–25 October 1930. W. Thornton Martin, "Simon Pure."

8 November 1930. Horatio Winslow, "Swelling the Purple Flood: Reminiscences of a Coach."

7 November 1931. Paul Jones, "The Tough Guy."

21 November 1931. Thomas Beer, "A Little Science."

22 October 1932. Harry A. Stuhldreher and W. Thornton Martin, "Bench Warmer."

19 November 1932. J. P. Marquand, "Fourth Down."

16–30 September 1933. Lucian Cary, "Saturday's Millions."

21 October 1933. Harry Stuhldreher and W. Thornton Martin, "The Gravy Game."

4 November 1933. Richards Vidmer, "The Swell Head."

29 September 1934. Richard Macaulay, "The Magic Toe."

24 November 1934. Harry Stuhldreher and W. Thornton Martin, "Off Guard."

21 September 1935. Brooke Hanlon, "End of Fanfare."

19 October 1935. George S. Brooks, "Block That Bride."

2 November 1935. George S. Brooks, "Clever Legs."

3 October–7 November 1936. Francis Wallace, "The Double Ride."

21 November 1936. Harold A. Fitzgerald, "Scrub: Based on the Diary of a Nameless Senior."

28 November 1936. W. Thornton Martin, "The Widow's Mite."

30 October 1937. George S. Brooks, "Itsy-Bitsy Halfback."

6–27 November 1937. Francis Wallace, "Razzle-Dazzle."

11 November 1939. Ben Peter Freeman, "A Ball Game for Delia."

18 November–2 December 1939. William Brent, "Yesterday's Heroes."

9 December 1939. Paul O'Neil, "Game Day."

16 November 1940. William R. Cox, "It's a Nice Day."

13 November 1943. William Fay, "Merry Widower."

24 November 1945. William Fay, "The Girl from Columbus."

4 October 1947. Frank O'Rourke, "Nothing to Do Till Next Fall."

6 December 1947. William Fay, "The Golden Arm."

4 September 1948. Joseph E. Shaner, "I Love You, Coach."

29 October 1949. William R. Scott, "The Kidnapped Quarterback."

3 December 1949. William Fay, "Touchdown Crazy."

23 September 1950. Jim Hendryx, Jr., "The Boy Who Hated Football."

7 October 1950. Tom Morrow, Jr., "The Psychological Halfback."

4 November 1950. John Fante, "One-Play Oscar."

2 December 1950. William Fay, "Throw the Bum Out!"

6 October 1951. Willard H. Temple, "Touchdown Play."

17 November 1951. Booton Herndon, "Football Punk—That's Me."

1 December 1951. Dan Gallery, "The Secret of the Great Upset."

18 October 1952. Booton Herndon, "Dirtiest Game of the Year."

17 October 1953. Robert Meyer, "He Learned Her about Love."

28 November 1953. William Fay, "The Fainthearted Fullback."

25 September 1954. Emmett Watson, "The Quarterback Who Couldn't Take It."

9 October 1954. Willard Temple, "A Bench Warmer Named Smith."

17 September 1955. Willard Temple, "You're a Real Nice Kid."

19 November 1955. James Kalshoven, "The Halfback and the High-Brow."

31 December 1955. William Heuman, "I'm Back, Coach."

22 December 1956. William R. Cox, "Playoff Game."

18 October 1958. Robert Daley, "The Touchdown Makers."

5 September 1959. Earlyne S. Browne, "Yesterday's Hero."

29 October 1960. Nancy Burrage Owen, "Second-String Star."

Collier's

14 February 1920. Meade Minnigerode, "Jimmy Repays."

4 September–18 December 1920. Wadsworth Camp, "The Guarded Heights."

18 September 1920. Jonathan Brooks, "Bills Playable."

23 October 1920. Jonathan Brooks, "Roll, Jordan, Roll."

1 October 1921. Jonathan Brooks, "Toes Up."

12 November 1921. Lawrence Perry, "David Harmon's Quarterback."

30 September 1922. William Almon Wolff, "Right About Face."

21 October 1922. Jonathan Brooks, "Square Heads."

18–25 November 1922. Wadsworth Camp, "The Victor."

13 October 1923. James Hopper, "The Photograph."

17 November 1923. Jonathan Brooks, "One Bad Turn."

22 November 1924. Jonathan Brooks, "Brothers under the Pigskin."

6 December 1924. Jonathan Brooks, "True Bills."

31 October 1925. Lawrence Perry, "Bull Pup and Tiger Cub."

16 October 1926. Lawrence Perry, "Barbed Wire."

5 November 1927. Lawrence Perry, "Straight-Arm Stuff."

1 December 1928. Clarence Budington Kelland, "Two Minutes to Play."

28 September 1929. Francis Wallace, "Pig Iron Dugan."

12 October 1929. William Almon Wolff, "Captain Courageous."

29 November 1930. Frederick Hazlitt Brennan, "This Football."

10 October 1931. Lucian Cary, "One to the Button."

24 October 1931. Frederick Hazlitt Brennan, "Beyond the Goal Line."

14 November 1931. Damon Runyon, "Hold 'Em, Yale!"

28 November 1931. James Hopper, "'My Quarterback.'"

22 October 1932. Dwight Mitchell Wiley, "Beat 'Em, Boy!"

12 November 1932. Quentin Reynolds, "He Could Take It."

26 November 1932. Talbert Josselyn, "No Alibi."

2 December 1933. Paul Jones and Louis F. McCabe, "Redheads Never Quit."

9 December 1933. George S. Brooks, "The Last Season."

13 October 1934. David Garth, "The Boy Who Sold Himself."

17 November 1934. George Brooks, "The Pie Slinger."

24 November 1934. Damon Runyon, "Undertaker Song."

8 December 1934. Frederick Hazlitt Brennan, "Hero's Son."

5 October 1935. Lucian Cary, "Out of the Shadows."

12 October 1935. Brassil Fitzgerald, "Gallagher's Game."

26 October–14 December 1935. Francis Wallace, "The Odds against Honor."

10 October 1936. Lucian Cary, "Scoring Play."

7 November 1936. Frederick Hazlitt Brennan, "Sorority Hero."

20 November 1937. Frederick Hazlitt Brennan, "The Girl Who Saved the Game."

4 December 1937. Corey Ford and Alastair MacBain, "Second Try."

18 December 1937. Eustace Cockrell, "Pep Talk."

12 November 1938. Harry Sylvester, "Orders Disobeyed."

19 November 1938. William Fay, "Uptown Boy."

11 November 1939. Ben Peter Freeman, "Right of Conquest."

18 November 1939. William Fay, "Strictly for Sweeney."

19 October 1940. Frank Fenton, "The Flying Dutchman."

23 November 1940. Harry Sylvester, "Return of the Hero."

30 November 1940. William Fay, "The Daughter of the Dean."

14 December 1940. Stanley Frank, "Gravy Train."

15 November 1941. William Fay, "Willy's Place."

22 November 1941. Harry Sylvester, "The Captain of the Team."

29 November 1941. Stanley Frank, "Second Wind."

6 December 1941. Edward Shenton, "Beyond the Game."

19 October 1946. Frank O'Rourke, "The Hard Way Home."

16 November 1946. Nick Boddie Williams, "Off the Reservation."

11 October 1947. Harry Sylvester, "All Honor to Old Appleby."

8 November 1947. Willard H. Temple, "Baby in the Backfield."

22 November 1947. Joel Reeve, "The Pigskin Heart."

16 October 1948. James Atlee Phillips, "Saturday Fever."

30 October 1948. Eustace Cockrell, "Beauty and the Drop Kick."

27 November 1948. Harry Sylvester, "Double or Nothing."

15 October 1949. W. C. Heinz, "Man's Game."

7 October 1950. Norman R. Jaffray, "Football Strategy."

14 October 1950. William R. Scott, "Son of the Coach."

11 October 1952. Willard H. Temple, "Halfback Hoodoo."

1 November 1952. B. M. Atkinson, Jr., "I'm a Snake."

8 November 1952. William R. Scott, "Operation Bench."

13 November 1953. Willard H. Temple, "Eleven Guys Named George."

27 November–11 December 1953. Adela Rogers St. Johns, "Goal to Go."

15 October–12 November 1954. Bonner McMillion, "The Big Win."

25 November 1955. W. L. Heath, "Most Valuable Player."

12 October 1956. William Heuman, "Fall Tryout."

Notes

Articles from newspapers are given full citations here and do not appear in the bibliography. Short stories from the *Saturday Evening Post* and *Collier's* are cited with their year of publication, to locate them in Appendix C; all other magazine fiction and nonfiction receive brief citations here and appear in the bibliography.

All radio broadcasts are from the Library of Congress, Motion Picture, Broadcasting and Recorded Sound Division.

Universal newsreels are from the National Archives, College Park, Maryland; Hearst newsreels (*Metrotone News* and *News of the Day*) are from the Film and TV Archive at UCLA. Information on *Fox Movietone News* is from an in-house database of surviving footage, and information on Pathé and Paramount newsreels is from a database on CD-ROM owned by Raymond Fielding, dean of the Florida State University Film School.

ABBREVIATIONS

AC	*Atlanta Constitution*
AH	*American Hebrew*
CD	*Chicago Defender*
CT	*Chicago Tribune*
DMN	*Dallas Morning News*
DW	*Daily Worker*
LAT	*Los Angeles Times*
NYAN	*New York Amsterdam News*
NYDN	*New York Daily News*
NYHT	*New York Herald Tribune*
NYT	*New York Times*
OWH	*Omaha World-Herald*
PC	*Pittsburgh Courier*
PO	*Portland Oregonian*
SEP	*Saturday Evening Post*

INTRODUCTION

1. Harris, *King Football*; Wechsler, *Revolt on the Campus*.

2. "Hail, King Football!"; Trevor, "King Football Answers the Depression"; "Here Comes King Football," *PO*, 2 September 1934; Sullivan, "Football Is King"; "To All Colleges"; Smick, "King Football"; and Ronald J. Kidd, introduction to Ratliff, *Autumn's Mightiest Legions*.

3. Watterson, *College Football*, 93–98, 120–40.

4. See Jable, "Birth of Professional Football"; and Peterson, *Pigskin*, 23–44.

5. "War Football," *NYT*, 23 November 1919.

6. See, for example, Towers, "Athletics' Aid to War"; and Tuthill, "Football and War."

7. See "What the Draft Should Teach Us"; Lewis, "World War I"; O'Hanlon, "School Sports as Social Training"; Mennell, "Service Football Program"; and Pope, *Patriotic Games,* 121–55. For the larger context of sports and the military, see Wakefield, *Playing to Win.*

8. *Historical Statistics of the United States,* 379 (the percentage of high school graduates increased to 63 percent by 1960). Surveys in the 1930s showed from 86 to 99 percent of high schools fielding football teams, with 17 to 19 percent of boys participating. See Brammell, *Intramural and Interscholastic Athletics,* v; O'Hanlon, "School Sports as Social Training," 7; Morley, "Report of the North Central Association Committee"; Morley, "Report of the Committee on Athletics"; and Rivett, "Relation of Athletics."

9. Wagenhorst, *Administration and Cost,* 21–23, 72, 81. See also O'Hanlon, "Interscholastic Athletics."

10. Rogers, *Future of Interscholastic Athletics,* 12; Brammell, *Intramural and Interscholastic Athletics,* 121–22.

11. Stephen Epler devised the game in 1934, and it spread to 156 schools in ten states by 1935, but the six-man game fully took off when the juvenile magazine, *American Boy,* began promoting it in 1937 and national magazines subsequently reported on it as a new craze. See Epler, "Safer Football," "Six-man Eleven," and "Six-man Football"; Reck, "Play Six-Man Football" and "Pigskin Revolution"; "Six-man"; "Six-Man Football for Vacant Lot and Rural High School"; and Lee, "Adaptation on the Plains."

12. Peterson, *Pigskin,* 67–83.

13. Quirk and Fort, *Pay Dirt,* 334–41.

14. Smith, "Outside the Pale," 276–77; Fox, *Big Leagues,* 322.

15. The most comprehensive history is Watterson's *College Football.*

16. *Historical Statistics of the United States,* 210.

17. Steiner, *Americans at Play,* 86–94.

18. Goldstein, *Ivy League Autumns,* 129–30, 143.

19. Notre Dame did not integrate until 1944—even then not without protests from southern alumni (see "Negroes at Notre Dame")—and the football team not until the 1950s. As a national university, like the service academies, Notre Dame had to take southerners into account, but the Catholic Church, as an immigrant church, also had its own problems with racism. See McGreevy, *Parish Boundaries.* The *Catholic Digest,* on the other hand, reprinted Heywood Hale Broun's 1939 denunciation of segregation in the NFL and racism in college football. See Broun, "'Color' in Football."

20. Smith, "Outside the Pale," 271; Spivey, "Black Athlete in Big-Time Intercollegiate Sports," 121; Will Robinson, "Every Team in Big Ten Has Negroes Listed," *PC,* 15 October 1955.

21. Paul, McGhee, and Fant, "Arrival and Ascendance of Black Athletes"; Pennington, *Breaking the Ice.*

22. The definitive history of black-college football is yet to be written, but see Chalk, *Black College Football,* Ashe, *Hard Road to Glory,* Hurd, *Black College Football,* and Saylor, "Black College Football."

23. Jones, *Recreation and Amusement*, 73.

24. Films in which football figured incidentally include: *Corsair* (1931), *Primrose Path* (1931), *Deception* (1932), *Ann Carver's Profession* (1933), *Gift of Gab* (1934), *Romance in the Rain* (1934), *She Had to Choose* (1934), *Adventurous Knights* (1935), *Annapolis Farewell* (1935), *Born to Gamble* (1935), *Roberta* (1935), *Love before Breakfast* (1936), *The Payoff* (1936), *Small Town Girl* (1936), *Times Square Playboy* (1936), *West Point of the Air* (1936), *The Jones Family in Big Business* (1937), *The Lady Escapes* (1937), *Murder Goes to College* (1937), *Rosalie* (1937), *There Goes the Groom* (1937), *The Lady Objects* (1938), *Convict's Code* (1939), and *Sorority House* (1939).

25. "Time Out for Love."

26. MacCambridge, *Franchise*.

27. See "Baseball and Football" and "Football as Our Greatest Popular Spectacle."

28. Grafton, "Million Dollars for Football!," 582.

29. Hobsbawn and Ranger, *Invention of Tradition*.

30. Hutchison, "Football: Symbol of College Unity."

31. Lerner, *America as a Civilization*, 815.

CHAPTER ONE

1. Only *$1000 a Touchdown* even warranted a review in the *New York Times,* where Frank S. Nugent on 5 October 1939 called it "a painfully witless farce of almost fantastic unoriginality."

2. See Dick Hyland, "Behind the Line," *LAT,* 3 January 1940; Stub Nelson, "World's Toughest Football League," *PO,* Magazine Section, 31 December 1939; and Frederick Ware, "General Ability of Big Six Reaches New High Level," *OWH,* 27 November 1939.

3. See John T. Czech, "Sixth Annual Pole-America Eleven Picked," *Narod Polski* (Chicago), 28 December 1939; Leo Fischer, "Pick Zontini on All-Italian Football Team," *L'Italia* (Chicago), 3 December 1939; Danny Erwin, "The Local Sports Scene," *Jewish Times* (Philadelphia), 5 January 1940; and Paddy Driscoll, "Football Facts," *New World* (Chicago), 8 December 1939.

4. This is the story told in my *Reading Football.*

5. Evensen, "Jazz Age Journalism's Battle," 234; McChesney, "Media Made Sport," 54, 57, 66; Bent, *Ballyhoo,* 49; Savage, *American College Athletics,* 266–70; Nugent, "Sports Section," 338; and Lever and Wheeler, "*Chicago Tribune* Sports Page," 301.

6. *Problems of Journalism* 5 (1927); Evensen, "Jazz Age Journalism's Battle," 230; *Continuing Study of Newspaper Reading* (1946), 11, 14, 17, 19; *Continuing Study of Newspaper Reading* (1951), 10, 13, 16; Woodward, *Sports Page,* 35; Savage, *American College Athletics,* 288.

7. Emery and Emery, *Press and America,* 245–48; Lee, *Daily Newspaper,* 523–40, 595.

8. On the feature syndicates, see Lee, *Daily Newspaper,* Chapter 15 and 531–36; Walsh, *Adios to Ghosts;* and Wheeler, *I've Got News for You.* On cartoonists, see Becker, *Comic Art in America,* 246–61; and Olderman, "Sporting Life."

9. "Who Reads the Tabloids?"; Emery and Emery, *Press and America,* 282; Bessie, *Jazz Journalism,* 85–86, 224–28; "Tabloid Poison"; "Are Tabloid Newspapers a Menace?"; Weyrauch, "The Why of the Tabloids"; Miller, "New York Tabloids," 37.

10. Miller, "New York Tabloids," 38; Murphy, "Tabloids as an Urban Response," 58.

11. Chapman, *Tell It to Sweeney,* 172; Evensen, *When Dempsey Fought Tunney,* 67–69; Bessie, *Jazz Journalism,* 92, 104, 124.

12. Forty-three percent of male readers read their local sports columnist, while only 27 percent read a syndicated one. See *Continuing Study of Newspaper Reading* (1946), 54. Rice alone among the sportswriters of the era has been the subject of multiple book-length studies: Fountain, *Sportswriter;* Inabinett, *Grantland Rice and His Heroes;* and Harper, *How You Played the Game.*

13. Littlewood, *Arch,* vii; Prell, in Holtzman, *No Cheering in the Press Box,* 140.

14. On women's preferences, see *Continuing Study of Newspaper Reading* (1946), 19, 54.

15. Walker, *City Editor,* 115–33; Rice, *Tumult and the Shouting,* 317; Frank, *Sports Extra,* 37, 169; Woodward, *Sports Page,* 60.

16. *Problems in Journalism,* 99; Savage, *American College Athletics,* 273.

17. For numerous examples see my *Reading Football.*

18. Dick Hawkins, "Georgia Tech Triumphs Over Notre Dame," *AC,* 21 October 1928.

19. Frederick Ware, "Nebraska and Pittsburgh Battle to Scoreless Draw," *OWH,* 18 November 1928.

20. Lipsyte, *SportsWorld,* 172–73.

21. Parker, "So You Want to Be a Sports Editor," in Drewry, *More Post Biographies,* 243.

22. Savage, *American College Athletics,* 278.

23. Lipsyte, *SportsWorld,* 179.

24. Red Smith, "Views of Sport," *NYHT,* 17 November 1953.

25. Ibid., 20 November 1953.

26. Even the widely admired Smith was accused by Seymour Krim of producing "a cute sweet poisonless narcotic." See Berkow, *Red,* 157.

27. Adamic, *My America,* 238. Besides Adamic's chapter, "The Immigrant Press," 238–47, for basic information on the ethnic press see Miller, *Ethnic Press in the United States.*

28. Parry, "Good-bye to the Immigrant Press," 56–60; Woofter, *Races and Ethnic Groups,* 223; Adamic, *My America,* 244.

29. Under the heading *"Allerlei Sportneuigkeiten"* (News Briefs of Various Sports) the Sunday editions of the *Westliche Post* covered local professional teams (the short-lived independent St. Louis Gunners football club as well as the baseball Cardinals), local and national college football teams (St. Louis University, Notre Dame, Yale, the Big Six Conference), and local sports ranging from boxing and wrestling to the activities of the *Deutscher Sportklub.* See the Sunday editions for October and November (*Mississippi Blätter*) beginning in 1931. The *New Yorker Staats-Zeitung und Herold*

published a similar sports page. See, for example, the coverage of local amateur and professional sport on 28 November 1940.

30. See Ralph C. Wilcox, "The Shamrock and the Eagle: Irish Americans and Sport in the Nineteenth Century," in Eisen and Wiggins, *Ethnicity and Sport*, 55–74; and Daley, "American Irish in Sports."

31. John Billi's daily columns in *Il Progresso Italo-Americano* appeared in Italian, but Sunday editions of the paper printed an English section, with sports (including articles with titles such as "Sturdy Italian Gridiron Heroes" on 14 November 1937). Billi selected an All-Italian team in 1937 (November 26). Frank X. Briante regularly selected Italian All-America teams for *Corriere d'America,* usually in Italian: see 29 November 1932, 5 December 1933, and 13 December 1936. The Chicago weekly *L'Italia* (daily beginning in 1938) dealt mostly with local club and professional sports, as did *American Citizen* (Omaha), *La Tribuna Italiana d'America* (Detroit), and *La Voce del Popolo* (Detroit), the last including a column in English beginning in 1938, J. A. Rosati's "The Sportcaster."

32. On the Jewish press, see David Wolf Silverman, "The Jewish Press," in Marty, *Religious Press in America,* 123–72; Singerman, "American Jewish Press" and "Jewish Press"; and Arthur A. Gordon, "The Jewish Press," in Miller, *Ethnic Press in the United States,* 203–88. On sports in the Jewish press, see Riess, *Sports and the American Jew;* and Levine, *Ellis Island.* On the Jewish Telegraphic Agency, see Silverman, 161. Among the papers I surveyed, the *Jewish Examiner* (Brooklyn) and the *Jewish World* (Boston) virtually ignored sports in the fall, but the others—the *Jewish Daily Bulletin* and *American Hebrew* (both New York), the *Sentinel* (Chicago), *Jewish Advocate* (Boston), *Jewish Times* (Philadelphia), *American Jewish Outlook* (Pittsburgh), *Detroit Jewish Chronicle, Jewish Independent* (Cleveland), *Jewish Press* (Omaha), and *California Jewish Voice* and *B'nai B'rith Messenger* (both Los Angeles)—paid much attention to football.

33. George Joel named his first All-America team in 1926; see *The Sentinel,* 17 December 1926, or *Detroit Jewish Chronicle,* 10 December 1926. Morris Weiner took over the selection in 1934. The Jewish Telegraphic Agency's All-America appeared in the *Jewish Independent* in 1927; in the *B'nai B'rith Messenger* in 1930, 1931, and 1935; in the *Jewish Daily Bulletin* in 1934; in the *Detroit Jewish Chronicle* from 1926 through 1933; and in the *Jewish Advocate* in 1930 (I surveyed only 1930, 1933, 1936, and 1939 of this paper). Irv Kupcinet's selections for Seven Arts appeared in the *Jewish Independent* in 1935, in the *B'nai B'rith Messenger* in 1935, 1936, and 1937, in the *Detroit Jewish Chronicle* in 1936 and 1937, and in the *Jewish Advocate* in 1936. The *Messenger's* Jule Zeid selected his own teams in 1932 and 1933, Barney Glazer in 1935 and 1936. Henry Levy presented his 1937 team in *American Hebrew.* Danny Erwin selected a team for the *Jewish Times* in 1939. I have supplemented Levine's identification of All-Jewish teams in *Ellis Island,* 209.

34. On the Polish press, see A. J. Kuzniewski, "The Polish-American Press," in Miller, *Ethnic Press in the United States.* Among the papers offering extensive coverage of Polish-American football players, see *Kuryer Polski* and *Nowiny Polskie* (both Milwaukee), *Rekord Codzienny* and *Dziennik Polski* (both Detroit), *Nowy Swiat* (New York), and the major dailies and weeklies in Chicago, the unofficial Polish-American

capital—*Dziennik Chicagoski, Dziennik Zwiazkowy, Dziennik Zjednoczenia,* and *Narod Polski.*

35. See John T. Czech, "Sport Cycle," 7 November 1931; "Sixty-Eight Poles in College Lineups Last Saturday," 12 November 1932; and Czech, "Sport Cycle," 18 November 1932, all in *Dziennik Zjednoczenia.* For the consensus All-Polish, All-America teams, see *Dziennik Zjednoczenia* for 27 December 1934, 21 December 1935, 19 December 1936, 22 December 1937, and 24 December 1938. When the paper folded in November 1939, Czech took his column, and the All-Polish team, to *Narod Polski.*

36. In 1930, the Jewish press noted with satisfaction that three Notre Dame players, including backfield stars Marchmont Schwartz and Marty Brill, were Jews (see Levine, *Ellis Island,* 209). The Jewish Telegraphic Agency's George Joel claimed Schwartz and Brill, then had to surrender Brill as non-Jewish but insisted that, contrary to some claims, Schwartz was indeed Jewish. See "The Sporting World," *Jewish Advocate,* 4, 11, and 18 November 1930. A profile in the *Saturday Evening Post* in 1947 finally explained that Schwartz was in fact half-Jewish. See Monroe, "Stanford's Storybook Coach."

37. Archdeacon, *Becoming American,* 125.

38. On the Catholic press, see John G. Deedy, Jr., "The Catholic Press," in Marty, *Religious Press in America,* 65–121; Real, "Trends in Structure and Policy," 265–71; and Barnes, "Catholic Press."

39. Maraniss, *When Pride Still Mattered.*

40. My example is the Fort Wayne, Indiana, edition of *Our Sunday Visitor.*

41. Among the papers I surveyed, the *Tablet* (Brooklyn), *Pilot* (Boston), *Catholic News* (New York), *Pittsburgh Catholic, Catholic Review* (Baltimore), *Catholic Standard and Times* (Philadelphia), *Michigan Catholic* (Detroit), *New World* (Chicago), *Monitor* (San Francisco), and *Tidings* (Los Angeles) all reported on Catholic football, both high school and intercollegiate. Only the *Catholic Herald Citizen* of Milwaukee did not.

42. See Gems, "Prep Bowl," and the annual coverage in the *New World.*

43. Anderson, *Industrial Recreation,* 53.

44. I found bits of football in the *Labor Advocate* of Nashville, Tennessee, and the *Labor World* of Spokane, Washington, but none at all in the following: *The Unionist* (Omaha), *The Labor News* (Omaha), *Oregon Labor Press* (Portland), *Labor Newdealer* (Portland), *Union Herald* (Raleigh, N.C.), *Labor Age* (New York), *Catholic Worker* (New York), *Labor World* (San Francisco), *Labor World* (Duluth), *Industrial Unionist* (New York), *Weekly People* (New York), *Industrial Worker* (Seattle), *Tacoma Labor Advocate* (Tacoma), and *Union Labor Record* (Philadelphia). Some of these papers had political affiliations; others were published by the local labor councils.

45. Among those that ignored sport were *The Militant, Class Struggle, Workers Age,* and the *Socialist Review.* The *Student Advocate* printed several articles in 1936 and 1937 that were both critical of college football as a reactionary force and hopeful that football players were slowly becoming aware of their own exploitation.

46. On worker sport, see Arnd Krüger, "Worker Sport Around the World," appendix to Krüger and Riordan, *Story of Worker Sport.* For criticism of "bosses' sports," see for example "Workers' Sports," *Young Worker,* 1 November 1926 (on Red Grange

turning pro); columns in the *Young Worker* for 7 November 1930, 20 December 1930, and 2 November 1931 (on charity football games for the unemployed that merely evaded governmental responsibilities); and columns on 23 November 1931 and 18 December 1934 (on the grim employment prospects for even college football heroes).

47. Naison, "Lefties and Righties," 132. See also Levenstein, "Worker, Daily Worker."

48. Naison, 135, 137. In his discussion of sports in the *Daily Worker* Naison excludes football, commenting that baseball, basketball, and boxing were "the sports most popular with 'Daily' readers" (137–38). Whether the *Worker*'s readers liked football as well as baseball or boxing, however, its sports pages during the fall months were full of the sport. Naison judges the Party's Popular Front embrace of spectator sport a sacrifice of Communist principles to liberalism, a failure that "was the price of the most minimal political influence" (142).

49. Among the major youth publications that covered football and other spectator sports more positively, the *Young Worker* ((1922–1936) was succeeded by *Champion of Youth* (1936–1937), then *Champion* (1937), then *Champion Labor Monthly* (1937–1938). The *Young Communist Review* (1936–1939) became *The Review* (1940–1941), then the *Weekly Review* (1941–1943). For details on all of these papers and their political affiliations, see Conlin, *American Radical Press.*

50. After no sports coverage from 1932 through 1936, another Communist paper, the *Western Worker* of San Francisco, introduced in 1937 a sports column with a similar Popular Front slant, "No Holds Barred" by "Lefty."

51. Lester Rodney exchanged insults with the *Daily News*'s Ed Sullivan over Kenny Washington in 1939. See *DW*, 14 December 1939, and 2 January 1940. In addition, occasional skirmishes with red-baiting sportswriters were waged in the postwar period. See Rodney's columns on 9 November 1948, 23 November 1948, 25 November 1948, 19 November 1951, 6 December 1951, and 12 November 1954. On the positive side, in a column eulogizing the sportswriter Heywood Broun on 19 December 1939, Rodney claimed that Broun was a regular reader and admirer of the *Worker*'s sports page.

52. See, for example, The Bug, "Sports," *DW*, 23 October, 13 November and 20 November 1926; Edward Newhouse, "Sports," *DW*, 12 October 1933; Jack Hardy, "Sports," *DW*, 19 October 1933; Hardy, "Sports," *DW*, 31 October 1933; and Newhouse, "Sports," *DW*, 6 December 1933.

53. Bill Mills, Bill Mardo, and Roosevelt Ward were at various times the black sportswriters on the *Daily Worker* staff.

54. Detweiler, *Negro Press in the United States,* 1–6; Wolseley, *Black Press, U.S.A.,* 10–11. See also Kreiling, "Commercialization of the Black Press"; Dates and Barlow, *Split Image;* Pride and Wilson, *History of the Black Press;* and Emery and Emery, *Press and America,* 227–31.

55. See Hogan, *Black National News Service;* Lee, *Interesting Athletes.* All-American News was distributed to some 400 black theaters in large cities during the 1940s and into the 1950s. See Baechlin and Muller-Strauss, *Newsreels across the World,* 61. *Ebony* appeared in 1946, *Jet* in 1951.

56. Hogan, *Black National News Service,* 28.

57. Ibid., 22; Kessler, *Dissident Press,* 40. On middle-class objections to the *Defender's* sensationalism, see Kreiling, "Commercialization of the Black Press," 184.

58. Young, "Study of Reader Attitudes toward the Negro Press," 148–52.

59. Despite a six-fold increase in enrollments at black colleges between 1917 and 1927, the total in 1927 was a mere 13,580, which combined with the 1,500 in integrated colleges added up to just 15,000 out of a black population over 11 million. See Wolters, *New Negro on Campus,* 17, 313.

60. The *Courier's* "Football Roundup" appeared in 1956 and 1957, following its introduction in the *Afro-American* in 1955. The *Chicago Defender* ran similar articles beginning in 1955.

61. At least one football game was broadcast earlier, over a noncommercial station: Texas vs. Texas A&M on Thanksgiving Day, 1920, over Texas A&M's WTAW. See McDonald, *Don't Touch That Dial,* 5.

62. Greenfield, *Radio,* 131.

63. Kurian, *Datapedia of the United States,* 299–300; McChesney, "Media Made Sport," 59. There were 28.5 million sets by 1940, 40.7 million by 1950.

64. Greenfield, *Radio,* 20–28; Goldsmith and Lescaboura, *This Thing Called Broadcasting,* 166–71.

65. McDonald, *Don't Touch That Dial,* 9; Banning, *Commercial Broadcasting Pioneer,* 110–11; Emery and Emery, *Press and America,* 275; "Millions Listen in on Rose Festival," *NYT,* 3 January 1928; "Bill Stern Broadcasts a Harvard Football Game."

66. Ronald Smith's forthcoming study of intercollegiate athletics and radio will document universities' handling of broadcast rights. In order to reach and increase its following around the country, Notre Dame offered radio rights to every radio station and network that wanted them, on a noncommercial basis, until 1941, when broadcasters were given the option of purchasing rights or continuing to carry games without a fee. See Sperber, *Shake Down the Thunder,* 279, 452–53.

67. For an anecdotal history of these and other broadcasters, see Poindexter, *Golden Throats.*

68. The NBC collection at the Library of Congress includes four games from 1935, two from 1936, six from 1938, and eleven more through 1945, then nearly weekly games from 1946 through 1954 (except for 1951). The twelve games from the late 1930s are Navy–Notre Dame (10/26/35), Notre Dame–Northwestern (11/9/35), Harvard-Yale (11/23/35), Rice-TCU (11/23/35), College All Stars–New York Giants (9/8/36), Ohio State–Pitt (10/10/36), College All Stars–Washington Redskins (8/31/38), Army-Columbia (10/8/38), Notre Dame–Illinois (10/15/38), Princeton–Penn State (10/15/38), Fordham-Oregon (10/22/38), and Army-Navy (11/26/38).

69. Greenfield, *Radio,* 134.

70. Douglas, *Early Days of Radio Broadcasting,* 59, 121–23; Greenfield, *Radio,* 134; "Sport"; and College All Stars vs. New York Giants, 8 September 1936.

71. Dunning, *On the Air,* 628; Bach, "Hold 'Em Husing!" Donald Paneth, "Pigskin Pundit," *NYT,* 7 October 1945; Husing, *Ten Years Before the Mike,* 267–678. Red Barber credited Husing's assistants for his accuracy. See Barber, *Broadcasters,* 30.

72. Gator Bowl, 1 January 1949.

73. Dunning, *On the Air*, 632; Buxton and Owen, *Big Broadcast*, 223–24; Glickman, *Fastest Kid on the Block*, 68. Glickman also challenged Husing's reputation for accuracy (67).

74. Douglas, *Early Days*, 125; Barber, *Broadcasters*, 21, 38. Barber's second chapter ("The Pioneers") has portraits of McNamee, Husing, Stern, and several other early sportscasters.

75. "Football Games by Radio," *NYT*, 12 October 1924; "Football Games Heard on the Radio Play By Play," *NYT*, 17 October 1926; broadcast of SMU-TCU football game, 29 November 1947.

76. McNamee, *You're On the Air;* 143–45; Douglas, *Early Days*, 122; Husing, *Ten Years Before the Mike*, 164–65; Husing, *My Eyes Are in My Heart*, 163–64.

77. See "Yankees Win, 2 to 1, While 63,000 Watch, 15,000,000 Listen In," *NYT*, 2 October 1926.

78. "Stenographers Take Oregon-Washington Game Over Radio," *PO*, 10 October 1926.

79. In 1926, the *Dallas Morning News*, for example, announced games not only over local stations WFAA, WRR, and KRLD, but also over stations as far away as New York, Chicago, Minneapolis, Omaha, and San Francisco. The *Omaha World-Herald* in 1926 used the term "Silent night" to indicate airwaves free from local programming, open to distant stations, and it offered readers a "Radio Atlas" to locate their signals (such a Radio Log continued to appear as late as 1934).

80. These dates are based on the listings in the *New York Times, Chicago Tribune, Portland Oregonian, Dallas Morning News, Omaha World-Herald, Los Angeles Times,* and *Atlanta Constitution.*

81. In Omaha, weekly pro games on radio began in 1946, on television in 1951 (and the title game in 1950). In Dallas, weekly radio started in 1947, television in 1953 (the title game in 1952, and partial games or highlights in 1950); in Atlanta, radio arrived in 1949, television in 1952 (the title game in 1950). In Portland, weekly pro football arrived on television in 1953 (the title game in 1952) without ever having been on radio (only the NFL title game, beginning in 1943).

82. Fountain, *Sportswriter*, 196; Dunning, *On the Air*, 162–63. Stern's *My Favorite Sports Stories*, a collection of his scripts, includes a section on football.

83. *Sports Stories* is not listed in Dunning or in other compilations, but episodes from 1943–45 are at the Library of Congress, including three football stories: "The Story of Minnesota Thorgins" (5 February 1944), originally published as "Second Chance" by Stanley Frank in *Collier's;* "Rackety Rax" (9 September 1944) by Joel Sayre, originally published in *American Mercury;* and "Football Brains" (13 January 1945) by Harrison Hendricks, originally published in the pulp magazine *Sports Winners.*

84. See Dunning, *On the Air*, 352–55. See Dunning also for the information for *The Adventures of Frank Merriwell* and *The Adventures of Dick Cole.*

85. Fielding, *American Newsreel*, 3, 132; Baechlin and Muller-Strauss, *Newsreels across the World*, 60–61; Sugrue, "Newsreels," 9; Cumming, "History of American Newsreels."

86. Fielding, *American Newsreel*, 9, 57–58; Dale, *Literature of Cinema*, 200; Baechlin

and Muller-Strauss, *Newsreels across the World,* 36, 61. There were other sports films as well, most notably Grantland Rice's one-reel (ten-minute) productions for his Sportlight Films, produced once a month beginning in 1925 and distributed by Pathé to more than seven thousand theaters nationally. Over time, Rice discovered that spectator sports were less successful with viewers, particularly women, than "novelties." See Fountain, *Grantland Rice,* 196–98; Rice, *Tumult and the Shouting,* 259.

87. McGrath, "Newsreel Football Specials"; Thomas M. Pryor, "Shooting from the 50-Yard Line," *NYT,* 23 October 1938; and Greenwald, "You Can't Outguess the Quarterback."

88. Pryor, "Shooting from the 50-Yard Line."

89. "Dear Old Sing Sing Goes Collegiate," 18 November 1931; "Big House Opens Football Season," 22 September 1935; "Midget Football Championship," 16 November 1938; "Middies Play Football in 'Gay Nineties' Style," 10 October 1935; "Boys' Town Gridders Go to Town," 23 November 1938. All are from *Metrotone News* and *News of the Day.* The Universal newsreels included a similar range of comical "human-interest" football features.

90. *Fox Movietone News* covered a regular-season NFL game as early as 1931, but except for the championship (first covered by *Metrotone News* in 1934 and by the other four newsreels by 1937) and the late-summer contest between the College All Stars and the NFL champions (beginning in 1937), the pros were all but ignored until after World War II. Beginning in 1946, the newsreels began covering a pro game or two in December, after the college season ended, in addition to a divisional playoff and the championship game, then in 1949 Pathé finally featured either an NFL or an AAFC game each week. By the mid-1950s the other newsreels did as well.

91. Still the best introduction to the periodical press is Mott's five-volume *History of American Magazines.* Volumes 4 and 5 provide profiles of the magazines discussed in this chapter. Also useful are Peterson, *Magazines in the Twentieth Century;* Nourie and Nourie, *American Mass-Market Magazines;* and Wood, *Magazines in the United States.*

92. *Continuing Study of Magazine Audiences* (1946), 28; and *NYT,* 6 November 1947, 27 (a full-page ad placed by *Look*).

93. MacCambridge, *Franchise.*

94. On *Time,* see Elson, *Time, Inc.,* but Elson has nothing to say about sports coverage.

95. *N. W. Ayer* (1960), 730. Unless otherwise noted, circulation figures throughout this book are from the annual Ayer directories.

96. Tebbel, *George Horace Lorimer,* 286.

97. On the *Post*'s nonfiction see ibid., 246; and Wood, *Magazines in the United States,* 161.

98. Mott, *History of American Magazines,* 4: 470.

99. From 1923 until the Depression shrunk the size of the magazines, the *Post* and *Collier's* together published between 500 and 600 stories each year. See the tables in *The Best Short Stories,* edited annually by Edward J. O'Brien from 1915 through 1941.

100. For an overview of the sports pulps, see Dinan, *Sports in the Pulp Magazines.*

101. Subscriptions to *Boys' Life* grew from 200,000 to 300,000 over the 1930s (before leaping to more than 500,000 by 1950, then to almost a million in 1955 and

1.8 million in 1960). The circulations of individual pulp magazines in the 1930s were smaller—about 150,000 for *Sport Story*, for example (Dinan, *Sports in the Pulp Magazines*, 36). Pulp publishers marketed magazines in a range of genres, and the only circulation figures made public were for a publisher's entire group, the basis on which advertising was sold. The circulation for the Popular group in 1940, for example, was 1.5 million for fifteen titles, two of them sports pulps. By 1945, circulation had nearly doubled, to 2.9 million. See the annual volumes of *Ayer* directories. The typical football pulp likely had a circulation between 100,000 and 200,000.

102. On this bare structure a number of story lines were developed in the 1920s. Heroes fell into dissipation or became entangled with dangerous women, then found their senses in time (*The Plastic Age*, 1925; *Brown of Harvard*, 1926; *College Days*, 1926). Others were falsely accused or nobly took the blame for a misguided teammate, but again were exonerated, and again just in the nick of time (*College Days*, 1926; *The Kick-off*, 1926; *The Quarterback*, 1926; *The Drop Kick*, 1927; *College Love*, 1929). The football stars lured to the school by a "college widow" discover her ruse but are persuaded to stay and win the big game (*The College Widow*, 1927, a remake of a 1915 film, remade again with sound as *Maybe It's Love* in 1930).

103. Wheeler and Woolsey (a third-rate Abbott and Costello) win the big game in *Hold 'Em Jail* (1933) with the help of a chloroformed towel. One of the goofy Ritz Brothers (second-rate Marx Brothers) catches his own pass to win the game in *Life Begins in College* (1937). An utterly inept Joe Penner (a fourth-rate—make that fifth-rate—Harold Lloyd) in *Mr. Doodle Kicks Off* (1938) boots the winning field goal as a spasmodic reflex when the band plays "Pop Goes the Weasel." Wide-mouthed Joe E. Brown is tossed over the goalposts for the winning score in *$1000 a Touchdown* (1939). Mickey Mouse, the Three Stooges, and Our Gang also had their moments of unlikely football stardom in football shorts. In the 1950s, a chimp wins the big game in *Bonzo Goes to College;* a mule gives the winning halftime pep talk in *Francis Goes to West Point;* the Bowery Boys win the game for Ivy College in *Hold That Line;* and Jerry Lewis offered an updated version of *The Freshman* in *That's My Boy*.

104. *Sunny Skies*, 1930; *College Humor*, 1933; *Pigskin Parade*, 1936; *Life Begins in College*, 1937; *Over the Goal*, 1937; *Start Cheering*, 1938; *Up the River*, 1938; and *Too Many Girls*, 1940. The college-football musical made a brief comeback after the war in *Good News* (1947) and *Yes, Sir, That's My Baby* (1949).

105. A series of films including *Hold 'Em Navy* (1937), *Navy Blue and Gold* (1937), and *Touchdown, Army* (1938) established the service academies as the places where such old-fashioned values still prevailed. This image of Army and Navy football was also appropriated for *Arizona* (1931), *Annapolis Farewell* (1935), *West Point of the Air* (1936), the Nelson Eddy–Eleanor Powell musical *Rosalie* (1937), and *Come On, Leathernecks* (1938), which used football only in the opening scenes as a sort of shorthand to establish their heroes' impeccable credentials. The biopics following *Knute Rockne* included *Harmon of Michigan* (1941), *Smith of Minnesota* (1942), *The Spirit of Stanford* (1942), *The Iron Major* (1943), *The Spirit of West Point* (1947), *Jim Thorpe—All-American* (1951), and *Crazylegs* (1953).

106. Wallace's novels in order of publication were *Huddle!* (1930), *Stadium* (1931), *O'Reilly of Notre Dame* (1931), *That's My Boy* (1932), *Big Game* (1936), *Autumn Madness*

(1936), and *Razzle-Dazzle* (1938). *Big Game* was serialized in *Collier's* in 1935 as "The Odds against Honor," *Autumn Madness* in the *Post* in 1936 as "The Double Ride," and "Razzle-Dazzle" in the *Post* in 1937 under the same title. *Huddle!* was produced as a film in 1932, *Stadium* adapted for *Touchdown* in 1931, *O'Reilly of Notre Dame* adapted for *Rose Bowl* in 1936, *That's My Boy* made into a film in 1932 (with the same title but a considerably changed plot), and "The Odds against Honor" made into *The Big Game* in 1936.

107. See, for example, the ad for Quaker Oats on the back cover of the *Saturday Evening Post* for 29 September 1900; and another for Cream of Wheat (the brand's familiar black cook serving four players) in *Woman's Home Companion,* November 1900.

108. Heller and Fili, *Cover Story,* 15–17. See also Best, *American Popular Illustration;* Reed, *Illustrator in America; Century of American Illustration;* and *Magazine Covers.*

109. Heller and Fili, *Cover Story,* 15.

110. The *New Yorker* had twenty-one football covers between 1927 and 1960 (see Lorenz, *Art of the New Yorker*). *Life* had sixteen between 1923 and 1936; *Judge,* twenty between 1922 and 1936.

111. For a sampling of these covers, see Heller and Fili, *Cover Story.*

112. Sperber, *Onward to Victory,* 102–4, and chaps. 10, 29, and 45 passim.

CHAPTER TWO

1. See, for example, "East Carries Grid Honors," *DMN,* 1 December 1925.

2. All of the stories are from 5 December 1926.

3. Dorman, *Revolt of the Provinces,* xi–xii.

4. See Ibid.

5. Stone, "Sport as Community Representation," 230. See also Schwartz and Barsky, "Home Advantage"; and Mizruchi, "Local Sports Teams."

6. See particularly, Hardy, *How Boston Played* and "Sport in Urbanizing America"; and Riess, *City Games* and *Sport in Industrializing America.*

7. On football and fraternities see Fass, *Damned and the Beautiful;* and Horowitz, *Campus Life.*

8. "Baseball and Football."

9. See Ingham et al., "Professional Sports and Community"; and Danielson, *Home Team.*

10. Paxton and Sylvester, "Hungry Young Coach of Nebraska"; and Rader, *American Sports,* 172.

11. Gems, *Windy City Wars,* 179, 211.

12. On high school football in Texas, see Reinert and Winningham, *Rites of Fall.* More recently, Bissinger's *Friday Night Lights* describes football at Permian High in Odessa, Texas, in the 1990s as something closer to a collective pathology than a sport.

13. I compared coverage in these papers in 1925, 1935, 1946 (the first fully post-war season), and 1955.

14. Following the Lynds, other sociologists conducted similar studies of "Yankee City," "Plainsville," "Elmtown," "Jonesville," and many other such places. In none of

these studies does football, or sport more generally, receive more than passing mention, but this oversight seems less an accurate measure of football's importance than an instance of this generation's scholars' unwillingness to take games, particularly schoolboys' games, seriously. In *Elmtown's Youth*, A. B. Hollingshead did, however, note that the football and basketball teams commanded considerable public interest, particular the games against nearby rival communities. See Hollingshead, *Elmtown's Youth*, 193. See also Warner and Lunt, *Social Life of a Modern Community;* West, *Plainsville, U.S.A.;* and Warner, *Democracy in Jonesville.*

15. Lynd and Lynd, *Middletown in Transition*, 292.

16. Lynd and Lynd, *Middletown*, 283–85.

17. Lynd and Lynd, *Middletown in Transition*, 378–79.

18. See Bob Barnet, "Punts and Passes," *Muncie Morning Star*, 21 October 1935.

19. See "Punts and Passes," *Muncie Morning Star*, for 10 October, 15 October, and 18 October 1935.

20. Bob Barnet, "Bearcats Are Victors," *Muncie Morning Star*, 29 September 1935.

21. Bob Barnet, "Punts and Passes," *Muncie Morning Star*, 29 October and 15 October 1935.

22. Bob Barnet, "Punts and Passes," *Muncie Morning Star*, 29 October 1935.

23. Wallace, "This Football Business."

24. In *Shake Down the Thunder*, Murray Sperber documents this development at Notre Dame.

25. George White, "West Point Noses out Mustangs, 14–13," *DMN*, 7 October 1928; Frederick Ware, "Cornhuskers Win First Big Six Football Championship," *OWH*, 30 November 1928.

26. Paul Warwick, "A Piece for the Paper: Invasions Are Worth While," *AC*, 12 November 1923.

27. Doyle, "Foolish and Useless Sport," 328.

28. George White, "Sport Broadcast," *DMN*, 15 December 1928; and 11 December 1931. See also his column for 12 December 1928.

29. *Gallup Poll*, 3: 1699–1700 (the poll was from 1961); and Hollingshead, *Elmtown's Youth*, 192–93.

30. The Carnegie Foundation reported alumni recruiting at thirty percent of the colleges and universities studied. See Savage et al., *American College Athletics*, 237–38.

31. George White, "Sport Broadcast," *DMN*, 3 October 1928, and 4 October 1930; "Big Crowd Will Follow Ponies for Scrap with Navy," *DMN*, 9 November 1930; and "S.M.U.-Syracuse, Texas-Oklahoma Games Next Saturday," *DMN*, 9 October 1932. On weekly wages, see U.S. Bureau of the Census, *Historical Statistics of the United States*, 92.

32. Thelin, *Games Colleges Play*, 68–90.

33. See Lester, *Stagg's University*.

34. On Northwestern, see Watterson, *College Football*, 162–64.

35. Ibid., 147–49.

36. Servin and Wilson, *Southern California and Its University*, 123–24, 172, 191 203; and Rappoport, *Trojans*, 142–43. In a foreword to Servin and Wilson's book, Carrie McWilliams mentions the emphasis on football in the 1920s (xv).

37. Riess, "Power without Authority," 74. On the Chandlers as community boosters, see Berges, *Life and* Times *of Los Angeles,* 41.

38. Servin and Wilson, 172. See, for example, Paul Lowry, "Football Players in Perfect Shape for Do-or-Die Argument Between North and South," *LAT,* 5 November 1921. The two Bay Area schools briefly severed athletic relations with USC in 1924. See the exchange of charges in "California, Stanford and U.S.C. Present Their Case," *LAT,* 5 November 1924. Three years later, a Stanford All-American, Dick Hyland—ironically to become one of the most abrasively chauvinistic of Los Angeles sportswriters after joining the *Los Angeles Times*—infuriated the Trojan players with a short story in *College Humor* magazine, "The Front Runner," that mocked USC star Morton Kaer as a "dumb-bell." For the Trojans' response, see Braven Dyer, "Dick Hyland's Story Makes Trojan Footballers Fighting Mad," *LAT,* 10 October 1927. Hyland later recalled that in the next Stanford-USC game the USC players "half killed me on the field." See Dick Hyland, "Hyland Fling," *LAT,* 7 August 1956.

39. The PCC was formed in 1915 by the University of California, University of Oregon, Oregon Agricultural College, and University of Washington. Washington State joined in 1917, Stanford in 1919, then USC and Idaho in 1922, Montana in 1924, and finally UCLA—originally just the southern branch of the university in Berkeley—in 1928. Montana dropped out after the 1949 season, but Idaho retained full voting power, despite playing only three or four conference games a season, until the PCC was dissolved on 30 June 1959.

40. Ed R. Hughes, "Thundering Herd Humbles Oregon Aggies," *LAT,* 12 November 1926.

41. Major episodes included USC's successful challenge to the eligibility of Oregon's Joe Lillard in 1931, to end a promising season for the Ducks; and the conference's bypassing Oregon for the 1949 Rose Bowl bid, in favor of California. See Gregory's responses in his "Greg's Gossip" columns for 9, 14, and 15 October 1931; and 22, 23, 24, and 26 November and 5 December 1948. In the 1950s, Gregory groused about Los Angeles sportswriters' persistence in mispronouncing "Oregon" as "Or-e-GON," as a seemingly intentional insult. See his "Greg's Gossip" columns for 2 January 1952 and 2 January 1953.

42. The breakup of the PCC over the slush-fund scandals is thoroughly described in Thelin, *Games Colleges Play.* For a brief version see Cohane, "Inside the West Coast Football Scandal."

43. See Cary, "Saturday's Millions," *SEP* (1933); Garth, "Boy Who Sold Himself," *Collier's* (1934); Cary, "Out of the Shadows," *Collier's* (1935); Fitzgerald, "Gallagher's Game," *Collier's* (1935); Wallace, "Double Ride," *SEP* (1936); Wallace, "Razzle-Dazzle," *SEP* (1937); and Brent, "Yesterday's Heroes," *SEP* (1939).

44. Thomas, *Southern Methodist University,* 86. Selecman was satirized in a 1929 football novel, *Pigskin,* by Charles Ferguson, a former editor of the campus newspaper.

45. Quoted in Terry, *"From High on the Hilltop,"* 23. The account of the controversy is taken from Thomas, *Southern Methodist University,* 85–91.

46. Thomas, 87, 89, 150; Terry, *"From High on a Hilltop,"* 35–37.

47. George White, "Sport Broadcast," *DMN,* 12 October 1930; "Seek Big Football

Attractions for Texas Centennial," *DMN,* 15 December 1934. On the Texas Centennial, see Ragsdale, *Year America Discovered Texas.*

48. "Record Breaking Special Train Movement Will Take Texans to Rose Bowl," *DMN,* 15 December 1935; and "Record Special Train Movement Carries Texans," *DMN,* 22 December 1935.

49. Ragsdale, *Year America Discovered Texas,* 142–43 and Chapter 10.

50. Schecter, *I Live on Air,* 123.

51. See, for example, Elkin, *City and Regime;* and Pelissero et al., "Urban Regimes."

52. Jabs and counter-punches by Gregg McBride, John Bentley, and Floyd Olds in the *World-Herald,* and by Cy Sherman in his "Brass Tacks" column in the *Lincoln Star,* ran from 22 November to 9 December 1945. The controversy is discussed in Denney et al., *Go Big Red.*

53. "Gregg McBride" (the title of McBride's own column), *OWH,* 4 December 1945.

54. Doyle, "'Causes Won, Not Lost,'" 237, 244–45.

55. See Pouncey, *Mustang;* Ratliff, *Power and the Glory;* and Tips, *Football—Texas Style.*

56. Savage, *American College Athletics,* 305.

57. "Ray Morrison Tells New York about Southwestern Gridders," *DMN,* 19 October 1935; Grantland Rice, "Grantland Rice Says 'Real Football' Is Played by Southwestern Elevens," *DMN,* 2 December 1935; Stub Nelson, "What's the Matter with Pacific Coast Football?" *PO,* Sunday Magazine, 3 October 1937.

58. Tips, *Football—Texas Style,* 31; Ratliff, *Power and the Glory,* 36.

59. Doyle, "'Causes Won, Not Lost,'" "Foolish and Useless Sport," and "Turning the Tide"; Miller, "Manly, the Moral, and the Proficient," 298, 300; Sumner, "John Franklin Crowell."

60. In the most famous "boner" in football history, Cal's Roy Riegels ran sixty-seven yards the wrong way with a fumble, leading to a safety that provided the margin in an 8–7 Georgia Tech victory. The *Atlanta Constitution* claimed a great southern victory; the *Los Angeles Times* claimed a fluke.

61. Dan Magill, "Athens Regards Yale-Georgia Game as Greatest Civic Aid," *AC,* "Georgia-Yale Section," 12 October 1929.

62. Ralph McGill, "Fighting for an Ideal Gave Georgia Victory," *AC,* 13 October 1929.

63. Meany, "Dixie Plays for Blood."

64. Ralph McGill, "Break o' Day," *AC,* 16 October 1937; Stanley Frank, "South Needs No War Ballyhoo," *New York Post,* 17 October 1935.

65. See, for example, Ralph McGill, "Georgia Crushes N.Y.U., 25–0," *AC,* 29 October 1933; Jimmy Jones, "Tech Was South's 'General Johnston,'" *AC,* 4 December 1933. Jones, "Bulldogs Make Grid History in Yale Bowl," *AC,* 11 November 1934; and Trammell Scott, "A Guest Column," *AC,* 20 December 1937.

66. Ed Danforth, "Mawnin'!" *AC,* 3 January 1931. See also Scott, "Guest Column."

67. Paul Zimmerman, "Sport Postscripts," *LAT,* 2 January 1943.

68. Braven Dyer, "Sportsmanship and Courtesy Make Alabama Team Popular," *LAT,* 28 December 1925; George Trevor, "Catfish Smith Stops Yale," *New York Sun,*

14 October 1929; Trevor, "Southern Football's Challenge"; Paul Gallico, "Moaning Monday," *NYDN,* 22 October 1934; Damon Runyon, "35,000 See Southerners Dash Bowl Hopes of Rams," *New York American,* 22 November 1936; and Left Wing, "Public Enemy No. 64B."

69. Tom Meany, "The Monday Morning Quarterback," *New York World-Telegram,* 9 and 16 October 1939; Bob Considine, "NYU Tops Georgia, 14–13; Players Fight," *New York Sunday Mirror,* 29 October 1939; Harry Forbes, "NYU Tops Georgia, 14–13," *NYDN,* 29 October 1939; "South Beats North 33 to 20 on Grid," *New York Journal-American,* 31 December 1939; Bob Bumbry, "First Down for Hollywood," *NYDN,* 27 December 1939; Grantland Rice, "Vols Drove Like Pickett at Battle of Gettysburg," *AC,* 2 January 1940.

70. See, for example, Horace McCoy, "Vanderbilt Defeats Texas Longhorns in Bitterly Fought Game, 14 to 6," *DMN,* 11 October 1925.

71. Harry McNamara, "Irish Upset Texans in 4th Period," *Chicago Herald and Examiner,* 5 October 1930.

72. "Big Games on Day's Program," *DMN,* 24 October 1931 (from the Associated Press); and John Kieran, "Sports of the Times," *NYT,* 24 October 1931.

73. "Crickard Writes New Alamo for Longhorns to Remember," *Boston Herald,* 25 October 1931; Bill Cunningham, "Harvard Puts 35–7 Brand on Texas Steers," *Boston Post,* 25 October 1931; "Texas Longhorns Routed by Powerful Harvard Eleven 35–7," *DMN,* 25 October 1931.

74. Will Stevens, Jr., "Southern Methodist Team Due Here Today," *San Francisco Chronicle,* 4 December 1931; Prescott Sullivan, "T.C.U. Arrives Today for Bronc Contest," *San Francisco Chronicle,* 6 December 1935; George Dixon, "Methodist Pony Gallops to 26–14 Victory Over Rams," *NYDN,* 29 October 1934.

75. Grantland Rice, "S.M.U. Earns Right to Battle Stanford—Rice," *LAT,* 2 December 1935; Joe Williams, "Flashy Football Is Tops," *New York World-Telegram,* 2 December 1935; Paul Gallico, "Best in the Land," *NYDN,* 1 December 1935; Bill Cunningham, "So. Methodist Winner, 20–14," *Boston Post,* 1 December 1935; "So. Methodist Sets Back T.C.U. with Late Aerial," *NYT,* 1 December 1935. Unfortunately, the sound has been lost from the newsreel coverage for Universal, the one newsreel in Dallas for the game.

76. See Braven Dyer, "Mustangs Tamed by Stanford's Line"; Jack Singer, "'Laughing Boys' Make Merry after Struggle"; Dick Hyland, "Texas Has New 'Alamo'"; and Grantland Rice, "Methodists Get Jitters"; all in *LAT,* 2 January 1936.

77. See, for example, Grantland Rice, "Baugh Ends College Grid Career in Blaze of Glory," *LAT,* 13 December 1936; Frank Finch, "Mustang Passes Down Bruin Eleven, 26–13," *LAT,* 21 November 1937; and L. H. Gregory, "'Bowl-Slighted' Longhorns Trounce Oregon Team; Massacre Score, 71–7," *PO,* 7 December 1941.

78. Charles Burton, "Covering Sport," *DMN,* 2 November 1941.

79. McLemore, "Texas Grid Fans Call the Plays"; and "Texas A. & M. Footballers"; Bill Rives, "The Sport Scene," *DMN,* 1 October 1950; Fay, "It's Hard-Ridin'"; "Meredith Will Be Ready for Tech," *DMN,* 20 October 1958.

80. Bill Rives, "The Sport Scene," *DMN,* 30 September and 27 October 1952.

81. Charles Burton, "The Inside Story," *DMN,* 9 November 1952; Bill Rives, "The Sport Scene," *DMN,* 16 November 1952.

CHAPTER THREE

1. For overviews of the key episodes of failed reform, see Thelin, *Games Colleges Play;* and Watterson, *College Football.*

2. See, for example, *NYT,* 28 December 1921; 29–31 January, 1 and 4 February 1922; and 2 November 1923. On the invention of the amateur ideal, see Pope, *Patriotic Games,* 18–34.

3. See Grange, *Red Grange Story;* Carroll, *Red Grange;* "Grange's Gold Quest on for 6 More Weeks," *NYDN,* 19 December 1925; "Red Grange's Team May Play in Dallas," *DMN,* 13 December 1925; and my own "Home Teams."

4. H. C. Hamilton, "Sportively Speaking," *AC,* 5, 6, 15, and 20 December 1925; Chauncey Brown, "The Branding Iron," *DMN,* 23 November 1925.

5. *NYT,* 7 December 1925; *OWH,* 8 December 1925; *LAT,* 11 December 1925, 1.

6. "Trying to Get Some of 'Red' Grange's Easy Money," *American Weekly,* in *Seattle Post-Intelligencer,* 3 January 1926.

7. "Grange Turns Professional," *NYT,* 24 November 1925, 24. In another editorial, on 3 December, the *Times* identified the Harvard *Crimson* and the *Yale News* as the leaders of the anti-Grange campaign (24).

8. Paul Gallico, "50 Weeks to Vacation," *NYDN,* 8 December 1925; and "Harold, How Could You?" *NYDN,* 9 December 1925.

9. Ted Vosburgh, "Subsidizing of College Athletes Is Bared," *AC,* 24 October 1929, 1. On the Carnegie report and its impact, see Thelin, *Games People Play,* 13–37; and Watterson, *College Football,* 158–76.

10. Westbrook Pegler, "Carnegie Probe Seems to Be a Waste of Time," *CT,* 25 October 1929; and "Nobody's Business," *OWH,* 24 November 1929.

11. Frederick Ware, "The Sportolog," *OWH;* George White, "Sport Broadcast," *DMN;* Ed Danforth, "Mawnin'!" *AC;* Ralph McGill, "Carnegie Foundation Fires Another Blank," *AC*—all of these on 24 October 1929; and "College Amateurism," *CT,* 25 October 1929.

12. Watterson, *College Football,* 174–75.

13. Ed Danforth, "Mawnin'!" *AC,* 24 October 1929.

14. Owen, "Football—Pleasure or Grind?"; Fish, "In Defense of Modern Football"; Reed, "Is College Football Doomed?"; Prince, "Hand Back the Game to the Boys"; "Demoting the Half Gods of College"; "Editor Steps Down"; Tunis, "Great God Football"; and Cagle, "Football as a Vocation."

15. See "Red Grange in Business"; Littell, "Ice Man Remembers"; "Open Market for Galloping Ghosts"; and "Yelping Alumni."

16. See Prince, "Hand Back the Game to the Boys"; Sinclair, "Killers of Thought"; "To Make Football a Sport"; "College Football"; Grafton, "Million Dollars for Football!"; Summers, "Football Business"; and Tunis, "Football and Fiction."

17. See "Twenty-Seven Deaths"; Trevor, "Brutal Truth"; "First Down for Yale"; Left Wing, "Men Who Make America's Gods" and "Public Enemy No. 64B"; "The Week" (1931 and 1936); and Bliven, "Bleeding Kansas."

18. See Wallace, "Hypocrisy of Football Reform"; Broun, "It Seems"; Cason, "Football Hero Rebels"; and Schoonmaker, "Pity the Poor Athlete."

19. Tunis, "Great God Football" and *$port$ Heroics*.

20. Tunis, "More Pay for College Football Stars" and "What Price College Football?" For the earlier articles, see "Football on the Wane?" "Slump in Football Common," and "Maguire"; as well as "Portrait of an Intellectual," "Eddie Stands for Good Clean Sport"; "Fellow Alumni of Mammoth," "College President," and "Honoris Causa" on the larger situation in higher education.

21. "Football Controversy" and Lardner, "What Price Whaddyacallit?"

22. Wallace, "Hypocrisy of Football Reform."

23. Wallace, "Pigskin Preview" (1937 and 1938) and "Football's Black Market."

24. See Hutchins, "Gate Receipts and Glory." The *Post* also reported on the Pacific Coast Conference's attempt to purify itself; see Neuberger, "Gridiron G-Man."

25. Charles Bartlett, "Harvard Backs Parade against Maroons, 61–0," *CT*, 15 October 1939; Bartlett, "Illinois Finds Par against the Maroons Is 46," *CT*, 26 November 1939; McLemore, "McLemore's All-America."

26. "Ohio State Players Get Wages of Sport from the State."

27. Wallace, "Test Case at Pitt" and "Football Laboratory Explodes." See also "News of Pitt Football Player Revolt Was Suppressed," *DW*, 3 December 1937; and Watterson, *College Football*, 180–82, 188–89.

28. The Associated Press covered the freshman revolt thoroughly. See "Pitt Freshmen Ask Help," *NYT*, 17 November 1938; "Pitt Set to Cancel Freshman Tuition," *NYT*, 24 November 1938; "Sutherland Not to Quit," *NYT*, 29 November 1938; "Pitt Code Permits Big-Time Football," *NYT*, 1 December 1938; "Pitt Freshmen, Saying They Were Misled, Demand Showdown on Aid from University," *NYT*, 2 December 1938; "Pitt Policy Explained," *NYT*, 3 December 1938; and "Bowman Tells Alumni Pitt Seeks 'Football Team Above Critics,'" *NYT*, 6 December 1938.

29. See Wallace's "Pigskin Previews" for 23 September 1939, 21 September 1940, and 19 September 1942.

30. Foree, "Archangel and His Bible"; Broeg, "Oil Makes the Hurricane Roar."

31. Little, "1946 Football Forecast"; and Olson, *G.I. Bill*, 43, 109. See also Andrews, "G.I. Bill and College Football."

32. Wallace, "Pigskin Preview" (1946) and "Football's Black Market"; Russell, "Big Bad Bulldog from Dixie," and Roberts, "One-Man Team" (both on Charlie Trippi); Frank, "Buddy Totes the Ball" (on Buddy Young); Small, "Football's Demon Deacon" (on Peahead Walker); Frank, "Big Ten's Surprise Package"; Fay, "Dixie's No. 1 Gridnaper" (on Bear Bryant); and Shallett, "Maryland's Busiest Byrd."

33. The fullest account of this period and these issues is Sperber's *Onward to Victory*.

34. Watterson, *College Football*, 209–18 and 227–28 (quotations from 209 and 228); Sperber, *Onward to Victory*, 227–36, 369–76; Thelin, *Games Colleges Play*, 101–3, 107–13; and Lawrence, *Unsportsmanlike Conduct*, 41–49.

35. Wallace, "Pigskin Preview" (1947); "Pigskin Preview" (1948), "Francis Wallace's 10th," "Francis Wallace's 11th," and "Francis Wallace's 12th."

36. See Sperber, *Onward to Victory*, 344–57.

37. Pro football at the movies, for example, was corrupted, not just threatened, by gamblers. This was an element in *The All-American* (1932), *Sport Parade* (1932), and *King of the Gamblers* (1948).

38. See, for example, "Atlanta Gambling Injures Football," *NYT,* 31 October 1921, which reported that gamblers in Atlanta approached Rutgers players and coaches for information before their game with Georgia Tech.

39. See Red Grange's twelve-part serial, *The Galloping Ghost* in 1931, as well as feature films ranging from *Horse Feathers* (1932), *70,000 Witnesses* (1932), and *Saturday's Millions* (1933) to *The Big Game* (1936), *Two Minutes to Play* (1937), *The Quarterback* (1940), *While Thousands Cheer* (1940), and *Pardon My Stripes* (1942).

40. "Football: Mid-season"; Tunis, "More Pay." See also Tunis, "Never Give a Sucker"; Martin, "Pig-Skin Game"; and Frank, "Easy Picking?"

41. Gamblers' attempt to bribe the New York Giants' Merle Hapes and Frank Filchock was front-page news in the *New York Times.* See Alexander Feinberg, "'Fixer' Jailed Here for Bribe Offer to Football Stars," 16 December 1946.

42. See "Student Accused of Attempt at Maryland Football Bribe," *NYT,* 30 October 1952; "2 Seized in Attempt to 'Fix' Florida Game by Bribing Star," *NYT,* 25 September 1960; and "Brooklyn Teacher Named in Alleged Attempt to Bribe an Oregon Halfback," *NYT,* 1 October 1960. The hoax involved two players at Fordham, who reported an attempted bribe before their game against NYU, in order to fire up their teammates. See Maraniss, *When Pride Still,* 45–46; and "Fordham Uncovers Hoax in 'Bribe' to Throw Game," *NYT,* 30 November 1935.

43. Woodward, "Next on the Sports Fix List."

44. Wallace, "Francis Wallace's 13th"; "Francis Wallace's 17th."

45. Guthrie, "No More Football for Us!"; Cherry, "Why I Quit Coaching"; Group, "I'm Through with High-School Football"; Cravath, "Hypocrisy of College Football"; and LaBrucherie, "Big-Time Football Is Not for Him!"

46. See Stump, "Football's Biggest Bargain"; Mullins, "I Like Small-Time Coaching"; "Dreams of Glory Come True"; Cohane, "Yale vs. Harvard: College Football's Last Stand"; Clasby, "I'll Take Harvard Football"; LaBrucherie, "Big-Time Football Is Not for Him!"; "Good Time in the Small Time"; and "Eastern College Football's Big Giant and Little Giant."

47. "Football Is a Farce"; see also Smith and Oulahan, "Football Is Pricing Itself Out of Business."

48. See Cohane, "How Maryland Became a Football Power," "College Football's Greatest Folly," "Inside the West Coast Football Scandal," and "Panther on the Prowl." For like-minded articles that Cohane published as editor, see Woodward, "Next on the Sports Fix List"; Polzer with Herndon, "Football Made a Gentleman Out of Me"; Star, "The Big New Battle in the Big Ten"; Star and Mollenhoff, "Football Scandal Hits the Big Ten" and "Exclusive"; Kaplan, "Case for Big-Time Football"; Arnett with Durslag, "Why Should We Be Scapegoats?"; and Kaplan with Cohane, "To Football Coaches."

49. See Woodward, "Is College Football on the Level?"; Parker, "College Football Cleanup?" and "My Case against the Bowl Games"; Clowser, "Janowicz on the Auction Block"; Danforth, "South vs. the Sanity Code"; Burton, "Truth about Charlie

Justice"; Stump, "Football College That Turned Pro," "Ronnie Knox," and "What Knox and Knox Are After"; Powers, "Case against the Bowl Games"; Watson, "Mighty McElhenny"; Olderman, "Railroaded Out of West Point"; Devine, "Michigan State Construction Job"; "Confessions of a Dirty Football Player"; and Bisher, "College Football's Public Enemy No. 1."

50. See Frank, "Big Ten's Surprise Package"; Shallett, "Maryland's Busiest Byrd"; Fay, "King of the Football Forest"; "Two Big M's"; Cohane, "How Maryland Became a Football Power"; Gleason, "Merry Maestro of Michigan State"; and Malette, "Jim Tatum of the Tarheels."

51. Kieran, "Rockne Made Football What It Is Today."

52. See Byers, *Unsportsmanlike Conduct*, for an account by the man who headed the NCAA in these years.

53. In his "Wake" columns during or after the 1947 (8 and 9 January), 1950 (30 January), and 1951 (29 January) NCAA conventions, Ward made brief comments supporting the reforms sought by the Big Nine/Big Ten conference. Ward criticized the "hypocrisy" of the NCAA in censuring Notre Dame, Michigan State, and Arizona State (19 August 1953), picking on schools that investigated and reported their own abuses. And in 1953–55 he several times denounced "the little men" of the NCAA's television committee for blocking the Big Ten's proposal for regional control of television rights (see, for example, 14 December 1953, 11 January 1954, 10 September 1954, and 27 January 1955).

54. Arch Ward, "In the Wake of the News," *CT,* 20 September 1951 and 14 January 1952.

55. See *OWH,* 11 January 1948, 6 January 1949, 11 December 1951, 9 January 1952, 13 January 1952, 11 January 1953, 16 January 1953, and 10 January 1954; *AC,* 7 January 1947, 8 January 1947, 14 December 1947, 12 January 1948, 10 January 1949, 12 December 1949, 11 January 1950, 17 January 1950, 19 January 1950, 7 January 1952, 8 January 1952, 14 December 1952, 9 January 1953, 12 January 1953, 10 January 1954, and 10 January 1955; *DMN,* 22 January 1947, 16 January 1950, 9 January 1951, 12 January 1951, 10 January 1952, 12 January 1952, 13 January 1952, 13 January 1953, and 20 May 1955.

56. Bill Rives, "The Sport Scene," *DMN,* 17 January 1953.

57. See Thelin, *Games Colleges Play,* 128–54.

58. Dick Hyland, "The Hyland Fling," *LAT,* 20 June 1949; Paul Zimmerman, "Sport Scripts," 14 January 1950; Braven Dyer, "Sports Parade," 17 January 1950; Hyland, "Hyland Fling," 16 January 1950.

59. Dyer, "The Sport Scene," *LAT,* 11 January 1951; Zimmerman, "Sportscripts," 19 November 1951, 12 December 1951, 9 January 1952, 12 December 1952, and 6 December 1954; Hyland, "Hyland Fling," 12 December 1951 and 17 January 1954; Zimmerman, "Sportscripts," 6 December 1954.

60. Thelin, *Games Colleges Play,* 128–54; Cohane, "Inside the West Coast Football Scandal."

61. See Ned Cronin, "Cronin's Corner," *LAT,* 20 May, 22 May, 24 May, 10 July, 5 October, 7 October, 8 October, and 19 November 1956; Hyland, "Hyland Fling,"

23 May and 10 July 1956; Zimmerman, "Sportscripts," 22 May, 24 May, and 11 July 1956; and Dyer, "Sports Parade," 23 May and 11 July 1956.

62. "Red Sanders Dies of Heart Attack" (AP), *PO*, 15 August 1958. The *Times* covered the story with its own staff, on the front page on 15 August, and Paul Zimmerman, Dick Hyland, Ned Cronin, and Al Wolf paid tribute to Sanders in their columns over succeeding days (Braven Dyer was on vacation).

63. Watterson, *College Football*, 287.

64. Frank, "He Doesn't Have to Win"; and Cohane, "Uncle Lou Little."

65. Guthrie, "No More Football for Us!"

66. Watterson, *College Football*, 285–86.

67. *Gallup Poll*, 2: 1017–18. This survey was reported on 29 October 1951.

CHAPTER FOUR

1. Among the five cities besides Chicago whose radio listings I surveyed, only in New York were Illinois games included in the radio listings—the contests with Michigan, Penn, and Chicago in 1925—but certainly Grange's games over WGN were picked up throughout the Midwest.

2. Edgar Munzel, "Sports Showup," *Chicago Herald and Examiner*, 1 November 1937.

3. *Hearst International News*, 24 November 1925; 6 December 1925; 9 December 1925; and *Pathé News*, 7 October 1925; 4 November 1925; 24 November 1925; 1 January 1926; 27 July 1926; and 18 September 1926.

4. See the movie ad in the *Chicago Daily News*, 2 November 1925, and compare to the photograph of Grange in the *Daily News* Rotogravure Section, 7 November 1925.

5. Sherman, *One Minute to Play;* and Snell, *Galloping Ghost*. On his favorable reviews for *One Minute to Play*, see Carroll, *Red Grange*, 131.

6. Ryan's comments came in a 1937 interview reported in Carroll, *Red Grange*, 70.

7. See "Lo! The Poor Tackle," "College Game Is Easier," "Easy Way to Score?," "Outguessing Them," "Future Football," and "Little Things Make Big Touchdowns" (all of these were written "with" George Dunscomb); and Dunscomb, "77." My thanks to Dennis Lien at the University of Minnesota's Wilson Library for tracking down Dunscomb's serial.

8. Rockne's most recent biographer, Ray Robinson (*Rockne of Notre Dame*), draws on material uncovered by Murray Sperber, but the best study of Rockne remains Sperber's *Shake Down the Thunder*.

9. See Sperber, *Shake Down the Thunder*, 34, 44–45, 139, 144–47, 164–65, 194–95.

10. Sperber (ibid., 181) claims that Strickler also gave Rice his "Four Horsemen" lead, accepting Strickler's own account in Holtzman's *No Cheering in the Press Box*, 146–48. Rice's most recent biographer argues that Rice came up with the lead himself, having recently used the image in other contexts. See Harper, *How You Played the Game*, 366–70. The details about Francis Wallace and Rockne's other press assistants are from *Shake Down the Thunder*.

11. Rockne, *Autobiography;* Brown, *Rockne;* Harron, *Rockne;* Hurt, *Goals;* Lovelace, *Rockne of Notre Dame;* Stuhldreher, *Knute Rockne*. In addition, a volume of Rockne's

writings was published as *Knute Rockne on Football*, and the following year appeared Huston's *Salesman from the Sidelines*, on Rockne's career at Studebaker.

12. On the film's role in deifying Rockne, see Sperber, *Onward to Victory*.

13. I explore this development more fully in *Reading Football*, and see Mrozek, *Sport and American Mentality*, 73–80.

14. Camp, "Walter Camp's Sports Page"; Savage, *American College Athletics*, 275; Prince, "Hand Back the Game to the Boys"; Reed, "Football for Sportsmen"; "To Make Football a Sport"; Tunis, "Whose Game Is It?" and "Player Control in Football."

15. Small, "Coaches' Graveyard." The controversial negotiations at Texas were covered by the *Omaha World-Herald* from 16 January to 22 January 1937, then in a final comment by sports editor Frederick Ware on 30 January. The *Saturday Evening Post* then gave the incident a positive spin in Foree, "Archangel and His Bible."

16. On the development of the rules, see Nelson, *Anatomy of a Game*. On the debate over two platoons, see, for example, "Platoon System" and "Notre Dame's Frank Leahy."

17. Sperber, *Shake Down the Thunder*, 115, 174, 260; Gallico, *Farewell to Sport*, 275–76; *Problems of Journalism* 5 (1927): 97, 101–2; Corum, *Off and Running*, 122; Rader, *American Sports*, 112–13, 184.

18. Tunis, "College Praise Men"; Williams, "All-Americas"; "Golden Goal Posts." Also see Stump, "Ballyhoo Boys." Before press agents became common, newspapers typically contracted with students on each campus to provide information, another practice criticized by the Carnegie report. See Savage, *American College Athletics*, 283.

19. Rice, *Tumult and the Shouting*, 192; Russell, *Bury Me in the Old Press Box*, 37; Wallace, "I Was a Football Fixer"; Cohane, *Bypaths of Glory;* Blaik and Cohane, "Red Blaik Speaks."

20. Kennedy, "Halfback of Notre Dame"; Heisman, "Signals," "Thundering Herd," "Fast and Loose," "Hold 'Em!," "Look Sharp Now!," "Rules Rush In," "Between Halves," "Their Weight in Gold," "Hero Stuff," "Rough Humor," and "Here Are Men"; and Warner, "Indian Massacres," "Heap Big Run-Most Fast," "Red Menaces," "Battles of Brawn," "What's the Matter with Football," and "Here Come the Giants!"

21. Stagg, "Touchdown!"

22. See Thompson with Stout, "Referee's Whistle," "Praying Colonels," "That's My Story," and "Villain of the Piece"; Cunningham, "Man Who's Always Wrong"; Reynolds, "Official Business"; Friesell, "I'm Always on the Spot"; Friesell with Reed, "How to Watch a Football Game"; Perry, "I Know We're Dumb"; Goebel, "I Cheer the Referee"; Crowley, "Man with a Horn"; and Henry, "We Call the Penalties."

23. Crichton, "Steaks and Punts" and "I'll Take Both." For the rest of Crichton's celebrity profiles in *Collier's*, see the bibliography.

24. See Forsythe, "Block That Kick!," "Wails of St. Mary's," and "Tragedy in the Yale Bowl"; and Crichton, "For Glory and Keeps," "For Love and Money," and "Quick, Harlow, the Needle!" For Crichton's use of "Robert Forsythe" as a pseudonym, see *Contemporary Authors*, 114.

25. Spencer, "He Clowns to Touchdowns."

26. Lowenthal, "Triumph of Mass Idols," 111–16; Susman, *Culture as History*. See also Cawelti, *Apostles of the Self-Made Man*.

27. Spencer, "He Clowns to Touchdowns"; Danforth, "Flatfoot Frankie the Fireball."

28. See *Popular Magazine*, 1 November 1909; *Century*, November 1909; *Collier's*, 28 November 1914 and 18 November 1916; and *SEP*, 14 November 1908; 30 November 1912, 15 November 1913, 21 November 1914, 24 November 1928, and 4 November 1933. For brother Frank's original *Post* cover, see 28 October 1899.

29. For Kuppenheimer ads featuring ruggedly handsome football players, see the inside cover of *SEP* or *Literary Digest*, 19 November 1921; and *SEP*, 29 October 1927, 108–9.

30. Schau, *J. C. Leyendecker*, 20.

31. *Collier's*, 14 October 1916.

32. Cooper, *Sexual Perspective*, 131–33; Gifford, *Dayneford's Library*, 17–18, 117–22.

33. *Collier's*, 12 October 1929, 18 October 1930, and 5 December 1931; and *SEP*, 19 November 1932 and 4 November 1933.

34. On Walker as cover boy, see Stump, "Ballyhoo Boys." Walker's covers included *Look* (14 September 1948), *Life* (27 September 1948), and *Collier's* (10 December 1949).

35. Fitch, "Ole Skjarsen's First Touchdown."

36. Hellman, "Rough and Rah-Rah" (*SEP*, 1925) and "Offside" (*SEP*, 1928); Winslow, "Swelling the Purple Flood" (*SEP*, 1930); Brennan, "Girl Who Saved the Game" (*Collier's*, 1937); Fenton, "Flying Dutchman" (*Collier's*, 1940); and Frank, "Second Wind" (*Collier's*, 1941).

37. Thurber, "University Days."

38. On the connections between child psychologists, physical education reformers, and sport in this period, see Cavallo, *Muscles and Morals*.

39. Sears, "Sixty Days of Football," discussed in my *Reading Football*, 198–201.

40. Johnson, *Stover at Yale*, 139.

41. O'Connor, *Jack London*, 76, 152.

42. Hopper, "Strength of the Weak." See also "The Freshman," "The Redemption of Fullback Jones," and "The Long Try."

43. Griswold, *Fatherhood in America*, 90–91, 98.

44. Young, "Touchdown Technic."

45. For coaches named Biff, see Hall, "Sixty-Minute Man"; Horton, "Pigskin U" and "Run, Kick and Pass"; Rober, "Fumble"; and Scholz, "Gridiron Dancer." For coaches named Pop, see Carleton, "Bouncing Back" and "End Run"; Cohane, "Gridiron Assassin"; Frank, "But Not So Dumb"; Garth, "Kid Brother" and "Third Alarm Strategy"; Litten, "Rebel Yell"; MacLauchlan, "Assigned to Stardom"; and Vickers, "Fighting Scotts." In both "But Not So Dumb" and "Gridiron Assassin" Pop is emphatically not a "Pop," the authors working against the stereotype. For coaches called "the Old Man," see Carver, "Fire with Fire"; Ford, "Cleat Warriors" (not a Pop) and "Lorenzo the Great" (an anti-Pop); Pierce, "Old Navy Fight"; and Whitman, "Son of Thunder McLeod." In more than two dozen additional stories, coaches fit the stereotypes of Biff or Pop.

46. Jones, "Tough Guy" (*SEP*, 1931); Stuhldreher and Martin, "Gravy Game" (*SEP*, 1933); Wallace, "Razzle-Dazzle" (*SEP*, 1937).

47. Josselyn, "No Alibi" (*Collier's*, 1932); Sylvester, "Orders Disobeyed" (*Collier's*, 1938); Brennan, "Beyond the Goal Line" (*Collier's*, 1931); and Brooks, "Last Season" (*Collier's*, 1933).

48. Brooks, "Bills Playable" (*Collier's*, 1920); "Toes Up" (*Collier's*, 1921); and "Square Heads" (*Collier's*, 1922).

49. See Stagg, "Touchdown!" (6 November); Heisman, "Between Halves"; and Rockne, "Coaching Men." See also Thornhill, with Taylor, "Head First"; and Crowley, "Go in There and Fight!"

50. "Coach's Tongue-Lashing" and "Lashing a Team to Do or Die." See also Kipke and Fitzgerald, "Dying for Dear Old Rutgers"; Thornhill with Taylor, "Head First"; and Crowley, "Go in There and Fight!" On the impact of *Knute Rockne—All-American* on the mythology of Rockne, see Sperber, *Shake Down the Thunder*, 464–83.

51. See Howell and Howell, "Myth of 'Pop Warner'"; Oxendine, *American Indian Sports Heritage*, 188–90; and Adams, *Education for Extinction*, 324.

52. Examples of the former include Hopper, "Father and Son" (*SEP*, 1924); Jones and McCabe, "Redheads Never Quit" (*Collier's*, 1933); Macaulay, "Magic Toe" (*SEP*, 1934); and Ford and MacBain, "Second Try" (*Collier's*, 1937). Examples of the latter include Brooks, "Bills Playable" (*Collier's*, 1920) and "Brothers Under the Pigskin" (*Collier's*, 1924); Perry, "David Harris' Quarterback," (*Collier's*, 1921); Hellman, "Soft and Sappy" (*SEP*, 1927); Cary, "Saturday's Millions" (*SEP*, 1933); and Fitzgerald, "Scrub" (*SEP*, 1936). These plots about fathers and sons were also a major concern in 37 of the 279 stories and serials in the pulp magazine *Sport Story*.

53. Hellman, "Soft and Sappy"; Reynolds, "He Could Take It" (*Collier's*, 1932).

54. For stories about dumb jocks, see Morrow, "Psychological Halfback" (*SEP*, 1950); Temple, "Touchdown Play" (*SEP*, 1951); Meyer, "He Learned Her About Love" (*SEP*, 1953); and Kalshoven, "Halfback and the High-Brow," (*SEP*, 1955). The stories of fathers and sons were Scott, "Son of the Coach" (*Collier's*, 1950); and Herndon, "Dirtiest Game of the Year" (*SEP*, 1952). The story about winning the girl through toughness was Watson, "Quarterback Who Couldn't Take It" (*SEP*, 1954).

55. For stories of the ex-GI, see O'Rourke, "Hard Way Home" (*Collier's*, 1946); Temple, "Baby in the Backfield" (*Collier's*, 1947); Sylvester, "Double or Nothing" (*Collier's*, 1948); and Scott, "Kidnapped Quarterback" (*SEP*, 1949); as well as the film comedy *Yes, Sir, That's My Baby* (1949). For the ordinary guy who becomes a hero, see Temple, "Halfback Hoodoo" (*Collier's*, 1952), "Eleven Guys Named George" (*Collier's*, 1953), and "Bench Warmer Named Smith" (*SEP*, 1954); and Scott, "Operation Bench" (*Collier's*, 1952). And for the coach, see O'Rourke, "Nothing to Do Till Next Fall" (*SEP*, 1947); Heinz, "Man's Game" (*Collier's*, 1949); Scott, "Son of the Coach" (*Collier's*, 1950); Atkinson, "I'm a Snake" (*Collier's*, 1952); and the film *Father Was a Fullback* (1949).

56. See, for example, Small, "Coaches' Graveyard"; and Kuechle, "Can Any Football Coach Win at Wisconsin?"

57. Small, "Football's Demon Deacon"; "You Coming Up Here with Me, Son?"; Grimsley, "Football's Craftiest Recruiter"; Hickman, "Confessions of a Football Re-

cruiter"; Fay, "Dixie's No. 1 Gridnaper"; and Siler, "Football's Jittery Genius." Sper-ber places Bryant, along with Jim Tatum, at the top of the list of the era's buccaneer coaches, and Maryland's Curly Byrd as the chief of the postwar booster presidents who sacrificed educational values to big-time football. See *Onward to Victory*, Chapters 24 and 34.

58. Holland, "Coach."

59. Reeve, "Pigskin Heart" (*Collier's*, 1947).

60. Russell and Tiller, "Georgia Plays for Keeps"; Fay, "Dixie's No. 1 Gridnaper"; Siler, "Football's Jittery Genius"; Clowser, "Phooey on Popularity!" (on Hayes); Malette, "Jim Tatum of the Tarheels." On Bryant, see also "Rugged Shakedown for a Tough Team."

61. Knoll, *Prairie University*, 115.

62. Paxton and Sylvester, "Hungry Young Coach of Nebraska."

63. See Russell, "Gay Deceiver of Georgia Tech" (on Dodd); Garrison, "Fun-Loving Frank from Dixie," (on Howard); Fay, "King of the Football Forest" (on Munn); and Gleason, "Merry Maestro of Michigan State" (on Daugherty). The first of the fun-loving coaches to be celebrated in the *Post* or *Collier's* was Stanford's Tiny Thornhill, in 1936. See Thornhill, with Taylor, "Football Follies."

64. Wallace, "Gridiron Gallahad" (on Wilkinson); Paxton, "That Gentlemanly Coach at Wisconsin" (on Williamson); Russell, "New Wonder Boy of Notre Dame" (on Brennan). The ultimate executive coach of the era was the professional Cleveland Browns' Paul Brown; see Brown, as told to Paxton, "I Call the Plays for the Browns." The *Post* named "the brisk new young-executive breed" in contrast to Jess Neely, a throwback to an earlier type. See Paxton, "Football's Most Underrated Coach."

65. See Russell, "They're All Rooting for Red" (on Sanders); Paxton, "Look Who Coaches Navy"; Going, "He Always Says 'We'll Win,'" (on Taylor).

66. Paxton, "That Gentlemanly Coach at Wisconsin."

67. Gregg McBride, "35 Players Say Glassford Inspired Fear," *OWH*, 15 January 1954.

68. McBride, "Better Than 'Mr. Roberts,'" *OWH*, 16 January 1954.

69. "Smith Says Players Hurt 'Physically and Financially,'" *OWH*, 17 January 1954.

70. Byers, *Unsportsmanlike Conduct*, 97–98. For a detailed account of the battle over substitution rules from 1953 to 1965, see Nelson, *Anatomy of a Game*, 253–322.

71. Russell, "Pigskin Preview" (1953); Wallace, "Francis Wallace's 14th Football Preview"; Fay, "Play's the Thing." See also the pro-and-con forums: "Platoon System" and "Notre Dame's Frank Leahy vs. Oklahoma's Bud Wilkinson."

72. Norris Anderson, "The Firing Line," *Lincoln Star*, 18 January 1954.

CHAPTER FIVE

1. "Football Takes Over All Over," *Life*, 7 November 1955.

2. I explore this aspect of early football more fully in *Reading Football*.

3. "Football as Our Greatest Popular Spectacle."

4. "Football: Mid-Season." *Time* put "Football's Public" on its cover again for the 11 November 1935 issue.

5. Marvin, "Big Business of Football."

6. In two of the encyclopedic overviews of American civilization in the 1920, Ring Lardner and Stuart Chase both lamented the passivity of the masses drawn to spectator sports. See Lardner, "Sport and Play"; and Chase, "Play."

7. Gallico, *Farewell to Sport,* 267–68; Rice, *Tumult and the Shouting,* 219; Riess, "New Huddle Muddle." "How to Watch Football" by Oklahoma coach Bud Wilkinson was the latest in a long tradition.

8. Paul Gallico, "Let Us Overemphasize," *NYDN,* 12 November 1928; and "Rain, Cold and Color," 30 November 1930.

9. Horowitz, *Campus Life,* 131–32; Fass, *Damned and the Beautiful,* 236–37.

10. Rice, "Pigskin Ballyhoo"; Cannon, "I'd Die for Dear Old Dollars!"

11. Maureen M'Kernan, "New Illinois Stadium Riot of Color and Noise as Grange Runs Over Wolverines," *CT,* 19 October 1924; Beverly Burgess, "Big Game Focus of Gay Social Whirl for Younger Set," *AC,* 15 November 1925; Rhea Seeger, "Grid Fashions Have Warmth and Swagger," *CT,* 5 October 1935.

12. Susman, *Culture as History,* 154, 159.

13. Fiedler's classic essay appeared in *No! In Thunder.*

14. The covers of *Good Housekeeping* were for October 1932 and September 1936; *Country Gentleman*'s was for November 1933, *Liberty*'s for 13 October 1945. For cute kids on *Collier's,* see 5 November 1921, 25 October 1924, 12 November 1927, and 2 November 1929. For the *Saturday Evening Post,* see 24 November 1923 (a boy hawking pennants), 21 November 1925, 23 October 1926, 12 November 1927, 17 November 1934, 27 November 1937, 26 October 1940, 14 November 1942, 13 November 1943, 17 November 1951, 15 November 1952, and 5 October 1957.

15. See "Shoeless Wonders Grid Aces," *Universal News,* 2 December 1937; "Midget Football Champions," *Metrotone News,* 16 November 1938; "Tiny Tots in Grid Thriller," *Universal News,* 11 October 1939.

16. Considine, "Death on the Gridiron."

17. See Dooley, "Making Football Safe" and "How Dangerous Is Football?"; Hyland, "It's a Tough Game"; Lea, "Is He Hurt?"; Considine, "No Holiday for Death"; Locke, "My Son versus Football"; Henry, "Do You Fear Football?"; Stuhldreher, "Should Your Boy Play Football?"; Grieve, "Should Your Boy Play Football?"; Morris, "High School Football Can Be Made Safe"; and Weinstein, "Can Junior Football Hurt Your Boy?" *Look* and *Collier's* contributed to this genre as well. See Cunningham, "Doctor Watches Football"; Little, "What Football Does to You"; Schneider, "Should Your Boy Play Football?"; and Stevens, "Will High School Football Hurt Your Boy?"

18. See *Thrilling Love,* November 1932, December 1933, December 1934, and December 1935; *Love Story,* 22 October 1938, 9 November 1940, 15 November 1941, and 7 November 1942; *Exciting Love,* Fall 1941, Winter 1943, Fall 1954, and Fall 1957; and *Popular Love,* January 1941 and November 1941. In addition, *Popular Love* had three covers with lovely fans alone (October 1947, December 1948, and Fall 1951). The accompanying handful of football stories in the love pulps were conventional romances that placed the heroine at the center and subordinated football to the course of true love. See Ahern, "Gridiron Hearts" and "Those Double Dates"; Anderson, "Cupid's Forward Pass"; Elvay, "Hero of Her Heart"; Manners, "Cupid Wins the

Game"; and Thomson, "The Captain Was a Redhead," "A Kiss for the Coach," and "You Can't Coach a Redhead."

19. On Lorimer's censoring of artwork "to keep the Post a family magazine," see Tebbel, *George Horace Lorimer,* 114.

20. See my *Reading Football,* 247–57.

21. "College Co-eds Cheer Gridiron Teams When Season Opens in Portland," *PO,* 16 October 1927.

22. Andrew Doyle uncovered this aspect of southern football in his dissertation, "Causes Won, Not Lost."

23. Bob Bowen, "Future All-Americans Run in Fritz Orr's Grid Carnival," *AC,* 8 December 1940; Al Sharp, "Blue Birds Defeat Red Devils in Fritz Orr Gridiron Battle," *AC,* 14 December 1941; Bob Christian, "Future Stars Sparkle in Fritz Orr Grid Games," *AC,* 4 December 1949.

24. Bessie, *Jazz Journalism,* 192.

25. See *Chicago Sun-Times,* 1 February 1957.

26. Gallico, *Farewell to Sport,* 245–46.

27. Fullerton, "Yells That Win Games"; Watterson, *College Football,* 201; Hanson, *Go! Fight! Win!*

28. "Pretty Girl Tulane's Voice," *Chicago Herald and Examiner,* 24 October 1925; "Coach Trains Girl Football Cheer Leaders," *Chicago Herald and Examiner,* 27 October 1925. See also the back page of the *Chicago Tribune* for 24 October 1925.

29. "We Want a Touchdown!"; Watterson, *College Football,* 201; Kane, "From Rah"; "Debut of 'Da Beauts,'" *AC,* 13 October 1940; "Feminine Touch," *DMN,* 18 November 1945. By 1934, the plot of a girls' novel could center on winning selection as head cheerleader, as "the highest honor for girls in high school." See Singer, *Cheer Leader,* 13.

30. The January 1930 cover of *Snappy* (painted by E. K. Bergey), December 1931 cover of *Film Fun,* and November 1933 cover of *Streets of Paris* gave cheerleaders tight sweaters and bare legs not seen at real games.

31. Bill Henry, "Mustang Air Forces Bombard Bruins," *LAT,* 12 November 1935, and "Bill Henry Says—," 23 December 1935; "Southern Methodist Band to Share Honors with Game," *LAT,* 20 November 1937.

32. *News of the Day,* 5 January 1934.

33. "Prancing Majorettes Win Heavy Share of Applause," *LAT,* 2 January 1940; "High Spots and Sidelights on Pasadena's Pageant of Flowers and Music," 2 January 1941.

34. "Snappy Reply from Beauty Cools Ardor," *LAT,* 2 January 1951; and see *LAT* for 2 January each year from 1946 through 1948 and 3 January 1949.

35. "Festival Spirit Shines Forth from Majorettes," *LAT,* 2 January 1957. Similar sentiments were repeated in 1959. See "Majorettes Still Here, but Under New Name," *LAT,* 2 January 1959.

36. See "Majorettes Sparkle Like Living Tinsel," *LAT,* 2 January 1953; and "Prancing Majorettes Give Special Thrill," 3 January 1955.

37. "It's Not All Work as Stars Prepare for Bowl Games," *CT,* 27 December 1936.

38. *AC,* 22 December 1947.

39. "Football Was Never Like This," *OWH,* 12 December 1949; "Orange Bowl Candidate Hopeful," *OWH,* 25 December 1949; "Big Bear and a Little Miami Cutie," *OWH,* 30 December 1951; "Orange Bowl Queen Greets Cornhuskers in Miami," *OWH,* 27 December 1954; "Oklahoma Co-ed Does Bit to Entertain Football Players," *OWH,* 1 January 1956; "Clemson Coach Howard . . . focuses attention on brunettes instead of football," *OWH,* 31 December 1956; "Happy to See the Princess," *OWH,* 30 December 1958.

40. "Uranium or Football," *LAT,* 9 November 1954; "Best Seat in the House," *LAT,* 8 December 1958; "How's This Form?" *LAT,* 7 December 1959.

41. See "Rangerettes"; Frankie Waits, "Deep in the Hearts of Texas," *American Weekly,* 22 November 1953 (my example appeared in the *Oregonian*); "Famed Rangerettes Prepare for Cotton Bowl Entertainment," *OWH,* 31 December 1951; and the front page of *DMN,* 1 January 1955; and 2 January 1956. The Rangerettes later appeared on the 5 October 1963 cover of the *Saturday Evening Post,* which folded out into two pages.

42. Shrake, "Trouping the Colors."

43. *Esquire,* November 1947, and "Esquire Girl," *Esquire,* September 1949; "Look's All-Service Girl," *Look,* 1 December 1942; *Play,* October 1944; and *Cartoon Humor,* Fall 1948.

44. Banner, *American Beauty,* 283. For magazine covers, see *Look,* 9 September 1952 (Monroe); *Coronet,* November 1952; and *American Weekly,* 16 November 1952. For full-page, full-color ads, see *SEP,* 28 October 1950, 41 (Lucky Strikes); and *Life,* 24 October 1955, 132 (Texaco). Barbasol shaving cream ran several small ads with a curvy cheerleader on tip-toes, stroking the football hero's smoothly shaved chin. See, for example, *SEP,* 8 October 1949, 132. The December 1951 cover of *Titter,* a pinup magazine far removed from mainstream respectability, also featured a cheerleader pinup.

45. "Football's Girls"; "Beauty and the Bowl"; "Happy Moods of Football"; Parker, "Saturday's Moods"; and Brown, "Babes, Brutes and Ole Miss."

46. Gonzales, "First College Cheer."

47. See "What, a Drum Majorette Hide Her Knees? And They're Such Dimpled Darlings, Too!" *Philadelphia Record,* 4 November 1939; and the Wide World photo in *LAT,* 17 November 1939, of "Dimpled Darling" Elsie with players squatted around her in their football stances.

48. "'Golden Girl' Cuts Down on Hula Wiggles," *CT,* 2 November 1958; "Women in Motion."

49. McLemore, "Sex Appeal in Sports."

50. Kozol, *Life's America,* 17.

51. "Bill Stern . . . Picks." The 1940 team was presented as student-athletes.

52. *Look,* 28 October 1947, 14 September 1948, 13 September 1949, 12 September 1950, 20 October 1953, and 2 November 1954; and *Collier's,* 13 December 1941, 10 December 1949; and 15 December 1951.

53. "Evansville Express" and "Jimmy Conzelman."

54. The view of the coach's wife was introduced in the anonymously written "I Can Take It" in 1934, then became a minor genre in the late 1940s and 1950s,

as the pressure on coaches became a major theme in magazine journalism. See Stuhldreher, "Football Fans Aren't Human"; Brennan, "Wife's View of Notre Dame Football"; and "Wife's Saga of Coach's Ordeal" (about Mrs. Murray Warmath). Variations include the story of a referee's wife (Goebel, "I Cheer the Referee"); of a coach's daughter (Jones, "Father Is a Football Coach"); of an entire family, except for the mother, involved in football ("Tennessee Touchdowns on the Family Plan"); and by a mother with five sons in big-time college football ("I'm a Football Mother"). "The Sight a Mother Could Not Watch" described the agony of a woman (Mrs. Bobby Dodd) when her husband's team (Georgia Tech) plays her son's (Florida). On kids' football, see "Life Goes to a Kids' Football Game" (1938, 1939); Tolbert, "Mighty Mites"; Graham, "Bantam Football"; and "Kids' Football."

55. The pageantry of college (and high school) football was part of virtually every photo-essay in *Life* and *Look* on big games, but also was its own subject in numerous features. See Clark, "Everybody Up!"; "Cheering Co-eds"; "Speaking of Pictures" (1937, 1938, 1954); "Football Fun"; McLemore, "Sex Appeal in Sports"; Crichton, "Mustang Magic"; "U.C.L.A. Makes Animated Cartoons"; and "Queen's Choice."

56. Reynolds, "Football Town." *Life* also featured Green Bay in "Little Wisconsin Town."

57. Breslin, "Town That Spawns Athletes"; "Cradle of Pro Football"; Martin, "Football City"; Biemiller, "Football Town"; "Look Goes to a High-School"; "Amarillo's Golden Sandies"; Martin and Carroll, "Whole Town Made the Team"; "Football Crazy Town"; "Championship High-School Football." See also "Menominee vs. Marinette"; "High-School Football"; "Texas Blows Its Top"; "High-School Football at Night"; and "High School Fevers."

58. See Clowser, "42 Colleges Wanted Him"; "Al Pollard"; "High-School Hero."

59. Frank, "Woes of an All-American"; Cohane, "College Football Tragedy"; Group, "I'm Through with High-School Football."

60. "Life Goes to a Football Game"; "Rambling Wreck Barbecues Duke"; "It Spells Big Campus Weekend"; "Texas Blows Its Top over Football"; and Betz, "How to Behave." Photo-essays in *Life* and *Look* on big college games also routinely captured the spirit of the football weekend, while bowl games were like more extravagant football weekends; see "U.S. Goes Bowl Crazy."

61. See May, *Homeward Bound*.

62. "Tennessee Touchdowns on the Family Plan." See also "The Sight a Mother Could Not Watch."

CHAPTER SIX

1. L. H. Robbins, "As Millions Cheer—or Groan," *NYT Magazine*, 8 October 1939.

2. Robert F. Kelley, "Pro Football: It's Different," *NYT Magazine*, 15 October 1939.

3. Arthur J. Daley, "Sports of the Times," *NYT*, 12 December 1938.

4. Pathé was the first, followed by the other major newsreels by the mid-1950s.

5. Arthur J. Daley, "Bears Overwhelm Redskins by Record Score to Capture World Football Title," *NYT*, 9 December 1940.

6. When the Bulldogs folded after the 1926 season, pro football disappeared from the *Evening Repository* as suddenly and completely as the team did.

7. See "Coaches Hostile to Pro Football," *NYT,* 28 December 1921; "College Team Men in $100,000 Game," *NYT,* 29 January 1922; "Accused Football Men Have Alibis," *NYT,* 30 January 1922; "Eight Notre Dame Players Confess," *NYT,* 31 January 1922; "Illinois Declares Players Ineligible," *NYT,* 1 February 1922; "Mohardt Played in Pro Football Game," *NYT,* 4 February 1922; and "Pro Elevens Hurt Sport, Says Stagg," *NYT,* 2 November 1923.

8. In Chicago, for example, the AFL's Bulls outdrew the Bears and Cardinals only when Grange and the Yankees were in town, the Yankees-Bulls game on 17 October drawing 16,000 while the Bears-Cards attracted 12,000 (See *CT,* 18 October). The Bulls' next largest crowd was 7,000, and attendance fell as low as 1,500.

9. "Professional Football," *NYT,* 8 December 1925, 24.

10. "In the Wake of the News," *CT,* 4 October 1925.

11. The Bears topped Northwestern the first time in 1937, when they drew 44,000 for the Packers a day after Northwestern drew 42,000 for Illinois. The Bears did not regularly attract such crowds, however, until the postwar years. In 1946, the four weekends that Northwestern and the Bears both played at home, the Bears outdrew the Wildcats twice. Beginning in 1954, as Northwestern suffered through its third straight losing season, the Bears consistently drew bigger crowds.

12. Edward Prell, "The Story of the Big Bad Bears," *CT,* 21–28 October 1941; and *CT,* 26 October–1 November 1948 (each installment with its own title).

13. See "Boom in Professional Football Is Picked as 1934's Most Striking Trend in Sports," *NYT,* 23 December 1934; and "Growth in the Popularity of Pro Football Voted as Year's Outstanding Sports Trend," *NYT,* 22 December 1937.

14. Westbrook Pegler, "Coaches Find Pro Football Is Good Game," *CT,* 17 October 1933.

15. "College Football Attendance for 1933 Rose 13%," *NYT,* 7 December 1933.

16. Allison Danzig, "Giants Defeat Notre Dame All-Stars, 22–0, in Charity Game before 50,000," *NYT,* 15 December 1930.

17. John Kieran, "Sports of the Times," *NYT,* 25 October 1929; "Is It Sport or Business?" *NYHT,* 24 October 1929; Paul Gallico, "Big Explosion! Pffft," *NYDN,* 24 October 1929; Frank Wallace, "32 Athletes Paid by N.Y.U. Carnegie Foundation Finds," *Daily Mirror,* 24 October 1929; Wallace, "Carnegie Bombshell Proves Dud," *Daily Mirror,* 25 October 1929; and Jimmy Powers, "Pure and Scarlet Mingle on Grid," *NYDN,* 26 October 1929.

18. John Kieran, "Yellow Jackets Trample Giants," *New York American,* 19 October 1925.

19. *Saturday Evening Post,* 5 December 1959. I know of but one other pro football cover, from *Judge* for September 1934, in which a player sits huddled on the bench among balding teammates, reading *Life Begins at Forty* in wide-eyed astonishment.

20. Grange, with Dunscomb, "Lo! The Poor Tackle," "Easy Way to Score," "Outguessing Them," "College Game Is Easier," and "Future Football."

21. Dunscomb, "$6000 for a Touchdown!"; Halas and Dunscomb, "Hold What Line?"; Marshall, "Pro Football Is Better Football"; Murray, with Riordan, "The Foot's Back in Football"; and Caldwell, "After the Ball Is Over."

22. Friedman, "Professional Touch"; Crichton, "For Glory and for Keeps" and "For Love and Money"; Kelly, "Football for a Living"; and Friedman, "Pro and Con."

23. Lewis, "Pass Master"; Reynolds, "Block and Tackle."

24. Brooks, "One Bad Turn" (*Collier's*, 1923); Hanlon, "End of Fanfare" (*SEP*, 1935).

25. Fay, "Uptown Boy" (*Collier's*, 1938); Freeman, "Ball Game for Delia" (*SEP*, 1939); Fay, "Strictly for Sweeney" (*Collier's*, 1939); Fay, "Daughter of the Dean" (*Collier's*, 1940); Cox, "It's a Nice Day" (*SEP*, 1940); Fay, "Willy's Place" (*Collier's*, 1941); Frank, "Second Wind" (*Collier's*, 1941).

26. Costello, "Wee Willie—Wow!"

27. The exceptions to this plot: Fay's "Touchdown Crazy" (*SEP*, 1949) celebrated the triumph of an undersized substitute blocking back; in Heuman's "Fall Tryout" (*Collier's*, 1956), the hero finds redemption in football as work; in "The Touchdown Makers" (*SEP*, 1958), by Robert Daley, a naïve, eager rookie is misunderstood and discarded by a ruthless owner. Of the pro football movies from 1948 to 1951 — *King of the Gamblers, Triple Threat, Easy Living,* and *The Guy Who Came Back*—the last two followed the plot of the bum redeemed. In *Easy Living,* a football star with a heart condition must face life outside the game, and the hero of *The Guy Who Came Back* is a football bum out of William Fay's early stories. (*King of the Gamblers* dealt with a murdered player who was fixing games, *Triple Threat* with an arrogant star's discovery of team spirit.)

28. On this resistance, see May, *Homeward Bound,* 10–11; Corber, *Homosexuality in Cold War America,* 5–8.

29. Crichton, "Passing Fancy"; Spencer, "He Clowns to Touchdowns"; Danforth, "Flatfoot Frankie"; Russell, "Big Bad Bulldog"; Cohane, "Levi Jackson of Yale."

30. Frank, "Bronko Bucks Again"; Crichton, "Whambam Man"; Costello, "Wee Willie"; Frank, "You Have to Baby the Pros"; Fay, "Meanest Man in Football" and "Bingo Bingaman"; Durslag, "Pro Football's Brat"; Layne, as told to Olderman, "This Is No Game for Kids."

31. "Life Visits Lions in Training"; "Savagery on Sunday"; "Hefty Pros Get Even Heftier." For Graham's accusations, see Graham, "I'm Through with Football."

32. "Pro Hazing for a Rookie"; "Fighting Irish Look Tough Again" and "Sequel." See Sperber's discussion in *Onward to Victory,* 481–82.

33. "Greetings to Our Victims in Play-off" and "Fans Go Ga-Ga Over Pro Football."

34. "Los Angeles Rams: Pro Football's Most Hectic Team"; "Pride of Lions"; "Man's Game"; "Pro Football"; "Violent Face"; Layne, "This Is No Game for Kids."

35. "Charlie Conerly" and "Old Passer Has His Last Fling."

36. "Quarterback and His Lady"; "Frank Gifford"; Paxton, "Fancy Dans"; "Nine Sticky Fingers."

37. Camerer, "Gladiators"; O'Brien, "Brutal Art"; Kahn and Schwartz, "Highlights of a Golden Decade."

38. Wakefield, "In Defense of the Fullback"; Schlesinger, "Crisis of American Masculinity"; Morgan, "Wham in Pro Football."

39. "Pro Football."

40. Mrozek, "Cult and Ritual of Toughness," 261; Griswold, "'Flabby American,'" 323–48; Kennedy, "Soft American."

41. Nelson, *Anatomy of a Game,* 260; Bill Rives, "The Sport Scene," *DMN,* 30 November 1952.

42. Paxton, "Terror of the Big Ten"; Fay, "Case for Rough Football"; "Terror and His Twin."

CHAPTER SEVEN

1. Burke, *Conundrum of Class,* xi–xii.

2. Marchand, *Advertising the American Dream,* xvii, 166. For a sampling of football "social tableaux" in the *SEP* (in addition to the Leyendecker ads cited in note 27 to Chapter 4), see the ads for Oldsmobile, 12 November 1921, 76; Overland Champion, 24 November 1923, 76–77; Holeproof Ex Toe Hosiery, 13 October 1928, 1; and Hudson, 3 November 1928, 135. Leyendecker's ads for Kuppenheimer, 4 November 1922, 2; Hart, Schaffner & Marx, 10 November 1928, 2; and Kuppenheimer, 9 November 1929, 184 (two of them in the prime location, the inside front cover) portray the ideal of the upscale gentleman fan.

3. See my *Reading Football,* 155; Riesman and Denney, "Football in America," 323; and Smith, *Sports and Freedom,* 184–87.

4. See Hopper "Strength of the Weak," "Boy Who Lost Weight," "Freshman," "Redemption of Fullback Jones," "Peewee Peters," and "Long Try."

5. Hughes, "Exquisite Thug." See also Pier, "Game by Wire"; Ward, "Thumbs Up"; MacArlarney, "Aaron Luckett's Gridiron Gloat"; and Perry, "Spoiled Boy."

6. Ross, *Working-Class Hollywood,* xii–xiii.

7. Camp, "Guarded Heights" (*Collier's,* 1920). See also Camp's "Victor" (*Collier's,* 1922), as well as Perry, "David Harmon's Quarterback" (*Collier's,* 1921), "Barbed Wire" (*Collier's,* 1926), and "Straight-Arm Stuff" (*Collier's,* 1927); and Wolff, "Right About Face" (*Collier's,* 1922).

8. Sombart, *Why Is There No Socialism;* Ross, *Working-Class Hollywood,* 175, 180; "Fortune Survey"; Centers, *Psychology of Social Classes,* 77–78; Vanneman and Cannon, *American Perception of Class.*

9. See my *Sporting with the Gods,* 16–28.

10. See, for example, "First All-American Iceman" and "Football History as Made by the Illinois Iceman." The second article contrasts Grange's innocent "iceman" days to his tumultuous defection to the pros.

11. Paul Gallico, "End of a Fine Friendship," *NYDN,* 19 December 1925.

12. Bill Cunningham, "Red Grange, on Trail of the Dollar, Has Lost His Campus Prestige," *DMN,* 10 January 1926.

13. "Bleachers" (1926). From 1920 through 1932, 81.3 percent of NFL players were collegians. For the period 1933–1946, 98 percent attended college. See Riess, "Social Profile of the Professional Football Player," 231.

14. "Flanagan Is First Gift of Stevedoring to Grid," *NYDN,* 15 November 1926.

15. Paul Gallico, "Motives? Motives?" *NYDN,* 11 November 1927; "Some Thoughts on Football," *NYDN,* 12 November 1927.

16. Rice, "Good Little Man"; Noel Busch, "Booth Earning Way through Yale,"

NYDN, 1 November 1929 (the middle of the three installments); Westbrook Pegler, "Here It Is, Folks, Life Story of Little Albie and Big Al," *CT*, 2 November 1929.

17. See McGill, "Paul Gallico," 123.

18. Paul Gallico, "Whew! Another Week-End!" *NYDN*, 15 November 1926; and "Congratulations in Order," *NYDN*, 22 November 1926.

19. Westbrook Pegler, "Yale Democracy Comes to Light in Game with Georgia," *CT*, 15 October 1928.

20. Paul Gallico, "Princeton after Dark," *NYDN*, 25 November 1928; "The Game of Games," *NYDN*, 23 November 1930; and "Via the Spy-Glass," *NYDN*, 27 November 1932.

21. Dan Parker, "Few of Them Innocent," *Daily Mirror*, 25 October 1929; "Football—Cursed Again," *NYDN*, 25 October 1929; "College Sport Held Tainted by Subsidies," *NYHT*, 24 October 1929.

22. Warner, "What's the Matter with Football?"; Frederick Ware, "Readers Write In," *OWH*, 23 November 1936, and "Ballad of the Lost," *OWH*, 15 November 1936.

23. Wallace, "Double Ride" (*SEP*, 1936); and see "Odds against Honor" (*Collier's*, 1935).

24. Garth, "Boy Who Sold Himself" (*Collier's*, 1934); Brooks, "Pie Slinger" (*Collier's*, 1934).

25. See Garth, "Battling Sixteen"; Horton, "Run, Kick, and Pass"; Ford, "Cleat Warriors," "Captain Crash," "Heir to Touchdown," and "Stadium Slaves"; and Miller, "Feud" and "Denshawe of Army."

26. Vanneman and Cannon, *American Perception of Class*, 41.

27. Ted Benson, "Diogenes Benson Finds Honesty," *DW*, 29 October 1936.

28. See Lester Rodney, "With Pencils and No Brains," *DW*, 14 November 1936; "Minnesota Gridders on Way Back to Top Rank," *DW*, 17 October 1937; and Dave Farrell, "UCLA Proletarians Are Headed for the Rose Bowl," *DW*, 27 October 1942. Farrell celebrated the Bruins' assault on Jim Crow throughout the 1939 season, and in his 1942 article called UCLA "the poor boy's college" and the "CCNY of the Coast."

29. Bill Newton, "The Pinch Hitter," *DW*, 28 October 1940; Ted Benson, "Footballers Join Grid Union," *DW*, 2 December 1936.

30. "Howard Strike Gains Support," *DW*, 21 November 1936. The *Chicago Defender* and the *Pittsburgh Courier* also covered the Howard strike thoroughly, but the only mention of it in the *New York Times* was a trivializing letter printed on 21 November.

31. "Michigan Will Not Renew Kipke's Contract as Head Coach," *NYT*, 10 December 1937; "Michigan Grid Coach Sends Players into Ford's to Aid Union-Busting," *DW*, 18 November 1937; and "Michigan Coach Who Aided Ford Removed," *DW*, 10 December 1937.

32. "News of Pitt Football Player Revolt Was Suppressed," *DW*, 3 December 1937; "Pitt Double Crosses Frosh Grid Stars on Subsidies," *DW*, 18 November 1938; "'Quit Because Pitt Stopped Aiding Players'—Sutherland," *DW*, 27 October 1939.

33. "Small Subsidies behind Grid Troubles," *DW*, 8 November 1938; "Stanford Players to Get Bowl Cut," *DW*, 11 December 1940; Lester Rodney, "On the Score Board," *DW*, 2 December 1948.

34. Bob Phillips, "Harrison and Whatley Quit," *Birmingham News,* 3 November 1938; "Auburn Ends Quit School; Blame Coach," *Birmingham Post,* 3 November 1938; and Paul Zimmerman, "Sport Post-Scripts," *LAT,* 23 December 1940. My thanks to Bill Plott for locating the Birmingham sources.

35. See Ted Benson, "Pro Football Is an Honest Game," *DW,* 19 October 1936; Doc Daugherty, "College Football Faces Dark Future," *DW,* 15 November 1936; Lester Rodney, "Scoreboard," *DW,* 23 November 1938, and "On the Score Board," *DW,* 24 October 1939.

36. Lester Rodney, "On the Score Board," *DW,* 7 December 1941.

37. See T. P. Flynn, "Football Hero," *Sunday Worker,* 29 November 1936; and James Dugan, "Football Millions," *Sunday Worker,* 16–30 October and 6–13 November 1938. Two anti-Red serials by Dabney Horton in *Sport Story* were the silliest of all. See "Run, Kick, and Pass" and "The Red Guard."

38. Lester Rodney, "On the Scoreboard," *DW,* 10 October 1946 and 21 October 1946.

39. Lester Rodney, "On the Scoreboard," *DW,* 13 November 1947 and 20 November 1947; and "Say We," *DW,* 17 November 1948.

40. In New York, the *Post, World-Telegram, Herald Tribune, Journal-American, Daily News,* and *Daily Mirror* offered no comment (although columnist Harold Weissman in the *Daily Mirror* on 2 December reported on San Francisco owner Tony Morabito's likely reprisals). In Chicago, the *Tribune, Sun-Times,* and *Daily News* were also silent (except for the wire-service report), but Davis J. Walsh, the INS columnist in the *Herald-American,* on 1 December mocked the players for backing down. For the AP story, see "Forty-Niners Reconsider Strike Threat on Bonus Demand," *NYT,* 1 December 1949.

41. "49ers Demand Playoff Pay," *DW,* 1 December 1949; "49ers to Play, but Resentment Is High," *DW,* 2 December 1949; Bill Mardo, "In This Corner," *DW,* 2 December 1949; Arthur Daley, "Sports of the Times," *NYT,* 4 December 1949.

42. Prescott Sullivan, "The Low Down," *San Francisco Examiner,* 1 December and 2 December 1949; Bill Leiser, "As Bill Leiser Sees It," *San Francisco Chronicle,* 3 December 1949.

43. Riess, "Social Profile of the Professional Football Player," 224.

44. Arthur Daley, "Sports of the Times," *NYT,* 11 December 1949; Bill Corum, "Sports," *New York Journal-American,* 11 December 1949; Joe Williams, "Football Peace Ends Honeymoon for Players," *New York World-Telegram,* 10 December 1949; Dan Parker, "Pro Grid Picnic for Fans and Players Ends," *Daily Mirror,* 11 December 1949. Jimmy Powers had no immediate comment in the *Daily News,* but a year earlier he took a position identical to Parker's, on behalf of the players and fans against the monopolistic owners. See "Powerhouse," *NYDN,* 7 November 1948. Red Smith mocked the owners and predicted that the players would not readily agree to reduced salaries but took no position on the issue. See Red Smith, "Views of Sport," *NYHT,* 13 December 1949. The *Post* offered no comment.

45. In Chicago, Davis Walsh had no sympathy for the players, John Carmichael took a pro-management view, Arch Ward admitted that salaries had gotten out of hand but warned the owners against returning to slave wages, and the *Sun-Times*

offered no comment. See "Davis J. Walsh," *Chicago Herald-American*, 10 December 1949; John P. Carmichael, "The Barber Shop," *Chicago Daily News*, 12 December 1949; and Arch Ward, "In the Wake of the News," *CT*, 12 December 1949. In San Francisco, Prescott Sullivan and Bill Leiser welcomed the merger for both parties. See "The Low Down," *San Francisco Examiner*, 10 December 1949; and "As Bill Leiser Sees It," *San Francisco Chronicle*, 11 December 1949. Paul Zimmerman expressed no concern for the players; see "Sport Scripts," *LAT*, 11 December 1949.

46. See Scranton, "Varieties of Paternalism"; and Tone, *Business of Benevolence*.

47. See Fay, "Strictly for Sweeney" (*Collier's*, 1939), "Merry Widower" (*SEP*, 1943), and "Throw the Bum Out" (*SEP*, 1950); and Edward Prell, "The Story of the Big Bad Bears," *CT*, 21–28 October 1941; and *CT*, 26 October–1 November 1948.

48. Bill Leiser, "As Bill Leiser Sees It," *San Francisco Chronicle*, 3 February 1957; Prescott Sullivan, "The Low Down," *San Francisco Examiner*, 4 February 1957; Joe Williams, "Players Threaten Pro Grid Bosses," *New York World-Telegram*, 7 February 1957; Dan Parker, "Going Around the Sports Course in Short Pars," *Daily Mirror*, 3 February 1957. Departing from his more typical pro-owner stance, John Carmichael judged the owners silly in refusing to recognize that unions had become a part of pro sport. See "The Barber Shop," *Chicago Daily News*, 5 February 1957.

49. Lester Rodney, "On the Scoreboard," *DW*, 4 December 1957.

50. Vanneman and Cannon, *American Perception of Class*, 61.

51. L. H. Gregory, "Greg's Gossip," *PO*, 31 January 1956.

CHAPTER EIGHT

1. Mitchell, "Racial Traits in Athletics," 93–99; 147–52; 197–206.

2. Ibid., 97–98, 148–50, 150–51, 197–99.

3. Ibid., 203, 97, 151, 203.

4. Ibid., 204.

5. This story is retold by virtually every study of immigration in the United States. The classic study, and my primary source, is Higham, *Strangers in the Land*.

6. Ibid., 319.

7. Archeacon, *Becoming American*, 118.

8. Jacobson, *Whiteness of a Different Color*, 78; Reed, *Class Notes*, 140.

9. Handlin, *Uprooted*, 223–24; Riess, *City Games*, 99–100, 122. See also Riess's *City Sport in Industrial America* and *Sports and the American Jew;* Gems, *Windy City Wars;* Levine, *Ellis Island to Ebbets Field;* and Mormino, "Playing Fields of St. Louis." Studies of minority ethnic groups in other countries confirm this pattern: that local clubs playing the group's traditional sports fostered ethnic identity, while embrace of the host country's popular sports fostered assimilation. On the Irish in Australia, see Daryl Adair, "Conformity, Diversity and Difference in Antipodean Physical Culture," and Joseph M. Bradley, "Sport and the Contestation of Cultural and Ethnic Identities in Scottish Society," in Cronin and Mayall, *Sporting Nationalisms*. Murry R. Nelson's "Basketball as Cultural Capital," in the same volume, describes the basketball played by German, Irish, and Jewish immigrants in New York early in the twentieth century on similar terms.

10. On this campaign see Hartmann, *Movement to Americanize the Immigrant*.

11. On their racial thinking see Higham, *Strangers in the Land,* 140; on their football thinking see my *Reading Football.*

12. Franklin Gordon, "A Collegeful of Topnotchers," *AH,* 20 December 1929.

13. Jacobson, *Whiteness of a Different Color.*

14. Lorimer's editorials in the *Post,* which embraced the racial theories of Madison Grant, helped build the popular base for attacking the foreign-born during World War I and for limiting immigration afterward. See Cohn, *Creating America,* Chapters 3 and 4. After quotas were established in 1924, his editorials and selection of articles from 1925 through 1935 repeatedly called for preserving America's primary Nordic stock and for accepting only those immigrants who fully embraced "Americanism." For his editorials, see the bibliography. Articles sharing Lorimer's view included Carroll, "Alien Workers in America" and "Americans or Aliens First?"; Child, "Whose Country Is This?"; Crawford, "Six Years of Immigrant Quotas" and "Visitor on Business"; Curran, "New Immigrant" and "Smuggling Aliens"; Dies, "Immigration Crisis"; England, "Through Uncle Sam's Back Door"; Garis, "Lest Immigration Restriction Fail"; Marcosson, "Alien and Unemployment"; and Stevens, "Laborers East and West."

15. Tunis, "Great God Football."

16. Dick Hawkins, "Irish Down Jackets, 26–27," *AC,* 30 October 1927; "Lumpkin, Former Leopard Ace, Stars as Georgia Tech Beats Micks," *DMN,* 21 October 1928; "Notre Dame Head Replies to Coast Writer's Criticism," *Tidings* (Los Angeles), 15 December 1931; Sperber, *Shake Down the Thunder,* 79–83. On the anti-Catholic nativism faced by Notre Dame, see Sperber, *Shake Down the Thunder,* 149, 158–62, 200–203; Robinson, *Rockne of Notre Dame,* 207; and Hennessey, *American Catholics,* 235, 237.

17. For details on the Notre Dame–Army series and its reception in New York, see Sperber, *Shake Down the Thunder.*

18. "Notre Dame Head Replies to Coast Writer's Criticism," *Tidings,* 15 December 1931.

19. John Billi, "U.S. Sports Firmament Is Dotted with Many First Magnitude Stars of Italian Origin," *Il Progresso Italo-Americano,* 9 November 1930.

20. Steven A. Riess, "Sports and the American Jew," in Riess, *Sports and the American Jew,* 14–16.

21. Edward A. Ross, *The Old World in the New,* quoted in ibid., 14.

22. Ibid., 35, 37.

23. Henry Paull, "Benny Friedman—Gridiron Hero," *AH,* 18 December 1925; Ned Goldschmidt, "They Starred on Many Gridirons," 21 December 1928; Henry W. Levy, "The College Sports Roundup," 16 December 1932; Franklin Gordon, "A Collegeful of Topnotchers," 20 December 1929; Levy, "An Athletic Galaxy," 20 December 1929; Levy, "Sports," 30 September 1938; and Levy, "Topnotchers in Intercollegiate Sport," 18 December 1931. The *B'nai B'rith Messenger* also made much of Alabama All-American Fred Sington's election to Phi Beta Kappa in 1930. See Harry Glantz, "Our Own Athletes," *B'nai B'rith Messenger,* 9 January 1931.

24. Henry W. Levy, "An Athletic Galaxy," *AH,* 20 December 1929; Gordon, "Collegeful of Topnotchers"; Paull, "Benny Friedman—Gridiron Hero"; Goldschmidt,

"They Starred on Many Gridirons"; Levy, "The College Sports Roundup," *AH,* 16 December 1932; and Levine, *Ellis Island to Ebbets Field,* 194–205.

25. Higham, *Strangers in the Land,* 89.

26. Chestochowski, *Gridiron Greats,* 19.

27. Unfortunately, no broadcasts before 1935 survive. The broadcasters of the Pitt–Ohio State game in 1936 (with Pitt's Marshall Goldberg and several Polish teammates), Army-Columbia in 1938 (with Columbia's Sid Luckman), and Fordham-Oregon in 1938 (with Fordham's typically ethnic lineup) almost ignored ethnicity completely. See Pitt–Ohio State, 10 October 1936; Army-Columbia, 8 October 1938; and Fordham-Oregon, 22 October 1938.

28. El Casey, "Fair or Foul," *Dziennik Zjednoczenia,* 26 November 1929.

29. See John T. Czech, "Sport Cycle," *Dziennik Zjednoczenia,* 9 November 1935; and George Joel, "The Sporting World," *Jewish Advocate,* 4, 11, and 18 November 1930; John Billi, "U.S. Sports Firmament Is Dotted with Many First Magnitude Stars of Italian Origin," *Il Progresso Italo-Americano,* 9 November 1930; and "Polish All-American," *Dziennik Zjednoczenia,* 13 December 1930.

30. Henry Archacki, "Klick, Rodak, Maretk, et al.," *Nowy Swiat,* 15 December 1935; John T. Czech, "Sport Cycle," *Dziennik Zjednoczenia,* 22 October 1937. On Nagurski, see Britz, "Of Football and Frontiers."

31. "Thirty-Letter Man," *Dziennik Polski,* 19 November 1936; Henry Archacki, "Polling the Polish All-American," *Nowy Swiat,* 4 December 1938.

32. Henry Archacki, "A Short History of Polish American Football," *Nowy Swiat,* 22 November 1942; and "An All-Time Eleven," *Nowy Swiat,* 8 November 1942. Rockne's supposed comment appeared in several versions over the years. See "Polish Grid Stars Feted," *Dziennik Zjednoczenia,* 28 November 1927; "All Polish-American Gridders 1939," *Nowy Swiat,* 3 December 1939.

33. Henry Archacki, "An All-Time Eleven," *Nowy Swiat,* 8 November 1942. This column elaborates on a comment Archacki made in 1939, where he attributed Ed Danowski's success to "his Polish stolidity inherited from centuries of sturdy soil tillers." See Archacki, "So Long! Ed!," *Nowy Swiat,* 17 December 1939.

34. Henry Archacki, "About Big Ed and Joe Jerwa," *Nowy Swiat,* 18 December 1938.

35. Child, *Italian or American?,* 85, 127.

36. Articles about Notre Dame's Frank Carideo and Marchy Schwartz, and Michigan's Harry Newman, ignored their ethnicity. See Carideo, "Rockne's Quarterbacks"; "Marchy Schwartz and Notre Dame's Victory March"; Schwartz, "All-American Recants"; and Kipke, "Punt, a Pass and a Prayer." An article by Benny Friedman did relate an anecdote of a former Notre Dame player calling out to him in Yiddish in his first game as a pro (see Friedman, "Professional Touch"), but none of Friedman's articles explored his ethnic background.

37. Rockne, "From Norway to Notre Dame."

38. See, for example, Allison Danzig, "Players of the Game," *NYT,* 10 December 1929. Danzig's profile of Rockne opens, "From Norway, the land of sagas, there came to America shortly after the turn of the century an immigrant boy who was, in the course of time, to write a saga of success as vivid in its appeal to the youth of today as

the Icelandic exploits of Leif, the son of Eric the Red." The biographies published immediately after Rockne's death, noted in Chapter 4, offered additional versions.

39. Cunningham, "How to Build a Football Business."

40. "Life Goes to a Football Game"; "Sid Luckman Is New York's Football Hero"; "Great Panthers Spring from Tower of Learning"; "Marshall Goldberg"; Miley, "Galloping Goldbergs"; and Terrill, "Man in Motion." Coverage of Goldberg in the *Pittsburgh Press* in 1936, his sophomore year when he first became a star, ignored both his Jewishness and his Polishness (the Pitt lineup, like those of the other Pittsburgh schools, Duquesne and Carnegie Tech, was overwhelmingly ethnic).

41. Rice, "All-America Football Team."

42. Quoted in Marannis, *When Pride Still Mattered*, 48–49.

43. Grahame, "How Carnegie Tech Plays Football"; "Bleachers" (1929).

44. Tunis, "More Pay for College Football Stars"; Henry Archacki, "Poles in the Rose Bowl," *Nowy Swiat*, 6 December 1936; Neuberger, "Gridiron G-Man."

45. A study of stories published in 1937 and 1943 found that only 9 percent of the characters were of non-Nordic stock (that is, blacks and new immigrants), and that they were much more likely to be "disapproved characters." See Berelson and Salter, "Majority and Minority Americans," 241.

46. Andrews, "Panski of the Irish"; Russell, "Latin from Manhattan." See also Standish, "Vagrant Lineman"; Ford, "Gridiron Goats"; Horton, "Touchdowns, Inc."; Miller, "Background"; and Russell, "Payoff in Pasadena."

47. See also Nichols, "Hooley's Unmentionables," in which a scrub team with representatives from ten equatorial nations outshines the varsity on hot days.

48. Scholz, "Prima Donnas," "Tackling the Townies," "Missing Halfback," and "Gridiron Crooner."

49. The American Film Institute's volume on *Ethnicity in American Feature Films, 1911–1960* lists just six football movies, in addition to the few with Indian or African American major characters: *Hold 'Em Yale* (1928), *Sunny Skies* (1930), *Huddle* (1932), *Knute Rockne—All-American* (1940), *Too Many Girls* (1940), and *Saturday's Hero* (1951). In *Hold 'Em Yale*, an Argentinian becomes a football star at Yale and wins a professor's daughter; in *Sunny Skies*, the hero has a Jewish roommate who does not play football; in *Too Many Girls*, Desi Arnaz plays a Latino football star at an American college whose distinctiveness is ignored until his conga number in the grand musical finale. In other words, none of these three has anything to do with the European immigrants transforming college football. See Gevinson, *Within Our Gates.*

50. Henry Archacki, "Wojciechowicz an All American Name," *Nowy Swiat,* 22 November 1936.

51. Brennan, "This Football," *Collier's* (1930); Kofoed, "Pappa Morelli's Boy."

52. Graham, "Climax Game"; see also Edgar, "All-Americanized." In Ralph Cannon's less complicated 1933 novel *Grid Star*, a lower-class Italian boy, a member of a gang of "lawless youths," learns loyalty and fair play through college football.

53. Frank, "Woes of an All-American"; Cohane, "College Football Tragedy."

54. Sperber, *Onward to Victory*, 126–36.

55. Fante, "One-Play Oscar" (*SEP,* 1950).

56. "High School Football."

57. Sperber, *Onward to Victory*, 318; Bee, *Touchdown Pass*, 204. Gantner's "Fighting Coach" was the last, as well as the first, integrated football story in *Boys' Life* in the 1950s. In two other stories from *Boys' Life* at the end of the decade—Jackson Scholz's "Gridiron Milkman" (November 1958) and Ross L. Crozier's "The Forlorn Fullback" (September 1960)—the teams are again ethnically mixed. None of these stories directly addresses the ethnicity of the characters.

58. Fay, "Football Bombardier"; Trevor, "Greatest Backfield in History?"; "Crusaders & Slaves"; Monroe, "Stanford's Storybook Coach"; Russell, "Big Bad Bulldog from Dixie"; Polzer with Herndon, "Football Made a Gentleman Out of Me"; Cohane, "Panther on the Prowl."

59. Frank, "Man Who Saved the Day for Yale."

60. Breslin, "Town That Spawns Athletes."

61. Jacobson, *Whiteness of a Different Color*, 110; Kantowicz, "Ethnicity," 1: 461; and Lipsitz, *Time Passages*, 41.

62. Riess, "Social Profile," 229.

63. Marion E. Jackson, "Sports of the World," *Atlanta Daily World*, 3 January and 4 January 1956.

64. Jacobson, *Whiteness of a Different Color*, 6–8.

CHAPTER NINE

1. Mitchell, "Racial Traits in Athletics," 198–99.

2. Ibid., 151–52.

3. On the continuing reporting on sports in highly racialized ways, see Hoose, *Necessities*.

4. On Carlisle football, see Bloom, *To Show What an Indian Can Do*, 1–30 passim; Steckbeck, *Fabulous Redmen;* Newcombe, *Best of the Athletic Boys;* and Oxendine, *American Indian Sports Heritage*, 184–93. For a discussion of the popular reception of Carlisle football, see my *Reading Football*, 233–47.

5. See "Differences Between Red and White Football Material"; and Warner, "Indian Massacres," "Heap Big Run-Most-Fast," and "Red Menaces."

6. See, for example, Berkhofer, *White Man's Indian*.

7. Peterson, *Pigskin*, 82; Deloria, "I Am of the Body," 333.

8. On Haskell, see Bloom, *To Show What an Indian Can Do*, 37–51, 57–61; and Oxendine, *American Indian Sports Heritage*, 193–202 and 261–64. Simply to reconstruct its football seasons, see the *Indian Leader,* the weekly paper published at the school.

9. See, for example, the photo of George Levi in the *Boston Herald*, 11 October 1925; the photo of Indians in traditional dress sitting on the sidelines in the *Pittsburgh Press*, 24 November 1929; and the photo of Louis Weller in the *Philadelphia Record,* 20 October 1931.

10. See Herbert M. Dustin, "Martineau Returns to Gophers as Graham Is Put Out with Injury," *Minneapolis Tribune*, 11 October 1923; and "Visiting Band Appears in Tribal Regalia to Spur Warriors," *Minneapolis Tribune*, 18 November 1928.

11. See John J. Hallahan, "John Levi Hurls Long Forwards in Haskell Indians' Workout," *Boston Globe*, 31 October 1924; Ray McCarthy, "Heap Big Injun Hurls

Pass 50 Yards and Punts More Than 60," *New York Tribune*, 18 November 1923; and Daniel J. Lynch, "Boston College 27, Indians 0, Second Period," *Boston Globe*, 1 November 1924.

12. "Kiddies with Indian Suits Will Be Admitted to Haskell Game Free," *New Orleans Time-Picayune*, 6 November 1928; and Gwen Bristow, "Indian Fight Like Braves of Old but Fort Wolf Holds," 11 November 1928.

13. See Riley, "Trapped in the History of Film." *Braveheart* was a remake of *Strongheart* (1914) and was "the first truly major football film," according to Zucker and Babich in *Sports Films*, 185. Stereotypical Indians of football films were just a subset of those in films generally. In his survey of Indians in film, Michael Hilger has concluded that Indian characters were limited to Savages and Noble Red Men throughout this period; see his *From Savage to Nobleman* and Kilpatrick, *Celluloid Indians*.

14. Paine, "The Indian"; Berkhofer, *White Man's Indian*, 90. One other story—Mooney, "Polysynthetic Football" (*SEP*, 1922)—used the noble savage in shoulder pads for comic effect. The indecipherable language used by Indian players turns out to be Latin.

15. Sam Greene, "U. of D. Second Eleven to Face Haskell Tribe," *Detroit News*, 4 November 1927.

16. See "Swift Running Indians Will Clash with U. of D.," *Detroit News*, 8 November 1922; Stanley Woodward, "Haskell Indians Appear to Be Bigger and Better in Workout at Wigwam," *Boston Herald*, 9 October 1925; Max E. Hannum, "Indians Face Dukes in Local Grid Feature," *Pittsburgh Press*, 23 November 1929; and Gordon Mackay, "All-Western Back Arrives Tomorrow at Head of Haskell Indians," and "20,000 See Temple Beat Indians 6 to 0," *Philadelphia Record*, 21 and 24 October 1931.

17. W. E. Mullins, "Haskell Indians, Looking Fit and Feeling Cocky, Arrive in Town Ready for B.C. Battle," *Boston Herald*, 11 November 1926. Gigantic Theo Roebuck's Indian name (Little Boy) received much attention in 1924, as did Louis Weller's (Little Rabbit) in 1931.

18. "Haskell Indians Work out at Temple for Owl Game," *Philadelphia Record*, 23 October 1931; Stanley Woodward, "John Levi Comes Up to His Press Notices in Trial at Braves Field," *Boston Herald*, 31 October 1924. For another account that dwelt particularly on Indian bodies and appearance, see Mullins, "Haskell Indians, Looking Fit."

19. "Seek Scalps of Gopher Gridders," *Minneapolis Tribune*, 10 October 1923; "Haskell Indian Here for Game," *LAT*, 21 December 1923 (as well as articles on 23 December by Bill Henry and 25 December by Braven Dyer); "Real Braves Coming to Braves Field" and "Boston Will Be Invaded by Redskins Tomorrow, Ready to Start on the Warpath," *Boston Globe*, 29 October 1924; "Heap Big Indians Ready to Scalp Palefaces," *Boston Herald*, 9 October 1925; Milt Davis, "Haskell Team Massacred by Gophers, 52–0," *Minneapolis Tribune*, 18 November 1928.

20. Gene Thatcher, "Indians, Wolves Primed for Little Scalping Party Today," *New Orleans Times-Picayune*, 10 November 1928. See also "The Vanishing American" (a caption for the photo of a Haskell player), *LAT*, 18 December 1925; "Haskell Gridders Meet Mercury Eleven Today," *LAT*, 19 December 1925; and "Indians Battle Palefaces at Wrigley Park," *Los Angeles Evening Herald*, 19 December 1925.

21. "Rejuvenated Blues to Meet Haskell Today in Homecoming Battle," *OWH*, 2 November 1923; W. W. Edgar, "University of Detroit Romps Over Haskell Indians," *Detroit Free Press*, 6 November 1927; Tom Shriver, "Temple Favored to Defeat Light Haskell Indian Team," *Philadelphia Record*, 4 November 1932.

22. Bloom, "There Is Madness," reprinted in *To Show*, 37–50. During this "dark age" of Indian journalism (Murphy and Murphy, *Let My People Know*, 52), coverage of Indian football by Indian newspapers was sporadic and meager. On the Indian press see also Littlefield and Parins, *American Indian and Alaska Native Newspapers and Periodicals*.

23. See the *New Orleans Times-Picayune* in 1928 for 6 November ("Kiddies in Indian Suits Will Be Admitted to Haskell Game Free"), 7 November (Gene Thatcher, "Veteran Haskell Squad Starts Southern Jaunt Tonight"), 8 November (Thatcher, "Haskell Squad Arrives Tonight; Works at Loyola"), 9 November (Thatcher, "Thirty Haskell Indians Arrive for Loyola Game Saturday"), 10 November (Thatcher, "Indians, Wolves Primed for Little Scalping Party Today"), and 11 November (Gwen Bristow, "Indians Fight Like Braves of Old but Fort Wolf Holds").

24. Gordon Mackay, "20,000 See Temple Beat Indians 6 to 0," *Philadelphia Record*, 24 October 1931. See also Mackay, "All-Western Back Arrives Tomorrow at Head of Haskell Indians," and "Haskell Indians Work Out at Temple for Owl Game," *Philadelphia Record*, 21 and 23 October 1931. As late as 1931 in Omaha, where Haskell teams had been frequent visitors, a writer in the *World-Herald* produced another of these elaborate riffs on the wild-Indian-turned-football-player. See Howard Wolff, "Grid Sport Going Sissy, Dietz Says," *OWH*, 8 November 1931.

25. Paddock, "Chief Bright Path"; Warner, "Indian Massacres," "Heap Big Run-Most-Fast," "Red Menaces," and "Here Come the Giants!"; Rice, "First Fifty Years"; Crichton, "Good King Jim"; "The Mid-Century All-America"; "Thorpe Hailed as Greatest Player on Gridiron in Past Fifty Years," *NYT*, 25 January 1950; and "Jim Thorpe Named Greatest in Sport," *NYT*, 12 February 1950.

26. Fox, *Big Leagues*, 252.

27. Williams, "Off the Reservation" (*Collier's*, 1946).

28. Herndon, "Dirtiest Game of the Year" (*SEP*, 1952); McMillion, "Big Win" (*Collier's*, 1954); and Cox, "Playoff Game" (*SEP*, 1956). One comic story preceded our period: see Norton, "A Gentleman's Game."

29. Steppin Fetchit appeared briefly in *Salute* (1929) and in Red Grange's 1931 serial, *The Galloping Ghost*, and other black actors played roles that became synonymous with his name. Films in which black porters or servants briefly appeared include *Eleven Men and a Girl* (1929), *Huddle* (1932), *Hold 'Em Navy* (1937), *Navy Blue and Gold* (1937), *Saturday's Heroes* (1937), and *Francis Goes to West Point* (1952).

30. Tolbert, "Mighty Mites"; Jones, "Father Is a Football Coach"; "Taps Sound for Blind Negro Football Rooter at Ole Miss," *OWH*, 22 October 1955.

31. Heisman, "Signals."

32. Stagg, "Touchdown! No. 4—Go West, Young Man" (16 October); Rockne, "From Norway to Notre Dame."

33. See, for example, *Judge*, 1 December 1894, 23 November 1895, 29 October 1898, and 21 October 1899; and *Life*, 22 December 1904.

34. Pitt-Illinois, 21 September 1946; and Rose Bowl (USC-Illinois), 1 January 1947.

35. Fay Young, "The Stuff Is Here," *CD*, 23 October 1937.

36. "All-America Plays of 1938!" *News of the Day*, 24 October 1938; and UCLA-California, *News of the Day*, 4 November 1939.

37. "Colored Gals Get Football Fever," *Hearst Metrotone News*, 28 November 1931.

38. "The Champion Gridiron Fans!" *News of the Day*, 25 November 1936.

39. *Fox Movietone News* showed four segments on black football, two of them the same games covered by *Metrotone News*, but these are unavailable for viewing. There is no reason to assume that the narration for *Movietone News* was equally racist; *Metrotone News* was notorious for its reactionary propagandizing in its news segments. See Fielding, *American Newsreel*, 248.

40. "Tigers Star[t] Grid Practice," *Universal News*, 5 September 1938; "LSU Introduces Novel Grid Training," *News of the Day*, 1 September 1938; "L.S.U. Gridders Set for the New Season," *Paramount News*, September 1938 (no specific date identified). The release sheets, or program notes, accompany the collections at the National Archives and UCLA. My thanks to Bill Hennessey, of the Sherman Grinberg Library in New York, who located the Paramount newsreel for me and played me its soundtrack over the telephone.

41. See Gleason, *Leisure Ethic*, 219.

42. Much has been written about racism in football but little about the history of stereotyping. See Wiggins, "Great Speed but Little Stamina"; and Davis, "Myth of the Superspade." On the press coverage of a black athlete from an earlier era, see Zang, *Fleet Walker's Divided Heart*, 28–29, 37–38, 41–42, 45, 49, 51, 54, 58.

43. See L. H. Gregory's comments in the *Oregonian* on 21 September, 4 October, 7 October, and 11 October 1931; and "Just a Loyola Pass That Turned Out to Be 'Just a Pass,'" *LAT*, 22 October 1933.

44. Charles Bartlett, "Indiana Whips Chicago, 32–6, in Private Battle," *CT*, 25 October 1931; and Bartlett, "Air's Full of Footballs, but Maroons Win," *CT*, 23 October 1932.

45. See George Morgenstern, "Indiana Crushed by Maroons, 32 to 6" and "Maroons Defeat Indiana in First Conference Game, 13–7," *Chicago Herald and Examiner*, 25 October 1931 and 23 October 1932; "Indiana Beats Maroons 32–6, 2d Hoosier Win," and "Northwestern Beats Indiana 7 to 6," *Chicago Daily News*, 24 October 1931 and 14 November 1931.

46. "Indiana Talks About Beating Iowans Today," *CT*, 15 October 1932.

47. Boskin, *Sambo*, 10–11; Cripps, *Slow Fade to Black*, 274–75. See also Leab, *From Sambo to Superspade;* and Bogle, *Toms, Coons, Mulattoes, Mammies, and Bucks.*

48. Wolters, *New Negro on Campus*, 313–17; Levine, *American College*, 159.

49. See the accounts in the *DMN* (UP), *NYT* (AP), and *Minneapolis Tribune* for 31 October 1937; Jimmy Lee, "In the Sport Light," *Minneapolis Spokesman*, 5 November 1937; and the *Minnesota Daily* for 4 November.

50. On race and racism in football, see (in the order of publication) Henderson, *Negro in Sports;* Chalk, *Pioneers of Black Sport* and *Black College Football;* Rust, *Art Rust's Illustrated History of the Black Athlete;* and Ashe, *Hard Road to Glory.* The major aca-

demic historians of football and race have been David K. Wiggins, Donald Spivey, and Charles H. Martin, with important contributions also from Thomas G. Smith and Patrick B. Miller.

51. The Syracuse quarterback was adopted by the Hindu doctor who married his mother. As a Hindu, Sidat-Singh was an acceptable opponent for Maryland; as a black American—apparently not discovered by Maryland's coaches until the eve of the game—he was not. See the *Chicago Defender's* brief account in "Northwestern's Officials Stop Hotel Jim Crow of Bernie Jefferson," 13 November 1937.

52. On the Bates affair, see Spivey, "'End Jim Crow in Sports.'" On the benching of Willis Ward, see Behee, *Hail to the Victors!* and Martin, "Racial Change." The first black players in reintegrated professional football also experienced the indignity of benching. See Peterson, *Pigskin*, 185.

53. Miller, "Slouching toward a New Expediency."

54. Wilfrid Smith, "Iowa Running Attack Whips Purple, 20 to 7," *CT*, 7 October 1934; David W. Kellum, "Simmons Wins for Iowa," *CD*, 13 October 1934; Harry MacNamara, "Simmons Rips Purple Line as Iowa Wins, 20–7," *Chicago Herald and Examiner*, 7 October 1934.

55. Irving Vaughan, "Iowa Rallies, but Nebraska Wins, 14 to 13," *CT*, 14 October 1934; "Iowa State Stops Simmons and Crayne; Beats Iowa, 31–6," *CT*, 21 October 1934; "Minnesota Beats Iowa, 48–12," *Chicago Tribune*, 28 October 1934; "Indiana Ties Iowa, 0 to 0," *CT*, 4 November 1934.

56. "Simmons, a Star To Others, Just a Player to Himself," *CD*, 27 October 1934; David W. Kellum, "Simmons Injured; Iowa Drubbed by Minnesota," *CD*, 3 November 1934; "May Quit Iowa," *CD*, 24 November 1934.

57. See "Iowa Routs So. Dakota,. 47–2," *CT*, 6 October 1935; Wilfrid Smith, "Hawkeyes Tie Score on Pass, Then Drive 48 Yards to Goal," *CT*, 13 October 1935; Smith, "Simmons Gains 192 Yards to Dazzle Ilini," *CT*, 27 October 1935; French Lane, "Iowa Ties Indiana, 6 to 6, on Simmons' 58 Yard Run," *CT*, 3 November 1935; Smith, "Gophers Whip Iowa, 13–6, on 77 Yard Drive," *CT*, 10 November 1935; Charles Bartlett, "Purdue Defeats Iowa, 12 to 6, on M'Gannon's Run," *CT*, 17 November 1935; and Lane, "Hawkeyes Miss Chances after Heap Is Injured," *CT*, 24 November 1935.

58. Al Monroe, "Speaking of Sports," *CD*, 23 November 1935.

59. Dan Burley, "Iowa, Simmons Lose To Gophers," *CD*, 16 November 1935; Al Monroe, "Speaking of Sports," *CD*, 30 November 1935.

60. Harvey Woodruff, "N.U. Defeats Iowa, 18–7," *CT*, 4 October 1936; "Simmons Stars, but Iowa Loses, 18–7," *CD*, 10 October 1936; Ted Robinson, "Jealousy Jams Oze At Iowa," *CD*, 24 October 1936; Al Monroe, "Speaking of Sports," *CD*, 31 October 1936; "Duke Slater Home after Trip to Aid Iowa Prep for Season," *CD*, 17 October 1936.

61. R. W. Houston, "Refuses to Apologize," *CT*, 12 November 1936; James S. Kearns, "Peace at Iowa; Ozzie Simmons to Rejoin Squad," *Chicago Daily News*, 12 November 1936. The *Chicago Herald and Examiner* provided less coverage.

62. "Simmons Quits, Returns To Iowa Team All In One Day," *CD*, 21 November 1936; "Simmons Opens Up Off the Gridiron," *CD*, 21 November 1936; "Hits At-

tack on Oze Iowa Gridiron Star," *CD*, 28 November 1936; Al Monroe, "Speaking of Sports," *CD*, 19 December 1936.

63. See Marvin McCarthy, "Tittle and Tattle," *Chicago Daily Times*, 16 November 1936.

64. For a full discussion of the incident, see Martin, "Racial Change."

65. Martin, "Racial Change," 550–53. Georgia's games with integrated St. Mary's in 1950 and Penn in 1952, and Georgia Tech's with Notre Dame in 1953, were covered by the *Atlanta Constitution* without controversy.

66. The text of Griffin's statement was carried widely. I have quoted from the *Nashville Banner*, 2 December 1955, 1. Griffin's statement appeared on 3 December in morning papers.

67. "No Succession for Students," *PO*, 6 December 1955; "Outburst in Georgia," *NYT*, 4 December 1955. The *Philadelphia Inquirer, New York Daily News, Boston Record, New York Post*, and *Christian Science Monitor* were all quoted in "Press taunts Georgia governor," *Baltimore Afro-American*, 17 December 1955.

68. "The Issue in Georgia Is More Than Playing in Sugar Bowl," *Louisville Courier-Journal*, 6 December 1955; "Rambling Wreck," *Washington Post*, 8 December 1955; "Tech Will Honor a Contract," *Nashville Banner*, 3 December 1955; "Common Sense Wins a Victory," *AC*, 6 December 1955; Ed Danforth, "Future Tech and Georgia Sports Programs Involved," *Atlanta Journal*, 2 December 1955, 1; "Griffin's Teapot Tempest," *Atlanta Journal*, 4 December 1955, 1; "Regents Deserve Thanks," *Atlanta Journal*, 6 December 1955. The *Raleigh News and Observer* is quoted in "Press Taunts the Governor," *Baltimore Afro-American*, 17 December 1955.

69. Halberstam, *Fifties*, 437.

70. "Cancel That California Trip," *Jackson Daily News*, 6 December 1955, 1; "No Investigation Needed," *Jackson Daily News*, 10 December 1955, 1; and "The Low Down on the Higher Ups," *Jackson Daily News*, 7 December 1955, 1.

71. "Griffin Petty, Newspaper in Augusta Says" (UP), *AC*, 5 December 1955; Naylor Stone, "A Cruel Blow to Football at Georgia Tech," *Birmingham Post-Herald*, 7 December 1955; John Temple Graves, "This Morning," *Birmingham Post-Herald*, 5 December 1955; "Governor Griffin's Football," *Albany Herald*, 3 December 1955; and "Tempest in a Sugar Bowl," *Charleston News and Courier*, 6 December 1955.

72. Halberstam, *Fifties*, 684.

73. Marion E. Jackson, "Sports of the World," *Atlanta Daily World*, 7 December 1955.

74. "'Grier Plays!'—Pitt," *PC*, 10 December 1955; Bill Nunn, Jr., "Change of Pace," *PC*, 14 January 1956.

75. Sam Lacy, "From A to Z," *Baltimore Afro-American*, 10 December 1955. The rest of the paper's coverage on 10 December took a more typically positive view." See "2,500 Chase Governor of Georgia from Atlanta," 10 December 1955, 1, and the accompanying reports, "Tan Atlanta Is 'Amused,' Not 'Alarmed'" and "Here's How Ga. Tech Students Showed Wrath."

76. Hearst's newsreel coverage of the Sugar Bowl included the play on which Grier was penalized, but the cameraman picked up the ball too late.

77. Ralph McGill, "Fine Grid Battle Dims Race Issue," *AC*, 3 January 1956, 1; Fur-

man Bisher, "The Sociological Bowl," *AC*, 5 January 1956; Ed Danforth, "Pitt Toughest Meat for Tech Since Baylor," *Atlanta Journal*, 3 January 1956. See also Naylor Stone, "Bowl Warfare Gives Thrills with Surprises," *Birmingham Post-Herald*, 4 January 1956; and Bill Keefe, "Viewing the News," *New Orleans Times-Picayune*, 4 January 1956.

78. Marion E. Jackson, "Sports of the World," *Atlanta Daily World*, 7 December 1955.

79. Martin, "Racial Change," 559–60; Martin, "Integrating New Year's Day"; and Foreman, "Discrimination against the Negro."

80. See Wiggins, "Prized Performers"; and Spivey and Jones, "Intercollegiate Athletic Servitude."

81. Hoffman, *Race Traits*. George Frederickson calls Hoffman's book "the most influential discussion of the race question to appear in the late nineteenth century." See Frederickson, *Black Image*, 249.

82. Welky, "Viking Girls," 36–38.

83. A brief AP account of Cobb's research appeared in the *New York Times* on 28 July 1935, buried on the sixth page of sports. Cobb's studies were also cited in the black press but carried no weight with the wider public. See, for example, Henderson, "Negro Athlete," 78.

84. Mead, *Champion*, 47–74. On the response to Johnson, see Jaher, "White America Views Jack Johnson"; Wiggins, "Boxing's Sambo Twins"; Roberts, *Papa Jack;* and Al-Tony Gilmore, *Bad Nigger!*

85. Quoted in Evensen, "Jazz Age Journalism's Battle," 244.

86. Quoted in Mead, *Champion*, 105.

87. Red Marberry, "Iowa's Great Backs Crush Purple 20 to 7," *Chicago Daily Times*, 7 October 1934.

88. These tests were reported in the *Chicago Defender* with apparent approval and even pride. Theories of black athletic superiority could be seductive to those they seemed to honor. See "Simmons Gets Brain Test," *CD*, 16 November 1935.

89. Dick Hyland, "Miracle Eye Camera Shows How Jackie Robinson Does His Stuff," *LAT*, 28 October 1939.

90. Frederickson, *Black Image*.

91. George White, "Lions and Mustangs Split Cotton Bowl Honors, 13–13," *DMN*, 2 January 1949, 1; Sam Blair, "Huge Negro Defender Shines in Hornet Loss," *DMN*, 29 November 1954.

92. The coverage of Oze Simmons at Iowa in 1934–36 prominently noted his costly fumbles, and in 1938, the *Los Angeles Times* noted Washington's "current habit of fumbling at critical junctures of the game." See Frank Finch, "Powerful Bears Rout Bruin Eleven, 20–7," *LAT*, 16 October 1938.

93. Fay Young, "Fay Says," *CD*, 7 November and 21 November 1925; Al Monroe, "Oze Simmons, the Joe Louis of Football, Runs Illinois Dizzy," *CD*, 2 November 1935; Dan Burley, "Iowa, Simmons, Lose to Gophers," *CD*, 16 November 1935; "What Happened to Ozie Simmons Comes Out at Last as Coach Solem of Iowa Tells of His Great Star," *PC*, 17 November 1934; Romeo Daugherty, "Sports Whirl," *NYAN*, 2 November 1935; Leon Hardwick, "Fans Cheer as Ozzie Takes Fight to Gophers,"

NYAN, 16 November 1935; and "Being a One-Man Team Not Enough to Make All-American," *NYAN,* 24 October 1936.

94. See Bill Rives, "Brown Alone Worth Price of Ducat," *DMN,* 7 December 1956; "Syracuse, TCU Geared to Bowl Test; Horned Frogs Rated as Slim Favorite," *DMN,* 1 January 1957, 1; and "TCU Shades Syracuse Eleven, 28 to 27, In Spectacular Cotton Bowl Contest," *DMN,* 2 January 1957, 1.

95. Parker, "Skinny Terror of Illinois"; Fay, "Can't You Hear Them Calling Caroline"; Gross, "All-Around Jimmy Brown"; "Cleveland's Jim Brown"; "Brown's Run at Records"; Lipscomb, "I'm Still Scared"; "Big Daddy from Baltimore"; and "Prentice Gautt." *Sport* more openly criticized the racism in football; see Parker, "How Democratic Is Sport?" and Cobbledick, "Cleveland Browns."

96. *Ebony* was founded in 1945, but articles on football did not become frequent until the 1950s. See "Addison Hawthorne," "Texans Like Negro Grid Stars," "Football's Most Democratic Team," "Quarterback from Little Rock," and "New Texan to Brag About," all on milestones in integration. Other articles celebrated the achievements of black stars such as Johnny Bright, Tank Younger, J. C. Caroline and Mickey Bates, Ollie Matson, Emlen Tunnell, Prentice Gautt, Joe Perry, Willie Galimore, and Big Daddy Lipscomb on essentially the same terms as mainstream magazines. Only a couple of articles focused on black-college football: "Big Time Football at Florida A. and M." and "Alonzo 'Jake' Gaither." *Esquire's* "Time Out for Mayhem" by Booton Herndon followed an earlier attack on segregation, Riess, "May the Best White Man Win."

97. For the cover stories, see 27 September 1954 (Jones), 7 October 1957 (Matson), and 26 September 1960 (Brown). See also Maule, "Browns' Jim Dandy," "Why the Browns Will Win," "They Cry for Moore," and "George and his Dragons" (on Galimore).

98. "Day of the Bowls Is Here."

99. Schmidt and Fitzgerald, "New Open Game"; L. D. Hitchkiss, "Simmons Leads Iowa to 12–6 Win Over Colgate," *LAT,* 13 October 1935; Al Monroe, "Speaking of Sports," *CD,* 2 November 1935.

100. George, *Elevating the Game;* Riley, "Did O. J. Dance?"

101. See also Majors, "Cool Pose"; Kochman, *Black and White Styles;* and the contributions by Jeff Greenfield, Michael Novak, Arthur Ashe, John Edgar Wideman, and Michael Eric Dyson in Caponi, *Signifyin(g).*

102. William G. Nunn, "WGN Broadcasts," *PC,* 19 November 1932.

103. Quoted in Miller, "To 'Bring the Race Along Rapidly,'" 119.

104. "Sidelights on the Lincoln-Howard Game," *Afro-American,* 2 December 1921; Frank A. Young, "Lincoln, 13 Howard, 7 in Downpour," *CD,* 3 December 1921.

105. Frank Young, "Lions Are Winning as 20,000 Cheer," *CD,* 6 December 1924; "Annual Classic Was a Brilliant Social Affair," *Baltimore Afro-American,* 6 December 1924; "'Annual Classic' Viewed by Throng of 25,000 Who See Hard Fought Struggle," *CD,* 8 December 1924; Jones, *Recreation and Amusement,* 75; and Bill Gibson, "12,000 See Howard U. Defeat Lincoln 12–0," *Baltimore Afro-American,* 1 December 1928.

106. "Pollard Pulverizer Grinds Tigers, 33–0," *NYAN*, 31 October 1936. See also Carroll, *Fritz Pollard*, 200.

107. "Howard's New Plays Gave Crowd a Thrill," *Baltimore Afro-American*, 6 December 1924; "'Eleven Second' Legs!" *Baltimore Afro-American*, 24 November 1928.

108. See Sundquist, *To Wake the Nations*, 278–82; and Lhamon, *Raising Cain*, 3.

109. George, *Elevating the Game*, 49–50.

110. William D. Piersen, "African-American Festive Style," in Caponi, *Signifyin(g)*, 417–33.

111. Al Monroe, "Speaking of Sports," *CD*, 23 November 1935.

112. See Henderson, "Athletics" and "Sports" (1926 and 1927). On Henderson, see Wiggins, *Glory Bound*, 221–40.

113. For a full discussion of this issue, see Wolters, *New Negro on Campus*.

114. See W. Rollo Wilson, "Sports Shots," *PC*, 3 December 1932; Chester L. Washington, "Chez Sez," *PC*, 3 November 1934 and 3 October 1936, and "Sez Ches," 9 November 1940; Daniel, "Talkin' Out Loud," *NYAN*, 9 December 1939; and Frank Young, "Fay Says," *CD*, 27 November 1948.

115. See George Strickler's pregame coverage in the *Tribune:* "Bears Bolster Attack; Point for Negro Team," 21 September 1938; "Ray Kemp to Do Double Duty against Bears," 22 September 1938; and "Bears Battle Colored Star Eleven Tonight," 23 September 1938. The *Herald and Examiner* also ran a handful of small, unsigned pregame reports.

116. William G. Nunn, "All-Stars Fall before Battering Chicago Bears," *PC*, 1 October 1938. See also Frank A. Young, "All Stars Unable to Halt Bears; Lose 51–0," and John Lake, "All Star Players Complain about Division of Money," *CD*, 1 October 1938. For Strickler's derisive account, see "Bears Roll Up 51 Points and Stars Get None," *CT*, 24 September 1938.

117. Dan Burley, "Do All-Colored Teams Compare with Top Mixed Units?" *NYAN*, 23 December 1939.

118. Black-white exhibitions in New York included a Negro All-Star vs. New York Yankees contest on 30 November 1941, Inter-Racial Stars vs. New London Diesels on 7 November 1943, Tuskegee Warhawks vs. New London Undersea Raiders on 22 November 1945, North Carolina A&T vs. New London Undersea Raiders on 11 November 1946, and Wilberforce vs. Bergen on 27 November 1947. These games, drawing between 15,000 and 23,000, were covered by the *Daily Worker* as well as the black press.

119. "Can We Build Thinker-Thrower?" *PC*, 7 January 1956.

120. Ellison, *Shadow and Act*, 78–79.

CHAPTER TEN

1. Kimmel, *Manhood in America*, 206–9. For a full account of Terman's work in this context, see Pleck, *Myth of Masculinity*.

2. Terman, *Sex and Personality*, 457.

3. Guttman, *Erotic in Sports*, 67.

4. See Chapter 4 of my *Reading Football*, "Versions of Masculinity."

5. Cunningham, "Bringing 'Em Back to Life"; Dick Hyland, "Behind the Line," *LAT*, 13 November 1939.

6. Braven Dyer, "Pitt Favored by 12 Points," *LAT*, 13 October 1934; Sutherland and Maulsby, "Yea, Pitt, Sock It to 'Em"; Marshall Goldberg, with Norman Reissman, "A Bunch of Sissies, Us," *New York Journal-American*, Saturday Home Magazine, 28 October 1939; Arthur Daley, "Sports of the Times," *NYT*, 26 October 1947.

7. Bill Rives, "The Sport Scene," *DMN*, 30 November 1932 and 12 December 1953.

8. Rice, "What Football Pays For"; "Stuff Men Are Made Of"; "Spoil-Sports."

9. William Roper, "Roper on 'Soft Men,'" *NYHT Magazine*, 7 October 1928.

10. K. K. Rockne, "Isn't 1934 Football the Roughest Thing?," *Chicago Herald and Examiner*, 13 November 1924; Sperber, *Shake Down the Thunder*, 151–52; Allison Danzig, "Players of the Game," *NYT*, 10 December 1929; Rockne, "What Thrills a Coach."

11. Ed Danforth, "Mawnin'!," *AC*, 24 October 1929; Warner, "What's the Matter with Football?"; Rockne quoted in Sperber, *Shake Down the Thunder*, 152; Howard Wolf, "Grid Sport Going Sissy, Dietz Says," *OWH*, 8 November 1931.

12. Joe Boyd, "Listening Post," *Atlanta Journal*, 10 January 1953; Ed Danforth, "An Ear to the Ground," *Atlanta Journal*, 12 January 1953; Ned Cronin, "Cronin's Corner," *LAT*, 22 May and 10 July 1956.

13. See "Twenty-seven Deaths"; "Football's Death Roll"; "Football Deaths"; Trevor, "Brutal Truth"; "Football Casualties"; "Making Football Safe for Men on the Gridiron"; "Football and Health"; and Dooley, "Making Football Safe."

14. Braven Dyer, "Second-Half Burst Ruins Cal, 21–14," *LAT*, 21 October 1951; Paul Zimmerman, "Sport Scripts," *LAT*, 22 October 1951.

15. Guimond discusses *Life*'s "heavy use of innuendo" in *American Photography*, 153.

16. "Rough Day in Berkeley."

17. Braven Dyer, "Sports Parade," *LAT*, 30 October 1951; Paul Zimmerman, "Sport Scripts," *LAT*, 14 December 1951.

18. Rice, "Were the Old-Timers Best?"; Grange with Fay, "I Couldn't Make the Varsity Today"; Heffelfinger with Trevor, "Nobody Put Me on My Back" and "Football's Golden Age"; Hopper, "We Really Played Football in the Gay Nineties."

19. Arthur Daley, "Sports of the Times," *NYT*, 12 December 1938, 13 December 1953, 13 November 1955, 11 October 1956.

20. Arthur Daley, "Sports of the Times," *NYT*, 2 November and 3 November 1958.

21. Edward Prell, "The Story of the Big Bad Bears," *CT*, 21–28 October 1941.

22. See, for example, Donovan, *Fatso*; Huff with Shapiro, *Tough Stuff*; and Leuthner, *Iron Men*.

23. O'Neil, "Game Day" (*SEP*, 1939).

24. Freeman, "Right of Conquest" (*Collier's*, 1939).

25. Sedgwick, *Between Men* and *Epistemology of the Closet*.

26. See the "Locker Room" department for Second October Number, 1935; First December Number, 1935; Second November Number, 1936; First December Number, 1938, and Second December Number, 1938.

27. The "inferiority complex" was popularized in the late 1920s. The *Reader's Guide to Periodical Literature* listed "complexes" as a subject heading beginning in 1925, with articles both earnestly explaining and mocking the concept (such articles ended by 1940). See, for example, Lane, "Your Child and That Fashionable Complex"; and "Fighting Our Inferiority Complex." Some fifteen tales of inferiority and other complexes appeared in *Sport Story* between 1929 and 1937. In the stories, the hero does not learn to compensate for deficiencies, as the advice literature counseled, but discovers that he is actually *superior*, not inferior, after all.

28. See Pfister, "Glamorizing the Psychological"; and O'Donnell, *Origins of Behaviorism.*

29. Carleton, "End Run"; Whitfield, "Angel Face"; Sand, "Graceful"; Ford, "Pigskin Feud."

30. See Cutter, "Ken Tries for Quarter"; Elderdice, "Sentimental Barth"; Horton, "Drop-Kicker"; Bryan, "Nice Boy!," "Record Wreckers," and "Touchdown Apollo"; Carleton, "Fiddler from Philly"; Scholz, "Prima Donnas" and "Gridiron Dancer"; and Ford, "China Doll" and "Profile Guy."

31. On the cult of primitivism see, for example, Torgovnick, *Gone Primitive;* and Pfister, "Glamorizing the Psychological," 183.

32. Mumford, "Significance of Herman Melville."

33. Mumford, *Technics and Civilization,* 303.

34. Fitzgerald, "The Bowl" (*SEP,* 1928), Marquand, "Fourth Down" (*SEP,* 1932); Shaw, "Eighty-Yard Run." William Brent's "Yesterday's Heroes" (*SEP,* 1939; film, 1940) and the 1939 film, *Hero for a Day,* also addressed the plight of the former football star.

35. Burr, "Wolf Man"; Stone, "'Beef'" and "'Taters' Byers—Freshman."

36. Stone, "'Beef'"; Moses, "Thanksgiving Throwback"; Scholz, "Gridiron Dancer."

37. See Stone, "'Tater' Byers—Freshman"; Ferguson, "Runcie's Cowardice"; Carleton, "Last White Line," "Straight-Armed," and "Bouncing Back"; Dorsett, "Taskman"; Whitfield, "Fight"; Chandler, "Five-yard Line"; Brand, "Thunderbolt"; Ford, "Pigskin Pins" and "Lorenzo the Great."

38. Guttman, *Erotic in Sports,* 6, 64.

39. Titus, "Man Who Made 'Em Block."

40. Scholz, "Hero Yell"; Ford, "Key Man" and "Lorenzo the Great." Various versions of this male sentimentalism are conspicuous in some thirty stories.

41. Tompkins, *West of Everything,* 50. See also Schwenger, *Phallic Critiques,* 44–45; and Naifeh and Smith, *Why Can't Men Open Up?*

42. Scholz, "Flanders Backs the Line."

43. Kimmel, *Manhood in America,* 204.

44. Williams, "Scapegoat" (*SEP,* 1925).

45. Mrs. Conerly's articles appeared weekly through the 1960 football season, distributed by the North American Newspaper Alliance. The *New York Times* is among the papers that carried them. For the articles on kids' football and by coaches' wives, see Chapter 5, notes 17 and 54. See also Black, "Football Wife," a woman's account

of how she coped with her husband's passion for the "boring spectacle" of football; along with Philips and Wood, *Hold 'Em, Girls!*, and Watters, *Football for Feminine Fans,* football primers for women.

46. *American Pathé News,* 28 October 1922; 27 October 1927; and 17 October 1928.

47. See "She Powders Her Nose Wherever She Goes," *American Weekly,* in *PO,* 11 December 1938; "Gridiron Glamor," *NYDN,* 10 November 1940; "Girls of Miami U. in Ohio Play Rouge Bowl Game," *NYT,* 24 November 1946; "Cutes Meet Beauts in Waco Bowl," *DMN,* 12 December 1949; "Powder Bowl Foes in Shape for Annual Gridiron Tussle," *DMN,* 10 December 1950; "Who Says They're the Weaker Sex?" *PO,* 21 December 1953; Joe Goulden, "A Hank of Hair; Football?" *DMN,* 29 November 1959, 1; "Girls on the Grid"; and "Coed Football, Iowa Style."

48. Garber, *Vested Interests.*

49. "College Girls Take Up Football," *DMN,* 14 December 1924.

50. On the history of women's athletics, see Cahn, *Coming On Strong.*

51. A photograph on the 3 December 1927 cover of the *Mid-Week Pictorial,* published by the *New York Times,* introduced readers to "Captain La Ferve of the Women's Eleven of Colorado Teachers College" in the familiar pose of the punter who has just gotten off a kick. The caption teasingly announced "A New Field for Feminine Prowess: Now We Have the Girl of the Gridiron." A year earlier, the *Mid-Week Pictorial* had run a photo of another female punter on its 2 December cover, but this one was a powder bowl-type gimmick, the "player" a dancer and the daughter of a naval commander, shown inspiring the Navy team "by Donning Its Football Togs and Giving a Demonstration of High Kicking." A similar photo in the *Chicago Herald and Examiner,* 26 October 1925, showed a former Follies girl demonstrating her punting technique for a Creighton University football player.

52. Cayleff, *Babe,* 42, 109–10, 260, 309; "What a Babe!"; Farmer, "Babe Is a Lady Now."

53. "Powder Football," *News of the Day,* 26 January 1955. Paramount also covered this sorority game on 1 February 1955. For other newsreel powder bowls, see *Fox Movietone News,* 7 December 1931, 4 November 1932, 21 November 1946, 14 November 1947, 7 December 1950, and 14 January 1952; and *News of the Day,* 4 February 1948; and 2 December 1950. *Fox Movietone News* also did a piece, "Women War Workers Play Football" (21 December 1943).

54. "Girl, 14, Regular Center, Helps Her Team Triumph," *Louisville Courier-Journal,* 5 November 1935; "Girl Football Player Not Soft," *Boston Post,* 6 November 1935; Jack Munhall, "Co-ed Determined to Kick Despite Faculty 'No,'" *Washington Post,* 4 November 1937; "There Really Shouldn't Be a Kicker Here," *PO,* 1 November 1937; "Girl Football Star," *New York Daily Mirror,* 29 November 1938; "Alabama High Lets Girl Kick for Point after Touchdown," *OWH,* 17 November 1939; John Hix, "Strange As It Seems," *Hays Daily News,* 1 January 1940.

55. "Girl Tackle to Get Big Chance Friday," *DMN,* 13 November 1947; William C. Barnard, "Frankie Plays in Rough Tilt but Her Efforts Aren't Enough," *DMN,* 15 November 1947; Reinert and Winningham, *Rites of Fall,* 78.

56. "Girls Ready for Grid Game," *Toledo News-Bee,* 25 October 1934. The game

in Dayton had been played (on 21 October) and the Toledo game was to be played on Sunday (28 October), with the Newport and Detroit games already scheduled, for 4 and 11 November, respectively. Unfortunately, the microfilm of the *News-Bee* is missing the issues for 27–31 October, so whether the 28 October game received any coverage cannot be known. Universal's program notes for its story on 17 September describe a "struggle for the 1934 championship," but there is no indication that more than two teams were involved. See also "Girls' Eleven Opens Season," *Universal Newspaper Newsreel*, 17 September 1934; and "Girls' Football Team in East & West Battle," *News of the Day*, 5 November 1934. I found nothing in the *Toledo Blade*, the *Detroit Free Press*, or three Chicago newspapers, the *Tribune*, the *Herald and Examiner*, and the *Daily News*.

57. Johnson, *When Women Played Hardball*; LeCompte, *Girls of the Rodeo*, 114–23.

58. "Yea Team! No Sissies Here!" *Chicago Herald-American*, 25 June 1941; "A New Type of Football—but the Same Old Sort of Shiner," *Chicago Daily News*, 27 June 1941; "Mudders Day for Grid Gals," *Chicago Herald-American*, 29 June 1941. *Fox Movietone News* also ran a piece, "Women's Football Practice," on 6 June 1941, undoubtedly on these teams.

59. "Girls Use Irish Shift" and "Fancy Punting," *Los Angeles Evening Herald and Express*, 17 October and 18 October 1939; "Putting Some Oomph . . . ," *Los Angeles Daily News*, 18 October 1939.

60. Dick Hyland, "Behind the Line," *LAT*, 15 October 1939.

61. "Girls in Powder Bowl Grid Game; Play Rough" (AP), *AC*, 16 October 1939; "Fair Grid Teams Mix at Gilmore," *LAT*, 22 October 1939; and "Girlish Gridders," 1 November 1939; "DeSoto Girls in Victory," 2 November 1939; "Doerr's 'Kid Sister,'" 8 November 1939; "Ike Referees Girls," 8 November 1939; "Girls to Toss 'Em," 9 November 1939; and "Girl Grid Stars in Gilmore Game," *Los Angeles Evening Herald and Express*, 10 November 1939. For more wire-service pieces, see "Grid Gals in New Kind of Huddle," *Dziennik Chicagoski*, 24 October 1939; "Ladies of Gridiron," *San Francisco Chronicle*, 1 November 1939; "Girlies Try Mixing Football 'n Lipstick," *Seattle Post-Intelligencer*, 1 November 1939; and "Help! Lady Gridders Hurt," *Muncie Morning Star*, 17 November 1939.

62. "Girl Gridders Invade Football Realm," *American Pathé News*, 2 November 1939.

63. "Girls' Football." The *Life* text refers to similar games played in 1938.

Bibliography

Newspaper articles fully cited in the notes are not included here, nor are the short stories and serials from the *Saturday Evening Post* and *Collier's* from 1920 to 1960 that are listed chronologically in Appendix C.

NEWSPAPERS
Albany Herald (Georgia)
American Hebrew (New York)
American Indian (Tulsa)
Amerikos Lietuvis (Worcester, Massachusetts)
Atlanta Constitution
Atlanta Daily World
Atlanta Journal
Atlantis (New York)
Baltimore Afro-American
Biloxi-Gulfport Daily Herald
Birmingham News
Birmingham Post
Birmingham Post-Herald
B'nai B'rith Messenger (Los Angeles)
Boston Evening Transcript
Boston Globe
Boston Herald
Boston Post
Canton Evening Repository (Ohio)
Carlisle Arrow (Pennsylvania)
Catholic Herald Citizen (Milwaukee)
Catholic News (New York)
Catholic Review (Baltimore)
Catholic Standard and Times (Philadelphia)
Catholic Worker (New York)
Champion (New York)
Champion Labor Monthly (New York)
Champion of Youth (New York)
Charleston News and Courier (South Carolina)
Chicago Daily News
Chicago Defender
Chicago Herald-American
Chicago Herald and Examiner

Chicago Sun-Times
Chicago Times
Chicago Tribune
Class Struggle (New York)
Corriere d'America (New York)
Daily Worker (New York)
Dallas Morning News
Denni Hlasatel (Chicago)
Detroit Free Press
Detroit Jewish Chronicle
Detroit News
Draugas (Chicago)
Dziennik Chicagoski (Chicago)
Dziennik Polski (Detroit)
Dziennik Zjednoczenia (Chicago)
Dziennik Zwiazkowy (Chicago)
Ethnikos Keryx (New York)
Gaelic American (New York)
Gwiazda Zachodu (Omaha)
Hays Daily News (Kansas)
Helenikos Typos (Chicago)
Indian Helper (Carlisle, Pennsylvania)
Indian Leader (Haskell, Kansas)
Industrial Unionist (New York)
Industrial Worker (Seattle)
Irish World and American Industrial Liberator (New York)
L'Italia (Chicago)
Jackson Daily News (Mississippi)
Jednota (Cleveland)
Jewish Advocate (Boston)
Jewish Daily Bulletin (New York)
Jewish Independent (Cleveland)
Jewish Times (Philadelphia)
Kuryer Polski (Milwaukee)
Labor Advocate (Nashville)
Labor Age (New York)

Labor Newdealer (Portland, Oregon)
Labor News (Omaha)
Labor World (Duluth)
Labor World (San Francisco)
Labor World (Spokane)
Lincoln Star (Nebraska)
Los Angeles Daily News
Los Angeles Evening Herald
Los Angeles Evening Herald and Express
Los Angeles Sentinel
Los Angeles Times
Louisville Courier-Journal
Michigan Catholic (Detroit)
Militant (New York)
Milwaukee Leader
Minneapolis Spokesman
Minneapolis Tribune
Monitor (San Francisco)
Muncie Morning News (Indiana)
Nacodoches Daily Sentinel
Narod Polski (Chicago)
Nashville Banner
New Masses (New York)
New Orleans Times-Picayune
New World (Chicago)
New York American
New York Amsterdam News
New York Daily Mirror
New York Daily News
New Yorker Staats-Zeitung
New York Evening Journal
New York Herald Tribune
New York Journal-American
New York Post
New York Sun
New York Telegram
New York Times
New York World
New York World-Telegram
Nowy Swiat (New York)
Omaha-Posten
Omaha World-Herald
Oregon Labor Press (Portland)
Our Sunday Visitor (Fort Wayne, Indiana)

Philadelphia Record
Pilot (Boston)
Pittsburczanin (Pittsburgh)
Pittsburgh Catholic
Pittsburgh Courier
Pittsburgh Press
Portland Oregonian
Progresso Italiano, Il (New York)
Raleigh News and Observer (North Carolina)
Red Man (Carlisle, Pennsylvania)
Register (Kansas City)
Richmond Times-Dispatch
San Francisco Chronicle
San Francisco Examiner
Savannah Morning News (Georgia)
Seattle Post-Intelligencer
Seattle Union Record
Sentinel (Chicago)
Skandinaven (Chicago)
Student Advocate (New York)
Student Review (New York)
Svornost (Chicago)
Szabadsag (Cleveland)
Tablet (Brooklyn)
Tacoma Labor Advocate (Washington)
Tidings (Los Angeles)
Toledo Blade
Toledo News-Bee
Tomahawk (White Earth, Minnesota)
Tribuna Italiana d'America, La (Detroit)
Twin-City Herald (Minneapolis)
Union Herald (Raleigh, North Carolina)
Unionist (Omaha)
Union Labor Record (Philadelphia)
Voce del Popolo, La (Detroit)
Vorvärts (New York)
Washington Post
Weekly People (New York)
Western Worker (San Francisco)
Westliche Post (St. Louis)
Workers Age (New York)
Young Communist Review (New York)
Young Worker (New York)

BOOKS AND ARTICLES

Adamic, Louis. *My America, 1928–1938.* New York: Harper & Brothers, 1938.

Adams, David Wallace. *Education for Extinction: American Indians and the Boarding School Experience, 1875–1928.* Lawrence: University Press of Kansas, 1995.

"Addison Hawthorne." *Ebony,* October 1952.

Ahern, Helen. "Gridiron Hearts." *Thrilling Love,* December 1934.

————. "Those Double Dates." *Love Fiction Monthly,* October 1939.

Alfred Politz Research, Inc., *A Study of Four Media, Their Accumulative and Repeat Audiences.* New York: n.p., 1953.

"Alonzo 'Jake' Gaither." *Ebony,* November 1960.

"Al Pollard—High School Football Prize." *Look,* 14 October 1946.

"Amarillo's Golden Sandies." *Look,* 16 November 1943.

American Film Institute Catalogue of Motion Pictures Produced in the United States. 7 vols. Berkeley: University of California Press, 1971–1988.

Anderson, Jackson M. *Industrial Recreation: A Guide to Its Organization and Administration.* New York: McGraw-Hill, 1955.

Anderson, Ruth. "Cupid's Forward Pass." *Popular Love,* January 1941.

Andrews, Donald S. "The G.I. Bill and College Football: The Birth of a Spectator Sport." *Journal of Physical Education, Recreation and Dance* 55 (September 1984): 23–26.

Andrews, Maurice T. "Panski of the Irish." *Sport Story,* 10 December 1934.

Archeacon, Thomas J. *Becoming American: An Ethnic History.* New York: Free Press, 1983.

"Are Tabloid Newspapers a Menace?" *Forum* 77 (April 1927): 485–501.

Arnett, Jon, with Melvin Durslag. "Why Should We Be Scapegoats?" *Look,* 26 November 1957.

Ashe, Arthur. *A Hard Road to Glory: A History of the African-American Athlete.* 3 vols. New York: Warner, 1988.

Bach, Julian, Jr. "Hold 'Em Husing!" *Literary Digest,* 6 November 1937.

Baechlin, Peter, and Maurice Muller-Strauss. *Newsreels across the World.* Paris: UNESCO, 1952.

Banner, Lois W. *American Beauty.* New York: Alfred A. Knopf, 1983.

Banning, William Peck. *Commercial Broadcasting Pioneer: The WEAF Experiment, 1922–1926.* Cambridge, Mass.: Harvard University Press, 1946.

Barber, Red. *The Broadcasters.* New York: Dial, 1970.

Barnes, B. L. "Catholic Press, World Survey—20th-Century Newspapers." In *New Catholic Encyclopedia,* 3:323–25. New York: McGraw-Hill, 1967.

"Baseball and Football." *Nation,* 1 December 1920.

"Beauty and the Bowl." *Sports Illustrated,* 23 December 1957.

Becker, Stephen. *Comic Art in America: A Social History of the Funnies, the Political Cartoons, Magazine Humor, Sporting Cartoons and Animated Cartoons.* New York: Simon & Schuster, 1959.

Bee, Clair. *Freshman Quarterback.* New York: Grosset & Dunlap, 1952.

————. *Touchdown Pass.* New York: Grosset & Dunlap, 1948.

Beetle, David H. "The Secret All-American." *Saturday Evening Post,* 17 October 1942.

Behee, John. *Hail to the Victors! Black Athletes at the University of Michigan.* Adrian, Mich.: Swenk-Tuttle Press, 1974.

Bent, Silas. *Ballyhoo: The Voice of the Press.* New York: Boni and Liveright, 1927.

Berelson, Bernard, and Patricia J. Salter. "Majority and Minority Americans: An Analysis of Magazine Fiction." In *Mass Culture: The Popular Arts in America,* ed. Bernard Rosenberg and David Manning White, 235–51. Glencoe, Ill.: Free Press, 1957.

Berges, Marshall. *The Life and Times of Los Angeles: A Newspaper, a Family, and a City.* New York: Atheneum, 1984.

Berkhofer, Robert F., Jr. *The White Man's Indian: Images of the American Indian from Columbus to the Present.* New York: Alfred A. Knopf, 1978.

Berkow, Ira. *Red: A Biography of Red Smith.* New York: Times Books, 1986.

Bessie, Simon Michael. *Jazz Journalism: The Story of the Tabloid Newspapers.* 1938. Reprint, New York Russell & Russell, 1969.

Best, James J. *American Popular Illustration: A Reference Guide.* Westport, Conn.: Greenwood, 1984.

Betz, Betty. "How to Behave on Your First Football Weekend." *Cosmopolitan,* October 1950.

Biemiller, Carl L. "Football Town." *Holiday,* November 1949.

"Big Daddy from Baltimore, A." *Life,* 24 October 1959.

"Big Time Football at Florida A. and M." *Ebony,* January 1956.

"Bill Stern Broadcasts a Harvard Football Game." *Life,* 21 November 1938.

"Bill Stern, Top NBC Announcer, Picks His 1939 All-America Team." *Life,* 20 November 1939.

Bissinger, H. G. *Friday Night Lights: A Town, a Team, and a Dream.* Reading, Mass.: Addison-Wesley, 1990.

Bisher, Furman. "College Football's Public Enemy No. 1." *Sport,* November 1958.

Black, Virginia. "Football Wife." *Saturday Evening Post,* 21 November 1936.

Blaik, Col. Earl H. (Red), with Tim Cohane. "Red Blaik Speaks." *Look,* 27 October–24 November 1959.

"Bleachers." *Sport Story,* 22 October 1926.

"Bleachers." *Sport Story,* First December Number, 1929.

Bliven, Bruce. "Bleeding Kansas and Points West." *New Republic,* 4 December 1935.

Bloom, John. "'There Is Madness in the Air': The 1926 Haskell Homecoming and Popular Representations of Sports in Federal Indian Boarding Schools." In *Dressing in Feathers: The Construction of the Indian in American Popular Culture,* ed. S. Elizabeth Bird, 97–110. Boulder, Colo.: Westview Press, 1996.

———. *To Show What an Indian Can Do: Sports at Native American Boarding Schools.* Minneapolis: University of Minnesota Press, 2000.

Bogle, Donald. *Toms, Coons, Mulattoes, Mammies, and Bucks: An Interpretetive History of Blacks in American Films.* New Expanded Edition. New York: Continuum, 1989.

Booth, Albie. "Albie Booth Says Larry Kelley Is Wrong about Ivy League
Football." *Look,* 7 November 1939.

Boskin, Joseph. *Sambo: The Rise & Demise of an American Jester.* New York: Oxford
University Press, 1986.

Brammell, P. Roy. *Intramural and Interscholastic Athletics,* Bulletin, 1932, No. 17,
Monograph No. 27. Washington, D.C.: United States Department of Education,
1933.

Brand, Max. "Thunderbolt." *Sport Story,* 25 October–25 November 1932.

Brennan, Mrs. Terry. "A Wife's View of Notre Dame Football." *Look,* 4 October
1955.

Breslin, Jimmy. "The Town That Spawns Athletes." *Collier's,* 15 October 1955.

Britz, Kevin. "Of Football and Frontiers: The Meaning of Bronko Nagurski."
Journal of Sport History 20 (Summer 1993): 101–26.

Broeg, Bob. "Oil Makes the Hurricane Roar." *Saturday Evening Post,* 24 November
1945.

Broun, Heywood. "It Seems to Heywood Broun." *Nation,* 30 November 1927.

Broun, Heywood Hale. "'Color' in Football." *Catholic Digest* 4 (November 1939):
9–10.

Brown, Jim. "How I Play Fullback." *Sports Illustrated,* 26 September 1960.

Brown, Joe David. "Babes, Brutes and Ole Miss." *Sports Illustrated,* 19 September
1960.

Brown, Paul R., as told to Harry T. Paxton. "I Call the Plays for the Browns."
Saturday Evening Post, 12 December 1953.

Brown, Warren. *Rockne.* Chicago: Reilly and Lee, 1931.

"Brown's Run at Records." *Life,* 17 November 1958.

Bryan, Robert N. "Nice Boy!" *Sport Story,* 10 March 1933.

———. "Record Wreckers." *Sport Story,* 10 October–25 November 1933.

———. "The Touchdown Apollo." *Sport Story,* Second November Number,
1935–First January Number, 1936.

Burke, Martin J. *The Conundrum of Class: Public Discourse on the Social Order in
America.* Chicago: University of Chicago Press, 1995.

Burr, Harold C. "The Wolf Man." *Sport Story,* 8 October 1923.

Burris, Mrs. Paul, as told to Geraldine McClung. "I'm a Football Mother." *Saturday
Evening Post,* 19 October 1957.

Burton, Lewis. "The Truth about Charlie Justice." *Sport,* November 1949.

Buxton, Frank, and Bill Owen. *The Big Broadcast, 1920–1950.* New York: Viking,
1972.

Byers, Walter, with Charles Hammer. *Unsportsmanlike Conduct: Exploiting College
Athletes.* Ann Arbor: University of Michigan Press, 1995.

Cagle, Christian K. "Football as a Vocation." *Outlook and Independent,* 10 December
1930.

Cahn, Susan K. *Coming on Strong: Gender and Sexuality in Twentieth-Century Women's
Sport.* New York: Free Press, 1994.

Caldwell, Bruce. "After the Ball Is Over." *Saturday Evening Post,* 10 December 1938.

Camerer, Dave. "The Gladiators." *Esquire,* November 1950.

Camp, Walter. "Good Little Man." *Collier's,* 22 November 1930.

———. "Walter Camp's Sports Page." *Collier's,* 17 November 1923.

Cannon, Ralph. *Grid Star.* Chicago: Reilly & Lee, 1933.

———. "I'd Die for Dear Old Dollars!" *Esquire,* January 1936.

Caponi, Gena Dagel, ed. *Signifyin(g), Sanctifyin', & Slam Dunking: A Reader in African American Expressive Culture.* Amherst: University of Massachusetts Press, 1999.

Carideo, Frank. "Rockne's Quarterbacks." *Saturday Evening Post,* 14 November 1931.

Carleton, Warren Elliot. "The Bouncing Back." *Sport Story,* 25 February 1934.

———. "The End Run." *Sport Story,* 8 September 1924.

———. "The Fiddler from Philly." *Sport Story,* 25 October 1933.

———. "The Last White Line." *Sport Story,* 22 September 1925.

———. "Straight-Armed." *Sport Story,* 8 November 1926.

Carroll, John M. *Fritz Pollard: Pioneer in Racial Advancement.* Urbana: University of Illinois Press, 1992.

———. *Red Grange and the Rise of Modern Football.* Urbana: University of Illinois Press, 1999.

Carroll, Raymond G. "Alien Workers in America." *Saturday Evening Post,* 25 January 1936.

———. "Americans or Aliens First?" *Saturday Evening Post,* 11 April 1936.

Carver, Jess. "Fire with Fire." *Sport Story,* November 1940.

Cary, Lucian. "White Flannels." *Saturday Evening Post,* 27 June 1925.

Cason, Clarence E. "The Football Hero Rebels." *Nation,* 30 October 1929.

Cavallo, Dominick. *Muscles and Morals: Organized Playgrounds and Urban Reform, 1880–1920.* Philadelphia: University of Pennsylvania Press, 1981.

Cawelti, John G. *Apostles of the Self-Made Man.* Chicago: University of Chicago Press, 1965.

Cayleff, Susan E. *Babe: The Life and Legend of Babe Didrickson Zaharias.* Urbana: University of Illinois Press, 1995.

Centers, Richard. *The Psychology of Social Classes: A Study of Class Consciousness.* 1949. Reprint, New York: Russell & Russell, 1961.

Century of American Illustration, A. New York: Brooklyn Museum, 1972.

Chalk, Ocania. *Black College Football.* New York: Dodd, Mead, 1976.

———. *Pioneers of Black Sport: The Early Days of the Black Professional Athlete in Baseball, Basketball, Boxing, and Football.* New York: Dodd, Mead, 1975.

"Championship High-School Football." *Look,* 23 September 1952.

Chandler, Stedman. "The Five-yard Line." *Sport Story,* Second December Number, 1929.

Chapman, John. *Tell It to Sweeney: The Informal History of the New York Daily News.* 1961. Reprint, Westport, Conn.: Greenwood Press, 1977.

"Charlie Conerly: The Old Pro Grows Older." *Look,* 6 December 1960.

Chase, Stuart. "Play." In *Whither Mankind? A Panorama of Modern Civilization,* ed. Charles A. Beard, 332–53. New York: Longmans, Green, 1928.

"Cheering Co-eds." *Life,* 1 November 1937.

Cherry, Blair. "Why I Quit Coaching." *Saturday Evening Post,* 20 October 1951.

Chestochowski, Ben. *Gridiron Greats: A Century of Polish Americans in College Football.* New York: Hippocrene, 1997.

Child, Irvin L. *Italian or American? The Second Generation in Conflict.* New Haven, Conn.: Yale University Press, 1943.

Child, Richard Washburn. "Whose Country Is This?" *Saturday Evening Post,* 22 May 1926.

Clark, Kenneth S. "Everybody Up!" *Saturday Evening Post,* 12 November 1934.

Clasby, Dick. "I'll Take Harvard Football." *Saturday Evening Post,* 16 October 1954.

"Cleveland's Jim Brown: The Big Breakaway." *Look,* 24 November 1959.

Clowser, Jack. "42 Colleges Wanted Him." *Look,* 8 September 1942.

———. "Janowicz on the Auction Block." *Sport,* October 1949.

———. "Phooey on Popularity!" *Saturday Evening Post,* 12 November 1955.

"Coach's Tongue-Lashing That Sometimes Wins the Game, The." *Literary Digest,* 20 November 1926.

Cobbledick, Gordon. "The Cleveland Browns." *Sport,* November 1952.

"Coed Football, Iowa Style." *Sports Illustrated,* 27 October 1958.

Cohane, Tim. *Bypaths of Glory: A Sportswriter Looks Back.* New York: Harper & Row, 1963.

———. "College Football's Greatest Folly." *Look,* 15 November 1955.

———. "College Football Tragedy." *Look,* 11 November 1958.

———. "Gridiron Assassin." *Sport Story,* December 1940.

———. "How Maryland Became a Football Power." *Look,* 2 November 1954.

———. "Inside the West Coast Football Scandal." *Look,* 7 August 1956.

———. "Levi Jackson of Yale." *Look,* 25 October 1949.

———. "1957 Football Forecast." *Look,* 17 September 1957.

———. "Panther on the Prowl." *Look,* 16 October 1956.

———. "Uncle Lou Little, Football's Dale Carnegie." *Look,* 9 November 1948.

———. "Yale vs. Harvard: College Football's Last Stand." *Look,* 2 December 1952.

Cohn, Jan. *Creating America: George Horace Lorimer and the Saturday Evening Post.* Pittsburgh: University of Pittsburgh Press, 1989.

"College Football." *New Republic,* 19 October 1927.

"College Football Is a Racket." *Look,* 22 November 1938.

"Confessions of a Dirty Football Player." *Sport,* December 1955.

Conlin, Joseph R., ed. *The American Radical Press 1880–1960.* 2 vols. Westport, Conn.: Greenwood, 1974.

Considine, Bob. "Death on the Gridiron." *Good Housekeeping,* September 1936.

———. "No Holiday for Death." *Good Housekeeping,* October 1937.

Contemporary Authors, vols. 89–92. Detroit: Gale Research, 1980.

Continuing Study of Magazine Audiences; Report No. 8, August 15, 1946; The Geography of Reading. New York: Time, Inc., 1946.

Continuing Study of Newspaper Reading: 100-Study Summary. New York: Advertising Research Foundation, 1946.

Continuing Study of Newspaper Reading: 138-Study Summary. New York: Advertising Research Foundation, 1951.

Cooper, Emmanuel. *The Sexual Perspective: Homosexuality and Art in the Last 100 Years in the West.* London: Routledge & Kegan Paul, 1986.

Corber, Robert J. *Homosexuality in Cold War America: Resistance and the Crisis of Masculinity.* Durham, N.C.: Duke University Press, 1997.

Corum, Bill. *Off and Running.* New York: Henry Holt, 1959.

Costello, Al. "Wee Willie—Wow!" *Collier's,* 8 November 1941.

Cozens, Frederick W., and Florence Scovil Stumpf. *Sports in American Life.* Chicago: University of Chicago Press, 1953.

"Cradle of Pro Football Cheers for a Great High School Team, The." *Life,* 2 October 1939.

Cravath, Jeff, with Melvin Durslag. "The Hypocrisy of College Football." *Collier's,* 30 October 1953.

Crawford, Remsen. "Six Years of Immigrant Quotas." *Saturday Evening Post,* 29 October 1927.

————. "A Visitor on Business." *Saturday Evening Post,* 9 February 1929.

Crichton, Kyle. "Backs in Motion." *Collier's,* 2 December 1939.

————. "For Glory and for Keeps." *Collier's,* 14 October 1933.

————. "For Love and Money." *Collier's,* 1 December 1934.

————. "Good King Jim." *Collier's,* 14 November 1942.

————. "The Gospel According to Charlie." *Collier's,* 18 October 1947.

————. "I'll Take Both." *Collier's,* 15 October 1938.

————. "Mustang Magic." *Collier's,* 16 November 1934.

————. "Passing Fancy." *Collier's,* 11 November 1939.

————. "Pass Master." *Collier's,* 16 November 1946.

————. "Quick, Harlow, the Needle!" *Collier's,* 12 October 1935.

————. "Steaks and Punts." *Collier's,* 8 October 1938.

————. "Swivel Hips." *Collier's,* 12 October 1940.

————. "The Whambam Man." *Collier's,* 17 November 1945.

————. "Wolverine Express." *Collier's,* 29 November 1947.

Cripps, Thomas. *Slow Fade to Black: The Negro in American Film, 1900–1942.* New York: Oxford University Press, 1977.

Cronin, Mike, and David Mayall, eds. *Sporting Nationalisms: Identity, Ethnicty, Immigration and Assimilation.* Portland, Ore.: Frank Cass, 1998.

Crowley, Jim, as told to Arthur J. Daley. "Go in There and Fight!" *Collier's,* 5 December 1936.

Crowley, William R. "Man with a Horn." *Saturday Evening Post,* 6 November 1943.

Crozier, Ross L. "The Forlorn Fullback." *Boys' Life,* September 1960.

"Crusaders & Slaves." *Time,* 14 October 1946.

Cumming, Adelaide F. "A History of American Newsreels, 1927 to 1950." Ph.D. diss., New York University, 1966.

Cunningham, Bill. "Bringing 'Em Back to Life." *Collier's,* 18 November 1933.

————. "A Doctor Watches Football." *Collier's,* 22 October 1932.

————. "How to Build a Football Business." *Collier's,* 4 November 1933.

————. "The Man Who's Always Wrong." *Collier's,* 8 December 1934.

Curran, Henry H. "The New Immigrant." *Saturday Evening Post,* 15 August 1925.

———. "Smuggling Aliens." *Saturday Evening Post,* 31 January 1925.

Cutter, Robert Ahern. "Ken Tries for Quarter." *Sport Story,* 22 October 1927.

Dale, Edgar. *The Literature of Cinema.* New York: Macmillan, 1935.

Daley, Arthur. "The American Irish in Sports." *Recorder* 34 (1973): 95–103.

Danforth, Ed. "Flatfoot Frankie the Fireball." *Saturday Evening Post,* 10 October 1942.

———. "The South vs. the Sanity Code." *Sport,* November 1949.

Danielson, Michael N. *Home Team: Professional Sports and the American Metropolis.* Princeton, N.J.: Princeton University Press, 1997.

Dates, Janette L., and William Barlow. *Split Image: African Americans and the Mass Media,* 2d ed. Washington, D.C.: Howard University Press, 1993.

Davis, Timothy. "The Myth of the Superspade: The Persistence of Racism in College Athletics." *Fordham Urban Law Journal* 22 (1995): 615–98.

"Day of the Bowls Is Here, The." *Sports Illustrated,* 26 December 1955.

Deloria, Philip. "I Am of the Body." *South Atlantic Quarterly* 95 (Spring 1996): 321–38.

"Demoting the Half Gods of College." *Independent,* 22 October 1927.

Denney, James, Hollis Limprecht, and Howard Silber. *Go Big Red: The All-Time Story of the Cornhuskers!* Omaha, Neb.: Kratville Publications, 1967.

Detweiler, Frederick G. *The Negro Press in the United States.* Chicago: University of Chicago Press, 1922.

Devine, Tommy. "The Michigan State Construction Job." *Sport,* December 1953.

Dies, Martin. "The Immigration Crisis." *Saturday Evening Post,* 20 April 1935.

"Differences between Red and White Football Material, The." *Literary Digest,* 11 December 1920.

Dinan, John. *Sports in the Pulp Magazines.* Jefferson, N.C.: McFarland, 1998.

"Does Radio Cut the Football Gate?" *Literary Digest,* 16 July 1932.

Donovan, Arthur J. *Fatso: Football When Men Were Really Men.* New York: William Morrow, 1987.

Dooley, Edwin B. "How Dangerous Is Football?" *Parents' Magazine,* October 1933.

———. "Making Football Safe." *Woman's Home Companion,* November 1932.

Dorman, Robert L. *Revolt of the Provinces: The Regionalist Movement in America, 1920–1945.* Chapel Hill: University of North Carolina Press, 1993.

Dorsett, Edward A. "The Taskman." *Sport Story,* 22 September 1925.

Douglas, George H. *The Early Days of Radio Broadcasting.* Jefferson, N.C.: McFarland, 1987.

Doyle, Andrew. "'Causes Won, Not Lost': College Football and the Modernization of the American South." *International Journal of the History of Sport* 11 (1994): 231–51.

———. "Causes Won, Not Lost: Football and Southern Culture, 1892–1983." Ph.D. diss., Emory University, 1998.

———. "Foolish and Useless Sport: The Southern Evangelical Crusade against Intercollegiate Football." *Journal of Sport History* 24 (Fall 1997): 317–40.

———. "Turning the Tide: College Football and Southern Progressivism." *Southern Cultures* 3 (Fall 1997): 28–51.

"Dreams of Glory Come True." *Life*, 8 December 1952.

Drewry, John E., ed. *More Post Biographies: Articles of Enduring Interest about Famous Journalists and Journals and Other Subjects Journalistic.* Athens: University of Georgia Press, 1947.

Dunning, John. *On the Air: The Encyclopedia of Old-Time Radio.* New York: Oxford University Press, 1998.

Dunscomb, George. "*77.*" *College Humor*, October–December 1932 and January 1933.

———. "$6000 for a Touchdown!" *Saturday Evening Post*, 12 December 1936.

Durslag, Melvin. "Pro Football's Brat." *Collier's*, 4 September 1953.

"Eastern College Football's Big Giant and Little Giant." *Look*, 8 November 1960.

Edgar, Day. "All-Americanized." *Country Gentleman*, November 1933.

"Editor Steps Down, The." *Independent*, 5 November 1927.

Eisen, George, and David K. Wiggins, eds. *Ethnicity and Sport in North American History and Culture.* Westport, Conn.: Greenwood, 1994.

Elderdice, J. Raymond. "Sentimental Barth." *Sport Story*, First December Number, 1929.

Elkin, Stephen L. *City and Regime in the American Republic.* Chicago: University of Chicago Press, 1987.

Ellison, Ralph. *Shadow and Act.* New York: Random House, 1964.

Elson, Robert T. *Time, Inc.: The Intimate History of a Publishing Enterprise, 1923–1941.* New York: Atheneum, 1968.

———. *Time, Inc.: The Intimate History of a Publishing Enterprise, 1941–1960.* New York: Atheneum, 1973.

Elvay, Cylvia S. "Hero of Her Heart." *Popular Love*, November 1941.

Emery, Michael, and Edwin Emery. *The Press and America: An Interpretive History of the Mass Media*, 7th ed. Englewood Cliffs, N.J.: Prentice-Hall, 1992.

England, George Allan. "Through Uncle Sam's Back Door." *Saturday Evening Post*, 19 October 1929.

Epler, S. E. "Safer Football." *School and Society*, 31 July 1937.

———. "Six-man Eleven." *Scholastic*, 23 October 1937.

———. "Six-man Football." *Scholastic*, 29 October 1938.

"Evansville Express, The." *Look*, 22 September 1942.

Evensen, Bruce J. "Jazz Age Journalism's Battle over Professionalism, Circulation, and the Sports Page." *Journal of Sport History* 20 (Winter 1993): 229–46.

———. *When Dempsey Fought Tunney: Heroes, Hokum, and Storytelling in the Jazz Age.* Knoxville: University of Tennessee Press, 1996.

"Fans Go Ga-Ga over Pro Football." *Life*, 5 December 1960.

Farmer, Gene. "Babe Is a Lady Now." *Life*, 23 June 1947.

Fass, Paula S. *The Damned and the Beautiful: American Youth in the 1920's.* New York: Oxford University Press, 1977.

———. *Outside In: Minorities and the Transformation of American Education.* New York: Oxford University Press, 1989.

Fay, Bill. "Bingo Bingaman—Pro Football's Immovable Object." *Collier's*, 29 October 1954.

———. "Can't You Hear Them Calling Caroline?" *Collier's*, 1 October 1954.

———. "The Case for Rough Football." *Collier's*, 23 November 1956.

———. "Dixie's No. 1 Gridnaper." *Collier's*, 23 September 1950.

———. "Football Bombardier." *Collier's*, 17 October 1942.

———. "It's Hard-Ridin', Two-Gun Football, Pardner!" *Collier's*, 13 September 1952.

———. "King of the Football Forest." *Collier's*, 27 September 1952.

———. "The Meanest Man in Football." *Collier's*, 25 November 1950.

———. "The Pigskin Palookas." *Football Stories*, October 1942.

———. "The Play's the Thing." *Collier's*, 29 November 1954.

Ferguson, Charles W. *Pigskin*. Garden City, N.Y.: Doubleday, Doran, 1929.

Ferguson, W. B. M. "Runcie's Cowardice." *Sport Story*, 8 January 1925.

Fiedler, Leslie A. *No! In Thunder: Essays on Myth and Literature*. Boston: Beacon Press, 1960.

Fielding, Raymond. *The American Newsreel, 1911–1967*. Norman: University of Oklahoma Press, 1972.

"Fighting Irish Look Tough Again, The." *Life*, 29 September 1952.

"Fighting Our Inferiority Complex." *Literary Digest*, 11 June 1932.

"First All-American Iceman, The." *Literary Digest*, 15 November 1924.

"First Down for Yale." *Nation*, 15 June 1932.

Fish, Hamilton, Jr. "In Defense of Modern Football." *Saturday Evening Post*, 19 December 1925.

Fitch, George. "Ole Skjarsen's First Touchdown: A Siwash College Story." *Saturday Evening Post*, 6 November 1909.

"Football: Mid-season." *Time*, 11 November 1935.

"Football and Health." *Literary Digest*, 8 October 1932.

"Football as Our Greatest Popular Spectacle." *Literary Digest*, 2 December 1922.

"Football Casualties from a Medical Viewpoint." *Literary Digest*, 30 January 1932.

"Football Controversy, The." *American Mercury*, December 1939.

"Football Crazy Town." *Life*, 4 December 1950.

"Football Deaths: What Shall We Do to End Them?" *Literary Digest*, 26 December 1931.

"Football Fun . . . Alabama Boys and Girls Have Plenty." *Life*, 16 October 1939.

"Football History as Made by the Illinois Iceman." *Literary Digest*, 26 December 1925.

"Football Is a Farce." *Life*, 17 September 1951.

"Football's Death Roll." *Literary Digest*, 12 December 1931.

"Football's Girls." *Sports Illustrated*, 7 November 1955.

"Football's Most Democratic Team." *Ebony*, December 1955.

"Football Takes Over All Over." *Life*, 7 November 1955.

Ford, T. W. "Captain Crash." *Sport Story*, Second November Number, 1936–First January Number, 1937.

———. "China Doll." *Sport Story*, 10 April 1934.

———. "Cleat Warriors." *Sport Story*, First November Number, 1935.

———. "Gridiron Goats." *Sport Story*, First December Number, 1935.

———. "Heir to Touchdown." *Sport Story,* Second November Number, 1937.

———. "Key Man." *Sport Story,* November 1939.

———. "Lorenzo the Great." *Sport Story,* 25 November 1934–10 January 1935.

———. "Pigskin Feud." *Sport Story,* 25 October 1931.

———. "Pigskin Pins." *Sport Story,* 25 December 1932.

———. "The Pinch Kicker." *Sport Story,* 25 December 1933.

———. "Profile Guy." *Sport Story,* First March Number, 1937.

———. "Stadium Slaves." *Sport Story,* First December Number, 1937–Second January Number, 1938.

Foree, Kenneth, Jr. "Archangel and His Bible." *Saturday Evening Post,* 9 October 1937.

Foreman, Thomas Elton. "Discrimination against the Negro in American Athletics." M.A. thesis, Fresno State College, 1957.

Forsythe, Robert. "Block That Kick!" *New Masses,* 27 October 1936.

———. "Tragedy in the Yale Bowl." *New Masses,* 13 November 1934.

———. "The Wails of St. Mary's." *New Masses,* 29 October 1935.

"Fortune Survey: XXVII." *Fortune,* February 1940.

Fountain, Charles. *Sportswriter: The Life and Times of Grantland Rice.* New York: Oxford University Press, 1993.

Fox, Stephen. *Big Leagues: Professional Baseball, Football, and Basketball in National Memory.* New York: William Morrow, 1994.

Frank, Stanley. "The Big Ten's Surprise Package." *Saturday Evening Post,* 14 October 1950.

———. "Buddy Totes the Ball." *Collier's,* 23 November 1946.

———. "But Not So Dumb." *Sport Story,* First December Number, 1935.

———. "Easy Picking?: Betting on Football Games." *American Magazine,* October 1939.

———. "He Doesn't Have to Win." *Saturday Evening Post,* 16 November 1946.

———. "The Man Who Saved the Day for Yale." *Saturday Evening Post,* 10 October 1953.

———. *Sports Extra: Classics of Sports Writing.* New York: A. S. Barnes, 1944.

———. "The Woes of an All-American." *Saturday Evening Post,* 17 November 1951.

———. "You Have to Baby the Pros." *Saturday Evening Post,* 25 October 1947.

"Frank Gifford: Gridiron Glamour Boy." *Look,* 29 October 1957.

Frederickson, George M. *The Black Image in the White Mind: The Debate on Afro-American Character and Destiny, 1817–1914.* New York: Harper & Row, 1971.

Friedman, Benny. "The Professional Touch." *Collier's,* 15 October 1932.

Friedman, Benny, as told to John B. Kennedy. "Pro and Con." *Collier's,* 25 November 1933.

Friesell, William H. (Red). "I'm Always on the Spot." *Saturday Evening Post,* 14 October 1939.

Friesell, William H. (Red), with Robert H. Reed. "How to Watch a Football Game." *Saturday Evening Post,* 5 October 1940.

Fullerton, Hugh. "Yells That Win Games." *Liberty,* 11 October 1924.

Gallico, Paul. *Farewell to Sport.* New York: Alfred A. Knopf, 1938.

Gallup Poll, The: Public Opinion, 1935–1971. 3 vols. New York: Random House, 1972.

Gantner, John. "Fighting Coach." *Boys' Life,* September–December 1951.

Garber, Marjorie. *Vested Interests: Cross-Dressing and Cultural Anxiety.* New York: Routledge, 1992.

Garis, Roy L. "Lest Immigration Restriction Fail." *Saturday Evening Post,* 10 October 1925.

Garrison, Wilton. "Fun-Loving Frank from Dixie." *Saturday Evening Post,* 29 October 1949.

Garth, David. "Battling Sixteen." *Sport Story,* 15 November 1933–10 January 1934.

———. "The Kid Brother Was No Half Back." *Sport Story,* 25 February 1933.

———. "Third Alarm Strategy." *Sport Story,* 10 February 1934.

Gems, Gerald R. "The Prep Bowl: Football and Religious Acculturation in Chicago, 1927–1963." *Journal of Sport History* 23 (Fall 1996): 284–302.

———. *The Windy City Wars: Labor, Leisure, and Sport in the Making of Chicago.* Lanham, Md.: Scarecrow Press, 1997.

George, Nelson. *Elevating the Game: Black Men and Basketball.* New York: HarperCollins, 1992.

Gevinson, Alan, ed. *Within Our Gates: Ethnicity in American Feature Films, 1911–1960.* Berkeley: University of California Press, 1997.

Gifford, James. *Dayneford's Library: American Homosexual Writing, 1900–1913.* Amherst: University of Massachusetts Press, 1995.

Gilmore, Al-Tony. *Bad Nigger! The National Impact of Jack Johnson.* Port Washington, N.Y.: Kennikat Press, 1975.

"Girls' Football." *Life,* 13 November 1939.

"Girls on the Grid." *Sports Illustrated,* 22 November 1954.

Gleason, William (Red). "The Merry Maestro of Michigan State." *Saturday Evening Post,* 17 November 1956.

Gleason, William A. *The Leisure Ethic: Work and Play in American Literature, 1840–1940.* Stanford, Calif.: Stanford University Press, 1999.

Glickman, Marty, with Stan Isaacs. *The Fastest Kid on the Block: The Marty Glickman Story.* Syracuse, N.Y.: Syracuse University Press, 1996.

Goebel, Margaret Callam. "I Cheer the Referee." *Saturday Evening Post,* 28 November 1942.

"Golden Goal Posts." *Liberty,* 19 October 1935.

Going, Clayton. "He Always Says 'We'll Win.'" *Saturday Evening Post,* 27 October 1956.

Goldsmith, Alfred N., and Austin C. Lescarboura. *This Thing Called Broadcasting.* New York: Henry Holt, 1930.

Goldstein, Richard. *Ivy League Autumns: An Illustrated History of Football's Grand Old Rivalries.* New York: St. Martin's, 1996.

Gonzales, Arturo F., Jr. "The First College Cheer." *American Magazine,* November 1956.

"Good Time in the Small Time." *Life,* 24 November 1958.

Grafton, Samuel. "A Million Dollars for Football!" *North American Review,* November 1928.

Graham, Frank. "Bantam Football: Little Fellows Play, Too, in This Northeastern Ohio League." *Look,* 17 October 1944.

Graham, Jay C. "Climax Game." *Sport Story,* November 1939–January 1940.

Graham, Otto, as told to Harry T. Paxton. "I'm Through with Football." *Saturday Evening Post,* 6 October 1956.

Grahame, Arthur. "How Carnegie Tech Plays Football." *Sport Story,* First December Number, 1930.

Grange, Red. *The Red Grange Story: An Autobiography, as Told to Ira Morton.* Urbana: University of Illinois Press, 1993.

Grange, Red, with Bill Fay. "I Couldn't Make the Varsity Today." *Collier's,* 25 October 1952.

Grange, Harold, with George Dunscomb. "The College Game Is Easier." *Saturday Evening Post,* 5 November 1932.

———. "The Easy Way to Score?" *Saturday Evening Post,* 28 October 1933.

———. "Future Football." *Saturday Evening Post,* 20 October 1934.

———. "Little Things Make Big Touchdowns." *Saturday Evening Post,* 9 November 1935.

———. "Lo! The Poor Tackle." *Saturday Evening Post,* 8 October 1932.

———. "Outguessing Them." *Saturday Evening Post,* 25 November 1933.

Grant, D. C. (Chet). "They All Coach at Wabash." *Saturday Evening Post,* 15 November 1941.

Grant, Madison. *The Passing of the Great Race.* Rev. ed. New York: Charles Scribner's Sons, 1918.

"Great Panthers Spring from Tower of Learning." *Life,* 14 November 1938.

Greenfield, Thomas Allen. *Radio: A Reference Guide.* Westport, Conn.: Greenwood, 1989.

Greenwald, Sanford E. "You Can't Outguess the Quarterback." *International Photographer,* November 1949.

"Greetings to Our Victims in Play-off." *Life,* 14 December 1959.

Grieve, Andrew W. "Should Your Boy Play Football?" *Parents' Magazine,* October 1956.

Grimsley, Will. "Football's Craftiest Recruiter." *Saturday Evening Post,* 10 November 1956.

Griswold, Robert L. *Fatherhood in America: A History.* New York: Basic Books, 1993.

———. "The 'Flabby American,' the Body, and the Cold War." In *A Shared Experience: Men, Women, and the History of Gender,* ed. Laura McCall and Donald Yacovone, 323–48. New York: New York University Press, 1998.

Gross, Milton. "All-Around Jimmy Brown." *Saturday Evening Post,* 22 November 1958.

Group, Don, as told to Harry T. Paxton. "I'm Through with High-School Football." *Saturday Evening Post,* 11 October 1952.

Guimond, James. *American Photography and the American Dream.* Chapel Hill: University of North Carolina Press, 1991.

Guthrie, Very Rev. Hunter, S.J. "No More Football for Us!" *Saturday Evening Post,* 13 October 1951.

Guttman, Allen. *The Erotic in Sports.* New York: Columbia University Press, 1996.

"Hail, King Football!" (in "From the Bleachers"). *Sport Story,* 10 November 1932.

Halas, George, and George Dunscomb. "Hold What Line?" *Saturday Evening Post,* 2 December 1939.

Halberstam, David. *The Fifties.* New York: Villard, 1993.

Hall, Royal. "Sixty-Minute Man." *Sport Story,* 10 December 1931.

Handlin, Oscar. *The Uprooted.* 2d ed. Boston: Atlantic Monthly Press, 1973.

Hanson, Mary Ellen. *Go! Fight! Win! Cheerleading in American Culture.* Bowling Green, Ohio: Bowling Green State University Popular Press, 1995.

"Happy Moods of Football, The." *Sports Illustrated,* 9 November 1959.

Hardy, Stephen. *How Boston Played: Sport, Recreation, and Community, 1865–1915.* Boston: Northeastern University Press, 1982.

―――. "Sport in Urbanizing America: A Historical Review." *Journal of Urban History* 23 (September 1997): 675–708.

Harper, William A. *How You Played the Game: The Life of Grantland Rice.* Columbia: University of Missouri Press, 1999.

Harris, Reed. *King Football: The Vulgarization of the American College.* New York: Vanguard Press, 1932.

Harron, Robert. *Rockne, Idol of American Football.* New York: A. L. Burt, 1931.

Hartmann, Edward George. *The Movement to Americanize the Immigrant.* New York: Columbia University Press, 1948.

Heffelfinger, W. W. (Pudge), with George Trevor. "Football's Golden Age—and Moderns Who Rate with Ancient Greats." *Saturday Evening Post,* 29 October 1938.

―――. "Nobody Put Me on My Back." *Saturday Evening Post,* 15 October 1938.

"Hefty Pros Get Even Heftier." *Life,* 18 November 1957.

Heisman, John W. "Between Halves." *Collier's,* 17 November 1928.

―――. "Fast and Loose." *Collier's,* 20 October 1928.

―――. "Here Are Men." *Collier's,* 16 November 1929.

―――. "Hero Stuff." *Collier's,* 2 November 1929.

―――. "Hold 'Em!" *Collier's,* 27 October 1928.

―――. "Look Sharp Now!" *Collier's,* 3 November 1928.

―――. "Rough Humor." *Collier's,* 9 November 1929.

―――. "Rules Rush In." *Collier's,* 10 November 1928.

―――. "Signals." *Collier's,* 6 October 1928.

―――. "Their Weight in Gold." *Collier's,* 24 November 1928.

―――. "The Thundering Herd." *Collier's,* 13 October 1928.

Heller, Steven, and Louise Fili. *Cover Story: The Art of American Magazine Covers, 1900–1950.* San Francisco: Chronicle Books, 1996.

Henderson, Edwin B. "Athletics." *Messenger,* March 1925.

―――. "Sports." *Messenger,* February 1926.

―――. "Sports." *Messenger,* April 1926.

―――. "Sports." *Messenger,* May 1926.

―――. "Sports." *Messenger,* February 1927.

Henderson, Edwin Bancroft. "The Negro Athlete and Race Prejudice." *Opportunity*, March 1936.

———. *The Negro in Sports*. Rev. ed. Washington, D.C.: Associated Publishers, 1949.

Hennessey, James, S.J. *American Catholics: A History of the Roman Catholic Community in the United States*. New York: Oxford University Press, 1981.

Henry, Jim. "We Call the Penalties." *Saturday Evening Post*, 26 November 1960.

Henry, Mary H. "Do You Fear Football?" *Parents' Magazine*, October 1946.

Herndon, Booton. "Time Out for Mayhem." *Esquire*, October 1953.

Hickman, Herman. "Confessions of a Football Recruiter." *Saturday Evening Post*, 30 October 1954.

Higham, John. *Strangers in the Land: Patterns of American Nativism, 1860–1925*. New Brunswick, N.J.: Rutgers University Press, 1955.

"High School Fevers at Football Time." *Life*, 7 November 1960.

"High School Football." *Look*, 2 October 1945.

"High School Football at Night." *Look*, 12 November 1946.

"High-School Hero." *Look*, 5 October 1954.

Hilger, Michael. *From Savage to Nobleman: Images of Native Americans in Film*. Lanham, Md.: Scarecrow Press, 1995.

Historical Statistics of the United States, Colonial Times to 1957. Washington, D.C.: U.S. Bureau of the Census, 1960.

Historical Statistics of the United States, Colonial Times to 1970. Washington, D.C.: U.S. Bureau of the Census, 1975.

Hobsbawn, Eric, and Terence Ranger, eds. *The Invention of Tradition*. New York: Cambridge University Press, 1983.

Hoffman, Frederick L. *Race Traits and Tendencies of the American Negro*. 1896. Reprint, New York: AMS Press, 1973.

Hogan, Lawrence D. *A Black National News Service: The Associated Negro Press and Claude Barnett, 1919–1945*. Cranbury, N.J.: Associated University Presses, 1984.

Holland, Gerald. "The Coach." *Sports Illustrated*, 13 October 1958.

Hollingshead, August de Belmont. *Elmtown's Youth: The Impact of Social Classes on Adolescents*. New York: J. Wiley, 1949.

Holtzman, Jerome, ed. *No Cheering in the Press Box*. New York: Holt, Rinehart and Winston, 1974.

Hoose, Philip M. *Necessities: Racial Barriers in American Sports*. New York: Random House, 1989.

Hopper, James. "The Boy Who Lost Weight." *Saturday Evening Post*, 9 October 1909.

———. "The Freshman." *Saturday Evening Post*, 16–30 September 1911.

———. "He Could Take It." *American Magazine*, November 1933.

———. "The Long Try." *Saturday Evening Post*, 7 October 1916. Reprinted in *Pictorial Review*, November 1925.

———. "The Passing of the Vet." *McClure's*, November 1904.

———. "Peewee Peters." *Saturday Evening Post*, 20 November 1915.

———. "The Pony Trio." *Everybody's*, November 1918.

———. "The Redemption of Fullback Jones." *Saturday Evening Post,* 26 October 1912.

———. "The Strength of the Weak: The Story of the Full-back Who Got Used to It." *Saturday Evening Post,* 22 October 1904.

———. "We Really Played Football in the Gay Nineties." *Saturday Evening Post,* 13 October 1945.

Horowitz, Helen Lefkowitz. *Campus Life: Undergraduate Cultures from the End of the Eighteenth Century to the Present.* New York: Alfred A. Knopf, 1987.

Horton, Dabney. "The Drop-Kicker." *Sport Story,* 25 November 1932–10 January 1933.

———. "Pigskin U." *Sport Story,* Second October Number–First December Number, 1937.

———. "The Red Guard." *Sport Story,* 25 November 1933–10 January 1934.

———. "Run, Kick, and Pass." *Sport Story,* First October Number–Second November Number, 1935.

———. "Touchdowns, Inc." *Sport Story,* First October Number–Second November Number, 1936.

Howell, Reet A., and Maxwell L. Howell. "The Myth of 'Pop Warner': Carlisle Revisited." *Quest* 30 (Summer 1978): 19–27.

Huff, Sam, with Leonard Shapiro. *Tough Stuff: The Man in the Middle.* New York: St. Martin's, 1988.

Hughes, Rupert. "The Exquisite Thug." *Saturday Evening Post,* 11 December 1909.

Hunting, Jarvis. "The Feinting Four." *Sport Story,* Second December Number, 1929.

Hurd, Michael. *Black College Football, 1892–1992: One Hundred Years of History, Education, and Pride.* Virginia Beach: Donning, 1993.

Hurt, Hubert William. *Goals: The Life of Knute Rockne.* New York: Murray, 1931.

Husing, Ted. *My Eyes Are in My Heart.* New York: Random House, 1959.

———. *Ten Years Before the Mike.* New York: Farrar & Rinehart, 1935.

Huston, McCready. *Salesman from the Sidelines: Being the Business Career of Knute Rockne.* New York: Ray Long and Richard R. Smith, 1931.

Hutchins, Robert M. "Gate Receipts and Glory." *Saturday Evening Post,* 3 December 1938.

Hutchison, Ralph Cooper. "Football: Symbol of College Unity." *Christian Century* 69 (16 April 1952): 461–63.

Hyland, Dick. "The Front Runner." *College Humor,* November 1927.

———. "It's a Tough Game." *Good Housekeeping,* September 1934.

"I Can Take It." [By a Football Coach's Wife.] *Saturday Evening Post,* 22 September 1934.

Inabinett, Mark. *Grantland Rice and His Heroes: The Sportswriter as Mythmaker in the 1920s.* Knoxville: University of Tennessee Press, 1994.

Ingham, Alan G., Jeremy W. Howell, and Todd S. Schilperoort. "Professional Sports and Community: A Review and Exegesis." *Exercise and Sport Science Reviews* 15 (1987): 427–65.

"It Spells Big Campus Weekend." *Life,* 16 November 1959.

Jable, Thomas J. "The Birth of Professional Football: Pittsburgh Athletic Clubs

Ring in Professionals in 1892." *Western Pennsylvania Historical Magazine* 62 (April 1979): 313–47.

Jacobson, Matthew Frye. *Whiteness of a Different Color: European Immigrants and the Alchemy of Race.* Cambridge, Mass.: Harvard University Press, 1998.

Jaher, Frederic Cople. "White America Views Jack Johnson, Joe Louis, and Muhammad Ali." In *Sport in America: New Historical Perspectives,* ed. Donald Spivey, 145–92. Westport, Conn.: Greenwood, 1985.

"Jimmy Conzelman." *Look,* 6 October 1942.

Johnson, Owen. *Stover at Yale.* New York: Frederick A. Stokes, 1912.

Johnson, Susan E. *When Women Played Hardball: Professional Lives and Personal Stories from the All-American Girls Professional Baseball League, 1943–1954.* Seattle: Seal Press, 1994.

Jones, Jean Butts. "Father Is a Football Coach." *Saturday Evening Post,* 20 November 1954.

Jones, William H. *Recreation and Amusement Among Negroes in Washington, D.C.* Washington, D.C.: Howard University Press, 1927.

Kahn, Roger, and Daniel Schwartz. "Highlights of a Golden Decade." *Esquire,* December 1960.

Kane, Martin. "From 'Rah' to the Supersonic." *Sports Illustrated,* 7 November 1955.

Kantowicz, Edward R. "Ethnicity." In *Encyclopedia of American Social History,* ed. Mary Kupiec Cayton, Elliott J. Gorn, and Peter W. Williams, 1:453–66. New York: Scribner's, 1993.

Kaplan, Joseph. "The Case for Big-Time Football." *Look,* 11 December 1956.

Kaplan, Joseph, with Tim Cohane. "To Football Coaches—Clean House or Else." *Look,* 9 December 1958.

Kelley, Larry. "Poison Ivy League Football." *Look,* 26 September 1939.

Kelly, John S. "Football for a Living." *Collier's,* 24 October 1936.

Kennedy, John B. "The Halfback of Notre Dame: An Interview with Knute Rockne." *Collier's,* 19 November 1927.

Kennedy, John F. "The Soft American." *Sports Illustrated,* 26 December 1960.

Kessler, Lauren. *The Dissident Press: Alternative Journalism in American History.* Newbury Park, Calif.: Sage, 1984.

"Kids' Football." *Life,* 10 November 1947.

Kieran, John. "Rockne Made Football What It Is Today and the Fans Are Satisfied." *American Magazine,* November 1929.

Kilpatrick, Jacquelyn. *Celluloid Indians: Native Americans and Film.* Lincoln: University of Nebraska Press, 1999.

Kimmel, Michael. *Manhood in America: A Cultural History.* New York: Basic Books, 1996.

Kipke, Harry G. "A Punt, a Pass and a Prayer." *Saturday Evening Post,* 30 September 1933.

Kipke, Harry G., and Harold A. Fitzgerald. "Dying for Dear Old Rutgers." *Saturday Evening Post,* 17 November 1934.

Knoll, Robert E. *Prairie University: A History of the University of Nebraska.* Lincoln: University of Nebraska Press, 1995.

Knox, Harvey. "Why Ronnie Knox Quit California." *Sports Illustrated,* 6 September 1954.

Knox, Ronnie, with Melvin Durslag. "College Football Is Pro Football." *Collier's,* 12 October 1956.

Kochman, Thomas. *Black and White Styles in Conflict.* Chicago: University of Chicago Press, 1981.

Kofoed, Jack. "Pappa Morelli's Boy." *Sport Story,* November 1939.

Kozol, Wendy. *Life's America: Family and Nation in Postwar Photojournalism.* Philadelphia: Temple University Press, 1994.

Kreiling, Albert. "The Commercialization of the Black Press and the Rise of Race News in Chicago." In *Ruthless Criticism: New Perspectives in U.S. Communication History,* ed. William S. Solomon and Robert W. McChesney. Minneapolis: University of Minnesota Press, 1993.

Krüger, Arnd, and James Riordan, eds. *The Story of Worker Sport.* Champaign, Ill.: Human Kinetics, 1996.

Kuechle, Oliver. "Can Any Football Coach Win at Wisconsin?" *Look,* 11 October 1949.

Kurian, George Thomas. *Datapedia of the United States, 1790–2000.* Lanham, Md.: Bernan Press, 1994.

LaBrucherie, Bert. "Big-Time Football Is Not for Him!" *Saturday Evening Post,* 21 December 1954.

Laird, Tom. "Cut-Rate Touchdowns." *Look,* 19 November 1940.

Lane, Winthrop D. "Your Child and That Fashionable Complex." *Delineator,* October 1927.

Lardner, John. "What Price Whaddyacallit?" *Newsweek,* 23 October 1939.

Lardner, Ring W. "Sport and Play." In *Civilization in the United States: An Inquiry by Thirty Americans,* ed. Harold Stearns, 457–61. New York: Harcourt, Brace, 1922.

"Lashing a Team to Do or Die." *Literary Digest,* 27 October 1928.

Lawrence, Paul R. *Unsportsmanlike Conduct: The National College Athletic Association and the Business of College Football.* Westport, Conn.: Praeger, 1987.

Layne, Bobby, as told to Murray Olderman. "This Is No Game for Kids." *Saturday Evening Post,* 14 November 1959.

Lea, Mrs. Langdon (Biffy). "Is He Hurt?" *Ladies' Home Journal,* November 1935.

Leab, Daniel J. *From Sambo to Superspade: The Black Experience in Motion Pictures.* Boston: Houghton Mifflin, 1976.

LeCompte, Mary Lou. *Girls of the Rodeo: Pioneer Professional Athletes.* Urbana: University of Illinois Press, 1993.

Lee, Alfred McClung. *The Daily Newspaper: The Evolution of a Social Instrument.* New York: Macmillan, 1937.

Lee, Christopher H. "Adaptation on the Plains: The Development of Six-Man and Eight-Man Football in Kansas." *Kansas History* 12 (Winter 1989–90): 192–201.

Lee, George L. *Interesting Athletes: A Newspaper Artist's Look at Blacks in Sports.* Jefferson, N.C.: McFarland, 1990.

Left Wing. "Men Who Make America's Gods." *Nation,* 27 February 1935.

————. "Public Enemy No. 64B: The Football Broadcaster." *Nation,* 9 October 1935.

Lerner, Max. *America as a Civilization: Life and Thought in the United States Today.* New York: Simon & Schuster, 1957.

Lester, Robin. *Stagg's University: The Rise, Decline, and Fall of Big-Time Football at Chicago.* Urbana: University of Illinois Press, 1995.

Leuthner, Stuart. *Iron Men: Bucko, Crazylegs, and the Boys Recall the Golden Days of Professional Football.* New York: Doubleday, 1988.

Lever, Janet, and Stanton Wheeler. "The *Chicago Tribune* Sports Page, 1900–1975." *Sociology of Sport Journal* 1 (December 1984): 299–313.

Levine, David O. *The American College and the Culture of Aspiration, 1915–1940.* Ithaca, N.Y.: Cornell University Press, 1986.

Levine, Peter. *Ellis Island to Ebbets Field: Sport and the American Jewish Experience.* New York: Oxford University Press, 1992.

Lewis, Guy. "World War I and the Emergence of Sport for the Masses." *The Maryland Historian* 4 (Fall 1973): 109–22.

Lewis, Jerry. "Pass Master." *Collier's,* 5 November 1938.

Lhamon, W. T. *Raising Cain: Blackface Performance from Jim Crow to Hip Hop.* Cambridge, Mass.: Harvard University Press, 1998.

"Life Goes to a Football Game." *Life,* 6 November 1939.

"Life Goes to a Kids' Football Game." *Life,* 21 November 1938.

"Life Goes to a Kids' Football Game." *Life,* 9 October 1939.

"Life Visits Lions in Training." *Life,* 24 August 1953.

Lipscomb, Eugene (Big Daddy), as told to Robert G. Deinforfer. "I'm Still Scared." *Saturday Evening Post,* 12 November 1960.

Lipsitz, George. *Time Passages: Collective Memory and American Popular Culture.* Minneapolis: University of Minnesota Press, 1990.

Lipsyte, Robert. *SportsWorld: An American Dreamland.* New York: Quadrangle Books, 1975.

Littell, Robert. "An Ice Man Remembers." *New Republic,* 30 December 1925.

Litten, Frederic Nelson. "The Rebel Yell." *Sport Story,* 25 January 1935.

Little, Lou. "Good Scouts." *Collier's,* 3 November 1934.

————. "1946 Football Forecast." *Collier's,* 21 September 1946.

————. "The Team Moves West." *Collier's,* 17 November 1934.

————. "Tuning Up the Team." *Collier's,* 10 November 1934.

————. "What Football Does to You." *Collier's,* 3 November 1934.

————. "What It Takes." *Collier's,* 27 October 1934.

————. "What You Don't See." *Collier's,* 20 October 1934.

Littlefield, Daniel F., Jr., and James W. Parins, eds. *American Indian and Alaska Native Newspapers and Periodicals.* 2 vols. Westport, Conn.: Greenwood, 1984, 1986.

"Little Wisconsin Town Produces World's Most Famous Pro Team." *Life,* 18 December 1939.

Littlewood, Thomas B. *Arch: A Promoter, Not a Poet: The Story of Arch Ward.* Ames: Iowa State University Press, 1990.

Locke, Gordon. "My Son versus Football." *Ladies' Home Journal,* October 1940.

"Look Goes to a High-School Football Week End." *Look,* 18 November 1941.

Lorenz, Lee. *The Art of the New Yorker, 1925–1995.* New York: Alfred A. Knopf, 1995.

Lorimer, George Horace. "Arithmetic and Unemployment." *Saturday Evening Post,* 2 August 1930.

———. "Crime and Immigration." *Saturday Evening Post,* 9 August 1930.

———. "Do We Want More Mouths to Feed?" *Saturday Evening Post,* 19 May 1934.

———. "Do We Want More Unemployed?" *Saturday Evening Post,* 21 April 1934.

———. "Halfway Measures." *Saturday Evening Post,* 8 November 1930.

———. "High Percentages." *Saturday Evening Post,* 3 November 1928.

———. "Immigration and Unemployment." *Saturday Evening Post,* 19 April 1930.

———. "Immigration Vigilance." *Saturday Evening Post,* 2 April 1932.

———. "Keep Up the Bars!" *Saturday Evening Post,* 10 December 1932.

———. "Lasting Values." *Saturday Evening Post,* 26 September 1925.

———. "The Less the Better." *Saturday Evening Post,* 8 June 1929.

———. "More Deportations Needed." *Saturday Evening Post,* 3 April 1926.

———. "More Immigration-Law Tinkering." *Saturday Evening Post,* 9 June 1934.

———. "New Immigration Programs." *Saturday Evening Post,* 22 February 1930.

———. "Our Immigration Emergency." *Saturday Evening Post,* 2 March 1935.

———. "Self-Protection under Alien Fire." *Saturday Evening Post,* 13 February 1926.

———. "Shall We Weaken the Johnson Act?" *Saturday Evening Post,* 15 October 1927.

———. "A Sound Immigration Program." *Saturday Evening Post,* 1 November 1930.

———. "Time to Consider America First." *Saturday Evening Post,* 30 March 1935.

———. "Two Immigration Programs." *Saturday Evening Post,* 5 May 1934.

———. "Who Made America?" *Saturday Evening Post,* 17 February 1934.

"Los Angeles Rams: Pro Football's Most Hectic Team." *Look,* 27 November 1956.

Lovelace, Delos Wheeler. *Rockne of Notre Dame.* New York: G. P. Putnam's Sons, 1931.

Lowenthal, Leo. "The Triumph of Mass Idols." In *Literature, Popular Culture, and Society.* Palo Alto, Calif.: Pacific Books, 1961.

Lynd, Robert S., and Helen Merrell Lynd. *Middletown: A Study in Contemporary American Culture.* New York: Harcourt, Brace, 1929.

———. *Middletown in Transition: A Study in Cultural Conflicts.* New York: Harcourt, Brace, 1937.

Lyons, Kennedy. "One Last Fight." *Boys' Life,* October 1939.

MacArlarney, Robert Emmet. "Aaron Luckett's Gridiron Gloat." *American Magazine,* November 1912.

MacCambridge, Michael. *The Franchise: A History of Sports Illustrated Magazine.* New York: Hyperion, 1997.

McChesney, Robert W. "Media Made Sport: A History of Sports Coverage in the United States." In *Media, Sports & Society,* ed. Lawrence A. Wenner, 49–69. Newbury Park, Calif.: Sage Publications, 1989.

McDonald, J. Fred. *Don't Touch That Dial: Radio Programming in American Life, 1920–1960*. Chicago: Nelson-Hall, 1979.

McGill, William J. "Paul Gallico." In *American Newspaper Journalists, 1926–1950*, ed. Perry J. Ashley, *Dictionary of Literary Biography*, 29:121–31. Detroit: Gale Research, 1984.

McGrath, Warren. "Newsreel Football Specials." *International Photographer.* December 1938.

McGreevy, John T. *Parish Boundaries: The Catholic Encounter with Race in the Twentieth-Century Urban North.* Chicago: University of Chicago Press, 1996.

MacLauchlan, Don. "Assigned to Stardom." *Sport Story,* November–December 1940.

McLemore, Henry. "McLemore's All-America Football Teams Is . . . the University of Chicago." *Look,* 2 January 1940.

———. "Sex Appeal in Sports." *Look,* 24 October 1939.

———. "Texas Grid Fans Call the Plays." *Look,* 21 November 1939.

McNamee, Graham. *You're On the Air.* New York: Harper & Brothers, 1926.

Magazine Covers: Art for the People. New York: Games Magazine, Cooper-Hewitt Museum, and the Smithsonian Institution's National Museum of Design, 1981.

Majors, Richard. "Cool Pose: Black Masculinity and Sports." In *Sport, Men, and the Gender Order: Critical Feminist Perspectives,* ed. Michael A. Messner and Donald F. Sabo, 109–14. Champaign, Ill.: Human Kinetics, 1990.

"Making Football Safe for Men on the Gridiron." *Literary Digest,* 5 March 1932.

Malette, Mal. "Jim Tatum of the Tarheels." *Saturday Evening Post,* 2 November 1957.

Manners, Shirley. "Cupid Wins the Game: A Football Romance." *Thrilling Love,* November 1935.

"Man's Game, A." *Time,* 30 November 1959.

Maraniss, David. *When Pride Still Mattered: A Life of Vince Lombardi.* New York: Simon & Schuster, 1999.

Marchand, Roland. *Advertising the American Dream: Making Way for Modernity, 1920–1940.* Berkeley: University of California Press, 1985.

"Marchy Schwartz and Notre Dame's Victory March." *Literary Digest,* 28 November 1931.

Marcosson, Isaac F. "The Alien and Unemployment." *Saturday Evening Post,* 14 June 1930.

Marshall, George Preston. "Pro Football Is Better Football." *Saturday Evening Post,* 19 November 1938.

"Marshall Goldberg." *Look,* 25 October 1938.

Martin, Charles H. "Integrating New Year's Day: The Racial Politics of College Bowl Games in the American South." *Journal of Sport History* 24 (Fall 1997): 358–77.

———. "Racial Change and 'Big-Time' College Football in Georgia: The Age of Segregation, 1892–1957." *Georgia Historical Quarterly* 80 (Fall 1996): 532–62.

Martin, Pete. "Football City." *Saturday Evening Post,* 20 November 1943.

Martin, Pete, and Ben Carroll. "The Whole Town Made the Team." *Saturday Evening Post,* 22 November 1947.

Martin, W. Thornton. "The Pig-Skin Game: Football's Newest By-Product." *Saturday Evening Post,* 8 February 1936.

Marty, Martin E., et al., eds. *The Religious Press in America.* New York: Holt, Rinehart and Winston, 1963.

Marvin, George. "The Big Business of Football." *Outlook,* 3 October 1923.

Maule, Tex. "The Browns' Jim Dandy." *Sports Illustrated,* 10 November 1958.

———. "George and His Dragons." *Sports Illustrated,* 27 October 1958.

———. "They Cry for Moore in Baltimore." *Sports Illustrated,* 20 October 1958.

———. "Why the Browns Will Win." *Sports Illustrated,* 23 November 1959.

May, Elaine Tyler. *Homeward Bound: American Families in the Cold War Era.* New York: Basic Books, 1988.

Mead, Chris. *Champion: Joe Louis, Black Hero in White America.* New York: Scribner's, 1985.

Meany, Tom. "Dixie Plays for Blood." *Saturday Evening Post,* 18 November 1939.

Mennell, James. "The Service Football Program of World War I: Its Impact on the Popularity of the Game." *Journal of Sport History* 16 (Winter 1989): 248–60.

"Mid-Century All-America, The." *Collier's,* 9 December 1950.

Miley, Jack. "The Galloping Goldbergs." *Collier's,* 29 October 1938.

Miller, Douglass W. "The New York Tabloids." *Journalism Quarterly* 5 (1928): 36–41.

Miller, Franklin P. "Background." *Sport Story,* Second December Number, 1938.

———. "Denshawe of Army." *Sport Story,* First December Number, 1936.

———. "Feud." *Sport Story,* Second December Number, 1935.

Miller, Patrick B. "The Manly, the Moral, and the Proficient: College Sport in the New South." *Journal of Sport History* 24 (Fall 1997): 285–316.

———. "Slouching toward a New Expediency: College Football and the Color Line during the 1930s." *Proceedings of the North American Society for Sport History* (1996): 93–95.

———. "To 'Bring the Race Along Rapidly': Sport, Student Culture, and Educational Mission at Historically Black Colleges during the Interwar Years." *History of Education Quarterly* 35 (Summer 1995): 111–33.

Miller, Sally M., ed. *The Ethnic Press in the United States: A Historical Analysis and Handbook.* Westport, Conn.: Greenwood, 1987.

Mitchell, Elmer D. "Racial Traits in Athletics." *American Physical Education Review* 27 (March, April, May 1922): 93–99, 147–52, 197–206.

Mizruchi, Mark S. "Local Sports Teams and Celebration of Community: A Comparative Analysis of the Home Advantage." *Sociological Quarterly* 26 (1985): 507–18.

Monroe, Keith. "Stanford's Storybook Coach." *Saturday Evening Post,* 15 October 1947.

Morgan, Thomas B. "The Wham in Pro Football." *Esquire,* November 1959.

Morley, E. E. "Report of the Committee on Athletics in Secondary Schools." *North Central Association Quarterly* 8 (April 1934): 454–64.

———. "Report on the North Central Association Committee on Athletics in Secondary Schools." *North Central Association Quarterly* 5 (December 1930): 332–39.

Mormino, Gary Ross. "The Playing Fields of St. Louis: Italian Immigrants and Sports, 1925–1941." *Journal of Sport History* 9 (Summer 1982): 5–19.

Morris, Mortimer H. "High School Football Can Be Made Safer." *Parents' Magazine,* September 1959.

Moses, Kingsley. "A Thanksgiving Throwback." *Sport Story,* 22 November 1927.

Mott, Frank Luther. *A History of American Magazines.* 5 vols. Cambridge, Mass.: Harvard University Press, 1930–1968.

Mrozek, Donald J. "The Cult and Ritual of Toughness in Cold War America." In *Sport in America: From Wicked Amusement to National Obsession,* ed. David K. Wiggins, 257–67. Champaign, Ill.: Human Kinetics, 1995.

——. *Sport and American Mentality, 1880–1910.* Knoxville: University of Tennessee Press, 1983.

Mullins, Larry (Moon), as told to Harry T. Paxton. "I Like Small-Time Coaching." *Saturday Evening Post,* 4 November 1950.

Mumford, Lewis. "The Significance of Herman Melville." *New Republic,* 10 October 1928.

——. *Technics and Civilization.* New York: Harcourt, Brace, 1934.

Murphy, James E. "Tabloids as an Urban Response." In *Mass Media between the Wars: Perceptions of Cultural Tension, 1918–1941,* ed. Catherine L. Covert and John D. Stevens, 55–70. Syracuse, N.Y.: Syracuse University Press, 1984.

Murphy, James M., and Sharon M. Murphy. *Let My People Know: American Indian Journalism, 1828–1978.* Norman: University of Oklahoma Press, 1981.

Murray, Franny, with Leo Riordan. "The Foot's Back in Football." *Saturday Evening Post,* 21 October 1939.

N. W. Ayer & Son's Directory of Newspapers and Periodicals. Philadelphia: N. W. Ayer & Son, published annually.

Naifeh, Steven, and Gregory White Smith. *Why Can't Men Open Up? Overcoming Men's Fear of Intimacy.* New York: Clarkson N. Potter, 1984.

Naison, Mark. "Lefties and Righties: The Communist Party and Sports during the Great Depression." In *Sport in America: New Historical Perspectives,* ed. Donald Spivey, 129–44. Westport, Conn.: Greenwood, 1985.

"Negroes at Notre Dame." *Ebony,* February 1950.

Nelson, David M. *The Anatomy of a Game: Football, the Rules, and the Men Who Made the Game.* Newark and Cranbury, N.J.: University of Delaware Press and Associated University Presses, 1994.

Neuberger, Richard L. "Gridiron G-Man." *Collier's,* 19 November 1938.

Newcombe, Jack. *The Best of the Athletic Boys: The White Man's Impact on Jim Thorpe.* Garden City, N.Y.: Doubleday, 1975.

"New Texan to Brag About, A." *Ebony,* December 1960.

Nichols, Robert H. H. "Hooley's Unmentionables." *Sport Story,* Second October Number, 1929.

"Nine Sticky Fingers." *Life,* 7 December 1959.

Norton, Guy W. "A Gentleman's Game." *Collier's,* 16 November 1918.

"Notre Dame's Frank Leahy vs. Oklahoma's Bud Wilkinson on the Return of One-Platoon Football." *Look,* 6 October 1953.

Nourie, Alan, and Barbara Nourie, eds. *American Mass-Market Magazines.* Westport, Conn.: Greenwood, 1990.

Nugent, William Henry. "The Sports Section." *American Mercury,* March 1929.

O'Brien, Robert. "The Brutal Art of Red-Dogging." *Esquire,* October 1960.

O'Connor, Richard. *Jack London: A Biography.* Boston: Little, Brown, 1964.

O'Donnell, John M. *The Origins of Behaviorism: American Psychology, 1870–1920.* New York: New York University Press, 1985.

O'Hanlon, Timothy. "Interscholastic Athletics, 1900–1940: Shaping Citizens for Unequal Roles in the Modern Industrial State." *Educational Theory* 30 (Spring 1980): 89–103.

———. "School Sports as Social Training: The Case of Athletics and the Crisis of World War I." *Journal of Sport History* 9 (Spring 1982): 5–29.

"Ohio State Players Get Wages of Sport from the State." *News-Week,* 19 October 1935.

Olderman, Murray. "Railroaded Out of West Point." *Sport,* October 1952.

———. "The Sporting Life." *Hogan's Alley* 6 (1999): 4–16, 122–23.

"Old Passer Has His Last Fling." *Life,* 3 December 1956.

Olson, Keith W. *The G.I. Bill, the Veterans, and the Colleges.* Lexington: University Press of Kentucky, 1974.

"Open Market for Galloping Ghosts, An." *Outlook,* 2 December 1925.

Oriard, Michael. "Home Teams." *South Atlantic Quarterly* 95 (Spring 1996): 471–500.

———. *Reading Football: How the Popular Press Created an American Spectacle.* Chapel Hill: University of North Carolina Press, 1993.

———. *Sporting with the Gods: The Rhetoric of Play and Game in American Culture.* New York: Cambridge University Press, 1991.

Owen, George, Jr. "Football—Pleasure or Grind?" *Independent,* 7 November 1925.

Oxendine, Joseph B. *American Indian Sports Heritage.* Champaign, Ill.: Human Kinetics, 1988.

Paddock, Charley. "Chief Bright Path." *Collier's,* 5–26 October 1929.

Paine, Ralph D. "The Indian." *Sport Story,* 8 November 1924.

Parker, Dan. "College Football Cleanup? Phooey!" *Sport,* October 1947.

———. "How Democratic Is Sport?" *Sport,* September 1949.

———. "My Case against the Bowl Games." *Sport,* December 1948.

———. "Saturday's Moods." *Sports Illustrated,* 23 September 1957.

Parker, Fred. "The Skinny Terror of Illinois." *Saturday Evening Post,* 9 October 1954.

Parry, Albert. "Good-bye to the Immigrant Press." *American Mercury,* January 1933.

Paul, Joan, Richard V. McGhee, and Helen Fant. "The Arrival and Ascendance of Black Athletes in the Southeastern Conference, 1966–1980." *Phylon* 45 (1984): 284–97.

Paxton, Harry T. "The Fancy Dans of Pro Football." *Saturday Evening Post,* 8 October 1960.

———. "Football's Most Underrated Coach." *Saturday Evening Post,* 23 October 1954.

————. "Look Who Coaches Navy." *Saturday Evening Post,* 10 November 1951.

————. "Purity Dies at Pitt." *Saturday Evening Post,* 19 November 1949.

————. "Terror of the Big Ten." *Saturday Evening Post,* 20 October 1956.

————. "That Gentlemanly Coach at Wisconsin." *Saturday Evening Post,* 21 November 1953.

Paxton, Harry T., and B. F. Sylvester. "The Hungry Young Coach of Nebraska." *Saturday Evening Post,* 27 October 1951.

Pelissero, John P., Beth M. Henschen, and Edward I. Sidlow. "Urban Regimes, Sports Stadiums, and the Politics of Economic Development Agendas in Chicago." *Policy Studies Review* 10 (Spring/Summer 1991): 117–29.

Pennington, Richard. *Breaking the Ice: The Racial Integration of Southwest Conference Football.* Jefferson, N.C.: McFarland, 1987.

Perry, Jim. "I Know We're Dumb: Confessions of a Down-South Referee." *Saturday Evening Post,* 22 November 1941.

Perry, Lawrence. "The Spoiled Boy." *Everybody's,* November 1919.

Peterson, Robert W. *Pigskin: The Early Years of Pro Football.* New York: Oxford University Press, 1997.

Peterson, Theodore. *Magazines in the Twentieth Century.* 2d ed. Urbana: University of Illinois Press, 1964.

Pfister, Joel. "Glamorizing the Psychological: The Politics and the Performances of Modern Psychological Identities." In *Inventing the Psychological: Toward a Cultural History of Emotional Life in America,* ed. Joel Pfister and Nancy Schnog, 167–213. New Haven, Conn.: Yale University Press, 1997.

Philips, Judson P., and Robert W. Wood, Jr. *Hold 'Em, Girls!: The Intelligent Woman's Guide to Men and Football.* New York: G. P. Putnam's Sons, 1936.

Pier, Arthur Stanwood. "The Game by Wire." *Scribner's,* November 1907.

Pierce, Frank Richardson. "The Old Navy Fight." *Sport Story,* 8 October 1925.

Pitz, Henry C. *200 Years of American Illustration.* New York: Random House, 1977.

"Platoon System, The: Is It Ruining Football?" *Esquire,* November 1949.

Pleck, Joseph H. *The Myth of Masculinity.* Cambridge, Mass.: MIT Press, 1981.

Poindexter, Ray. *Golden Throats and Silver Tongues: The Radio Announcers.* North Little Rock, Ark.: River Road Press, 1978.

Polzer, John, with Booton Herndon. "Football Made a Gentleman out of Me." *Look,* 18 October 1955.

Pope, S. W. *Patriotic Games: Sporting Traditions in the American Imagination, 1876–1926.* New York: Oxford University Press, 1997.

Pouncey, Temple. *Mustang Mania: Southern Methodist University.* Huntsville, Ala.: Strode Publishers, 1981.

Powers, Jimmy. "The Case against the Bowl Games." *Sport,* January 1951.

"Prentice Gautt: Oklahoma's Quiet Powerhouse." *Look,* 13 October 1959.

Pride, Armistead S., and Clint C. Wilson II. *A History of the Black Press.* Washington, D.C.: Howard University Press, 1997.

"Pride of Lions, A." *Time,* 29 November 1954.

Prince, Morton. "Hand Back the Game to the Boys." *Forum,* December 1926.

"Pro Football." *Look,* 11 October 1960.

"Pro Hazing for a Rookie." *Life,* 8 September 1958.

"Quarterback and His Lady, The." *Look,* 25 November 1947.

"Quarterback from Little Rock, The." *Ebony,* January 1958.

"Queen's Choice." *Life,* 27 November 1950.

Rader, Benjamin G. *American Sports: From the Age of Folk Games to the Age of Televised Sports.* 3d ed. Englewood Cliffs, N.J.: Prentice-Hall, 1996.

Ragsdale, Kenneth B. *The Year America Discovered Texas: Centennial '36.* College Station: Texas A&M University Press, 1987.

"Rambling Wreck Barbecues Duke." *Life,* 10 November 1952.

"Rangerettes, The." *Life,* 29 October 1951.

Rappoport, Ken. *The Trojans: A Story of Southern California Football.* Huntsville, Ala.: Strode Publishers, 1974.

Ratliff, Harold V. *Autumn's Mightiest Legions: History of Texas Schoolboy Football.* Waco, Tex.: Texian Press, 1963.

———. *The Power and the Glory: The Story of Southwest Conference Football.* Lubbock: Texas Tech University Press, 1957.

Real, Michael R. "Trends in Structure and Policy in the American Catholic Press." *Journalism Quarterly* 52 (1975): 265–71.

Reck, Franklin M. "Pigskin Revolution: Six Man Football Teams." *Christian Science Monthly Magazine,* 5 October 1937.

———. "Play Six-Man Football." *American Boy,* September 1937.

"Red Grange in Business." *New Republic,* 9 December 1925.

Reed, Adolph, Jr. *Class Notes: Posing as Politics and Other Thoughts on the American Scene.* New York: New Press, 2000.

Reed, David P. "Is College Football Doomed?" *Outlook,* 23 December 1925.

Reed, Herbert. "Football for Sportsmen." *Outlook,* 22 December 1926.

Reed, Walt, ed. *The Illustrator in America, 1900–1960s.* New York: Reinhold, 1966.

Reinert, Al, and Geoff Winningham. *Rites of Fall: High School Football in Texas.* Austin: University of Texas Press, 1979.

Reynolds, Quentin. "Block and Tackle." *Collier's,* 4 November 1939.

———. "Football Town." *Collier's,* 6 November 1937.

———. "Official Business." *Collier's,* 14 October 1939.

Rice, Grantland. "The All-America Football Team." *Collier's,* 19 December 1936.

———. "The First Fifty Years." *Collier's,* 9 December 1939.

———. "Grantland Rice's Football Forecast." *Look,* 13 September 1949.

———. "Grantland Rice's Football Forecast for 1951." *Look,* 11 September 1951.

———. "1947 College Preview." *Look,* 16 September 1947.

———. "The Pigskin Ballyhoo." *Collier's,* 18 September 1926.

———. "The Spoil-Sports." *Collier's,* 18 December 1926.

———. "The Stuff Men Are Made Of." *Collier's,* 24 October 1925.

———. *The Tumult and the Shouting: My Life in Sport.* New York: A. S. Barnes, 1954.

———. "Were the Old-Timers Best?" *Collier's,* 21 November 1925.

———. "What Football Pays For." *Collier's,* 19 September 1925.

Riesman, David, and Reuel Denney. "Football in America: A Study in Culture Diffusion." *American Quarterly* 3 (Winter 1951): 309–25.

Riess, Curt. "May the Best White Man Win." *Esquire,* September 1941.

———. "The New Huddle Muddle." *Esquire,* November 1941.

Riess, Steven A. *City Games: The Evolution of American Urban Society and the Rise of Sports.* Urbana: University of Illinois Press, 1989.

———. "Power without Authority: Los Angeles' Elites and the Construction of the Coliseum." *Journal of Sport History* 8 (Spring 1981): 50–65.

———. "A Social Profile of the Professional Football Player, 1920–82." In *The Business of Professional Sport,* ed. Paul A. Staudohar and James A. Mangan, 222–46. Urbana: University of Illinois Press, 1991.

———. *Sport in Industrial America, 1850–1920.* Wheaton, Ill.: Harlan Davison, 1995.

———, ed. *Sports and the American Jew.* Syracuse, N.Y.: Syracuse University Press, 1998.

Riley, Clayton. "Did O. J. Dance?" *Ms.,* March 1974.

Riley, Michael J. "Trapped in the History of Film: Racial Conflict and Allure in *The Vanishing American.*" In *Hollywood's Indian: The Portrayal of the Native American in Film,* ed. Peter C. Rollins and John E. O'Connor, 58–72. Lexington: University Press of Kentucky, 1998.

Rivett, B. J. "The Relation of Athletics to the High School Program." *North Central Association Quarterly* 14 (January 1940): 275–79.

Rober, Eric. "Fumble." *Sport Story,* 25 September 1931.

Roberts, Andrew. "One-Man Team." *Collier's,* 26 October 1946.

Roberts, Randy. *Papa Jack: Jack Johnson and the Era of White Hopes.* New York: Free Press, 1983.

Robinson, Ray. *Rockne of Notre Dame: The Making of a Football Legend.* New York: Oxford University Press, 1999.

Rockne, Knute. *The Autobiography of Knute Rockne.* Indianapolis, Ind.: Bobbs-Merrill, 1931.

———. "Beginning at End." *Collier's,* 25 October 1930.

———. "Coaching Men." *Collier's,* 15 November 1930.

———. "The Four Horsemen." *Collier's,* 1 November 1930.

———. "From Norway to Notre Dame." *Collier's,* 18 October 1930.

———. "Gipp the Great." *Collier's,* 22 November 1930.

———. *Knute Rockne on Football.* New York: Individual Publications, 1931.

———. "To Shift or Not to Shift." *Collier's,* 29 November 1930.

———. "Turning Up the Team." *Collier's,* 8 November 1930.

———. "What Thrills a Coach." *Collier's,* 6 December 1930.

Roettger, Dorye. *Rivals of Rockwell.* New York: Crescent, 1992.

Rogers, Frederick Rand. *The Future of Interscholastic Athletics.* New York: Teachers College Press, Columbia University, 1929.

Ross, Steven J. *Working-Class Hollywood: Silent Film and the Shaping of Class in America.* Princeton, N.J.: Princeton University Press, 1998.

"Rough Day in Berkeley." *Life,* 29 October 1951.

"Rugged Shakedown for a Tough Team, A." *Life,* 23 September 1957.

Russell, Fred. "Big Bad Bulldog from Dixie." *Saturday Evening Post,* 2 November 1947.

———. *Bury Me in an Old Press Box: Good Times and Life of a Sportswriter.* New York: A. S. Barnes, 1957.

———. "The Gay Deceiver of Georgia Tech." *Saturday Evening Post,* 27 November 1948.

———. "The New Wonder Boy of Notre Dame." *Saturday Evening Post,* 25 September 1954.

———. "Pigskin Preview." *Saturday Evening Post,* 12 September 1953.

———. "They're All Rooting for Red." *Saturday Evening Post,* 11 November 1950.

Russell, Fred, and Guy Tiller. "Georgia Plays for Keeps." *Saturday Evening Post,* 5 November 1949.

Russell, Ross. "Latin from Manhattan." *Sport Story,* November 1939.

———. "Payoff in Pasadena." *Sport Story,* January 1943.

Rust, Art, Jr., and Edna Rust. *Art Rust's Illustrated History of the Black Athlete.* Garden City, N.Y.: Doubleday, 1985.

St. Johns, Adela Rogers, and Dick Hyland. "The Front Runner." *College Humor,* November 1927.

Sand, Paul. "Graceful." *Sport Story,* 22 November 1926.

Savage, Howard J., et al. *American College Athletics.* New York: Carnegie Foundation, 1929.

"Savagery on Sunday." *Life,* 24 October 1955.

Saylor, Roger B. "Black College Football." *College Football Historical Society Newsletter* 13 (May 2000): 4–7.

Sayre, Joel. "Rackety Rax." *American Mercury,* January 1932.

Schau, Michael. *J. C. Leyendecker.* New York: Watson-Guptill, 1974.

Schecter, A. A., with Edward Anthony. *I Live on Air.* New York: Frederick A. Stokes, 1941.

Schlesinger, Arthur, Jr. "The Crisis of American Masculinity." *Esquire,* November 1958.

Schmidt, Francis A., and Harold A. Fitzgerald. "The New Open Game." *Saturday Evening Post,* 5 October 1935.

Schneider, Charles J. "Should Your Boy Play Football?" *Look,* 28 September 1948.

Scholz, Jackson. "Flanders Backs the Line." *Sport Story,* First November Number, 1930.

———. "Gridiron Crooner." *Sport Story,* 10 December 1934.

———. "Gridiron Dancer." *Sport Story,* 25 December 1934.

———. "Gridiron Milkman." *Boys' Life,* November 1958.

———. "The Hero Yell." *Sport Story,* 22 November 1927.

———. "The Missing Halfback." *Sport Story,* 10 November 1934.

———. "Prima Donnas." *Sport Story,* 10 December 1933.

———. "Tackling the Townies." *Sport Story,* 10 January 1934.

Schoonmaker, Frank. "Pity the Poor Athlete." *Harper's,* November 1930.

Schwartz, Barry, and Stephen F. Barsky. "The Home Advantage." *Social Forces* 55 (1977): 641–61.

Schwartz, Marchmont. "The All-American Recants." *Saturday Evening Post,*
26 November 1932.

Schwenger, Peter. *Phallic Critiques: Masculinity and Twentieth-Century Literature.*
Boston: Routledge & Kegan Paul, 1984.

Scranton, Philip. "Varieties of Paternalism: Industrial Structures and the Social
Relations of Production in American Textiles." *American Quarterly* 36 (Summer
1984): 235–57.

Sears, J. H. "Sixty Days of Football." *Harper's Weekly,* 5 November 1892.

Sedgwick, Eve Kosofsky. *Between Men: English Literature and Male Homosocial Desire.*
New York: Columbia University Press, 1985.

———. *The Epistemology of the Closet.* Berkeley: University of California Press, 1990.

"Sequel: Here Are Formal Photos of Players in Story Notre Dame Has Criticized."
Life, 13 October 1952.

Servin, Manuel P., and Iris Higby Wilson. *Southern California and Its University:
A History of USC, 1880–1964.* Los Angeles: Ward Ritchie Press, 1969.

Shallett, Sidney. "Maryland's Busiest Byrd." *Collier's,* 9 December 1950.

Shaw, Irwin. "The Eighty-Yard Run." *Esquire,* January 1941.

Sherman, Harold. *One Minute to Play.* New York: Grosset & Dunlap, 1926.

"Should College Football Players Be Paid?" *Look,* 9 November 1937.

Shrake, Edwin. "Trouping the Colors for Gussie Nell Davis." *Sports Illustrated,*
16 December 1974.

"Sid Luckman Is New York's Football Hero." *Life,* 24 October 1938.

"Sight a Mother Could Not Watch, The." *Life,* 24 October 1960.

Siler, Tom. "Football's Jittery Genius." *Saturday Evening Post,* 3 November 1951.

Sinclair, Upton. "Killers of Thought." *Forum,* December 1926.

Singer, Janet. *Cheer Leader.* Chicago: Goldsmith, 1934.

Singerman, Robert. "The American Jewish Press, 1823–1983: A Bibliographic
Survey of Research and Studies." *American Jewish History* 73 (June 1984):
422–44.

———. "The Jewish Press." In *Jewish-American History and Culture: An Encyclopedia,*
ed. Jack Fischel and Sanford Pinsker, 514–19. New York: Garland, 1992.

"Six-man." *Time,* 11 October 1937.

"Six-Man Football for Vacant Lot and Rural High School." *Literary Digest,*
13 November 1937.

Small, Collie. "Coaches' Graveyard." *Saturday Evening Post,* 18 October 1947.

———. "Football's Demon Deacon." *Saturday Evening Post,* 8 November 1947.

Smick, Danny. "King Football." *Dow Diamond,* September 1947.

Smith, Page. *As a City upon a Hill: The Town in American History.* New York: Alfred A.
Knopf, 1966.

Smith, Marshall. "Sad News from the Campus: Nobody Loves the Football Hero
Now." *Life,* 11 November 1957.

Smith, Marshall, and Richard Oulahan, Jr. "Football Is Pricing Itself Out of
Business." *Life,* 16 October 1950.

Smith, Ronald A. *Sports and Freedom: The Rise of Big-Time College Athletics.* New York:
Oxford University Press, 1988.

Smith, Thomas G. "Outside the Pale: The Exclusion of Blacks from the National Football League, 1934–1946." *Journal of Sport History* 15 (Winter 1988): 255–81.

Snell, Roy J. *The Galloping Ghost.* Chicago: Reilly & Lee, 1933.

Sombart, Werner. *Why Is There No Socialism in the United States?* Trans. Patricia M. Hocking and C. T. Husbands. 1906. Reprint, London: Macmillan, 1976.

"Speaking of Pictures . . . Drum Majorettes Are Latest in Ballyhoo." *Life,* 10 October 1938.

"Speaking of Pictures . . . School Yells' Saucy Rhymes Inspire a Cheerleader's Exuberant Rhythms." *Life,* 25 October 1954.

"Speaking of Pictures . . . These Are 'Card-Stunt Cheers.'" *Life,* 15 November 1937.

Spencer, Emerson L. "He Clowns to Touchdowns." *Saturday Evening Post,* 27 September 1941.

Sperber, Murray. *Onward to Victory: The Crises That Shaped College Sports.* New York: Henry Holt, 1998.

———. *Shake Down the Thunder: The Creation of Notre Dame Football.* New York: Henry Holt, 1993.

Spivey, Donald. "The Black Athlete in Big-Time Intercollegiate Sports, 1941–1968." *Phylon* 44 (1983): 116–25.

———. "'End Jim Crow in Sports': The Protest at New York University, 1940–41." *Journal of Sport History* 15 (Winter 1988): 282–303.

Spivey, Donald, and Thomas A. Jones. "Intercollegiate Athletic Servitude: A Case Study of the Black Illini Student Athletes, 1931–1967." *Social Science Quarterly* 55 (March 1975): 939–47.

"Sport." *Time,* 25 October 1927.

Stagg, Amos Alonzo, as told to Wesley Winans Stout. "Touchdown!" *Saturday Evening Post,* 18 September–13 November 1926.

Standish, Burt L. "Vagrant Lineman." *Sport Story,* First January Number, 1936.

Star, Jack. "The Big New Battle in the Big Ten." *Look,* 25 June 1957.

Star, Jack, and Clark Mollenhoff. "Exclusive: The Big Ten's Secret Report." *Look,* 30 October 1956.

———. "Football Scandal Hits the Big Ten." *Look,* 21 August 1956.

Steckbeck, John S. *Fabulous Redmen: The Carlisle Indians and Their Famous Football Teams.* Harrisburg, Pa.: J. Horace McFarland, 1951.

Steiner, Jesse Frederick. *Americans at Play: Recent Trends in Recreation and Leisure Time Activities.* New York: McGraw-Hill, 1933.

Stern, Bill. *My Favorite Sports Stories.* New York: MacDavis Features, 1946.

Stevens, James. "Laborers East and West." *Saturday Evening Post,* 12 February 1927.

Stevens, Marvin A. (Mal). "Will High School Football Hurt Your Boy?" *Look,* 25 September 1951.

Stone, Gregory P. "Sport as Community Representation." In *Handbook of Social Science of Sport,* ed. Günther R. F. Lüschen and George H. Sage, 214–45. Champaign, Ill.: Stipes Publishing Company, 1981.

Stone, Leonard. "'Beef.'" *Sport Story,* 22 November 1923.

———. "'Taters' Byers—Freshman." *Sport Story,* 8 December 1924.

Stuhldreher, Harry. *Knute Rockne, Man Builder.* New York: Grosset & Dunlap, 1931.

Stuhldreher, Mary. "Football Fans Aren't Human." *Saturday Evening Post,* 23 October 1948.

———. "Should Your Boy Play Football?" *McCall's,* November 1951.

Stump, Al. "The Ballyhoo Boys of Football." *Saturday Evening Post,* 26 November 1949.

———. "The Football College That Turned Pro." *Sport,* November 1950.

———. "Football's Biggest Bargain." *Saturday Evening Post,* 20 November 1948.

———. "Ronnie Knox: A Football Case History." *Sport,* November 1955.

———. "What Knox and Knox Are After." *Sport,* September 1958.

Sugrue, Thomas. "The Newsreels." *Scribner's,* April 1937.

Sullivan, Frank. "Football Is King." *Atlantic,* November 1938.

Summers, Raymond L. "The Football Business." *New Republic,* 6 November 1929.

Sumner, Jim L. "John Franklin Crowell, Methodism, and the Football Controversy at Trinity College, 1887–1894." *Journal of Sport History* 17 (Spring 1990): 5–20.

Sundquist, Eric J. *To Wake the Nations: Race in the Making of American Literature.* Cambridge, Mass.: Belknap Press of Harvard University Press, 1993.

Susman, Warren I. *Culture as History: The Transformation of American Society in the Twentieth Century.* New York: Pantheon Books, 1984.

Sutherland, John Bain, and William Shipman Maulsby. "Yea, Pitt, Sock It to 'Em." *Saturday Evening Post,* 7 December 1935.

"Tabloid Poison." *Saturday Review of Literature,* 19 February 1927.

Tebbel, John. *George Horace Lorimer and the Saturday Evening Post.* Garden City, N.Y.: Doubleday, 1948.

"Tennessee Touchdowns on the Family Plan." *Life,* 12 November 1956.

Terman, Lewis. *Sex and Personality: Studies in Masculinity and Femininity.* New York: McGraw-Hill, 1936.

Terrill, John. "Man in Motion." *Collier's,* 25 October 1941.

"Terror and His Twin: Mike and Marlin McKeever of University of Southern California." *Life,* 16 November 1959.

Terry, Marshall. *"From High on the Hilltop . . .": A Brief History of SMU.* Dallas: Southern Methodist University Press, 1993.

"Texans Like Negro Grid Stars." *Ebony,* November 1952.

"Texas A. & M. Footballers Are Rugged, Rangy, Rough." *Life,* 9 September 1940.

"Texas Blows Its Top over Football." *Life,* 29 October 1956.

Thelin, John R. *Games Colleges Play: Scandal and Reform in Intercollegiate Athletics.* Baltimore, Md.: Johns Hopkins University Press, 1994.

Thomas, Frank. "The Passing Show." *Collier's,* 19 October 1934.

———. "Squads West." *Collier's,* 23 November 1934.

Thomas, Mary Martha Hosford. *Southern Methodist University: Founding and Early Days.* Dallas: Southern Methodist University Press, 1974.

Thompson, Mike, with Wesley Stout. "Praying Colonels—Golden Tornadoes." *Saturday Evening Post,* 17 October 1931.

———. "The Referee's Whistle." *Saturday Evening Post,* 10 October 1931.

———. "That's My Story." *Saturday Evening Post,* 24 October 1931.

————. "The Villain of the Piece." *Saturday Evening Post,* 31 October 1931.

Thomson, Ruby la Verte. "The Captain Was a Redhead." *Love Story,* 7 November 1942.

————. "A Kiss for the Coach." *Love Story,* 15 November 1941.

————. "You Can't Coach a Redhead." *Love Story,* 9 November 1940.

Thornhill, C. E. "Good Mixers." *Collier's,* 21 November 1936.

————. "Head First." *Collier's,* 14 November 1936.

Thornhill, C. E., with Frank J. Taylor. "Tiny." In "Football Follies," *Collier's,* 7 November 1936.

Thurber, James. "University Days." In *My Life and Hard Times,* 115–20. New York: Harper & Brothers, 1933.

"Time Out for Love." *Look,* 12 October–23 November 1937.

Tips, Kern. *Football—Texas Style: An Illustrated History of the Southwest Conference.* Garden City, N.Y.: Doubleday, 1964.

Titus, Harold. "The Man Who Made 'Em Block." *Sport Story,* 8 November 1923.

"To All Colleges." *Football News,* 14 September 1939.

Tolbert, Frank. "Mighty Mites." *Collier's,* 22 November 1941.

"To Make Football a Sport." *Outlook,* 30 March 1927.

Tompkins, Jane. *West of Everything: The Inner Life of Westerns.* New York: Oxford University Press, 1992.

Tone, Andrea. *The Business of Benevolence: Industrial Paternalism in Progressive America.* Ithaca, N.Y.: Cornell University Press, 1997.

Torgovnick, Marianna. *Gone Primitive: Savage Intellects, Modern Lives.* Chicago: University of Chicago Press, 1990.

Towers, Walter Kellogg. "Athletics' Aid to War." *American Boy,* October 1917.

Trevor, George. "Brutal Truth: 1931 Injury Epidemic." *Outlook and Independent,* 30 December 1931.

————. "Greatest Backfield in History?" *American Magazine,* November 1946.

————. "King Football Answers the Depression." *Literary Digest,* 16 September 1933.

————. "Southern Football's Challenge." *Outlook and Independent,* 12 November 1930.

Tunis, John R. "College Praise Men." *Esquire,* November 1938.

————. "College President." *Harper's,* February 1937.

————. "Eddie Stands for Good Clean Sport." *Harper's,* December 1933.

————. "Fellow Alumni of Mammoth." *Harper's,* November 1935.

————. "Football and Fiction." *Outlook and Independent,* 6 November 1929.

————. "Football on the Wane?" *Harper's,* November 1929.

————. "The Great God Football." *Harper's,* November 1928.

————. "Honoris Causa." *Harper's,* June 1937.

————. "Maguire, Builder of Men." *Harper's,* December 1931.

————. "More Pay for College Football Stars." *American Mercury,* November 1936.

————. "Never Give a Sucker . . ." *Esquire,* November 1940.

————. "Player Control in Football." *Outlook and Independent,* 20 November 1929.

————. "Portrait of an Intellectual." *Harper's,* March 1932.

————. "The Slump in Football Common." *Atlantic,* December 1932.

————. *$port$ Heroics and Hysterics.* New York: John Day, 1928.

————. "What Price College Football?" *American Mercury,* October 1939.

————. "Whose Game Is It?" *Outlook and Independent,* 13 November 1929.

Tuthill, Lieut. Harry. "Football and War." *American Boy,* October 1918.

"Twenty-seven Deaths This Fall." *Nation,* 9 December 1931.

"Two Big M's, The." *Life,* 3 November 1952.

"U.C.L.A. Makes Animated Cartoons with Football Cheer Cards" and "Girl Cheerleaders Specialize in Rhythm Gymnastics." *Life,* 10 November 1941.

U.S. Bureau of the Census, *Historical Statistics of the United States, Colonial Times to 1957.* Washington, D.C.: Bureau of the Census, 1960.

"U.S. Goes Bowl Crazy, The." *Life,* 12 January 1948.

Vanneman, Reeve, and Lynn and Weber Cannon. *The American Perception of Class.* Philadelphia: Temple University Press, 1987.

Vickers, Stanley. "Fighting Scotts." *Sport Story,* October 1940.

"Violent Face of Pro Football, The." *Sports Illustrated,* 24 October 1960.

Wagenhorst, Lewis Hoch. *The Administration and Cost of High School Interscholastic Athletics.* New York: Teachers College Press, Columbia University, 1926.

Wainwright, Loudan. *The Great American Magazine: An Inside History of Life.* New York: Alfred A. Knopf, 1986.

Wakefield, Dan. "In the Defense of the Fullback." *Dissent* 4 (Summer 1957): 311–14.

Wakefield, Wanda Ellen. *Playing to Win: Sports and the American Military, 1898–1945.* Albany: State University of New York Press, 1997.

Walker, Stanley. *City Editor.* New York: Frederick A. Stokes, 1934.

Wallace, Francis. *Autumn Madness.* Philadelphia: Macrae, 1936.

————. *Big Game.* Boston: Little, Brown, 1936.

————. "The Double Ride." *Saturday Evening Post,* 3 October–7 November 1936.

————. "The Football Laboratory Explodes." *Saturday Evening Post,* 4 November 1939.

————. "Football's Black Market." *Saturday Evening Post,* 9 November 1946.

————. "Football's Civil War." *Look,* 22 October 1940.

————. "Francis Wallace's 10th Pigskin Preview." *Collier's,* 24 September 1949.

————. "Francis Wallace's 11th Pigskin Preview." *Collier's,* 16 September 1950.

————. "Francis Wallace's 12th Pigskin Preview." *Collier's,* 15 September 1951.

————. "Francis Wallace's 13th Pigskin Preview." *Collier's,* 30 August 1952.

————. "Francis Wallace's 14th Pigskin Preview." *Collier's,* 18 September 1953.

————. "Francis Wallace's 15th Pigskin Preview." *Collier's,* 17 September 1954.

————. "Francis Wallace's 16th Pigskin Preview." *Collier's,* 16 September 1955.

————. "Francis Wallace's 17th Pigskin Preview." *Collier's,* 14 September 1956.

————. "Gridiron Gallahad." *Collier's,* 14 October 1950.

————. *Huddle!* New York: Farrar & Rinehart, 1930.

————. "The Hypocrisy of Football Reform." *Scribner's,* November 1927.

————. "I Was a Football Fixer." *Saturday Evening Post,* 31 October 1936.

————. "The Odds against Honor." *Collier's,* 26 October–14 December 1935.

———. *O'Reilly of Notre Dame.* New York: Farrar & Rinehart, 1931).

———. "Pigskin Preview." *Saturday Evening Post,* 26 September 1937.

———. "Pigskin Preview." *Saturday Evening Post,* 24 September 1938.

———. "Pigskin Preview of 1939." *Saturday Evening Post,* 23 September 1939.

———. "Pigskin Preview of 1940." *Saturday Evening Post,* 21 September 1940.

———. "Pigskin Preview." *Saturday Evening Post,* 20 September 1941.

———. "Pigskin Preview." *Saturday Evening Post,* 19 September 1942.

———. "Pigskin Preview." *Saturday Evening Post,* 21 September 1946.

———. "Pigskin Preview." *Saturday Evening Post,* 13 September 1947.

———. "Pigskin Preview." *Saturday Evening Post,* 18 September 1948.

———. "Razzle-Dazzle." *Saturday Evening Post,* 6–27 November 1937.

———. *Razzle-Dazzle.* New York: M. S. Mill, 1938.

———. *Stadium.* New York: Farrar & Rinehart, 1931.

———. "Test Case at Pitt." *Saturday Evening Post,* 28 October 1939.

———. *That's My Boy.* New York: Farrar & Rinehart, 1932.

———. "This Football Business." *Saturday Evening Post,* 28 September 1929.

Walsh, Christy. *Adios to Ghosts.* New York: n.p., 1937.

Ward, Herbert D. "Thumbs Up." *Harper's Bazaar,* December 1911.

Warner, Glenn S. "Battles of Brawn." *Collier's,* 7 November 1931.

———. "Heap Big Run-Most-Fast." *Collier's,* 24 October 1931.

———. "Here Come the Giants!" *Collier's,* 21 November 1931.

———. "The Indian Massacres." *Collier's,* 17 October 1931.

———. "Red Menaces." *Collier's,* 31 October 1931.

———. "What's the Matter with Football?" *Collier's,* 14 November 1931.

Warner, W. Lloyd. *Democracy in Jonesville.* New York: Harper & Brothers, 1949.

Warner, W. Lloyd, and Paul Sanborn Lunt. *The Social Life of a Modern Community.* New Haven, Conn.: Yale University Press, 1941.

Watson, Emmett. "Mighty McElhenny." *Sport,* December 1951.

Watters, Mrs. Len. *Football for Feminine Fans.* Scarsdale, N.Y.: n.p., 1933.

"We Want a Touchdown!" *Collier's,* 1 December 1928.

Watterson, John Sayle. *College Football: History, Spectacle, Controversy.* Baltimore, Md.: Johns Hopkins University Press, 2000.

Wechsler, James. *Revolt on the Campus.* New York: Covici, Friede, 1935.

"Week, The." *New Republic,* 9 December 1931.

"Week, The." *New Republic,* 2 December 1936.

Weinstein, George. "Can Junior Football Hurt Your Boy?" *Good Housekeeping,* October 1960.

Welky, David B. "Viking Girls, Mermaids, and Little Brown Men: U.S. Journalism and the 1932 Olympics." *Journal of Sport History* 24 (Spring 1997): 24–49.

West, James. *Plainsville, U.S.A.* New York: Columbia University Press, 1945.

Weyrauch, Martin. "The Why of the Tabloids." *Forum* 77 (April 1927): 492–501.

"What a Babe!" *Life,* 23 June 1947.

"What the Draft Should Teach Us." *Literary Digest,* 2 August 1919.

Wheeler, John. *I've Got News for You.* New York: E. P. Dutton, 1961.

Whitfield, Raoul F. "Angel Face." *Sport Story,* 22 October 1925.

———. "Fight." *Sport Story,* 22 November 1926.

Whitman, Vic. "The Son of Thunder McLeod." *Sport Story,* 10 December 1933.

"Who Reads the Tabloids?" *New Republic,* 25 May 1927.

"Wife's Saga of Coach's Ordeal." *Life,* 14 November 1960.

Wiggins, David K. *Glory Bound: Black Athletes in a White America.* Syracuse, N.Y.: Syracuse University Press, 1997.

———. "Great Speed but Little Stamina: The Historical Debate over Black Athletic Superiority." *Journal of Sport History* 16 (1989): 158–85.

———. "Prized Performers, but Frequently Overlooked Students: The Involvement of Black Athletes in Intercollegiate Sports on Predominantly White University Campuses, 1890–1972." *Research Quarterly for Exercise and Sport* 62 (1991): 164–77.

Wiggins, William H., Jr. "Boxing's Sambo Twins: Racial Stereotypes in Jack Johnson and Joe Louis Newspaper Cartoons, 1908 to 1938." *Journal of Sport History* 15 (Winter 1988): 242–54.

Wilkinson, Bud, as told to Harry T. Paxton. "How to Watch Football." *Saturday Evening Post,* 1 November 1952.

Williams, Joe. "The All-Americas." *Scribner's,* December 1938.

Wolseley, Roland E. *The Black Press, U.S.A.* 2d ed. Ames: Iowa State University Press, 1990.

Wolters, Raymond. *The New Negro on Campus: Black College Rebellions of the 1920s.* Princeton, N.J.: Princeton University Press, 1975.

"Women in Motion." *Sports Illustrated,* 10 November 1958.

Wood, James Playsted. *Magazines in the United States.* 3d ed. New York: Ronald Press, 1971.

Woodward, Stanley. "Is College Football on the Level?" *Sport,* November 1946.

———. "Next on the Sports Fix List: College Football." *Look,* 6 November 1951.

———. *Sports Page.* New York: Simon & Schuster, 1949.

Woofter, T. J., Jr. *Races and Ethnic Groups in American Life.* New York: McGraw-Hill, 1933.

"Yelping Alumni: The Matter with College Football." *Outlook,* 6 January 1926.

"You Coming Up Here with Me, Son?" *Life,* 19 September 1955.

Young, Consuelo C. "A Study of Reader Attitudes Toward the Negro Press." *Journalism Quarterly* 21 (1944): 148–52.

Young, Lou. "Touchdown Technic." *Saturday Evening Post,* 9 November 1929.

Zang, David W. *Fleet Walker's Divided Heart: The Life of Baseball's First Black Major Leaguer.* Lincoln: University of Nebraska Press, 1995.

Zucker, Harvey Marc, and Lawrence J. Babich. *Sports Films: A Complete Reference.* Jefferson, N.C.: McFarland, 1987.

Index

Galimore, Willie, 317, 318

Gallico, Paul, 28, 92, 95, 129, 133, 166, 179–80, 207, 234, 235, 236, 237–40, 245, 360

Galloping Ghost, The, 128

Garber, Marjorie, 354

Garth, David, 243, 244

Gauss, Christian, 110

Gautt, Prentice, 317

Gender roles: and masculinity, 13, 226–27, 299, 328–63, 365; and football, 19, 88, 175–88, 330–63, 365, 370; and powder bowls, 352–54; and females playing football, 354–63, 365, 370

George, Nelson, 320, 322

Georgetown University, 35, 116, 119, 124, 302

George Washington University, 301

Georgia, University of, 66, 75, 76, 77, 79, 87, 89–92, 106, 137, 155, 157, 169–70, 180, 239, 276, 279, 292, 301, 308, 309, 310, 312; integration of football team of, 10, 313

Georgia Tech, 23, 45, 66, 75, 76–77, 85, 89, 106, 157, 162, 169–70, 281, 283, 301, 370; integration of football team of, 10, 313; and controversy over 1956 Sugar Bowl, 308–13

Giel, Paul, 189

Gifford, Frank, 218, 334, 335

Glassford, Bill, 155, 156–61, 222

Glazer, Barney, 34

Glickman, Marty, 44

Goldberg, Marshall, 263, 264, 271, 331

Good Housekeeping, 53, 173, 175; football covers on, 171, 173, 174

Gordon, Franklin, 265

Grafton, Samuel, 13, 109

Graham, Frank Porter, 301

Graham, Otto, 214, 215

"Graham Plan," 124

Grambling State University, 11

Grange, Harold ("Red"), 11, 126–28, 130, 135, 137, 208–9, 336; as pro-fessional, 5, 103–5, 108, 109, 202–4, 236; as collegian, 7, 72, 169, 234–35

Grant, Madison, 258, 259

Grant, Vernon, 59

Great Alone, The, 286

Greene, Sam, 287–88

Gregory, L. H., 27, 80, 254

Grier, Bobby, 318, 319; Sugar Bowl controversy over, 281, 308–13

Griffin, Marvin, 308, 309–11, 312

Griswold, Robert, 149, 221

Grove, Frankie, 356

Grubb, Gayle, 44

Guglielmi, Ralph, 160

Gustavus Adolphus College: women's football at, 354–55, 356

Guttman, Allen, 329, 348

Guyon, Joe, 283

Halas, George, 205, 209, 214, 252, 271, 317, 318

Halberstam, David, 310, 311

Hall, G. Stanley, 146

Haller, Dick, 44, 46–47

Hamilton, H. C., 27, 103–4

Handlin, Oscar, 259–60

Hannah, John, 117, 118

Hardin-Simmons University, 96, 97

Harlem Globetrotters, 285, 322, 360

Harmon, Tom, 10, 143, 151, 188, 314

Harmon of Michigan, 151

Harper, William Rainey, 79

Harper's Monthly, 53, 54, 110, 261

Harper's Weekly, 146, 161, 228

Harris, Homer, 307

Harris, Reed, 1

Harrison, Don, 114

Harvard University, 3, 7, 8, 25, 45, 48, 51, 59, 74, 75, 77, 79, 94, 103, 108, 113, 130, 131, 146, 163, 164, 228, 238–39, 269, 286, 302; integration of football team of, 9

Haskell Institute, 333; football at, 285–91

Haughton, Percy, 128

ball, 7, 86, 87; and integration of
football, 8, 32
West, Charlie, 301
West Virginia University, 41, 153, 301
Western Conference. *See* Big Ten
Western Worker (San Francisco), 37
Westliche Post (St. Louis), 33
Wheeler, John, 25
While Thousands Cheer, 292
White, Byron ("Whizzer"), 66, 135,
209
White, George, 27, 75, 77, 78, 82, 106,
315
White Flannels, 233
Whitney, Caspar, 108, 228, 231, 260
Whyte, William, 157, 220
Wilkin, Wilbur ("Wee Willie"), 211
Wilkins, Roy, 305
Wilkinson, Charles ("Bud"), 157
Williams, Bob, 189
Williams, Chuck, 188
Williams, Ed, 301, 308
Williams, Joe, 28, 95, 133, 252, 253
Williamson, Ivan ("Ivy"), 157, 158
Willis, Bill, 6
Wilson, Don, 44
Wilson, George, 103
Winslow, Horatio, 145
Wire services, 25, 27, 66. *See also* Asso-
ciated Press; Associated Negro Press;
International News Services; United
Press
Wisconsin, University of, 31, 87, 180
Wister, Owen, 344

Wojciechowicz, Alex, 225, 261, 267,
269, 270, 271, 274
Wolfe, Tom, 369
Woman's Home Companion, 53, 175
Women's Professional Football League,
365
Wood, Barry, 137
Woodward, Stanley, 28, 29, 288
World War I, 332; and football, 2, 3
World War II, 221; and integration, 9;
and football, 116–17, 152
Wright, Elmo, 320, 365

Yale University, 3, 7, 8, 25, 45, 48, 50,
51, 59, 74, 75, 77, 85, 89–91, 103,
109, 130–31, 163, 164, 175, 202, 228,
236, 237, 238–39, 269, 280, 286,
336; integration of football team
of, 9
Yes, Sir, That's My Baby, 152, 153, 155
Yost, Fielding, 128, 129
Young Communist Review (New York), 37
Young Worker (New York), 37
Young, Buddy, 10, 39, 117, 294, 308,
311, 316
Young, Fay, 294, 321
Young, Lou, 149
Younger, Paul ("Tank"), 292
Youth's Companion, 56

Zied, Jule, 34
Zimmerman, Paul, 27, 91, 122, 123,
248, 334, 335
Zuppke, Robert, 103, 235